A Lifetime of SEX

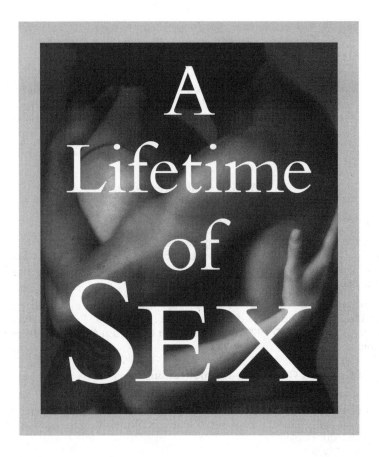

A Lifetime of SEX

THE ULTIMATE MANUAL ON SEX, WOMEN, AND RELATIONSHIPS FOR EVERY STAGE OF A MAN'S LIFE

by Stephen C. George, K. Winston Caine,
and the Editors of **Men'sHealth** Books™

*Reviewed by Shirley Zussman, Ed.D., a certified sex and
marital therapist in private practice in New York City, and James H.
Gilbaugh Jr., M.D., a urologist in Portland, Oregon,
and author of* Men's Private Parts

Rodale Press, Inc.
Emmaus, Pennsylvania

CREDITS

"How Are You Doing?" on page 63 is adapted from *Fighting for Your Marriage: Positive Steps for Preventing Divorce and Preserving a Lasting Love*, by Howard Markman, Scott Stanley, and Susan L. Blumberg. Copyright © 1994 Jossey-Bass Inc., Publishers. Reprinted by permission of the publisher.

"Going with the Flow" on page 234 was adapted with permission from Barry, M. J., et al., "The Urological Association Symptom Index for Benign Prostatic Hyperplasia" (*J. Urol.* 1992). Copyright © 1992 by the American Urological Association. Reprinted by permission.

Library of Congress Cataloging-in-Publication Data

George, Stephen C.
    A lifetime of sex : the ultimate manual on sex, women, and relationships for every stage of a man's life / by Stephen C. George, K. Winston Caine, and the editors of Men's Health Books.
       p.   cm.
    Includes index.
    ISBN 0–87596–424–9 hardcover
    1. Sex instruction for men. 2. Sexual hygiene. 3. Sex customs. 4. Man-woman relationships. I. Caine, K. Winston. II. Men's Health Books. III. Title.
HQ36.G42   1998
613.9'52—dc21   97–22722

Distributed in the book trade by St. Martin's Press

  4 6 8 10 9 7 5 3   hardcover

―――― OUR PURPOSE ――――
*"We inspire and enable people to improve
their lives and the world around them."*

Sex and Values at Rodale Press

We believe that an active and healthy sex life, based on mutual consent and respect between partners, is an important component of physical and mental well-being. We also respect that sex is a private matter and that each person has a different opinion of what sexual practices or levels of discourse are appropriate. Rodale Press is committed to offering responsible, practical advice about sexual matters, supported by accredited professionals and legitimate scientific research. Our goal—for sex and all other topics—is to publish information that empowers people's lives.

Notice

This book is intended as a reference volume only, not as a medical manual. The information given here is designed to help you make informed decisions about your sex life and health. It is not intended as a substitute for any treatment that may have been prescribed by your doctor. If you suspect that you have a medical problem, we urge you to seek competent medical help.

A Lifetime of Sex Editorial Staff

Editor: Neil Wertheimer

Contributing Editors: Jack Croft, Jeff Bredenberg

Principal Writers: Stephen C. George, K. Winston Caine, Kelly Garrett, Larry Keller

Contributing Writers: Doug Hill, Erik Kolbell, Kevin Cook

Assistant Research Manager: Jane Unger Hahn

Book Project Researcher: Jan Eickmeier

Editorial Researchers: Deanna Moyer, Teresa A. Yeykal, Staci Ann Sander

Copy Editor: David R. Umla

Art Director: Darlene Schneck

Cover and Interior Designer: Charles Beasley

Cover and Interior Photographer: Mitch Mandel

Layout Designers: J. Andrew Brubaker, Donna G. Rossi

Anatomical Illustrator: John W. Karapelou

Sexual Positions Illustrator: Julie Johnson

Manufacturing Coordinator: Patrick T. Smith

Office Manager: Roberta Mulliner

Office Staff: Julie Kehs, Mary Lou Stephen

Rodale Health and Fitness Books

Vice President and Editorial Director: Debora T. Yost

Executive Editor: Neil Wertheimer

Design and Production Director: Michael Ward

Research Manager: Ann Gossy Yermish

Copy Manager: Lisa D. Andruscavage

Book Manufacturing Director: Helen Clogston

CONTENTS

INTRODUCTION

We're taking a real chance with this book.

The risk has nothing to do with sex, of course. We know that men want books about sex—how to improve technique, how to give and get more pleasure, how to last longer, all that stuff. And if you want that, it's all here in exquisite detail.

No, the risk is that we wrote about *more* than sex. In the pages that follow you will find extraordinary wisdom and advice on dozens of topics that merely dance along the periphery of sex. Topics like intimacy, understanding women, relationships, mental toughness, aging, attitude, apartment decoration.

You see, we've come to some conclusions here at *Men's Health* Books regarding the beloved topic of men and sex. One of the key ones is this: You can talk about sex in isolation, but then you're missing the point. Because sex—in particular, good sex—is intricately linked with the rest of life. Ultimately, you can't have truly great sex if you don't know how to cultivate intimacy with a partner. Nor can you have great sex if your attitudes, your health, your life are in disarray.

This bit of wisdom didn't come off the top of our heads. Here at *Men's Health* Books, we take pride in knowing deeply the subject matters we cover. Over the past few years, we've conducted dozens of surveys, fax write-ins, focus groups with men just like you to figure out exactly what you know and don't know about sex. Then we've interviewed everyone who's anyone in the sex-research realm. We've read every study, heard every theory, seen every book. Yes, we even got paid to do that.

The result of all this research is that we have a uniquely thorough understanding about sex and the role it plays in men's lives. And you know what? The news is good.

For example, we can say with good certainty that the stereotype of men as perpetually horny frat boys is way off base. Sure, Hollywood and Madison Avenue and plenty of women like to pigeonhole us as nothing but sex-crazed ogres. And it's true that a guy of 16 to 22 years old may be a heat-seeking missile, overwhelmed by sexual desire. But his body is programmed to do that. As for the majority of us adult guys, well, let's tell you about us.

First, we prefer monogamy. We don't enter into relationships with the intent of breaking up. That's just stupid. We are surprisingly dedicated to our mates. When men do cheat on their partners—something we are absolutely against, of course—it is more to strike back against a bad relationship or situation than it is a need for more sex.

That said, we do love sex. Absolutely. Positively. But certainly not to the exclusion of everything else. Usually, by our late twenties, we've gained perspective. Intimacy, caring, giving as well as receiving—these are parts of our value systems, too. Making our partners happy is a high priority in our lives.

This brings us to one of our most important truisms: Sex when you are 20 is considerably different than sex at the age of 30, 45, or 60. How a man deals with sex—how he prioritizes it, feels it, thinks about it, reacts to it, needs it—changes steadily as one ages. So do his skill levels and his physical capacity for lovemaking. Sex is a lifelong path that goes through many terrains, some barren, some lush.

It's a simple concept, but surprisingly, few people have grasped it, even the experts. When you look at most sex books on the market, they deal with the topic as if all men are identical, as if sex was just one single terrain (usually, a hot, sweaty jungle). That's wrong.

Hence, a book concept was born: Provide advice and wisdom customized for men at every age level. Several thousand hours of researching and writing later, we have what we believe is the most relevant, useful sex book ever written for a man.

WHAT'S INSIDE

We open this book with several sections that look at universal themes—aspects of sex, women, and relationships that every man needs to know about, independent of age. Then, we go decade by decade, exploring the nuances of love and life from the perspective of a man at a unique point in his life.

This isn't to say that a man in his forties won't find chapters in "The Twenties" section relevant. In fact, we hope you bounce throughout the age-specific sections: Look ahead to see what you face in the years to come; look back to see if you met the challenges of earlier years with grace.

Indeed, it's important to acknowledge that these decade-by-decade divisions are wholly arbitrary. Who's to say that the topic of dating someone at work is solely the domain of men in their twenties? Or that disillusionment happens only in your fifties? As you know, the day you hit 30 (or 40 or 50) a switch doesn't get thrown and suddenly your body, your attitudes, your needs become different. Each man evolves in a uniquely linear path, independent of his years.

That said, we think we've done a nice job clustering topics in a way that makes sense. Read this book from beginning to end, and you will have tracked a pretty accurate path of the typical man's life. But if you find that the chapters relevant to you are spread between three or even four decades, congratulate yourself: It means that you are a complex, thinking, living adult.

Ultimately, this is a book about great sex and how to have it as soon as possible. And if that is what you get out of it, we'll be satisfied. But if we are *truly* successful, 20 years from now, you will still be reading this book. Now that would make us very happy indeed.

Neil Wertheimer
Executive Editor
Men's Health Books

1

RELATIONSHIPS

SEX VERSUS COMPANIONSHIP

Hands down, most men agree: Sex is among the most glorious, most fascinating, most beautiful, most enjoyable, most rewarding experiences in life.

Sex provides untold physical pleasures. Sex validates our manliness, no matter how old or young, rich or poor, weak or strong we are. Most of all, sex opens doors to the most intense intimacy a man and a woman can share. It can be the beginning of something incredible. Every time.

But sex alone will not sustain a relationship. Intimacy will. Intimacy fuels, enhances, and drives loving, long-term sexual relationships. So when we talk about a lifetime of sex, we also talk about a lifetime of intimacy. We talk about closeness—emotional closeness, physical closeness, and, if you will, a sort of spiritual closeness. And, of course, we talk about great sex. How to create it. How to keep it. How to ensure that it just keeps getting better. For life.

How do you do that? Here's the short version.

Know yourself. Know your partner. Communicate at the most lovingly honest, caring levels. Know what turns you on. Tell her. Show her. Learn what turns her on. Expect to learn something new every time. Never stop learning. Develop technique and control. These are secrets to a lifetime of sex.

Don't just take our word on this. Ask Barry McCarthy, Ph.D., a psychologist in Washington, D.C., and co-author with his wife, Emily, of the book *Sexual Awareness* as well as other titles. This is what he teaches his clients. This is the alchemy that transmutes sexual sparks and sexual coal into sexual fire and sexual gold, says Dr. McCarthy. This should not be a secret, he says.

In this book we share many secrets. We tell you guaranteed ways to turn on your woman, again and again. Guaranteed ways to squeeze the most pleasure from sex. To be sure, much of this book is devoted to techniques and behaviors that make you a better, more sensitive, more accomplished lover—at all phases in your life. We're here to help you perform at your peak. We're here to help you enjoy life to the fullest year after year, decade after decade.

That said, let's put sex in perspective. Important as it is, satisfying as it is, compelling as it is, sex is simply one aspect of a life of intimacy with the woman you love. The truth is that couples don't spend most of their time in bed, even if they'd like to. But what they do out of the bedroom has great bearing on those most special, private moments and hours we do spend behind closed doors. You want good sex? Take Dr. McCarthy's advice: Be a good companion.

Tʜᴇ Rᴏʟᴇ ᴏꜰ Cᴏᴍᴘᴀɴɪᴏɴsʜɪᴘ

For a lusty teen, it's hard to believe that sex isn't everything. But in the overall male scheme of things, sex isn't really all that much. A typical man thinks about sex for an average of 6 minutes of every hour—that's just 10 percent of the time. So, if we draw a pie chart of our lives and count every minute devoted to sex and sexy thoughts, for most of us, sex is a mighty thin slice. Maybe the best slice, but a skinny one for sure.

This is especially evident in strong, healthy, loving male-female relationships of long standing, says psychologist Harris Teller, Ph.D., assistant professor of special programs at National University in San Diego. Life with a partner is not one endless "sexcapade" in the literal sense. Sex, sexual attraction, and the rituals of romance draw us together in the opening act. Sex and romance add crucial spice and pleasure through the subsequent acts. But it is the dynamics of companionship and friendship—caring, trust, support, and communication—that truly keep the show on the road, Dr. McCarthy says.

You see, even purely sexual relationships rarely remain purely sexual, says Dr. McCarthy. "What gets people into a sexual relationship is the sense of newness, adventure. The excitement of whether it's going to work, whether you're going to be accepted, whether you're going to click or not click. But that kind of sexuality is going to fade at anywhere from a week to, at the most, two years into the relationship. If the relationship's going to continue to be sexual in a functional way, it is going to have to integrate some components of intimacy."

The bottom line is to develop the components of intimacy—the things that make people close emotionally—if you want a good, long-term sexual relationship.

The sentiment is echoed by Galdino F. Pranzarone, Ph.D., professor of psychology at Roanoke College in Salem, Virginia. Dr. Pranzarone draws from folk wisdom to illustrate the point: "There's a Pennsylvania Dutch saying: 'Kissing don't last; cooking does.' And what it's saying is that as you get older, the sexual attraction factors give way more to matters of companionship and looking for a good friend rather than just a lover."

Rᴏᴍᴀɴᴛɪᴄ ᴠᴇʀsᴜs Iɴᴛɪᴍᴀᴛᴇ Lᴏᴠᴇ

Sure, initial romantic attraction offers the *illusion* of intimacy—with kissing and cuddling and hand-holding and endless talks into the night. But such romantic love is largely based on deeply held love-fantasies that each partner unknowingly projects onto the other, notes clinical psychologist Polly Young-Eisendrath, Ph.D., clinical associate professor in psychiatry at the University of Vermont College of Medicine in Burlington and author of *You're Not What I Expected.*

True intimacy, Dr. Young-Eisendrath says, is built on trust, shared interests, and two-way communication.

In fact, the rites of romance involve hiding and ignoring differences and seeking and celebrating superficial similarities, says syndicated columnist Michael J. McManus, president of Marriage Savers in Bethesda, Maryland, and author of *Marriage Savers*. In this early, romantic phase of a relationship, there may be only partial sharing of each person's core beliefs, feelings, and expectations, McManus points out.

Couples often fool themselves, McManus says, by confusing physical intimacy and sexual intimacy with emotional intimacy. "Sex gives the illusion of intimacy and makes you feel close to the other person, but if you have not talked through the issues, it is kind of a hollow illusion," he observes. Physical intimacy does not at all guarantee long-term comfortable emotional intimacy, but it does tend to raise expectations, psychologists say.

Sometime not too long after the wedding bells toll, nearly every partner in a coupling awakens to the realization that they are married to someone they really don't understand very well and who doesn't understand them very well. And this comes as a surprise and a shock and a disappointment. Mc-Manus, Dr. Young-Eisendrath, and others describe this as an almost-universal process of disillusionment—simply a stage of marriage.

It is generally at a point of disillusionment that couples begin establishing incontestable emotional intimacy—if their marriages are to blossom into strong, healthy relationships, says Dr. Young-Eisendrath. Developing emotional intimacy means developing an inviolable trust, she says. It means that within the private bounds of the relationship, you and your partner can let down your guard and feel safe.

It means "with you I don't have to wear my armor," says psychologist Harville Hendrix, Ph.D., of Abiquiu, New Mexico, author of *Getting the Love You Want* and *Keeping the Love You Find*.

If emotional intimacy is not developed, sexual drive and interest wane, observes Daniel Beaver, a marriage and family therapist from Walnut Creek, California, in his book *More Than Just Sex*.

THE BENEFIT OF LOVE: GREAT SEX

Fortunately, notes Dr. McCarthy, couples who develop strong emotional intimacy enjoy a great payoff: much more pleasurable and intense sex. We'll look at ways to develop and enhance emotional intimacy in a few moments.

First, though, let's recognize that love *is* a many splendored thing. Love comes in flavors, suggests Naomi B. McCormick, Ph.D., a licensed clinical psychologist and visiting scholar in family studies and psychology at the University of Northern Iowa in Cedar Falls. One flavor, which she calls "companionate love," is essential for happy, well-adjusted, long-term relationships, she writes in her book *Sexual Salvation*.

Companionate love, according to Dr. McCormick, is rooted in trust, caring, shared experiences, similar values, and acceptance of one another's foibles and shortcomings.

If it were easy for couples to bridge the gap from romantic love to companionate love, marriage counselors would be paupers. Most marriages go through predictable stages, and a relationship's future depends upon how you deal with stage two, the withering of romance, notes Dr. Young-Eisendrath.

THE STAGES OF MARRIAGE

Most marriages are committed in a magical haze during the height of the feel-good days of romance, say McManus, Dr. McCarthy, and others.

This is a period, says McManus, when couples simply can't get enough of one another, when they are fascinated with each other's every word and thought and never tire of talking on and on and on, when nearly everything they do is fun and exciting and no matter where they are or go, it is as if a spotlight is on them that blacks out the rest of the world. If only those days could last forever. If only we could conjure them at will. They don't. We can't.

Stage two: Disillusionment sets in. The fantasy unravels. The cute little behaviors become irritating. Days seem filled with mundane routines, duties, and responsibilities. And little seems special anymore. We subconsciously start to blame the partner for not being the person we thought they were, for not living up to our expectations.

The process begins as soon as we surrender our identities as individuals and accept that we are part of a couple. We begin resenting the person we are tied to and/or the relationship that binds, says Dr. Young-Eisendrath. We see limits that the relationship places upon us, she notes, and start seeking a balance between requisite intimacy and independence, notes Dr. McCormick.

According to Dr. Pranzarone, what happens during the disillusionment phase is that we start discovering all the ways this person we have committed to share our life with does not fit our "Lovemap" as precisely as we had believed.

So, for many couples, this is where an ever-escalating cold war begins. And many go to their graves resenting one another. For others, it's Quitsville. For still others, it is a challenge to be met head-on. And the disillusionment phase is seen in retrospect as the seed from which a deep, intimate, companionate love blossomed. And for still others, a love-hate relationship emerges with shades of resentment and shades of companionate love.

The good news, teach Dr. Young-Eisendrath, McManus, Beaver, and others, is that no matter what stage of cold war a couple is in, a truce can be called, a treaty negotiated, and usually, a deep, loving, emotionally intimate relationship forged.

That stage, McManus says, comes when a troubled couple chooses to create joy in their lives and recognizes that "love is a choice. Feelings are flighty. Choices are decisive and under our control." When a couple "chooses love," he says, they begin taking responsibility for it. No longer do they view love as a mysterious state expected to manifest magically amidst glittering stardust and the scent of rose petals, but as a condition they create on their own through their actions.

Most couples do not recognize that disillusionment is a natural stage in a relationship and is needed so that the couple can develop true intimacy, suggests Dr. Young-Eisendrath. Take that long view and the process is not nearly as disheartening.

BUILDING THE BRIDGE

Want to breathe a little loving life back into your relationship? Could you use some how-to advice for negotiating the transition from romantic to companionate love? Or is romance so long dead that cardiopulmonary resuscitation seems hopeless? Want to be friends and lovers? Here are some of the techniques sexologists, psychologists, and marriage counselors recommend for building emotional intimacy. Most can be applied to both new and long-standing—and even damaged—relationships.

Recognize and alleviate envy. Envy and its many manifestations kill the kind of trust that couples need for pleasurable, uninhibited sexual encounters, says Dr. Young-Eisendrath.

Envy in its various forms causes sexual desire to evaporate. A man's desire

Unfold Your Lovemap

What we're looking for in a woman is imprinted on our subconscious. Psychologist John Money, Ph.D., named the imprint our "Lovemap." Clinical psychologist Polly Young-Eisendrath, Ph.D., clinical associate professor in psychiatry at the University of Vermont College of Medicine in Burlington and author of *You're Not What I Expected*, refers to it as our dream lover.

This imprint defines all the characteristics of the ideal woman for us. And is unique for each of us. It's all there. From the sound of the voice, color and length of hair, shape of teeth, to the types of activities and scenarios we find pleasant, enjoyable, and erotic. And it's all fantasy. Much of it was implanted in our minds by the time we were seven years old, says psychologist Galdino F. Pranzarone, Ph.D., professor of psychology at Roanoke College in Salem, Virginia.

Fantasy or not, conscious or not, we tend to gauge every woman we deal with by how closely she follows or fits the concept of our Lovemap/dream lover, says Dr. Pranzarone.

Men find it extraordinarily enlightening to realize that they have these rather indelibly printed mental impressions of the ideal mate, says Dr. Pranzarone. And they benefit from locating the impressions and analyzing them, he says. Some of the impressions may be in conflict, he notes. Those will need to be sorted out. It's not going to be a finger-snap process necessarily, but when we do it, we learn a lot about the qualities—physical, emotional, mental—that we expect and require for stimulation and satisfactory relationships. And that can

is destroyed when he feels shame and humiliation; a woman's when she feels fear and confusion, says Dr. Young-Eisendrath. Envy is subtly used to cut a partner down to size, she says. It's under way when one partner belittles the other's qualities and resources and abilities, withholding praise, trivializing, and diminishing the other person's worth, she says. Stop putting each other down. Now. If you want great sex. Healing the damage caused by envy requires consciously stopping those sorts of behaviors, honestly and openly recognizing the hurt they have caused the other, and asking for forgiveness. And the damaged partner must proudly reassert and reclaim the qualities that have been belittled, suggests Dr. Young-Eisendrath. Learn to express appreciation and admiration of your partner's strong qualities and abilities, she says, particularly those she takes pride in. Don't feel threatened by your partner's strengths.

Banish betrayal. Agree and promise that you and your spouse will not seek sexual intimacy outside your relationship. Even partners in open marriages suffer severely from loss of trust and intimacy when outside sexual relationships occur, says Dr. Young-Eisendrath. Marriages deteriorate even if one partner does not tell the other about an affair, she says. So if you want unin-

help us determine what to look for and what to avoid in a partner, he says.

How do you discover your Lovemap? Here are five steps that Dr. Pranzarone recommends. Expect these exercises to unleash long-suppressed or forgotten fantasies and memories, he says.

1. Men comfortable in shops that rent and sell adult videos can do some valuable research there, says Dr. Pranzarone. As a learning exercise, visit a shop just to review titles and covers of videos, he says. Pornographers, says Dr. Pranzarone, have found and mined every niche and cranny of male desire. Look at video cover after cover. Note what pleasantly draws your attention as well as what does not. Do the same with magazine covers. Note not just physical traits but also expressions and any activities depicted.

2. Analyze your fantasy turn-ons. In particular, the ones you return to often.

3. Recall your pubescent wet-dream fantasies.

4. Note media representations of sex and relationships and femininity that draw your attention favorably—and unfavorably.

5. Recall your boy-girl interactions between ages 5 and 8. You formed a lot of lasting opinions about what is comfortable and pleasant and what is not during those years. Who turned you on then? Who made you feel comfortable? And who turned you off? And why? What qualities were factors? Consider appearance, but go beyond that. Consider activities and environments and manner of dress.

hibited closeness and trust, make the commitment to monogamy, she advises. And then keep it. Because it's very difficult to rebuild trust if you don't, says Dr. Young-Eisendrath.

Face your fantasies. Accept that they are your own. Think back to the falling-in-love process, or analyze it carefully if you are going through it, and realize that a lot of what you find so appealing about the other person is a long-held fantasy of your idealized lover that you are projecting onto them. Figments of your imagination. They are only part of what you imagine them to be, notes Dr. Young-Eisendrath. And they can't be held to expectations and qualities and responses that really aren't theirs but products of your experiences and dreams and how you've filtered and processed them. Those are part of your Lovemap, or what Dr. Young-Eisendrath calls your dream lover. A real-life lover is going to be much more ornery and challenging than your fantasized dream lover, and that's as it should be, says Dr. Young-Eisendrath. Realize this and you will begin to appreciate your real-life lover as a unique individual and will be less likely to blame them for not being the person you imagine, suggests Dr. Young-Eisendrath.

Learn to communicate. Talking effectively about important and touchy subjects is crucial to a relationship, experts say. For tips on developing positive couples communication, see Communicating on page 38.

Make time for connecting. McManus and his wife find it early in the morning, before the kids and the rest of the world take over. Dr. McCarthy suggests that couples spend a few minutes together, just the two of you, after making love. Maybe take a short walk. Maybe share a cup of tea. To develop a trusting rapport, couples need to carve out some time—away from TV, newspapers, work, kids, and so forth—just to be together and talk a little, every day, if possible.

It's okay to institutionalize it, says McManus.

So much in a marriage becomes routine that it is important to have positive routines to look forward to, says Dr. Young-Eisendrath.

QUALITY VERSUS QUANTITY

Getting any?

Somebody somewhere, sometime, has asked you that. What were they really asking? They were really asking: Are you getting bonked? Often? With one steady, with a bevy of women, or with a secret sultry seductress on the side? And is it any good? That is, are you just getting bonked, or are you getting bonked royally?

"Getting any?" Two simple words. Such a complex query.

The common answer is, "Not nearly enough." But it's not the right answer. It's not the right answer because there is no mathematical or scientific formula that links *quantity* of sex with *quality* of sex, says psychologist Barry McCarthy, Ph.D., a psychologist in Washington, D.C., and co-author with his wife, Emily, of the book *Sexual Awareness* as well as other titles.

Stated more plainly, lots of quantity does not necessarily add up to a quality sex life. You could be getting a lot and still be getting not nearly enough, if you catch our drift. It's the quality of the individual episodes that add up to a quality sex life. This is a tough lesson for many men to learn. We're scorekeepers at heart, and quantity is easily measured and compared, not to mention genetically programmed, as we'll explain in a moment. Quality—well, it's hard to define and even harder to compare.

HOW INSTINCT CLOUDS JUDGMENT

We're all sex demons at heart, ready to do the nasty with anything sensuous that moves, notes Galdino F. Pranzarone, Ph.D., professor of psychology at Roanoke College in Salem, Virginia. This is a matter of male instinct, he says. Perhaps the strongest of the primal urges is this urge to propagate. And of course, that's exactly what sex with fertile females accomplishes if you do it enough without the intervention of birth control devices.

"Biologically, the purpose of life is to propagate," says Dr. Pranzarone. "And it doesn't take into consideration such things as people's feelings, society's norms, and ethics and morality. Basically, the biological message is just, 'Let's propagate.' So the way you're wired is, 'Choose the young, fertile women.' "

Men rarely say no to sex, says Dr. McCarthy. Even when they'd like to or even when they know that they should. And sometimes men have sex when all they really wanted was a hug because they know how to ask for sex but not for a hug, he says. And that's the crux of the matter.

Good sex involves soulful, loving, caring communication. It's not just thrusting and pumping. It is touching, laughing, exploring. It is validation and recognition and adoration and appreciation and unfettered fantasy and all sorts of "pleasuring," a verb that Dr. McCarthy may have coined. It seeks to meet both partners' needs, physically and emotionally, much of the time. And in a good, healthy sexual relationship, both partners understand that a certain percentage of the time—maybe 15 percent, says Dr. McCarthy—"the sex is going to be just so-so or blah." And that's okay. There should be no pressure or expectation that every encounter be nominated for an Oscar.

If you read that paragraph carefully, you'll have surmised that great sex is most easily accomplished with a steady partner, someone to whom you have some emotional bond. This flies in the face of our instinct to have sex with lots of women—good proof that our instincts are more for survival (the need

% Sex by the Numbers

So how often do the men of America have sex? Here are numbers from the biggest survey ever on the subject.

All Men

Four or more times per week . .8%
Two or three times per week . .26%
A few times per month 37%
A few times per year 16%
Not at all 14%

Married Men

Four or more times per week . .7%
Two or three times per week . .36%
A few times per month 43%
A few times per year 13%
Not at all 1%

Single Men Living Alone

Four or more times per week . .7%
Two or three times per week . .19%
A few times per month 26%
A few times per year 25%
Not at all 23%

SOURCE: *Sex in America*

to have children) than for personal satisfaction (the need for satisfying sex). There's an important message in this: Not only does quantity of sex not matter that much but neither does quantity of partners. We men hear a guy boast about the dozens of sexual partners that he has had the past year, and we automatically go "O-o-o-o-oh—wish it was me." You ought to think the opposite; that this boneheaded bed hopper should be jealous of the great sex *you* have had with your single, loving partner. Because chances are that your sex *has* been better.

WHERE QUANTITY DOES MATTER

We gasp, burning with fever, crawling on hands and knees across the barren sexual landscape for days, weeks, months. No food. No drink. No touch of a fair young maiden. It happens to most of us from time to time. We hit a dry spell.

It's at these times that we must make the painful realization that before you can have a quality sex life, there has to be a sex life, period. There has to be at least *some* quantity.

When we're single, the lean times are pretty commonplace. And those of us with an active fantasy life who are uninhibited about masturbating tend to weather them with little emotional damage, says Wendy Fader, Ph.D., a licensed psychologist and certified sex therapist in private practice in Boca Raton, Florida. Such men can go without a taste of the real thing for a year or even two and be none the worse for it, says Dr. Fader. "For some other men, going a just a week would drive them up a wall. It really depends on the individual."

Following a divorce, a man may go through a year or more of depression and self-realization during which he does not seek a sexual relationship, says Allan J. Adler, M.D., a psychiatrist in San Diego and co-author of the book *Divorce Recovery*. "Other men will overcompensate and become extremely sexual. They'll have rebound sex with a lot of people." The ideal, says Dr. Adler, is for a man to take some time off from sexually intimate relationships and to explore who he is, where he's going, and what he wants now that his life is changing drastically.

Dr. Adler and Dr. Fader agree that a drought in a marriage is a danger signal. "If you and your partner have gone a month without sex—and this is assuming that one of you is not in the Navy and off on a trip around the world—then you need to talk about it," says Dr. Adler.

Couples are, in fact, having less sex these days, and most are unhappy about it, says Dr. Fader. It has to do with two-income households, 60-hour workweeks, and such, she says.

"I'm seeing a lot of young, very healthy people who aren't having sex. They're very overworked, have a lot of stress, and have a lot of financial concerns. I hear people in sessions saying they'd rather get a good night's sleep, and they're really being serious about it," says Dr. Fader.

The problem with this, say Dr. Fader and Dr. Adler, is that so many super-serious emotional issues that foul couples' relationships get played out in the bedroom, with one partner withholding sex from the other. So, they say, when you feel that your sex life isn't what it should be, you need to talk about it. (For more on sexual communication, see page 38.)

GETTING TO QUALITY

When we take steps to improve the quality of our sexual experiences, often we discover a secret bonus: Quantity increases as well. After all, we all want more of a good thing. So how do you improve the quality of your sex? That's the point of much of this book, in particular, part two (Mental Mastery) and part three (Physical Mastery). But the question is on the table right now, so to start, here are some of the super sex secrets taught by the top sexologists—surefire ways to improve and maintain the quality of your sexual experiences. Many will be elaborated on further in the book.

Make time for making love. Too often we squeeze in sex only when we're tired and drifting off to sleep, exhausted and frazzled from the hectic day. When this becomes a pattern, is it any wonder that couples get bored or resentful and begin to view sex as an irritating obligation? No one enjoys any activity fully nor performs their best when they are exhausted. Lovemaking is no exception, notes Dr. McCarthy. Make time for it, he says. Devote quality time. And allow at least 30 to 45 minutes, he says. Don't rush. Allow time to relax.

Sexless in Seattle

Here are some warning signs that you've gone too long without sex, according to Wendy Fader, Ph.D., a licensed psychologist and certified sex therapist in private practice in Boca Raton, Florida (we took liberty with some of the language).

1. You're constantly thinking about it.
2. You can't keep your attention focused on anything else when an even remotely attractive female is within visual range.
3. Everything anyone does or says reminds you of sex. You see sexual metaphors everywhere, like pumping gas or driving through the Lincoln Tunnel.
4. You have trouble sleeping because, well, you're thinking about sex.
5. You're tense, irritable, and moody.
6. You have a hungry, desperate look in your eyes that scares off every attractive woman as well as (shame on you) young teenage girls, senior citizens, and some small domestic animals.

Bask in the afterglow. It ain't over when it's over, bud. Take advantage of the warmth and closeness you feel after orgasm with your partner and engage in some afterplay, recommends Dr. McCarthy. By afterplay he means talking, touching, cuddling, spending some close time together—maybe slipping on some clothes and taking a stroll together, maybe sharing a cup of tea. This, he says, really builds intimacy and extends the pleasure of sexual coupling. "It doesn't have to be heavy," he says. "The idea is just of staying with each other and staying connected with each other for a few minutes. At least 5 minutes. Not just rolling over and going to sleep."

Lose the erection. That's right. Let it ebb away. Let it rise and fall during a sexual encounter and don't worry about it, says Jack Morin, Ph.D., a psychotherapist and sexologist from the San Francisco Bay area and author of *The Erotic Mind.* An erection is only useful for a few specific sex acts. Don't let its presence determine the agenda. Go ahead and use it for a while if you want; then give it a rest and explore other possibilities.

"The more you can view sexuality as being more than genitals, intercourse, and orgasm, the better off you're going to be," says Dr. McCarthy. "Most intercoursing, per se, lasts less than 10 minutes. A big pitch we make to men is that there is much more to sex than thrusting. There are many kinds of stimulation."

Let your fingers do the walking. And the talking. Focus on the sense of touch. Touch and be touched—all over—particularly in nongenital regions, says Dr. McCarthy. Use your gentlest touch, then make it 10 times more gentle. Try stroking, rubbing, patting, massaging, squeezing. Explore the extremities. The insides of legs and arms, the neck. Get the focus off orgasm and away from the genitals and on to pleasant, sensitive sensations, he advises. Don't just touch during sex. Touch often, affectionately, intimately, and privately, he says. And don't make touch always a prelude to sex. Make it an expression of love.

Relax, relax, relax. You must unwind and let go in order to fully enjoy and experience sexuality, says Kevin Grold, Ph.D., a psychotherapist based in Del Mar, California, and author/producer of *Hypnosex*, an audiotape series. Practice deep breathing, and tensing and releasing muscles in various parts of your body for a few minutes if you're particularly uptight or frazzled, he advises.

Foster fantasy. "A lot of people's peak sexual experiences are naughty, kinky, or off-color," says Dr. Morin. "This is part of what makes it fun for many people. This is a natural part of human sexuality." Healthy couples play, he says. They encourage, entertain, and indulge one another's fantasies. They use toys, costumes, and other erotica, if they like. Fantasy is okay as long as the people playing them out are able to distinguish between fantasy and reality, says Dr. Morin.

One of the fascinating things about being a sex therapist, says Dr. McCarthy, is discovering the extraordinary range of scenarios that people find sexually stimulating. For some people a semiformal candlelight dinner is a hot prelude. For others it could be reading erotic tales aloud; slathering each other with oils and creams beneath a ceiling mirror, in front of a roaring fire, or while watching adult videos; stripping and masturbating for a partner; even engaging in games of bondage. This is what being a human sexual animal is all about. Don't suppress it. Enjoy it.

Vary it. "Sometimes it's nice to have a quickie," says Dr. McCarthy. "Sometimes it's nice to have a really lustful scenario. Other times it's nice to have a non-demand pleasuring that doesn't go to orgasm." Don't allow yourself to follow a routine in sex unless you want sex to become routine.

As long as you're making an effort to root out routines, realize and accept that sexual experiences are supposed to hit different marks, to achieve different levels of pleasure and satisfaction. This is natural. "Less than half of the time are both people equally desirous, equally aroused, and equally orgasmic," says Dr. McCarthy. "It's much more variable than that. And 5 to 15 percent of the time the sexual experiences are really blah, mediocre, or failures. You want to have positive expectations, but you also want to be realistic."

Do your sexual exercises. Easy-to-practice Kegel exercises (see instructions in Lasting Longer on page 184) strengthen and tone the muscles that contract and tickle and caress many pleasure centers deep in the groin during sex. So besides giving you more control and more forceful ejaculations, toning these muscles also increases pleasure throughout the act, notes Dr. Grold.

WHERE TO FIND WOMEN

Quick, look at your driver's license. Is your name Mick Jagger? Julio Iglesias? Sean Connery? Denzel Washington? Too bad. These guys don't need to find women. As we speak, women—beautiful women—*many* beautiful women—are plotting ways to slip past the guards and sneak into their homes.

As for the rest of us, the only women we have knocking at our doors are selling Girl Scout cookies or passing out religious pamphlets. If we want to meet women, we had best get out of the house and go looking.

Imperfect world that it is, there is no Women "R" Us shop at the mall where they all hang out, on display. You actually have to go into real-world environments where real women interact to find and meet them. We're going to tell you great ways to do that, and we'll tell you some things to avoid.

It helps to know who you are and what you need and desire in a partner. We help you explore those things in the chapters Sex versus Companionship (page 2) and How to Find the Right Woman—And Avoid the Wrong One (page 18). Once you know what you're looking for, then figuring out where to find that type of woman becomes a whole lot easier.

GO WHERE YOU SHINE

Where should you go to find a woman you're compatible with? Someone possibly right for you?

An opera singer doesn't perform at the Grand Ole Opry if seeking critical acclaim. Likewise, if you're a terrible dancer, hate dancing, and have no desire to get better, how comfortable are you going to be with someone you meet at a dance club? If you're not a verbal wizard, skip intellectual discussion groups. This is the biggest lesson for meeting women: Match your social activ-

---

Pickup Places

Here are five terrific places and five lousy places to meet women, courtesy of Sherry Singer, co-owner of Meet a Mate matchmaking service in Los Angeles.

Great Places	Not-so-Great Places
In a class	In a bar
At an outdoor festival	In a lingerie store
At a wedding	In an airport
While volunteering	On a vacation
At a great matchmaking service	At work

% **Sex by the Numbers**

Percentage of relationships that were launched through an introduction made by a mutual friend, family member, co-worker, classmate, or neighbor:

Married couples 63%
Unmarried couples living together 60%
Dating relationships of more than a month 55%
Dating relationships less than a month 49%

SOURCE: *Sex in America*

ities with your abilities, skills, and talents. You'll be much more likely to meet someone you feel comfortable with. Here are some ways to achieve this.

Enlist the help of your friends and family. An introduction from a trusted friend, co-worker, or family member remains the number one way for couples to meet. So go with the odds. Let your circle of contacts work for you. Let them know that you are interested in meeting attractive women you might enjoy spending time with and would appreciate any introductions they think might be appropriate. This is the way that most people meet compatible partners, says Galdino F. Pranzarone, Ph.D., professor of psychology at Roanoke College in Salem, Virginia.

Get out and about. To meet new women, you have to go where the women are. Look up the calendars of social activities in your area newspapers. You'll find gatherings for everything from flower-arranging clubs to support groups for UFO abductees. Go to ones that interest you, recommends Barbara Powell, Ph.D., a clinical and behavioral psychologist in New Canaan, Connecticut, and author of *Alone, Alive, and Well* and *Good Relationships Are Good Medicine*. If you're a single parent, take the kids to a playground on Saturdays. Look around. What do you see? Voilà! Other single parents, some of them women, with whom you have an immediately apparent shared interest.

Actually make a trip to a singles bar, advises Mindi Rudan in *Men: The Handbook*. But don't go any farther than the cigarette machine. Grab every free publication stacked there and displayed on "free, take one" racks. These, she points out, are chock-full of listings of organizations and activities and gatherings catering specifically to singles.

Do what you like. What do you really like to do? Think about it. Maybe think on paper. List all your top interests, hobbies, sports, skills, activities. Are there women who like to do these things? Where do they do them? Get the idea?

In *New Ways to Meet New People*, Isadora Alman, a sexologist and syndicated columnist of "Ask Isadora," writes of a shy client in his late thirties who

How to Talk to Strange Women

"Yo! Woman!" Guaranteed pickup line. Works every time—if you want to pick up nasty glares, cold shoulders, an evil reputation, or psychic leprosy.

Forget pickup lines. Open with almost anything friendly and sociable and within the bounds of politeness and decency. Talk about the here and now, if nothing else, suggests sexologist and syndicated columnist Isadora Alman in *New Ways to Meet New People*. Focus on who you are and why you're here, she says. Here are some other suggestions.

Don't be scared to initiate. The first step in meeting women is to get in the general proximity of women. The next step is to initiate contact. For most of us, the first is easier than the second. The second can seem downright terrifying. But it need not be so terrifying since, as Alman points out, often it's a stranger we're meeting.

If, in the initiation process, you commit the most hideous social blunder and realize the words "I'm an idiot" are written all over your forehead in neon, and flashing on and off, so what? This person is a stranger. You don't have to ever see her again. The key is to make the move, take the step, start the conversation. If you don't, it may never happen. If you do, it may blossom into something warm and beautiful.

So, make eye contact and if the woman seems receptive, say something. Maybe she'll respond in a way that indicates she's willing to talk a little more.

Show restraint. If you do get a conversation rolling, keep your language reined in, advises R. Don Steele in his book *How to Date Young Women for Men over 35*. Don't jabber about sex or use foul language, even if the lady's every other word starts with "f." She's having fun being bad. If you respond in kind, she'll see you as sleazy and possibly scary.

Let magic happen. If it's one of those rare meetings where the chemistry is perfect, where the attraction is mutual and electric, where the movie scorer would cue a thousand violins, it doesn't matter what your opening words are. You could say, "Bibbidi-bobbidi-boo," and it would be met with a rapturous smile, Alman says. And if the other person responded with, "Sometimes some

was divorced and wanted to meet a potential wife. He had little money and little free time, and most of his leisure activities were guy things, like tying flies and fishing. However, when he thought about what he liked to do, he realized that he was good with his hands.

He and Alman scoured the catalog of free local adult education night classes and settled on sewing. Okay, he didn't particularly like the idea either, Alman notes—that is, until he got into the class. He was the only heterosexual male in a class of 34 women. He was an instant celebrity.

Classmates invited him out after class for coffee, to weekend family gath-

seashells shatter," you no doubt would smile back in perfect glee. A heavenly band of angels would float overhead trilling, "Soul mates, soul mates, soul mates." And you and the especially skilled conversationalist you just met would exchange nonsense phrases happily ever after.

Mystical love aside, the principle at work here is valid in many encounters, says Alman. What is important are the sounds made in an interaction and the nonverbal expressions. The actual words often have no meaning.

Use your eyes. Eye contact. It's a pretty good predictor of how an opening comment will be accepted. It's a good thing to have before an opening gambit. That is, don't just start mumbling to the back of the woman's head in front of you in the grocery line.

Open nonthreateningly. You're a stranger, she's a woman. The first thing you have to do is convince her that you are not the Boston Strangler or Charles Manson. You don't do it by talking about the Boston Strangler, Charles Manson, or sex, or anything else suggestive. Remember that old saying about first impressions? Matchmaking authors and advisers Alman and Steele agree on this—in today's world, women often are frightened of strange men. You have to come on safely, gently, innocuously, suggests Steele. Talk about college, movies, TV shows, cars, skiing, your recent trip to Seattle—those sorts of things, Steele suggests. Show friendly, casual interest in her as a human being, he says. Your job in a first conversation is to show her that you are safe and interesting. Nothing more.

Reveal something about yourself—your name and a bit of opinion—and then ask about her take on the situation. Then do it again. And volley back and forth. Keep it simple and nonthreatening and help her through the first couple minutes, advises Steele.

And use common sense, says Steele. Don't ask her where she lives. She's still wondering whether you're the Boston Strangler, remember? Tell her your name; tell her what you do for a living; tell her where *you* live, if you want; talk about things you both might enjoy and have opinions about. Then move on. Really. Don't try to transform an introduction into an all-nighter.

erings, introduced him to single daughters and sisters, and so on. You could say that he has things sewn up in the meet-women department.

Steer past singles bars. Unless, of course, your interests are expensive public drinking and competing for sexual favors. Consider bars if you're in the greatest shape and love to strut and are shopping for noncommitted, primarily sexually based flings—one-nighters with little promise of a future, says Dr. Pranzarone.

Be a do-gooder. Your community needs you. Answer the call. Volunteer your talents and time to charity and service groups. Not only will you meet people, but chances are that you'll also meet people who are positive and caring, says Dr. Powell.

Play at it. Is there a sport or physical activity that you particularly enjoy? Volleyball? Sailing? Croquet? Are there any coed groups dedicated to the activity? This is just another twist on the do-what-you-like tip, suggested by Alman.

Exercise your options. Studies show that people with fitness routines who do them with others are more likely to stick with the program, says Jonathan Robison, Ph.D., executive co-director of the Michigan Center for Preventive Medicine in Lansing.

Consider joining an exercise group or class—or starting one, says Alman. Either way, you will meet people with whom you share a passion and goal and you'll be doing something physically healthy in the process.

Overcome shyness by role-playing. Have a hard time talking with strangers? Then take on a job role (volunteer, professional, or otherwise) that makes doing it perfectly natural. Be the person who hands out programs, collects tickets, passes out drinks, or the like. This draws people to you and gives you a license to talk to strangers, notes Alman.

Re-ignite an old flame. Sometimes, the woman of your future could be in your past. Look back on old loves and friendships. Consider the question, "Would I renew the relationship if I could?" If your answer is yes, here's what to do about it. Ask yourself, "Can I? Where do I start?" Then get on with it. And have fun tracking down and catching up. (This is a promising avenue that lonely people sometimes overlook, notes Alman.)

Consider a variation on this theme: Was there someone at some time who you felt great around and really wish you had initiated a relationship with but did not? Why not track them down and see what they're up to now, suggests Alman.

HOW TO FIND THE RIGHT WOMAN—AND AVOID THE WRONG ONE

Most of us would relish a romp with Sharon Stone, Kathleen Turner, or Glenn Close. Or, hey, all three at once, as long as everyone is willing. But we wouldn't for a moment choose to pay the price paid by the characters that Michael Douglas portrays in the movies *Basic Instinct*, *The War of the Roses*, and *Fatal Attraction*.

Sex by the Numbers

%

We tend to both date and marry women who, in a broad way, are most like us. That is, women from similar backgrounds: the same race, a similar education level, same age group, and similar religious beliefs. Similar religious beliefs, however, are the least important of the factors. Religious beliefs play a greater role in whom we marry (72 percent of married couples have a similar religious background) than in whom we live with (53 percent) or whom we date (56 percent).

SOURCE: *Sex in America*

No. Michael Douglas, bless his multimillion dollar heart, gets mired in the deepest vixen voodoo—again and again—when he rubs up against "the wrong woman" on the silver screen. You and I may not possess the dimple, the physique, the Aspen vacation home, or the bank account of Douglas. But we do have a sporting chance of finding ourselves sloughing off all sorts of sticky emotional slop after an unexpected bout with the wrong woman. How does this happen? And why? And just what can you do to avoid it?

It usually starts innocently enough, notes Galdino F. Pranzarone, Ph.D., professor of psychology at Roanoke College in Salem, Virginia. We rarely know what we're getting into until several months down the line. When we find our kid's pet rabbit simmering in the stew pot and some crazed crone charging down the hallway with a butcher's knife. Okay, so it doesn't have to be that bad to be bad. Most often, it's just this sinking realization that this really isn't the right person to be with and that you need to find a way to extricate yourself from this entanglement with as little psychological damage as possible.

LOOKS KILL

The eyes have it. Again and again and again.

"Most of us, you might say, are initially attracted on superficialities," says Dr. Pranzarone. "The superficialities are, of course, the looks. My grandmother in her infinite wisdom says that you have to eat a ton of salt with somebody before you get to know them." But men instinctively skip the salt and go for the sugar.

"If a man is initially attracted to someone—physically, sexually—very quickly he seeks a sexual relationship," notes Dr. Pranzarone. "That's what nature wants. Nature does not care for a long-term relationship. All that nature wants is for you to impregnate somebody. And looks are a mechanism that works well for quick impregnations. Whereas if you have to live with somebody for a long time, you need other characteristics that keep you there, such as character and personality. And those take some time to know."

The things that turn men on immediately are visual. But the visuals do

The Madonna versus the Whore

What women have you known who really, really turned you on? Your favorite, most sexy babes. The ones you can't quit fantasizing about. The ones you would die to sleep with. Is that the kind of woman you would marry? Is that the woman you did marry?

Sure. Uh-huh.

"Unfortunately, a lot of American males have this dichotomous conceptualization of women called the Madonna/whore syndrome," says Galdino F. Pranzarone, Ph.D., professor of psychology at Roanoke College in Salem, Virginia. "Basically, in this concept the male believes that he should select a Madonna for a wife and mother of his children and lifetime companion."

A Madonna is virginlike, is above sex, and must deny and repress sexuality. (Obviously, we are *not* talking about the pop singer, but the historical, Christian reference: the Virgin Mary.)

"You seek a Madonna for a wife because your culture tells you that an exciting, sexually active woman who fills all your desires would not be an appropriate stay-at-home mother for your children," says Dr. Pranzarone. "Whereas before you make this decision of settling down, you usually date the whore.

not tell you much about the total package. About what's under the hood. About whether this is the right woman or the wrong woman overall. About whether you will love or loath each other after the initial passion wears off.

"We should really instruct our young men that looking is okay, but they should get to know somebody first before getting involved with them," Dr. Pranzarone says. "It saves a lot of trouble. And you really do need to do a lot of talking to get to know someone. A *lot* of talking."

Jabbering is one of the keys to finding the right woman and avoiding disasters. And there are other steps we can take.

KNOW THYSELF

Forget Hollywood and *Playboy*. There is no perfect woman. No one-size-fits-all right woman.

Therefore, rule number one, says Dr. Pranzarone, is know what you need. To do that, you'll need to look at who you are. To find that out, determine your "Lovemap" (see "Unfold Your Lovemap" on page 6). Your Lovemap is your "concept of the idealized lover," he says. This ideal "is formed in childhood, like a native language, as a result of social and environmental experiences and input through the senses and becomes wired into your biology."

Your Lovemap, says Dr. Pranzarone, contains indelible mental imprints of your "idealized lover's face, figure, sex, activities, appearance, personality, and social characteristics and includes the activities that you engage in erotically."

You see her in all the passionate, exciting girls that turn you on and that you enjoy being with and that you have a lot of fun with and with whom you have the most intense orgasms and multiple orgasms and so on.

"Unfortunately, a lot of guys do make this distinction: One is the type of girl I have fun with, and the other is the type of girl I marry." But then in the marriage, because the sexual chemistry is not right or is inhibited, after a while "they find that their sex life wanes, that the excitement is gone, or that they are relatively impotent, or that their performance fails with this woman."

The ideal marriage partner, says Dr. Pranzarone, is one who has a combination of the physical/emotional/personality characteristics that most turn you on as well as the skills and traits needed to develop a stable, lifelong relationship and home life. In other words, a woman who offers the best aspects of both the whore and the Madonna.

But what if you married a Madonna and you're missing the whore? Most of us learn to adjust our preconceived turn-ons at least somewhat as we grow older. Otherwise, we might never be turned on by anything but 6-, 12-, or 19-year-old girls, Dr. Pranzarone says.

It includes a blend of physical characteristics, emotional characteristics, smells, even things like the sound of a voice, says Dr. Pranzarone. And women who exhibit the characteristics imprinted on your Lovemap are going to turn you on much more than women who do not.

Understanding just what about a partner makes you feel good and comfortable obviously will help you look for those qualities. And recalling and considering how things worked well in the past also can help. We've adapted this concept from Isadora Alman, a sexologist, syndicated columnist of "Ask Isadora," and author of *New Ways to Meet New People*, and call it writing the book of love. To do this, you'll need to do some amateur self-psychoanalysis at home, in your spare time. It will help you sort the past and figure out what worked and why—as well as what didn't—and why. Here's how to proceed.

1. Buy the book. Get a notebook and dedicate it to your quest.

2. List your loves. Start by listing the name of each partner you've had in every "couple" relationship in memory. Alman suggests just listing the good ones.

However, Dr. Pranzarone sees value in analyzing relationships that didn't work so well.

If you haven't had many relationships, or any, list the almosts or might-have-beens, such as "the woman I sat next to on the train from Los Angeles to San Clemente," suggests Alman.

3. Turn a new leaf. Give each partner a page to herself. Put her name at the top and then think about and answer the following questions, says Alman.

- Where did I meet her? How?
- Who initiated things?
- What was my first impression?
- What exactly was it that attracted me at first?
- What was the best thing in the relationship?
- What didn't I like?
- When and how long was the good part?
- How did the relationship end and who ended it?
- Would I renew the relationship if I could?

The answers to these questions, particularly over several relationships, should be revealing. Some patterns, both positive and negative, should be apparent. The exercise and the knowledge it provides should be empowering and confidence-building. Mentally replaying successes is particularly inspir-

When Wrong Is Right

This does happen. Some men and women require nasty, mean, cold interactions and are only excited by unpredictable, undependable, violent, or otherwise abusive partners.

Some men, says Galdino F. Pranzarone, Ph.D., professor of psychology at Roanoke College in Salem, Virginia, have a deeply embedded turn-on "that says, basically, 'I want an abusive woman. The more you humiliate me, the more I'm going to be attracted to you.' Some guys are into that. Abuse is a sexual turn-on to them. Whereas a nice, loving woman they could live with is a dull turn-on."

This is not healthy, says Dr. Pranzarone. If you find this is your pattern, you should talk it out, sort it out, and overcome it through psychological counseling, advises Dr. Pranzarone. You might not *want* to but probably should. Because how can you ever be happy if to be happy you must be unhappy? Or to put it another way, how can you ever be in a loving relationship if in order to feel loved you must be abused?

And then there are "drama queens." These are men—or women—who must constantly be on the verge of breaking up or reconciling in order for love to be real to them. Lots of tears, arguments, fights, and passionate reconciliations. The stormier the relationship, the better. For others, this would be sheer horror. But, says Dr. Pranzarone, if it's part of your turn-on scenario, you'll need a partner who doesn't abandon ship when the seas get choppy. You'll need to find someone who knows how to play the game. Or seek counseling and get over it, he says.

ing, says Seattle psychologist Arthur Wassmer, Ph.D., author of *Making Contact* and other books.

4. Detail your priorities. After analyzing all of your lists, list traits that you find important in a partner. One line per trait—things like good looks, sense of humor, professional career, religion, and so on. Think of everything that matters to you and list it, suggests Alman.

5. Take a tally. To the left of each item, rate on a scale from 1 to 10 how important the trait is to you in a partner.

6. Once you've completed that assessment, using the same numbering system, rate *yourself* on each item, putting your score on the right side of the sheet. That'll give you a clue as to whether you're being realistic and point out areas where you could use a little work.

Finally, where you look for your friends and lovers has a lot to do with what you find. (For some tips and clues about where to find your ideal lover, see Where to Find Women on page 14.)

THE RULES OF DATING

Suzy Mallery created quite a stir in 1979 when she founded an organization called ManWatchers. Among other things, members of the organization handed men cards informing the recipient that he was certified as a man "well worth watching" by the woman handing it to him. The woman then checked off what she liked about the guy—his eyes, his smile, whatever.

All this was such a novelty that Mallery became a minor media star, fielding interviews from reporters around the country and appearing on television shows such as *The Phil Donahue Show*. But today, ManWatchers's membership is a fraction of what it once was, and Mallery says that she's going to have to redesign those cards that women give to worthy men.

"Originally, everyone wanted ManWatchers cards," she says. "They thought complimenting men was exciting and kind of daring. Well, it's not a big thing now, and a lot of women do not like to compliment men. There's a little more animosity between the sexes. I see a terrific lack of communication between the sexes."

Welcome to the grave new world of dating.

PLANNING A DATE

Women do still want to meet and date men, of course. "We all know that women still want guys who are loyal, loving, trusting," says Timothy Perper,

Ph.D., biologist, co-editor of *The Complete Dictionary of Sexology*, and an independent researcher who has studied human courtship for two decades. But where do you take them? What do you do with them? There are some universal truths about dating that are pertinent whether you are 25 or 65. Further on in the book, we'll look at dating issues specific to men in various age groupings.

Do the prep work. If you've known for some time the woman you are asking out, chances are that you're aware of some of her interests. So plan accordingly. If she loves classical music, invite her to join you for a performance of the nearest orchestra.

If you don't know her well, you might offer her some options. "It's difficult when you say, 'What would you like to do?'" says Cathy Colbert Inman, a clinical social worker and owner of Professional Introductions in Champaign, Illinois. "If you can, give the person several choices of things that you think would be reasonable and that you'd be willing to do."

It's best, though, not to appear indecisive. "Women like men who have self-confidence," Mallery says. One venue to avoid on the first date is the movies. The idea is to talk and get to know each other better on this initial outing. Try doing that in a movie theater and you may find yourself with a black eye.

Consider a day date. "I think that a good first date would be a casual, informal setting for lunch or coffee," Inman says. "I think that an afternoon date is generally a better choice." She thinks that a day date is appealing because it gives both parties some control, especially if they arrive at the designated place on their own. That way, neither is dependent upon the other for bringing a bad date to a merciful end. Moreover, there is less chance of sexual tension getting in the way of a day date since it is implicit that both of you will go your own way and resume your day's activities afterward.

So how long should the first date be? Inman says that it can be as little as an hour or two. "That's another reason I think that lunch is a popular time for people to get together—because most people have to be back at work at a certain time," she says.

If lunch isn't your thing or you want to make a day date on the weekend, there are lots of other possibilities. Among them: a museum, a ball game, the zoo, an art gallery, a festival, the beach, or a park. All are relaxed settings in which you can talk easily.

This is not to say that a first date should not be in the evening. Some contend that a dinner date is preferable to lunch because you won't be rushed. And some of the casual day dates, such as a ball game or possibly an outdoor festival, can be done at night, too.

Spend smartly. As with so many things in dating, there are no set-in-concrete rules on how much to spend on the first date. Some women go gaga over ostentatious spending, while others feel uncomfortable.

"My feeling is that the first date should not be a display of money," Dr.

Perper says. "There are men for whom the first date is an opportunity to spend a lot of money and to show off. But most guys are not deeply attracted to women who seem to want a lot of money."

A lot of women, however, are impressed if a guy splurges on the first date, says Maria Elena Fernandez, an Atlanta newspaper reporter who is single. "A guy who's a little generous on the first date makes a lot of points."

Whether you spend a little or a lot, make the date an outing that you, too, will enjoy. If you hate music, don't ask her to a concert. "Don't do something you don't like, or it will come across as being contrived," advises Marilyn Fithian, Ph.D., a sex researcher and retired sex therapist in Long Beach, California. "And why should you do something you don't like? This is your date, too."

Sweat the details. Should you arrive at her door with flowers or some other small offering on your first date? You want to make an impression, but you don't want to overdo it. "The first date, it's nice, but some women might feel that it's a little pushy," says Deborah Pfeiffer, a professional matchmaker and founder of Love Search in Coopersburg, Pennsylvania. "Personally, I'm flattered."

Dr. Fithian says that flowers are okay but that an expensive gift is not on the first date.

If the woman you're asking out has children, should you offer to pay for a babysitter? "I think to offer is generous and nice," Inman says. "But I think he needs to think carefully about that. Is that setting a precedent?"

A guy may want to consider the woman's financial situation, if he knows it. If his date is struggling to make ends meet, his offer to pay for babysitting may be the only way she can afford to go out with him. On the other hand, she may feel uncomfortable with his paying because it makes her feel obligated to him. The solution may be for the man to simply ask her if he can help her with the babysitting cost.

THE DO'S AND DON'TS OF DATING

You may think now that you've gotten this woman to go out with you that the most challenging part is behind you. It's not. If you're like a lot of guys, you have a better chance of figuring out the quantum theory than dating etiquette.

With the gains in equality made by women in the boardroom and the bedroom, some of the old rules of dating seemed outdated. We thought women wanted to be our equals in romance, too. Then a book called *The Rules* was published. This best-seller advised women to revert to the games and manipulation of earlier generations, as in Rule 5: "Don't call him, and rarely return his calls." No wonder a lot of guys are clueless nowadays as to what is expected of them. And plenty of situations arise on a date where you have to make an instant decision that could mark you as a stud or a dud in your date's eyes.

Example #1: At dinner she offers to pay her portion of the tab. If you say nothing, she may be irritated because she was hoping that you would insist on paying the entire check yourself. But if you do insist on paying for both of your dinners, she may think that you're being chauvinistic. And she may genuinely want to pay because some women fear that a man thinks she owes him sex if he pays for the date.

Example #2: Should you open car doors or pull out your date's chair? She may dislike such chivalrous gestures, taking the attitude that she's not a child and she's capable of opening her own doors. But if you don't open doors for her, she might think that you are rude and crude for not doing so.

What's a guy to do? "Try and figure out what it is the woman wants and expects," says Dr. Perper. "We should be a lot more observant or attentive to the things that she's saying."

And while the rules of dating are in flux, you will have good times if you stay true to a few principles that never change.

- Be yourself.
- Be a good listener.
- Be creative in what you do and say.
- Don't treat dating like it's a life-or-death matter.
- Be punctual. Call her if you are running late.
- Use good manners. Refrain from demonstrating the armpit noises you are so good at.
- Be clean and dress nicely and appropriately for the occasion. You don't need to wear a tie to the zoo, but neither should you don jeans and go sockless to the symphony.
- Show an interest in your date's life and ambitions.
- Take the Beatles' advice—act naturally.
- Walk her to the door at the end of the date.

Easy enough. Now here are some things that dating pros say you should *not* do.

- Don't talk constantly about yourself. Show her how great you are rather than telling her.
- Don't talk a lot about an ex-wife or ex-lover.
- Don't use coupons when paying for anything.
- Don't steer the conversation to sex on initial phone calls or dates. "One of the mistakes that men make is that they're in such a hurry for the sexual part of a relationship that they don't form any friendship," Mallery says. "I think to a fairly intelligent woman, this is terrifically annoying."
- Don't wear out your welcome by phoning too often. Some 71 percent of single women under 35 polled by Great Expectations, a dating service chain, said that you should wait two to four days to call after a good first date.
- Don't say that you will call her unless you mean it.

DATE COMMUNICATIONS

Part of the problem between men and women is language, Dr. Perper says. "Men have a way of speaking to each other that is topic-oriented, fact-oriented." Women are less direct, more circuitous. They may say one thing and mean another.

In the best-seller *You Just Don't Understand*, Deborah Tannen, Ph.D., a linguistics professor from Georgetown University in Washington, D.C., discusses these verbal vexations. She concluded that men's conversation tends to focus on preserving their independence, while women's language promotes intimacy and relationships.

Dr. Tannen also notes that words and actions carry "metamessages" that often get crossed. For example, a guy who opens a door for a woman may be trying to send a metamessage of "I'm polite and refined and gentlemanly." The woman, however, may be getting a metamessage of "he's chauvinistic and thinks I'm subordinate to him." That's a lot of miscommunication without a word getting uttered.

If a guy is clever, he can figure out what a woman really wants during a date—read her metamessages, so to speak—even if it's not clear by what she initially says, Dr. Perper says. For example, after they've gone, say, to the theater, she says that she wants to go straight home. Now the guy may be wondering, is this an invitation to sex, or does it mean that she wants to get rid of me?

"He might have to ask her, not bluntly, but by saying, 'Are you tired? Do you want to call it an evening?'" Dr. Perper advises. "Then she has to say yes or no. I call this disambiguation. I think it's something that men have to do. Don't assume anything. Figure it out."

Dr. Perper gives another example. You go to a movie and ask your date where she would like to sit. She says anywhere. In fact, she may prefer sitting near the front, but by her vague response she's saying that she wants you to make the choice. So Dr. Perper suggests that you ask her instead if she has a favorite place to sit. If she says, yes, in the first 10 rows, then you (her manly and thoughtful date) can still decide precisely where the two of you will sit, and both of you are happy.

"What I'm suggesting is that guys can be inventive in trying to figure out politely and with curiosity exactly what this woman wants," Dr. Perper says. "Women appreciate that very much."

OTHER ISSUES OF CONDUCT

As for opening doors and other small courtesies, you can ask a woman her preference. Or you can do as many dating experts suggest and just do what feels right. Don't make a big show of sprinting around the car so that you can open her door for her. Don't trip over her trying to reach the door of a restaurant before she does. But if you like opening doors for women and it's something that you've always done, then do so unless she objects.

"A man should be himself," says Pfeiffer. "If the woman can't appreciate it, then that's not the right type of woman for him, or vice versa."

Who should pay for the date? "My feeling is the person who does the asking does the paying," Mallery says. A nationwide survey of more than 6,000 single people conducted by Great Expectations, found that most women agree with Mallery. Fifty-six percent of women questioned under the age of 35 said that the person requesting the date should pay for it.

By the end of a first date, a guy still has one more dating dilemma to resolve. Should he try and kiss the woman? Inman says that men have to pay attention to a woman's body language. If she lingers at the door or leans in toward him, these are positive signs.

If a guy still has doubts, Inman says that he ought to err on the side of caution. "There's nothing wrong with asking," she says. A woman who isn't inclined to give a kiss may do so anyway because she is so surprised by the question, Inman says.

It would be nice if women asked men out more so that they would have to grapple with these dating questions. But it is anybody's guess whether women are asking men out more than in the past. In the Great Expectations survey, only 7 percent of women over the age of 36 said that they prefer to do the asking.

Mallery thinks women have become more assertive in asking men out, but they aren't necessarily good at it. "Some women do it like some of the dumber men who do not take no for an answer and pursue someone like mad and make a general nuisance of themselves," she says.

Yikes. Sounds like *Fatal Attraction*. Maybe it's not so bad being the one responsible for making the first move after all.

THE FIRST TIME WITH A WOMAN

There's an old saying: You can't make love to all the women of the world, but you should die trying. Hardly anyone really lives by this maxim, but in its sexist absurdity lies a potent kernel of truth: that the first time with a woman can be an intoxicating, dizzying, enthralling experience.

As with life, there are those who relish the challenge of new sexual adventures and those who are deathly afraid of them. Most of us fall somewhere in between, both excited and nervous. But no one should see a first sexual encounter with a person as something to get over with so that you can get on to better sex later. While there are certainly risks to any new undertaking—

especially one as intimate as this—your overriding feelings should be of adventure and a mystical kind of wonder, not dread and anxiety. After all, this is not a crisis. This is an event. Once you have sex with a woman, you've reached a new level of understanding, peeled away a bit of mystery, and there's no going back. Not that you'd ever want to.

"It's a milestone, there's no doubt about that. It's something that should be special. And yes, there may be some nervousness and anxiety. But that doesn't mean that it can't be enjoyable," says Doreen Virtue, Ph.D., a relationship expert and psychotherapist in Newport Beach, California, and author of *In the Mood*.

As you'll see for yourself, the trick to overcoming first-time jitters is to focus on the thrill of the new, to revel in the pleasures that you had only heretofore imagined with this person, to be a man of wonder, not a man of anxiety. We've taken the liberty of providing some foolproof ways to make sure your first time isn't the worst time but just the beginning of the best time.

Take it slow. A man of anxiety feels compelled to get his first sexual encounter with a new partner over and done with. A man of wonder knows that this experience is a banquet of sensual delights, and he's not about to wolf it down. No, this is something to take a bit of time with.

"You'll certainly learn more about each other that way. And that will only make sex better for both of you," points out Dr. Virtue. Give yourself plenty of time to relax and get comfortable with one another. When the evening reaches the point that you're ready to get physical, don't just rip each other's clothes off and go at it. Undress each other—slowly. Kiss. A lot. Remember, you're a passionate explorer, not a mob hit man.

Lower your expectations. We're not saying you should go in anticipating a big, messy, awkward, frustrating, embarrassing time of it—although that certainly is one way of keeping your expectations low.

A better way might simply be to go in expecting that this evening, though special, is not necessarily going to be the be-all and end-all of sex. "That will start to create a lot of anxiety. You'll both try to bluff your way past the awkwardness of the moment," says Lonnie Barbach, Ph.D., a clinical psychologist in San Francisco and author of *For Each Other: Sharing Sexual Intimacy.* "And the thing is, there's really no way to prevent awkwardness in the beginning." So instead of expecting your first sex together to be the acme of carnal delight, expect some jitters and awkwardness. Go ahead—be nervous. Acknowledging those feelings is the first step to confronting and controlling them, says Dr. Barbach. Trust that you will both learn as you go, and each time will be better and less anxiety-ridden.

Don't focus on sex. Sounds self-defeating, doesn't it? You spend days or weeks to reach this magic moment, and now you have to drive it out of your mind?

"It's part of tempering your expectations," says Dr. Virtue. "The evening when you think sex is going to occur may not happen. If you focus on sex as the goal, you're just setting yourself up for potential disappointment." So instead of thinking ahead to sex, think ahead to the other good things that may happen: learning more about this wonderful person, discovering what pleases her, doing other physical things together, such as kissing or massaging or foreplay. "These are all great things in themselves, and having sex that night isn't going to make them better or worse," says Dr. Virtue.

Keep talking. Chances are that what got you to this point was not merely your winning smile nor flashy fashion sense but also your ability to woo her with words. Now that you've both talked yourself into this situation, let your words continue to buoy you up. "Keep the lines of communication open. Men are likely to focus on the job at hand; they're worried about performance issues. They're thinking, 'My God, this is my first time with her, I can't blow it,' " says Robert Birch, Ph.D., a psychologist in private practice in Columbus, Ohio, specializing in marriage and sex therapy. It's a bad habit to get into. Keep talking. Ask how this feels or that feels. And if the buildup to sex was based on your ability to laugh together, carry that into the bedroom. No one says that sex has to be serious. In fact, laughter often is the best way to evaporate the tension of first sex.

Communication also helps protect both of you. "If one of you feels you're going too fast, then by all means say so," says Dr. Barbach. And the other partner has to listen and respect those wishes. "You can always take a rain check and try again tomorrow night or next weekend."

Follow up. If there's a cardinal rule to first sex with a woman, it's this: "You *must* call her the next day. There is no excuse," says Dr. Virtue. This can be as low-key as calling her machine and leaving a message or as extravagant as sending her flowers at work.

Fair warning: If you don't contact her the next day, you better have a darn good reason and proof to back it up—a death certificate, an emergency room bill, a videotape of the evening news, clearly showing your apartment building burning to the ground. And even then, be ready with an apology—unless you want your first time with her to be your only time.

COPING WITH REJECTION

True story about two guys we know, Dick and Wally. In college, Dick would stand out in front of the student center and proposition every woman who passed by. He was a samurai in the art of rejection. Women would turn down his rude come-ons by the score. Bloodied but unbowed, he pressed on. And though it might take 50 or 75 or 100 rejections, eventually he'd find a woman receptive to his advances, and off they'd go to his room. We don't know where Dick is today—either he made his fortune in market research, or he's lying in a bed somewhere, ravaged by a disease without a name.

Meanwhile, Wally was shy around women, especially the girl of his dreams. He labored for weeks, working up the nerve to ask her out. And when he finally stammered out his invitation, she turned him down cold. He was two years getting over an incident that lasted all of 30 seconds. When he finally did get involved with a woman, it was only after she threw herself at him. He ended up marrying her, of course, and at his reception talked about how grateful and relieved he was to be out of the dating world, which he had experienced, remember, for less than a minute.

We all know a Dick and a Wally, the two emotional extremes of coping with rejection. How is it that one guy reacted by brushing rejection aside and the other internalized it to the point that it inhibited him?

"How you react to rejection is going to depend on a lot of things: how successful you are in other aspects of life, how much emotional investment you have in the person you've been rejected by, how confident you are, how you handle adversity in general," says Sherry Lehman, a sex therapist in Cleveland and author of *Seven Days to Better Sex and a More Loving Relationship*. Depending on what's going on in your life, you could react to rejection in any one of several ways. Here's just a handful of common reactions we have when our advances are spurned.

I'm a failure. Some guys pin all their hopes and well-being on asking a woman out. Putting all your emotional eggs in one basket is not necessarily the best move. "If you hang too much on this one event, you'll crush yourself," says Lehman. When we tend to have this reaction, we'd all do well to take a page from Dick's book and get right back in the saddle again. "It's certainly true that the more people you ask out and try to develop relationships with, the less likely you'll be to pin all your well-being on the acceptance or rejection of one person," says Lehman.

I wasted so much time and money on her. This is a not-so-uncommon reaction of men who wine and dine and lavish attention and resources on a woman, only to have her dump them after a few weeks. While it's natural to wonder if your effort wouldn't have been better spent on someone else, you should never think of resources expended in a relationship as a waste. Instead, think of it as a cost-benefit: In exchange for free meals and trips to the Bahamas, as well as numerous hours of your precious time, you got in return valuable experience in women. In this case, you learned what qualities you won't be needing in the perfect mate. "When we date, we're looking for the perfect match. You're almost never going to find that in the first person you date. So it follows that you're going to have to date around, to identify those qualities you want or don't want in a woman," says Galdino F. Pranzarone, Ph.D., professor of psychology at Roanoke College in Salem, Virginia.

I'll never find someone that good again. If rejection hits you hard, this may be an initial gut reaction. But the operative term here is "initial." It will pass. When your heart feels this way, you have to listen to your head, which knows the score: There is always someone else. Don't believe us? Then let Dr. Pranzarone offer the comfort of solid science. "Statistically speaking, it's highly unlikely that there's only one person in all of the billions in the world who has all the ideal characteristics you look for in a woman," he says. "You can safely assume that there are hundreds. Maybe even thousands."

Who needs her? Ah, now here's a positive reaction. Granted, you should never let rejection make you embittered about women in general. But it isn't bad if it thickens your skin a little. "If you're dating, you need a thick skin. Rejection is inevitable in relationships. If you can't bear up against it, if you give up now, how are you ever going to meet the woman of your dreams?" asks Lehman.

Who cares? The danger of a thick skin, though, is that you'll start to be hardened against any kind of feeling, which will make you cold and distant to women, which, in turn, will make them more likely to reject you. "Don't go overboard," warns Lehman. If you're starting to have a fatalistic sense about your relationships, maybe that's a hint to drop out of the dating game for a while, spend some time with yourself, instead of moving aimlessly through an unending stream of women you couldn't care less about.

STANDING UP TO TURNING DOWN

Now, there's the "I-failed-to-score-a-single-phone-number-at-the-bar-last-night" rejection, for which not much pity from the world will be forthcoming. All our lives are filled with low-level rejections. This is life, and we all cope. Then there's the "after-a-year-of-dating-bliss-the-woman-of-my-dreams-has-left-me-for-her-previous-boyfriend" rejection, for which the pain is real and deep and fundamental, and for which healing is vital.

"When rejection hits a man, the first thing he thinks about is loss," says Jeffrey A. Botman, Ph.D., a licensed psychologist in private practice in Cambridge, Massachusetts. Dr. Botman helps his patients cope with rejection using a problem-solving approach to therapy. He guides his clients through small, incremental changes in day-to-day matters that ultimately lead to a resolution of major problems—getting over a lost love, for instance.

"I help people to see the things they can do on their own, as individuals, rather than focusing on the things they did when they were part of a couple," says Dr. Botman. "Pursuing individual interests helps them toward overcoming their feelings of loss."

That's comforting news if you're coping with some of the harder-hitting aspects of rejection—the pain, the loss, the nagging sense of humiliation. When these sensations strike, you can deal with them. Here's how.

Go ahead—feel bad. If you're trying to cope with rejection, just about the worst thing you can do is try to numb yourself from the pain. Experiencing strong feelings is part of the healing process, says Harold Bloomfield, M.D., a psychiatrist in Del Mar, California, and author of *How to Survive the Loss of a Love*. Give in to your emotions a little bit, even the negative ones, the feelings that make you think you'll never love again. "It's okay to *feel* them, but to the degree you can, don't *believe* them."

Cool off. When a man has been rejected, sometimes he chooses his own brand of therapy: the old jump-back-in-the-saddle therapy.

"If he has been rejected, his masculinity has been called into question. He's feeling some need to prove to himself that he's still a man, still capable of having women," says Lehman.

And while this might seem like the perfect balm for your bruised ego, beware.

"The big danger in rushing into a new relationship lies in choosing badly," says Dr. Botman. "A man may set out to prove that he still has the magnetism to attract a woman rather than to find a partner with whom he can share his life. That's how men get trapped in patterns of broken, frustrating relationships—by looking for proof that they can still attract women. In the proving, they create new troubles for themselves."

So take a vacation from relationships for a while—at least a few months. Spend that time on you, not on someone else.

Focus on friends. Part of spending time on yourself means cultivating or reconnecting with friends.

"I think developing friendships with other men is important. After a breakup, a lot of men feel alone because they were focused so much on their partner and may not have many—or any—close friends," says Lehman.

In *How to Survive the Loss of a Love*, Dr. Bloomfield suggests working on developing your own personal support system. Call up that friend you haven't spoken to in months; visit relatives; gather your friends and co-workers around you.

Get involved. If your friends are few and far between, it's still a good idea to connect with people rather than retreating into your own shell of despair and self-pity.

"That's why I promote men getting involved in some volunteer work," says Lehman. "A lot of men get very self-involved, or get very involved in the relationship, but they haven't given out to others. Joining some community effort or doing volunteer work can be helpful both for your sense of worth and your confidence." Plus, you may make some new friends in the process.

Hit the gym. We couldn't call this a *Men's Health* book without suggesting some physical fitness. But this is not a gratuitous plea for physical betterment. Going to the gym and working out can be one of the most beneficial forms of therapy that you will find to nurse yourself through the pain of rejection.

"I will send a client to the gym not only because emotional well-being goes hand in hand with physical well-being but also because I want him to turn his attention to those needs, wants, and desires within himself that he can fulfill on his own, without being part of a couple," says Dr. Botman.

It doesn't have to be weight training in the gym. It could be the pursuit of any personal, self-improvement goal that you can accomplish as an individual. "Generally, you want to choose something that will become a source of pride and accomplishment for you. And that is what will make you feel better," says Dr. Botman.

Know what's good for you. One of the great traps we set for ourselves as we try to overcome the pain of rejection is that we often do things that make us feel better. Don't. Instead, Dr. Botman suggests, focus on doing things that are good for you. A mere semantic difference? Not at all.

Consider that going to the gym won't make you feel better instantly. Sitting on the sofa, watching football, noshing on pork rinds, swilling beer—now, that's pure comfort. But you have to ask yourself: Is it good for you?

"I'm not saying that you can't do things that feel comforting once in a while. But eventually, you're going to have to focus more on doing things that are good for you," says Dr. Botman. "It is true that going to the gym today may not make you feel better today. But if you go to the gym every day for two months, you will definitely feel better in two months. The rule is simple: If you do things that are good for you long enough, eventually you will feel better."

Talk to someone. Sometimes the pain of rejection seems too much, too prolonged, for us humble souls to bear. If you're finding that you're so overwhelmed that you don't do the simple things anymore—take out the trash, do the laundry—you might want to talk to someone about the pain you're in.

"There is no shame in seeking the help of a qualified counselor or therapist when you're in distress," says Dr. Botman. "Because emotional pain, just like physical pain, distorts perception, a man facing rejection may need an outsider's perspective to solve his problem." If you find that normal activities are getting harder rather than easier, get help. As a good starting point, check the benefits package where you work—most companies offer discreet counseling services or can refer you to a qualified therapist.

MAKING A COMMITMENT

Who says that men are incapable of commitment? Pick up any newspaper and check the wedding announcements—those women have to be marrying *somebody*. No, making the commitment is not our problem. Getting to the point where we're *ready* to make the commitment, though, that's a toughie.

"Really, it's tough for anyone," says Doreen Virtue, Ph.D., a relationship expert and psychotherapist in Newport Beach, California, and author of *In the Mood*. "The decision to commit yourself solely to one person is a momentous event, whether you're a man or a woman. And it takes some time before you feel ready to do it. That's only natural." But the fact remains that women seem to have a better time recognizing and coping with situations or conditions that may make them hesitate about commitment. Men, on the other hand, often have no idea why they're dragging their feet.

To that end, we offer some following rationales. They're not meant to be used as excuses. Rather, they're intended to help you understand why you might feel a hand closing around your throat when you hear the word *commitment*.

You're in uncharted territory. Men are not innately in touch with their feelings, at least not like women are. Emotions scare us; we don't know them very well. So when we come face-to-face with "the real thing," the woman who evokes the most powerful emotions of all from us, well, it makes us nervous.

"Powerful emotions are scary things. And we don't necessarily come out of the box knowing how to cope with them. Women seem to be a bit better-equipped in this regard," agrees Steve Manley, Ph.D., staff psychologist for the Male Health Center in Dallas. This may explain why they always seem to be the ones pushing for commitment. Women never have to go through the long dial-up process of getting in touch with their emotions; they're online 24 hours a day.

One word: genetics. You do the math: Women produce about 400 eggs in a lifetime. They can produce one offspring at a time, at significant expense of time and resources. In addition, they are afraid of that biological clock. Men can expel upward of 100 million sperm each time they ejaculate. Like the ancient pharaohs, we have the potential to sire hundreds, even thousands of children in a lifetime. We've been genetically coded to cast our seed as far and wide as possible. Our lowbrow forebears pledged allegiance to the flag of Wham-Bam-Thank-You-Ma'am. The relatively modern notion of committing—putting all our hopes for future generations on just one woman—clashes violently with the deeply embedded imperatives of species survival.

An important note: We're not telling you this as a way to justify rampant love-'em-and-leave-'em behavior. We're telling you this so that you can understand that you're up against an insidious and formidable foe. One that, as a modern man, you'll eventually have to surmount. Sorry, but you will—unless, of course, you want to die alone, in an unmarked grave. The only ones to mark your passing will be the archaeologists who stumble upon your remains centuries from now, deem your bones a historic find, and put you on display. You know, like a caveman.

Fear of boredom. Settling down also means settling for one person. Sud-

Make Her an Offer

As you make a commitment to that pulsing light of your sensate life, you may feel compelled to make some offering of commitment. It's not a bad idea; we're all for it. Typically, what you give and when you give it follows some predictable patterns. Here are some basic guidelines.

Stage 1: Early commitment
You give her:
- Favorite clothing, particularly jackets and sweatshirts
- The bottom drawer of your dresser
- The keys to your apartment

Stage 2: Moderate commitment, possible cohabitation
You give her:
- Expensive or extravagant gifts, such as electronic equipment or weekends in the Berkshires
- The rest of the dresser (you take the bottom drawer)
- The keys to your car

Stage 3: Serious commitment, future together is imminent
You give her:
- A sliver of pure carbon, dense enough to cut glass, set on a gold band—and you ask a certain question
- Carte blanche to buy bedroom furniture, so she throws out the old dresser
- The keys to your heart

denly, the great cereal aisle of your dating life, so rich with colorful packages and flavors, has been reduced to a single box of cornflakes. You ask yourself: Can man be expected to live on the same flavor cereal every day, with no hope of Froot Loops or Rice Krispies ever again?

Take heart, man. This reaction may actually be quite a noble thing. If you didn't care about this person, why would you care about whether you'd get bored later? In many ways, worrying ahead of time about boredom, about feeling tired or trapped in the relationship are all signs that you actually care about the relationship. At least you care enough that you hesitate to commit for fear that you'll do something clumsy, like going home with your secretary, or heading out the door for the paper and never coming back.

You're just not ready (no, really!). Maybe this is your first serious relationship. Maybe it isn't, but you've been there and still need some recovery time before you try to go there again. Maybe you just know—in the way that only you can know—that this relationship, this person, isn't the one for you (if so, we refer you to Breaking Up on page 57).

WHEN YOU ARE READY

You've been together for a while. You've actually begun to drop some of the facades we all put up when we're dating. She has learned that really you're not so well-mannered or well-groomed all the time. She knows about the tattoo, your brush with the law, the fact that you once voted Libertarian. And still she wants you. Come to think of it, you still want her. In fact, it's beginning to dawn on you that this may not be just any old lover. This may be the love of your life.

"Good Lord," you realize, "I'm ready to commit!"

Just then, anxiety steals over you. Now what? It's not like you do this every day. What if you blow it? Relax. To help you chart these deep and unfamiliar waters, we've provided a few suggestions to help you show your honey that you're ready to be committed...uh, to have yourself committed...well, you know what we mean.

Take a breather. We're not saying to break up and have a cooling-off period to test your love. We're saying to get away from whatever or whomever is pressuring you to commit. Take a day or a night or a couple hours to think things through on your own, says Lonnie Barbach, Ph.D., a clinical psychologist in San Francisco and author of *For Each Other: Sharing Sexual Intimacy*. Ask yourself if you're interested in playing the field. Ask yourself how you'd feel if she suddenly wanted out of the relationship. Try to imagine yourself with her five years from now, living together, being married, sharing a mortgage. Gauge your reactions. "How you'll feel after thinking things through—on your own—will put you on much firmer ground to make the next step, no matter whether that step is forward or backward," says Dr. Barbach.

Tell her. Only a cad would hang around, making her wonder every morning whether this will be the day she wakes up alone. If you want to be with her and just her, open your mouth and tell her, ya big lug.

"Nothing's more romantic to a woman than being told that she's wanted and desired, that someone wants to be with her and take care of her," says Dr. Virtue. You could do this the simple way: Just tell her that she's the one, that there's no one else for you in this wide world, and watch her face light up. Other options include poetry, serenading, and skywriting. The point is to be heartfelt about it. "If you're not sincere about it, she'll figure it out pretty quickly," says Dr. Virtue. And that would be worse than not telling her anything.

Follow through. You've thought it out; you've spoken your mind. But now you have to do more than say that you're committed to her. You have to show that you're committed. It won't take sweeping gestures of great expense.

"It's never the big things you do that matter; to her it's always going to be the little things you think to do that will show her your commitment," says Dr. Virtue. It's all well and good that you made a big show of burning your little black book, bought her a piece of meaningful jewelry, or transferred all your assets into her name. But it would be even better—and quite a lot easier—if you take time out of your day to call her and check in, for example.

Or ask her how her day was and then really listen when she tells you. Or get up and dance the hokey-pokey at her girlfriend's wedding, even though you never dance. Or simply hold her hand. Or just tell her you love her.

Now, was that hard?

COMMUNICATING

Some people talk good sex. Some people stutter; some people babble; some people choke up and say nothing at all.

Sexuality is a language—one of the many languages humans communicate with, notes Timothy Perper, Ph.D., biologist, co-editor of *The Complete Dictionary of Sexology*, and an independent researcher who has studied human courtship for two decades. We constantly send little signals back and forth, verbal and nonverbal, consciously and subconsciously, when we interrelate with others. Among those signals are cues about our sexual state of mind, arousal, desire, interest.

Most of us are hyper-tuned to these sex signals when we're first entering a relationship. But often we begin miscommunicating and misinterpreting messages and cues—on all levels, not just sexual—as a relationship progresses, say marriage counselors, psychologists, and sexologists.

And when any form of interpersonal communication deteriorates in an intimate relationship, sex suffers, notes Wendy Fader, Ph.D., a licensed psychologist and certified sex therapist in private practice in Boca Raton, Florida. "Everything gets played out in the bedroom," she says.

That's why it's important to talk good sex. And to develop good communication skills in our intimate relationships.

Commonly though, even couples who start out seemingly on the same wavelength before long find their communications lost in static. Here's how it happens.

Once the newness fades in a relationship, we no longer find ourselves on our best behavior. We no longer find ourselves utterly fascinated with everything that our partner may be thinking or feeling nor excited about doing everything our partner wants to do. We begin expressing frustrations—with each other, with the world. And we feel comfortable enough with the other to show anger, hurt, irritability, and other emotions. Emotions we kept in check during courtship. And that tosses a cantankerous monkey into our interpersonal communications because our partner probably isn't comfortable with us being angry or irritable and has little idea how to deal with this. So communications begin breaking down. We begin hurting each other, developing resentments, and closing off from each other, a little bit at a time. We

Sex Talk Quiz

You and your lovely. Can you talk the walk? We'll know in a second. This is a one-question, score-yourself quiz developed by Daniel Beaver, a marriage and family therapist from Walnut Creek, California, and author of *Beyond the Marriage Fantasy* and *More Than Just Sex.*

Be brutally honest. Answer this question: *Am I able to ask my partner to give me sexual pleasure in specific ways?*

Yes? Ooh la la.

No? It's time to brush up on sexual communication skills.

start taking for granted that we know what our partner likes and dislikes, wants and doesn't want, thinks and feels. And, pretty soon, as President Ronald Reagan might have said to Iran-Contra-gate Lieutenant Colonel Oliver North, "What a fine mess you've gotten us into, Ollie."

Sex is a thermometer in all this, says Dr. Fader. As communication deteriorates into miscommunication and assumptions and pain and resentment and defensive behaviors, the bedroom gets chillier. Sex becomes inhibited, more rote, and eventually less frequent. We lose our sense of adventure and our desire to risk. And the truth is that most of us aren't very good at talking about it. But talk we must, therapists say, if we are to enjoy lively, passionate sex for life.

Let's examine the communications problems that quench the fires of sex and, of course, see how the experts say we can avoid or overcome them. As they say in counseling, we all have issues we must deal with. These are the universal ones surrounding communication.

MISCOMMUNICATION

Say what you mean. Mean what you say. Far too often we don't deal straight on with sensitive and even less-sensitive matters, notes Seattle psychologist Arthur Wassmer, Ph.D., author of *Making Contact* and other books. If you want your partner to cuddle with you more, don't say, for instance, "You're not affectionate enough." Instead say, "I really like it when you lay your head on my shoulder and when you hug me and stroke my arms and chest." It doesn't hurt to add how it makes you feel, says Dr. Wassmer. For instance, "It makes me feel loved and appreciated."

Ask for what you want. You know what you need and want. Your partner knows what she needs and wants. She can help you get what you need, and you can help her get what she needs. But only if you each let the other know specifically what it is, says Dr. Wassmer. Politely. Positively. Encouragingly. You must communicate what you need and what you like in a positive, encouraging manner, if you truly want a positive response, notes clinical psychologist Polly Young-Eisendrath, Ph.D., clinical associate professor in psychiatry at the University of Vermont College of Medicine in Burlington and author of *You're Not What I Expected*.

Too often partners try to force the other one to love them by punishing them, insulting them, beating on them emotionally and physically, says psychologist Harville Hendrix, Ph.D., of Abiquiu, New Mexico, author of *Getting the Love You Want* and *Keeping the Love You Find*. You can do that, but it doesn't work. Okay?

Don't assume. Too often we expect our partners to be mind readers, the counselors say. And too often we read our partners' minds. That's another form of miscommunication.

"We make assumptions about what the other person is thinking or feeling," says Dr. Fader. "But I don't care how good you are, no one can read the other person's mind." So we end up misjudging what certain behaviors, cues, and signals mean.

Be open-minded. An open mind and direct communication are the keys to developing and enhancing healthy, lively sex between partners, teaches Richard Cohn, Ph.D., a sexologist, family therapist, and adjunct professor of psychology at Pepperdine University in Malibu, California, and National University in Los Angeles. Use these two keys to turn on your relationship's sexual engine if it is stalled.

"A man needs to take the attitude: 'I don't know everything. And I accept that I don't know everything. So I need to be able to ask my partner what she likes. And I need to be able to tell my partner what I like,' " says Dr. Cohn. Encouraging that kind of communication establishes an environment for sexual alchemy and lays the groundwork for breakthrough transformations, he suggests.

Apply the principle to your relationship beyond the bedroom, the counselors advise. Ask questions. Assume that everything you know about what your partner likes and dislikes about your relationship, your routines, your dreams and plans, your activities, is wrong, advises Dr. Young-Eisendrath. Become an open-minded, fascinated student and ask what may seem like the silliest, most basic questions. Regularly, from time to time, practice pretending that your partner is a fascinating stranger you want to know.

ATTACKING, BLAMING, HURTING

"Emotional closeness" is simply another definition of *intimacy*, says Daniel Beaver, a marriage and family therapist from Walnut Creek, California, and author of *Beyond the Marriage Fantasy* and *More Than Just Sex*. Emotional closeness is an essential ingredient in the recipe for mind-blowing sex. You can't develop and maintain emotional closeness if you're cutting each other up with words, putting each other down, blaming, complaining, withholding information, and otherwise challenging the other's right to be themselves, the experts say.

Those things compound and destroy sexual intimacy.

Don't put your partner down. And don't denigrate her actions or feelings. This does not mean that you cannot disagree, says Dr. Hendrix. It means that you learn to disagree while respecting your partner's feelings and positions as being as valid as your own.

How?

Practice "I" statements instead of "you" statements. That is, "I am angry that you didn't pick me up after work like you said you would," instead of, "You are an inconsiderate, self-centered, undependable airhead." The first approach, Beaver notes, tells your partner how you feel. The second attacks her character. Expressing feelings, as in the first approach, invites and leads to intimacy, he says. Attacking character destroys it and pushes the person away.

Learn the language of feelings. Learn, when upset, to say specifically how this makes you feel rather than call the person names or resent the person who makes you feel bad. And don't fall into the trap of saying how it makes you feel about the other person but, rather, how you feel when the other person does that. No matter how tempting it is to attack, realize that attacking won't win you more love. But venting frustrations positively will build closeness, says Beaver.

Men, in particular, have a tendency to listen to and respond to the words being spoken rather than to what feelings are being communicated, says Beaver. Often though, words are window dressing and the feelings are the point, he says. We need to make an effort to zero in on feelings and comment on them rather than on the words and concepts being communicated, Beaver advises.

An example? "You sound angry" will probably yield a quicker understanding and more positive resolution than "You've totally misinterpreted what I said." Why? That's because "You sound angry" acknowledges a feeling, while "You totally misinterpreted" escalates conflict through argument and attacks the other person's reasoning abilities.

Rule out envy. Finally, learn to admire your partner's talents, strengths, successes, popularity, abilities. Never envy your partner. Envy is sex poison, says Dr. Young-Eisendrath. (See more details on Dr. Young-Eisendrath's advice about envy in Sex versus Companionship on page 2.)

TRUST

While tied to all the others, trust may be the biggest issue of all, say Beaver, Dr. Hendrix, and Dr. Young-Eisendrath. You must be able to trust that your partner is committed to the relationship and won't suddenly run off with the butcher, the baker, and/or the candlestick maker. You must be able to trust that your partner will take responsibility for her own pleasure and will communicate to you when and what you can do to help, says Beaver.

You must be able to trust that you can let your guard down with your partner and it won't come back to haunt you. You must be able to trust that your partner won't share or reveal to others sensitive information you and she discuss intimately, advises Barry McCarthy, Ph.D., a psychologist in Washing-

Let's Talk Sex

You'd think we'd want to talk about something that's so much fun. But talking about S-E-X with the person who knows us naked is downright scary for a lot of us.

"People hesitate, blush, stammer just saying the word *sex*, let alone talking about what they need or desire," observes Wendy Fader, Ph.D., a licensed psychologist and certified sex therapist in private practice in Boca Raton, Florida. The verbal inhibition itself is a sex problem that needs to be dealt with, Dr. Fader says. And most other sex problems that couples deal with can only be resolved by acknowledging them and talking about them constructively.

What kind of sex problems often result from a frozen tongue and can be helped with a little heart-to-heart? For a quick sampler off the top of the list, try these on for size: lack of frequency, loss of desire, performance anxiety. Just talking about it is a first step toward resolving the problem. Here's how, in seven easy steps.

1. Acknowledge the truth. If either you or your partner feels there is a problem in your sex life, there *is* a problem in your sex life, says Dr. Fader. One partner may not even be aware of it. Gently, directly get it out in the open—but not in the bedroom, says clinical psychologist Polly Young-Eisendrath, Ph.D., clinical associate professor in psychiatry at the University of Vermont College of Medicine in Burlington and author of *You're Not What I Expected*.

Also, advises Dr. Fader, "Don't talk about the problem before or after any kind of sexual encounter." In other words, don't discuss it in the bedroom. Wait until you're both feeling relaxed over a glass of wine or while taking a walk.

2. No blaming. "Don't talk about what the other person is or isn't doing," says Dr. Fader. Instead, talk about how you feel and how it affects you and what you'd like: "I'd like to have my penis licked from time to time; it feels so great and makes me feel so close to you," rather than "I go down on you and you never go down on me."

3. Make notes. Do this before you initiate the talk, if this is something that has never been discussed. Think it through. And write down the things you want to cover, advises Dr. Fader.

4. Reassure your partner that you love her, care for her, and want to please

ton, D.C., and co-author with his wife, Emily, of the book *Sexual Awareness* as well as other titles.

You must be able to trust that your partner won't take advantage of things revealed in confidence to belittle or pressure you, says Dr. Fader. And you must be able to trust that your partner will not do things to hurt you.

her, advises relationships counselor John Gray, Ph.D., author of the series of mega-selling books with Mars and Venus in the titles.

5. Ask questions. Ask your lover how she likes to be touched, how she'd like to make love, and so on. And prepare to be surprised, says Dr. Young-Eisendrath.

6. Don't get defensive; don't get argumentative. Don't, don't, don't. Don't allow yourself to be hurt or angered by your partner's replies to your inquiries. Rather, positively negotiate ways to incorporate her needs and desires—along with your own—comfortably into your lovemaking scenarios, advises Dr. Young-Eisendrath.

7. Make it clear that your partner is welcome to masturbate herself to orgasm whenever she needs it and while in bed with you—especially when you're too tired for sex. And that, when you can, you'd like to help as she reaches climax, advises Dr. Gray. That way it's clear you aren't depriving her of sex or using sex as a weapon.

Then, moving sex communication into the bedroom, try this.

Talk during sex. Ask your partner, "Do you like this? Does this feel good? Is this better, or this?" Break the silence. Silence is deadly when it comes to sex. This doesn't mean that you must chatter like chimpanzees the whole time. But do practice making a comment here, a suggestion there, a sound of approval, a sound of pleasure, says Daniel Beaver, a marriage and family therapist from Walnut Creek, California, and author of *Beyond the Marriage Fantasy* and *More Than Just Sex*.

Lighten up. Make it clear that suggestions you make are for information purposes only. They are not requirements. Your partner is welcome to do with them as she pleases, says Beaver.

Make sex a fun, playful adventure. Encourage experimentation. An adventure is a situation in which you cannot predict the outcome and that contains an element of surprise or danger. Encourage your partner to join you in devising and playing out adventuresome scenarios. Be open to new possibilities. Be willing to try things your partner presents or suggests. Be willing to suggest things to your partner. This opens up sex and makes it much more intimate, says Beaver.

Now, reverse all those statements. Your partner needs to feel the same way about you.

How do you accomplish that? Practice, practice, practice, say the counselors. Just do it, as the Nike commercial says.

How do you repair broken trust? With much difficulty, the experts say.

Sex by the Numbers

"We need to talk."—What 43 percent of the women who want more sex said they say to their lover, according to a survey of 715 women

SOURCE: *Mademoiselle*

The transgression must be acknowledged openly. The hurt it caused must be recognized and communicated. There must be sincere, heartfelt apology. There must be sincere forgiveness. It must never, ever happen again. And you must give the wound lots of time to heal. Expect that trust will be rebuilt one baby step at a time, says Dr. Young-Eisendrath.

How do you increase trust? Start by sharing secrets, says Dr. McCarthy. Your partner needs to feel completely confident that what she confides to you will be respected and will remain confidential. And you need to feel the same with her.

Be each other's absolute confidantes. No matter what. Have secrets from the rest of the world. Feel free to share your deepest fears and insecurities with your mate, and to ask for comfort and reassurance, and you won't need Ed McMahon to inform you of the payoff. It'll be obvious in the bedroom. If you can be "emotionally vulnerable" with your partner, says Beaver, then you'll naturally feel inclined to let go of all inhibition and restraint in sex as well. Letting go is essential for super sex, he says.

RESOLVING CONFLICT

It's hard to be excited sexually and lovingly with someone you're angry at or while unresolved conflict with them gnaws at your consciousness, notes Beaver. It's hard to be excited sexually with someone who's always trying to prove that you're wrong and they're right. It's hard to get excited about sex with someone you feel doesn't listen to you or understand you. "Simply put," says Beaver, "unresolved conflicts inhibit a couple's sexual frequency."

Looking for a miraculous quick fix? Practice using the "I" statements and the other advice taught in the discussions of issue given earlier in this chapter and, for starters, you'll have fewer unresolved conflicts to deal with, say the experts.

What else can you do?

Encourage sharing deep personal feelings by respecting them when they are expressed, say Dr. Hendrix and Beaver. Do this—when talk is sensitive— by showing that you have heard what the other person said. Repeat it or paraphrase it as best you can and ask if you got it right, advises Dr. Hendrix. Don't argue about it or challenge how your partner feels, he says. Your partner feels the way your partner feels. This is true. Always. Understand how your partner feels. And acknowledge its validity.

This is active listening, says Beaver. It requires some discipline. That is, you must keep your mouth shut and your mind focused while your partner is talking. Don't interrupt. Don't start silently rehearsing your counterargument. Listen. And then prove that you have heard and understood what was said by restating it—without prejudice.

Love does not mean that you have to agree on everything, says Dr. Hendrix. It does mean that you seek ways to meet both your and your partner's needs and seek acceptable compromises when that is not possible, he says.

Compromise, however, does not mean one partner must always give in, cautions Beaver. What it means is that trade-offs are negotiated, are fair, and are clearly understood.

Conflict resolution needs to be a nonadversarial process in which both sides are respectful of the other and are mindful of each other's needs. The process can take minutes, days, or weeks. It's accomplished when both parties feel that the solution reached is fair to both, says Beaver. (For more on how to improve and rebuild communication, see Reinventing Romance on page 406.)

SUSTAINING INTEREST

So you've been married for a while. A long while. Or you've been dating so long that it seems like you're married. Or you're just thinking about embarking on a lifelong course with that special someone, but the longevity of the whole enterprise is daunting. You are committing to be with this one person—and this one person only—for a long time, perhaps even the rest of your life. How in the name of creation are you going to keep any kind of interest in her over the long haul?

If this thought has crossed your mind and you're feeling guilty because of it, relax. Interest is a tricky thing—even the Federal Reserve can't keep interest consistent over time. When interest is of a personal and sexual nature, sustaining it over a long period of time is trickier still. And while you may be wondering how you're going to stay interested in her, it's also not unheard of to worry how you're going to sustain her interest in you. Either way, don't fret. Pondering these concerns is a healthy sign that you'll actually do something to keep your interest level and hers high enough that you'll both be able to enjoy a rich and diverse love life.

Relationship expert Ellen Kreidman, Ph.D., is no stranger to this notion. In fact, she has made a career of helping couples sustain interest through *Light Her Fire* and *Light His Fire*, a series of inventive books and seminars designed to help couples keep the flames of passion well-kindled.

Start Sustaining Interest Tonight

Want to increase your chances of a warm reception when you hit the hay? Here are the things you can do—or not—to secure her amorous interest in you this very night.

Do...	Don't...
Seek her out as soon as you walk through the door	Root through the mail or roll around with the dog first
Give her a kiss when you find her	Ask, "Hey, when's dinner?"
Make dinner together	Go near the TV or the sofa
Ask her about how her day went	Get that glazed look when she actually starts to tell you
Wash the dishes	Forget to take out the trash, too
Rub her feet while you watch TV	Tell her they stink (even if they do)
Shower or shave before heading for bed	Go near the bedroom without at least brushing your teeth

"The first step, of course, is that you both have to want to change. I've seen plenty of people come to my seminars who said they were pressured into going," says Dr. Kreidman. "They were resistant at first. But then when they saw that it was actually possible to rekindle their love lives, they got interested in making a change for the better. Once you're interested, you're motivated. And once you're motivated, nothing can stop you."

KEEPING YOUR INTEREST HIGH

For the moment, let's assume that you're the one with the interest problem. Visually stimulated as men tend to be, it's completely natural for us to get a little bored surveying the same scenery year after year. It's okay to admit this. What's not okay is to alleviate your boredom by jetting off to Barbados with that 23-year-old from sales and marketing. Or to take out your sense of tedium on your partner by constantly criticizing her.

What you really need to do is to shift your perspective, just a tiny bit, just a hair. To do that, you'll need to turn some old behavior and conventions on their collective ear. You can start doing that with just a few simple steps.

Look for the new. Thought for the day: *To know her is to never stop discovering her.* Deep, eh? We picked that up from a commercial, but it's a wonderful thought—the idea that the person you've chosen to be with is, in fact, this vast, unexplored territory, replete with assets, qualities, and virtues you haven't even found yet. Well, it's not just a nice idea. It happens to be the truth.

"People are always changing. They're always going to surprise you if you give them the chance," says Dr. Kreidman. What you want to do, however, is minimize surprises like your coming home and finding your bags on the front step.

So, your first change-of-perspective assignment is to find the newness in that same old someone. Don't think about what you know about her, how you expect her to react. Think of what you don't know about her. What historical figure does she admire the most? What was her favorite candy as a child? Where was she when Kennedy was shot? When John Lennon was shot? Even simple, seemingly stupid questions like this can spark discussions that will lead you to aspects of her personality you never knew existed.

Don't criticize—encourage. As time marches on, you may be startled to notice how many imperfections your once-perfect partner is starting to develop (incidentally, she's noticing the same thing about you, too). Quirks and characteristics that were once endearing are now nagging at you. Physical qualities so textbook-perfect in their youth may now be succumbing to the forces of time and gravity. You may feel that your years of easy familiarity now entitle you to comment or pass judgment on even the tiniest of flaws. And she's doing the same to you.

You might find it easier and far more life-affirming if, instead of harping on her, you encouraged her in a more positive fashion. "It's surprising the nasty things people can say to one another after they've been together for years. Most people don't even realize how cruel they can be to one another," says Dr. Kreidman. Before you say something, ask yourself how that would have sounded coming out of your mouth during your dating years. "If you're cringing, then it's a sign that you should be rephrasing whatever you were going to say," she says.

Spend some selfish time. The longer the two of you are together, the more likely you both are to spend time apart pursuing your own interests. That's perfectly normal—healthy, in fact. We encourage you to keep doing that. That keeps you both active in your own goals, which is only going to make you more positive and attractive when you come together.

"It's good to pursue individual interests. Just make sure that you also spend time with her, sharing your passion for whatever is occupying you, whether it's your hobby or your career," says Robert Birch, Ph.D., a psychologist in private practice in Columbus, Ohio, specializing in marriage and sex therapy.

Look inward. And while you're spending some of that quality time with yourself, it wouldn't hurt to take stock of your own quirks, qualities and characteristics. Ask yourself some hard questions: What are you doing to make her life better, more fulfilled? What behaviors are you exhibiting that may be bugging her? "Remember that you're in a partnership and that often people behave one way because other people in their lives are behaving another way," says Dr. Birch. Take some responsibility for your own actions, and you may find her taking responsibility for hers.

KEEPING HER INTEREST

Now, it could very well be that you like her just as she is—except that she keeps nagging at you all the time to get off the couch once in a while, or to be more responsible once in a while. Or maybe she has lost interest in love-making, and you can't for the life of you figure out why. Sustaining interest in the bedroom—in any room—requires sustaining interest in each other as people, as individuals. If you're trying to hold up your end, trying to be the man of boundless diversity she always thought you were, here are some simple methods to keep her interest alive and flourishing.

Keep talking. Remember when you first met? How you found each other so interesting? How you were able to spend hours together without ever tiring of one another?

"What do you suppose most couples were doing during all those hours they couldn't keep away from each other?" asks Dr. Kreidman. The answer's not what you think. "Most of the time, they were talking nonstop."

And we're not talking sexy talk. We're talking any talk. "Women are verbal," says Dr. Kreidman. "Talk excites them." Conversation was your original pathway to engaging one another's interest, and it's still the best method we know. Here's why. The more you discuss things—whether it's the day's news or your day at work—the more you'll keep in touch with one another as thinking, feeling beings. And that will enable you to sustain interest in one another more than anything else.

Keep listening. To point out the obvious for a moment, talking gets neither of you anywhere if one of you isn't willing to listen while the other speaks.

"This is an especially important skill for men to keep sharp because, over the years, they're more likely to tune their partners out," says Dr. Kreidman. Don't give in to it, and don't think that she doesn't notice when you're listening with half an ear. "The main way women deal with feelings and emotions, including feelings of intimacy with you, is through talk. If you're shutting down on her when she opens her mouth, then what you're really doing is shutting her out," says Dr. Kreidman. How long is she going to keep interest in a situation like that?

Try new things together. In her books and seminars, Dr. Kreidman suggests looking for new projects you can tackle as a couple. Sign up for a ballroom dancing class. Take a course together at the local community college (you can pass each other notes during class). Join a health club and exercise at the same time. Or do something as simple as setting a time each evening where the two of you take a walk together. The point is to inject some new and exciting outside stimuli into your partnership. And by doing it together, neither one is left out of the fun.

Look after yourself. As they get older, men, too, can suffer the effects of time and gravity. Not to mention the ravages of unwanted body hair, infrequent bathing, and excessive halftime "snackage."

Just to clue you in: Being a physically attractive and appealing partner is not entirely up to her. "It's important to women that the men in their lives take care to look nice and to stay fit and healthy. This sends a message that you care about them enough to look good for them," says Dr. Birch. This impression doesn't change as women get older; in fact, it only intensifies. So if you want to keep her interest in you alive, make it look like you have some interest in your own appearance. Wash up before you come to bed. Keep your errant whiskers, wisps, and hairs neat and tidy. And do some kind of exercise three or four times a week. Not only will it make you look better; exercise will help you live longer, too.

Be on the lookout for ruts. In any long-term undertaking, always remember that complacency is the killer of enthusiasm, the birth mother of boredom. But if you can spot the ruts in your life together, you can then work to fill in those low spots with new fun and excitement of every stripe. Keep your eyes peeled for the danger signs: when your conversations start to follow familiar patterns—even including the same phrases and retorts you use on one another. Or in the bedroom, if your lovemaking seems formulaic and mechanical, that, too, is a classic sign of a long-term relationship rut. Don't let things reach the danger point where you're not talking or you're actively thinking about being with someone else.

The world is full of happy couples celebrating 50th anniversaries and higher. They don't have any special advantages over you; they just chose to work together to sustain a lifetime level of interest and wonder about each other. There's no reason you can't do it, too, if you're interested.

INFIDELITY

Two people stand up in front of an altar. In full view of God and a roomful of their closest friends and family, they look each other square in the eye and make promises. They enter into a compact and draw a magical circle around themselves. Their promises underscore an implicit truth: from now on, no one else shall be allowed in the circle. No one shall come between us. The compact has been sealed. The promises they make become sacred, inviolate.

Except something happens. Someone falters. The perfect geometry of their union is flawed; the circle becomes a triangle. Now, two people stand amid the fragments of a shattered compact, wondering how this could have happened. And whether they can redraw the circle.

Sometimes they can't. According to the "1990 Kinsey Institute New Report on Sex," extramarital affairs are responsible for fully 20 percent of all di-

Sex by the Numbers

Percentage who say an affair is always harmful to a marriage: 70

Percentage who think affairs can sometimes be good for a marriage: 22

SOURCE: *Newsweek* poll

vorces. If it doesn't end the marriage, infidelity can still cause months and years of heartache and mistrust. Whether it's yours or hers, infidelity is one of the most corrosive forces ever inflicted on a relationship. Any relationship.

"People think that affairs are a function of a bad marriage, but that's not true," says Scott Stanley, Ph.D., co-director of the Center for Marital and Family Studies at the University of Denver and co-author of *Fighting for Your Marriage*. Infidelity can occur in the best of marriages, in the best of men. Dr. Stanley points out that being unfaithful is not a cause of marital discord so often as it's a symptom of some underlying problem or deficiency in the relationship. "There can be a lot of reasons for cheating on someone, but it boils down to this: You're not getting something you need inside of the relationship, so you go outside the relationship to find it," he says.

Imperfect creatures that we are, we often mislead ourselves into thinking that we can find what we're looking for in the arms of another. "That rarely happens, though," says Sherry Lehman, a sex therapist in Cleveland and author of *Seven Days to Better Sex and a More Loving Relationship*. "Ultimately, many people who've had affairs learn—the hard way—that the only way to deal with inadequacies in the relationship is to deal with them from within the relationship."

BREAKING YOUR FALL

Unless he's truly amoral, a man does not enter into marriage or a long-term relationship intending to be unfaithful. And rarely does he choose infidelity overnight.

"If anything, it's a gradual change. It sneaks up on you. A thought here, a fantasy there. Little by little, year by year, you can find yourself drawn away from your partner and toward someone else. I've seen it happen," says Lehman.

Since statistics tell us that men are almost twice as likely to have affairs as women, we're aiming the following information squarely at you, guy. Our goal is to help you track the feelings and avoid the actions that may put you on the slippery slope that leads to infidelity. "Preventive medicine is always better and easier than dealing with the aftermath of an affair," says Lehman. If you can spot the behavior that might lead you to stray, you'll be in much better control of yourself and your relationship. Here are some questions to ask yourself.

Is your definition of* infidelity *accurate? One of the hardest questions to answer in a relationship is this: What constitutes infidelity? "Some wives would consider it unfaithful if you went to a topless bar. Others only consider it adultery if you've had sex. I counseled a man who insisted he wasn't being unfaithful because he was only having oral sex with his lover—they never had intercourse," says Lehman. That man was kidding himself. Don't you do the same.

A good barometer of impending infidelity is this: If you're doing something that you don't want your mate to find out about; if you're doing something that you know would upset her if she caught you, then you're on pretty dangerous ground.

Are you bored? Even in the best of marriages—with solid communication and good sex all around—men still stray, says relationship expert Ellen Kreidman, Ph.D., author of *Light Her Fire* and *Light His Fire*, a series of inventive books and seminars. One reason? Boredom.

"It's the thrill of something new, the variety that causes them to have affairs," says Lehman. If you're the kind of guy who shifts jobs every couple of years, likes to take up new things at the drop of a hat, it's a possibility that one day the new hobby you'll take up is Betty in accounts receivable. Keeping yourself occupied with nonadulterous pursuits that interest you would be preferable. And if there's boredom in your sex life, why, there are dozens, hundreds, even thousands of ways you can breathe new life into old relationships. (And you'll find a bunch of them among these pages. Check out Sustaining Interest on page 45 for starters.) Make sure that you've made every effort to solve your issues of ennui from within the marriage first.

Are you suffering midlife madness? As we stagger toward the half-century mark, men get to a point where they are just a little scared that there may be fewer years ahead of them than behind them. This makes guys do crazy things. Like buy hair. Or cars. Or the affections of a handy, willing youngster.

"Often, this is no reflection on the marriage," says Lehman. "But men will look at their wives—who are usually as old as they are—and they think, 'My God, I'm getting older. I need to do something to make me feel alive and young.' A lot of them will do things impulsively to stop their fear." Hint: If it comes down to buying a sports car or renting a suite at the Hilton Towers for a nooner with your secretary, for the love of God, buy the car. In the long run that car will be a bargain compared to the emotional and financial cost of a fling. Trust us on this.

Are you lonely? Most affairs grow out of a sense of loneliness, observes Dr. Stanley. Even if you see your wife every day of the week and all day on weekends, you may still feel a lack of connection, a genuine loneliness.

Don't let this continue, says Lehman. "People can spend so much time together that they actually get out of touch with one another. And out of loneliness, the partner who feels neglected may go outside the relationship to try to fulfill his needs."

A better solution would be talk about your loneliness. "If you're feeling this way, you have to speak up. Sometimes we get so wrapped up in our own lives, we don't notice that our partner's suffering. Or we do notice and block it out. Either way, it's important for you to speak up if needs aren't being met," says Lehman.

Are you acting out of character? As men, we are by design creatures of fantasy. But consider it a danger sign if some of your day-to-day fantasies start spilling over into your day-to-day reality and you start doing things strikingly out of character.

"Wanting to do things with your single friends more and more, making dates with someone at work for after-work drinks, trying to arrange situations where you can be alone together with someone, even planning whole trips with someone else. These are not things a man does if he's well-satisfied in his long-term relationship," says Lehman.

Do you have someone to talk to? This isn't a warning sign, but if the answers to any of the previous questions are making you squirm uncomfortably in your chair, it's probably a good idea to talk with someone other than your partner, or the someone you may be having adulterous thoughts about. We're talking a trusted friend, relative, or co-worker. "Getting an outside perspective can be very helpful in situations like this."

COPING WITH YOUR INFIDELITY

It happened.

Much as you might wish otherwise, you gave in to temptation and broke the seventh commandment—you committed adultery. We warned you, and now look at you. Guilt rules your mind and body, possessing you like a demon.

Or maybe not. Maybe you've suppressed your guilt and you're functioning just fine, thanks, walking that tightrope between your honey and your wife. But you know, in your heart of hearts, something's got to give. You're going to have to tell. You're going to get found out. You're going to have to do something.

If you decide to end your marriage and go off with your lover, there's not much advice we can give, except to get a good divorce lawyer. And by the way, don't expect your new lover to be the love of your life—statistically speaking, only a very small percentage of men ever stay in the relationships they left their wives for.

If you opt to continue in your committed relationship, however, there are many ways you can go, not all of them fun. Or easy. But then, this isn't about fun; this is about redemption. If you want it, you're going to have to work for it. Hard. But you'll find that it's oh, so worth it. Here's what you need to do.

Put a stop to it. Regardless of whether you tell your partner (and we'll get to that in a minute), if you want to have any kind of intimate and lasting relationship with the woman you've been unfaithful to, you're going to have to call it quits with your lover.

Everyone's Doing It?

From the cover lines in women's magazines and the lineups on TV talk shows, you'd think that every man on the planet was divvied into two categories: the guys who screwed around on their wives, and the guys who are about to.

Popular media and, yes, even some scholarly sex surveys seem to reinforce that notion. According to *The Hite Report on Male Sexuality*, for instance, 72 percent of men married two years or more said they had sex outside the marriage. This is the sort of datum that gives manhood a bad name.

In the interest of fairness, we thought we'd hype the results of other surveys, which put the numbers on male infidelity at somewhat more modest levels. How do you know which numbers to trust? You can't always: A study is only as good as the sample of people used to get the data. Plus, who knows how many men lie when they give an answer? But we know one thing: Once we started digging around, we found a lot more data that put male infidelity on the low side than in the 70 percentile range. Here's what we found.

The Kinsey Institute New Report on Sex
Percentage of married men who admitted to having at least one extramarital affair: 37
General Social Survey
Percentage of men who reported ever having sexual relations with a person other than their wives while they were married: 21
Sex in America
Percentage of men who reported they had *no* partners other than their wives while they were married: 65 to 85

In her book, *After the Affair*, Janis Abrahms Spring, Ph.D., a clinical psychologist in Westport, Connecticut, says that continuing an affair without the consent of both partners only perpetuates a bad relationship and absolutely hobbles any hopes you'll have for a good one. "If you're an unfaithful partner who is serious about reconnecting, you must, I believe, give up your lover," she writes.

Lehman seconds that. "Even if the other person doesn't know about it and never does, you are spending time and emotions and energy—and have an intimacy—that is taking away from what you could give to your mate."

Get some professional help. If you're wrestling with an affair and its effects on your relationship, it's probably not a good idea to rely on your own judgment. "When you're looking at sticky issues, such as whether to confess an affair or how to rebuild your relationship, it's really a situation where you need to proceed under the guidance of a professional counselor," says Lehman.

Give it plenty of time. If you commit to staying in the relationship, don't think this is all going to blow over in a couple weeks. Or even a couple years. Instead, be prepared to do some serious penance.

"There's no specific time limit. It takes as long as it takes. Rebuilding trust is not an overnight process. You have to stick with it. Every day, you have to work at it. And if you have to sleep on the couch during that time, then that's what you have to do," says Lehman. As the injured party, she's going to need some time to get past this. If you're truly repentant and truly want to save what you have, you'll give it to her.

TO TELL OR NOT TO TELL?

In general, experts say that honesty is the best policy. And if you want to save your marriage and regain some intimacy with your partner, you probably ought to come clean. That said, there may be certain situations where you may be better off keeping your mouth shut.

Note well: This is not an excuse to keep an affair secret. "But you do have to examine the particulars of the situation," cautions Lehman. "What if it truly was a one-time thing, six years ago, and you've been faithful ever since? It's arguable that confessing the affair could actually destroy the relationship you're trying to save. Her reaction might be that she'll never trust you again. Each situation, each couple, is highly individualized. You need to think very carefully about the whens and hows and whys before you tell."

Incidentally, if you decide to keep your mouth shut, remember the gospel according to country singer Hank Williams: Your cheatin' heart may still tell on you. In other words, even if you don't say a word, some action, some behavior, some thing may just register on her psychic radar and spill the beans for you. If that happens, if you're confronted, admit to it. Own up. You owe her that much.

And when you do own up, expect that she's going to react. It may be loud and violent or quiet and weepy or all of these in quick succession, but it will happen.

"Every woman is different, of course, but there are common stages of reaction," assures Lehman. These may occur in the space of a few seconds (in that case, take cover) or they may play out over weeks and months. Here's what to expect (although not necessarily in this order).

Shock and physical reaction. For most people, both men and women, the moment of discovery is a trauma. And humans react to trauma by going into shock. She may seem in a daze or she may behave irrationally. Coupled with the shock, Lehman says, is a physical reaction. She may get physically sick, or she may lash out at you. If she is physically violent toward you, certainly don't let her injure you. But don't keep her from venting either.

Disbelief. Faced with a situation beyond her control—she can't stop an affair that's already happened—your partner may go into denial. "For a time anyway, the reality of the situation is too painful to deal with, so she may block it out or be in a state of disbelief," says Lehman. Don't expect this to last very long. It'll be followed quickly by anger.

Anger. If she didn't lash out at you during the initial phase of shock, now's the time. You thought you'd get angry if you ever found out someone was cheating on you? Lehman assures us that hell hath no fury like a woman scorned.

"They get just as angry—and sometimes as violent—as men," she says. Lehman has counseled women who punched and kicked their husbands, then went out, found their husbands' lovers, and kicked their butts, too. Or they vented in other ways, destroying prized possessions, kicking unfaithful spouses out of the house, jumping in bed with their husbands' best friends. Again, your job in this drama is to take it, to absorb her rage without any finger-pointing of your own (she won't hear it, even if your claims have merit). And, of course, you want to make sure that no one is physically harmed at this explosive point in time. Try not to confess your affair in the kitchen, the workshop, or while she's piloting a moving vehicle. We're serious.

Loss. Once she unleashes her anger at your infidelity, the next phase of her reaction will be loss. While this is a natural phase, it can be a dangerous one. She could sink into depression or make decisions that will ultimately not be in anyone's best interest. If you're truly repentant and want to save your marriage, now is the time to reiterate that fact.

Regrouping. Having gone through the basic phases, she'll reach a rebuilding point where she'll try to recover what has been lost—her security, her self-confidence, and maybe even her marriage to you. This is a turning point. Once she gets here, the two of you can begin to work together on salvaging your relationship.

COPING WITH HER INFIDELITY

You bucked the odds. You were the straight arrow in the relationship. You kept your word; you were good and faithful and true.

And she cheated on you.

And you found out.

Now what are you going to do?

"This is a hard area for men to deal with because it really strikes a blow to their masculinity. At the same time, it's emotionally overwhelming, and men have a hard enough time dealing with their emotions as it is," says Lehman.

Can you and your sense of manhood survive a woman who has been untrue? Of course; it takes more than a woman to make you a man. But facing the infidelity of a partner does force you to ask some tough questions and face some harsh realities. Here are a few guidelines to help you through what could arguably be one the most trying times in a man's life.

Control your anger. Of course, an affair is going to make you angry. Angry like you've never been before—red-faced, steam coming out of your ears, veins sticking out of your forehead, the whole works. It's okay to have anger. What's not okay is to let anger have you.

"A first impulse may be blind rage and jealousy. The man will want to retaliate physically against his partner and her lover," says Lehman. Let's be frank for a moment: You may well have thoughts of harming or killing your partner or her lover. While it's common to have such thoughts, we also hope those visions of mayhem scare you a little.

Don't give in to violence. Don't raise a hand to the people who've hurt you—it will just compound things. Worse still, you might come out of this looking like the bad guy. "If you're seeing red, if you don't feel like you can control yourself, then go off by yourself until you feel like you're in better control," says Lehman. Go find a friend to talk to; go beat the crap out of your trash cans; run down the street howling at the moon if you have to. But don't give in to the heat of the moment and retaliate against the people who have hurt you.

Don't play tit for tat. After the initial shock and anger has worn off, your mind may still be working along two specific lines: getting back at her somehow and soothing your ruffled masculine ego. Efficient fellows that we are, many men immediately see an economical course of action that can kill two birds with one stone: jump in the sack with another woman.

"It may seem like a great idea at the time: You pick up someone at a bar, have a one-night stand, and reassert your masculinity. But most men who do this almost always regret it," says Lehman. Never mind that you may have inadvertently exposed yourself to disease, you've also just stooped to the level of the person who hurt you. And did it erase her transgression? "No. And what's more, this is the sort of thing that can drive a wedge further between you and make it more difficult for you to resolve anything," says Lehman.

Take stock. During your cooling-off phase, try to look back across the landscape of your relationship and see what led to this moment. "As I said earlier, affairs are often symptoms of another problem in the relationship. You may have played a role in that," says Lehman. We're not saying the affair was your fault, but these things don't happen in a vacuum. "Hard as it may be to accept, sometimes the injured partner has played a role in the events leading to an affair."

Dr. Kreidman points out that sometimes men are so driven by the demands of their career that they often ignore their partners and don't give them the attention or affection they crave. "I tell the men in my seminars, 'If you don't have a love affair with your wife, someone else will,'" she says.

The second part of taking stock of what has happened concerns not looking back but looking forward. Specifically, now's the time to start asking yourself: Do you want to continue in this relationship? "Your gut reaction might be no. But think again. In my experience, an affair does not have to mean the end of the marriage," says Lehman.

Get past the blame. If you resolve to at least try to salvage your relationship, a crucial factor in this salvage operation is in getting past the finger-pointing phase, suggests Dr. Spring.

"It's too easy to constantly be lording it over someone that they cheated on you, that you're in the morally superior position. When I work with couples, I tell them that I'm not there to assign blame, I'm there to help them to work together to rebuild trust, to work on the second marriage within their marriage," echoes Lehman. As long as you hold blame, or she holds blame that you drove her to infidelity, you'll have a difficult time moving forward and rebuilding your life together.

BREAKING UP

People can part for many reasons, falling out of love being just one of them.

Maybe you've hit a time in your life where relationships only make you feel encumbered. Or some tic of her personality—so cute when she exhibited it the first thousand or so times—is now seemingly intolerable. Or you've finally decided to show the real you, to let your guard down. Only it turns out that she doesn't want the real you; she wants you always on your best behavior, the way you were when you first met. Maybe deep down you just know that the two of you aren't right for each other, and it's not fair for either of you to stay together. So you don't.

People break up all the time. The act of breaking up is like a force of nature—neither good nor bad, at times a source of terrible destruction or a brief, rejuvenating storm. Ultimately, even though it sounds contradictory, breaking up is a natural, even necessary part of an evolving life of relationships.

"Think about it. You're not really going to know what kind of woman you want to be with until you start dating a few. And in the process, you're going to find that there are some people you're just not interested in, compared to others. What are you going to do? Stay in the unsatisfactory relationship and make each other miserable? No, you move on, you find someone else who more closely matches your perceptions of the ideal," says Galdino F. Pranzarone, Ph.D., professor of psychology at Roanoke College in Salem, Virginia.

Eventually, says Dr. Pranzarone, the idea is that you find someone who so closely matches your internal picture of the perfect woman that you stop there and start the rest of your wonderful lives together. But until then, you have to go through the trial-and-error process of meeting—and leaving—various examples of the opposite sex. Women do this, too, by the way. They even have a clinical phrase for the process: "kissing a lot of frogs."

Relationship Repo

Relationships are predicated on the notion of give and take. You give her your prized hand-knitted Irish sweater to keep her warm one night in the park; she brings over a stack of CDs for your party next week. You exchange books and clothing; leave jewelry on one another's dressers. Then comes the day when you break it off. While it might be time to leave each other, you're not quite ready to part with that sweater, or any of a dozen personal items still in her possession.

Unless you're careful, recovering prized possessions after a breakup can seem like hostage negotiations—tense, bitter, full of recriminations, the risk of never seeing your loved ones again remains a distinct possibility. Of course, in that event, you get to keep her stuff in trade. But really, what are you going to do with four pairs of panties, a couple of size-5 pumps, and a charm bracelet? Meanwhile, we know guys who've lost treasured books and albums, comfortable sweatshirts (which take years to break in!), expensive leather coats, and a wide selection of household appliances.

Whatever it is, if you want it back so badly, it's worth contacting your ex one last time to get it. At the same time, if there's anything you owe her, it speaks well of your virtue, dignity, and self-respect if you make an honest effort to return what's rightfully hers. Here's how to handle the negotiations, according to several experts we consulted with.

Give, then take. If you ever want to see that collection of Grateful Dead bootlegs again, call her up and get the ball rolling. Give her a reason to meet and make the exchange. Say, "Listen, I have a bunch of your things here. I'm

MAKING THE BREAK

As men, we don't have a problem with the kissing part. It's the leaving part that trips us up. It's not that we can't do it but that we have a particularly hard time initiating a breakup in a genteel and civil fashion that doesn't leave emotions, reputations, and apartments in tatters. The truth is that when it comes to breaking up, we'd rather just skip town, erase all chance of contact with our former lover, make a clean break.

But—and here's the reason breaking up is hard to do—if you want to leave, some way, somehow, you have to communicate with the person that you want to leave. Specifically, you have to tell someone else that you don't want to be with them anymore. That's a hard thing for anyone to do. No one wants to hurt someone else deliberately, and no one wants to have someone else think ill of them. Recognize, however, that this is bound to happen when you tell a girlfriend you're moving on. So if you're going to make an exit, make it with grace, dignity, and self-respect all intact. Here's how.

Don't waffle. If you're on the fence about her, get clear with your feelings before you voice them. Nothing looks worse than an indecisive guy

sure you'd like to have them back. When's a good time for me to bring them over?" Not only do you come off sounding like a decent guy, you're also giving her a not-so-subtle reminder that she has a few things of yours. If she's so obtuse that she doesn't take the hint, you can then baldly ask for your possessions back when you get to her place.

Don't ask for gifts back. Anything you gave her in the course of your relationship that was not wrapped or offered with the words "Here. Keep it. It's yours." is considered a loaner and still belongs to you. You are therefore entitled to ask for it back. If you gave her something as a gift, do not lower yourself by asking for it back, even if she really burned you. One exception is an engagement ring. If she won't take the man, she can't keep the rock.

Return all keys. Only a cad would make her change the locks.

Pay all debts. You're an honest man. You pay your bills, and you expect people to do the same. So, if she ever floated you a loan—for the rent, for a car payment, for bail money—make it clear at the end of the relationship that you intend to repay her in full. Same deal for any charges you might have made on her credit card. If you loaned her any money, you're certainly within your rights to ask for it back. But don't harass her for it. No one wants to be one of those guys standing in a darkened apartment courtyard screaming, "You owe me money, woman!" In the end, if all she stiffed you for was a few hundred bucks, then you've gotten off cheap, friend. You've also learned a valuable lesson about the kind of woman she is—before it was too late.

who breaks up with his woman and then decides maybe they should try again.

"If you're having problems, then try to work them out—every couple has problems at some point," observes Robert Birch, Ph.D., a psychologist in private practice in Columbus, Ohio, specializing in marriage and sex therapy.

But if you're to the point where no amount of problem solving will work and you've resolved to get out of the relationship, then get out. All the way out. Don't tell her you're thinking about it. Don't change your mind two weeks after the fact. Just do it. Be firm, not mean. Sometimes there's something to be said for making a clean break.

Pick a time and place. Sometimes relationships end in a sudden explosion. Bang!—and you're propelled out the door. Sometimes breakups are long, slow, painful affairs, ultimately tapering off to nothing—and both of you are left wondering what ever happened. Neither extreme is a good note to end a relationship on. Instead, Dr. Birch says, there should be a reckoning, a moment of truth, something that will give you both closure. Often, all that is needed for you to create this moment is to say, "We have to talk." Then speak

your piece. Before you do, be sure that you're both on an even keel emotionally. You don't want to break up right after a big fight or, say, the day she gets
back from her uncle's funeral. And while you may not want to take her to
dinner at a four-star restaurant in order to drop the bomb on her, sharing a
meal or a drink in a neutral environment (not, for example, the romantic
restaurant you went to when things were hot and heavy) is certainly appropriate. So is a quiet conversation in your living room. Wherever you plan,
make sure that there's opportunity for each of you to retreat after it's done.
For example, breaking up on the first day of a week-long cruise or halfway
through a hiking trip in the Sierras is not recommended.

Keep it simple. Once you've made up your mind and decided to end it,
don't get into long protracted reasons and justifications. In the end it won't
make a bit of difference, except you might end up talking yourself out of it
and thereby get sucked into the trap of waffling (see earlier tip on page 58).

"If you're going to end a relationship, be as honest and straightforward as
possible, without being hurtful and mean," says Steve Manley, Ph.D., staff psychologist for the Male Health Center in Dallas. Don't tell her she's fat or that
you just don't love her anymore. But if you don't see a future with her, and
you think you'd both be better off with other people, make no bones about it.

Don't make her do it. Funny thing, the human animal. Sometimes we so
dislike being the instigator of sticky situations that we behave badly to get others to instigate the sticky situation for us. Let's say, for example, you're itching to
get out of a relationship but are so disinclined to be the bad guy that you begin
misbehaving in the hope that she'll get sick of you and dump you. Problem
solved. Except, of course, that it isn't. Technically, she ends the relationship. But,
in reality, you did because your deliberately pathetic behavior drove her to it.

"If you find yourself doing things and behaving in ways you know she
won't like or approve of, that's a warning sign," says Dr. Manley. "At that
point, you really want to ask yourself, 'Why am I trying to provoke her?' Try
to identify the real issue that's making you behave this way." At that point you
can sit down and discuss the situation—openly, without the subtle provoca-
tions—and decide whether things are worth salvaging.

Don't forget her. For most guys, it's common for us to try to put former lovers out of our minds, says Dr. Birch. The breakup was painful enough;
why keep thinking about her? First, if you were in a relationship with her,
and now it's over, that's something you're entitled to mourn—even if you initiated the breakup. Second, even though you may not want to be with her
anymore, you probably had genuine feelings for her—maybe still do. It's
worth sorting those feelings now that you've broken up.

Also, remembering old relationships will help you when you finally do
find the love of your life, says Dr. Pranzarone. Those old relationships you
may have seen as mistakes or as failures actually do have some positive benefit: They helped you—both of you—gain valuable experience about the
kind of person you are interested in, what parameters you can handle in a re-

lationship, and so on. That way, when you do meet the great love of your life, you'll be more likely to recognize it when it happens and less likely to fall into the same old traps.

DIVORCE

With perhaps the exception of Hollywood actors, those veritable members of the Wife-of-the-Month Club, most men do not enter into marriage expecting it to fail.

Like the other big decisions in our lives—buying a house, having children—we expect the marriage decision to have legs. Our emphasis is on the long term. We assume that the house will last at least as long as the 30-year fixed mortgage that came with it. And kids—well, that's for life. Same deal with marriage. We want it to go the distance. We want it to work.

How mystifying, then, that so many marriages don't. As social diseases go, divorce has hit epidemic status. Just look at the numbers: According to U.S. statistics, there are more than 7.3 million men who are divorced. In any given year, there are going to be more than a million newly dissolved marriages. And it wasn't always like this. For people born in the 1930s and early 1940s, the odds that they would be divorced by their 10th anniversary was one in five. Statistics tell us that about half of all marriages will fail. One out of two is scary odds—your chances of surviving most major diseases are better than that. Your chances of avoiding divorce can be better, too, if you and your wife can spot and control the behavior that all too often takes couples from the altar to the lawyer's office.

DODGING THE BIG D

This chapter covers two key areas: how to sidestep divorce and how to deal with its aftermath. What we *don't* cover is how to get a divorce. For that, you'll need expert, detailed help beyond the scope of this book. And besides, when it comes to divorce, every particular case calls for its own unique breakup process.

Still, if you're in the midst or on the far-side of marital breakup, you'll find plenty of information to help you through, or at least to understand how your breakup could have happened. That way, you'll be better able to avoid future breakups when you begin the process of meeting someone new.

There's also plenty of useful advice here for the rest of you—the happily married guys who wonder...and worry, just a little bit. What you'll find in the next few pages can help you steer your marriage well clear of divorce's craggy shoals.

"In fact, if you are worried a little bit about your marriage, it's a good sign, not a bad one. For a marriage to go the distance, you have to be vigilant—you have to constantly work at it. Men who don't worry, even a little bit, don't work at it," says Scott Stanley, Ph.D., co-director of the Center for Marital and Family Studies at the University of Denver and co-author of *Fighting for Your Marriage.*

Dr. Stanley and his co-author Howard Markman, Ph.D., have spent more than 20 years studying the dynamics of married couples. To say their experience has given them keen insight into the sacred institution would be an understatement. They've observed so much interaction between couples that they say they can predict, with 93 percent accuracy, which couples will stay together and which are headed for divorce. Because, like a physical illness, divorce has its symptoms, and Dr. Stanley says that certain couples are in higher-risk categories than others. Here are some of the biggest indicators that your marriage could end up on the rocks.

Marrying young. Couples who get married in their teens or early twenties often have difficulties because neither of them has finished growing up. "You're always going to change as you get older, but changes you make at this age—where you're really on the cusp of adulthood—can be radical and profound. A lot of early marriages can't handle the strain. Or when people reach an age where they've matured a little bit, they may find that they've grown apart from the person they married at 18 or 20," says Dr. Stanley.

Coming from divorce. If you or your spouse have parents who split, that family history puts you at risk of divorce. "Having parents who divorce sends a message that this is acceptable, that marriage is temporary," says Dr. Stanley. It makes it a lot easier for you to justify leaving when your own marriage hits a trouble spot. People who come from families where there is no divorce are much more likely to stay in the marriage and try to work at it."

Religious or cultural differences. From his work, Dr. Stanley has found that interracial unions or marriages where the couple come from widely diverse religious or cultural backgrounds are often problematic. "There's nothing wrong with diversity, but sometimes people can have such diverse beliefs and values that it can cause problems that are hard to reconcile. This is not an argument for marrying within your race, religion, or cultural background. But it's a valid research finding," says Dr. Stanley.

Avoiding conflict. Many couples believe that, if they're truly meant for each other, they'll never have disagreement. Hogwash, says Sherry Lehman, a sex therapist in Cleveland and author of *Seven Days to Better Sex and a More Loving Relationship.* "Conflict is inevitable. People are going to fight. It's a healthy part of marriage," she says.

If, on the other hand, you find yourself anxious about talking with your spouse because you always seem to end up fighting, that, too, is a warning sign. "But it's not a sign that you have to stop fighting; it's a sign that you have to learn better conflict-resolution skills," says Dr. Stanley.

How Are You Doing?

How is *your* marriage going? To help get a bead on the status of your relationship, in their book *Fighting for Your Marriage*, Scott Stanley, Ph.D., co-director of the Center for Marital and Family Studies at the University of Denver; Howard Markman, Ph.D.; and Susan Blumberg, Ph.D., have couples ask themselves the following questions. If you answer "yes" to one or two every now and then, that's fine. Everyone goes through a rough patch. But if you're consistently answering "yes" to a lot of these questions, it's a good idea to start working on better communication and conflict resolution with your partner.

1. Do routine discussions often erupt into destructive arguments?
2. Do you or your partner often withdraw or refuse to talk about important issues?
3. Do you or your partner often disregard what the other says, or do you often use put-downs?
4. Does it seem as if the things you say to your partner are often heard much more negatively than you intended?
5. Do you feel that there has to be a winner and a loser when you disagree?
6. Does your relationship often take a backseat to other interests?
7. Do you often think about what it would be like to be with someone else?
8. Does the thought of being with your partner a few years from now disturb you?

Unfair expectations. Too often, when we marry, we unconsciously put heavy expectations on our spouses—expectations they could never possibly fulfill. "Expecting someone to always make you happy. Or to give you the kind of respect and attention your parents never gave you. To solve all your personal problems. These are very real needs people grapple with. And when they get married, sometimes they assume that their spouse is going to be the magical prince or princess who resolves all unresolved issues," says Dr. Stanley. Such an impossible situation just invites friction and conflict.

Failure to communicate. Like the proverbial bad penny, poor communication turns up time and again as the root cause of many marital troubles.

"And it manifests itself in a lot of different ways," says Lehman. For example, not telling your spouse when you have a problem or concern, but instead letting it back up on you as resentment. Or sharing a problem you have but not listening to her needs and concerns. Or simply reaching a point where you both start tuning each other out. "By and large, the single best predictor of a couple's marital health is how well they communicate," says Dr. Stanley. "This is the foundation."

Divorce Fact

According to *The Divorce Sourcebook*, the first recorded divorce in the United States happened in 1639. A Massachusetts court granted the divorce to a woman—turned out her husband already had a wife. (The court fined him, sent him to prison, then exiled him.)

WHAT YOU CAN DO

Some of the factors given in this chapter are what Dr. Stanley calls static symptoms—things you can't change, so you just have to learn to live with them. Others are dynamic symptoms—factors that the two of you can work on to stave off an impending divorce, or to help minimize the risk factors you can't change. Here's what you need to focus on to do both.

Know when to talk and when to listen. Understanding that it's okay to disagree and have conflict is only the beginning. Dr. Stanley says next you have to learn to fight fairly, in such a way that you both manage to air your grievances and feel that the other has heard you. In his PREP (Prevention and Relationship Enhancement Program) system, Dr. Stanley and his colleagues teach couples these skills. One of the most important is simply giving one another time to talk, without interruption. Using what's called a speaker-listener technique, the person listening can paraphrase what the speaker has just said. Then, the listener gets the floor and it's the speaker's turn to listen. "It seems forced and artificial at first, but it helps couples who are having trouble talking problems out," says Dr. Stanley. "It reassures that people have a chance to talk about what's bothering them, and by paraphrasing what was just said, the speaker is reassured that the listener really heard and understood her."

Look behind the little things. She yells at you because you always go out with the boys on Thursday night. You crab at her every time you find panty hose in the shower. "We all snipe about little things, but pay attention if you're constantly harping on one another about little things. Often, couples fight about small, petty stuff to avoid talking about the bigger issue behind it," says Dr. Stanley. Maybe she yells at you for going out, not because she doesn't want you to have any fun but because she's feeling like the two of you aren't spending enough time together. She misses you. Try to see past the moment and you may be able to get at the root of a real issue that the two of you can solve. "And often, simply finding the real issue is helpful in itself. Couples feel like they've come closer together just because they've gotten to the root of something," says Dr. Stanley.

Leave no stone unturned. When couples have difficulties with each other, sometimes the impulse to cut bait and run is almost overpowering. "When you hit some serious obstacles in your marriage, or if you're feeling like it's time to throw in the towel, that's when it's important to ask yourself—

have I really tried everything I could to save the marriage? Have I tried to talk it out? Have I sought counseling? Have I done all I can?" says Dr. Stanley. When framed in that context, most couples usually find they haven't reached the end of their rope yet. "Which is good. It means that there are still options available to them," says Dr. Stanley.

Know when to ask for help. Some situations are just intrinsically harmful in a marriage, and you may not be able to resolve them on your own. If one of you is abusing drugs or alcohol. If your arguments turn to physical violence. If the bad in your marriage has so outweighed the good that you don't love or hate one another—you just feel ambivalent. In these cases, it's time to seek help. "Don't wait until it is an emergency situation," suggests Shirley Zussman, Ed.D., a certified sex and marital therapist in private practice in New York City.

"You may find that the marriage can't be saved. But at least you will have tried and you will have gotten an outside opinion on the problem from an impartial observer," says Lehman.

AFTER THE DIVORCE

After you've exhausted every venue of help, you may find that there's only one option left—divorce. Whether you've had one, are contemplating one, or are in the midst of one, you have our sympathies and good wishes. You also have a new set of issues to be concerned with—issues you don't want to neglect. We've provided a brief outline below to help you focus on some essentials during this difficult time.

Set new priorities. If your marriage is ending, don't dwell on it, or pore over it, trying to rethink past actions. "What's done is done. The important thing is to get past the blame and try to learn from what has happened," says Lehman. That means setting new priorities for yourself and your future. It also means setting goals that you can achieve as an individual, not as a couple. "Sometimes writing down a list of things that are important to you can help you focus on what's ahead rather than what's behind you," suggests Lehman.

Protect everyone's interests. No matter how amicable your parting may be, it would be wise of you to consult a lawyer before signing on the dotted line. Yes, it could be seen as provocative or a sign that you're out for blood. Try to spin it differently: You're protecting everyone's interests, especially the kids', if you have them. In her book, *The Divorce Sourcebook*, Dawn Bradley Berry, J.D., points out that divorce is not just an emotionally wrenching event but a complex legal issue, too. For a free list of divorce lawyers in your area, contact the American Academy of Matrimonial Lawyers at (312) 263-6477. Remember, no one ever got upset because an agreement was spelled out too closely.

Spend time smartly with your kids. If you have children—and a lot of divorced couples do—then the emotional ante on divorce is even higher.

"It's going to take a toll on you and the kids. Most of the time, children end up living with the mother, and men don't realize how much they miss the kids until they're gone," says Lehman. If you have visitation rights or a joint custody situation, be sure to spend that time wisely with your kids. "Make sure they know that they can ask you questions about what's going on. Don't ever let them doubt that you love them," says Lehman. As hard as this is for you, it's twice as hard for them. How you treat them now could very well effect how they cope with their own marriages in the future.

Be civil when seeing your ex. Sooner or later, you're bound to be in the same room with her again. Dealing with your ex can be a vexing situation. It's hard to know how to be around someone whom you once shared a life with. If your parting was acrimonious, you may be tempted to fire a few shots across her bow; or you may feel compelled to respond to one of her not-so-subtle digs.

Or maybe you'll behave the best way: in a civil manner, with mutual respect.

"No one says that you have to be friends with your ex-wife, but if you have to deal with her on a regular basis, there's not much point in being antagonistic," says Lehman. That's true even if she is antagonistic—in fact, especially then. Try to rise above it; don't respond to any invitations to re-open old wounds. "For you to get on with your life, you need to get past the blame. What's done is done. Even if she can't move on, you should," says Lehman.

Walk—don't jump—back in. Finally, remember that man was not meant to be alone. After your marriage has ended, you may feel like the whole event was something you never want to get into again. This may lead you to become a bit of a social hermit. Or you may go just the opposite route; you may jump in the sack with the first willing woman you can find, if only to erase the memory of your ex.

We're not saying that you should become a ladies' man or a monk. "What's probably a better idea is to take a few months off from women. Spend that time adjusting to single life, or being with your kids, if you have them," says Lehman. Divorce, regardless of whether you initiated it, is going to hit you like a death in the family. In other words, you should allow yourself time to grieve and come to terms with what has happened. Be patient with yourself. "It may take a year or more, but by then you may feel ready to get back into a relationship, this time a bit wiser than you were before," says Lehman.

2

MENTAL MASTERY

YOUR SEXUAL FOUNDATION

There is no mystery to how a man's sexual parts develop. Testosterone rushes in during puberty and—voilà!—we become mature, fertile sexual beings. It's preprogrammed. It's basic plumbing and chemistry. We can understand this. But what is it that shapes a man's *attitudes* about sex? What is it that gives each man a unique perspective on what is erotic, attractive, exciting, comforting—or vulgar, lewd, out of bounds? Hard, rational science has no clear response.

The superficial answer, of course, is personal experience. But it goes much deeper than that. The way you think right now about sex is the culmination of a myriad of events, the majority of which happened many years past in your life. In fact, by the age of 14, much of your sexual foundation, your fundamental attitudes and preferences regarding sex, is already established for life. Understand those distant events, forces, and incidences that shaped your sexual attitudes and you'll have a far better grasp of how to make sex better for you now and tomorrow.

Assessing Your Foundations

Laugh a lot during sex? Have a hard time talking about the whole subject? Obsessed with large breasts? Chances are that events occurred during your adolescence that helped shape these traits. Here are some questions to ask yourself to help you learn why you are as you are sexually.

- Did my parents talk to me about sex?
- Did I see physical affection between my parents?
- Was there affection toward the children?
- Was I exposed to pornography at a young age, and if yes, how did it affect my thoughts about sex?
- Were my social advances routinely rejected by girls, or did I have some successes as well?
- Did I lie or brag excessively about sexual exploits to friends? If yes, why?
- Were my initial sexual experiences successful or embarrassing?
- Did any traumatic event occur in my youth that affected my thinking about sex?
- What sexual memories from my adolescence stand out most strongly? Why? How did these experiences affect my sexual attitudes?

Where's Teacher?

The first thing to understand is that when it comes to sex, you are self-taught. There is no sex school for boys or girls. We don't take any final exams. For the most part, we men learn to "do it" through trial and error. And each of us develops a unique curriculum of lessons and experiences.

Some of the lessons are forced on us, such as learning to cope with the uncontrollable, persistent, and ever-so-evident erections we experience at puberty. Some lessons we choose, such as working up the courage at age 13 to call pretty Betty Bonner and ask her to a community center dance and then getting over her rejection.

Ideally, men proceed on a course of lifelong sexual learning and earn continuing education credits regularly. But not everyone does. Some men remain 14 years old sexually for life, says psychologist Harris Teller, Ph.D., assistant professor of special programs at National University in San Diego. Teller operates a private practice and has spent 30 years working with teens at Sweetwater Union High School District in Chula Vista, California.

The problem with that is that boys don't need partners or guides to discover or enjoy the pleasures of sexual stimulation and release, says Barry McCarthy, Ph.D., a psychologist in Washington, D.C., and co-author with his wife, Emily, of the book *Sexual Awareness* as well as other titles. To some boys, sex means a well-handled penis and the selfish joy of orgasm, and not much else. So from a sexual standpoint, these pubescent boys may view women as interchangeable objects to use and discard. Obviously, that attitude, if sustained into adulthood, leads to poor relationships.

While the recipe for healthy, mutually satisfying sexual coupling does involve physical stimulation and release, it adds the ingredients of sharing and emotional interplay and a sort of spiritual connectiveness, suggests Dr. McCarthy.

Those ingredients are things that can be learned, at any time. Some boys come by them relatively effortlessly, some don't. We can grow beyond our 14-year-old perceptions, whatever they are. Society can help, but it can hinder as well; pervasive nudity, lewd advertising, even the celebrity status of supermodels contribute to the objectifying of women. If all the images around you reinforce this juvenile attitude, why grow up? And so many men don't.

Adolescence, Puberty, and Attitudes

If real life is where we learn about sex, then the lessons begin the moment we join the planet, says psychologist Galdino F. Pranzarone, Ph.D., professor of psychology at Roanoke College in Salem, Virginia. Through our infant and childhood years we are bombarded with sexual images and incidents. This is the time when the foundations for love and intimacy are laid. We play "doctor" with schoolmates. We watch our teachers, our parents, our

Are You Sexually Mature?

Answer yes or no to the following questions:

1. Is the primary question in your mind most of the time, "Am I or am I not going to get laid?"
2. Can you regularly engage in hugging, caressing, touching, cuddling, and/or intimate communication with your sexual partner without insisting that it culminate in intercourse or feeling disappointed if it doesn't?
3. Do you worry that your penis is smaller than average?
4. If a sexual encounter turns out poorly—you misfire or can't get it up or don't come explosively—are you devastated?
5. Are you constantly thinking about sex, pursuing sex, or engaging in sex, nearly to the exclusion of all else?
6. Do you engage in fantasies of completely socially unacceptable sexual acts?
7. Have your views, attitudes, and approaches to sex changed substantially since you were 20 years old?

Now analyze your answers.

1. A yes answer is a sign of youth. If you are older than 25 and answered yes, chances are that you need to get a life. And chances are that the reason you aren't getting much sex is because you have "desperate" written all over you.
2. A yes answer indicates sexual maturity, says Barry McCarthy, Ph.D., a psychologist in Washington, D.C., and co-author with his wife, Emily, of the book *Sexual Awareness* as well as other titles. A sexually mature man "has many sexual gears," has developed and enjoys many modes of sexual communication, and is able to give, receive, and enjoy "sexual pleasuring" of all sorts, he says.
3. Trick question. This has little to do with sexual maturity since surveys show that 75 percent of all men believe this, says Dr. McCarthy. Obvi-

neighbors interact. We see lovers kissing in the park. We observe salacious billboards. We get told to leave the room when something "dirty" comes on television, and then when we peek, we see that "dirty" means two people bouncing while naked. These sexual images are "wired into our brains by age 7 or 8," says Dr. Pranzarone. And these impressions become part of our sexual fantasy life when we hit puberty.

It is these building blocks, coupled with the experiences of puberty, that mold our lifelong sexual persona, says Dr. Teller.

Of course, puberty is among the most tumultuous times in any person's

ously, 75 percent of men's penises can't be smaller than average, or "average" would mean nothing. And besides, says Dr. McCarthy, size really, really, really doesn't matter. Really. Technique and attitude are *so* much more important—and you can do something about them.

4. Men, as well as women, have negative sexual experiences from time to time, says Dr. McCarthy. This is normal. "People are going to have bad sex experiences," he says. "Learning to accept those, learn from them, recover from them is part of good sexuality." The sexually mature man is resilient and is not devastated by a less-than-perfect performance or experience. "The truth is," says Dr. McCarthy, "that less than half of the time are both people equally desirous, equally aroused, and equally orgasmic. And 5 to 15 percent of the time the sexual experiences are really *blah*—mediocre or failures. Positive expectations are fine, but you need to be realistic."

5. Or does it just seem that way? About 15 to 20 percent of a sexually mature man's life is devoted to the sexual pursuit—mentally, physically, or both, says Dr. McCarthy. That's a lot, if you do the math—about 4 hours a day. And most of that is pursuing rather than doing.

6. Sexually healthy, mature men and women do fantasize and are comfortable with fantasy, says Dr. McCarthy. What makes fantasies sexually exciting usually is that the subject matter is illicit or forbidden in nature and often involve people other than your regular partner. Fantasies are healthy so long as you are able to distinguish between fantasy and reality, between imagined and actual behavior, he says.

7. The man who still views and approaches sex the way he did when he was 20 is immature, says Dr. McCarthy. Our sexual sensibility should become more sensitive and sensuous as we grow older, and our thinking much less penis-oriented, he suggests. The sexually mature male is more concerned with loving and sharing pleasure than he is with just getting off, he says.

life, all flux and motion, making this a chancy time to be establishing lifetime values and preferences.

Imagine you are on a roller coaster. You dip, you dive, you're flung around curves, you zip up steep mountains and then, losing all momentum, roll almost to a stop. With gravity tugging you backward, you inch—clack, clack, clack—ever so slowly, just a bit higher, just a tiny bit more. Then whoosh, you're plunging again.

That's how Dr. Teller views puberty—a time when hormones soar and plunge and scream and fade unpredictably.

As a result, puberty also is a time when your world is spinning socially. Your daddy doesn't hug you anymore. Your mommy doesn't kiss you. Your friends taunt you about your cracking voice and anything and everything else they can latch onto, and yet you wouldn't be caught dead without your friends. A time when you lose all train of thought the instant a particular pretty girl—or any girl or reasonable facsimile thereof—smiles, sighs, pouts, or just breathes in your vicinity or crosses her legs or brushes against you. Boing! Your penis springs to attention and warm, fuzzy feelings overwhelm you and you tingle all over and drift into sexual dreamland. You jolt back to reality, and your face flushes red. You squirm in embarrassment, hoping some-how to disguise or deflate the tent in your lap that you're sure everyone is staring at and snickering about.

These are the days when you start thinking differently and for yourself, says Dr. Teller. You feel this great need to be independent, and at the same time, you feel extreme pressure to fit in. You begin to question all authority and wonder why you should or shouldn't do anything anyone tells you—because your mind is developing new thinking skills. You're physically awkward, enduring cruelly inconsistent growth spurts. And you're extraordinarily self-conscious and cer-tain everyone is whispering behind your back because, no contest, you are the silliest looking creature and biggest fool that ever walked the earth. You know it. You look in the mirror every morning and ask God why.

"The roller-coaster years," Dr. Teller calls them. And it's during this period of physical, sexual, social, and psychological development and discovery that your essential sexual personality and self-esteem shake out. And by age 14, it's pretty much set, says Dr. Teller.

THE PARTICULAR INFLUENCES

What specifically shapes your sexual mindset during these years? Here are some key themes.

Genetics. First up, of course, is the luck of the draw, the unique gene combination we are encoded with. It determines nearly everything about us physically—and some things about us emotionally. Our gene coding deter-mines how strong a sex drive we are blessed or cursed with and, scientists in-creasingly are coming to believe, our dominant sexual preference, says Dr. Teller. The best advice here is that we should maximize the hand we are dealt.

Our parents. Extreme behaviors by parents can warp kids, says Dr. Mc-Carthy. And that warping can last a lifetime. Examples include "parents who are sexual in front of their kids or who coerce the kids to be sexual or the other extreme—parents who won't talk at all about sex."

Kids have a harder time with sexual expression if they come from a household where nudity and bodily functions were treated as shameful and embarrassing, adds Dr. Teller. The opposite is true, too: A respectfully open, loving, hug-filled family can give a child the sexual knowledge and confi-dence needed to overcome lots of negative external influences.

God Only Knows

A wise woman, his grandmother, assisted San Diego psychologist Harris Teller, Ph.D., in unraveling the mysteries of sex.

She was, he says, "my mentor, the one who told me everything about the world, whom I trusted absolutely. She had made it very, very clear very early on that there wasn't anything that we couldn't talk about. So when I first discovered masturbation and discovered sexual thoughts and all these other things, and being at the same time highly religious, I thought absolutely that the devil had taken me over and I was an evil person.

"In one of my down moods, my grandmother said, 'What's wrong?' And I said, 'Well, I am really ashamed,' and I told her what was going on. She began to explain to me that sexual feelings are a natural part of life. That sex is a natural part of the way in which we express ourselves. That everybody is sexual, but some people choose not to act on it. Others do. That sexual feelings come at different times.

"Then with a kind of smile on her face she asked me if I believed in God. I told her that I did. She said, 'Then I can tell you a little secret. The secret is this: If God made anything better than sex, he's kept it for himself.' "

The first time. If your first sexual experience with a partner is seriously traumatic, it can have long-lasting negative effects, say Dr. McCarthy and Dr. Teller. Otherwise, it probably has little influence. "For most males, the first intercourse is a big, important learning, and they often brag about it. But even so, it's often not great sex—they come fast or before penetration. Or they get scared or don't get an erection or have trouble or whatever. Of course, they never admit that to their friends. For most males, that first time is just something they sort of just check off the list." Been there, done that, got the T-shirt, on to the next big-ticket thrill ride.

On the other hand, if you were raped or injured or berated severely during the first encounter, it could have quite a chilling or distorting effect on how your sexual persona develops, note Dr. Teller and Dr. McCarthy. Being berated sexually by a woman is one of men's greatest fears, says Dr. McCarthy.

The media and culture. "In the movies, sex is always intense and nonverbal and always perfect, and you never have to worry about HIV or contraception," says Dr. McCarthy. "The media's presentation of sexuality is very unrealistic and makes people feel inadequate. I think that it has a harmful effect on how boys develop sexually. It promotes unrealistic expectations—the idea that you are a performing machine, that what matters sexually is how big your penis is and how self-confident you are and that you are a perfect-looking person under 30. It sets up a performance criterion for male sexuality that is unrealistic and far too rigid. And that's tough on people. The reality in life for people is that they are not movie stars."

The timbre of our times and social pressures. Our view of sexuality is colored by the tone of the decade in which we came of age and of the community in which we lived and of the people we hung with. These factors affect the sorts of conflicting pressures and expectations our friends, parents, and teachers put upon us.

Just consider some of the sexual and moral clichés and icons attached to recent eras and it becomes obvious how the sexual clime of our place in time can affect our perceptions. Were the 1950s Ozzie and Harriet and Marilyn Monroe? The 1960s: JFK, swinging, and love-ins? The 1970s: bra burning and Annie Hall? The 1980s: "Just Say No" and safe sex? Unquestionably, the times you were born in helped shape your sexual preferences and thinking.

UNDERSTANDING WOMEN'S NEEDS

So maybe you aren't from Mars and your lover isn't from Venus, despite what those books say. Maybe the two of you are from Pluto and Saturn. Or Phoenix and Paris. Or First Street and Third Street. The fact is that men and women *are* different in at least a few crucial ways. Biologists can prove this. They know your lady has different stuff in her DNA than you do. She has different hormones and different biological needs and purposes. And, consequently, different emotional needs.

"A woman needs to feel emotionally close to make love. A man needs to make love to feel emotionally close," declares Daniel Beaver, a marriage and family therapist from Walnut Creek, California, and author of *Beyond the Marriage Fantasy* and *More Than Just Sex.* Yogi mystics cite paradoxes like this as evidence of "Maya," the great cosmic joke inherent in all existence.

So if you want good loving, we suggest that you develop a sense of Maya. And learn to give women what they need. Then you'll get what you need.

Women, in particular, have a need for romance—the sort of close, loving attention usually found early in dating, notes Beaver. When they don't get it, they often become depressed, withdrawn, sexually frustrated, and eventually angry. And through anger, they finally get the attention they want. Better we give them positive attention regularly, notes Beaver. How? Since this book is about sex, we'll start our advice in the bedroom. Then we'll discuss ways to fulfill a woman's broader emotional needs.

SATISFYING HER SEXUALLY

Women's sexual needs are not universal, any more than men's needs are. Each woman is unique and deserves respect for that. Nor do a woman's needs stay the same from day to day, year to year, even moment to moment, notes relationships counselor John Gray, Ph.D., author of the series of mega-selling books with Mars and Venus in the titles.

You want to be a great, sensitive lover? Your best strategy here is *not* to memorize a half-dozen routines and formulas. Rather, put on the safari hat and treat each sexual encounter as a new expedition into uncharted territory. We're not telling you to forget what your woman has told you she likes. We're saying don't get mired in techniques to the point that you become a rote performer.

There *are* some physical and mental skills to learn, like ejaculation control and passionate foreplay. But forget routines; that is, set patterns in your lovemaking sessions. Routines are routines, says Beaver. She'll catch on and get bored, no matter how skilled you are. And you'll quit relaxing and enjoying yourself. You'll start performing. Performing the routine. You don't need to be a performer. Next thing you know, you'll have performance anxiety. And you'll start competing. Competing with yourself, competing with movies and all kinds of imaginary standards. Sex is not a sport, sport. Sex is not a sport. Don't keep score. Don't rush the goal line.

You want to meet your woman's sexual needs? Remember this: She's different from any other woman you've ever seen or known. She's different today than she was yesterday. *Vive la différence!* Get into the moment and you'll get into your woman in a way she likes, advises Beaver. Forget about intercourse, he says. Focus on sensuality, on loving, on intimate communication—with words, looks, touch. That is sex play. That is foreplay. That is the stuff that the hottest sex of your life will be made of.

Sex is free verse. Sex is jazz improvisation. Learn enough skills and techniques to play the melody and then make up the music as you go, and you'll be playing her song.

Foreplay. It's a clinical term. It's essential. Women need it. Men do, too. But a lot of us don't realize it, says Barry McCarthy, Ph.D., a psychologist in Washington, D.C., and author of *Male Sexual Awareness*, among other titles. We may have gotten overly focused on orgasm at puberty by furiously getting off quickly when masturbating so as not to get caught. Well, now we want to get caught. Get caught up in the act. Women most of the time need a gentle, loving warmup. And a warm cooldown afterward, too. And when we get into the spirit of that, we find incredible pleasure there, too, says Dr. McCarthy.

Take your time. Stroke your penis while you talk to her and kiss her neck and trace the inside of her arm, and enjoy the sensations *you* feel. This is being responsible for your own pleasure. This is giving pleasure. This is getting the

How to Make Love to a Woman

Writers Lucy Sanna and Kathy Miller surveyed hundreds of women about matters of romance, love, and lovemaking. They reported their findings in the book *How to Romance the Woman You Love—The Way She Wants You To!* Women told them that they wanted men to take their time, establish a strong sensual connection, and clearly desire to give love and pleasure.

Women, according to the survey, view lovemaking as an ongoing, 24-hours-a-day process—not just something that takes place in the bedroom. If we want them to feel really hot in the bedroom, here are some things they say we must do out of the bedroom.

1. Flirt playfully. Frequently. Not just when you want sex. But in the market. In the restaurant. In front of friends. In the car. In the living room. It's fun. It's reassuring.
2. Make touching a way of life. Nonsexual touching. Cuddling, kissing, caressing, hugging. Run a hand along her cheek. Gently move a hair from her eyes. Put your arm around her shoulder. And many women report appreciating loving, unexpected, and tactfully executed secret intimate touches (under the table, in the cloakroom, and so on) while in public.
3. Smile at her with your eyes. Notice her in a complimentary, admiring way from across the room. Appreciate how she moves. Appreciate her like you would any attractive woman.
4. Compliment her while smiling at her.

Then, when you wish to seduce your lover:

5. Set a mood. Turn off the TV. Dim the lights. Light the candles. Put on the romantic music. And put the focus on her.
6. Relax. Talk sweetly. Spend some time just caressing her with your lips, your breath, your sensuous words, your touch. And don't rush the undressing business.
7. Tell her things you love about her.
8. Touch her. Gently. All over. Keep touch tender. If you go with the flow, you will alternate heavy with light when things get hot and the act is really rolling. But at first, light is almost always best. And clumsy is never cool.
9. Take your time, say Sanna and Miller. Slow down when you're getting overheated. She appreciates that.

focus off intercourse. This is showing your woman that she is important to you. That it excites you to touch her, to gaze upon her, to give her pleasure, says Beaver. "This is also telling her that you know that it takes her longer to get aroused—about 15 to 20 minutes—and that you're willing to spend the time for her," adds Shirley Zussman, Ed.D., a certified sex and marital therapist in private practice in New York City.

And, hey, don't rush to her crotch. Pretend that her crotch is too hot to touch. Pretend that if you touch it for more than a second, you'll burn. So only touch it around the edges until you're really sure she's turned on. Don't rip off her panties, advises Dr. Gray. Don't pull her panties down too quickly, he says. Take them off slowly. And only when you can feel she's wet, or when she thrusts against your hand each time it's in the vicinity. In fact, tease her sometimes, says Dr. Gray. Start to pull them down, then pull them back up, and devote more attention elsewhere.

This is a woman's need. She needs to be romanced. She doesn't want you rushing things. She doesn't want to be treated like the same ol' same ol'. She wants to believe that you're there for her. So be there.

CONNECTING OUTSIDE THE BEDROOM

A woman wants to feel loving support from her partner, says Dr. Gray. She wants good communication. She wants to feel that you and she are in touch and encouraging and supporting one another, he says. She needs to feel these things in order to enjoy sex with you. She can only feel those things if they are true.

One huge mistake men make with women is that we fall into the role of Mr. Fix-It, suggests Dr. Gray. And women find this terribly frustrating. They feel that we aren't listening to them when they bring us a problem and we give it thought and offer advice, he says. We think we're supporting and helping them by doing that. They think we're not really hearing them, says Dr. Gray. What they really want is empathy, he says. They want to know that we understand what they are going through. They don't want advice—usually. When they specifically ask for advice, they may want advice, he says. Or it may be that they simply have learned a proven way to get our attention. Because we men generally love to be Mr. Fix-It. It makes us feel needed and useful. And we aren't always really patient about listening to our partner rattle on and on. Especially about things that could be oh, so easily fixed.

But, says Dr. Gray, always remember: Saying that something can be oh, so easily fixed belittles its importance, its significance, and communicates to the woman that you don't respect her or understand her.

Here's another generality that tends to hold true, says Dr. Gray: Women work off frustration and anger and stress by talking things out. We need to learn how to let them do that without critiquing, criticizing, solution-izing, or flipping on the TV and surfing through the channels. We do that by actually paying some attention and expressing empathy, says Dr. Gray.

How can a man communicate empathy?

One way, taught by numerous therapists, is to practice what is called active listening or mirroring. Here's an example.

She says: "It just infuriates me that Johnny leaves his dirty clothes strewn all over the floor for me to pick up and never, ever makes his bed or cleans his room. And I have to do these things after I come home from working hard in the office all day."

He says: "You're frustrated with Johnny. He leaves his clothes on the floor and doesn't clean his room. And you work hard all day at the office."

And, in her mind, the message clicks, "He gets it; he understands where I'm coming from, what I'm feeling."

This sort of technique can degenerate into being just a technique or a mind game, warns Wendy Fader, Ph.D., a licensed psychologist and certified sex therapist in private practice in Boca Raton, Florida. And this isn't the way people in the real world tend to talk. But it often is taught in therapy so that people can learn and practice the art of listening to their partners, hearing what they are saying, and checking that they've gotten it right. Listening, hearing, and checking, regardless of technique or form used, is a positive way of communicating understanding and empathy, she says. Improvise your own

10 Ways to Stay in Touch

We communicate a lot with little actions. Here are a few that tell your lady that you really do care about her, really do think about her, really do appreciate her. Little gestures like this go a long way and help her feel like you two are really connected.

Do the oral thing. Tell her you love her. Now. And again. Several times a day. And mean it. We know, you told her back in 1985 and you've been proving it ever since. Sorry. That doesn't count. You have to say it—lots.

Consult her. Ask her for advice and really listen to it.

Buy cut flowers. Cut flowers. You'll find them at most grocery stores, and they don't cost an arm and a leg. Buy pretty ones. We know, a potted plant seems so much more practical and lasting. Don't even think about it, says relationships counselor John Gray, Ph.D., author of the series of mega-selling books with Mars and Venus in the titles. Only cut flowers will do. The kind that wilt, wither, and die in five days. That's romance. Because then you must go out and buy more and show her again that you're remembering her and think she is special. And you do need to do that. The potted plant problem, says Dr. Gray, is that she sees it as just so much more work. Something else she's expected to tend to. The cut flowers say, "You're special and deserve an atmosphere of beauty." And don't just bring the flowers when you're dating. Make cut flowers a part of your weekly love budget. Every week.

Order for her occasionally. At the restaurant, ask her what she's going to have. Ask her how she likes it. Then when the waiter or waitress comes to your table, order it for her. We suggest that you then turn to her and ask something like, "Is that right? And would you like anything else?" before placing your own

natural style of positive ways to show that you are hearing what your partner is saying, she recommends.

Another approach to listening to your woman and communicating empathy is recommended by writers Lucy Sanna and Kathy Miller who surveyed hundreds of women about what they find romantic. In their book, *How to Romance the Woman You Love—The Way She Wants You To!*, Sanna and Miller write that a woman wants you to listen to, appreciate, and understand her situation. So, they say, instead of trying to provide an answer, hold her. Offer comfort. Sympathize. Thank her for sharing with you. Let her know that you support her.

Women, say Sanna and Miller, want to know that you value them enough to set aside quality time just for being with them. So do it. Regularly. It is crucial for couples to set aside a few minutes each day to be with each other and talk about their day, says syndicated columnist Michael J. McManus, president of Marriage Savers in Bethesda, Maryland, and author of *Marriage Savers*. We haven't talked to a psychologist or marriage counselor who disagrees with that advice.

order. This proves to her that you really do pay attention to her, says Dr. Gray. That you really do listen (at least once in a while).

Report your findings. Any time you notice something lovely or delightful about her (the smell of her hair, the sparkle in her eyes when she laughs), tell her, say Lucy Sanna and Kathy Miller in their book *How to Romance the Woman You Love—The Way She Wants You To!*

Surprise her. Love notes, I-miss-you phone calls, unexpected niceties—the sappy stuff you did when you were first falling in love. Keep it up if you want to keep falling in love, recommend Sanna and Miller. Keep it up and keep it changing. A surprise is not a surprise unless it's unexpected.

Greet her. Forget the Ward Cleaver, "Honey, I'm home" holler. Find her. Face her. Hug her. Warmly. Make encountering her a high spot in your day any time you've been apart, say Sanna and Miller.

Work on your voice. Play with a tape recorder. Get the whine, the nag, the bitchy (sorry, but yeah, you can be a bit bitchy, bud) tones out of there whenever you're talking to the lady you love. Work on sounding pleasing. The tone of the voice means so much, says Isadora Alman, a sexologist, syndicated columnist of "Ask Isadora," and author of *New Ways to Meet New People*.

Hang up tauntingly. Learn this phrase, advise Sanna and Miller. And develop variations of it. Use it when you need to get off the phone with your beloved. Don't say, "I'd better get back to work now." Say, "I can't wait to see you later. Bye for now." Whew! Hot, hot, hot.

Be there. Offer to help when she is tired or overworked, advises Dr. Gray.

UNDERSTANDING YOUR NEEDS

What does a man need to truly enjoy sex? Sorry, the answer is *not* merely a live female body. Certainly, men can be selfish about sexual pleasure; it's the old stereotype, and it's partly true—most any partner will do for a guy if the goal is merely an orgasm. But for sex to be meaningful and rich for the typical man, according to Daniel Beaver, a marriage and family therapist from Walnut Creek, California, and author of *Beyond the Marriage Fantasy* and *More Than Just Sex*, he must:

- Feel emotionally at ease with the woman
- Not harbor resentments toward the woman
- Feel that the woman wants him and cares for him
- Relax and let go of anxiety
- Feel free of performance expectations—self-set or otherwise
- Not be self-conscious about how he looks, feels, sounds, and smells from second to second
- Feel free to express pleasure as he feels it (a woman needs the same)

And if those things just aren't clicking, the conversation will go something like this: "Look, do you want to talk about it?"

SHORT COURSE IN "OUTERCOURSE"

So how do we obtain these things? All it takes is a mindset, says Hollywood psychologist and sexologist Rachel Copelan, Ph.D., author of *100 Ways to Make Sex Sensational and 100% Safe*. And this is the mindset: In our sexual relationships, outercourse is just as valid as intercourse. Always. Outercourse is essential. Develop lusty sensuality. Get the emphasis on loving and giving pleasure and sex will sizzle and the threat of performance anxiety will evaporate, she says. There's absolutely nothing wrong with intercourse, she says. But it's only a piece of the pie. It's only a corner on this thing called sex. Learn to give and receive sexual pleasure without intercourse, and your ability to sense all sexual pleasure will multiply manifold—and so will your lady's.

Get the focus off your penis and off orgasm, agrees Barry McCarthy, Ph.D., a psychologist in Washington, D.C., and author of *Male Sexual Awareness*, among other titles. No obligation to even get hard. Just enjoy yourself. This is what is called nondemand pleasuring. His prescription is to practice, practice, practice. And if your partner is tired, you can love yourself. Honest. Relax and enjoy it. Doctor's orders.

Why learning this is so important, explains Beaver, is that another male quality is to transform everything into a competition—including sex. We set targets and goals, and if we can't find anyone else to compete with, we compete with ourselves. But when we do this in sex, we wipe out pleasure. Pleasure we need. Pleasure we want. Pleasure we deserve.

Lesson: A man needs to remind himself that sex is not a competition. It's not a spectator sport. We need not constantly be observing, critiquing, and judging our technique. Orgasm is not the goal. The only points awarded are for how well we lose contact with the outer world and how deeply we immerse and converse in the lively, loving, lusty language of touch and feel. Points do not flash on a backlit board. These points we feel. Deeply. Forever, traces reside in our memory when we get to this place, says Dr. Copelan. She calls it spiritual sex.

KEEP THE LINES OPEN

We need signals. We need encouragement. A man needs to feel that his partner enjoys having sex with him, says relationships counselor John Gray, Ph.D., author of the series of mega-selling books with Mars and Venus in the titles.

When a man feels that his partner enjoys their sexual adventures, then he will feel comfortable initiating sex, says Dr. Gray. But if his efforts to initiate sex meet frequent, unexplained rebuffs, or often require a serious sales job, in time he is likely to quit trying and lose interest. Sad, sad story.

A man needs communication. Open, clear communication.

Lesson: Ask for it. Ask for open, clear supportive communication about sex with your partner. And give it. Make it happen. That's your assignment. (For beginner's tips on how to effectively accomplish this task, see "Let's Talk Sex" on page 42.)

Let your woman know that you will not feel rejected or take it personally if, when she needs to say "not right now" she also makes it clear that she enjoys sex with you and will want it again, soon. Let her know that that kind of message will encourage you to try again, to continue initiating, says Dr. Gray.

Men need lots of reassurance from their partners, says Wendy Fader, Ph.D., a licensed psychologist and certified sex therapist in private practice in

Ask the Sex Doc

"Most men are so goal-oriented and competitive that they don't see the sexual experience as an experience but as a goal," says Wendy Fader, Ph.D., a psychologist and sex therapist in private practice in Boca Raton, Florida. "And the orgasm is the prize, rather than making love and sharing a sensual experience. A lot of times when couples come in here, I lay down an opening rule: no orgasms. Just enjoy one another. And that's a hard concept for a lot of guys to get."

Boca Raton, Florida. "It's important that women tell their partners that they find them attractive, that they're turned on by them, that they find them sexually exciting," says Dr. Fader. "Most men are pretty insecure about that." Men as well as women often are insecure naked, uncomfortable about how their partner perceives their body, she says.

Obviously, we feel better about our bodies when we exercise them, feed them right, and keep them in shape. That's part of good, healthy self-esteem, notes Seattle psychologist Arthur Wassmer, Ph.D., author of *Making Contact* and other books. But, even when we do all that, even in the best case, we still need to know that our lover looks beyond whatever we perceive to be our physical flaws and does find us sexually attractive, says Dr. Fader. How do you explain this need to your partner? You might ask her to read this section and ask her what she thinks about it all. Communicating "I feel loved when you..." messages, positively, appreciatively (not in any kind of blaming manner) also help get the message across.

TIME OUT

Men need time off, time to ourselves. We need to withdraw and mull things over or just have good, clean fun with buddies or go crawl under the hood of a car or climb a mountain from time to time, notes Dr. Gray. We simply cannot handle full-on, full-time, full-press, full-court intimacy. In fact, we begin to lose our delicate intimate feelings and get irritable and rather unlovable if a high level of continuously exhibited and expressed intimacy is demanded.

Men recharge by automatically alternating between intimacy and autonomy, says Dr. Gray. When we understand that about ourselves and make room for it in our relationships, we make our relationships stronger.

Dr. Gray explains it this way: Men have a hunger for intimacy. And after fulfilling it, they have a hunger for independence. And after fulfilling it, they have a hunger for intimacy. He uses a rubber band as an analogy. A man stretches away and springs back, stretches away and springs back. This is not a flaw. This is the nature of the beast.

What we need to understand, Dr. Gray says, is that women are different. They require a bit of wooing and soothing and reassurance before they again can feel close to someone who has pulled away. Pulling away feels like rejection to them. For us, absence makes the heart grow fonder. For them, there has been a break in the connection. And we have to redial their number and start the conversation all over again if we want to hear the tinkle in their laughter, see the sparkle in their eyes, feel the warmth in their touch.

Lesson: A man has a built-in thermostat. His intimacy engine is designed to alternately run hot and cold. That's how it maintains its equilibrium. When the engine is on the cold cycle, the man is not upset. He's just not talkative or touchy-feely. For relationship equilibrium it is important to practice graceful transitions between cycles. And when on cold cycle, to encourage our lover to talk some about her experiences and feelings when it's clear she's desiring more intimacy. That way she feels connected to us, even though we don't feel like talking. And we show we care about her by being there and listening and encouraging. This requires minimal effort and goes a long, long way, says Dr. Gray.

An important caveat: Not all sex experts agree with Dr. Gray's theories on intimacy. Nor do they agree that men and women are so vastly different in their need for intimacy. We all have need for intimacy, notes Dr. Zussman, but express it in different ways and at different times. We all have a need for space, too. And again, there are tremendous variations in how much space we need and under what circumstances. What we can all agree on: Get to know yourself, what gets in the way of your being intimate with your partner, how to get close, and how to know when you feel too closed in.

MAKE A FRIEND

Many men are so emotionally needy, says Dr. Fader. And they do not express emotion well, do not talk intimately with other men, and expect to get absolutely all their needs filled through their relationship with their lover. Whoa! That's a lot to expect.

"This is a problem we have especially in the United States," says Dr. Fader. "We don't teach our little boys to have close, communicative relationships with their friends. It's all competition, beating the other, snickering together about girls. But basically it doesn't have to do with revealing themselves to one another. Men don't have intimate friends. They have what I call sports buddies."

"Men," says Dr. McCarthy, "are taught not to express emotions, and often the only way they know to experience closeness and feelings of intimacy is through intercourse."

"What happens," says Dr. Fader, "is that men end up becoming very emotionally needy in their sexual and emotional relationships. Because they expect to get everything from their partner. And they can't. It's impossible. So, overwhelmingly, I see a lot of loneliness in men."

Lesson: Take up tribal drumming. Just joking. But we do need to find and cultivate some male friends we can trust and really, truly can express fears and feelings with, advise Beaver and Dr. Fader and others.

We're beginning to make strides here. "I think some recognition needs to be given that men, especially younger men, are changing and are learning to express their emotions verbally more than they have in the past," adds Dr. Zussman.

LIGHTEN UP

Stop being so damn serious. We have to stop doing things that cause us pain, says Beaver. Learn to have fun. We need to have fun. Real fun. Men need to experience pleasure that is not work- or competition-related, says Beaver. But, he says, we pretty much have to retrain ourselves to do it.

Sex by the Numbers

Eighty-nine percent of men say their wife is their best friend.

SOURCE: *The Janus Report on Sexual Behavior*

Lesson: Find activities that provide pleasure and that you can be passionate about that are not performance- and achievement-oriented, Beaver advises. Break the "I have to be producing something in order to have fun" syndrome, he says. Learn to just sit on the beach and relax and enjoy it, he says. Most of us can't, he says, because we think we need to be "doing" something.

Learn to have pure, simple fun for fun's sake, advises Beaver. And that's a big order, he admits. But learn it, and we see benefits in all facets of our life.

ACHIEVING A BALANCED LIFE

Sorry I'm late, boss, but my wife really needed it this morning. We just stayed at it for a while. Lost all sense of time. I'm kinda wobbly on my feet now."

For the record, that is not an approach *Men's Health* recommends. Sex may make the world go 'round, but we suggest that you offer a better excuse for missing work or an important meeting or a court appearance.

In fact, missing work, falling behind on important duties, failing to keep commitments, consistently skipping sleep just so you can spend a bit more time dipping your candle are signs your sex life may be tipping out of balance, notes Wendy Fader, Ph.D., a licensed psychologist and certified sex therapist in private practice in Boca Raton, Florida. Balance is a touchy matter, she says. But you know that, right?

"No one should be too hard on themselves and think they are abnormal if they are thinking about sex 24 hours one day and then not thinking about it for four months or a couple of weeks," says Dr. Fader. For instance, she says, if you're having a blast learning to inline skate, you may forget about sex altogether for a while. Then you may brush knee pads with an inline skating cutie and start imagining all kinds of intriguing and possibly dangerous scenarios.

When is too much too much, or not enough not enough?

"If a person is psychologically healthy, they know when it feels right," says Dr. Fader. "They know their own balance."

ASPECTS OF BALANCE

Sex suffers unless we can keep its emotional, natural, and technical aspects in balance, says sex educator Sari Locker in her book *Mindblowing Sex in the Real World*.

Let's look at each of those aspects briefly and ask ourselves, "Could we use a little brushing up here?"

• Emotion. If we're emotionally healthy, says Locker, then we're aware of feelings, moods, desires—ours and our partner's—in sex, around sex, before sex, after sex, about sex. We talk about our feelings, moods, and desires with our partner. We ask our partner about her emotions and emotional needs. We trust our partner and feel trusted in return. We respect our partner and ourselves. We're comfortable giving and having "space," and we avoid smothering or being smothered.

• Nature. Here we're talking about accepting our gender, our orientation, our body. We aren't self-conscious about how our body looks, moves, or smells during sex. In general, we're comfortable with our sexual nature, with sexuality. We know how to relax during sex, how to make it fun and pleasurable, says Locker.

• Technique. Healthy awareness of technique involves understanding our sexual physiology and our partner's, what feels good, and how to produce good feelings, says Locker. It involves developing sexual skills and pacing, and protecting against unwanted pregnancy and sexually transmitted diseases.

Beyond that, balance means being able to see our partner as the whole person they are and not just as a sex object, or as a hag or nag or helpless maiden, notes clinical psychologist Polly Young-Eisendrath, Ph.D., clinical associate professor in psychiatry at the University of Vermont College of Medicine in Burlington and author of *You're Not What I Expected*.

Lots of marital conflicts are the result of couples viewing their partners too narrowly, says Dr. Young-Eisendrath. A man may idealize the woman he is with as a mistress-lover, for instance, and have difficulty accepting the parts of her that are more than that. That she is also, perhaps, a mother and a house decorator and a homemaker and a financial partner and a person with a full range of emotional and physical needs and responses, and talents and skills, and increasingly likely these days, a career-woman with many responsibilities outside the home.

Our partners need to know that we see and appreciate them for who they are, not who we idealize them to be, counselors say. Actively making an effort to do that is a positive exercise in attaining and maintaining balance in the relationship.

10 Signs You're Tipping out of Balance Sexually

The following symptoms may indicate you are devoting too much or too little attention to your sexual needs, according to Wendy Fader, Ph.D., a licensed psychologist and certified sex therapist in private practice in Boca Raton, Florida. (One caveat: These symptoms could be pointing toward other addictions or imbalances in your life, so if they exist, don't immediately assume that it's your sex life that's in trouble. Think things through; analyze all aspects of your life.)

1. Lack of sleep
2. Oversleeping
3. Overeating
4. Headaches
5. Muscle strains
6. Irritability
7. Moodiness
8. Nocturnal emissions
9. Driving to the streetwalker side of town and striking up conversations with scantily dressed women leaning against bus-stop signposts
10. Rushing to adult book and video stores after work

BUT HOW MUCH IS NORMAL?

A "normal" guy makes love 3.2 times a week for 40 minutes per session and fantasizes about sex 320 times a week for 4 seconds per session. No, no, no. Those are *not* real numbers. We made them up. But they got your attention. We guys want numbers. We want to compare ourselves with the average and see how we stack up.

We don't mean to be mysterious about this or to frustrate you. You want to know how much time should be devoted to sex, both in and out of a relationship. Is there any benchmark? Bluntly, the answer is no. Sex surveys provide some averages. But sex survey averages do not address the greater issue of "normalcy." Frequency of sexual activity and thoughts—as Dr. Fader said—is an individual matter. And, for most of us, it tends to be fluid. It changes with the emotional and hormonal weather and the busy-ness and stress in our lives.

Enough clever talk, you say. What's *normal*? Okay, we'll give you two sets of statistics to ponder. Researchers asked 4,420 individuals if they had thought about sex in the past 5 minutes. Interviews were dispersed throughout the day—morning, afternoon, and evening. Of males ages 14 to 25, 52 percent said yes. Of males ages 26 to 55, 26 percent said yes.

In another study, 103 men were asked to estimate the amount of time they spent thinking about sex. Fifty-five percent said more than 10 percent of the time.

When are you out of balance? The answer has nothing to do with statistics like these. You're out of balance when there is no time or desire for sex, says Dr. Fader. You're out of balance when everything else in your life suffers because of sex—good sex, bad sex, excessive sex, or no sex.

When are we out of control? When we become aware that a behavior is interfering with our normal functioning and we are unable to control it, says Dr. Fader. This applies to sexual expression as well as to drugs, alcohol, chocolate, or sports. Whether sexual addiction is a true addiction or just another variety of what the head doctors call obsessive-compulsive behavior is a matter that psychology clinicians and researchers are puzzling out. In any case, if sexual fantasizing and/or behavior seems beyond your control and other things are going haywire as a result, that sounds like a problem, says Dr. Fader. You probably should talk to a counselor about it, she advises.

What can a man do to maintain balance?

Take responsibility for your own sexual pleasure, says Dr. Fader. Enjoy your body. By yourself. With a partner. Regularly spend quality time enjoying and appreciating sexual pleasure and you'll likely maintain balance.

SEX APPEAL

Just what is it women look for in a man in those first 3, 10, 30, 60 seconds of an encounter? And how do we manufacture more of it?

Science does have some clues and theories—and even some hard evidence—about the laws of lust, the ABCs of animal attraction, the DNA of delightfulness, in short, the secrets of sex appeal. We won't linger too long in the laboratory, but we will consider what science has to say and from there explore the seven proven ways each of us can multiply our microbes of magnetism a millionfold.

THE SCIENCE OF ATTRACTION

Social scientists, biologists, and psychologists share three basic views about what draws us to potential partners and how we size them up in the process, observes psychologist Harville Hendrix, Ph.D., of Abiquiu, New Mexico, author of *Getting the Love You Want* and *Keeping the Love You Find*. Rarely is any one of the theories solely at play in the total interaction; rather, all three crisscross back and forth, possibly hundreds of times a second, Dr. Hendrix says. The three theories of attraction? These are not the precise terms Dr. Hendrix uses to describe them, but these are the factors that he says are generally believed to be at play in sexual attraction and mate selection.

Survival of the species. This is the Darwinistic, purely biological component of sexual attraction. It purports that men are drawn to beautiful, bright-eyed, healthy young women of childbearing age. The more physically perfect, robust, and beautiful, the better. Those factors signify a woman most likely to produce a strong, healthy, attractive child. From a propagation of the species standpoint, men are supposed to feel lust whenever they see a fine female specimen. And, we all know, so it is.

Women, the theory continues, are drawn to strength, power, and resourcefulness—signs of a good protector and provider. They're looking for the man with the courage and wherewithal to kill the charging boar and bring home the bacon consistently. With women, the man's age is not so important. A physically ugly, but powerful, successful, wealthy man in his fifties may be more appealing than a 25-year-old lifeguard/fashion model.

Of course, these are just theories that ignore things like billboards, prime-time television, locker rooms, and the rest of real-life existence. This conscious input obviously shapes sexual preferences independent of biological programming.

Current studies are also suggesting that we are drawn to mates whose immune systems most oppose ours—a factor which results in the best possible genetic coupling for producing strong, healthy, hybrid offspring.

Meet me in the middle. We make hundreds of instantaneous calculations when we meet a potential mate to determine whether we play in the same league. We look for equals and equivalents in terms of education, background, attitudes, preferences, upbringing, and so on, this theory goes.

See me, feel me, touch me, heal me. We are drawn to members of the opposite sex who most enhance our sense of self-worth, our self-esteem, who make us feel most complete, in this theory.

Dr. Hendrix further asserts, and many sex counselors agree, that in addition to the above, we subconsciously look for a perfect parent—for *us*. Someone who will love us in all the ways we felt unloved as a child, heal our hurts—that is, counter and correct all the real and imagined abuse, emotional trauma, terror, and deprivation our parents subjected us to—and trigger greatness. Certainly a tall order and one that never can be fulfilled, he says. It's a subconscious setup that sabotages relationships, he contends.

OUT OF THE LAB, INTO THE BARS

Here at *Men's Health* Books we like to cite doctors and authorities of similar repute. Now John Eagan's not a doctor, but he is an authority. And maybe we should recognize him as an honorary "doctor of mixology." Besides mixing thousands of drinks in his job as nightclub bartender, this guy has watched thousands and thousands of people mix and mix it up. And he made it his mission to study beautiful women. He convinced 2,000 to fill in a ques-

Does Love Make Scents?

The smell of your sweat, buddy, turns some women on.

Scientists proved this at the University of Bern in Switzerland. They took 49 female students and 44 male students, all in their mid-twenties, who presumably did not know each other, and conducted serious smell tests.

First they profiled each person's immune system based on their genes.

Then they had the men wash their bedding with a perfume-free detergent. And instructed them to wash their bodies only with the perfume-free soaps provided; to skip all aftershaves, perfumes, and deodorants; to stay out of smelly environments; to avoid sex and certain odor-producing foods; and more. Each man was given a 100 percent cotton, untreated T-shirt to sleep in two nights in a row. The T-shirts were stored in plastic bags between wearings and, after the two nights, turned over to the researchers. Each was placed in a cardboard box and coded.

The next day the women were brought in. Each sniffed six T-shirts through a triangular hole in each box, (sniffing an unworn, neutral T-shirt between each whiff). Each woman was unknowingly provided three T-shirts from men whose immune system coding was similar to theirs and three from men whose immune system coding was quite different from theirs. They were instructed to rate the smells based on their pleasantness and sexiness, among other factors.

The results? The women preferred the scent of men whose immune systems most differed from their own. And, in fact, related those odors to the smells of current or former partners.

Authors speculate from their studies with mice that this preference could have evolved as a mechanism for inbreeding avoidance or as protection from pathogens. A child produced by a physiologically diverse couple would gain the genetic coding of both parents and, therefore, would have a stronger immune system than a child born of a couple with similar immune coding. The inference: Women subconsciously use smell to help choose a mate. (An intriguing aberration: Researchers found that birth control pills, which alter body hormonal activity, seem to interfere with natural mate choice.)

tionnaire and then discuss their answers in person.

Eagan asked questions like, "What part of the body do you first look at when you meet a man? What draws you to a man? What turns you off when you meet a man? What's the nicest first thing a man has ever said to you?" Plus lots of ultra-specific multiple-choice questions. He tabulated the results and self-published his findings in the 100,000+-selling book *How to "Pick Up" Beautiful Women*. And he consented to share his findings with us fortunate guys at *Men's Health*. And we, of course, are passing on the goods to you. To whet the appetite, we'll give the answer to the first question we mentioned:

What part of a man's body does a woman check out first? The response was overwhelmingly focused on one place. And it has nothing to do with pumping iron or stuffing a salami in our shorts. Women get their first sense of a man by looking into his eyes. And they decide in a split second whether they're interested in looking any further.

They look for warmth. For sincerity. For inner confidence. For trustfulness. And they see all those things in our eyes, says Eagan.

We project all that—and more—with our eyes, agrees Hollywood psychologist and sexologist Rachel Copelan, Ph.D., author of *100 Ways to Make Sex Sensational and 100% Safe*. Poets are right, says Dr. Copelan. The eyes truly are the windows to the soul.

"My eyes? What can I do about my eyes?" you ask. Lots, says Seattle psychologist Arthur Wassmer, Ph.D., author of *Making Contact* and other books. Start by paying attention to your eye contact. Practice developing relaxed, extended eye contact. If you have difficulty with this, take it a step at a time. Make an effort to hold eye contact in all your interactions for at least 15 seconds continuously. Whenever that becomes comfortable—and it will be within days or weeks, Dr. Wassmer says—double it. Practice until that's comfortable and then add 15 seconds more.

In intimate, warm early contact—where only the eyes are touching—a man's eyes briefly will wander ever so slightly away from the woman's eyes and journey around her face delicately, appreciating her cheeks, her mouth, her forehead, her hairline, says Timothy Perper, Ph.D., biologist, co-editor of *The Complete Dictionary of Sexology*, and an independent researcher who has

Real Voices

"I think men go for the brute strength. They think if they pump up and are very muscular, the women are going to like that. And sure, there are always going to be those couple of men who are so knockout gorgeous that everybody is going to look at them and go, 'Wow!' But that's not the case most of the time.

"The things that women find attractive are very basic," says Wendy Fader, Ph.D., a licensed psychologist and certified sex therapist in private practice in Boca Raton, Florida, speaking both firsthand and from clinical experience. Things like hygiene, being neat, not being the greatest dresser but being presentable, smiling a lot, making eye contact is really important, listening to the person, remembering things about the other person. Basically, why we like other people is how they make us feel about ourselves. So if someone shows interest, well, we're going to be inclined to like that person. Some other factors? A good sense of humor is high on everybody's list. Not taking yourself too seriously, not being an egomaniac—that's a big one."

studied human courtship for two decades. During these breaks in direct eye contact, the man's eyes stay focused on the woman—on her features above her neck, most of the time, says Dr. Perper—if the developing interaction is to continue escalating.

As for projecting honesty and sincerity and trustfulness with your eyes, that's easy. Be honest, sincere, and trustworthy, says Eagan. Don't use silly canned lines or try to con a woman into liking you. If you're sincerely interested in her, exhibit that with your demeanor and your words and your questions and your actions. And your eyes will follow and sometimes even scout ahead.

WHAT WOMEN FIND ALLURING

What are some other things that turn women on when they first see a man? There are seven big ones. Let's let Eagan talk for a while.

Keep it clean. "I tell a man to be super-clean, from the top of his head down to the tips of his fingernails and the tips of his toes whenever he approaches a woman because they have a function in their mind for detail that we don't have," says Eagan. If a man and a woman meet and you asked the man to describe the woman right afterward, he won't be able to do it in detail. But if you ask the woman to describe the man, she'll do it right down to the last detail. They have razor eyes for detail."

Dr. Wassmer backs this up. To be sexually appealing, says Dr. Wassmer, you must feel good about yourself and your appearance. Appearance is an initial factor in pairing, but it can be quite fleeting. And we don't have to be Greek gods or have the chiseled face of Kirk Douglas to be physically appealing. But we do need to make the most of what we have. Smiling helps, says Dr. Wassmer. And, yes, being neat and clean is particularly important.

We should regularly perform an appearance inventory and make sure that we are putting forth our best, says Dr. Wassmer. And that's not just to impress people but so we feel attractive and good about ourselves. Here's Dr. Wassmer's personal appearance inventory checklist: hair, teeth, skin, odor, weight, and clothes. Each of those areas requires regular monitoring and maintenance.

Eagan asked women about how a man should dress. The good news is that most said it doesn't matter and that casual is fine, so long as it's appropriate to the occasion. You don't have to be a fashion plate. But you should appear neat and clean. Women don't admire rumpled, sloppy, or street urchin looks.

Lighten up. Among the most common things that turned off Eagan's women was when the man was "full of himself." By this they meant the men were cocky and egotistical, that they only wanted to talk about how great and important they are, says Eagan. Can the crap, says Eagan. They've heard it all. Forget the lines, the bragging. Listen more, talk less. Ask questions. Don't do the guy thing of topping each of her anecdotes with one of yours. She tells a story, respond with admiration.

How to Be More Appealing to Your Lover

Want to increase your sex appeal with your lady? Learn three simple phrases and use them in lovemaking, says Hollywood psychologist and sexologist Rachel Copelan, Ph.D., author of *100 Ways to Make Sex Sensational and 100% Safe*.

The magic words?

1. "We have plenty of time."
2. "I enjoy giving you pleasure."
3. "Tell me what you want me to do."

Smile. This is a biggie, guys. Ninety-seven percent of the women responding to Eagan's survey said that a man who wants to win their attention should be smiling. But, he cautions, it must not be forced. The women were adamant about that. It must be natural and heartwarming. Not hard to do, says Eagan. Just thinking about beautiful women makes most of us smile. Release the inhibition and beam pleasantly.

Dr. Wassmer concurs. A smile brightens everybody's face, he says, and helps brighten the room. (How can you tell a fake smile? A real smile usually affects the whole face—the forehead, eyes, and cheeks all crease up. A fake smile usually involves just the mouth. Try it in the mirror.)

Have fun. Kid. Tease. Women love a humorous approach. Eagan asked, "Should a man you just met be serious, comical, or romantic?" Hands down, guys, Seinfeld gets the girl. They want you to be fun-loving and fun. Sense of humor is the key. They do not, repeat, do not want long jokes or a practiced stand-up routine. Just some light-heartedness and some laughs. Second, and barely in the running, was romantic. Serious didn't even show.

Emphasize resourcefulness and ambition. Don't come on gangbusters about the yacht, the sports car, and the chateau in the Alps. But women do need to know that you are a serious worker with ambition and a future and the wherewithal to make it happen.

"A man needs to verbalize the times he has been industrious, successful, resourceful, those kinds of things, not in a full-of-himself way, but factually," says Eagan. "Casually work these things into the conversation when you can. Women aren't looking for losers, okay? They're looking for guys who are going to rise. And they're looking for clues to the future."

This is part of the evolutionary biological survival factor in attraction that we discussed earlier. "It goes all the way back to Wilma Flintstone," says Eagan.

Be sensitive. Women want to know that you have feelings. You don't have to cry for them to prove it. But you do need to notice things and care about things and express some emotion, says Eagan.

Forget the macho act, says Eagan. "Women today demand sincerity, honesty, mutual respect, a guy in touch with his feelings. You have to be a man, don't get me wrong," he says. "You can't be a doormat for anybody. You have to keep your manly qualities."

Sensitivity means paying attention, being aware of the woman and how she is feeling and what she is doing. Be considerate and responsive.

"I don't care if it's the first date or if you've been married 100 years—you knock on the door and she looks beautiful, you have to tell her," says Eagan. "I mean, she's worked hard on that. I mean, women have worked *hours* on that, and they've made it plain to me that they expect a man to be intelligent enough to appreciate the fact that they've put a lot of time in on themselves."

That's part of being sensitive.

Project a personality. Women, Eagan says, are drawn to good-looking men, much as men are drawn to good-looking women. But for women, the greater draw is not classic good looks. And classic good looks fail quickly—as soon as a conversation starts—if there isn't warmth, sincerity, and general likeability to back them up. And, lucky for us, women say that warmth, sincerity, and likeability can easily overcome less-than-perfect looks.

"Men have what I call eyegasms, and women have what I call eargasms," says Eagan. "If you want to reach a woman, you have to learn how to verbally communicate with her. It has to pass through her ears first. That's how she becomes attracted to you. That's charm and charisma. We're not born with charm and charisma. That's actually a skill we have to learn."

FOREPLAY

Dictionaries tell us that foreplay is the erotic stimulation that occurs before intercourse. Makes it sound a bit like a chore, doesn't it? After all, how much stimulation do you, the guy, really need to be prepared for intercourse? Usually, the mere presence of a naked female body is all we need to be ready for action.

Women, on the other hand, need plenty of physical and emotional stimulation to get aroused, lubricated, and primed for orgasm. This is why many a man sees foreplay as an obligatory task to perform to prepare a woman for sex. So they turn foreplay into a rote sequence: 5 minutes of stroking this, 10 minutes of licking that, a couple rubs here, a few kisses there, then—bam!—intercourse.

Absolutely, positively wrong attitude. Our message: Foreplay is more than mere stimulation. Foreplay *is* sex.

If you want to be a world-class lover, get this into your head—flirting, joking, touching, caressing, kissing, tongue work, penetration, intercourse, orgasm—these are all points on one sexual continuum. Formal definition aside, foreplay is not merely a combination on the door to intercourse. It is no more and no less than the sex that occurs during intercourse. It is something as much for the pleasure of men as it is for women.

BEING FOREMOST AT FOREPLAY

To be a master of foreplay, you already have the two most important tools you need—your mind and your body, says Doreen Virtue, Ph.D., a relationship expert and psychotherapist in Newport Beach, California, and author of *In the Mood*. The trick is using those tools to cultivate skills that will make you a virtuoso in the symphony of sex. For advice on physical technique, turn to the next part (Physical Mastery, page 121). But if you want the secret to hitting the opening notes on-key every time, here's what you need.

A willingness. You knew this was the first criterion, didn't you? Yes, if you're going to see foreplay as a part of sex, not apart from sex, you have to be open to new possibilities.

"One of the most important parts of my workshops is getting men to apply their creativity and imagination to pleasing and romancing their wives," says relationship expert Ellen Kreidman, Ph.D., author of *Light Her Fire* and *Light His Fire*, a series of inventive books and seminars. "For men, that means being open to her needs and essentially being her fantasy," says Dr. Kreidman. This might be as simple as being more attentive and complimentary to her than usual, or as complex as renting a tux and becoming her romance-novel hero.

"The key is to be imaginative and you'll open yourself to all sorts of possibilities," says Dr. Kreidman.

An all-day attitude. As we said, foreplay is not some activity that occurs 15 minutes or an hour or 2 hours before intercourse. To tell you the truth, foreplay—the events and actions that stimulate you and make you want to have sex with one another—can encompass whole days.

"There's an old saying that if you want to make love in the evening, you have to start in the morning," says Robert Birch, Ph.D., a psychologist in Columbus, Ohio, specializing in marriage and sex therapy and author of *Oral Caress*. "It's a bit of folk wisdom that really holds up." Spending a day together, complimenting your wife first thing in the morning, giving her a phone call at work—all these events are building blocks that lay the foundation for intimacy between you and, of course, good sex.

A few kind words. You probably already know that women are more verbal than we visual guys. Talking is one of the best ways to arouse a woman, says Dr. Virtue. More important, talking is also a way of letting your partner know that she can take all the time she needs.

In Defense of the Quickie

In the meteorology of sex, the quickie is a tornado: touching down with little warning, blowing through with dizzying power and velocity, disappearing as quickly as it comes, leaving you with rumpled clothes, tousled hair. Your senses are alive with feelings of excitement and impending danger. Some part of you is overwhelmed with the thrill of it; some part of you is grateful simply to have survived the experience.

So even as we make the case that longer sex is better sex, we do feel compelled to point out that the spontaneous, banzai form of sex known the world over as the quickie also has its time and place.

"A quickie now and again is a wonderful way to inject a little variety into your sex life. It's a promise of more to come," says Robert Birch, Ph.D., a psychologist in Columbus, Ohio, specializing in marriage and sex therapy and author of *Oral Caress*.

Whenever it happens, wherever it happens, most sex educators are in favor of getting out of public view and giving in to the impulse. Here are a couple guidelines for getting years of enjoyment out of great, quick sex.

Don't let it replace romance. Remember, a quickie is just that—a quick sex snack, an amorous appetizer. "Agree that this is a once-in-a-while thing where you simply give in to carnal lust. It's meant to fuel your passion for more prolonged lovemaking later," says Dr. Birch.

Seize the moment. If the urge hits you, try to respond to it as fully and quickly as possible. In his book *Secrets of Better Sex*, Joel D. Block, Ph.D., a clinical psychologist and sex therapist at the Human Sexuality Center of Long Island Jewish Medical Center in New York, tells couples to "be open to erotic opportunity." Postpone a quickie for a more convenient time and you've missed the point—and the fun—of the whole enterprise.

Be selfish. As the quickie is a celebration of the carnal activities of our forebears—who were too busy hunting and gathering to worry about such niceties as foreplay—agree that this is a sexual free-for-all. Don't worry about pleasing her; don't let her worry about pleasing you. Each of you focus on yourselves for those few minutes. Remember that you'll have time to spend on each other later.

"During foreplay, women are often thinking about how they look, whether they can please you, whether they're desirable. On top of this, both of you are focusing on her orgasm. It can be pretty stressful and counterproductive," says Dr. Virtue.

So listen up, men. Here are the three best words you can say to a woman during foreplay: "Take your time."

"It sounds silly, but just by saying, 'Take your time,' or 'It really turns me on when you're turned on,' you're giving her permission to relax and enjoy herself. It's very effective, and she'll appreciate you for saying it," says Dr. Virtue.

A clean body. Dr. Birch points out that a woman's sense of smell and touch tends to be more sensitive than our own. An essential part of foreplay, therefore, is presenting yourself clean and well-shaven—no smoking or alcohol breath either. "Not only will you be more appealing to her but you're also sending the message that she's worth getting cleaned up for. That's very seductive," says Dr. Birch.

A giving gesture. While Dr. Virtue was compiling her book *In the Mood*, she polled hundreds of women to determine what their most romantic moments were. "Overwhelmingly, these moments all had a common denominator: Their lover was giving them something—a flower, a back rub, a glass of champagne, a compliment," says Dr. Virtue. So make some gesture of giving, especially if you're giving of herself. "The act of giving is a sign of caring, of providing, of serving her needs. These are all important for a woman to feel intimate," she says.

A willingness to be corny. Here's a rule of thumb for foreplay—if it feels corny, do it.

"That applies to both men and women, but in different ways," says Dr. Virtue. "For women, it feels corny to dress up in lingerie or erotic costumes, but men find it highly stimulating." By the same token, the things that men feel corny doing—lavishing compliments on their women, snuggling and cuddling, waiting on them hand and foot—are highly effective forms of foreplay. "So many men say they don't know what to do to make their wives happy. Well, they really do. They just can't imagine doing or saying it. If you feel embarrassed or corny saying something, you now know that it's probably the thing that's going to make her day," says Dr. Virtue. "Now you're turning a negative feeling into something positive."

A willingness to receive. You may not need to be rubbed and licked to be ready for intercourse. But that doesn't mean that you don't need erotic stimulation, particularly in a long-term relationship. Foreplay in this broader, around-the-clock sense is as useful to keeping a guy's long-term interest in sex as it is for piquing a woman's short-term interest. So happily receive it. Acknowledge that those back rubs, fine meals, and sudden hugs and kisses and tickle attacks are her way to keep *you* sexually motivated, and be grateful for them. Looked at from this perspective, you might be surprised to find out how much foreplay you're actually receiving.

DIVERSIFYING YOUR LOVEMAKING

While it's nice to have sex in an environment where you're totally comfortable, totally at ease, we can't warn you too often about the danger of complacency. Sometimes it's healthy to shake up the sexual status quo, to turn the lights on once in a while.

Here's why: The human animal loves to be comfortable. We like to get into routines. But sometimes, for some people, routines become ruts. And that's a problem. Get too complacent in your sex life, you'll start to get bored.

"In general, human beings have incredibly short attention spans. We need variety in all aspects of our lives—in our jobs, in the foods we eat, and even in our sex lives," says Doreen Virtue, Ph.D., a relationship expert and psychotherapist in Newport Beach, California, and author of *In the Mood*. And there's the rub: It's tricky having diversity in a sex life that involves the same two people, year in and year out. Tricky, but not impossible.

"Sometimes what's needed is to simply recognize that you're in a rut. A lot of people are afraid to admit it. They think that there's something wrong with them or that they're being hurtful to the other person to admit it," says Steve Manley, Ph.D., staff psychologist for the Male Health Center in Dallas. Trust us, it's more damaging in the long run not to say anything.

MAKING A FRESH START

Even if your sex life is going along just fine, thanks very much, it never hurts to administer a little shock to the system now and again.

"Making a conscious decision to try different things is positive," says Dr. Manley. It makes you a more well-rounded, more spirited, more adventuresome sort who's that much more likely to keep a desirable partner interested in him. It's also just as likely that you'll inspire some creativity in your partner.

But first, you'll require some basic elements to diversify your lovemaking repertoire.

An open mind. Sounds like a catch-22, huh? To develop an open mind, you have to have an open mind. Not really.

"The first step to any kind of growth is the willingness to accept something new and different, even if you have doubts about it in the beginning," says Dr. Virtue. Given the opportunity, you may find that you like something new; and if you don't like it, well, at least you've started down a path of exploration. Keep at it, keep plugging away, and pretty soon you will find something you do like. Remember that the innovators of this world have always been the ones who questioned the status quo, who asked, "How can I make

Plagued by Complacency?

Worried that you're stuck in a sexual rut? Here are the top warning signs.

- You have sex in just one or two different positions, dismissing all the ones you used to use as "too much work."
- Like meat loaf on Tuesdays, you have sex on one night of the week, same place, same time.
- You actually believe that some things are more interesting than sex. Televised golf, for example.
- Sex? Hmmmm, come to think of it, you can't quite remember the last time you had sex.
- Two words: Twin beds. Or its modern reincarnation—a king-size bed, which keeps the two of you far apart.

this better?" Be a Leonardo of love; don't be afraid to think big and daring and even, yes, just a little weird.

Improvisational skills. In the theater of life, sex is not a scripted play; it's a madcap, bombastic improvisational comedy of manners and errors.

"It's really important to get away from the idea of sex as this formula that you have to stick to because it always worked in the past," says Dr. Virtue. Throw out the repertoire.

A willing accomplice. Sex is a bicycle built for two. If your partner likes her sex in one flavor only, you'll first have to work with her so that you can both diversify. Talk. Be open. Express your fantasies, your desires. Get the ball rolling. The more you can talk about what you'd like to try, the closer you can be to actually trying it. And if you don't like it, you try something else.

"If one of you is hesitant, then the other one has to take the initiative. And always, you want to encourage the other person to come up with ideas, too. Don't force; don't get impatient. Lead by example," says Dr. Manley.

VIVE LA DIFFÉRENCE

So you want to lead by example, but you're suffering stage fright? That's okay. If you're seeking a sexual jump start to diversity, you've come to the right place. After polling our experts, we've come up with the perfect program for your diversity training. Here are several easy ways you can start innovating—tonight.

Talk to her. Whoa—talk about starting at the deep end. Seriously, though, when was the last time you talked? "Lack of communication is often the first step toward a stale relationship," says Dr. Manley. Go out on a limb; trade fantasies. You may pleasantly surprise one another.

Light some candles. If diversity and change are going to thrive, they're going to need the right atmosphere in which to grow. You can be the master of that atmosphere. Strike a match. Or put some romantic music on the stereo. One of the quickest ways to break up routine sex is with just a little tweak to the environment. "Making an effort to be just a little bit romantic can go a long way," says Dr. Virtue.

Give her a massage. Routine sex is usually quick sex, without a lot of frills. Make an effort to prolong things, suggests relationship expert Ellen Kreidman, Ph.D., author of *Light Her Fire* and *Light His Fire*, a series of inventive books and seminars. A long, sensual massage will certainly do that. Or you can take a shower together. Give yourselves time to focus on each other, not the daily routine of your life.

Use no less than three different positions. Setting fun rules can help you spice up your sex life, says Dr. Virtue. Instead of a three-position rule, designate tonight as Sex Standing Up Night.

Impose restrictions on your old favorites. As you set rules to help you explore new lovemaking techniques, so can you impose sanctions on those comfortable old favorites, says Dr. Virtue. For example, no more missionary position for three months (we offer plenty of others on page 168); or no sex on any surface resembling a bed until autumn comes around. The point with any rule is to design them not to restrict your love lives but to coax you toward different ideas that will expand your sexual awareness.

And of course...leave the lights on.

FANTASIES

Sometimes it's hard having so many women vying for your attention. On the way to work, for example, that blond in the really short dress and the really fast car sidled up alongside you, peered over the tops of her Wayfarers, and asked if you wanted a ride. That's the second time this week!

You're still thinking of her when you strut into the office, hardly noticing that all the heads of your female co-workers are turning.

Later, as you try to get some work done, your secretary comes in wearing a slinky, scoop-neck number. She slides herself onto the edge of your desk. When she leans forward, you can see down to her navel. She's chewing on her pen. She's talking about taking some dictation. She's...

Wait a second. You don't even have a secretary.

MAN: THE FANTASY MACHINE

All right, so maybe your fantasy tastes run less to secretaries and more toward that pert little sister-in-law of yours; or the buxom teen you saw hitch-

What's on Her Mind?

Think you're the only one with a fantasy life? Dream on. Women have them, too (84 percent have said they've had fantasies during sex). But the fantasy world of women may seem like an alien landscape to men, with good reason. For starters, the fantasies that turn a woman on are generally far less explicit but sometimes far more elaborate than what men fantasize about. "In my seminars, I say that man is X-rated, woman is PG-rated. Sometimes her most powerful fantasies don't even involve sex," says relationship expert Ellen Kreidman, Ph.D., author of *Light Her Fire* and *Light His Fire*, a series of inventive books and seminars.

If you were to peruse a transcript of many female fantasies, it would likely read less like a porn script and more like a romance novel. Because for women, romance, not sex, is the most arousing part of sex itself.

Still confused? To give you a clearer picture, here's a head-to-head comparison of likely male and female fantasies. See the difference?

Him	Her
Sex	Cuddling
Sex on the beach	Walking hand-in-hand on a moonlit beach
Sex on the kitchen table	A candle-lit dinner laid out on the table
Sex in a public place	You, holding her hand or kissing her in public
Sex with a supermodel	Sex with a movie star
Phone sex	You, telling her how much you love her, how beautiful she is
Oral sex	Oral sex
Her, waking you up with oral sex	You, waking her up with a massage
Tearing each other's clothes off and having sex like rabbits	Getting dressed up and dancing to love songs
Her, in a Wonder Woman costume, having sex with you	You, as Superman, keeping her safe from evil

hiking on the highway last night; or this week's hot supermodel. Maybe it's not the partner you fantasize about but the scenario—it doesn't matter who she is, so long as you end up hog-tied and she's wearing a chicken mask; or you're a spy on the run and she's the stranger you met on the train to Prague;

or you're a Presidential advisor and she's a well-paid call girl with a big mouth; or...well, you get the idea.

It comes down to this: Every man has a dream, a cherished fantasy or two he keeps in the recesses of his mind, like guilty secrets. Except we shouldn't feel guilty about our fantasies, even when they incorporate the unusual, the immoral, and the illegal. Because by and large, your sexual fantasies—yes, even the really twisted ones you'd never admit to having—aren't an indication that you're evil or sick. In fact, fantasies are a sign of *good* mental health.

FANTASY: THE ULTIMATE SAFE SEX

Fantasies can be a kind of test area, a private place where we play out certain aspects of our daily frustrations and desires without doing anything that might be unseemly or wrong.

"Fantasies help keep us out of trouble," says Galdino F. Pranzarone, Ph.D., professor of psychology at Roanoke College in Salem, Virginia. They're the perfect playground for notions and practices that might be highly arousing but also highly imprudent to pursue in the waking world. "It's human nature to be drawn to things that are forbidden or taboo," says Dr. Pranzarone. "Of course, you don't want to act some things out in real life, things that are hurtful to you or other people. In your fantasies, though, you can explore some of these forbidden practices, get them out of your system." Thus, an active fantasy life can be a kind of steam valve, a safe way to relieve the pent-up pressures of life.

And men tend to keep that valve wide open at all times of the day. According to some surveys, more than half of all men spend about 10 percent of their time having sexual fantasies. It has been estimated that most of us think about sex 6 or 7 times a day, or more than 2,500 times a year.

MAKING YOUR DREAMS COME TRUE

With such varied sexual scenarios sizzling in your brain, it may occur to you at some point to try bringing your favorite fantasies to life.

Giving birth to a dream is tricky business. After all, not every fantasy translates into a good reality. Look at Dr. Frankenstein—he tried to make his dream come true and ended up creating a monster.

That said, fantasies are a wonderfully creative part of you, and they can provide some fun and exciting ideas that will supercharge your sex lives. Here are some safety guidelines for discussing, and possibly living out, your fantasies.

Talk first, act later. Again, we feel compelled to counsel caution when it comes to exploring your fantasies in the real world. You want to enhance your sex life, remember, not weird anyone out or frighten them off.

"Common sense dictates that there are some fantasies you just want to keep to yourself, and replay them only for you, say, during sex when you want a little boost," says Robert O. Hawkins, Ph.D., professor emeritus of health sciences at State University of New York in Stony Brook. But in a relationship where there's mutual trust and respect, you and your partner may want to talk with one another about some aspects of your fantasy life.

"It's always a good idea to be communicating with your partner, sharing your feelings, your desires, and your expectations. Sharing your fantasies can be part of that," says Dr. Pranzarone. "You'll never know if your partner has a similar fantasy unless one of you broaches the subject."

Take turns. As with any part of your relationship, sharing—and satisfying—one's fantasies is a give-and-take process.

"You're two different people. Different ideas and scenarios are going to arouse you than are going to appeal to her," says Doreen Virtue, Ph.D., a relationship expert and psychotherapist in Newport Beach, California, and author of *In the Mood*. "If you want her to do something for you, you have to be open-minded enough to do things that are going to please and arouse her, even though they might not be much of a turn-on for you." Don't expect her to do all the work; meet each other halfway.

Don't overanalyze. Finally, a word of comfort for those of you who might be a little surprised or shocked by the scenarios your imagination dreams up: Try not to read too much into them.

"It's a mistake to make interpretations about the kind of person you are simply on the basis of sex fantasies and daydreams," says Dr. Hawkins. "Fantasies don't mean anything. It's just a way your body arouses itself to enjoy sex more."

FANTASY FAVORITES

As different as we all are, our fantasy lives do revolve around some common themes. We decided to list some of the most common sexual fantasies men enjoy. We'll tell you why you might be aroused by a particular scenario and, where applicable, how you might use that fantasy to spice up sex in the real world.

Another woman. Whether it's a babysitter, a prostitute, an unattainable actress, or a total stranger, fantasizing about sex with anyone other than your usual partner is the most common type of erotic daydream we can muster. Often, though, it's also the most guilt-inducing, especially when those fantasies include people you and your wife both know, such as her best friend or that pert sister-in-law we mentioned earlier.

If you're in a committed relationship, this is not the sort of fantasy you want to live out. You shouldn't feel too guilty about having such adulterous thoughts, though. "Fantasizing about other women is a safe way to inject a little variety into your life," says Dr. Pranzarone. "Of course, you're going to be attracted to other women—just because you're in a relationship doesn't mean you're blind." Fantasies of this stripe help throttle back the primitive male drive to sleep with every woman we see, satisfying our polygamous urges while keeping us out of divorce court at the same time.

A lot of other women. Right next door to the sleeping-with-every-woman fantasy is the sleeping-with-every-woman-at-once daydream. It doesn't take a rocket scientist to figure out the appeal of group-sex scenarios: First, it's a way of reaffirming your attractiveness to the opposite sex (you're so desirable, they're willing to share you). Second, there's a certain anonymity to group fantasies. "The focus is off you. You don't have to do all the work either. You can sit back and just enjoy it," points out Dr. Pranzarone. Indeed, a common male fantasy is watching two women make love.

All tied up. Restraining someone and then having your way with them—it's a powerful, and powerfully naughty, fantasy for many men. Dr. Pranzarone says the fantasy of tying your partner down is typically an offshoot of the standard male desire to dominate and hold power over someone, piggish and chauvinistic though it sounds. "It can be very appealing to have someone who's powerless to resist your advances; there's no chance of rejection in this fantasy," he observes.

Trying to make this daydream a reality is tricky and not advisable in all cases, though. As you can imagine, many women—especially if you've just met them—are going to be highly resistant to putting themselves entirely into your control. Even if you've been together for years, don't be surprised if she raises an eyebrow when you raise the subject. But if it's something you're really interested in, talk it over with her. Better yet, volunteer to be the guinea pig—let her tie you up. This will help reinforce trust between you and make her more likely to submit to your wishes.

If you're lucky enough to get her to agree, go gently into that new world. Start with loose bonds, and don't use anything rough. Think scarves and bathrobe belts, not rope and clothesline.

Being dominated. Day to day, we have lots of stress, power, and responsibility in our lives. At home, in the bedroom, we may want to let go of the reins a little bit, let someone else take charge. That's why a lot of men, especially men of great power and responsibility, get their kicks by being kicked around—not physically, but mentally. Being submissive, being dominated by your woman, serving her needs, obeying her every command, living as her perfect lapdog—some men just can't get enough of this.

"Powerful executives, cops, politicians—these are the men who tend to enjoy being dominated because exerting power and influence is old hat. It's not exciting for them anymore—just the opposite," says Dr. Pranzarone. Plus, letting her take the reins relieves you of the considerable task of being the one with the initiative. It's a great relief for many men and a source of great arousal.

Pleasure with pain. Other fantasies might revolve around so-called sadomasochist, or SM, practices—slapping, tickling, spanking, and so on.

Technically, SM isn't about pain so much as it is about creating intense sensations that heighten your awareness and sexual arousal. For example, some people enjoy being spanked because the slap on the butt makes the skin more sensitive to the touch, and the action can stimulate nerve endings in their more erogenous zones. If you've ever enjoyed a woman raking her fingernails up and down your back, maybe you have some inkling of how pain can be a pleasure, too.

If you want to explore this kind of fantasy in your life, tread very carefully. Talk with your partner about it, and proceed slowly. Remember, your fantasies should never injure, but enhance.

Another man? While we wouldn't call it a favorite fantasy among heterosexual men, it's not at all uncommon, unhealthy, or unnatural if 1 or 2 of those 2,500 fantasies a year happens to involve a sexual encounter with another guy. Dr. Hawkins says that if you're straight, having a homosexual fantasy every now and again does not necessarily mean you have latent homosexual tendencies. At the most, it's a let's-try-it-on-for-size notion of a vividly creative mind; or a quick reality check, a way for you to look at something and say, "Yup. That's not for me." If in the midst of your fantasy life your mind throws a homosexual image at you, don't let it bother you. Dream on.

MATURE GAMES

According to many reports, the major sexual problem in our culture is sexual boredom. Same partner. Same place. Same time. Same way. Next stop: abstinence. If your diet were like that, you'd stop eating.

You don't accept a third straight day of tuna casserole. Instead, you book a table at some restaurant with an unpronounceable name and order up your first-ever portion of honey-lime salmon with black bean and mango sauce.

And for sexual boredom? The solution is just as obvious. Beckon your honey and challenge her to a rousing game of Nude Indoor Volleyball.

Still with us?

In fact, we're serious. Or rather *not* serious, and that's the point. Just listen to Gerald Schoenewolf, Ph.D., a psychoanalyst and director of The Living Center, a therapeutic cooperative in New York City. "All sex really is is adult play," he says. "The more you can be a child during sexual activity, the better. So a silly game like nude volleyball challenges you to let go of the tensions of middle-age life."

Dr. Schoenewolf should know. He literally wrote the book on adult sexual play. His *Erotic Games* is an adult compendium of dozens of mature diversions with names like "Reverse Headache," "Indecent Proposal," "Massage Poker," "The Last Person on Earth," and, of course, the aforementioned "Nude Indoor Volleyball."

There's a message to this mirthful approach. The games, many of them essentially scripted role-playing, are designed to address specific impasses in a relationship. Passive-aggressive couples, for instance, might try their hand at "The Master and the Maid," in which she seduces him in a deliberately provocative way designed to provoke active, rather than passive, aggression.

"The idea is to get stuff to the surface," Dr. Schoenewolf says. "Playing the games brings up the feelings and conflicts that led to the impasse."

Take Nude Indoor Volleyball. (Please.) As far as we know, there's no rules committee, but here's how you play: Blow up a balloon, tie a string across your bedroom or living room, close the shades (this is decidedly *not* a spectator sport), mark some out-of-bounds points, and take off your clothes. You each get three taps to get the balloon over the string. Play to 15. There's one key rule: You're allowed—in fact, encouraged—to distract your opponent by touching and fondling her. And she employs the same tactic. All erogenous zones are eligible for this diversionary touching.

"Of course, this leads to sexual play," Dr. Schoenewolf points out. "If you give up the game entirely and fall to the floor in sexual passion, then you both win."

You may just as likely fall to the floor in hysterical laughter, but no matter. You can't say your sense of play wasn't stirred, if only for a few spikes and squeezes. One way or another, says Dr. Schoenewolf, sex games will shake things up in a stale marriage.

Role-playing games are particularly effective for middle-age couples, according to Dr. Schoenewolf. In "Seduction Surprise," you greet her at the door in a tuxedo with the lights low, the music wafting, table set, the whole nine yards. She's queen for the day, you're the sophisticated seducer, and you keep it up until she gets into the spirit of the thing and the seduction is consummated. Here you're doing an exaggerated version of the kind of romancing you know you should have been doing all along. But because it's a role, a shtick, almost a caricature, you can do it. "And she'll be bowled over by it," promises Dr. Schoenewolf.

There are all kinds of fantasy scenarios you can create for good, clean fun—"The Nude Cleaning Lady," "The Prostitute and the John"—but Dr. Schoenewolf stresses that those back-of-the-classifieds, "Helga-the-Dominatrix" encounters aren't beneficial for couples. "Those games tend to maintain one's neurotic way of life," he says. "They prevent you from having a genuine relationship with somebody."

GETTING STARTED

Whether it's because couples are more bored these days or more liberated, there's something of a cottage industry springing up in mature games. Dr. Schoenewolf's book focuses on psychotherapy-derived games, but less therapeutically minded titles such as Laura Corn's *101 Great Nights of Sex* or Michael and Barbara Jonas's *The Book of Love, Laughter, and Romance* are sourcebooks for the saucy. Or try some of the board and card games out on the market, ranging in raunchiness from the mild *Getting to Know You Better* to *Dirty Minds.* The Jonases' Games Partnership Limited (800-776-7662) has sold almost 800,000 boxes of *An Enchanted Evening*, which takes a suggestive, leave-it-up-to-you approach ("Gently caress something your partner has two of"). And this is not just a mail-order phenomenon. You can buy your "foreplay in a box" at department stores—in the lingerie department, of course.

Want to play? Here's how to get started.

Take a chance. Even occasional bouts of "Gender Reversal" or "Erotic Cards" aren't something you can wander into casually. "You have to make a commitment to do it," says Dr. Schoenewolf. "You have to both say you're going to do this thing no matter how long it takes."

Bribe her. It may be the understatement of the decade to say that it could take some convincing to get her to play "One Night Stand" or "Politically Correct Sex" with you. Do it the old-fashioned way: Bribe her. "You know by now what it will take," says Dr. Schoenewolf. "Everybody has her price."

You may have to go see *Cats* or sit through a Julio Iglesias concert. But a deal's a deal.

Stick with it. Let's face it. Playing "Deserted Island" doesn't come naturally. The temptation will be to say, "This is unbelievably idiotic," and chuck the whole project before you get to first base. Hang in there. Remember, you're doing this for your sex life, and the rewards can be big. "It may take several weeks," says Dr. Schoenewolf. "At first, you both may just take off your clothes and argue about how stupid it is. That's part of working through the process."

And if things never leave the ground, don't worry. Sometimes games just don't do it for a couple. The ultimate goal, of course, is fun and creative sex and intimacy, and there are many other roads to take to it.

AFTERPLAY

Afterplay—let's be clear about this—is not anything that occurs after you've ejaculated. For example, if she has not yet had an orgasm, and you magnanimously decide to help reach the glory land, that is not afterplay, pal—you're still having sex.

Once the two of you are satisfied, though, chances are that you are both going to feel a crashing sensation come over you, a wave of euphoria that leads women to want to snuggle and be close to you and leads men straight into a coma. Overpowering as the urge may sometimes seem, however, afterplay is not the act of rolling over and going to sleep. Instead, afterplay is the happy ending to the story of sex. Without the finishing touches of a little postcoital tenderness, you are essentially leaving a job undone. You are also missing out on a great opportunity for some quality time with your sweetie.

"Afterplay is a logical, proper follow-through for foreplay and intercourse. Men don't feel that they have a lot of opportunities in life to be truly relaxed, to let their guard down. Afterplay gives you that chance," says Doreen Virtue, Ph.D., a relationship expert and psychotherapist in Newport Beach, California, and author of *In the Mood*.

BASKING IN THE AFTERGLOW

Most men would love to take advantage of a chance to spend quality time with a gorgeous, naked woman who thinks he's the greatest. But the fact is that many guys do feel sleepy and exhausted after a good bout of lovemaking. What gives? Is this physiological or psychological? Well, a little bit of both.

First, let's look at the physiology. While people vary greatly in the duration and intensity of their responses to sexual stimulation, what is remarkable, notes Shirley Zussman, Ed.D., a certified sex and marital therapist in private practice in New York City, is the similarities between men and women rather than the differences. There are four distinct physiological phases of sexual intercourse: *Arousal* is the very opening gambit of sex, where you start to become excited. You get an erection; her vagina starts to lubricate. Then follows *plateau*, where you both reach a prolonged state of arousal—this is usually when intercourse occurs. Then comes the point when you've become stimulated so much that *orgasm* occurs. Then comes *resolution*, when things cool down.

After you ejaculate, the sudden relaxation triggers responses all over your body, sending you into a pleasure-filled, dreamlike stupor. You relax from your exertions, catch your breath, return to "normal" (meaning that your penis goes flaccid, your heartbeat resumes its regular pace, and other basic body functions resume business). As the tension unwinds from your body, you're likely to be pitched over the edge of consciousness into the dark chasm of blissful sleep. This shift from sexual ecstasy to a flaccid, calm state typically takes just 2 minutes for a man.

Then there is that glorious creature, woman. It can take nearly four times as long for women to be stimulated to orgasm as men. And more important to our discussion here is that after climax, women take quite a while to descend from sexual tension to a pre-arousal state—often as long as 15 or 20 minutes. Some scientists point to this physiological difference as a major cause of tension between women and men. Women, they say, hate it when they are left to pass through resolution alone. They want some tenderness, caressing, intimacy.

MAKING A PLAY FOR HER

There are some biological functions occurring that may make it easier for a guy to fall asleep immediately after sex, acknowledges Dr. Virtue. "But it's not an absolute that you will," she says. "I think there's a big psychological component at work here. For men, sex is a way of stress relief, and after they have an orgasm, they allow themselves to relax, give themselves permission to drift off." By the same reasoning, we ought to be able to exert enough mental control that we can keep ourselves awake long enough to find out what's going on on her side of the bed.

And as we said, as women come down, they need soothing words, gentle touching, and a sense of warmth and affection—all of which is incumbent upon you to generate.

"This is a time when women want to feel loved and close and intimate, and it doesn't take much for a man to help her feel that way," says Robert Birch, Ph.D., a psychologist in Columbus, Ohio, specializing in marriage and sex therapy and author of *Oral Caress*. But that little bit means an awful lot. "You don't want sex to become an all-or-nothing deal where you're just having the physical contact of intercourse. Women need the talking, the holding, the reassuring, the close time. If they don't have that, then over time you're going to have a problem. She's not going to feel valued, and you're not going to know what's going on with her," says Dr. Birch.

Yes, we know you're probably tired after sex. Yes, we know you'd like nothing better than to drift off to sleep filled with the knowledge of a job well done. "Except you're not quite finished—the sex is not yet over," says Dr. Birch. Now's the time when you can follow through on what has just happened and reinforce to your partner how good she is, how desirable you find her, how much you care for her.

"It only takes a couple minutes, and it's so worth it," says Dr. Virtue. And by giving her a little attention right after you've had sex, you're basically guaranteeing more sex for yourself in the future. Here are some tried-and-true methods that will not only put a satisfying ending to this bedtime story but also leave open the possibility of a sequel.

Tell, don't show. Talk about how great she was. Don't give a blow-by-blow account, but don't just leave it at "Baby, you're the greatest" either. Tell her how sexy she is, how good it was, how incredible she makes you feel. It's not enough to be delirious about how great you feel—make it clear that you feel so good because she made you feel so good. A few well-chosen words are all you need. Don't babble.

Show, don't tell. Now that you've said your piece, take her in your arms. Hold her close. Grunt in contentment. This takes—what?—30 seconds? A minute? "You can stay awake that long. Just don't roll away. Roll toward her," says Dr. Virtue.

Be gentle with her. As you're showing your affection and appreciation of her, don't be ham-fisted and clumsy about it. After orgasm, many of her more erogenous zones are probably a little too sensitive to be handled, and what felt good at the height of ecstasy may be too intense during resolution. Caress her lightly, using a featherweight touch. Give her a light massage, no deep-muscle kneading.

Be her waiter. Perhaps you're one of those lucky men who can naturally avoid the urge to fall asleep right after sex. Perhaps you get up, go the bathroom, come back to bed, then fall asleep. When you get up, ask if she wants anything—a glass of water, for example. "You're showing some extra bit of attention to her, demonstrating an added concern for her needs. That extra effort can go a long way," says Dr. Virtue. Whatever she asks for, whether it's a cup of tap water or a plate of appetizers, bring it to her.

Do something else together. Once you've trained yourself to stay awake for a while, Dr. Virtue suggests sharing some other activity besides sex. Depending on the time of day, you could go for a walk or cook a meal together. "Of course, you don't have to leave the bedroom," she says. Watch a movie in bed. Read to each other. The point is to continue sharing with one another to maintain that closeness your lovemaking has built.

Afterplay on the day after. If you don't live together, call her up the next day. If you do live together, call her up the next day. Or you could just make a passing reference. "Last night was really wonderful." Extra credit: Once in a while, send her a rose at work. "You'll be her hero," says Dr. Virtue. But at this point, are you participating in afterplay, or is it really foreplay? Pretty soon you'll start to see just how true it is that terms like *foreplay* and *afterplay* only describe parts of the much larger whole of your sex lives together.

SOCIETAL PRESSURES

It's a crusty, old, manly man expression: "Pressure makes diamonds." And in the realm of sex and relationships, pressure can indeed take a man and twist him into something unrecognizable.

Like it or not, how we conduct relationships is informed by numerous outside forces. This is pretty much unavoidable. We are, after all, social creatures. Part of what shapes us is how we interact with society—our friends, our family, our society at large. Much as we want to be our own person and think our own thoughts, on some level we want to conform, too.

And so, without even realizing it, we give in to certain myths and messages, allowing them to shape or warp not only our aesthetic sense but also how we make sense of our world, our society, and our relationships.

MAN AGAINST SOCIETY

Books, magazines, movies, newspapers, and advertising all work in concert to spoon-feed us a rather odd view of life. Under the influence of the media, we are told, for example, that "beauty" is a painfully thin woman with gigantic breasts and long legs. "Handsome" is a man six feet tall with a full head of hair, six-pack abs, and a butt as hard as a bowling ball. And if we want either to be these people or to attract them into our lives, we have to wear the right clothes, drink the right beer, eat the right diet supplements, buy the right hair-replacement system, use the right deodorant.

Sometimes, though, the messages are less subtle but more conflicting—a study in paradox. On one hand, the sheer amount of sex depicted in American movies and TV shows tells us that sex is an endlessly hot, endlessly passionate, endlessly sweaty free-for-all where a man can leapfrog from partner to partner—even if he's married—and get away with it. But flip a channel or a page and suddenly there's a public service announcement about safe sex or a story lambasting a prominent man for having a mistress—or even just a foot fetish. Whatever your view of morality or sexual correctness, you can't deny the mixed messages.

Psychologists and anthropologists say that when we see these sorts of conflicting messages every day, we ourselves become conflicted. About what's right and wrong in the realm of sex and relationships. About how we should conduct ourselves in those relationships. About how we should discuss these issues with one another. Men are especially guilty of this. We can joke about sex, even brag about specific events or endowments. But we can't bring ourselves to talk seriously about it.

"That highlights another contradiction. As permissive as the media makes us out to be, in fact, Americans are really quite prudish when it comes to dealing with sexual issues," says Helen Fisher, Ph.D., research associate in the department of anthropology at Rutgers University in New Brunswick, New Jersey, and author of *Anatomy of Love*. If we could learn to filter out some of these messages, or at least recognize when we're being influenced by outside forces, we'd be far less conflicted and probably have a lot less trouble in our relationships.

FIGHTING THE FORCES OF FAMILY AND FRIENDS

As powerful as the media and popular culture are, there's an even greater external force at work in our lives: the obvious and subtle social forces exerted on us by family and friends. Our capacity for love and intimacy is developed in our earliest years. From birth, our families taught us how to interact with people, says Dr. Fisher, and thereafter they continue to influence us. We all remember how our parents tried to impose their opinions on our lives and our choices about jobs, friends, and lovers, always wondering when we were ever going to "settle down and grow up/get married/start a family."

Friends, meanwhile, are in many ways our benchmarks: We're constantly comparing what we're feeling and how we're doing with what they're feeling and doing. Looking back over your life, you may also have noticed how most of your pals—you included—seemed to get married or have kids or get divorced all within a few years of each other. Some of that is a result of you being the same age or on similar tracks in life, certainly. But we're also willing to bet that among your acquaintances, you know a guy who looked around and said, "Gee, Jake's settling down. I guess it's time for me to do that, too."

THRIVING UNDER PRESSURE

If hearing about the pervasiveness of societal pressure on our love lives makes you a little angry, well, maybe it should. In a world full of sheep, we all like to imagine that we're the one in the black wool. Or better yet, we see ourselves as the wolf in sheep's clothing, adopting the veneer of conformity when beneath that docile exterior beats the heart of a powerful predator. To hear that we're secretly being brainwashed by the actions of our friends and our culture, well, it's annoying.

"That's good, though. It should bother you. Any time we start to give in to messages from the outside, we should have some awareness of it so that we can control what's happening," says Lonnie Barbach, Ph.D., a clinical psychologist in San Francisco and author of *For Each Other: Sharing Sexual Intimacy.*

As Dr. Barbach explains, awareness is the first step to avoiding outside pressures on the natural progress of your relationship. And there are other ways to make sure that you don't succumb to peer pressure, Hollywood-ized reality, or the weight of your cultural norms. Here's how.

Question your drives. First, you have to ask yourself: What's pushing you? "If you're feeling the pressure to do or not do something, try to identify the source of that pressure," says Dr. Barbach. If it's coming from within, if this is how you genuinely feel, then do it. If it's coming from outside, watch out.

Avoid countermoves. One danger to recognizing when you're being pushed by someone or something is the instinctive reaction to dig in your heels and fight it. It's what makes men men: As soon as we realize a force is controlling us, it's a knee-jerk reaction to fight. Just on principle.

Of course, another way to look at it is that you're acting out of spite. Doing the exact opposite because that will show the forces arrayed against you. This can be especially destructive in relationships.

"When you feel the urge to react this way, it's always a good idea to take a time-out to ask yourself: What do I want?" says Steve Manley, Ph.D., staff psychologist for the Male Health Center in Dallas. Just touching base with yourself in this way can give you the strength to resist external pressure and do exactly what it is you feel you need to do.

Don't believe the hype. A good rule of thumb: If you see sex on a TV or movie screen, it's not real sex. Trust us, it's not. Think actors, think special effects, think fantasy. Is it realistic that you're both going to have perfect bodies, that the lighting is going to be that flattering, that John Williams is going to be scoring a soundtrack in the background?

"It's important to sensitize yourself to when you're getting outside input, messages that are influencing you," says Dr. Barbach. Try this exercise: Count the number of minutes of the average on-screen sexual encounter, before they cut away to the morning after. Do you want all your sexual encounters to be that short?

Count off. Here's another exercise. Watch a prime-time soap opera—any one, it doesn't matter. Now, in the space of that hour of fine programming, count the number of sexual references you see—it could be a kiss, a racy double entendre, or outright coitus. This exercise accomplishes two purposes. First, it opens your eyes to just how often you're exposed to sex through the popular media. Second, it helps build up your resistance to the influence of such a bombardment of highly idealized sexual information.

Third, it also makes you realize just how much crap is on TV these days.

Don't keep up. As living, breathing testosterone factories, it's our nature to be competitive, even with friends. Especially with friends. When an old pal gets a vice presidency while you're still languishing in Cubicle City, you suddenly feel the itch for career advancement. This sort of competitive spirit extends beyond the workplace and into relationships, too. When a pal's getting married, getting divorced, having kids, or having an affair, for a lot of guys, the first impulse is to try to play catch-up. But what's good for your friend is not good for you.

"Ultimately, it boils down to one thing: We're the only ones who can decide for ourselves what is good or bad for us," says Dr. Manley. "Friends and family can be helpful and provide support and advice, but they cannot live your life for you." Only you can do that. You're on your own, big guy.

PORNOGRAPHY

Okay, pretend you're the Supreme Court. Today, you have to render a decision on the burning question: What is pornography? Is it:

a.) The stash of girlie magazines your dad kept in the back shed
b.) The triple-X videos they showed at your bachelor party
c.) The steamy novels your wife keeps in the nightstand
d.) The seamy, hard-core stuff involving exploited children, animals, or other perversions too terrible to mention in a family book
e.) All of the above

Technically, you could argue the answer is "e"—it's all pornography. We almost hate to say that, though, because "pornography" is such a dirty word these days. Webster's broadly tells us that pornography is any material that describes or depicts erotic behavior with the intent of causing sexual excitement. It makes no distinction between the tamest and the wildest of racy material and makes no judgment call about its inherent goodness or badness.

That's a little too all-encompassing to suit us. We prefer to think that, like art, like beauty, pornography is in the eye of the beholder. Heck, even the real Supreme Court can't make up its mind what truly constitutes pornography, but they know it when they see it. You probably do, too.

For the most part, pornography is not an illegal or necessarily immoral offshoot of our culture. Like other controversial entertainment (e.g., boxing, hunting, radical talk radio), pornography can be a valuable resource when done and consumed in a civilized manner. And it can be a destructive force when used improperly—when you use it to the point that it becomes more satisfying to you than a flesh-and-blood relationship, for example. The experts we spoke to say that, contrary to some prevailing notions, buying and enjoying pornography does not mean you secretly hate women, or that over time you'll come to respect the female sex less.

"There's no doubt that erotic material can be used to enhance a couple's sex life," says Anne Semans, one of the owners of the adult store Good Vibrations in San Francisco and co-author of *The Good Vibrations Guide to Sex*. "It can be a very positive, enhancing thing. Where it's bad is when you start relying on it to 'fix' a relationship. Or if it's being used to the point that it makes one or both of you uncomfortable." The bottom line: If you're a discriminating, intelligent, and thoughtful fellow, you should be able to use and enjoy pornography without guilt.

MEN: BORN TO LIKE PORN

When you peer beneath the surface of the medium, though, it's clear that pornography has more to do with primal instinct and genetic wiring than intelligence or thought.

"Men almost can't help but respond to pornographic material. This is not a weakness; this is how men are built," says Doreen Virtue, Ph.D., a relationship expert and psychotherapist in Newport Beach, California, and author of *In the Mood*. As Dr. Virtue explains, men are creatures of visual stimuli. There's a wire that travels from our eyes to our genitals. Flash us an image of a centerfold and an arousal process begins south of the belt buckle. On this basic impulse is built a billion-dollar industry of books, magazines, videos, and other media all catering to that pump-priming need to see sex with our own eyes.

And perhaps because it's so image-based, men's pornography gets the lion's share of negative attention and scrutiny. Women's pornography, meanwhile, barely registers on any social critic's radar.

Wait a sec—women's pornography? Can there be such a thing?

Porn Policies

If you enjoy pornography regularly, or are planning on it soon, here are a few basic guidelines to save you any potential pain or embarrassment.

Keep out of reach of children. If you have children in the house, take appropriate precautions. Store erotic videos separately from any others in the house. And as an extra measure of safety and privacy, keep them physically out of reach—in a high cupboard or locked cabinet, just like the liquor.

Be aware of the law. A prudent man knows it pays to check local laws to see what crimes or misdemeanors he might or might not be committing by, say, ordering videos from out of state or bringing home a little "gift" for the wife in his overnight bag. Not all lawmakers are as liberal as you, remember.

Be appropriately discreet. For reasons of local standing or political correctness, you may feel uncomfortable going to the adult shop that's just off the airport highway. In that case—and assuming you've followed the rule above—order your material from any number of discreet and reputable firms. Here are our favorites.

Access Instructional Media (educational tapes)
16161 Ventura Boulevard #328
Encino, CA 91436
(800) 772-0708

Good Vibrations
938 Howard Street
San Francisco, CA 94103
(800) 289-8423

Eve's Garden
119 West 57th Street #420
New York, NY 10019
(800) 848-3837

Xandria Collection
165 Valley Drive
Brisbane, CA 94005
(800) 242-2823

"Of course, and it's perhaps even more pervasive than men's pornography," says Galdino F. Pranzarone, Ph.D., professor of psychology at Roanoke College in Salem, Virginia. It's available in any supermarket or convenience store—and not behind the checkout counter either, but right out on the shelves. Even the most refined booksellers devote millions of square feet to the thousands of volumes of pornography women buy and devour in droves.

We're talking, of course, about the romance novel.

Oh, it sounds wonderfully innocent. According to experts, though, the steamy scenarios of a romance novel are to women what the Playmate of the Month is to men.

"Where men need visual stimuli for arousal to occur, women respond to verbal stimuli. Explicit words, either spoken or written, can ignite a strong sexual response—even stronger than the response men get from seeing explicit images," says Dr. Pranzarone. Consider that the biggest selling genre of books is the romance novel. Women can't get enough of them. Why? Certainly not because it's great literature but because it depicts scenarios that arouse women, subtly, in a way that's not terribly graphic. "The two are at opposite ends of the spectrum. She sees the *Playboy* and says 'Ugh!' He sees the Harlequin romance and says 'Ugh!' Visual versus verbal," says Dr. Virtue.

PORNO FOR PARTNERS

As opposite as these two types of pornography seem, there are ways to merge the two, to find erotica that will satisfy both you and your partner at the same time. And that's a good thing.

"About the best way to use pornography is to use it together. When couples share it, it can be a great way to spice up their sex lives, to get ideas and inspiration," says Semans. The trick is to find the right kind of erotic material, which features the best of both visual and verbal content. Here are our suggestions for the proper perusal and procurement of partner pornography.

Movies. You may not be aware of this—we were surprised to learn this ourselves—but many X-rated movies today actually contain plots. That may not matter much to you, but it will definitely matter to your partner. "Seeing 90 minutes of mindless screwing isn't going to do much for her. On the other hand, movies with some story line, some erotic language, are going to arouse her," says Semans. Some champions in this genre of video include the classic *Behind the Green Door* and *The Devil in Miss Jones*, and the more contemporary "Emmanuelle" series available on video and cable.

Incidentally, who says the movie has to be X-rated? Some of the steamiest movies around carry an R or NC-17 rating and have a nice balance of plot and graphic nudity (see our list on page 116 for some examples).

Books. You already know about the romance novel and its erotic power over women. There are somewhat steamier and more explicit literary choices, too. No, we're not talking *Penthouse Forum* (although some of those "real-life" letters do have a certain crude appeal). We're referring to erotic literature—works by Anais Nin, Marco Vassi's *The Vassi Collection*, or *Erotic Interludes* and other explicit anthologies edited by Lonnie Barbach, Ph.D. No pictures, but powerful, page-turning, seductive writing. Take turns reading the stories—or at least the hottest parts of the stories—to one another.

Instructional media. Sex manuals and videos can be terrific turn-ons, once you get past the clinical veneer or the chatty how-to format of these

Critics' Choice

Some of the best pornographic movies on the market aren't even X-rated yet feature plenty of sex for your satisfaction and plenty of plot for her pleasure. Recently, *Men's Health* polled top movie critics for their picks of the steamiest, sexiest movies. The following choices are available at your local mainstream video store.

- *Body Heat* (1981): Kathleen Turner and William Hurt make it hurt so good in this steamer. Watch for the ice cube scene!
- *Carnal Knowledge* (1971): Jack Nicholson and Ann-Margret set the screen ablaze in this tale of erotic obsession at the dawn of the women's liberation movement.
- *Casablanca* (1942): Who could forget that scene where Ingrid Bergman slips out of her gown and—wait a minute, there's no sex in *Casablanca*! Still, when you see the sexual chemistry between Bogart and Bergman and feel the sheer romanticism of this wartime love story, you'll understand why we put it on the list.
- *The Last Seduction* (1994): Linda Fiorentino has raw, passionate sex again and again with Bill Pullman. Did we say *has* raw, passionate sex? She *is* raw, passionate sex.
- *Last Tango in Paris* (1973): Available in both R- and X-rated versions, Marlon Brando broke new ground and a few taboos making this sexually intense and realistic movie about a man trying to forget his dead wife by entering into a no-questions-asked sexual liaison.

products. *Joy of Sex*, by Alex Comfort, M.D., D.Sc., remains a classic both for its nice illustrations and also its great writing, which describes numerous positions and practices in a way that is both titillating and useful. On the video side, the Good Vibrations folks recommend *Dutch Sex: A Lifelong Pleasure* as well as the popular *Better Sex* series advertised in most magazines.

Other media. If you want to transcend the conventional modes of pornographic arousal, there are other forms of media you can enjoy. Audiotapes, like Cyborgasm, boast a stereo recording of 16 different sexual vignettes full of groans, moans, and even a few cracking whips. Several CD-ROM products can also turn your computer into a sex machine. Or if you have Internet access, you can log on to various sex newsgroups and get access to true, fictional, wild, and weird stories and images (for more information, see Cybersex on page 310).

Live entertainment. Although it's not something you would probably partake of together, strip clubs can also provide a healthy jolt to the libido. If you decide to head off to a strip joint while she gets her kicks from Chippendale's, that's fine—so long as you have full disclosure with one another about what you're doing.

In fact, that's good advice for any pornography you use. "It's always best if you're open with your partner," says Sherry Lehman, a sex therapist in Cleveland and author of *Seven Days to Better Sex and a More Loving Relationship*. "If you're each using pornography separately, it's okay, as long as there's an understanding that you're using it to bring something back to the relationship."

And if you have a partner who just wouldn't understand about that stash of girlie magazines or videos you have? Don't worry too much about keeping it a secret. "It's not ideal," says Lehman. "But it's not really a problem, so long as a secret use of pornography isn't a crutch, isn't something meant to take the place of the relationship." If you find that you are relying on pornography in place of real flesh-and-blood excitement, then you might be ignoring some important issues in your relationship that need more tending to than your video collection.

PROSTITUTION

We live in a society of commerce. Our lives and our livelihoods depend on the exchange of goods and services. In certain situations, in certain circles, sex is the coin of the realm.

When you view it a certain way, sex is a marketplace all its own. It's all about negotiations. An exchange of looks, the trading of pleasantries, a delicate commerce where kisses and touches and caresses are the currency. Sometimes this form of emotional commerce leads to sex; sometimes negotiations break off.

In its own fashion, prostitution takes the abstracts of sexual exchange and renders them in concrete terms: erotic acts and services in exchange for hard cash. These transactions occur in a range of venues. At the low end, it can be as simple and as unsavory as oral sex in a back alley for 20 bucks. More commonly, you could shell out $100 or more for a hand job or fellatio in the more "respectable" climes of a massage parlor. And for a chosen few with the money to spend, you could pay $1,000 or more for an evening with the best an escort service has to offer.

We're not here to teach you the art of negotiations in any of these worlds. This is not a how-to chapter. You won't find any insider tips for engaging in what is, after all, an illegal act in 49 states.

But it's important to talk about prostitution honestly. In the history of sex, the concept of sex for money has a long—and sometimes noble—tradition in many societies. In ancient Mesopotamia, prostitution was considered an essential service industry. Early Greek writings give prostitution a religious aspect: The historian Herodotus talks about holy temples where women served as prostitutes to any stranger who made a donation to the temple goddess.

Even today, the world's oldest profession has no shortage of customers. In the comprehensive *Sex in America* study, 16 percent of men reported having paid money for sex; and many more have certainly thought about it. Even the most law-abiding and morally conservative single man has asked himself, "Who needs the hassle, the ups and downs, the emotional roller coaster of dating, the hellish half-life of trying to meet women and impress them enough to get them into the sack?"

"Therein lies one of the most basic reasons to pay for sex," says Norma Jean Almodovar, who was a prostitute for about 15 years. Now she's an activist, executive director of the southern California branch of COYOTE (Call Off Your Old Tired Ethics), a group devoted to promoting prostitute rights and the decriminalization of prostitution. "Why go through all that trouble, and have no guaranteed outcome, when you could save yourself time and energy by simply seeking out a professional, negotiating a fee, and having your needs met in a perfunctory, businesslike fashion?"

Why indeed?

WHY WE DO IT

At first glance, it just doesn't add up. Statistics tell us that there are more women on this planet than there are men. Why can't a guy just get a date? Then he can have sex for free.

"You know better than that," says Almodovar. "It's not about ratios. It's not because a man is shy or socially inept—not always. It's not because he's sick or has some sort of sexual addiction. There are many, many reasons why someone is going to go to a prostitute." And many different kinds of men who will proposition a sex worker.

"We've arrested plenty of guys who are confident, powerful, successful men. They're married or dating these gorgeous women—and still they go to prostitutes," says Lt. Det. Robert O'Toole, former director of information services for the Boston Police Department. O'Toole spent seven years working the vice detail. "I've posed as a john, and I've posed as a male prostitute. I've seen the broad range of clients."

While O'Toole and the prostitutes we interviewed may disagree on the legality of prostitution, they all agree on one thing—the clientele come from all walks of life: rich men, poor men, married, single, gay, straight, outgoing thrill seekers, and shy nebbishes alike.

"And for every different type of man, there's going to be a different reason for going to a prostitute," says Carol Leigh, a prostitute/activist who runs the Prostitutes' Education Network on the Internet. As we mentioned earlier,

Leigh says that some men would genuinely rather pay for sex than deal with all the interpersonal agonies and potential disappointments the dating world entails. For some men—married or single—it's the thrill factor, pure and simple. "Some people get off on danger and the fear of getting caught."

Still others find themselves in stagnant relationships and feel that they have no other outlet. "They're not getting what they want at home, so they go to a place or a person where they know they can get it," says Almodovar.

And there is a small but significant portion of physically disabled clientele for whom Almodovar says prostitution is a godsend. "They may be physically undesirable to a partner. Or if they do meet someone, they may wonder whether this person is really interested in them, or if she is just taking pity on them. They have enough problems in life that they don't want to worry about attracting a partner and wondering if she is sincere. Meanwhile, they have the same sexual needs and desires as other men. This is where my work is especially satisfying. We provide a genuine therapeutic service to these men."

Almodovar points out that in Europe, some doctors have gone so far as to solicit prostitutes on behalf of disabled patients, recognizing that some sexual contact benefits their patients' well-being.

IF YOU'RE CONSIDERING IT

Perhaps you're one of the 16 percent who spends his hard-earned dollars on sexual services. Perhaps you're one of an untold number who's just toying with the idea. In either case, we urge you to think twice before proceeding any further. Entering a business relationship with a prostitute is like entering any other relationship where sex is involved. Take a moment to consider what you're doing before you go in. In the heat of sexual frustration, chances are that you're not thinking clearly. So now, while you have a calm, clear moment, we'd like to remind you of a few facts about prostitution as it exists today.

It's illegal. In 49 states, soliciting a prostitute is a misdemeanor, a real embarrassing, career-damaging one, at that, unless your name happens to be Hugh Grant. You could be looking at fines, jail time, and public exposure.

"In Boston, we sentence convicted johns to sweep the streets," says O'Toole. "Then we invite the media to come and take photos and video of the johns while they're serving their sentences. It sends a clear message to guys who are thinking about hiring a prostitute. They think: That could be me on TV."

It's unregulated. The funny thing about an illegal activity is that there's no committee or governing body to ensure the quality of the merchandise you're buying. You run all sorts of risk to yourself and your property.

Prostitutes themselves are the first to point out this fact. "One of the reasons we're involved in efforts to decriminalize prostitution is to make it safer for everyone—clients and prostitutes," says Almodovar. And while the vast majority of prostitutes insist on safer sex, "Where there's sex, there's always the risk of disease," she says.

Conflicts of interest. If you happen to be married and using a prostitute, we'd like to remind you of a clause in the standard marriage contract—see Section 4, under "Forsaking All Others." Put simply, you already gave your word that this was the sort of thing you weren't going to do within the bonds of matrimony. Are you really the sort of man whose word is no good?

And whether you're married or dating, take a hard look at why you're leaning toward paying for sex. Ask yourself some important questions: What's missing? Try to find out what needs aren't being met—not just physical needs but emotional ones, too.

3

PHYSICAL MASTERY

UNDERSTANDING SEX DRIVE

What is it that sparks a man's hunger for sex? Don't try to count the ways. How can you count to infinity? The desire for sex is kindled by a complex mix of internal chemistry and external triggers as subtle as a smile, as blunt as a porno film. By the smell of a perfume or the sound of a song's lyrics. By touching another's body or our own. By a thought. A meal. A dream.

Just as the cause of sexual hunger varies with the wind, so does the amount of sexual appetite a person has at any given moment. While men and women may have a yearning for sex throughout their lifetimes, that hunger can vary enormously day by day, year by year, not unlike the wild undulations of a stock market. For some, sex drive can take a downturn from which they never recover. (Talk about a great depression.) Others, however, can look forward to being bullish in bed for a lifetime. One way to end up in the latter camp is to invest a little time in learning the intricacies of sex drive—yours and hers. It can pay big dividends.

First of all, know this: There is no typical or average sex drive or libido. "There is a very wide range," says Domeena Renshaw, M.D., director of Loyola Sex Therapy Clinic at Loyola University in Chicago and author of *Seven Weeks to Better Sex*. "It's uniquely individual."

So men who have low libido needn't feel that they are inadequate. "If they're perfectly content, it shouldn't become a problem," Dr. Renshaw says. "It's a problem when in a committed relationship, the partner is discontented. Then we see them."

In the pages ahead, we'll cover the physiological factors first, then take up the role of the mind. Then we'll explore how the two mesh.

THE ROLE OF HORMONES

Women might want to think twice the next time they make cracks about the male sex hormone testosterone when commenting on some guy's supercharged sex drive. That's because testosterone also revs up their own sex engines. It's just that all eight of our cylinders are pumped with this potent fuel. The women's motors get just a small amount. Testosterone and other hormones are the stuff that create "a vague unrest," says Ted McIlvenna, Ph.D., president of the Institute for Advanced Study of Human Sexuality in San Francisco. That unrest is your sex drive—a deep-rooted feeling that does not need erotic stimulation but upon which further sexual stimulation then builds. It is affected, for better or worse, by physical and emotional factors.

"It's testosterone that gives you the ability to sexually function," says Dr. McIlvenna. It does so by acting as a conduit between nerve cells and the brain and creating desire. Without desire, having an erection is like being given the keys to a Ferrari that has no gas.

Testosterone is produced in our testicles and then flows into our bloodstreams, where it is omnipresent. The amount of testosterone a man has in his blood varies not only throughout his life but also during the course of a day. When we win an argument or a tennis match, or when we have sexual thoughts or intercourse, our testosterone rises. Combine this testosterone with a mental stimulus, and the next thing you know, blood is rushing into our penis and—tah-dah!—we have an erection. Preferably in the bedroom, not on the tennis court.

Oddly, testosterone also has a "loner profile" that, among other things, increases a guy's urge to masturbate rather than his desire for intercourse, says sex therapist Theresa Crenshaw, M.D., author of *The Alchemy of Love and Lust.* It's that quality in the hormone that also makes guys want to head to another room after intercourse, often to the chagrin of their partners, she says.

Of course, testosterone is much more than a sex hormone. It also is responsible for the following:

- Shaping our penis, scrotum, and testicles when we were embryos
- Promoting development of our muscle mass, bones, and cognitive skills
- Making us aggressive, assertive, confident—it's because of testosterone that we are more likely to get enraged by a rude driver or go to war
- Being a natural antidepressant—for both genders

A man's sex drive and his ability to get an erection or to ejaculate can be affected if he has a hormonal imbalance that causes a deficiency in his testosterone, says Dr. Renshaw. Tumors in the pituitary gland, for example, can cause an imbalance, as can radiation treatment for prostate cancer, says Dr. Renshaw. Fortunately, hormone imbalances are rare, particularly in younger men, and treatable.

But a guy with a normal testosterone level and a sex drive stuck in neutral will not benefit by infusions of more testosterone. In fact, it could harm him by interfering with his normal hormonal cycles. That's what happens when bodybuilders and athletes take anabolic steroids. These synthetic hormones, among other things, shrivel guys' testicles and destroy their fertility.

In truth, you probably don't want to have too much testosterone. A guy who does "is more self-centered, selfish, and has a personality profile not unlike a psychotic," writes Dr. Crenshaw.

A Pennsylvania State University study of hormone levels of more than 4,000 men seems to support her. The study found that men with high testosterone levels were less likely to get married. Those who did marry were more

Testosterone's Helpers

Testosterone has help from several other chemicals in playing a key role in sex drives. Among its cohorts are the following:

• LH-RH (luteinizing hormone–releasing hormone). A gorgeous babe sits on the bar stool next to you and smiles seductively. Wham! This hormone is released, and it, in turn, tells your testicles to come up with some more testosterone—fast. LH-RH also acts as testosterone's safety valve. If your testosterone level dips, LH-RH prompts the testicles to produce more. When testosterone reaches a sufficient level, the brain receives a message to stop LH-RH secretion.

• Serotonin. Low levels of this hormone intensify sex, and it seems to always be low when testosterone levels are up, increasing our sexual appetite and our aggression, says sex therapist Theresa Crenshaw, M.D., author of *The Alchemy of Love and Lust*. But extremely low levels of serotonin could have dire consequences. Animals in which the hormone has been depleted will torture, kill, and sometimes devour their mate during sex. Some will even mount dead animals, according to Dr. Crenshaw. We humans don't go to such extremes. But low levels of serotonin in men does increase their aggression, especially if they are hard drinkers, she says.

• Dopamine and PEA. Dopamine is a neurotransmitter that makes you seek and pursue pleasure, and yearn for the pleasure of sex. PEA, or phenylethylamine, is sometimes called the molecule of love. A natural amphetamine produced by our bodies, it produces feelings of giddiness and elation. Not surprising, high levels have been found in the bloodstreams of lovers.

apt to have affairs, physically abuse their wives, and dump them because they could not get along with them.

THE ROLE OF THE MIND

"People think sex drives are largely biological," says Al Cooper, Ph.D., clinical director of the San Jose Marital and Sexuality Centre in California. "They are mainly psychological events."

While acknowledging that testosterone is important to fueling one's sex drive, it's only one part of the equation, Dr. Cooper and other sex therapists stress. The other is that 3-pound lump of gray matter inside our skulls.

It is our minds that convert a scent, a sight, even a sound into a desire for sex. Each person is triggered differently, based on preferences and attitudes that have accumulated since childhood. Some guys are aroused by legs, others by breasts, others by the sight of a bare back and long hair. This is not physiological; this is mental programming.

Are there commonalities among men? Certainly. Guys are justly fa-

- Oxytocin and vasopressin. These are peptide molecules—chemicals that interact with our hormones—that are sometimes known as the monogamy molecules. That's because oxytocin in women is thought to promote the bonding or commitment of partners, while vasopressin is believed to have the same effect in men.
- DHEA (dehydroepiandrosterone). This is the most abundant hormone that men and women have. Produced mainly by the adrenal glands above the kidneys, it increases sexual desire, perhaps more so in women than men. And it is thought to produce pheromones that give off our scent through the skin, perhaps influencing whom we are attracted to. But we have to enjoy its effects quickly. Its production peaks by age 25 and drops steadily thereafter.

Women's sex drives react differently to some of the same chemicals we have in our bodies. Take serotonin. While this hormone heats up aggression and sexual appetite in guys, it has the opposite effect on women, Dr. Crenshaw says.

When serotonin was lowered in female rodents, they became really amorous, but they weren't picky about whom they coupled with. They mounted other females and smaller males. And some even made humping gestures like those of males ejaculating. We don't know that women would necessarily react this way. But Dr. Crenshaw says that women who are abusers of amphetamines—which lower serotonin—have an increase in promiscuity, compulsively masturbate, engage in prostitution, and have sado-masochistic fantasies.

mous—or infamous—for needing very little mental spark to ignite their sexual engines. And the top stimuli for men are visual—the sight of something arousing, usually an attractive female body. "Men are more tuned into visual cues," says Dr. Cooper. "A man may not feel sexual toward his wife, but if he sees Pamela Lee on *Baywatch*, then he might feel very sexual toward her. The women won't get the same sort of charge out of looking at something." Skeptical? Just compare the sales of *Playboy* and *Playgirl* magazines, Dr. Cooper suggests.

In fact, our minds are so powerful that in some cases you can remove a man's testicles—where testosterone and sperm are produced—and he still will be interested in sex and become aroused, says licensed psychologist William R. Stayton, Th.D., professor of human sexuality at the University of Pennsylvania in Philadelphia and president of the American Association of Sex Educators, Counselors, and Therapists (AASECT). For that reason, proposals to castrate sex offenders are ludicrous, he says. "All that means is that they can't have children."

Upping Your Octane

You know that sex drive varies among men. You know that a low libido is nothing to stew about. Still, you want more boost in your rocket, more tiger in your tank. What do you do?

See a doctor. He can tell you if there is a physical reason why your putter isn't a-flutter more often.

Work out. Researchers think that exercise boosts testosterone levels.

Improve your appearance. Lose weight. Buy a new sport coat. How you feel about your body affects your sexuality.

Compartmentalize your life. Put financial worries, work-related stresses, and the like out of your mind during romantic interludes.

Get out of the house. Take a vacation—even for just a weekend. And take the woman in your life with you. A change of scenery and less structured time can put the zing in your thing.

See a therapist. When all else fails, a therapist may help you discover personal issues that are stymieing your drive. Check his or her credentials before committing.

Conversely, a guy with a high level of testosterone might have little sexual desire if he has been taught to dislike sex, says Dr. Stayton. "You take three different men with the same testosterone levels, and they're going to respond three very different ways. A lot of it is going to come from how they were socialized."

Worry, stress, and depression can also impair one's sex drive as can illness, fatigue, and many drugs. Job pressures, mortgage woes, and anger at one's spouse or children are examples of the sorts of things that can run a man's libido off course, says Dudley Seth Danoff, M.D., senior attending urologist at Cedars-Sinai Medical Center in Los Angeles and author of *Superpotency*. "What happens between your ears definitely reflects what happens between your legs," he says.

"The old stereotype was the 365-day headache for women," says Dr. Renshaw. "But we've seen as many 'headaches' in the man as in the woman."

And yet some men who seek professional help don't really have deficient libidos, therapists say. Sometimes it's simply a matter of a guy's partner wanting sex more often than he. Or a wife complains that her husband isn't interested in sex, but it turns out that he is routinely masturbating in secret. The problem is not with his sex drive but with his relationship.

"What I hear over and over is that it's less hassle doing it with yourself rather than going through the business of foreplay and everything else," Dr. Renshaw says. "It becomes another job to do."

HOW HORMONES AND THE MIND MESH

Like Astaire and Rogers or pigs and mud, your hormones and your mind are an inseparable duo. Each is dependent upon and connected to the other in the urge we call sex drive. Your testosterone is just sitting there in your blood minding its business when something—a touch, a fantasy, a smell—triggers the old arousal switch. Then the chemicals kick in. Testosterone and

The Smell of Love

Some experts think that in addition to visual cues, erotic thoughts, and being touched, there is another stimulus that triggers sexual desire—chemical signals called pheromones.

The theory is that a half-inch inside our noses we have something called a vomeronasal organ—VNO for short—that detects pheromones. We know that other animals and insects have pheromones, but their existence among humans is less clear.

If we do emit pheromones, it's believed that we do so through our sweat, skin, hair, saliva, and urine. Licensed psychologist William R. Stayton, Th.D., professor of human sexuality at the University of Pennsylvania in Philadelphia and president of the American Association of Sex Educators, Counselors, and Therapists (AASECT), is a believer. "I think we get this from our animal background," he says. "I think as we evolved, we lost a lot of this, but not all of it. You have to ask why some people get really attracted by some other people, and it could be that it's in the pheromones. What turns on one man doesn't turn on another man. We call it chemistry. I think it is chemistry."

An experiment with pedophiles lends credence to the pheromone theory, Dr. Stayton says. Pedophiles generally are attracted to children in a two-year age range, say, ages 5 to 7, he says. The experiment placed pedophiles in a room, face to a corner, while a child in his preferred age range entered the room out of his field of vision. The pedophile would know the child was present. But when a child entered the room that was either younger or older than those desired by the pedophile, he was unaware of their existence, Dr. Stayton says.

"That's sort of a glowing example, I think, that there is something in our chemistry that we put out that attracts," says Dr. Stayton.

Others, however, are unconvinced. "It's still controversial as far as research goes," says Domeena Renshaw, M.D., director of Loyola Sex Therapy Clinic at Loyola University in Chicago and author of *Seven Weeks to Better Sex*. "Of course, we make pheromones, but we don't have a heat the same way our mammalian cousins do."

Besides, Dr. Renshaw sniffs, "We use deodorants to the point of being without any odor," all but losing our natural scent anyway.

neurotransmitters such as dopamine create the urge to pursue pleasure. The brain then messages the penis ("Wake up, penis!") via the nervous system to prepare for an erection. Blood vessels expand and blood swooshes in. Congratulations. You have an erection.

To what extent our hormones or our minds influence our sexual behavior often depends on who is doing the interpreting. Men are often portrayed—probably accurately—as complaining that their partners have lower sex drives, while women say that men want sex too much, says Dr. Cooper.

Blame our brains, says Dr. Stayton. "Males are socialized that they are interested, ready at any time with anybody under any circumstances. Females are socialized much more that they're not sexual, that their interests and desires are going to come out of pleasing a man."

Unless the couple is married. Then the stereotype—again probably accurate—is of a husband who is shirking his marital duties in the bedroom, à la Al Bundy in the sitcom, *Married with Children*, Dr. Cooper says. One reason for this discrepancy is that men want variety, women want romance, he adds.

Blame our hormones, says Dr. Crenshaw. Testosterone creates men's craving for sexual variety or novelty. Estrogen makes women want intimacy.

How Women Differ

You had better communicate well with your woman or be an awfully good mind reader in trying to determine when she's in the mood for sex. Because of their menstrual cycles, a woman's sex drive or desire is far more complex and varied than that of men, Dr. Crenshaw says. She contends that women experience four types of lust of varying intensity, depending on which of their hormones are ebbing and flowing. She identifies them as aggressive, passive, seductive, and resistant. Men (being the primitive brutes that we are) generally have just one type of lust—aggressive, she says.

The trick then for men is to figure out when, hormonally speaking, a woman is most apt to be in the mood for sex during her 28-day cycle. Dr. Crenshaw provides help there, too, by summarizing the results of nearly four dozen studies on this very subject. While each woman has a unique pattern of sexual desire, these studies show some commonalities. Grab a calendar and follow along (for our purposes, the start of menstruation is day one of a woman's cycle).

- Women generally report their most intense sex drives on days six and seven after a period begins.
- A close second in terms of sex drive is just before a woman starts her period—days 25 through 28.
- A distant third is around the time of ovulation—when an egg is released from an ovary. This is days 13 through 15.
- Few women have strong sexual desire during their periods (the first few days of their 28-day cycle).

- Finally, the time of least sexual interest appears to be the second half of her cycle—the time between ovulation and the days immediately before the start of menstruation.

While testosterone is crucial to a woman's sex drive, estrogen is her most important hormone. This is her counterpart to testosterone in a man. Estrogen is responsible for:

I'm So Hot, and She's So Cold

It's a complaint that sex therapists hear all the time: One-half of a couple wants sex a lot more than the other. It has long been a staple of sitcom jokes, but it's no laughing matter.

"I think it's really important that when people partner, they try to partner with somebody whose level of interest is similar," says licensed psychologist William R. Stayton, Th.D., professor of human sexuality at the University of Pennsylvania in Philadelphia and president of the American Association of Sex Educators, Counselors, and Therapists (AASECT).

"If you have a person who likes to have sex five days a week and they partner with somebody who likes to have sex twice a month, it's going to be horrendous. Almost invariably, the person with the lower interest wins. What happens then is that the person with the higher drive becomes agitated, upset, unfulfilled, frustrated. So while the person with the lower interest wins, it really turns out to be a lose-lose situation."

Here are some solutions for men in such a prickly predicament.

Compromise. If you want sex five times a week and your partner prefers it once a week, see if you can settle on three times a week. "Sometimes your needs take precedence, sometimes mine. That's the way we give and take in a relationship. It's called altruism," says Domeena Renshaw, M.D., director of Loyola Sex Therapy Clinic at Loyola University in Chicago.

Masturbate. Either masturbate by yourself or ask your partner to stroke you. "There is no demand on the partner other than to work up the muscles in her arm," notes Dr. Stayton.

Resolve anger. Sometimes the person who wants little sex is repressing anger at his or her partner.

Treat physical problems. Excessive drinking, tranquilizers, hormonal imbalances, and reactions to blood pressure and other medications are but a few of the physical factors that can diminish a person's sex drive. Depression, stress, and fatigue can also be factors.

Become a better lover. If the partner with the lower interest is interested in increasing his or her sex drive, "that could mean just that they need a better lover," Dr. Stayton says.

- Shaping a female's primary sexual characteristics—the vagina, uterus, and ovaries—while she is still in her mother's womb
- Causing mood swings, budding breasts, rounder hips, and other dramatic changes during puberty
- Generating the need for intimacy during sex
- Promoting lubrication of the vagina and sustaining or improving tissue and texture of sex organs

Just as women have some testosterone, men have a little estrogen. But it does not have the impact on their sex drives that testosterone has on women's sex drives.

More men masturbate than women, and they do so more often. We also think about sex a lot more than women. So are women's sex drives weaker than our own raging beasts? No, say some sex therapists.

Women's libidos are just different. Disparities in sex drive are more prevalent within genders, not between them, says Barbara Levinson, R.N., Ph.D., a licensed marriage and family therapist and director of the Center for Healthy Sexuality in Houston. "Men are just more verbal about sex," she says.

Women actually have a greater capacity for sex than men, notes Shirley Zussman, Ed.D., a certified sex and marital therapist in private practice in New York City. Men's erections are more vulnerable to disease than women's sex organs, she says. Unlike men, women don't need to rest from an orgasm before resuming sex again.

Complicating matters more, the conventional wisdom has long been that while men reach their sexual peak in their late teens or early twenties, women don't reach theirs until they are in their thirties. No wonder men want to do it when women don't, and vice versa. Only not everybody buys it. "For me, that doesn't ring true anymore," Dr. Zussman says.

That perception about women may have come about in prior generations when there was more of a stigma attached to women being sexual when they were young and unmarried, Dr. Zussman believes. "I would say that young women between 15 and 20 probably have a high sexual drive. I think masturbation is much more common among young girls today, enabling them to learn much more about their bodies."

DECADES OF DALLYING

One tip-off as to whether you will be amorous as you age is how horny you were as a kid. Studies have shown that both men and women who had a strong interest in sex at a young age were also more inclined to have a high level of interest in their later years, says Dr. Zussman.

That said, men and women both face hurdles to having a lifetime of sex, but most aren't insurmountable. With the onset of menopause, women suddenly and dramatically lose a large amount of one of their most vital hormones—estrogen. This can result in a number of physical and emotional symptoms that can curtail their sex drives—such as a dry, sensitive vagina—that often make intercourse painful. Happily, there are treatments available. And for some women, menopause is a boon to their sex lives.

A man's decline in sex drive is so gradual that some continue to have an active sex life into their eighties and nineties, says Dr. Danoff, who estimates that he has seen more than 100,000 penises in his medical practice.

Indeed, while men gradually produce less testosterone as they age, most of us continue to manufacture this sex drive hormone, along with sperm and semen, until the end of our lives.

"One of the things we believe is that if a person stays sexually active through their early adult and middle years, their testosterone level is not going to go down as much," says Dr. Stayton. Use it or lose it? "Absolutely a truism," he says.

Actually, it's not diminishing testosterone per se that should concern men as they age, says Dr. McIlvenna. It's a decline in what he calls bioavailable-free testosterone that can affect men's sex drives. As we age, he says, more and more of our testosterone becomes bound to blood coagulates. That which doesn't is the good stuff that keeps us interested in sex.

For this reason, a doctor who rules out testosterone deficiency in a man with a flagging sex drive after reviewing his testosterone level may be in error unless the test includes a measurement of his unencumbered testosterone.

Certain medications and illnesses can also take their toll on a man's sex drive as he gets older. But most of these can be corrected. As long as men and women remain interesting partners to each other, many will be able to continue to enjoy sex—albeit less often—into their later years.

"You don't stop having sex because you get old," Dr. Danoff advises. "You get old because you stop having sex."

A WOMAN'S SEXUAL PARTS

Nature, at its pinnacle of beauty, is the female body. From the sculptures of ancient Greece to the paintings of the Renaissance masters to the best of modern-day photography, the flow and shape and softness of the naked female body has captivated artists—and mankind, for that matter—like no other vision.

Of course, that is keeping the zoom lens away. From afar, the rounded breasts, narrow waist, curved hips, and V-shaped mound of the pubis all speak of hidden pleasures and maternal fulfillment. But focus in on the female genitalia—and that's another matter. Not too many artists messing with *that*. Of course, that's because much of female genitalia is internal. It's not like a penis and testicles, dangling out there for all the world to admire. But it's more than that. Female genitalia are hard to understand for many men. Vaginal lips? A

"G" Marks the Spot

If disagreements make life interesting, then the G-spot has kept the community of sex scientists *very* interested the past few decades. The primary question, of course, has been: Does it or doesn't it exist? And if it does, is it the magic button to orgasm that many therapists—and women—would have you believe?

Actually, if all the sex therapists and researchers in America were to vote today on whether the G-spot exists, the yes's would probably overwhelm the no's. Still, doubt lingers, primarily because researchers remain unable to find an actual physical G-spot when inspecting a woman's private parts.

"It's controversial because it's a relatively new kind of concept," says licensed psychologist William R. Stayton, Th.D., professor of human sexuality at the University of Pennsylvania in Philadelphia and president of the American Association of Sex Educators, Counselors, and Therapists (AASECT). "It's difficult for people to accept that we've had medical schools and cadavers being cut into for hundreds of years and this area hasn't really been located."

The reason for that, Dr. Stayton says, is that the G-spot is erectile tissue that only swells and becomes apparent when stimulated. Hence, it would not appear in a cadaver. Nor are gynecologists apt to encounter the G-spot. Because when they conduct pelvic examinations of women, they do not touch their patients in such a way as to stimulate their G-spots, he says.

The G-spot, as most agree, is located on the upper wall inside the vagina, 1 to 2 inches behind the back of the pubic bone. Named for German obstetrician Ernst Grafenberg who described it in the 1940s, the G-spot consists of nerve endings and blood vessels that may grow anywhere from the size of a dime to a half-dollar when stimulated, according to the authors of the book *The G-Spot and Other Recent Discoveries about Human Sexuality*.

This, in turn, provides an intensely good feeling—even leading to orgasm—to some women. Sensitivity varies greatly, however, with some women saying that they have little feeling in the G-spot area. And many women say that they can't even find the G-spot.

"Mainly, they don't know where to look," says Marilyn Fithian, Ph.D., a sex researcher and retired sex therapist in Long Beach, California. And some women, she says, simply don't have much feeling in the vagina.

Some sex experts, such as Barbara Levinson, R.N., Ph.D., a licensed marriage and family therapist and director of the Center for Healthy Sexuality in Houston, remain skeptical that G-spot stimulation can produce orgasms. It's more likely that women who report orgasms when their G-spot is being

clitoris? The vulva? We just don't relate. It's *their* plumbing. Well, perhaps it's time to zoom in. You may discover that even up close, the sexual parts of a woman are a work of art.

stimulated also are receiving clitoral stimulation at the same time, says Dr. Levinson.

Some women, however, insist not only that they have orgasms when their G-spot is stimulated but also that they ejaculate a fluid.

Women sometimes feel like they have to urinate if their G-spot is aroused, and those who ejaculate a fluid do so through the urethra, the very tube through which a woman passes urine. But it's a mistake to think that female ejaculators are women with weak pelvic muscles who accidentally urinate when aroused, Dr. Stayton says.

"In fact, these women tend to have very good control of the muscle system in the pelvic region," Dr. Stayton says. Some researchers have found that the female fluid is not urine but a liquid with the same chemistry as male ejaculate, minus the sperm, he adds.

Other tests have shown, however, that it indeed is urine that these women are releasing, says Dr. Fithian. "Probably what happens is that the intensity of the arousal gets to a point that it's so exquisite that there's a relaxation of the internal sphincter, and when that happens, the urine just comes out," she says. Whether anything else is being secreted with the urine is a matter of ongoing study, she says.

To guys frantically searching for their partner's G-spot, relax. There's nothing magical about a G-spot orgasm, Dr. Fithian says. "Orgasm is orgasm. If you rub an elbow and a woman has an orgasm, it's going to look just like it does if you stimulate the clitoris. It's going to feel different because you're stimulating a different area. What you're talking about is a difference in nerve endings in a specific area."

So how do you and your partner find her G-spot? Joel D. Block, Ph.D., a clinical psychologist and sex therapist at the Human Sexuality Center of Long Island Jewish Medical Center in New York and author of *Secrets of Better Sex*, says that a man and woman should lie face to face. With his palm facing him, the man should push his lubricated index finger and middle finger gently in the outer third of the vagina's top region until he finds a rougher patch than the surrounding skin. The spot can be stroked, he says, by making the "come hither" gesture with the fingers. The four o'clock and eight o'clock points in the vagina seem to work best, adds Dr. Fithian.

The G-spot is a lot harder to stroke with your penis during intercourse. Best bets for success are rear-entry doggie style or with the woman on top.

THE VAGINA

As impressive as having an erection may be, it doesn't even come close to matching the physiological feats of a woman's vagina. If there were a sexual Olympics, the penis would win at best a silver medal in the expanding organ event.

The winner, of course, would be the vagina. In an adult woman it is only about 3 or 4 inches long, yet it can expand during intercourse to receive a man's thrusting penis that typically is quite a bit longer. More remarkably, the vagina expands to far greater dimensions in order to become the birth canal during childbirth. (The biggest baby ever born was a 30-inch-long, 23-pound, 12-ounce behemoth to a Canadian woman in 1879, according to *The Guinness Book of World Records*.)

The walls of the vagina contain deep folds that allow it to do its neat expanding trick, growing deeper and wider during intercourse and childbirth.

These walls are lined with muscles, connective tissue, and a mucous membrane that secretes a fluid that helps lubricate it during intercourse. The cervix—the opening of the uterus at the deep end of the vagina—also secretes mucus that lubricates the vagina. And the vagina is loaded with blood vessels, which become engorged with blood during sexual arousal.

Like men, women are aroused by touch or erotic thoughts. Also like men, testosterone is what kicks in their sex drive, though women have less of the hormone. Whereas a guy's erection is the most surefire sign he is aroused, the best such indicator among women may be those vaginal secretions.

But this isn't a foolproof signal. A woman's lubrication is affected by fluctuating female sex hormone levels, and she may be sexually aroused even if she's dry. Older women in particular tend to have difficulty producing enough vaginal lubrication for sex.

The vagina was long the source of one stubborn misconception. Many men believed that if a woman did not have a hymen—a thin fold of tissue that partly covers the vagina—then she was not a virgin. Sexual intercourse can, in fact, tear a hymen. But so can lots of other things, like riding a bicycle or inserting a tampon.

Another male fallacy is that we have to be equipped with a howitzer between our legs to make a woman happy. "Most all of the erotic nerve endings are in the first third of the vagina," says licensed psychologist William R. Stayton, Th.D., professor of human sexuality at the University of Pennsylvania in Philadelphia and president of the American Association of Sex Educators, Counselors, and Therapists (AASECT). "That's why penis size doesn't matter. Size is a real myth."

A woman's vagina can be totally satisfied with an erect penis as modest as 3 inches, Dr. Stayton says. "The problem comes if it's a really large penis"—generally, more than 8 inches, he says. "What happens when they're having intercourse is that the penis tends to hit up against the cervix area, which doesn't have any give to it," Dr. Stayton says. End result: The guy with the long dong can't go in all the way, he says.

But as is often the case in sex research, there are contrary views. Some researchers, while agreeing that the outer third of a woman's vagina is the most sensitive, have found that some women do have orgasms from deep vaginal penetration. Whether these sensations are produced by pelvic muscles, uterine contractions, or the G-spot is not clear. Some researchers even speculate that the cervix may have nerve endings that respond to a thrusting penis.

THE CLITORIS

This is the closest thing a woman has to a penis. Like the glans or tip of a penis, the clitoris is packed with sensitive nerve endings. Like a penis, it has two corpora cavernosa, the spongy tubes that become engorged with blood. And like a penis, the clitoris becomes erect when this occurs. But a penis has the dual function of passing semen and urine. The clitoris simply makes a woman happy. Its only known purpose is to provide sexual pleasure—the sole organ in human anatomy so designed.

That makes it the most sexually potent spot on a woman. Less than a third of women can reach orgasm without clitoral stimulation, writes Joel D. Block, Ph.D., a clinical psychologist and sex therapist at the Human Sexuality Center of Long Island Jewish Medical Center in New York and author of *Secrets of Better Sex*.

The problem for many men is finding the little bugger. This bashful pink love button is above the vaginal opening where the top of the inner lips meet. It ranges from a dainty ¾ inch to 2 inches long, but it appears even tinier. That's because most of the clitoris is nestled inside a woman's body, leaving just the tip visible above a flap of skin called the clitoral hood.

It is this tip, not the entire clitoris, that swells during arousal. When erect, the rate of swelling varies considerably among women, with some of their organs doubling in size, while others hardly change. Yet its size has no bearing on the degree of pleasure it gives.

And unlike a penis, which strains to be seen when erect, the clitoris is apt to demurely hide below its hood of skin just as a woman becomes sexually aroused. Nobody said sex was easy.

So how do you stimulate the clitoris? Well, that varies from woman to woman. Ask your partner what she likes. Or have her show you.

It is difficult to rub the clitoris during intercourse. But if that's your goal, the woman on top position is probably the best, sex experts say. Of course, you or your partner can also stimulate her clitoris manually at the same time you are having intercourse.

Or you can use your tongue. Dr. Block suggests trying different techniques, such as circling the clitoris, to moving up and down along the shaft, letting your mate's responses be your guide.

Sigmund Freud, among others, said that an orgasm induced through vaginal stimulation was more intense and "mature" than an orgasm reached through clitoral stimulation. Sex experts now reject that view as nonsense. You fail to become intimately acquainted with the clitoris at your own peril.

THE VULVA

No, this is not a Swedish automobile. The vulva is what we actually see when a woman is naked, rather than her vagina. It is the visible, external genitalia. Here are the key components.

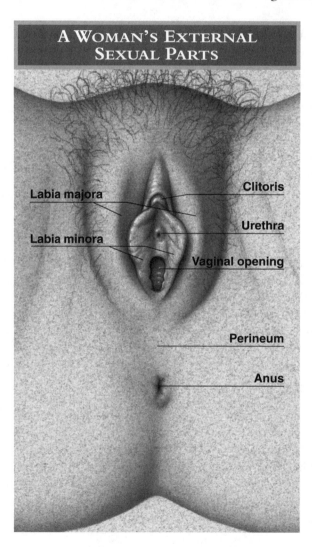

A WOMAN'S EXTERNAL SEXUAL PARTS

Labia majora

Labia minora

Clitoris

Urethra

Vaginal opening

Perineum

Anus

• The Labia Majora: These are the outer lips of the vagina. They consist of two fleshy folds of skin and fatty tissue. When a woman becomes sexually aroused, the lips become engorged with blood and swell.

• The Labia Minora: These inner lips of the vaginal opening are mostly covered by the outer lips. The inner lips usually cover up the opening of the urethra and the vagina. They vary in size, shape, and color among women and have nerve endings that make them highly sensitive and a source of sexual stimulation.

There is an opening between the lips of the labia minora called the vestibule. Glands secrete a lubricant into this area when a woman is sexually aroused. The lubricant reduces skin friction, easing the way for you to penetrate the vagina during intercourse.

• The Urethra: This is the tube through which women pee. Unlike a man's urethra, which also carries semen, a woman's has only this one function. A woman's urethra is wider than a man's but a whole lot shorter—about 1½ inches versus 8 inches. Its opening is above the vaginal opening and below the clitoris.

The Cervix

Our tour now leaves the exterior body and proceeds inward, part by part. At the back of the vagina is a cylindrical mass of tissue and muscle called the cervix. Located at the neck of the uterus, the cervix is a woman's gatekeeper. It allows sperm to pass through a small opening into the uterus, and menstrual blood to flow out through the vagina.

The mucus secreted by the cervix changes throughout a woman's men-

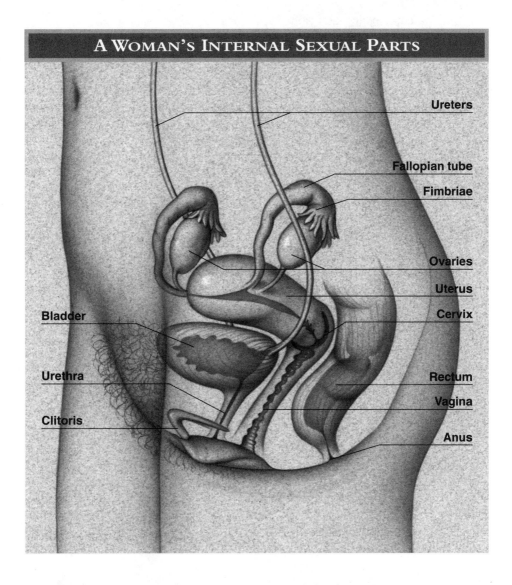

A Woman's Internal Sexual Parts

Ureters

Fallopian tube

Fimbriae

Ovaries

Uterus

Cervix

Bladder

Urethra

Rectum

Vagina

Clitoris

Anus

That Time of the Month

It's called "The Curse" and worse. A woman's period. About every 28 days it happens. Some cultures have believed that menstrual blood was tainted and that a man who had sex with a woman during her period would be poisoned. Some societies have prohibited sex with menstruating women.

In fact, a woman's period is nothing more than nature telling her that she has not conceived a child. Every month a woman produces an egg that eventually wends its way to her uterus. The walls of the uterus become lined with blood and tissue with which to nourish a fetus. But if the woman's egg has not been fertilized by sperm, it soon dies and this extra blood and tissue get shed. That's menstruation.

The female hormones estrogen and progesterone regulate this process, and they and other hormones and body chemicals oscillate throughout a woman's cycle. Depending on the mix, she may be moody or horny. It differs from woman to woman. (A prediction: If you ask your partner if she's "on the rag," her mood will rightfully get a whole lot uglier.) Because the makeup of this hormonal brew is constantly in flux, many women report heightened sexual desire at certain points during their cycle, such as just before or just after their period.

Having sex with a menstruating woman won't poison you unless she is HIV-positive. In that case, you are indeed taking a huge risk. If you aren't certain of your partner's HIV status, it makes it all the more imperative to wear a condom when she is having her period.

But there are plenty of pluses about menstrual sex, provided that you and you partner don't mind a little extra mess. For one, a woman's chances of get-

strual cycle and aids the passage and survival of sperm during ovulation—the time when a woman releases an egg. And it is the cervix that opens up to allow the baby to advance into the birth canal during the final stages of labor.

THE UTERUS

This is the womb, that nice warm place where we hung out before birth, kicking our moms periodically so that they wouldn't take us for granted. Shaped like an upside-down pear, the uterus is behind the bladder and 3 to 4 inches long.

If an egg is fertilized, it will embed itself in the uterine wall, where it will be nourished. If the egg is not fertilized, it will be shed when a woman has her menstrual period. During pregnancy, the uterus expands and adds muscle to contain the developing baby. These are the same muscles that produce mighty contractions during labor, propelling us bawling into our brave new world.

ting pregnant are remote. That, in fact, is one reason why some women find sex during menstruation a turn-on—because the fear of pregnancy is gone, says Domeena Renshaw, M.D., director of Loyola Sex Therapy Clinic at Loyola University in Chicago and author of *Seven Weeks to Better Sex*.

There's another time each month when some men would be safer teasing a rattlesnake than trying to seduce their partners. It's when women are suffering PMS—premenstrual symptoms or premenstrual syndrome.

Premenstrual symptoms are experienced by as many as 90 percent of women in their childbearing years. A couple of weeks before their period begins, they get bloated, moody, irritable, and the like.

That's bad enough, but pity the poor woman—and the guy in her life—who has premenstrual syndrome. This disorder has been severe enough in some cases to break up marriages, contribute to child abuse—even murder.

Researchers have found that the symptoms and the syndrome most often occur when women undergo rapid hormonal changes, such as at puberty, after a pregnancy, when oral contraceptives are discontinued, and just before the onset of menopause.

If you are involved with such a woman, urge her to do the following to try and lessen the severity of her symptoms.

- Cut back on her intake of caffeine, salt, and nicotine.
- Get regular exercise.
- Eat a nutritious diet.
- Keep a menstrual calendar to chart symptoms and when they occur.

OVARIES

Shaped like almonds, but the size of large walnuts, the ovaries rest in the lower abdomen, one on either side of the uterus. They accomplish three important tasks. First, they produce the hormones estrogen and progesterone, which shape a woman's sexual characteristics—the counterpart of a man's testicles. Second, they cause the walls of the uterus to thicken with blood-rich cells to receive a fertilized egg. Third, the ovaries produce the eggs, which, when fertilized by sperm, create human life.

The eggs develop in sacs called follicles. During each menstrual cycle only one egg normally pops out of its follicle and is escorted by fingerlike frills called fimbriae on a little trip over to the nearest Fallopian tube.

FALLOPIAN TUBES

This is the destination of those hardy sperm that survive the grueling journey after we ejaculate inside a woman's vagina. And it is here where conception usually occurs.

Their Bodily Concerns

Women fret about their figures. Even actresses and models renowned for their beauty have admitted battling bulimia and other eating disorders. Women's top five body issues, says Joel D. Block, Ph.D., a clinical psychologist and sex therapist at the Human Sexuality Center of Long Island Jewish Medical Center in New York, in *Secrets of Better Sex*, are the following:

1. Weight: Most think they are 5 to 10 pounds overweight
2. Breast size: Either too small or too large
3. Signs of aging: Sagging skin, drooping breasts, varicose veins
4. Thighs: Too heavy
5. Scars from pregnancy and childbirth: Stretch marks, cesarean scars, stretched vaginas

The Fallopian tubes are about 3 inches long and attached to the upper end of the uterus. From either of these tubes the egg is then carried along into the uterus.

MORE ON ORGASMS

How we envy women and their orgasms. For guys, it's a couple of quick spurts of semen and we're spent—for a matter of minutes, perhaps, when we're teenagers, to hours or days as we grow older. Not so for women. Not only do they not need a refractory period in which to recharge their sexual batteries, but some are capable of having one orgasm after another, like an earthquake followed by strong aftershocks.

And women's climaxes seem so all-encompassing, I-feel-the-earth-move powerful. Admit it. You like being a guy, but for one lust-laden night, you'd like to bend your gender. Then again, maybe you wouldn't. After all, women have a harder time reaching orgasm than we do. It's the second most common complaint of women visiting sex therapists. Lack of desire is first.

Paradoxically, there are some women whose orgasmic ability is awesome. "A woman can have an orgasm without even touching genitalia," says Marilyn Fithian, Ph.D., a sex researcher and retired sex therapist in Long Beach, California. "Women can fantasize to orgasm."

One reason for the difficulty many women have is that penis-in-the-vagina intercourse doesn't provide much direct stimulation to a woman's clitoris.

But that can't be the only reason. Ten to 15 percent of women never reach orgasm at all—not even when they masturbate, Dr. Block says.

The way they were raised may be a factor. Boys are raised to be ready for sex at all times, but women are taught to suppress their sexuality, Dr. Stayton says. Remember that much of sex is in the brain. If it's not interested in or wired for sexual pleasure, all that stroking and poking will go for naught.

Then, too, women simply aren't ready to do the deed at the drop of a panty, like us guys. "We'll stick it in anything," says Ted McIlvenna, Ph.D., president of the Institute for Advanced Study of Human Sexuality in San Francisco. "We're inserters."

To repeat a key lesson mentioned many times in this book: Women want romance, conversation, and a partner they like and who they believe likes them, says Al Cooper, Ph.D., clinical director of the San Jose Marital and Sexuality Centre in California. "Men are into sex; women are into relationships. Women's sex is usually in the context of a relationship. Men's sexuality is in the context of sex," Dr. Cooper says.

Even under those circumstances, orgasms are slow-going for most women. They need more stimulation and more time than men—15 minutes on average—devoted to kissing, nibbling, talking, and the like before penetration, says Barbara Levinson, R.N., Ph.D., a licensed marriage and family therapist and director of the Center for Healthy Sexuality in Houston.

After all these physical and psychological hurdles, when a woman does have an orgasm, it's a wondrous event. For some, the sensations cascade throughout their entire bodies. Their heart rates will increase—and the faster the pulsing, the more intense the orgasm. The muscles in the lower third of the vagina contract involuntarily and repeatedly. The anus may also have contractions. And the uterus, too, similar to that during birth. In fact, during the final stage of delivery, some women actually have orgasms.

Some women also say that orgasms relieve their menstrual cramps by dumping blood from the uterus. So now you have a new argument to present your partner when negotiating sex. Honey, it's for your benefit, not mine.

A Man's Sexual Parts

Men, like women, become shorter with age. Some of us think this shrinkage extends to that most precious of appendages, our penis. Happily, it doesn't. "The length of the penis does not change in your whole life," says Dudley Seth Danoff, M.D., senior attending urologist at Cedars-Sinai Medical Center in Los Angeles and author of *Superpotency*. One caveat: If you put on some pounds as you get older, it may *appear* that you've shrunk because the base of your organ is obscured by layers of abdominal fat, Dr. Danoff says.

If penis size stays constant through life, not much else does. We are not stable creatures; over the years, the male body goes through a myriad of

Our Bodily Concerns

We may act like we're above worrying about our looks, but guys are sensitive about certain perceived physical shortcomings. Here are men's top five body issues, according to Joel D. Block, Ph.D., a clinical psychologist and sex therapist at the Human Sexuality Center of Long Island Jewish Medical Center in New York and author of *Secrets of Better Sex.*

1. Penis size: Few men think they are big enough.
2. Balding: As all those commercials for the "Hair Club for Men" attest, hair loss can be harrowing.
3. Aging signs: Gray hair and wrinkles are no longer as acceptable for men as they once were, especially in the workplace, where executives may feel pressured to maintain a youthful appearance.
4. Stomach size: In women, weight shows up in the butt and thighs; for men, weight goes first to the belly.
5. Height: Women still prefer a man who is a bit older, richer, and taller than they are.

changes, cycles, traumas. Our internal chemistry changes as hormones surge and recede. Our muscles and bones gradually weaken. Our hair and skin go from full and smooth to sparse and wrinkled. Our tubing gets nicked, clogged, worn. Of course, to what extent any of this happens depends mostly on you—the way you eat, exercise, live.

Given that this is a book on sex, we are primarily interested in your sexual apparatus. What follows is a primer to the most important parts of your sexual equipment: what they do, how they work, what you need to know to be a truly informed guy.

THE PENIS

No physical attribute so defines male virility as the penis. Indeed, some men and their partners are so enamored of the little fellow that they give it a pet name, as if it were a separate being. And since so many of us want to believe we are endowed like a Clydesdale, those nicknames often reflect this. Goliath. Whopper. Jumbo. And so on.

In slang, it's sometimes called a boner, but the penis has no bones. It's also called the love muscle, but the penis doesn't have any muscles to speak of, other than the small ones that help regulate blood flow through the vessels. So what makes an erect penis hard? Blood. Lots of blood.

Essentially, the penis is comprised of one long tube and three inflatable cylinders. The tube is the urethra. Extending from the bladder to the tip of your penis, this dual-purpose tube passes urine when you pee and ejaculate when you climax. The urethra runs through the corpus spongiosum, which, as the name implies, is made up of spongelike material that is filled with blood vessels and minuscule chambers or caverns.

The other two cylinders are the corpora cavernosa. These, too, are made up of spongelike material. The corpora cavernosa separate near the base of the penis like two branches of the letter "Y."

So let's say that you're at the beach slathering suntan oil all over Cindy Crawford when you start to feel that old familiar stirring—an erection. What forces are at work that transform your modest member into such a manly rod?

Here's the short version: Something—a thought, a sensation, the sight of something enticing, any of an infinite number of stimuli—sexually arouses your brain. The brain sends signals to the lumbar region of the spinal cord; from there, the signals are zipped along a network of nerves to the penis. These signals tell the arteries in the corpora cavernosa to become dilated. Blood pours into the tiny caverns of spongy tissue in these two cylinders. This increases by several times the amount of blood that routinely flows into and out of the penis.

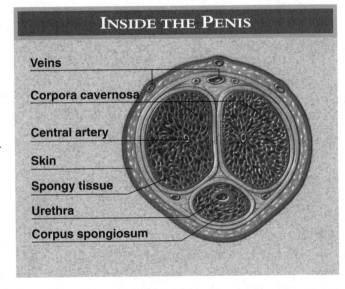

INSIDE THE PENIS

Veins

Corpora cavernosa

Central artery

Skin

Spongy tissue

Urethra

Corpus spongiosum

An erection would vanish as quickly as it appeared if this increased blood flow quickly poured right back out. But it doesn't because the expansion of the spongy caverns in the corpora cavernosa compresses tiny exit veins, trapping the blood.

What ends the erection? Usually, one of two things: First is the departure of the stimulus. You lose interest, and your brain signals the penile arteries and caverns to contract, enabling blood to flow back out of the penis again. Second is ejaculation. You've gone through the full sexual cycle of arousal and orgasm, at which time the penile arteries get the same signal from your brain as above: Contract and let the blood out.

As you can see, our minds have the real control over when to pump blood into the erectile chambers and for how long. If we are tense, nervous, or discouraged, the penis will go limp or not become hard in the first place.

Nor are erections limited to when we are aroused. Men of all ages have them while they sleep. These nighttime erections are longest during teenage years and taper off with age. But even healthy men in their eighties have three or four erections a night, Dr. Danoff says. "All of which means that on the average, the penis of a medically fit man is erect more than 100 minutes a night," the doctor adds.

This is good because nocturnal erections nourish your happy organ with oxygen-rich blood, says Al Cooper, Ph.D., clinical director of the San Jose Marital and Sexuality Centre in California. A minimum of two or three erections a week is necessary for good penis health, Dr. Cooper says.

The angle at which an erection points at attention varies from man to man, based primarily on the strength and tightness of the ligaments that connect the penis to your pelvis. In older men, the erection may tilt downward as these ligaments stretch.

Finally, there is the outside of the penis. The glans is the name for the head of the penis. Why do we have one? Well, like a woman's clitoris, the glans is packed with highly sensitive nerve endings. And the penis and the clitoris are identical in early form, but the penis was later enlarged in the male fetus due to testosterone.

Whatever the reason for the head of a penis, when born, it is sheathed in a protective layer of skin called the foreskin. For health and religious reasons, more than half the men in America have had their foreskin removed (the procedure is called a circumcision; for more on this, see "The Foreskin Flap").

Most of the skin on the penis is sensitive, but one part is more sensitive than the rest: the frenulum, the skin on the underside of the penis where the glans meets the shaft.

THE TESTICLES

Like the penis, testicles are closely identified with manliness. When somebody—even a woman—demonstrates courage, we say he or she has balls. Pretty lofty stuff for these egg-shaped ornaments, but not unjustified. Testicles produce two things vital to mankind's existence: sperm for which to procreate and testosterone for which to develop as a man.

Way back when we were still embryos, the testicles were already pumping the male hormone testosterone into our bloodstream. This helped form sexual features such as our penis. At puberty our brains told our testicles to dramatically step up production of testosterone and to start making sperm. Like some incredibly efficient assembly-line plant, our two testicles will continue to manufacture 50,000 sperm per minute, every hour, every day, well into old age.

If you were to cut a testicle open—admittedly a scary thought—you would find a mess of stringy tubes resembling a ball of yarn. It is within these tubes that we make sperm. Between the tubes, cells called Leydig's cells produce testosterone.

The sperm travel from each testicle through yet another pair of tubes,

The Foreskin Flap

One of the great debates among men in recent years has been whether it's wise to wear a hood. On your penis, of course.

It's called a foreskin, the sheath of skin that forms a hood over the penis. We're all born with one. But a lot of us have it snipped away right after we are born.

Sometimes this is done for religious reasons, such as among Jews and Muslims. But people in Western societies also follow this practice because it makes it easier to clean the area around the glans, or tip of the penis. More than 60 percent of male babies born in the United States every year are circumcised.

Circumcision proponents say that the practice cuts back on urinary tract infections among infants, and infections of the foreskin and tip of the penis in young boys. And they point to studies showing that uncircumcised men are more likely to contract sexually transmitted diseases than guys who are circumcised, and more apt to suffer from penile cancer.

Opponents insist, however, that foreskin-related infections and diseases are rare among boys and men who regularly retract the skin and wash with soap. They also argue that foreskin is highly erogenous since it rubs against the ultra-sensitive frenulum during sex.

In fact, routine circumcision of infants was introduced by the British more than a century ago in a futile attempt to prevent masturbation, says Jim Bigelow, Ph.D., a retired psychologist and clergyman from Pacific Grove, California, and leading opponent of circumcision.

The opponents' arguments seem to be gaining favor. The American Academy of Pediatrics and the American College of Obstetricians have found no medically valid reasons for routine circumcisions of newborns. In fact, the practice is declining in the United States. It is far less common in Canada, Great Britain, and Western European nations.

Dr. Bigelow even formed an organization, UNCIRC—Uncircumcising Information and Resources Center—as an information exchange for men in what he calls the foreskin restoration movement. And he wrote a book, *The Joy of Uncircumcising!* in which he advocates a skin-expansion program for men who want to reverse their circumcisions. This involves pulling and taping skin from the penis shaft over the glans, and eventually attaching weights to the overhang.

"It comes as quite a shock to many American males to realize that 85 percent of the male population of the world is intact," says Dr. Bigelow. "That often shocks males who assume that all sorts of civilized people do this to their males because it's better for them."

called the vas deferens, and are stored in the seminal vesicles. The sperm are mixed in these pouches with other seminal fluid, which helps move the sperm along when they are ejaculated.

A MAN'S SEXUAL PARTS

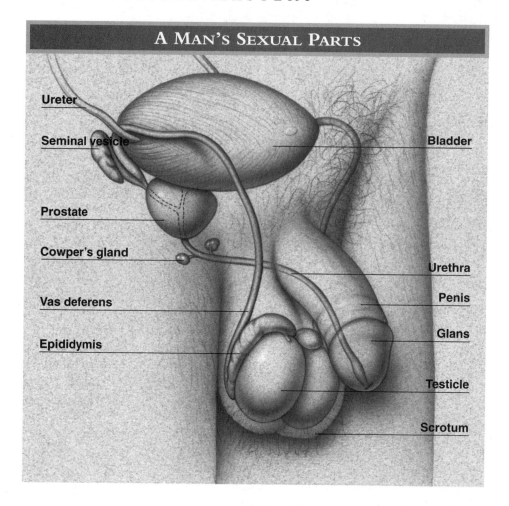

Ureter

Seminal vesicle

Prostate

Cowper's gland

Vas deferens

Epididymis

Bladder

Urethra

Penis

Glans

Testicle

Scrotum

Unless, perhaps, you have suffered a swift kick or other blow to the testicles. Not only is this unbelievably painful, but it can inhibit sperm production. One study found that about one out of six men with infertility problems had received an injury to the testicles.

On the other hand, if you want to ensure that you don't make babies, have a doctor cut and block off each vas deferens, which will then prevent sperm from leaving the testicles. The procedure is called a vasectomy.

Your testicles are nestled in that scraggly sack of skin called the scrotum. The scrotum keeps our testicles away from the body, allowing them to remain a few degrees cooler than our body temperature, which better enables them to produce vast quantities of sperm. That's why boxer shorts are favored by some men over briefs if they are trying to start a family. The loose-fitting boxers allow testicles to remain cooler.

The scrotum also allows your balls to rise and fall, depending on the temperature.

You needn't worry if one testicle always droops lower than the other. One always does—usually the left one.

THE PROSTATE

In terms of basic functionality, the prostate is a relatively inconsequential organ. But it takes on far greater proportions when looked at from the big picture, for two reasons. First, it is covered with nerve endings, making it a highly sensitive and sensual organ. Second, and of far greater importance, is its propensity to cause serious health problems.

This walnut-size gland resides at the front of a man's rectum, beneath his bladder and surrounding his urethra. It has two functions: produce, along with the seminal vesicles, the fluid that makes up the seminal fluid that helps whoosh sperm on to its destination. This uniquely male sex organ also helps stop the flow of urine from the bladder so that when a man is aroused, only semen enters the penis.

When you are aroused, but before you ejaculate, you may notice that your penis secretes a few drops of what appears to be semen. In fact, this is fluid from the Cowper's glands, two pea-size glands just below the prostate, on each side of the bulbous part of the urethra. This fluid helps protect the sperm by neutralizing the acidity of the urethra and may serve as another means of lubricating the vagina.

Made up of nerve-rich glandular matter and muscular fibers, the prostate sometimes is referred to as the male G-spot. The main reason is that it is so decadently sensitive and, like the female G-spot, not so easy to reach. In fact, the female G-spot and the prostate are both believed to originate from the same embryonic tissue.

You can have your partner stimulate your prostate by inserting a lubricated finger into your anus. If either of you is uncomfortable with that idea, another method is to apply pressure to the perineum, that area between the scrotum and the anus.

So what's the big deal with the prostate? As we age, the prostate usually grows larger. Since the prostate surrounds the urethra, this can put the squeeze on the tube, making urinating difficult and painful. This condition is called benign prostatic hyperplasia—BPH for short. A common symptom is feeling an urge to pee several times a night. It used to be that one in four elderly men needed surgery to correct the problem. But now there are new medications such as terazosin (Hytrin) and doxazosin (Cardura) that relieve their symptoms.

More serious is that about 12 percent of men develop prostate cancer, making it the most prevalent form of cancer in men. More than 80 percent of prostate cancers occur in men over the age of 65. African-Americans and men with a family history of prostate cancer are especially at risk. Since the early stages of prostate cancer are often symptomless, the disease often doesn't get caught until the cancer has spread to other parts of the body. This is why the medical community is being so vocal and adamant about men over 40 getting their prostates checked regularly. Depending on how a prostate tumor is treated, it can result in diminished sex drive, trouble having erections—even impotence and incontinence. Advances are being made on these side effects, however.

Good news: Too much or too little sex has no effect on the gland. In fact, an active sex life, whether with a partner or going solo, is good for the prostate, Dr. Danoff says. Why? Because each ejaculation keeps the gland's ducts open and fluids from becoming stagnant.

SEMEN

This is what you ejaculate. About 95 percent of semen is composed of fluids from the seminal vesicles and the prostate gland. The rest is sperm and fluid from the testicles that nourishes the sperm. We typically ejaculate about a teaspoonful of the stuff, says Domeena Renshaw, M.D., director of Loyola Sex Therapy Clinic at Loyola University in Chicago and author of *Seven Weeks to Better Sex.*

Normally, the neck of a man's bladder opening closes to prevent semen from entering the bladder. But for some men the neck doesn't close and they have what is called retrograde ejaculation. These men do not ejaculate during orgasm because their semen goes into their bladder.

Sometimes this occurs in men with diabetes or multiple sclerosis, or who have had surgical removal of their colon or rectum. This is bad news if you want to be a dad. No surgical technique can reverse this, but some men have found medications to be of some help. And if they don't help, sperm can be retrieved from the bladder for use in artificial insemination.

Sperm are those amazing chromosome-carrying, microscopic cells resembling tadpoles that not only can impregnate a woman but also can determine whether the baby will be a boy or a girl, and what many of its features will be.

Estimates range on the number of sperm released every time we ejaculate—from a paltry 80 million to 300 million. At little more than $\frac{1}{1,000}$ inch long, they are so small that they all can fit inside a space the size of a pinhead. (And you thought Manhattan was crowded.) It takes the little devils four or five days to learn to swim, and then at a leisurely 1 to 2 inches an hour until they reach one of a woman's Fallopian tubes. If they are to create life, they have to act fast. Sperm die within three days, and as early as 2 hours, in a woman's reproductive tract.

And what if you abstain from sex? Where does your ever-growing pool of seeds go? Forget those childhood "sperm-on-the-brain" jokes. Old sperm just dissolves and gets reabsorbed by your body.

PUTTING IT ALL TOGETHER

Truly, the process that allows the pure pleasure of getting an erection and ejaculating is one of nature's great engineering feats. We know you want to share with others your newfound knowledge. Here's the short version of how it happens.

Either through touch or thoughts, a guy gets sexually aroused. As we discussed earlier, the brain sends a signal to the penis to commence erecting. Arteries in the penis open wide, allowing a flood of blood to rush into the spongy caverns of the expanding organ.

As your excitement continues to build, the muscles in the perineum—the area between your scrotum and your anus—contract, closing the neck of the bladder and opening ejaculatory channels. This prevents semen from entering your bladder, and urine from going into your semen. Your testicles, like your penis, become bigger with an infusion of blood as they get ready for ejaculation by lifting themselves up higher into the scrotal sac.

As stimulation grows, the prostate, seminal vesicles, and vas deferens all contract, sending sperm and seminal fluid surging into the urethra. These contractions, along with those of the pelvic muscles, propel the semen onward, and we quickly reach a point where nothing—not even the unexpected appearance of your lover's hotheaded, gun-wielding ex-husband—can stop you from ejaculating.

This is what sex researchers call ejaculatory inevitability—a purely reflexive action that is a point of no return in a guy's orgasm. When we reach that point, we ejaculate a milky fluid the length of the urethra and out the tip of the penis.

A rather clinical discussion of an orgasm, no? In fact, doctors have a hard time understanding why it is such a pleasurable, intense experience. But some things are certain—orgasms are remarkably similar from person to person, and they involve the whole body, not just the sexual organs. Involuntary muscle contractions and spasms may occur in the arms, legs, and back. Nipples may become erect; much of your body becomes flushed. Your heart races, blood pressure soars, skin breaks a sweat. Interestingly, during orgasm, your pelvic muscles contract at pretty much the same pace as for every other guy—every 0.8 second. Kind of a universal constant.

Two other truths: You can ejaculate and not have an orgasm—that is, not have the intense bodywide rush of feeling that usually accompanies ejaculation. Seems like a waste, though. More interesting, you can orgasm but not ejaculate. You can teach yourself the latter and use it as a tool to become multiorgasmic, in fact (for instructions, see Becoming Multiorgasmic on page 187).

Unlike women, men cool down quickly after an orgasm. When the contractions subside and the stimulation ends, those little exit arteries in the penis open up again, allowing blood to flow back out of our penis, which promptly goes limp.

After that, many of us will have an overwhelming desire to go right to sleep. But if we were with a partner and not masturbating when the sexual feat occurred, this may be perceived as a selfish act. But that's the subject of another chapter.

MASTURBATION

It's the universal guilty secret. We've all done it. We'd just rather not admit it—to anyone.

As pleasurable as masturbation can be, it's often accompanied by latent guilt, a nagging worry that "real men" don't do this, or a vague sense that we're doing it in spite of ourselves. It's these sorts of back-of-the-mind notions that contribute to the broad view of masturbation as a topic best left undiscussed.

That can be dangerous, leading to a kind of ignorance and hypocrisy that is a lot more detrimental to society than a little self-love in the bathroom. As a cautionary tale, consider the case of U.S. Surgeon General Joycelyn Elders, who neither advocated nor admitted to the practice of masturbating—nothing so obvious, no. All she did was merely suggest that masturbation might be a topic worth educating kids about. For her plain speaking, she was made a "former" U.S. Surgeon General—and proved, we suppose, that being a public servant is indeed a wankless job.

In a society that was more accepting and honest about masturbation, this sort of reaction would never occur. Don't get us wrong: We agree that one should be discreet about self-stimulation. We just don't think that it's a taboo topic. Or one that will lead to your ruination. You already knew that masturbation is not a means of going blind, losing your mind, sprouting hair on your hands, or going to hell. But self-stimulation is more than simply "not harmful." We can make a stronger recommendation than that: It's a good thing.

Now, if your upbringing or sense of morality tells you that masturbation is inherently wrong, we'd have to agree that it probably *is* wrong—for you. If self-pleasuring truly makes you feel unbearably guilty and uncomfortable with yourself, then maybe you're better off adopting a hands-off policy for now. But you might be interested to know that most sex experts today regard masturbation as a valuable tool for everything from relieving stress to perfecting ejaculatory control to ultimately becoming a better lover—and most important, giving yourself pleasure. And it doesn't have to be something you do by yourself—mutual masturbation with your partner is one of the cornerstones of foreplay. "It's a wholly natural, safe, healthy, pleasurable, and accessible form of sexual stimulation," says sex therapist Kathleen Gill, Ph.D., a clinical psychologist in Wellesley, Massachusetts, and author of *Sexuality after Spinal Cord Injury*.

HANDS-ON TRAINING

Understanding that masturbation is good for you is the first, biggest step to truly *making* it good for you, says Harold Litten, author of that masturbation magnum opus, *The Joy of Solo Sex*, and *More Joy...An Advanced Guide to*

Sex by the Numbers

Single men who admit to masturbating once a week or more 48%
Married men who admit to masturbating once a week or more 44%
Divorced men who admit to masturbating once a week or more .. 68%
Men with graduate degrees who admit to masturbating......... 80%
Men who never finished high school who admit to masturbating... 45%

SOURCE: *The Janus Report on Sexual Behavior* and *Sex in America*

Solo Sex. Once you've bridged that gap, you can begin to think about how best to engage in the act, to use it to your advantage (besides the obvious advantages, we mean) either by yourself or with a partner.

What follows is not Masturbation 101—at this late date, we hope that you have figured out what works for you and what doesn't. Instead, we would just like to offer some suggestions and mind-easing encouragements. It's our way of letting you know that in the realm of self-pleasuring, we're, uh, pulling for you.

Take your time. In a *Men's Health* magazine article, readers were asked how long they spent masturbating. One man had his routine down to about 90 seconds. "Three minutes maximum," said another. Impressive though those numbers are, masturbation isn't about setting land-speed records. A quickie always has its time and place, of course. If you can't sleep or you're feeling tense, many men find that taking the express route is often just what they need to settle down. For the most part, though, masturbation should be a leisure activity, that is, something to take your time with. So sit back, relax, enjoy what you're doing.

Ditch the distractions. Not surprisingly, masturbation is a pastime you'll likely want to focus on exclusively, without being sidetracked. We understand. So take appropriate precautions, even if you're indulging in a quickie. Phone off the hook? Doors locked? Room dimly lit? Accessories (tissues, lubricant, and the like) close at hand?

Be unfaithful. Some sex experts suggest that masturbatory guilt may stem from the fact that we often let our fantasies run riot while we're performing self-service—instead of, say, fantasizing about our partners. But as long as these fantasies stay firmly implanted in your mind, you're not doing anyone harm. In fact, you're probably doing the relationship some good. "I hate to demean masturbation by calling it a coping strategy, but in a sense, that's what it is," says Martin Cole, Ph.D., a sex therapist in private practice in Birmingham, England. "It provides an opportunity for fantasy and arousal outside the relationship, which is enough to keep many men faithful." If, however, you find yourself repeatedly fantasizing about clearly taboo subjects,

such as coercive sex, blatant violence, or pedophilia (sex acts involving children), Dr. Gill recommends that you not repress those fantasies but explore
them with a therapist.

Keep your piston lubed. Although some men prefer a dry-handed approach, you'll probably prefer it more—and chafe your equipment less—if
you use a modicum of lubricant. Famed sex educator and masturbation instructor and author of the book *Sex for One* Betty Dodson, Ph.D., considers
lubricant a key part of the masturbation ritual. Massage oils and water-based
lubricants designed for sex (K–Y jelly and Astroglide, for example) are favorites. Don't be afraid to experiment with different lubricants and lotions to
see what you like.

Learn what you like. Instead of going through the motions, take some
time to explore your genitals. The goal is to see what arouses you more or
less. For example, you may like it when your scrotum is cupped or tugged
lightly (or it may be excruciatingly uncomfortable). Or you'll likely learn that
the V-shaped spot on the underside of your penis, right where the shaft and
the head meet, is one of the most sensitive spots on your body (it's called the
frenulum, by the way). Gathering this sort of information can only help you
when you're engaged in sex with someone besides yourself. By knowing
what feels good and what feels *too* good, you can vary positions, angles, and
thrust speed to minimize sensations on the hot spots and thus better control
when you ejaculate.

Put your body into it. Don't just focus on your sexual equipment,
though. See what other parts of your body are more or less sensitive. Instead
of going straight for your penis, try touching other parts of your body first:
nipples, chest, thighs, buttocks—even your anus (this area is rich with nerve
endings, and many men enjoy stimulation there). You might even try "teasing" yourself with several finger forays near your genitals but not on them. As
you're going through this wondrous exercise in self-love and self-discovery,
keep two things in mind. First, remember that no part of your body is off-
limits. If you can reach it, try playing with it. Second, keep in mind that your
explorations may yield discoveries that can be useful not only now but also
in the future, when you want to communicate to a partner what really turns
you on.

Switch positions. Have we mentioned yet that masturbation should be
an exercise in experimentation and exploration? Try stroking your penis with
just your thumb and forefinger. Try isolating one part of it, maybe by running
your finger slowly along the back of the shaft. Maybe covering the head with
your well-oiled fist feels good to you. Caress yourself with just your fingertips or fingernails in light, feathery motions. Wander around a little bit; see
what feels good. Try a variety of positions, grips, strokes, degrees of pressure,
speeds, even methods of fantasizing until you discover which ones, in what
combinations work best for you. Remember: When you're wondering how
best to please yourself, the answer is in your hand—and your head.

KISSING

A kiss is to sex what a key is to a car. It ignites the motor, sets off that first spark for what you hope will be a long and wonderful journey. And along the way, after the rest stops, a kiss is the key to restart the engines.

But if kissing is a key, remember that it must ignite two engines—yours *and* hers. This is where men can get into trouble with kissing. Her key may be a soft, elegant lip brush; yours might be a big, slobbering, tongue-in-cheek affair. You may be off to the races, but she is left in the garage, engine flooded out.

Men of style kiss well, with their partner's arousal always in mind. Here's how to proceed.

AT THE START

When kissing, most women will say, the biggest mistake we make is the first mistake we make. We move too fast, too aggressively, too intimately, especially with the first kiss.

"In my lectures and workshops on kissing," adds William Cane, professor of English at Boston College and author of *The Book of Kisses*, "the single most common complaint I hear from women is that a man's first kiss is less a peck than a pounce, and boy, you can bet that turns them off like a hot bath in hell."

Here's the deal. For women, kissing is pleasure. For men, it's prelude. To her, the kiss (especially the first one or two) is a playful, intimate form of communication that's meant to tell you "I like you, I like this, I'm pretty satisfied." That's why she tends to approach it gently, slowly, without all the heavy breathing and tongue whipping guys are likely to be hot for. Your best advice, according to Cane? Pay attention to these cues. Let her lead. Take your time. Be patient. Enjoy it for what it is. At least initially, keep them brief, closed-mouthed, and soft on the lips. Don't be scheming your next "move" because there may not be one. "*If* things are going to accelerate, let them happen gradually. And let *her* do the accelerating."

INCREASING THE HEAT

Okay, let's say you've avoided mistake number one and learned to do it her way. Admit it, now, she's right, isn't she? Slow *is* good, isn't it? But eventually, you're both ready to torque things up a bit. So what's next?

Once the two of you have gotten beyond the jitters of the first kisses past you, it's time for exploring. The key to kissing is technique, and the key to technique is variation.

Continue to take things slowly, gradually, but begin to play around a little. Try long, sustained kisses, which women generally like, says Cane, sometimes with your lips really locked on one another and other times with them barely

Five Basic Tips for Better Kissing

1. Alternate heavy kissing with light pecking, playfulness with arousal.
2. Keep variety in your kissing life; avoid the same old tricks in the same old order.
3. Sometimes kiss each other just for the sake of kissing.
4. Any part of her body might welcome your lips; you don't know until you go there.
5. Kissing can include licking, sucking, and nibbling as well. Use your imagination, and don't hold back.

touching. Alternate that with little, staccato pecks on the lips. Quick, hummingbird nips. Move your hands around suggestively but not threateningly. Up and down her back, her side, fingers through her hair.

Remember, too, that it can be great to "kiss for no other reason than to kiss," adds Victoria Lee, Ph.D., a clinical psychologist and sex therapist and author of *Soulful Sex*. In other words, don't treat it as prelude, even when you're turning up the heat. Enjoy the act itself without necessarily using it to help you get you from the love seat to the bedroom.

ACCELERATING FORWARD

Moving along nicely, eh? It's time to introduce your tongues to one another. And when you do, keep in mind that most women aren't looking to have a dart shoved down their throats. "It's a pretty intimate gesture," Cane notes, "with potent symbolism to boot. The tongue is phallic, the mouth vaginal. Quite a come-on. You want to be gentle and easy here, too. Probe a little bit. Make sure she's willing to receive your tongue. See if she wants the two of them to do their own little dance. Play 'my place or yours' with her. Invite her tongue over to your mouth for a while." Keep in mind that women like to kiss back.

And don't be dull. Use your imagination. Tongue on tongue is nice, but you can also get the little fellow to dance around her lips, her gums, even her teeth. Let it do a little exploring on its own. Gently run it along the outside of her lips and down inside her mouth, between her cheek and her gums. Scoot it along her teeth the way a street sweeper might clean a road, with swirling, spinning motions from one side to the other. Try sucking each other's lips simultaneously—she on your top lip and you on her lower. While you're at it, see what moves elicit reactions from her, what turns her on. And don't become too obsessed with your work; ease off sometimes. Vary your pace. Most specialists find that the movement from intense to easy, from sexual to playful and back again, only heightens the excitement and adds to your pleasure.

ULTIMATE KISSING

No need to confine kissing to her lips and mouth. Use your mouth, as Cane suggests, like one of those metal detectors that beachcombers use to look for coins. In other words, probe.

As arousing as the mouth is, a lot of women get even jumpier when they have their earlobes kissed, tongued, sucked, or lightly nibbled. One good technique is to gently tug on the lobe with your lips, then slowly work your way up to the ear itself and insert your tongue, like a swab, with slow circular motions. Soft breathing into her ear can also be quite a turn-on.

Another pleasure point is her neck, usually in the front, near the base. Again, try gentle kissing, followed by sucking, licking, and soft biting. If she picks her neck up a little bit, she's telling you that you've hit a good spot, so stick around a while. If she lowers it, move on.

A little unpredictability never hurt either. After kissing her lips for a while, start to move elsewhere on her body, but nowhere in particular. The mystery may intrigue her. Try what Cane calls sliding, that is, kissing and licking your way down her body, perhaps down her arms or stomach, or down her back to where the back meets the buttocks, perhaps to her fingers or toes, or the nape of her neck. Pay particular attention to crevices: the back of the knee or elbow, the crook of the neck, the spaces between toes.

And when at any point in your journey her lazed pleasure gives way to a hot twitch or a brow-furrowed moan or tweet, plant a mental flag. Chances are that you're gonna want to remember that spot and pay it another visit some other time.

And again, mix it up. Even in high gear it's good to mingle a little playful, even timid kissing with the hot sexuality of overdrive. Remember that she likes things gradual.

PROBLEM AREAS

Since kissing is both wonderful in and of itself and a kind of gateway to other sexual pleasures, you want to keep in mind some of the snags that come

Do's and Don'ts

1. Avoid bad breath, especially smoker's breath. Keep mints, gum, even toothpaste handy.
2. Let her set the pace with the first couple of kisses; take all your cues from her. Take your time.
3. Don't ramrod your kisses, especially when you use your tongue.
4. Use your kisses to communicate to her. Let them tell her you like her, not just that you're horny.

up between men and women and what to do about them.

As we mentioned earlier, first kisses can be real problems for women who feel as though the guy is really putting the oral screws to her. Likewise, according to Shirley Zussman, Ed.D., a certified sex and marital therapist in private practice in New York City, when a couple has been together for a long period of time, women begin to complain that kissing gets all but eliminated from their sex life, and with it a lot of the intimacy they've always enjoyed.

Women need kissing, Dr. Zussman points out, because they are slower to get their appetites whetted. Men, on the other hand, are eager to pass on the hors d'oeuvres and go straight for the main course. Perhaps because it's so readily available to us, Dr. Zussman ponders, it loses its thrill.

So if the plugs are wet and you want to refire that kissing machine, you might try any or all of the following:

• Get back to kissing one another with absolutely no possibility of sex to follow. Let it be an end in itself instead of a means to an end.

• When you kiss, occasionally fantasize that she's someone else. Imagine her a complete stranger or some other object of your desire whom you're kissing for the first time.

• Try arousing her and bringing her to orgasm without using your hands or penis at all; just your tongue, lips, mouth, and so on.

• When you do this, try it some time without her doing anything to you in return. Just service her needs and wants. You'll be excited both by your own ingenuity and by the sheer one-sided pleasure she gets from it.

EROGENOUS ZONES

Erogenous zones are like Zen realities: They exist, but then again, they don't. What you need to know is that erogenous zones—spots on the body that are particularly sexually sensitive—are anchored as much between the ears as between the legs. Here's why.

"In essence," says Shirley Zussman, Ed.D., a certified sex and marital therapist in private practice in New York City, "the entire body holds the potential to be an erogenous zone; any part of the body equipped with nerve endings can arouse pleasure. The question becomes, 'Which parts will we *permit* ourselves to enjoy?' That's what ultimately determines whether a neck or a knee or a navel is or isn't an erogenous zone."

Dr. Zussman offers some examples: "Many women can be aroused by a good body massage, while most men, perhaps because they're conditioned to reject passive-receptive behavior, tend to be more or less indifferent to the idea. On the other hand, women, perhaps because of irrational fears that they're overweight, are often loath to have their stomachs and other parts of their bodies touched. Men are rarely burdened in this way." And, Dr. Zussman adds, differences from one person to the next are as common in guys as they are in women. Both sexes report a wide and wild diversity of sexual trigger points, literally from head to toe.

Finally, as Joel D. Block, Ph.D., a clinical psychologist and sex therapist at the Human Sexuality Center of Long Island Jewish Medical Center in New York and author of *Secrets of Better Sex*, adds, "Though erogenous zones don't necessarily change as we age, over time we do have the capacity to discover previously unidentified sensuous areas in ourselves and our mates. So we should be open to these discoveries." In other words, says Dr. Block, the 60-year-old Valentino with 40-plus years of sex under his belt could still make the claim, "I'm getting juiced up in places I didn't even know I had."

So remember, no single "Lovemap" covers all women at all times. But, like a treasure hunt, those sensors are scattered throughout her entire body, just beneath the surface, waiting to be discovered. So learn to enjoy the hunt as much as the find. After all, part of the allure of sex is its mystery.

THE PHYSIOLOGY OF PLEASURE

Having said this, there are some neighborhoods of the human body often more eager to receive visitors than others, and—big surprise—they, too, are different for men than for women.

We guys are a pretty predictable lot. Our erogenous zones tend to be limited to the genital area. Our most sensitive point is the frenulum (underneath and behind the head of the penis), followed by the rim of the glans (the head of the penis), the urethra (the hole), the shaft, the perineum (the stretch of skin between the scrotum and the anus), and finally, up the road a bit, the nipples. If none of these areas turn you on, you need to be reading another book. If they do, keep reading this one.

Women, by contrast, are much more versatile and can present a veritable smorgasbord of physical pleasure, with the most obvious areas being the breasts and genitalia. Miriam Stoppard, author of *The Magic of Sex*, notes that breasts and nipples are almost universally erogenous, as are the labia minora (the inner lips of the vagina), the entrance to the vagina itself (actually, only the outer couple of inches, which are just loaded with nerve endings), and that queen bee of sexual receptors, the clitoris (a small, pea-shaped nodule located at the top of the vagina, where the labial lips join). A wondrous little gift, the clitoris is wholly a sensation receptor. It transmits nothing and performs no function other than to arouse the woman. Like any true specialist, it is a function that, with the proper assistance, it performs pretty well. When you're looking for it, remember that you have to work a little bit because it's covered with a sheath of skin. But like any treasure hunt, it's well worth the effort.

Stating Your Preferences

There are three things to keep in mind when trying to communicate with your partner about your respective erogenous zones, from Joel D. Block, Ph.D., a clinical psychologist and sex therapist at the Human Sexuality Center at Long Island Jewish Medical Center in New York and author of *Secrets of Better Sex.*

1. Physical mastery is best preceded by verbal mastery. The ability of two people to openly and candidly communicate their peeves and pleasures to one another can be the greatest single asset in your quest to play to one another's erogenous zones. Try to gauge the sensitivity of the issue for both of you, and then be as candid as that sensitivity will allow.
2. Communication can be forceful even when it's nonverbal. In exploring for one another's erogenous zones, listen carefully for unspoken cues, which often manifest as little more than a sigh, a twitch, or a carefully placed hand.
3. Sometimes the best directions are nondirect. That is, if talking seems too difficult, find a list of "positive turn-ons" and casually share it with one another. Many women's magazines and/or books contain such lists. (A good place to start: Have her read this chapter.)

And lest we forget, there is the matter of the fabled G-spot, that spot inside the vagina that is extremely sensitive to deep pressure. The Atlantis of female anatomy, it lies in the anterior wall of the vagina about 2 inches from the entrance and is named for Dr. Ernst Grafenberg, the first modern physician to describe it. Like the lost continent, no one's sure if it really exists. But if it does, it's quite an extraordinary terrain and is well worth the visit. Evidence is mixed, but if the proper stimulation brings pleasure to your partner, who are you to argue? (For more on the G-spot, see A Woman's Sexual Parts on page 131.)

Finally, let's keep in mind the more remote, less obvious regions as well. The mouth, the back of the neck, earlobes, and inner thighs are common hot spots, to which Alex Comfort, M.D., D.Sc., author of *The New Joy of Sex*, throws in the even lesser-expected feet, toes, and armpits.

Remember that these are just the *typical* zones; in fact, any area on her body may be glorious grist for the pleasure mill.

READING THE SIGNALS

So, short of looking for a road map, how can you find out which buttons to push? Ask her, of course. Remember, you're not in this thing alone. There's a better-than-even chance that she'll have some information you might find handy.

Either because of misplaced pride or entrenched embarrassment, you may be edgy about broaching the subject. Understandable. But the bottom line is that no one knows the ecstasies and eccentricities of a human body quite like the one who's living in it, and there's no surer way of benefiting from that knowledge than by asking for it.

Easier said than done, right? Of course. "Sexual preferences can be an extremely sensitive subject; that sensitivity should be respected," says Dr. Block. Maybe one of you is simply too shy to bring it up. Or maybe you dig the mystery of the search. Or maybe one of you isn't fluent in the knowledge of your own pleasure points. No big deal. Whatever the reason, keep in mind that we have a variety of ways of communicating with one another. If you ever watch a rowdy crowd at a lousy ball game, you know that we can do it without ever uttering an intelligible word.

So let's say you're running your hand down your lover's thigh and she's lying prone with a languid look of subdued pleasure on her face. You make your way to the back of her knee and suddenly—wham!—body taut, brow furrowed and beaded with sweat, teeth biting the pillow with the tenacity of a young jaguar going in for its first kill. She just might be communicating with you here. Maybe something along the lines of "Yeah, well, that feels pretty good; you can do it some more."

Of course, body language is often a good bit more subdued than this, Dr. Block acknowledges. Sometimes the discovery of a pleasure point is more likely to be met with a contented sigh or a passing twitch than an eye-popping shriek of carnal delirium. But you get the idea, which is: When you're probing each other's bodies, be attentive to one another. Be patient. Listen closely. Some clues might come with no more than the of the force of a hint.

Others may be more explicit, like her guiding your hand—a particularly effective nonverbal, nondemanding way to communicate desires, suggests Dr. Zussman.

TOOLS OF THE TRADE

It doesn't do you much good to find a door you want to go through unless you have the right key. There's more to this game than just where you and your partner touch one another, Dr. Zussman notes. You also want to figure out how. And when you have that figured out, there's the matter of how fast or slow, with what part of your body, and with what kind of stroke.

The best advice here is to be as creative as you will allow yourselves to be. You like feathers? Then use feathers. She likes being licked on her lower back? You love licking lower backs. You don't need to be rocket scientists to send each other into orbit.

Cathy Winks, co-author of *The Good Vibrations Guide to Sex*, encourages a mixture of creativity and common sense. "Remember that what turned her on last night might leave her flat tonight," Winks says. "Be ready for some of those zones to shift."

Having said that, Winks continues, "once you've hit a hot spot, work it. Go to and fro. Leave it for a while, and then come back to it." If she's loving the way you're fingering the back of her knee tonight, tease her a little with it. Stay there for a while, wander off, but come back to it later. After all, it's not going anywhere.

To this, Winks adds that we shouldn't underestimate the power of versatility. Let's say that she's humming when you're fondling her breast with your left hand. Great. Now start tickling her buttocks with your right. Congratulations, she goes from hum to moan. Good, now how about your penis along her thigh. Moans become muffled screams. Now we're getting somewhere. Your tongue on her clitoris. Screams give way to ecstatic hollers rarely heard outside of revival tents and sci-fi movies. Keep it up, shift positions, let the tongue trade place with one hand and the penis with the other. Let different parts of your body simultaneously crank up different parts of hers.

Or maybe the part of your body you employ isn't as important to her as how you employ it. Does she like her thighs stroked gently or vigorously? Would she rather have her breasts kneaded, rubbed, or perhaps probed with your fingertips? Or does she want her nipples toyed with by your penis? In other words, though you have the equipment to provide her with an immense amount of pleasure, you want to learn how to use it properly.

And again, with all of this, keep in mind that unless the two of you discuss such intricacies explicitly, you're probably going to have to discover how best to satisfy one another through trial and error. Even so, to paraphrase the poet Rilke, you can learn to love the process itself.

MASSAGE

Contact. We need it; we can't live without it. The human animal is a skin-hungry creature. We crave the loving touch, the gentle caress, the comforting hand.

Most people believe that the ultimate expression of touch is the act of making love. If that's so, then the penultimate expression must surely be the act of massage. In many ways, though, massage can be more intense, more intimate than mere intercourse. Between two lovers, a rubdown becomes a sexual act, too—a seduction visited upon tens of thousands of nerve endings; a languorous lovemaking experience encompassing the largest sexual organ on your body—the skin.

Like intercourse, though, being a good maker of massage is a skilled profession, requiring plenty of experience in the field, a willingness to explore and be playful, and an understanding of the rudiments. Oh yes, and oil. Lots of great, slippery, glistening oil.

A TOUCH OF LOVE

We hope that you already use massage as a regular part of your lovemaking. As you may have discovered, massage is more than a handy widget in the toolbox of foreplay. It's a bridge to greater physical intimacy and a great method of learning your way around a partner's body says Gordon Inkeles, a masseur in Bayside, California, and author of *The New Sensual Massage*. It also happens to ease tension, reduce stress, and even cure headaches—regardless of whether it leads to sex.

Here, we're not going to focus on massage as a home remedy but as an erotic device. As such, we'll be draping it in a certain mystique, elevating it to a ritual. Our goal is to show you the sensual pleasures that lie beyond the old "honey-will-you-rub-my-neck-a-minute" school of massage many of us are enrolled in. Here, we're going to graduate you to a higher level of tactile pleasure. This chapter is your diploma.

First, though, we need to lay some ground rules, some core requirements, if you will. If you're going to be a world-class lover and masseur, you need to know what the experts know about creating the right atmosphere of sensual pleasure and relaxation. Here are some basic first steps.

Get loose. Since so much of massage revolves around creating a relaxed mood, begin by cultivating that atmosphere. Dim the lights. Crack open a bottle of wine. Get some soft jazz on the stereo. Slip into a warm bath or shower together. Taut muscles begin to uncork, furrowed brows iron out, shallow breaths give way to deepened, languid, satisfied sighs.

Check the oil. If there's an essential tool for a good massage, it must be the oil; make sure that you have an ample supply on hand. Not only is it highly sensual; oils lubricate the skin and eliminate the painful friction that will inevitably occur if your try to give someone a dry rubdown. You can start with something as elementary as baby oil or massage oil (which many health food stores carry). You can make your own, too, using pure oils like almond or coconut oil, or more exotic ones like avocado or lemon-scented sesame oil. There are also many body lotions to choose from. Whatever you use, be sure to warm it by rubbing it between your hands.

Get naked. Did we need to tell you this? A massage while wearing clothes is no massage. This is an all-body, tactile experience, much like sex itself. So don't let garments get between you and the experience. Shed those clothes, along with your tension and your inhibitions.

Create the right feeling. Make sure that your bedroom is as prepared for what's about to ensue as you are. "Think of it as theater," recommends Inkeles. "Set up a space that establishes a mood." The candles and soft music you used to relax should extend into here. On a practical note, make sure the massage surface (bed, floor, table) is warm—between 70° and 75°F (cold surfaces will make her tense up). Have your oils close at hand. Have a large towel laid out on your bed or mat to catch the runoff of those oils.

How to Give Good Foot

Among women, it's one of the most powerful erogenous zones on the body, a sensitive, wiggling thing loaded with nerve endings. Because it's "down there" and sometimes considered dirty or malodorous, it may gross some unenlightened guys out. But if you're a man who knows what women want, you'll quickly learn your way around this part of her anatomy. Touch it with a masterful hand and you'll have her writhing in pleasure.

We're talking, of course, about her foot.

We have no survey data to back us up on this, but we've heard from scores of women that, when it comes to an explosively pleasurable sensory experience, a good foot rub ranks right up there with nipple stimulation, oral sex, and eating frosting from the can. If you want to be a man who knows how to please women, you'd better learn to give good foot. Here's how, according to Gordon Inkeles, a masseur in Bayside, California, and author of *The New Sensual Massage*.

1. Take her foot in your hand, begin kneading with your fingertips, and work your way from the ankle to the toes, all the while kneading both the inside and the outside of the foot.
2. When you're through with that, push the tip of your thumb or all four knuckles into the depression of her arch, again with gentle pressure.
3. Same again, this time using your thumb or knuckle to put pressure on her heel.
4. One by one, take each toe and give it a slow, delicate tug.
5. No tickling!

RUBBING HER THE RIGHT WAY

While there's no single prescription for a good, sensuous massage, there are some techniques and styles of handwork that the professionals swear by. You probably use some of them already, but it never hurts to add a few more moves to your repertoire. Just remember that massage is an improvisational art, that you're free to pick and mix whatever techniques might be particularly appealing to the two of you. And with that in mind, experiment with these techniques.

The opening. Have her lie on her stomach, hands at her side, head turned to one side. Kneel down on the bed, at her head, facing her, with your knees on either side of the head, suggests Dr. Andrew Yorke, a British masseur and author of *The Art of Erotic Massage*. Drop some oil all the way down her back, on either side of her spine, and begin to massage it in with both hands in big, circular motions. Try making big circles with your hands one after the other, each overlapping the track of the previous hand. Keep your hands flat, fingers spread. This is a practical stroke, serving to spread the oil around the area you're about to rub as well as check for areas of tension in the muscles (which you'll feel as knots or rigid areas in the muscles).

Kneading. After the initial stroking, you'll naturally want to start working the tension out of her using deep, firm strokes. The French call this *petrissage*. For our purposes, let's just call it kneading. As Inkeles describes it, kneading is just what you think it is: You take a small bit of skin in your hands and push down on it while circling, the way you might knead bread dough, or Play-Doh, for that matter. This is a simple squeeze-release action, with the fingers on one hand squeezing while fingers on the other are simultaneously releasing. It's great for the shoulders and the neck. Try it and you'll start to get into a rhythm.

Stroking. This is just as it sounds: lightly caressing her body. You wouldn't think it would have much effect on her, but a light touch can actually be more stimulating than deep kneading, especially on sensitive areas of her body, or places where the bone is close to the skin. Stroking makes a nice counterpoint to kneading, so you should mix the two where appropriate. For example, knead her buttocks, then stroke gently between her legs. If she's on her back, you can rub her sides, shoulders, or legs, but stroke her breasts, face, or scalp.

Friction. When you spot a specific area that you want to work on—to loosen tension at a joint, to get at deep tissue, to ease a knot—you'll want to direct pressure in a very narrow area. You can do that using friction. Using the pad of your thumb, press down and move your thumb in a circular motion. This penetrates the tension and concentrates the massage. It's great for small concentrated areas, like the neck. To cover a wider area of tension, use the flat of your hand instead of the pad of your thumb. For fleshy areas like the buttocks, make a fist and use your knuckles. Be sure to ask for feedback from her to make sure you're not pushing too hard.

Wringing. When you're working on arms or thighs, you can try "wringing." This entails having both hands on one side of her thigh, let's say. Have your palms open and pull in one direction with one hand and the other direction with the other, all the while applying gentle pressure and a slight twisting motion. If it feels a little like you're wringing out a wet towel, you're doing it right. Work your way up and down both the inner and the outer thighs and then, with her leg bent in an "L" position, do the same for her calves.

Pulling. Here's an easy technique that's always a favorite. It's simply called pulling, in massage lingo. What this entails is grasping what Inkeles calls the natural handles—the feet, hands, and their attendant appendages. Take her right wrist in your left hand, put your right hand on her shoulder, and slowly pull the arm taut. Hold that pose, and then release it. Try this a couple of times, and then move on to the other arm. Next try the ankles (although she may need to hold on to something in order to give proper resistance), and after that, try pulling on her head. We're serious—it's a human handle, too.

Cup her head in your open palms, lift it, tug it ever so gently (never yank or jerk any of her handles). Then gently turn it from side to side.

Improvising. Okay, now you're on your own. The rest of the evening's yours. Just remember two more things. First, keep in mind that you can always glide from one massage point to another and back again at any time. There's no need to follow a specific regimen so tightly that once you finish, say, massaging her thigh, you feel as though you can't return to it later. Second, take turns. As much fun as running your hands all over her slick body was, you may find it pales in comparison to having her sit astride you and give you a proper rubdown. Just make sure she tugs on all of your handles.

ORAL SEX

Illegal in some states. Condemned in some religions. Vulgar, unheard of in some cultures. No wonder oral sex is such a turn-on.

Funny how mankind finds evil in all the things we most enjoy. And when it comes to oral sex, no question, we enjoy it. Women, too. While about one-third of women can reach orgasm from intercourse, nearly one-half claim that oral sex can do the trick, according to one survey. So what's the big thrill?

To begin with, men can devote more attention to the specific genital areas, like the clitoris and the labia, that excite their women when they're closer to the action with their tongues and fingers, says sex therapist Kathleen Gill, Ph.D., a clinical psychologist in Wellesley, Massachusetts, and author of *Sexuality after Spinal Cord Injury*. A penis is a great stimulus, but it doesn't allow for the precision you get from a flicking tongue. Think of it as the difference between performing delicate surgery with a scalpel and a sledgehammer. What matters is not the size of your tool but your ability to wield it carefully in a tight space.

In addition, many women are just flat-out jazzed by the idea of laying back, relaxing, and having their man do all the work. Imagine, for instance, how she might feel while luxuriating on a soft bed as her modern-day equivalent of the temple slave supplicates between her legs for the sole purpose of delivering her into the stratospheres of erotic ecstasy. "The gesture itself," Dr. Gill notes, "is exciting." Exciting indeed.

THE OBLIGATORY WARNINGS

We may agree in theory that oral sex is a wonderful thing. Action is trickier than theory, however. Here are a few things you and your partner need to be clear about.

When She's Not Interested

Men love fellatio. Every survey, study, poll, and talk show confirms this. If only the feeling was reciprocated. But the truth is that many women are not exactly fond of performing the act. The older the woman, the less the interest, according to studies. So what do you do if you want your flute played and your partner refuses to toot?

Give to receive. It certainly helps when you are eager and willing to perform oral sex on her. Sometimes there is an unspoken bargain involved: You give to her, she gives to you. But don't keep score; sex is not a game of points. Nothing you do earns you the *right* to get oral sex. She controls the decision.

Talk, don't beg. As always, communication is the key. Discuss her feelings. Take them seriously. Perhaps it's that she's afraid of gagging. Or that she hates the smell and taste of semen. Or that she finds it insulting or demeaning. All of these are rational and reasonable—and relatively easy to overcome.

Respect her decision. If she is still adamantly opposed, live with it. Not getting oral sex is a small sacrifice to make in exchange for an otherwise healthy, happy relationship.

• It's not for everyone. For some, it's religion. For others, it's squeamishness. Or laziness. Or a sense of vulgarity. The truth is that not everybody is predisposed to oral sex. Either one of you might not want to place your mouth on the other's sexual apparatus—for any number of reasons—and, as Dr. Gill recommends, "if necessary, talk it to death, preferably outside of the bedroom. Have an agreement with one another, and make sure that neither one of you is feeling any pressure to do anything you don't want to do."

• How far it should go. Now if you're both up for it, you also ought to discuss the role it should play in your sexual encounters. For example: her bringing you to orgasm. Do you want her to? Does *she* want to? Will she swallow your semen? Is her decision cool with you? Because when you're allowing yourselves to get swept up in the ethereal raptures of oral sex, the last thing you want to be doing is second-guessing your actions or her responses. So, as Dr. Gill put it, talk it to death if you have to.

• The funk factor. Finally, there's the ticklish matter of vaginal odors. A number of guys report really enjoying performing oral sex but only if they don't have to contend with what is by most standards an aroma you wouldn't want bottled as an aftershave. So, what are your options? Well, *if* you want to perform oral sex and *if* she has a vaginal odor and *if* you find it's really getting in your way, your only choices are to accept and learn to live with it, reluctantly eliminate oral sex from your repertoire, or diplomatically ask if she wouldn't mind bathing before you hop in bed together. It may be a tough subject to bring up, but it serves you both in the long run if you do. You can even make the most of it by incorporating a shared bath as a part of your sexual ritual. What woman wouldn't be enticed by an invitation to shower on the premise that you want to make sure that *nothing* is out of bounds in the ensuing encounter?

GETTING IN POSITION

As we mentioned, performing oral sex on a woman lets her mind wander to wonderful places. This idea of her fantasizing while you're performing is something to keep in mind when you're considering what pose to strike for oral sex, because the position itself can be a big part of the action for her. If, for instance, you're not into any role-playing but just looking to be comfortable, you may simply want to have her lie on her back with her legs opened and you nestling in between her legs (she can keep her feet on the bed or rest her legs on your shoulders). Alternatively, you can be kneeling at her side, facing her feet, and approaching her vagina, as it were, from the north instead of the south.

But remember too that form follows function, so in addition to comfort, you want to be thinking about what it is you plan to be doing down there. For instance, you probably want to be set up so as to be able to get your tongue onto her clitoris without really straining. You also might want to be in a position that allows your tongue to reach either her anus or that sensitive strip of skin between the anus and the vagina (the perineum, for you Latin buffs). And while we're at it, are you planning on using your fingers as well? If so, you may find it easier when you bend down over her genitals, facing her feet rather than reaching up from between her legs, facing her head.

Yet another consideration is whether this street's going one-way or two. If the two of you want to perform oral sex simultaneously, you'll need to strike some variation of the pose we commonly call "69." Here, you're both orally locked on to the other's genitals at the same time. There are many ways to accomplish this; here are some of the favorites.

• First, you lie on your back with your legs spread. She then descends, facing your feet, on her knees, with her legs open and straddling your body and your penis level with her mouth. This is a favorite with a lot of guys because from here men can more easily sustain an erection without reaching orgasm prematurely.

• Another variation is simply the reverse, with you in the so-called superior position.

• Last, there's the more democratic version in which neither of you is "superior." You both just lie on your sides, facing each other head to toe, her with her legs slightly spread and, if possible, gently wrapped around your body.

Latin Lesson of the Day

You may call oral sex by any number of crude and funny nicknames. Be mature anyhow and use these.

Cunnilingus (cun-eh-LING-ges) comes from the Latin word *cunnus*, for "vulva," and *lingere*, "to lick." It's the clinical name for oral stimulation of a woman's genitals.

Fellatio (feh-LAY-she-o) comes from the Latin word *felare*, meaning "to suck." It's the clinical name for oral stimulation of a man's genitals.

THE PERFECT TECHNIQUE

Now, once you get where you're going, what is it she wants you to do? The first thing you may want to keep in mind is that there's no hurry. Take your time, get comfortable, and work your way in slowly, recommends Dr. Gill. You may want to start off by working your tongue into her vagina, up and down the inside lips (labia minora), gradually finding your way to her clitoris. Then try gently flicking your tongue against it for a few moments, up and down or side to side.

Now, back off a little. Explore a bit. Try gently thrusting your tongue in and out of the vaginal opening, rotating it around the rim of the opening itself, and again licking the labial walls. Then, maybe return to the clitoris again. Keep licking it in different directions. Vary your speed and the amount of pressure you apply. In other words, *diversify*.

By now, she may be getting pretty worked up, so if you're both interested in her coming to orgasm, you may want to gradually zero in on the clitoris, eventually giving it your undivided attention. You won't be sorry. And when you notice her gripping your hair with sweaty palms and heaving like a weight lifter on the clean and jerk, you realize that neither was she.

But as good as this sounds, it can be even better, if only because you have still other options. For instance, while scintillating her with your tongue, you can also be teasing her with your fingers, working them slowly up and down the labia while the tongue is penetrating her vaginal opening. You also may discover that as much as she likes your licking action, a little kissing and gentle sucking thrown in can only add to her pleasures.

One thing you should *never* do is blow air into her vagina, warns Dr. Gill. It's rare, but it could cause an air bubble to enter her bloodstream. That's called an embolism, and it is extremely dangerous.

Finally, for the more adventurous among you, you might want to wander a little far afield and try what is popularly known as rimming, or positioning your tongue around the rim of her anus, gently swabbing it and perhaps thrusting your tongue in as far as it will penetrate.

Rimming can be a real thrill for both of you, but you'll want to keep a couple of things in mind if you're going to go that route.

Be clean. Obviously, you want her to be as clean as possible, says Dr. Gill. This bears repeating: If you are about to launch into a nothing-is-taboo sexual encounter, consider suggesting a shower together to start it off.

Keep her clean. Once your tongue or fingers start snooping around her anus, you can't put them back in or even near her vagina without washing them first—even if you have showered, Dr. Gill cautions. Sure, sure, it seems like a drag, but not as big a drag as the infection she'll be looking at if you're careless. Remember that a vagina is warm and moist, making it a haven for germs. So be smart, says Jack Morin, Ph.D., a psychotherapist and sexologist from the San Francisco Bay area and author of *Anal Pleasure and Health*.

Position smartly. You may find that rimming requires a different position than genital-oral sex. Try having her lie on her stomach with her legs slightly spread, or, from the same position, up on her knees so you can then kneel down behind her and be about eye level with her buttocks, suggests Dr. Morin. This may allow for greater maneuverability for you and comfort for both of you.

SEXUAL POSITIONS

Let's say you go dancing three times a week. Now stop laughing and play along with us because we need to make an important point. You do hours of dancing each week, but you know just one dance step, this kind of lame rock-and-roll shuffle. So you do it, over and over and over, whether the music is fast or slow, samba or blues, Springsteen or polka. Your partner is pleased to have a guy who dances, sure. But she is also bored, slightly embarrassed, unamused—maybe even looking for a new partner.

Sexual positions. They're like dances. A good lover knows how to adapt to the changing music of passion. A dull lover applies the same technique to all occasions.

This is no minor issue. A man in a committed relationship could have sex thousands of times with the same partner as the years pass. To maintain some sense of growth or adventure, variety is essential. And part of variety is trying new positions for intercourse. Need more convincing? Here are more reasons to vary your approach.

• Better pleasure. Don't think that intercourse feels just one way. By varying positions, you stimulate different parts of your penis and, even more so, her vagina.

The Art of Thrusting

The beauty of sex is in the friction. But as with so many things, quantity doesn't necessarily equate to quality. Here are some tips on maximizing the pleasure for both of you during intercourse through thrusting technique.

1. One common complaint is that men begin too vigorously. Women often prefer a gradual buildup.
2. Avoid stopping and starting unless she is prone to orgasm during intercourse (in which case you may be helping induce it). Instead, women prefer a rhythmic pattern to your thrusts.
3. Don't pull out unless it's necessary (to change positions, for instance). Once joined, women prefer staying that way.
4. If intercourse goes on too long, she can become dry, in which case your thrusting is only going to irritate her. Know when to stop.
5. Remember that there are positions in which she can control your thrusts more effectively (such as female superior), so let her. She'll work you both up into a rhythm that feels right to her.
6. There's not just in and out, of course. Play a little with up and down. Side to side. Small circles. Even as you go in and out. Ask her if you have reached any interesting spots.
7. Faster is not always better. This is not a race. Find out her preferred speed and cruise comfortably at it.
8. Mix up short, quick thrusts with long, slow thrusts. See if this diverse approach rings any bells. Maybe yes, maybe no.
9. Always read the signals. Is she liking what you are doing? If you can't tell, ask. Just as there is a world of positions to try, so are there many thrusting techniques to try. Communication, my friend, communication.

• Delaying orgasm. By sequencing your lovemaking, changing the sensations, taking short pauses in the action to readjust, you can add minutes to each lovemaking session. Is this not a good goal?

• Sense of adventure. Doesn't it add a sense of excitement not knowing what is going to happen during a lovemaking session, not knowing where you'll start or where you'll end or what position you'll be in when orgasm arrives? Or think of it from the other side: Isn't it rather dull knowing that you will start and finish in the same position that you used just the other night?

In the chapter Diversifying Your Lovemaking (on page 97), one suggestion we give is to make each lovemaking session include at least three different intercourse positions. Try it for a few weeks and see if the sparks don't increase. Here's how, both in words and illustrations. (This chapter covers the

(continued on page 172)

POSITIONS: A VISUAL MENU

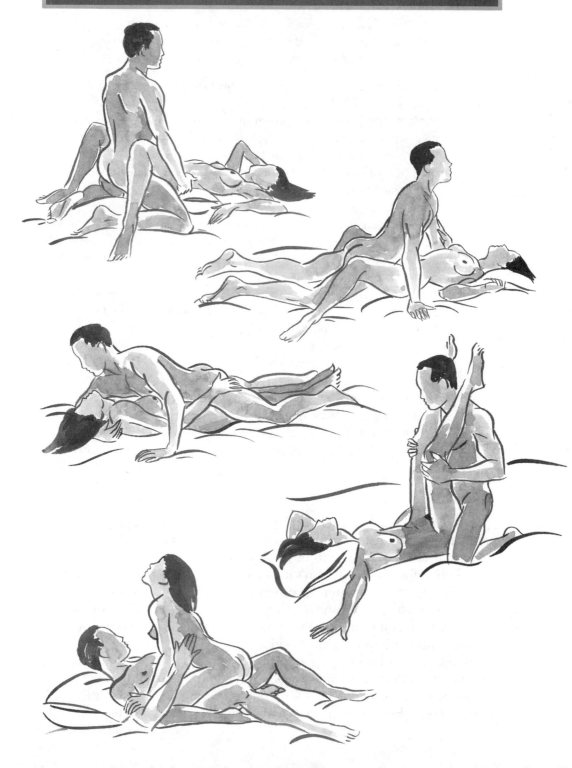

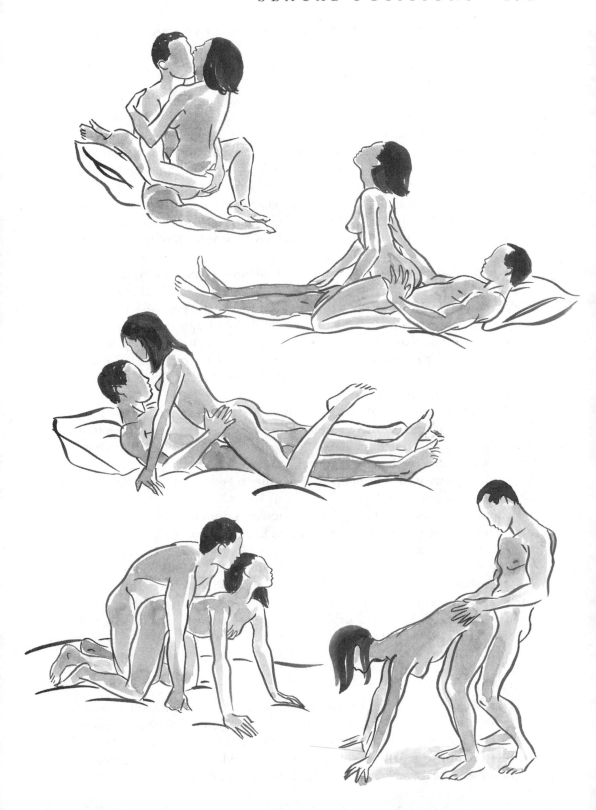

basic positions; for more advanced positions, see Advanced Positions on page 176.)

WITH MISSIONARY ZEAL

The "classic" position of sex is you on top, she on her back, the two of you facing each other, her legs open and yours closed with your penis inserted. This is called the missionary position. In case it ever comes up for discussion, the name derives from European conquerors hundreds of years ago instructing Polynesians to have intercourse only in this manner because all other positions were considered barbaric and pagan. It does have a bit of a conquering theme to it because when you're in this position, you're pretty much in control. You dictate both the timing of your thrusts and the depth of penetration. She, on the other hand, doesn't have a whole lot of room to maneuver.

Of course, there must be some real advantages to missionary, seeing as how commonly it's employed. And as Barbara Keesling, Ph.D., author of *How to Make Love All Night*, points out, the first would be that it's user-friendly. You can get yourselves into position without a whole lot of squirming around. In this way, it's particularly good for beginners. But it's also intimate. When you're making love in missionary, you can look at and kiss one another, making the whole experience sweeter. It can also be very relaxing for her since you wind up doing most of the work.

On the other hand, it can have its drawbacks. It can quickly become routine and thus boring. Also, if you've been to the local restaurant more often than the local gym, you could be too heavy for her to support comfortably. And, as we alluded to above, if she wants to do a little moving and shaking herself, she's pretty well constrained from doing so. You're in charge here, and she might not always like that.

There are lots of variations of the missionary position, of course. If your partner lies with her buttocks close to the edge of the bed, you can enter her from a semi-standing position, a position perfect for more assertive thrusting. Another take is for her to pull her knees to her chest and hook her ankles over your shoulders while you support your weight on your hands. This gives you greater penetration and stimulates the back walls of her vagina. Best of all worlds: Combine these two variations. Have bring her bottom to the edge of the bed, enter her while standing up, and have her raise her legs so they rest against your chest.

HER ON TOP

The mirror image of missionary is female superior, where she becomes the driver and you the passenger. You're on your back, legs together, she's on top of you, legs spread. You're stomach to stomach, and her hands are probably on either side of your arms. Now she's in charge, which means she controls the movement, frequency of thrust, and depth of penetration.

This position is great for couples that want the woman to assume some of the "work" of intercourse. It allows you to be in the passive role for an enjoyable change while she takes the active role. It also can be a major turn-on for her because it can allow your penis to penetrate more deeply into her. In addition, it frees your hands up, so why not put them to good use? It's a perfect opportunity for you to stimulate her breasts, buttocks, or clitoris while she's busy gyrating. And on top of all this, female superior will probably bring you to orgasm a little more slowly than in the missionary position. For men who come quickly, this helps give you better control.

You also might want to keep in mind a couple of variations on this particular theme. If she mounts you kneeling instead of lying down, you may get even deeper penetration, meaning that what this variation sacrifices in your maneuverability it more than makes up for in ecstasy. A second twist is for her to turn around and mount you with her face toward your feet and her buttocks toward your face. She then moves up and down by pushing off on your knees. Now, while you can't kiss each other from this position, some guys are really jazzed about it nonetheless. Not only is the sensation different, but if fantasy is your thing, when you can't see each other, you're both freer to let your minds wander wherever they will.

FROM BEHIND

This is the one we so delicately refer to as doggie-style, although we could also call it kitty, skunk, or for that matter elephant style since it's an almost-universal pose in the animal kingdom. So here it is in its most common form.

She's on her hands and knees, like she's looking for a lost contact lens. Her legs are spread a little bit. You're on your knees, upright, between her spread legs. From this position you insert your penis, then gently lie your chest across her back or remain erect and hold the cheeks of her buttocks. And away you go.

What's great about rear entry is that both of you have some real wiggle room and can maneuver either on your own or in tandem. You also have access to other intriguing pleasure zones, including her clitoris, anus, and breasts, all of which are within arm's reach. Dr. Keesling notes that on top of all this, men and women both report a heightened sense of stimulation from this position, he because of the friction it brings to the back of the penis shaft (a very sensitive erogenous zone), and she because it allows for deeper penetration and more direct pressure on her G-spot.

So with all this going for us, why don't we use it more often? Well, it does have a few drawbacks, Dr. Keesling argues, not the least of which is the fact that some women just flat out don't even want to try it. Some say it excludes intimacy, and they have a point. It allows for no kissing, nothing for her to look at, and nothing to do with her hands. Others feel degraded by the thought of it, perhaps because of the animal connotations attached to it. They

The Wisdom and Folly of the *Kama Sutra*

Still obsessing about making your penis bigger? Try mixing the hairs of an insect called a shuka with oil and rub your penis with this balm for 10 nights. When it swells, sleep face down on a wooden bed, letting your penis hang through a hole.

Want to ensure that your woman is faithful to you? Sprinkle a potion that includes monkey excrement on her head. She'll never love another.

Your woman is unhappy with her pale lips? Surprise her with a delightful mixture of sweat from the testicles of a white horse diluted in yellow arsenic. When she applies it to her lips, they will redden.

These remedies and much more are found in that famous bible of eroticism, the *Kama Sutra*. Sure, the advice is a little dated. But people are still buying the book.

Walk into any bookstore nowadays and you find dozens of fly-by-night books about sex: how to get it, how to do it. But rare is the bookstore that doesn't have one or more editions of the *Kama Sutra*. Written at least 1,600 years ago, this venerable old classic still holds its own against the handsome young upstarts. Now that's staying power.

Indeed, the *Kama Sutra* may well be the world's oldest and most widely read sex manual. It has been published in hardback and softcover. With nothing but text, and with illustrations. At least one edition features male and female models demonstrating various positions. There is even a *Kama Sutra* book for cats, a pop-up *Kama Sutra*, a *Kama Sutra* in 3-D, and at least two gay *Kama Sutra* books.

Then there are the other offshoots. *Kama Sutra* on videotape and CD-ROM. And, of course, the oils, creams, and soaps bearing the *Kama Sutra* name.

All of this from a compilation written in India by a Brahmin and religious scholar named Vatsyayana that was not translated to English until the late nineteenth century. And when it was, much of it was censored. So what is the key to the book's longevity?

have a point here, too. After all, we've all caught glimpses of hot little mutts going at it in the town square, haven't we? If she doesn't want that imagery floating by her screen when she's making love, who's to argue? Finally, it requires a little dexterity. If your gymnastic skills aren't what they once were, you may find your penis slipping out of her from this position, making it difficult to consummate. It's a wonder, you think, that there are so many dogs in the world.

But if you both do enjoy it, keep in mind a few variations on the theme. For instance, she can lie flat on her stomach, supported by her elbows. This might not be as stimulating, but it allows for greater intimacy because you can

"I suppose it may be the mystique of something Eastern," says Rebecca Manring, Ph.D., a visiting professor of religious studies and India studies at Indiana University in Bloomington. "I think that it's a curiosity as much as anything." What else? Well, the book is without a doubt naughtily explicit. Also, it's one of the few sex manuals where therapists aren't preaching to you on every other page. And for the literate among us, there is the exotic beauty of the language itself.

The *Kama Sutra* is more than a sex book. It is a treatise on many aspects of living, such as the proper behavior of an educated man or how to cope with lovers' quarrels. But it is the extensive passages on sexual positions and subjects ranging from lesbianism to bestiality for which the book is famous.

Much of the advice would elicit accusations of misogyny if advocated by an author today. For example, one learns that "all parts of the body are suitable for biting, except for the upper lip, the tongue, and the eyes," and that a man and woman can increase each other's sexual pleasure by scratching and hitting each other.

Of the latter, the *Kama Sutra* advises guys to strike a woman in the space between her breasts at the moment he enters her, if she is on her back. "Begin gently, then, when she starts liking it, strike harder and harder, finally striking in other places," the book recommends.

No sex therapist today is likely to concur with that advice. We certainly don't advocate it. But the *Kama Sutra* does describe a myriad of positions that the sexually adventurous and physically fit may want to try. For example, "When the girl crosses her raised legs, it is known as the tight position."

It's that sort of information that makes the *Kama Sutra* still relevant today.

"I felt that it was valuable in terms of learning more about sex," says Marilyn Fithian, Ph.D., a sex researcher and retired sex therapist in Long Beach, California. "People need to evaluate it themselves in terms of how many different kinds of positions you want to try."

get your faces close to one another. A second variation finds her on her knees and elbows, with her legs together and her buttocks higher in the air. You straddle her legs and keep your hands on her back or buttocks and control the action by gyrating her hips and waist. Again, it takes some dexterity, but it can produce a real primal sense of pleasure.

SEATED POSITIONS

Last, you can do it by the seat of your pants, so to speak. There are a few ways to proceed. One is to be on a bed or mattress. You sit down with your legs in front of you, crossed at the ankles. She then straddles you, with her legs wrapped around your hips. Then as far as the action is concerned, she leads, you follow.

People often like this pose because it's visually stimulating. You both get to watch what's going on, so you're spectators and participants at the same time. It also allows for the intimacy of the missionary position and keeps your hands free to wander, fondle her breasts, and massage her clitoris. Be careful, though, because this one too requires some dexterity. It's kind of tricky to get your rhythm going when there's little to push off on. Why don't you suggest practicing a few hundred times?

And if you want a change of pace or posture, try moving from the bed to a chair. The deal's pretty much the same, except you're sitting down instead of sitting on your ankles. If you try this one though, remember that choosing the right chair is not unlike choosing the right condom: You want it to be comfortable, but you need it to be sturdy.

ADVANCED POSITIONS

What is an "advanced" sexual position anyhow? Let us be pleased that there is no organization or committee that rates such things. In truth, for the young and limber and free, many of what follows are natural and easy to achieve. Rather, these are positions that take a bit more creativity to dream up or extra maneuvering to get to. We'll start with some intermediate positions, then graduate to advanced. We'll describe many with words, and we'll show some more in illustrations. Enjoy the journey.

SIDE BY SIDE

This one is good if the two of you are pretty beat but still want to get it on, or if she's pregnant and still interested in some action. Simply put, you lie down facing one another, and she slings her legs around your hips. You then move in and insert your penis, which will then allow the two of you to get a slow, continuous rocking motion going, leading to a very gradual buildup of excitement. You'll notice that penetration isn't too deep in this pose, and it may take some work to stay engaged. But think of it the way you'd think of a snifter of fine sipping brandy as opposed to a quick shot of potent whiskey. It makes for a mellow high, stretched over time.

There are a couple of twists on this theme. First, there's "spoons." In this one, you lie like spoons in a silverware drawer, on your sides and both facing the same direction. You're behind her and you're both slightly curled up in a kind of semi-fetal position. From here you can put your free arm over her stomach and make a rear entry into her vagina, whence you can both supply the movement to get each other off. This is a good pose because it's quite relaxing and intimate, your arm is free to massage her breasts or clitoris, and she shouldn't have to lift her leg up in order for you to penetrate her. She's also free to use her hands to stimulate herself.

A more intricate variation on this theme is the "scissors." Here you're lying down, let's say on your right side. She lies next to you, on her back. She puts her right leg between your thighs and throws her left leg up over both your legs. You'll see that her legs are like scissors, with your one leg caught between them. You enter her vagina from a side angle, and away you go.

THE "X" POSITION

Okay, you've made yourselves into spoons and scissors. Now how about an X? Here's how Alex Comfort, M.D., D.Sc., author of *The New Joy of Sex*, maps it out.

You sit down with your legs extended and slightly spread. You're leaning back slightly, arms supporting your torso. She then straddles you, with her legs outside of yours (and her buttocks slightly off the bed until your penis is fully inserted). She's leaning back, too. With your penis in, the two of you can then hold each other's hands and get into a slow, coordinated rocking rhythm, kind of like one of those hand pumped railway cars you see in old Charlie Chaplin movies. It's a great rhythm, though, and you should be able to sustain it for an incredibly long period of time.

REAR WINDOW

Here's another maneuver from Dr. Comfort, one he calls the *négresse*. She kneels down on the bed, with her hands clasped behind her neck. Her breasts and face are resting on the bed. You then kneel down behind her and position yourself to enter her. Now, here's where it gets interesting: She hooks her legs and feet behind your thighs and pulls you in toward her. You, meanwhile, put one hand on each of her shoulder blades and press down. It makes for a very deep, very tight connection for both of you.

STANDING POSITIONS

You're at an incredibly tedious lecture on, say, the molting habits of South American water rats. You can't leave because your old college roommate is giving the lecture. So instead, you and your lady duck out for just a few minutes. Luckily, the two of you find an empty storage room. You lock the door. Time to make something about the evening worthwhile.

The problem is that the room is little more than a closet with high ambitions. There's barely room for the two of you. So, can you handle standing up?

If you are taller than she, she may need to wrap her legs around your hips tightly enough to hold herself up with the help of your hands clasped under

(continued on page 180)

ADVANCED POSITIONS: A VISUAL MENU

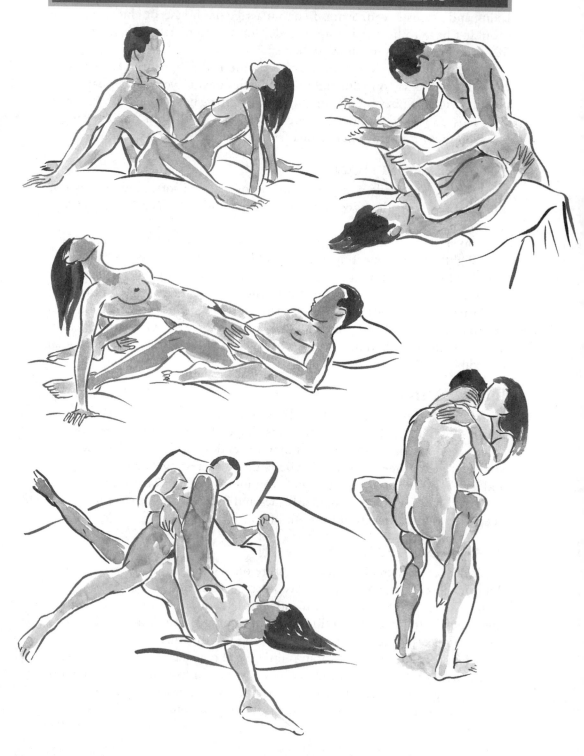

her buttocks. But if she's tall enough, you may be able to enter her by having her stand in place while you crouch down just a little. In this case the two of you can choose between rear and front entry.

Now standing entry may not become your position of choice, but in the "any port in a storm" category, it's pretty hard to beat. It adds versatility and spontaneity to your repertoire, adds the excitement of getting it on in forbidden places (just don't get arrested), and even makes boring lectures bearable.

ADAPTATIONS

Like tried-and-true recipes to which you add a little more spice, here are a few "adaptables" you might be interested in.

• Dr. Comfort's *pompoir* is an adaptation of the woman superior position, with one interesting twist. Here you're on your back, and she mounts you with her buttocks facing you. While she's moving up and down, she alternately constricts and relaxes her vaginal muscles, so your penis gets massaged both from the up and down thrusting action *and* from the squeeze play she's putting on. She's in complete control of the situation, so sit back and enjoy yourself.

• Here's a variation on the sitting position. Use a sturdy chair. You might prefer a cushioned seat as well. Now, instead of her straddling you, have her take the sitting equivalent of the spoons position. She's on your lap, with her back facing you. You enter her from the rear, and now have your hands free to hold her, massage her, or wander pretty much anywhere on her body the two of you want to go. If her legs are long enough (that is, the chair's legs are short enough), she can supply some of the thrust, but if not, the two of you will have to get yourselves into a coordinated rhythm of push and pull.

• Even the missionary has its own slant, literally. Try this on a bed that's fairly close to the floor, maybe 18 inches or so. She lies down with her middle back on the edge of the bed and her legs on it. She leans back until her head touches the floor (you might want to put a pillow down for her) and you enter her in the normal missionary position, being careful not to push her over the edge. She can either put her hands up behind her head or, if her arms are long enough, reach up and hold onto your buttocks for stability. Because of the pressure that comes when she stretches herself in this way, she's likely to get a more intense feeling of your penis inside of her. Let's assume she wouldn't object to that.

• Finally, there is the potpourri approach, which simply suggests that you change from one position to another throughout the sexual encounter, in some cases without ever having to disengage. Or, if you want to remain in one position, modify it yourselves. If, for instance, you're in the missionary pose, roll around a little, let her move her legs up and down your back, maybe one at a time. If you're in the female superior position, then you move *your* legs up and down *her* back. Standing rear entry? Maybe she can bend over and grab onto her ankles without bending her knees.

And keep a few of things in mind when you're sequencing from one position to another.

1. You don't need to go through every move in your repertoire; it's not a performance. Most couples employ one or no more than two or three positions in any given encounter.
2. You probably want to start yourselves out with a fairly conventional pose, gradually working up to the more advanced ones.
3. Take your time between positions. Move slowly and gracefully from one to the next. The complaint most women register in this area is that men can be too clumsy in their rush to "get things done," at the risk of changing a passion-charged encounter into a no-passion wrestling match.

ANAL SEX

In researching this book, we looked at lots of other sex manuals for background. And what we found on the topic of anal sex was, well, very little. Go to the index and look it up, and you find that the few entries that are there likely point you either to the "safe sex" or "AIDS" discussion. Nothing about the many acts that make up anal sex—how many people partake, why they do, how to do it right, whatever.

You don't have to think deeply to figure out why. For so many Americans the subject of anal sex is strictly taboo. Some consider it vulgar, violent, unnatural, demeaning. Some wrongly place homosexual connotations on the act, no matter who is partaking. Others just think it's dirty, literally, and not worth the effort.

The truth is that anal sex is not at all deviant. Roughly 1 in 4 of us have done it, and roughly 1 in 10 of us have done it in the past year, according to the landmark *Sex in America* survey.

THE IMPORTANT DISCLOSURES

We suspect that some of you, maybe a majority of you, are put off by the concept of anal sex. Even if you are not interested in anal sex and intercourse, self-exploration of the anus and rectum are vital to all over good health, says Jack Morin, Ph.D., a psychotherapist and sexologist from the San Francisco Bay area and author of *Anal Pleasure and Health*. "It is important for everyone to learn and explore their bodies, including the rectum and anus. This is especially important if you are planning on experimenting with anal pleasures as you need to know what you like and don't like, what relaxes your rectal muscles, what feels good and what doesn't. For those of you who wish to partake in this pleasure—and if done right, it *is* a pleasure—there are a couple of things you need to know first.

• Safety. Unless you've spent the last 15 years of your life on the dark side of the moon, you know that AIDS (as well as any number of other sexually transmitted diseases) is transmitted through the exchange of bodily liquids. There is an incredibly rich blood supply in the anal area, and if small capillaries in the surface break or tear, which they are prone to do, microscopic access to the blood supply is the result. And even a little tear, undetectable to the naked eye, is sufficient to invite the transfer of a virus between two bodies. This is why the anus is such a vulnerable location for the transmission of the AIDS virus.

So, what do you do for safety's sake? No question: Wear a condom, says Dr. Morin.

• Lubricants. There's simply no way your penis is going to slide in and out of her anus and provide *any* degree of pleasure for either one of you unless you can, as they say, grease the skids. The friction's just too great, says Dr. Morin; the anus doesn't generate its own lubricant as does the vagina. So to make it work, you need to apply a generous portion of a lubricant (preferably not petroleum-based since the petroleum eats away at condoms), according to sex therapist Kathleen Gill, Ph.D., a clinical psychologist in Wellesley, Massachusetts, and author of *Sexuality after Spinal Cord Injury*. Apply to both to your penis *and* to the opening of her anus in order to get that movement comfortable. (And, no, your saliva is not a sufficient substitute.)

• Hygiene. Finally, a word about cleanliness. And that word is *bathe*. We don't have to go into gruesome detail explaining the anus's primary function. Suffice it to say if the two of you expect to maximize the degree of pleasure and minimize the threat of bacterial infection, you'll both jump in the shower before crawling under the covers. In fact, the bath can even become a part of your ritual foreplay, as Dr. Morin points out.

BACK-DOOR TECHNIQUE

Want to dally in the netherworld? Here's some important advice.

Ask first. Obviously, the first and most important thing you need is a willing partner. Keep in mind that anal sex very well might not be to her liking. Always ask first. If she says no, you must go along with her decision. She feels the pain, not you. Any guy who tries too hard to persuade his woman to engage in anal sex is behaving like the thing he's trying to get into.

Listen to her pain. Many women who engage in anal sex report that it does indeed hurt sometimes but that there's pleasure to be had as well, according to Dr. Gill. Your job as a sensitive partner is to know if and when you're nearing that threshold of pain that's going to shut her down and turn her off. Remember that the receiver should be in control of the action here, and she's depending on you to see to her comfort.

There should never, ever be any pain associated with anal intercourse, says Dr. Morin. If it hurts, she is simply not ready. She needs to be relaxed enough and lubricated enough for a pain-free entry.

You need to be communicating with one another. If in the heat of action she looks as though it's getting a little tough for her, you probably want to pull out, take a break, and check in with her. If she tells you she could've gone a little longer or a little harder, keep that in mind for the next time. But figure that it's better to have stopped too early than too late.

Get her ready. Because there is a potential for pain with anal intercourse, relaxation and awareness are extremely important. First, remember that like the vagina, the anus can be explored and its muscles relaxed with gentle finger penetration. Again, keep in mind that you'll need the lubricant even here, and you want to work your way in slowly, perhaps beginning by just massaging the outer rim before you actually penetrate, says Dr. Morin.

Make a good start. When you're both ready for penetration, Dr. Morin reminds you that different receivers like different approaches. Like vaginal sex, there is no right or wrong way to do it. Some women like you to slide your penis about halfway into their anus and then take it out and repeat for a smooth entry the second time around. Others will like you to penetrate and keep very still. Others like it slow and gentle, while some will opt for a rockin' good time. Make sure to take time and learn the shape of the receiver's rectum and her likes and dislikes and earn her trust.

Having gone in and out once, you can now begin to work up to a more regular thrusting rhythm for as long as the two of you can enjoy it.

Position for comfort. There are many different ways to position yourselves for anal sex, says Dr. Morin. The most popular position is the side-by-side or "spoons" position, which allows for greater exploration and participation by both. Another popular position is the woman on top, as it allows greater freedom of movement and gives her a lot of control. And of course, there is the man-from-behind position, in which the woman is on hands and knees and the man kneeling behind her.

Want something more daring? Try it with her standing, bent over a table at a 90-degree angle, so that penetration can be easy for you while standing up. Dr. Morin recommends experimenting with these and other positions to determine what feels good for the both of you.

Ask the "O" question first. Regardless of whether you're wearing a condom, it makes sense for you to know if she does or doesn't want you to ejaculate during anal sex. Don't play a head game with this, so to speak. Discuss it outright beforehand.

Always clean up afterward. This brings us back to the subject of hygiene. After having spent time in her anus, either with your finger or with your penis, don't go anywhere other than the bathroom sink. *Especially* stay away from her vagina. Clean yourself up, says Dr. Gill, because no matter how well you both scrubbed initially, there are still zillions of tiny little bacteria that can wreak big-time havoc if they find their way into a neighboring orifice.

LASTING LONGER

It's not the quantity of time you spend making love; it's the quality. Sure. That's like saying, "I'd love to go to a really great baseball game, even if it only lasts two innings." The truth, in sex, is that quantity is a part of quality because it's a quality sexual experience only if it lasts as long as the two of you want it to last.

Many things can affect the length of a lovemaking session, but above all else, we're talking about delaying ejaculation. If you've been reading this book carefully, you know that after a man ejaculates, his body shifts from ecstatic tension to sleepy relaxation in as fast as 2 minutes. Yes, we are advocates of no-erection sex, in which you use mouth and hands and words and everything else available to pleasure your partner. Do this as much as you can. But in an excellent lovemaking session, there is no question that an erect penis gets marquis billing.

We're not talking about premature ejaculation, by the way. That's covered starting on page 242. We're assuming here that you already can last a reasonable length of time before reaching orgasm. Our goal is take you to that next level of skill, in which you have control over the timing of your ejaculations. And, in fact, with the proper mental training, along with some physical practice, most any man can gain far greater control than he ever expected. Now why didn't they teach you *that* in high school?

STEP ONE: RELAX

Jack and Jane are about 10 minutes into the throes of a heavy lovemaking session. The temperature's rising and so is Jack. The only problem is that his heat's so high he thinks his thermometer is about to blow, and it's way too early. So what does he do? He "desensitizes," in the words of the late Helen Singer Kaplan, M.D., Ph.D., founder and director of New York Hospital–Cornell Medical Center's Human Sexuality Program in New York City and author of *How to Overcome Premature Ejaculation*. Interpretation: He starts frantically thinking about anything that might get his mind off the sex itself. Baseball scores, mowing the lawn, leafing through the recent copy of

The Sears Guide to Perfect Plumbing. Nice idea, Jack, but it doesn't work, does it? That's because, as Dr. Kaplan wrote, desensitizing thoughts are aimed at *reducing* pleasure, when what you're really looking to do is *prolong* it, by learning to stay in control when highly aroused. So what can Jack do to get himself past the second inning?

For starters, he needs to realize that frantic, anxiety-laced efforts to delay orgasm usually have the opposite effect. They pull the trigger prematurely. Rather, relaxation is the first key toward mastering the all-night erection, according to Kathleen Gill, Ph.D., a clinical psychologist in Wellesley, Massachusetts, and author of *Sexuality after Spinal Cord Injury.* As Dr. Gill suggests, think of engaging in whatever exercises best calm you down; be it yoga, jogging, soft music, deep breathing, whatever. Relax your mind. Relax. Gain control over your thoughts. Then you can optimize the conditions under which you perform best.

STEP TWO: MASTER THE STOP-START

Calming your mind during sex does more than give you a mental boost; it relaxes muscles, lowers blood pressure, soothes your pulse. That in itself can help delay ejaculation, but it is hardly enough. The next element in lasting longer has to do with knowing your own body as it functions sexually. In other words, at what point during sexual stimulation do you become so excited that you're ready to blow your cork? What does it feel like when you're just moments from crossing that mind-bending threshold?

Four Myths about Lasting Longer

1. *If I think about other things when I'm sexually excited, I'll be able to delay my orgasm.* Wrong. Diverted thoughts only remove the pleasure from sex; they don't prolong it.
2. *If I try really hard, maybe I'll stay really hard.* Wrong. One indispensable key to sustained sex is your ability to relax yourself and remain relaxed.
3. *When I'm gone, I'm gone. I can't hold back ejaculating when the time has come.* Wrong. There are stages of excitation, the last one being orgasm. You have complete control over all the stages, right up to the seconds before you ejaculate. You can orgasm without ejaculating.
4. *Lasting longer is all up to me.* Couldn't be more wrong. It's not a matter of you or her, or you against her. It's a matter of the two of you enjoying one another over a sustained period of time. Consequently, her doing what she can to help you prolong your erection is in both of your best interests. So don't be at all surprised if she's more than eager to lend a hand, so to speak.

To better frame this, Dr. Kaplan recommended that you think of a scale from 1 to 10, with 1 being wet noodle limp and disinterested and 10 being full-fledged orgasm. What you want to do is learn what it feels like to be at point 7 or 8, because that's where you're maximizing your pleasure but still in control.

To do this, Dr. Gill recommends that you practice by yourself a few times. Slowly masturbate and pay close attention to what you're experiencing throughout the process. Get to where you can reach that crux, that 7 mark, and then stop. Take a break. You remain erect, but you notice that your elevator is slowly descending from the seventh floor down to the sixth, fifth, and so on. Don't let it hit the basement, though. Re-stimulate yourself while you're still erect and see if you can't hit 7 or 8 again. And again, when you do, pause.

After you've gotten a handle on your sexual stimulation levels, so to speak, the next step is to engage your lover in the process.

The most effective way for her to help is by stimulating your penis with her hand the way you've been doing it with yours. Go ahead and show her how hard to grip it, how deep the strokes should be, how fast or slow. Meanwhile, pay attention to your levels of excitement. Watch them climbing and know precisely when you should gently signal her to stop for a while. The first time out, have her stop at 3 or 4. Then, after waiting, have her take you to 5 or 6, then to 7. And keep in mind that you don't have to sit around making small talk between bouts. You just might want to shift the emphasis from your genital stimulation to any other form of sex play.

If she's comfortable with this approach, your next step toward longer-lasting erections is to switch from manual stimulation to actual intercourse. Have her take the female superior position, that is, with her on top (this is generally a less stimulating position for your penis). Begin by joining, but not moving. Then, have her begin to move, slowly, but with you controlling the pace and depth of the thrust. (You might simply want to have your hands on her buttocks while gently pushing and pulling. This gives her the message without you having to engage in a lot of traffic cop choreography.) Again try stopping, resting, and starting up again, at least three times, with the fourth cycle bringing you to orgasm.

After you've mastered this pose, repeat the whole thing from the classic missionary, or male superior position. Is this working? Congratulations. You have crossed an important bridge toward understanding and controlling your sexual performance.

STEP THREE: MASTER YOUR LOVE MUSCLE

Okay, you've learned to relax, and you've learned how to pace your love-making to delay orgasm. But we're not done. The final step in learning to last longer is to strengthen a sneaky little muscle called the pubococcygeus. This is the muscle located directly behind the testicles that we tense up when we're urinating and want to stop the flow. The PC, as it's commonly called, can do the same for semen as it does for urine, provided it's strong enough, explains Barbara Keesling, Ph.D., author of *How to Make Love All Night*.

You see, just like your abs or biceps, the PC needs to be exercised if it's going to have any power in it. So Dr. Keesling and others recommend that you work it out daily. How do you do that? Well, first, you find it. Take two fingers and place them just behind your testicles. Now, do what you would do to stop a urinary flow. Feel the muscle tense up? Say hello to your PC.

The next step is to make sure that you can tense it without at the same time tensing the muscles in your buttocks, thighs, or stomach. Have you gotten that far? Okay, next, what you want to do is flex it 20 times, in 1- or 2-second segments. Do this three times a day for three weeks, Dr. Keesling suggests. It sounds like a lot of work, but keep in mind that you can do it pretty much anywhere, anytime, and each round takes only about a minute or so. See that guy in his car at the red light smiling? He's probably flexing his PC muscle.

Now, if you want to have the Arnold Schwarzenegger of pubococcygeus muscles, the next thing you'll need to do is increase the workout. To do this, add to your regimen 10 more tensors, each 15 seconds in duration, Dr. Keesling prescribes. Spend 5 seconds gradually tensing the PC, 5 seconds fully tensed, and then 5 seconds easing back into relaxed position. These exercises, by the way, are called Kegels.

So, do you think your PC muscle is ready to be put to use? Then give it a try. Go to the bathroom and masturbate. When you are beginning to feel the start of an orgasm, clench your PC muscle hard, and hold it down for 10 seconds or so. If your PC is strong enough, and your timing just right, you will cut yourself off from ejaculating, Dr. Keesling says. This is very hard to do at first. It takes practice, practice, practice. But in time, you'll find that you can prevent yourself from ejaculating—which, as you will learn in the very next chapter, is what becoming multiorgasmic is all about. Life has just become considerably sweeter.

BECOMING MULTIORGASMIC

Remember those adolescent bull sessions in which some self-proclaimed Romeo would go on and on about how many times he popped his wad while making love the other night? Well, you can finally let go of the secret lust-envy you harbored over his Herculean feats. You see, the goal isn't multi-ejaculations; it's multiorgasms.

The term *multiorgasmic* usually refers to women, not men. Some lucky women are capable, if properly stimulated, to have several orgasms in quick successions. A mature man, on the other hand, ejaculates, goes limp, and if lucky, is able to become erect for a second round.

Is a multiorgasmic evening a possibility for most men? You bet it is. But is a multi-ejaculatory evening possible as well? Well, yes, but for far fewer men. Confused? You're not alone. Here's the deal.

Most of us equate orgasm with ejaculation, according to Barbara Keesling, Ph.D., author of *How to Make Love All Night*. In fact, they're two distinct but closely related experiences. The key to multiorgasms for men is learning how to pry the two apart. So let's first take a look at the difference between them and then consider how to enjoy them independently.

ORGASM VERSUS EJACULATION

An orgasm is a powerful, almost mystical physical reaction, the pinnacle moment after progressive sexual arousal. It involves a kind of full-bodied rush in which your heart races like an Arabian steed, your muscles flex, your neurons start break-dancing all over your body, your temperature soars like hell at high noon, and your mind drains of any other thoughts or concerns that might have once remotely mattered to you. Nipples become erect, toes curl, your skin flushes. And, oh, yes, it feels really good.

Ejaculation, on the other hand, more closely resembles a kind of internal bartender mixing and pouring a sex cocktail (pardon the pun). In it, different internal organs contribute ingredients to the semen stream and pour them into your urethra, whence they are dispensed by a bunch of pelvic muscles that steadily contract to shoot the semen out the head of your penis. (Interestingly, these contractions are nearly always 0.8 second long, identical to the rate of contractions of a woman's uterus and vaginal muscles during a female orgasm.)

In most cases, orgasm and ejaculation coincide. It's hard to tell one from the other. The key to multiorgasmic evenings lies in your ability to bring yourself to orgasm but not ejaculate. So how do you do this?

HOW TO DO IT

For starters, go back and review the previous chapter (Lasting Longer, page 184) because the techniques described there are the key to becoming multiorgasmic.

We covered three skills in that chapter. Here's a recap: First, you need to learn how to relax yourself. Think of your body as you would one of those jumpy, frenetic little ankle-nipping dogs you see in the park. The smart way to control that dog is to calm it down, soothe it, get its heart pumping slowly, get it to rest and sit still. The more agitated the little beast gets, the more unpredictable it is. The calmer you make it, the more apt you are to be able to manipulate it, have it do what you want.

Second, you need to take yourself, either alone or with your partner, through the arousal-pause exercises that edge you along close to orgasm without crossing over into its rarefied air of wanton bliss. In mastering this little ritual you can accomplish two things: You come to a clear understanding of exactly when you are on the brink of orgasm, and, with a cool head on your shoulders, you use that understanding to control the hot head between your legs.

Third, you want to strengthen your pubococcygeus (PC) muscle. It's that tiny muscle situated behind the testicles that you've flexed any time you've tried to cut off your urine stream. The PC is the guardian of the gate to multiorgasms; it needs to be strong to allow you to have that orgasm without ejaculating. All the relaxation and self-awareness techniques in the world will do you absolutely no good unless this little guy has the power to keep that gate shut until you want it opened. So start flexing!

So, equipped with a relaxed attitude, a tough-as-nails PC muscle, and a zenlike awareness of your various stages of arousal, how do you then stretch 30 minutes of sensuous rapture into hours? How do you go from "The Big O" to "First in a Series"? The answer is deceptively simple.

When you're making love—be it through intercourse, hand stimulation, or oral stimulation—pay attention to how close you're getting to orgasm. Go through the pattern of stimulation and pause two or three times, as taught in the previous chapter. Then allow yourself to reach orgasm. But here's the crucial point: As you begin to orgasm, tighten that PC muscle as if it were holding the purse strings to the national mint, Dr. Keesling explains. What you'll discover is that your body will still go into orgasm—your heart will rush, your muscles will tense, those waves of pleasure will wash over you—but you'll not have ejaculated. Better yet, you'll remain erect. Lie calmly for a moment or two, and then feel free to jump back into the evening's activities. Try this two or three times and see how it works. Then, when you're both ready, allow the orgasm to give way to ejaculation and call it a night. An extremely long and pleasurable night.

OTHER APPROACHES

Don't be surprised (or disappointed) if you don't quite split the difference between your orgasm and ejaculation the first few times out. This is not a test but a process, and, like learning the lines for a school play, what you're looking to do is become familiar enough with the cues and clues of your own body so that what feels like a foreign exercise becomes, with enough rehearsal, second nature to you. So be patient.

There is another approach that doctors sometimes recommend for stopping an ejaculation. It's called the penile squeeze. The squeeze play involves much of the same ritual cited earlier in this chapter, but now, when you're just about to climax, either you or your mate gently, gently, gently grips the head of your penis with two fingers and the thumb and squeezes it like you might a garden hose whose water you're trying to stanch. Keep it pinched until the potential ejaculation subsides, and then let go. And did we mention you want to do this gently?

MULTI-EJACULATORS

Of course, there are some men who needn't bother with all of the above. They are the ones who can indeed ejaculate several times in relatively quick succession. How do they do it? Simple, says Dudley Seth Danoff, M.D., senior attending urologist at Cedars-Sinai Medical Center in Los Angeles and author of *Superpotency*. They're young. "It's fairly common in young, healthy men," he says. "If they have a willing partner and the appropriate stimulus, they can ejaculate a lot."

The period of time that elapses between an ejaculation and the next time a guy is able to become sexually aroused is called the refractory period. Its purpose is to allow the seminal vesicles to fill up again with seminal fluid, says Dr. Danoff. If that's so, how can some guys come within minutes of their first ejaculation?

The answer is that most men don't completely empty their seminal vesicles after the first ejaculation, says Dr. Danoff. Any ejaculations that follow shortly after the first one will have less volume, he says.

"Can a 20-year-old kid do it five times between midnight and 8:00 in the morning? Probably. But the fifth time he does it, the volume of the ejaculate will be very small," says Dr. Danoff.

Not surprising, men have a wide range of refractory periods—from a matter of minutes to as long as 30 days.

The two factors that most determine how long this interval is are age and frequency of sexual activity, Dr. Danoff says. The older you are, the longer the refractory period. And the guy who has ejaculated 10 times in the past three days will have a longer refractory period than one who has not ejaculated at all.

These aren't the only things, however, that can affect the refractory period. Fatigue, the quality of the relationship with his partner, even the environment can have an impact. People probably feel sexier in balmy Hawaii than in frozen Alaska, Dr. Danoff surmises.

A man's overall health is also extremely important. "If you have someone who is obese and diabetic, neurologically impaired and taking drugs, he's going to be more impaired in terms of his ejaculatory function and his refractory period than somebody who's a well-conditioned athlete," says Dr. Danoff.

Finally, a lot more men can have multiple orgasms during a lovemaking session than they realize, says Marilyn Fithian, Ph.D., a sex researcher and retired sex therapist in Long Beach, California. After they come, most men assume that they have nothing left, she says. This becomes a self-fulfilling prophecy.

But if more men were like the Little Engine That Could ("I think I can. I think I can."), it would be a different story, Dr. Fithian says. After ejaculating, men often will get another erection—and sometimes another orgasm—if they continue stroking, rubbing, kissing, and the like with their partner, she says. A lot depends on the physical condition and energy level of the man in question. The key is to enjoy what you're doing and not make another erection or orgasm the focus of your activities. "Don't quit," Dr. Fithian advises. "If you want to go on, go on."

4

SEX AND HEALTH

Fitness and Sex

Sex is not an Olympic event. It doesn't require years of practice and training to handle its physical requirements, lucky for us.

But sex is still an intensely physical act. And when done to its full capacity, it requires no small amount of sweat, muscle, and flexibility.

"It's true that you don't have to be a physical marvel to enjoy good sex. But I also think it's true that the more you are physically fit, the more you'll enjoy sex," says Tommy Boone, Ph.D., an exercise physiologist at the College of St. Scholastica in Duluth, Minnesota.

Here's a quick quiz. Can your arms and back comfortably support your body during a full-length lovemaking session in the missionary position? If you need to change positions solely due to muscle fatigue, then, well, let's just say you might be in need of a date with a barbell.

Obviously, we don't mean that you have to gain 10 pounds of muscle and push your body fat percentage into the single digits to enjoy mind-blowing sex. With just a modicum of fitness training, though, you'll enjoy sex longer and better than ever.

Exercise or Sexercise?

If you need an incentive to hit the gym, here's one: Exercise is a powerful aphrodisiac. James White, Ph.D., professor emeritus and former director of the Exercise Physiology and Human Performance Laboratory at the University of California, San Diego, studied the sexual behavior of a group of middle-age men who were placed on a regular exercise program of three to four days a week, 1 hour per exercise session. Then, Dr. White compared their sexual activity against a group of similar men who didn't exercise.

In the study, the exercisers reported a significant boost in sexual performance and activity. They had a 30 percent increase in the frequency of sex with their partners as well as an increase in the amount of orgasms they experienced. Meanwhile, the couch potatoes—the guys who didn't exercise—reported no such increases in their sexual behavior or performance.

"There's certainly a link between sex and physical fitness," says Jean Miller, D.O., a holistic medical practitioner in private practice in New York City. "First, there's a mental component—exercise and fitness training raise your energy levels, make you feel better about yourself. That's going to make you more confident and more attractive to your partner. Then, because you've been exercising, you'll have the physical capability to enjoy sex longer and better."

Aerobic Amore

To be fit for sex, your exercise regimen has to have plenty of the right kind of exercise, chiefly aerobics.

Sex before Sports

It's an age-old warning to players on the eve of "the Big Game": No drinking, no drugs, no sex.

So *that's* why professional athletes always look so surly.

Oh, there's no doubt that drinking alcohol and taking drugs can hamper your sports performance. But no sex?

"Somewhere along the line, coaches and players got it in their heads that sex before a big game would diminish their performance, sap them somehow," says Tommy Boone, Ph.D., an exercise physiologist at the College of St. Scholastica in Duluth, Minnesota. Dr. Boone set out to test this belief by studying the performance of athletes who had sex and those who abstained on the eve of a competition. "We found no difference in performance. The two sets of athletes were pretty similar, except that one group got to have sex the night before."

So if you're gearing up for the company softball game or training for a corporate 10-K, don't martyr yourself for the sake of performance. "If you want to have sex, go ahead and have it. It might even help you by taking the edge off any anxiety or stress you're feeling the night before a big competition," says Dr. Boone.

Now, when we say "aerobics," we don't mean you have to join the Sweatin'-to-the-Oldies, neon-leotard, jumping-up-and-down crowd. But you do have to perform an exercise that gets your arms and legs moving, and gets your heart and lungs pumping and blowing. Plenty of activities fit this bill: running, cycling, cross-country skiing, stairclimbing, rowing, hiking, brisk walking. Whatever exercise you choose, make sure you do it three or four times a week, for 30 minutes or so. That will ensure that your cardiovascular system is getting revved up to fat-burning speed.

Stay at it, and pretty soon you'll find you have plenty of stamina for marathon lovemaking.

Not only will aerobic exercise add hours of pleasure to your sex life; it'll tack on years of quality time to your life.

"Aerobics are good for your body, no question of that," says Dr. Boone. They help keep your heart and lungs in tip-top shape. Plus, aerobic activities burn off excess fat, which can cause heart problems or low-back pain and contribute to other health problems, such as diabetes, later in life.

MAKING LOVE MUSCLES

In addition to aerobic exercise, you may feel compelled to build some bulk, add some tone to an otherwise tone-deaf body. If that's the case, you need to start lifting weights.

"Muscle building and toning, even if you're just working with dumb-bells, can be very good for your body in general," says Dr. Boone. The reasons are manifold: The more toned your muscles are, the better you can perform and excel in any physical activity, be it a pickup game of hoops or a quickie in the laundry room. No matter what's required, your svelte, toned self will be ready for action.

Also, muscle has great advertising value. If you have decent pecs, some nice development in the arms, and a belly that doesn't hide your belt buckle, you're going to be sending a message to potential partners that you are a guy who knows how to take care of himself—and you probably know how to take care of her, too. What can a larded-over broad-belly do? Show her that chin trick he does? Stretch his shirt across his stomach and talk affectionately about his "food baby"? In the circus of life, you can be either the strong man in the center ring or just another geek in the sideshow tent. Take your pick.

If you make the smart choice, you'll need to dedicate three or four days a week to weight training, says Carlos DeJesus, world champion bodybuilder and fitness trainer in Richmond, Virginia. You can do this after your aerobic work-out, when your muscles are warmed up and ready to do some lifting. Start with a simple pattern: Monday, do legs and abs. Tuesday, work the upper body—the chest, back, shoulders, and arms. Rest on Wednesday, then repeat the same routine for Thursday and Friday. Start out with 8 to 12 reps of a fairly light weight. After a few weeks, start building inroads. When you can lift a weight easily for 12 reps, increase the weight by 5 percent or 5 pounds, whichever is less, then lift for 8 to 12 reps again. Keep following this pattern. In a month, you'll notice some tone. In six weeks, you may even spot new muscle.

FLEXING FOR SEX

As manly as weight training is, it's really not the most important aspect of physical training for better sex.

"Lifting weights is all well and good, but strength isn't what counts in bed. Flexibility is what counts," says Bob Anderson, flexibility consultant and author of the bible of flexibility books, *Stretching*.

As Anderson observes, sex is not a sport of power; it's a gymnastic pursuit of grace and fluidity. "You have a lot of different muscles working together in a variety of different positions, which are changing all the time. In this sort of activity, what good is a strong muscle if it's so tight that it won't function—or worse, might get injured?" he asks.

Unfortunately, the majority of men never spend any time doing flexibility training. "But these are the same guys who are going to wonder why their back hurts or why they got a cramp in their leg or why they pulled a groin muscle when they should have been enjoying themselves," says Anderson.

For better flexibility, you don't need to become a yoga fanatic. But it sure wouldn't hurt to spend a few minutes doing some simple stretches every day. "The muscles you want to focus on are in the low back, the groin, the backs of the legs," says Anderson. Keeping these muscles supple not only will help you during all your sexual contortions but also will help you resist day-to-day perils such as low-back pain. Anderson suggests the following stretches, which can be done in the comfort of your very own bed, by yourself or with a partner. "If you do it with a partner, you can even make the stretches part of foreplay, if you want. They won't even seem like exercise then," he says.

Groin Stretch

To keep your groin muscles limber and flexible, lie on your back, knees bent, feet flat on the bed. Pull your heels toward your butt; turn your ankles so that the soles of your feet are touching. By now, your knees should be pointing out to the sides.

Let your knees slowly drop toward the bed. Gravity will pull them in that direction, but you may want to put your hands on your inner thighs and apply slight downward pressure. Relax and stretch for about 30 seconds.

To make this stretch a twosome, have your partner kneel in front of you, knees barely touching the tops of your ankles (this keeps them from moving). Then have her put her hands on either thigh and apply downward pressure until you feel the stretch in your hips and groin—it should not feel painful. When you feel the stretch, have her apply steady, gentle pressure to hold a comfortable stretch for about 30 seconds. Switch positions.

Low-Back Stretch

To stretch your lower back and hips, lie on your back. Hold the back of your left knee with your left hand and pull your knee toward your chest. Hold the stretch for 30 seconds. Switch legs and repeat. Now do both legs at the same time.

Your partner can help with this stretch by putting her hand on your leg, just below the knee, and gently pushing your knee to your chest. When you feel the stretch, have her hold for 30 seconds, then release. Do the same with the other knee. Then have her push both knees to your chest, for a full stretch across the lower back.

APPRECIATING YOUR BODY

Body image isn't something that men admit to readily, oh no. Yet it does play a role in the lives of our sexual selves, especially as we get older. The body that makes us look and feel like a stud on some days also seems like it's surrendering to the excesses of a life well-lived on others. Meanwhile, the messages we get from popular culture confirm our worst suspicions. Commercials, movies, and magazines tell us that we have to have hair, have to have six-pack abs, have to have a chest as wide as the hood of a car if we want to have any kind of sex life. Or any kind of life, for that matter.

Our message to the pop culture gods: Cut the crap, will ya?

As the riptide of modern life sucks us under, sometimes it's hard to remember that the human ideals Madison Avenue foists upon us are simply not realistic, nor even worthwhile. When you watch the latest avatar of manhood swagger across the screens, covers, and billboards of the world, bear this is mind: It's make-believe. What you are seeing is little more than a puppet of light and shadow, held together by hair dye, anabolic steroids, and cosmetic surgery.

"Some of the things we're told we have to have—bulging muscles, white teeth, a full head of hair, and so forth—really aren't a natural part of the body's development over time," says Tommy Boone, Ph.D., an exercise physiologist at the College of St. Scholastica in Duluth, Minnesota. "Of course, it's to your advantage to be in good physical shape. But that's quite a different thing from looking like a bodybuilder."

As Dr. Boone explains, there are some completely natural physiological consequences from spending life on a planet that has gravity and orbits a sun. These include wrinkles, sagging, spots, and other skin imperfections. And yes, even a little bit of paunch around the middle is a completely natural, and not necessarily unhealthy, hallmark of the man who has paid his dues in the great game of life. If you have any or all of these qualities, you shouldn't get down on yourself about it. And you certainly shouldn't believe that your body is falling apart.

"At any given point in life, there are things going on in the body that we may not like or that we may think is unattractive. It doesn't just happen when you hit middle age," says Dr. Boone. Consider that when you were a kid, you may have felt too short or had no muscle or had a perpetual cowlick. As a teenager, you had rotten skin, greasy hair, a voice that squawked like a police radio. Compared to those anatomical indignities, what's a few wrinkles or gray hairs?

IMAGE IS NOTHING

So now you know about the great conspiracy that society and the media are playing upon you. Now you're not going to be fooled by their mind games, made to believe you're a smelly, unsavory, unattractive old man. Are you?

Okay, maybe you're buying a *little* into the cultural pressures that say you have to look this good, have this tight a butt, have that much hair or muscle.

Guess what? Your partner probably isn't.

"I've counseled a lot of couples, and I don't hear women complaining very often about the physical appearance of their husbands," says Robert Birch, Ph.D., a psychologist in Columbus, Ohio, specializing in marriage and sex therapy and author of *Oral Caress*.

As Dr. Birch explains, men are tuned to react to visual stimulation much more than women. In other words, we tend to put more importance on the

Hairy Situations

As you get older, it seems like your hair is migrating from the places you wanted it to places you don't need it.

"Ear hair, nose hair, male-pattern baldness—these can all be legitimate image concerns. And they may well be things that some woman might find unattractive," says Steve Manley, Ph.D., staff psychologist for the Male Health Center in Dallas.

If your hairline's on a retreat, grooming experts say that you're better off keeping your coiffure trimmed short—growing a ponytail only makes that bald spot look like the dot on an exclamation point. And growing wisps that you can comb over your bald spot never works. A far better tack is to adopt a short, close cut, which seems to minimize any obvious signs of balding. And if you are bald, then revel in it. Make Sean Connery and Patrick Stewart your patron saints. Perpetuate the idea of bald men being more virile. Who are we to say they're not?

If your problem revolves around unwanted hair, just remember this: If it grows, it can be cut. Next time you shave, pass the razor—gently—along the edge of your earlobes, snipping off any long wisps that might be sprouting. If the hair is growing from within a body cavity like your ears or your nostrils, don't use scissors—you'll likely end up stabbing yourself. Instead, you can buy a battery-powered clipper shaped to fit these hard-to-reach spots—almost any variety store sells them.

physical appearance of our partners than they do on us. Consequently, we're more likely to assume that, because some physical imperfection is a big deal to us, it's going to be a big deal to them. Not so.

Women, as it happens, are more aroused by intangibles, like your wry personality or the aura of power and self-assurance you generate or just by the very idea of being intimate with you. "If you have a personality that she finds attractive, she's not going to worry so much about your acne scars or your love handles," says Dr. Birch.

Knowing women are more interested in making love with their minds may not stop you from worrying about some offensive aspect of your body, though. And in fact, women are beginning to put more emphasis on having a male partner who is fit and sexy, due, in part, to changing male images in the media, notes Shirley Zussman, Ed.D., a certified sex and marital therapist in private practice in New York City. So let's take a look at some of the most common bodily concerns men have.

WORKING OUT IMAGE ISSUES—LITERALLY

Of course, there's always the chance that you feel self-conscious about your body because it really is flabby and corpulent. One couch-bound Sunday too many, one weekday workout too few—that's all it takes to put you on the slippery slope between fit and fat.

"Or it doesn't have to be a fat issue," points out Steve Manley, Ph.D., staff psychologist for the Male Health Center in Dallas. "Some men may feel self-conscious because they're underweight—they feel scrawny."

You can stare in lament at your stooped-over, unmuscled frame, or you can get off your duff and do something about it. We're not saying that you have to drop a few hundred bucks on a club membership and become a spandex-clad gym rat. But getting out and getting some exercise—any exercise—three or four times a week for 30 minutes can do you a world of good, physically and mentally.

"The point is not to try and recapture the body you had when you were 18. You're trying to feel better about yourself," says Dr. Manley. Exercise can certainly help. Even if you never get washboard abs or a huge chest, you can derive pleasure from the fact that you're working on it, man; you're making some effort to improve yourself. And don't think that's going to be lost on your partner either. She'll notice your efforts, and she'll appreciate that fact that you're trying to take care of yourself, not just for your own benefit but for hers, too. (For more detailed information about the way a good fitness regimen can rev up your sex life, see Fitness and Sex on page 194.)

COMING CLEAN

Some image problems men wrestle with may have less to do with images, and more to do with a different type of sensory input—smell. You may be Mr. Universe and Brad Pitt rolled into one, but if you have body odor (B.O.) or bad breath, no woman's going to want your hard body bench-pressing her.

To a certain degree, there's nothing wrong with having a manly scent about you, says Dr. Manley. "Some women may like you a bit sweaty," he says. But if your daily activities have left you smelling like a dumpster in the middle of July, it's time to attend to some hygiene.

"Women tend to be more sensitive to smell than men," says Dr. Birch. "That's why how you smell—whether you have nicotine or alcohol breath or just a bad case of B.O.—can be a real turnoff." If you're going to smell for her, you might as well smell good.

Let this be your watch word—make that wash word. Bathe before bed. Even if you normally take a shower in the morning, consider washing up at night, suggests Dr. Birch, especially if you're looking for some action in the bedroom. And when you're washing, be a sergeant who cares for his privates. Get a good lather going and suds up your pubic hair and all surrounding equipment.

"And if you're uncircumcised, be particularly careful to pull back the foreskin and wash the head of your penis," says Dr. Birch. All too often, a cheesy, smelly substance called smegma can build up under there, making for an unpleasantly aromatic experience for almost any woman who gets a whiff.

As a rule, you don't need to wear deodorant to bed. In fact, Alex Comfort, M.D., D.Sc., in his famous *Joy of Sex* and *The New Joy of Sex*, says that, in bed, deodorant should be "banned absolutely." Instead, men and women should rely on the seductive powers of their own clean, natural smell. "Wash and leave it at that," he suggests.

FIGHTING PERCEPTION WITH REALITY

While it's nice to think you can control or eliminate all of the unappealing aspects of your body, you may have some imperfections that you feel you can never eliminate.

"There may be things you've always been sensitive about, perceptions about yourself that seem impossible to change," says Dr. Manley. Often, these perceptions are born in our youth—a cutting remark in the locker room, an overly critical parent, a personal event that embarrassed you deeply. All could lead to self-perceptions that back up on you for a good chunk of your life. No exercise routine or change of grooming habits will make them disappear instantly.

"But if you have this kind of anxiety—and most of us do about one thing or another—the best way to eliminate it is to stop carrying it around with you, to share it with somebody," says Dr. Manley.

"Bottom line: If you're worried that she's going to be turned off by some physical quality about you, there's only one way to find out. You guessed it: You have to ask her," says Dr. Manley. "Communication is just about the only way to find out what she likes and doesn't like. It's also a way for you to feel better about your body.

"Just the act of talking, of saying, 'Look, I have a little anxiety about this,' can be wonderfully freeing. You finally get this great weight off your chest," says Dr. Manley. "And one of two things will happen. Either she'll acknowledge your concern—maybe even agree with it—and you two can talk together about improvements, or you'll discover that what concerned you so much wasn't even an issue for her." In either event, you're in a win-win situation: By opening up to her, you've not only begun the process of facing down personal demons; you've also become closer as a couple.

SAFER SEX

Imagine, for the moment, that your mind is a skyscraper. Up in the rarefied air of the observation deck, there lives your politically correct, eminently responsible self. He can see the entire sexual landscape from here, and safe sex takes up a lot of the view. A real fin de siècle type of guy, he accepts this fact with grace and élan.

Meanwhile, a hundred levels below, there's the sweaty troglodyte in the basement who keeps the boilers stoked at a feverish pitch. He's shaking his head every time he hears the words "safe sex." And he's admitting with gusto what his upstairs counterpart would never contemplate.

For the moment, let's descend to the basement and admit it, too: Safe sex just doesn't feel as good as barrier-free intercourse.

Safe sex advocates argue that this narrow, selfish concept is all in your mind. Of course it is—that's where all our feelings and sensations are interpreted. This doesn't change the fact that, no matter how you use it, latex just can't compare to the delicious sensation of slippery, uncovered body parts sliding against one another.

There. Now that we have that off our collective chests, let's face facts.

1. Safe sex—or safer sex, for no sex is truly 100 percent safe—is an inextricable and unavoidable necessity of life for virtually every man on the planet. Possible exceptions include your dad and the Pope.

2. Safer sex feels a lot better than no sex.

3. Safer sex feels one heck of a lot better than the painful or even fatal complications of a sexually transmitted disease (STD), including AIDS (for the gory details, see Sexual Diseases on page 253). This is what you risk every time you engage in unprotected sex with a new partner.

Here's what happens: When your point A slides into her slot B, a connection is made, like plugging into a wall socket. Fluids secreted by your body and hers meet and mingle. If she has an infectious disease, cells carrying that infection can quickly and easily make the short hop from her fluids to the tip of your penis or tongue, or into any microscopic opening on your skin that they come in contact with.

If you're the one carrying an STD, it's the same process, except the bugs that you're carrying are going to take to her body like a couch potato to a wide-screen TV. As you may have noticed, a vagina is a warm, moist environment; it's the sort of place where germs thrive. Plus, the walls of the vagina, though elastic, can tear microscopically when stretched, which only opens more doors for opportunistic viruses to make the jump from you to her. The same thing happens in anal sex, only tearing in the delicate membranes of the rectum is far more frequent (unlike a vagina, that part of the body has no natural lubrication). In general, the same principles apply whenever you bring genitals into contact with bodily fluids or skin that can tear. If there's unprotected contact, there's a danger of infection. The trick, then, is to throw up a barrier between your cells and her cells, cutting off any unwanted exchange.

For years, the guardians of society have had themselves in a lather making sure we practice safer sex, and with good reason. According to the Centers for Disease Control and Prevention, men account for nearly 400,000 new cases of STDs every year in the United States.

Sex by the Numbers

Percentage of men who reported that their condoms were too tight: 19

Percentage of men who reported that their condoms were so tight that they actually split on occasion: 68

SOURCE: *British Medical Journal*

And those are just your run-of-the-mill STDs like gonorrhea and non-specific urethritis (NSU). AIDS, we don't have to tell you, is a full-blown pandemic all by itself. At press time, the number of AIDS sufferers in the United States alone totaled more than a half-million people. You, on the other hand, can avoid being one of the numbers with a few simple precautionary measures.

If you're already practicing safer sex, good for you. Keep it up; keep it on. But if for whatever reason you find yourself starting out in the brave new world of sex with a new partner or partners, there are effective—even enjoyable—methods you'll want to try. No, safer sex may not feel as great as bare-naked, full-contact sex, but it could spare you or your partners a whole lot of misery. And that alone should make you feel pretty good.

BIRTH OF A CONDOM NATION

Rubbers. Skins. Trojans. Plonkers. Raincoats. For most men, safer sex is primarily about condoms—when to wear them, how to wear them, and how to enjoy wearing them.

Hold on—where constrictive rubber sleeves are concerned, is such a thing as enjoyment really possible? Sure it is, says Carol Queen, a San Francisco sex educator and author of *Exhibitionism for the Shy* and a book of essays on sex and culture, *Real Live Nude Girl*.

"Yes, safe sex can really be erotic," Queen insists. But you have to have the right attitude. For example, don't think of condoms as protection from all the nasty diseases out there; think of them as sex toys. "Putting on a condom isn't a medicinal chore," she says. "It's a promise, a sign that lovemaking has escalated to the point of penetration."

Sounds good to us. So, in the interest of helping you reach that point safely, we offer the following suggestions. They should make it easier for you when it comes time to acquire and, most important, to use condoms.

Sample the range. There was a time when a man had only one kind of condom available to him—the thick, dry, no-frills "rubber," acquired only by visiting some dingy truck stop rest room or summoning the nerve to ask the neighborhood pharmacist for a pack. Nowadays, even the smallest convenience store has several different sizes and shapes of latex condoms for sale. What's more, virtually every major city in this country has a store that specializes in condoms and safer sex accessories (check the Yellow Pages under "Condoms").

How do you know which kind to buy? There are so many—ultra-thin, super-thin, extra-large, extra-long, ribbed for her pleasure, lubed for yours. With these kinds of options available, it's next to impossible to choose. So don't—try a variety instead. Queen recommends being a kid in a candy store. Go crazy—buy a selection. Then, in the privacy of your home, you and your partner can see which ones you like best.

Check the ingredients. We don't want to dampen the enthusiasm of a good shopping spree. But for safest sex, make sure that the condoms you buy share some key elements, chiefly, latex construction, which blocks transmission of disease; spermicide, which can also help kill viruses; and some kind of expanded or reservoir tip, which makes a condom less likely to split when you ejaculate. If you or your partner are allergic to latex (a small percentage of men and women are), there are polyurethane condoms available for men and women. However, these condoms may not be as effective as latex at stopping the spread of disease, according to Nancy Alexander, Ph.D., former chief of the Contraceptive Development Branch of the National Institutes of Health in Bethesda, Maryland.

Condoms to avoid are those made of animal intestines; they're too porous to stop the microscopic critters that can cause disease. Also, beware of novelty condoms—the kind that change color or glow in the dark, for example. Fun, yes, but these may not be effective in preventing diseases. Make sure that the ones you use are latex, labeled "for disease prevention."

Call for condoms. Perhaps you're a tad wary about lingering in the "family planning" aisle of the local drugstore, reading labels. If so, Queen says that there are any number of reputable catalog or mail-order companies who will be happy for your condom custom. Often, these companies have more options than what you'll find down at the corner drugstore, too. One of the largest venues, Condomania, accepts both telephone and Internet orders at (800) 926-6366 or http://www.condomania.com. Or check the back of any men's magazine for those ads selling 100 condom samplers for $9.95. That should give you plenty of options to choose from.

Keep 'em handy. One of the best ways to ensure that you'll practice safer sex is to keep condoms close to hand. Make them ubiquitous in your life. Store them in the drawer of your nightstand. Keep a few in your shaving kit so that you'll always have a supply when you're on the road. And if you're out on the prowl, keep a couple in your jacket pocket. Do *not* store them in your wallet—your own body heat will deteriorate the condom, making it more likely to break at a critical moment.

Don't drink and drive. This last tip has more to do with common sense than condom sense. Specifically, the more you consume mind-altering substances, the less likely you are to make sensible choices about whom to spend the night with—and what to wear when you do. The Alcohol Research Group in Berkeley, California, conducted a study to measure the effects of alcohol use on sexual behavior. They found that the men in the study who drank the most were also the least likely to use condoms consistently.

WEIGHING THE RISKS

While condom wearing is one of the most important parts of safe sex, it's not all there is to safe sexual behavior.

"Kissing, body contact, touching, talking, using your hands, mutual masturbation...most safe sex behavior doesn't involve barriers and spermicide," says Queen. These are all activities you can and probably do enjoy as part of your sexual repertoire, and it can all be done safely.

That said, there are other ways besides intercourse to transmit disease. According to the Institute for Advanced Study of Human Sexuality in San Francisco, some sexual behavior is considered safer than others. Here's a quick review of the realm of sexual behavior, and how each activity stacks up in terms of safety.

• Nonsexual touching. From holding hands to an oily massage, most touching—provided it doesn't involve the transfer of bodily fluids—can be totally safe. Incidentally, it can also be incredibly erotic. "Holding hands can be incredibly sexy. It can be a way to be intimate. Remember that there's a whole body out there; it's not just genitals," says Robert Birch, Ph.D., a psychologist in private practice in Columbus, Ohio, specializing in marriage and sex therapy.

• Kissing. This is still considered relatively safe, provided you go easy on the deep, tonsil-swabbing French kisses. In that situation, you're swapping a lot of saliva, which can carry viral agents. Dry kisses on any part of the body is also considered pretty safe, says Dr. Birch.

• Sexual touching. Generally speaking, any touching or caressing above the waist is pretty safe, provided no bodily fluids are going into any openings. Queen points out that even masturbating one another can be safe—make sure that you or your partner has no open cuts on your hands. Also, with mutual masturbation, it's only natural to want to use some form of lubrication, so go ahead—just don't use saliva. Massage oils and lubricants like K-Y jelly or Astroglide are all safe options.

• Oral sex. "Although increasingly risky, oral sex can be done safely," says Dr. Birch, author of *Oral Caress*. Men, wear a condom. Experiment with flavored ones (though some taste pretty bad) or let her top you with chocolate sauce, whipped cream, and the like. If you want to perform oral sex on a woman safely, she can wear a vaginal pouch or female condom—just make sure that the outer rim fully covers her genitals. Or you can use a dam, a rubber device used to cover the genitals.

• Anal sex. This is perhaps the riskiest of all because the walls of the anus are incredibly rich in blood vessels. Anal intercourse, without proper lubrication, can cause microscopic tears or openings in the anal walls, says Jack Morin, Ph.D., a psychotherapist and sexologist from the San Francisco Bay area and author of *Anal Pleasure and Health* and *The Erotic Mind*, allowing infected semen to pass readily into the bloodstream. If you're going to engage in anal sex, it is crucial to wear a condom with plenty of lubrication.

• Monogamy. As sex practices go, this is probably the safest of all. But practicing it can be tricky, as you may have already discovered.

"If you and your partner are committed and exclusive to one another, you'll be far less likely to contract a disease than someone with a ongoing relationship with numerous partners," says Dr. Alexander. Even after you decide to be monogamous in a relationship, though, safe sex advocates suggest that you continue to practice safer sex for several months. After that, both of you should get tested for STDs. If you have a clean bill of health, at that point, you can more safely and smartly make the decision to choose mutual commitment and trust as your safe sex method of choice.

CONTRACEPTION

Centuries of human development have layered sex with numerous functions and meanings. Sex can be fun, angst-ridden, a thrill, a danger, a method of stress relief, an expression of intimacy. But pare it down to the basics and suddenly you're cheek to cheek with one inescapable, stupendously obvious fact: Sex is the leading cause of children.

In fact, perpetuating the species is the original job description of sex. Our primordial forebears were not overly concerned with such modern concepts as lasting longer or locating their partner's erogenous zones. Their sexual goals were much less complicated—get in, get out, move to the next one. Men were designed to be the Johnny Appleseeds of DNA and, like most species on the planet, they came equipped with an undeniable urge to procreate.

We don't have to tell you how powerful the sex drive remains today. But the single-minded purpose of that primitive drive is often in conflict with the broader goals of the modern world. To put it bluntly, we don't want to worry about having a kid every time we have sex.

If you're a person of certain religious or personal beliefs, there aren't many ways to get around this. Every time you have sex with your partner, you're accepting a very good chance that you'll find yourself on the receiving end of fatherhood. Working without a net requires incredible grace and composure, and we respect that. As for the rest of us, a more feasible option to child-free sex is the judicious application of birth control.

PROPHYLACTIC PROSPECTS

Contraceptives come in a cornucopia of styles and formats—pills, jellies, foams, barriers, inserts, implants, and injections. Some work better than others, some have more side effects than others. But one thing is certain: For every method of contraception that exists, you'll find someone who thinks that method is the most complicated, least comfortable, messiest form of birth control known to man, and someone who wouldn't think of using any other form of contraception.

"Which is to say that birth control is a highly subjective area. The best method for you or your sexual partner is going to depend on many things," says Nancy Alexander, Ph.D., former chief of the Contraceptive Development Branch of the National Institutes of Health in Bethesda, Maryland. For example: how long you've been in your current relationship, how concerned you and your partner are about getting pregnant, what methods you consider "messy" or "problematic," or other personal issues.

The hassles of cost and doctors also play a role in contraception choices. Not everyone wants to go to a doctor for so much as a prescription, let alone a procedure where injections or implants are involved. Nor can everyone justify the expense. Luckily, birth control has a price scale. Condoms, for example, can be had for less than a dollar each—even free at some clinics. Meanwhile, newer forms of birth control like the under-the-skin Norplant can exact a much larger cost in time and money—and not many insurance plans cover its use.

"Personal preference and convenience—as well as efficacy—are some of the reasons that there are so many different forms of contraception out there and why there will be more in the future. The idea is to offer a method of contraception that's going to satisfy everyone," says Dr. Alexander.

Finally, men, we must point out that virtually all methods of contraception—condoms excepted—put the onus on the lady. And with few exceptions, she has to deal with complicated procedures or strict timetables if her methods are going to be effective. Frankly, it's not fair for her to do all the work or for you to expect it of her. So do your part and always have a condom ready, just in case. Not only is this a matter of modern etiquette and a sign of respect for your partner, Dr. Alexander says; it's also a matter of common sense and self-preservation.

Odds are that you and your partner already have a favored method of birth control. If that works for you, great. But it might be worth knowing how that method stacks up against other forms of contraception. Here, then, is a lineup of the tried and true and the latest and greatest in temporary contraception. We'll tell you how they work, how well they work, and what possible advantages and disadvantages exist. (If you're thinking about permanent contraception, see Vasectomy on page 214.)

Condoms

One of the few birth control measures a man can use, condoms are among the most widely accepted forms of contraception. According to Planned Parenthood, condoms can be 88 percent effective at preventing pregnancy when used correctly.

How to use: Put a drop of water-based lubricant (like K-Y jelly or Astroglide) into the tip of the condom—this will reduce friction (and the possibility of tearing) while increasing sensation. As soon as your penis is erect, unroll the condom down over it, leaving about a half-inch space at the tip. Smooth out any air bubbles and you're ready to ride. When you're withdrawing, be sure to hold the condom against the base of your penis. Otherwise, it could slip off while you're pulling out, creating a hazardous spill.

Advantages: Besides their ready availability—what all-night convenience store or gas station rest room doesn't carry them?—condoms also have a useful advantage for men. Because of the constrictive nature of condoms, they can trap blood in the penis more effectively, making you harder. Also, condoms can decrease sensitivity, which may help you last longer, too.

Disadvantages: Well, that decreased sensitivity can work against you. Many men complain that sex just doesn't feel the same with a condom on. Also, many men are allergic to latex. If you're one of them, you'll be pleased to know that condoms made out of tough polyurethane are now available, but Dr. Alexander warns that these may not be as effective as latex condoms.

The fact that there's such a wide variety of condom shapes and styles these days can also be a bit of a drawback. No one wants to linger overlong in the "family planning" aisle of the local drugstore. In general, don't be distracted by flashy colors or amazing claims (larger for large men; ribbed for *her* pleasure). Keep it simple: Look for something made with latex, with a reservoir tip (helps keep condoms from splitting), and with lubrication. Also, be aware that some condoms will just feel thicker than others. Trial and error is your best guide. When you go shopping for the first time, buy 3-packs, not 12-packs. That way, if you don't like what you bought, you won't have to waste much money or endure uncomfortable sex—you can just go back to the store and try another flavor.

Female Condoms

Also known as a vaginal pouch, the female condom works similarly to its male analog but is made of polyurethane, which is considered almost as effective as latex.

How to use: One end of the pouch has a soft plastic ring at the base, which is inserted into the vagina. A wider outer rim at the other end stays outside the body and covers your partner's genital area (which also makes this

Shots and Pills for Men?

For decades, men have only had a few methods of birth control available to them exclusively: condoms, withdrawal, or a vasectomy.

"It's a pretty limited choice, with a lot of extremes," says Nancy Alexander, Ph.D., former chief of the Contraceptive Development Branch of the National Institutes of Health in Bethesda, Maryland. "But that's it—and that's how it has been for a long time."

Perhaps not for very much longer.

The World Health Organization (WHO) conducted a study of men who received regular injections of testosterone as a method of reducing the overall amount of sperm being produced. Unfortunately, subjects had to get their shots weekly, which was more than some men could stand. By way of comparison, Depo-Provera, the birth control shot for women, only has to be administered every three months.

In the end, the results from the trial were promising indeed—WHO researchers tabulated a 98.6 percent rate of effectiveness, comparable to female contraceptive drugs.

Dr. Alexander says that scientists are also looking hard at ways to target androgen receptors in the male body. Among other things, these receptors tell the body when to start making more sperm. By isolating the correct receptor, researchers can develop a shot or pill that will shut down that receptor temporarily, thus stopping sperm production.

"We've developed an injection that can be given every three months, and it has been shown to be effective," Dr. Alexander says. But this form of contraception is still in the research stage. It could be a couple of years yet before the male shot—and quite a few years before the male pill—are available widely.

method useful for safe oral sex). The condom naturally follows the contours of the vagina.

Advantages: Female condoms have all the convenience of traditional condoms. There are no constrictive sensations, and *you* don't have to wear it.

Disadvantages: The outer lip of the female condom has been known to slip into the vagina. Also, sex with a female condom on is, um, awfully noisy. Not howling-like-a-cat-in-heat noisy; more like cat-trapped-in-a-garbage-bag noisy. Suffice it to say, the distinctive squishing and gulping sounds take some getting used to.

Spermicide

Whether it's a foam, cream, suppository, or jelly, spermicides like nonoxynol-9 are designed to kill sperm on contact. Used on its own, spermicides aren't the most effective form of birth control, says Dr. Alexander, but they can be very effective when used with other forms of contraception, such as condoms or diaphragms and caps, which depend on spermicide for their efficacy.

How to use: Foams, creams, and jellies depend on an applicator, which you fill and insert into the vagina before intercourse. With a suppository, simply insert it; it will dissolve in the vagina.

Advantages: Besides increasing the effectiveness of other forms of contraception, spermicides also offer an extra lubrication.

Disadvantages: Most spermicides are pretty smelly and messy. Also, many men and women are sensitive to the active ingredient in spermicides. If you or your partner notice a rash, itching, or genital pain while using a spermicide, stop using it and try something else.

The Pill

One of the most popular options for women, birth control pills offer convenience and a 97 to 99 percent rate of effectiveness. The pills contain estrogen and progestin, hormones that prevent an egg from being released, being impregnated by sperm, or attaching to the uterus.

How to use: Your partner takes one pill every day throughout the course of her monthly cycle.

Advantages: Aside from being incredibly hassle-free, birth control pills may offer women some health benefits. Birth control pill use has been linked with reducing a woman's risk of certain types of cancer. The Pill has also been shown to help prevent against pelvic inflammatory disease and anemia. On top of that, it usually makes a woman's monthly period easier to bear, reducing cramps, menstrual flow, and premenstrual tension.

Disadvantages: If your partner is over 35 or smokes or has a history of heart problems, the Pill may not be for her. Oral contraceptives like the Pill have been shown to increase blood pressure and the risk of circulatory problems, including heart attack and stroke. Also, it's a prescription that should be taken at the same time every day, which some women have difficulty remembering.

The Implant

Better known by the brand name Norplant, this relatively new form of contraception releases progestin—a hormone that helps prevent an egg from implanting in the uterine wall—over a period of five years.

How to use: Your partner's doctor implants a grouping of six matchstick-size straws under the skin of her upper arm. The procedure is considered minor and is done with a local anesthetic.

Advantages: Implants can be among the most carefree forms of birth control, requiring no daily pills to swallow nor messy preparations every time you and your partner want to have sex. "Because it's effective for up to five years, Norplant is good if you're looking for long-term contraception, but still plan to have children at some point in the future," says Phillip Galle,

M.D., director of Reproductive Endocrinology Associates in Springfield, Illinois.

Disadvantages: Some women have reported troublesome side effects, not the least of which are irregular bleeding, headache, sore breasts, and nausea. Also, the nature of implants has caused some painful scarring where the straws are placed under the skin.

The Shot

Known commercially as Depo-Provera, this method has women being injected with synthetic progesterone, which stops ovulation. Planned Parenthood rates Depo-Provera as 99 percent effective.

How to use: Your partner's doctor administers the shot (usually in the arm or the buttocks). The effects of the shot last for 12 weeks.

Advantages: Like Norplant, Dr. Galle points out, Depo-Provera is a good form of contraception for couples who want to be free of the day-to-day hassles of birth control.

Disadvantages: Women have reported several health problems linked to Depo-Provera, including weight gain, irregular bleeding, mood swings, and even hair loss. Moreover, since the effects can't be reversed until the shot wears off, the symptoms could persist for three months.

The Insert

There are actually a few types of vaginal inserts: the diaphragm is a wide, shallow latex cup of soft plastic; the cervical cap is similar, but it's deeper and made of harder plastic. These devices are tailor-made, meaning your partner's doctor will have to fit her for it first.

A third option is a vaginal ring that, when inserted, releases pregnancy-preventing hormones.

How to use: Cervical caps and diaphragms work the same way. First, you coat them with spermicide, then you insert them in the vagina. Because they're fitted for your partner, the device will fit snugly over the cervix, providing a barrier that keeps sperm from entering the uterus, where one might inseminate an egg. Rings, which don't require you to apply spermicide, are also inserted vaginally.

Advantages: Diaphragms and caps are ideal for women who can't or won't take contraceptive drugs. Plus, these barrier devices can last for several years. Vaginal rings, meanwhile, offer similar benefits to injections or Norplant without any invasive procedures or as many long-term side effects.

Disadvantages: Diaphragms and cervical caps are slightly less effective than other barrier methods, such as condoms. Also, using this form of contraception has been known to increase a woman's risk of bladder infection. As with any contraception drug, vaginal rings may cause irregular bleeding, cramping, or other symptoms.

The IUD

Unlike diaphragms and cervical caps, intrauterine devices (IUDs) are inserted in the uterus for long periods of time—up to 10 years, in some cases. IUDs have gotten a bad reputation over the years, ever since the faulty Dalkon Shield IUD caused infections, sterility, and even death in a few cases. "Today's IUDs are much safer," says Dr. Alexander. "And they are very effective. We're starting to see women using them more."

How to use: A doctor has to insert the T-shape device, which is made of copper and plastic, into the uterus. A string hangs down from it so that your partner can check to make sure it's still in place. Although some IUDs can be inserted for up to 10 years, others—which contain progesterone, a pregnancy-preventing hormone—have to be replaced annually.

Advantages: As with injections or Norplant, many women appreciate IUDs as a form of convenient, long-term birth control that can be up to 99 percent effective, says Dr. Alexander.

Disadvantages: IUDs still carry a stigma, and they can cause internal bleeding and infection in some instances. Usually, though, side effects are no more serious than heavier menstrual flow or increased cramping.

STAYING IN CONTROL OF BIRTH CONTROL

While perusing the catalog of contraceptive options, you may have noticed that no method of birth control was listed as 100 percent effective.

"That's because none of them are," says Dr. Galle. "There's always room for human error—you forget to take a pill, or you don't use a diaphragm properly." And there's always a chance, despite whatever drugs are coursing through your partner's system, that one of your guys will slip past every defense. An egg gets inseminated, it implants in the uterine wall, and suddenly you're faced with some life-changing decisions.

Before you reach that point, however, you may be interested to know there are ways great and small to increase the odds of contraception in your favor. Here are a few suggestions.

Double your efforts. Use two forms of birth control. Wear a condom and use spermicide, or use a condom even if she is using a diaphragm. "Two are always better than one," says Dr. Alexander. And she points out that many forms of contraception already mix more than one medium of birth control. For example, many brands of condoms come treated with spermicide. "And diaphragms and caps are intended for use with spermicidal foams and jellies," she says.

Play an active role. As we mentioned earlier, it's hard not to notice that many forms of contraception are dependent on the woman using them. "Unfortunately, this circumstance has also created the assumption in the minds of many men that birth control is somehow the woman's responsibility," says Robert Birch, Ph.D., a psychologist in private practice in Columbus, Ohio, specializing in marriage and sex therapy.

% Sex by the Numbers

Wondering how your method of birth control stacks up? Here are the rates of effectiveness.

Spermicide (without diaphragm or cervical cap) . . . 72%
Withdrawal. 77%
Natural family planning (rhythm method) 80%
Cervical cap 82%
Diaphragm. 82%
Condom. 88%
Birth control pill 97%
Intrauterine device (IUD). 97%
Depo-Provera 99.7%
Sterilization (vasectomy, tubal ligation) 99.6%
Norplant. 99.96%
Abstinence 100%

SOURCE: Planned Parenthood

Don't buy into that. And don't expect her to bear all the responsibility for contraception. There's any number of things you can do to show your participation. This can be as simple—and as simply erotic—as helping her apply the spermicide or insert the diaphragm, or as practical as reminding her to take her pill (or get her shot) at regular intervals.

"The point is that even though the contraception might have to be applied to her, you're doing everything possible to show your support, to try to play a part in this. It's a sign of responsibility and commitment to her, and it'll make the two of you closer for your efforts," says Dr. Birch.

Avoid withdrawal penalties. Some of the older and more conservative forms of birth control aren't, in the truest sense, birth control methods at all. A better term for them might be "gambling."

The riskiest of those methods is the withdrawal method, wherein you, the man, withdraw from your partner's vagina before ejaculating. The idea is that you deposit your seed on less fertile ground—the bedspread, for example—than in her womb. Never mind that this is an awfully messy and inelegant form of contraception; it also doesn't happen to work.

"If your penis is inserted in her vagina and neither of you has any protection, then you can get her pregnant, even if you haven't ejaculated," says Dr. Galle. The reason is that your penis is already leaking sperm by the thousands in the form of pre-ejaculate fluid, which lubricates the inside of the penis in anticipation of the seminal fusillade to come. By the time you're ready for withdrawal, you've already made a good-size sperm deposit. And as you know, it takes only one sperm to hit the egg and start that nine-month clock ticking.

Don't plan on family planning. The other traditional form of birth control is the rhythm method, also known these days as natural family planning.

"Oh, natural family planning is a wonderful method—for making babies," says Dr. Alexander.

The theory behind natural family planning is that, by checking her temperature and the thickness of various fluids she emits, a woman can determine when she's ovulating. When she is, you abstain from sex. When she's not, you go at it like rabbits.

Temperature checks, measuring internal fluids—it sounds like she's a well-calibrated car engine, something subject to factory specs and recommended maintenance cycles. Except of course, that she's a human being, unique in this universe, right down to the internal workings of her body.

"The problem with family planning is that it assumes there's a set window of time in which every woman ovulates, and the same set of clues that tells you when she's ovulating applies to everyone. Well, it doesn't," says Dr. Galle. A rise in temperature may mean she's ovulating, or it may mean she has a fever. Or she's simply hot. Some women may be fertile for three days; others for four or five. It's even possible that she could be ovulating during her menstrual cycle—there's nothing that says her body can release only one egg in any given month.

Starting to see the chanciness of this whole business? "It's better than doing nothing," says Dr. Galle. But unless you have a good reason—strongly held personal beliefs, or a medical condition that would make other forms of birth control a health risk—don't use natural family planning as a form of contraception, Dr. Galle recommends.

VASECTOMY

Despite what you might think, a vasectomy is not the unkindest cut of all. Yes, there's cutting of sensitive parts—of your scrotum and the vasa deferentia, the tubes that carry sperm from your testicles to the rest of your reproductive equipment. But the procedure doesn't affect your masculinity, at least not physically. Your testicles are still producing testosterone, the hormone that makes you a man. Remember, you're getting sterilized, not castrated.

But try telling that to some men. If you're like most guys, reading the above probably caused an immediate, involuntary contraction of various lower abdominal muscles in some subconscious attempt to protect your boys from harm. As surgical procedures go, however, vasectomies are fast and simple and have few potential complications. There are far more harmful procedures that one could undergo.

Just ask any woman who has had her tubes tied.

"When you compare the two different types of sterilization, a tubal ligation is far more complicated than a vasectomy," says Phillip Galle, M.D., director of Reproductive Endocrinology Associates in Springfield, Illinois. A tubal ligation involves abdominal surgery, under a general anesthetic, which carries a greater risk of complication than a vasectomy. By contrast, getting your vas "ectomized" involves a local anesthetic, a couple of small snips, and 20 minutes of your time, at most. It's also half as expensive as a tubal ligation.

When you look at it that way, a vasectomy is pretty beneficent. It makes you a genuine hero—keeping your woman from harm and misery by virtue of your own determination and sacrifice. Plus, it may help you enjoy sex more.

This, when snip comes to cut, is the best thing about a vasectomy. No, it won't increase the sensitivity of your equipment or enable you to enjoy marathon sex for hours and weekends at a time. But it does mean that you won't have to mess around with sloppy birth control methods and provides peace of mind that you and your partner won't have an unwanted pregnancy. As you'll see, it's not for everyone. But if you and your partner are at a stage in life in which you're ready for serious, permanent contraception, a vasectomy may be your best option. It's relatively easy to undergo, too, once you know what's involved.

SCALPEL OR NO-SCALPEL?

When it comes time to get a vasectomy, it turns out that there are two ways about it.

"No matter what you do, you have to sever the vas deferens to prevent sperm from mixing with semen when you ejaculate," says Michael Warren, M.D., chief of the division of urology at the University of Texas Medical Branch in Galveston. "But there are a couple different procedures for severing the vas."

The most common method usually involves two incisions, made above each testicle. The urologist reaches in, cuts out a piece of the vas deferens, then stitches, ties off, or cauterizes the ends of the vas with an electrical device (warning—you may see sparks and smoke coming from between your legs). Then he sutures the holes closed with dissolving stitches.

A newer, less complicated procedure is the no-scalpel vasectomy (NSV) and some doctors think that it should become the standard way vasectomies are performed. With an NSV, the doctor makes one hole—a puncture actually—in the scrotum, using a special tool. From this single opening, he's able

Reversing Course

A vasectomy is not to be done lightly. It's a serious procedure. You shouldn't get one thinking that it can be easily undone. It can't.

Some doctors are performing vasectomy reversals, where they reattach the vas, but it's not exactly like having the plumber patch a few pipes to get hot water running to the shower again.

"There are plenty of complications. Vasectomy reversal is complex and expensive microsurgery. A surgeon has to go in, open the vas and reconnect the tubes," says Phillip Galle, M.D., director of Reproductive Endocrinology Associates in Springfield, Illinois. That's tricky to do since the original procedure involved removing chunks of the vas that can't be replaced.

Even if you do get your tubes untied, no surgeon in the world will guarantee that you can have kids again. Some experts put your odds at around 50-50. "Your odds can be worse, if it has been long time since you had the vasectomy—better if it has only been a few years," says Dr. Galle. Either way, it's yet another reason to spend plenty of time thinking it through before you decide to have a vasectomy in the first place.

If you decide to pursue a reversal, choose your surgeon carefully, suggests James H. Gilbaugh Jr., M.D., a urologist in Portland, Oregon, and author of *Men's Private Parts*. Find out how may reversals the doctor has done and what his success rate has been.

to draw out each of the vasa deferentia—one at a time—and make the necessary cuts to render you sterile. The puncture requires no stitches to close, takes less time to perform, and to date offers men a reduced risk of infection and excess bleeding.

For years, the NSV has been the standard way of performing vasectomies in China, but it has only been available in the United States since the late 1980s. Since it's considered relatively new—and many urologists see nothing wrong with the old two-cut vasectomy they've always performed—you may have to shop around before you find a doctor versed in the procedure. But it's worth investigating. The Association for Voluntary Surgical Contraception International (phone: 212-561-8000), a nonprofit organization devoted to improving access to all kinds of contraception, can provide more information about NSV, including a list of doctors in your area who know how to do it.

SHOULD YOU MAKE THE CUT?

Now that you know what you're in for, the pressing question you have to answer is this: Is a vasectomy right for you?

"There is an ideal candidate, and there are men on whom I'd never perform a vasectomy because their profile is all wrong," says Dr. Warren. "A good urologist will ask plenty of questions, learn something about his patient before proceeding."

If all you can think about is freeing yourself from the worry of impregnating your partner and you're hell-bent on getting a vasectomy, you can find someone who'll do the job. Ideally, though, don't start thinking about submitting to such a significant surgical procedure unless you meet one or more of the following criteria.

You're old enough. Most doctors are uncomfortable performing vasectomies on men in their early thirties or younger. "For example, there's no way I'd perform a vasectomy on a young, single man in his twenties. He has too much time and too many experiences ahead of him. He could change his mind," says Dr. Warren.

You've sown your seeds. Of course, if you've had three kids by your 30th birthday and you've decided enough is enough, most doctors would think you a fine candidate for the procedure. "But that's because you've met one of the most important criteria—you've had kids. Most vasectomies we perform are on men who have had all the kids they want to have and don't want to have any more," says Dr. Warren.

If you've never had kids, though, many doctors will raise an eyebrow before agreeing to do the procedure. "I would be wary of performing a vasectomy on a man who had no children, even if he assured me he didn't want any. There's always a chance you or your partner may have a change of heart," Dr. Warren adds. That holds true even if you think you've had enough children. Take some time to think about it. Make sure that you don't want any more.

You have a good reason for not having children. Thinking that you might not want to have children is one thing. Knowing that you shouldn't have children is something else. "If you or your wife has a hereditary disease that could be devastating to pass on to a child, or if you know that getting pregnant could be harmful or life-threatening for your wife, these are certainly reasons to consider sterilization," says Nancy Alexander, Ph.D., former chief of the Contraceptive Development Branch of the National Institutes of Health in Bethesda, Maryland.

The Fluid Truth

Myth: After a vasectomy, you ejaculate less fluid, which makes orgasm feel different.

Fact: Nearly all of the seminal fluid you ejaculate comes from the seminal vesicle and the prostate, which aren't affected by a vasectomy. Sperm accounts for an infinitesimal amount of semen. It's impossible to notice a difference.

You've played the field. Most urologists agree that the best candidates for a vasectomy are married men, or men who've been in the same relationship for several years. "If you're still single, or you think there's any possibility that you're not going to be with the person you're currently with, then that's another reason to think twice before having a vasectomy. You do not know what future partners will want. If what they want is to carry your children, and you've had a vasectomy, then you're going to have a problem that you could have avoided," says Dr. Galle.

GETTING FIXED

If you've made it this far, we're assuming you're a prime candidate for a vasectomy, or that you're at least committed to the decision. Either way, if you're considering getting a vasectomy in the future, there's any number of things you should and shouldn't do. Here's a quick primer.

Think it through. We really can't say this enough: Don't go off to the urologist without asking yourself some hard questions. Are you *ever* going to want more kids? Is she? Are you sure you're going to be with this person for the rest of your life? If you're not sure, how do you know the next person won't want children—your children?

How you answer these questions should help tell you to proceed...or turn back. "Even though it's possible to reverse a vasectomy, for all intents and purposes you should consider this a permanent life change," reminds Dr. Galle.

Talk it out. Sure, it's your vas deferens they're snipping, but in deference to your partner, talk about the procedure up front. "It'll iron out a lot of problems. If she's pushing you to get this done, talking about what's involved will help you make up your own mind about it," says Dr. Warren. And it will certainly ease the natural anxiety you're feeling. It's a way of getting comfortable with the idea.

Shop around. Once you've decided to get one, ask your family doctor for information about the procedures available. Which method do you want? Scalpel or no-scalpel? Then, set about finding a urologist who will do the job. Your family doctor can provide referrals; so can friends who've had it done (you may be surprised how many of them are out there).

Make an appointment to meet the doctor. Explain that you have lots of questions, says Dr. Warren. Then ask them. How many vasectomies does the doctor perform? (A dozen a year should be the minimum. Fifty a year would be better.) How long does it take? How much does it hurt? What about complications?

Get it done on a Friday. Typically, a weekend of sitting on the couch with some ice and lots of personal attention should be enough for you to recover from a vasectomy. That's why you should schedule the procedure for a Friday afternoon or evening, then go home. Prop yourself up on the sofa, keeping the remote within easy reach. Ask to be brought food and drink at regular intervals. Wince from time to time. Bask in the resulting sympathy. You're her hero—milk that for all it's worth.

Put yourself on ice. Soreness and tenderness for a few days should be the extent of the damage. Most doctors recommend keeping an ice pack in your pants to help prevent pain and swelling. Wrap the pack in a fairly thin towel or washcloth and apply for 20 minutes, then take it off for 20 to 30 minutes and apply again. Do not apply ice directly to your genitals—that could cause frostbite, which would hurt even worse than a vasectomy. If you notice sharp pains, swelling, or discoloration of the testicles or penis, don't wait to see if it'll pass—call the doctor, suggests James H. Gilbaugh Jr., M.D., a urologist in Portland, Oregon, and author of *Men's Private Parts*. Odds are that you've developed a minor infection, which can happen even in a very small percentage of cases.

Take it easy. You probably won't feel like it anyway, but we wanted to warn you against a couple activities: no heavy lifting and no sex for the first few days after a vasectomy says Dr. Gilbaugh.

Keep the protection on. This may come as a surprise, but even though you've had a vasectomy, you won't be shooting blanks for a few weeks yet. "It takes about 15 to 20 ejaculations to clear the system of active sperm," says Dr. Warren. Until you hit that number, keep using another method of birth control. Then see your doctor for a follow-up. They'll take a semen sample and check for active sperm. Even if it's clear, they'll want another sample in couple weeks, just in case. After that, you can have as much unfettered, spontaneous, worry-free sex as you can stand. In more ways than one, you'll be fixed for life.

PENIS SIZE

We'll keep this short.

Excuse us—not short, no. Brief. We'll keep this discussion brief.

When you're talking about penis size, you have to choose your adjectives carefully. Among men, few issues are more sensitive, few subjects are heavier with anxiety—both repressed and expressed—than the topic of penile dimensions.

In this world, success is measured by the number of digits in a paycheck. Smarts are tabulated by percentages of correct answers on countless tests. Strength is marked by the number of pounds a man can bench. With such dimensions at issue in this life, it's amazing that we spend as much time as we do obsessing about a few inches of flesh that most people never get a good look at anyway. Such is the mystery of man.

Don't Overextend Yourself

By now, you've heard the buzz in men's magazines and the media about penile enlargement, surgical procedures that purport to lengthen and thicken your penis—all for $6,000 or so. It sounds like the answer to an age-old concern, but you should think twice before you put your penis under the knife.

"Unless you have a penis that's so short that you have trouble urinating or inseminating a partner, you shouldn't even consider having the surgery," says Irwin Goldstein, M.D., professor of urology at Boston University Medical Center. "These procedures involve snipping ligaments in the abdomen that anchor the penis to your pubic bone. The surgeon then pulls the shaft out of the body, so you look a little longer. But they're not adding length. The shaft was already there." Dr. Goldstein likens the procedure to exposing the foundations of a building and saying it's taller as a result.

"On a more serious note, snipping those ligaments means that you'll have a more wobbly erection—a greater chance for buckling and fracture," says Dr. Goldstein.

Of course, not everyone agrees that penile enlargements are inherently unnecessary or unsafe. When done correctly, penile extensions aren't more wobbly and could do wonders for a man's self-esteem, says E. Douglas Whitehead, M.D., a urologist and president-elect of the American Academy of Phalloplasty Surgeons.

It's a lively debate. Dr. Goldstein notes that as with any surgical procedure, scar tissue could develop at the base of the penis and pull the shaft back in. Voilà! Your penis is shorter than when you started.

True, Dr. Whitehead counters, but only if the patient fails to use a penile stretching device or penile weights as he should after such a procedure.

Thickening, meanwhile, involves transplanting fat from some other part of your body—your butt or your groin, usually—into the shaft of the penis, thus making it wider.

"If you had widening by liposuction fat transfer, over time the fat cells can migrate down the shaft, or bunch up in odd places," says Dr. Goldstein. "In the end, you could have a lumpy penis."

TAKING THE MEASURE OF A MAN

The perennial concern about penis size isn't such a mystery to experts of the male psyche, though. "There has always been a fascination with the penis. Going back to primitive times, it was worshipped as an object of fertility," explains Robert Birch, Ph.D., a psychologist in private practice in Columbus, Ohio, specializing in marriage and sex therapy. "There's plenty of evidence of this in primitive art. At some ancient sites, you'll find mammoth stone penises erected as totems of fertility and prosperity. From the stand-

Some men have learned the sad truth already, and they learned it the, um, hard way. In California, where penile augmentation is a booming industry, thousands of men submitted to the treatment of one surgeon and found themselves not with longer and thicker penises but with extreme pain, obvious scarring, and a loss of sensitivity in key spots. Complaints became so numerous and serious that the state medical board finally stepped in and revoked the surgeon's license, calling the doctor's practice a danger to public health and safety.

But not all surgeons use these risky procedures. "Some of us do what's called a transverse incision and a dermal fat graft," says Dr. Whitehead, who is also director of the Association for Male Sexual Dysfunction and associate clinical professor of urology at the Albert Einstein College of Medicine, both in New York City. "These procedures are safer and more effective." The transverse incision heals well and has a less noticeable scar. And in the dermal fat graft, the fat moved to the penis is attached to the skin and so remains alive and evenly spread.

It's more difficult to do, however, so it costs more—about $8,000 when coupled with penile enlargement.

If you're thinking about getting a penile enlargement, make sure that you have realistic expectations. "We can't give you an additional 3 to 6 inches, but we can often increase your penis length by ½ inch to 1½ inches and permanently increase your width by 30 to 50 percent with the dermal fat graft technique," Dr. Whitehead says.

But all surgical procedures have risks. That's why the best way to deal with your size problem may be to talk with a therapist, not a surgeon. "Most men who have size issues tend to have average or even above-average dimensions," says Steve Manley, Ph.D., staff psychologist for the Male Health Center in Dallas. "Their problem isn't penis size. Usually, their feelings of inadequacy are generated by some other aspects of their lives. Talking it over with a professional counselor can help you make some sense of things and help you feel better about yourself."

point of our ancestors, bigger was always seen as better, in terms of the potential to fertilize."

Down through the years, that thinking has become deeply ingrained upon the male psyche, says Dr. Birch. "Now, we have come to the point where men base their feelings of masculinity and their self-confidence on the size of their penises. And since we live in a society that encourages the bigger-is-better mentality, that's only going to reinforce men's concerns about penis size."

Chances are that you're not going to change society any time soon. But if you're having questions about how you measure up to your fellow man, well, we can change that right now. We've polled the penis experts and learned some truths that may help dispel the phallic fallacies society has placed upon you.

KNOWING THE AVERAGES

"Everyone wants to know what the average length is," says Isadora Alman, a sexologist, syndicated columnist of "Ask Isadora," and author of *New Ways to Meet New People.* "If there was one question I hear so often I could answer it in my sleep, this is the one."

For years, the most any sex expert would dare give you was a broad range. But Irwin Goldstein, M.D., professor of urology at Boston University Medical Center, wanted a more precise average. So he got hundreds of selfless men to go into a laboratory and have their penises subjected to every kind of scientific measurement.

And the average erect penis length is...

"Five and one-half inches—that's across all ages and races in our study," says Dr. Goldstein. And erect penis length is really the only number that counts, he says, because flaccid length—yours and everyone else's—can vary widely, depending on the time of day, how you're feeling, and how hot or cold the weather is.

WHEN SMOKE GETS IN YOUR SIZE

Whatever your measurements are, there's not much you can safely do to extend them. However, we feel compelled to point out that some personal habits may shorten your dimensions. For instance, it turns out that smoking not only takes years off your life but takes inches off your penis as well.

"I'm dead serious," says Dr. Goldstein. In his study of penis size, Dr. Goldstein correlated penis length with a number of health factors, including problems like diabetes, hypertension, and smoking. "Smoking especially seems to affect elastin—the ingredient that makes your skin supple and flexible." This flexibility is especially important when it comes to penis size. "If the skin of your penis isn't elastic enough, or starts to become less stretchy because of smoking, for example, then that's definitely going to affect how long an erection you're going to get," says Dr. Goldstein. As if there weren't enough reasons to give up smoking already.

SHORTER IS BETTER

So you whipped out the ruler and it happens that your penis is just a little below the average. Don't sweat it. In fact, we'll let you in on a little secret: You're a lucky guy.

"It's no advantage to have a long penis. Statistically speaking, men with long penises are more likely to be quite narrow. And impotent," says Dr. Goldstein.

Here's why: The longer something is, the thicker it has to be to remain rigid. "Typically, though, long penises are not very wide. Therefore, they're less rigid. That's bad for sexual performance," says Dr. Goldstein.

And if a long penis were to be rigid, there's a greater likelihood that it would buckle or break during intercourse—and no one's going to enjoy that. "No, the ideal penis is a nice, short, thick one. It'll stay the most rigid," says Dr. Goldstein. Plus, it's more likely to please your partner than a longer, thinner version.

"A short, wide penis is going to stretch and stimulate the outer area of the vagina more than a narrow penis," says Dr. Goldstein. "And that's more likely to be more pleasurable. Women have very few nerve endings in the vagina. It's the outside that's really sensitive."

Meanwhile, if you still harbor doubts about your size, there are a few steps you can take to combat that perception. Here's how.

Look in a mirror. If you haven't done so lately, then you're probably not getting an ideal view of your penis and its actual length. When we usually inspect our equipment, we're looking down at it.

"This bird's-eye view perspective tends to make the penis look shorter," observes Steve Manley, Ph.D., staff psychologist for the Male Health Center in Dallas. To beat this optical illusion, Dr. Manley suggests checking yourself in the mirror next time you get out of the shower. "That will give you the best view of your penis." What's more, you may be surprised to find that it looks bigger than you actually thought. And remember that this is the view your partner is seeing, too.

Get a haircut. When it comes to assessing your own dimensions, many men truly can't see the tree through the forest. "In many cases, pubic hair can obscure a good bit of the penis," says Dr. Birch. If you want to make sure you expose the most of your measurement, keep your pubes well-trimmed.

Ditch the gut. Another great robber of penis size is the ubiquitous pad of fat that hangs on the pubic bone at the base of the penis. We need some of that fat as cushioning during the vigorous thrusting of sex, but most men have far more of it than they need.

"As you get older, that fat pad will hang more and more off the pubic bone, and it can start to obscure the base of the penis. Obviously, the less fat you have there, the more you'll be exposing your true length," says Dr. Goldstein. The best way to avoid this problem is by following a proper diet and exercise regimen. Try to get at least 30 minutes of aerobic exercise three or four times a week. This will help burn the fat off your frame. At the same time, stay off the high-fat foods like red meat, eggs, and nuts. Stick with pastas and leaner meats like fish and poultry; this keeps more fat from building up down there.

5

SEXUAL STRUGGLES

ERECTION PROBLEMS

Impotence is a word with such creepy connotations that a bunch of doctors recently decided that just *saying* it was dangerous to your self-esteem. Let's not call it impotence anymore, they said. Let's call it erectile dysfunction.

Sure, the new name's not too catchy, but it does have advantages. "Impotence" implies a permanent state, when, in fact, many men have only occasional problems achieving erections. "Impotence" also implies an all-encompassing loss of manhood, when, in truth, lots of men begin experiencing erection problems when they're at the height of their powers in almost every other respect.

The fact is that, thanks to increasing understanding about psychology and the physiology of the erection, even temporary dysfunction needn't be a recurring issue. "Any man in this country can get an erection," says Steve Manley, Ph.D., staff psychologist for the Male Health Center in Dallas. "All he has to do is decide to deal with the problem."

The vast majority of men who need to deal with the problem are in their forties or older. A major study of nearly 1,300 men by the New England Research Institute found that the probability of complete impotence tripled between 40 and 70 years of age. "By the age of 55 the line on the graph begins to go up exponentially," says John J. Mulcahy, M.D., Ph.D., professor of urology at Indiana University School of Medicine in Indianapolis.

That's because most long-term, chronic erectile problems are now thought to be primarily physical rather than psychological in nature, and the kinds of physical conditions that cause impotence are the kinds of conditions men begin to develop as they get older.

Men in their teens, twenties, and thirties can have erection problems, too. But the origin of their troubles is far more likely to be in their minds. Of course, erectile problems have mental and emotional repercussions no matter what age they hit, which is why both body and mind need to be taken into account when dealing with them. Here's what to watch for on both fronts.

GETTING OLD, STAYING HARD

Let's face it, there are consequences to getting older. Our skin wrinkles, we need reading glasses, and our 10-K times aren't quite what they used to be. So why are we surprised to learn that our penises slow down, too? "As men age, erections occur less frequently with less rigidity and less duration," says E. Douglas Whitehead, M.D., director of the Association for Male Sexual Dysfunction and associate clinical professor of urology at the Albert Einstein

College of Medicine, both in New York City. "That's absolutely normal." But not entirely inevitable.

The main reason our penises tend to get less sprightly as we get older is cardiovascular. The mechanics aren't complicated. Our penises get hard because they get engorged with blood. They won't get hard if the arteries and vessels that provide that supply of blood get blocked. Blockages occur when excess cholesterol builds up on arterial walls. It's the same problem that causes heart attacks. And the same good health habits—eating a low-fat diet and exercising regularly—will help prevent both.

Staying in good cardiovascular shape is by far the most important thing you can do to prevent the onset of impotence with age. The New England study found that men being treated for heart disease, diabetes, or high blood pressure were much more likely to become completely impotent later in life than men without those problems.

Here are some specific pointers for keeping your equipment and you happy, healthy, and ready for action as you get older.

Get tested. The best way to find out if you're at risk of cutting off the blood supply to your penis is to get a reading of your cholesterol level. All it takes is a simple blood test. Make sure to keep an eye on your high-density lipoprotein (HDL, or "good") cholesterol as well as your low-density lipoprotein (LDL, or "bad") cholesterol. HDL helps remove the gunk that clogs up your arteries, which is why the New England study found that the lower a man's HDL level, the higher his risk of impotence. You can build up the amount of HDL in your system by exercising, which also happens to be a great way of reducing your LDL level.

Stop smoking and watch the booze. You might still think that smoking makes you look romantic, but it doesn't do your penis any good. Men who smoke two packs a day for 25 years are 65 percent more likely to have erection problems than men who don't smoke at all, according to Steven K. Wilson, M.D., clinical associate professor of urology at the University of Arkansas in Little Rock.

Alcohol is another staple of romantic fantasies that can hinder romance in real life. A few drinks relax the inhibitions; a few too many will put your penis to sleep.

Take a medication inventory. A wide variety of medications can contribute to erection problems, from hypertension medications to Prozac to antihistamines. If you're having a little trouble getting it up, take an inventory of the pills you're taking. Harin Padma-Nathan, M.D., director of the Male Clinic in Santa Monica, California, and associate professor of urology at the University of Southern California School of Medicine in Los Angeles, recommends that you read the literature that comes with your medications to see if erectile dysfunction is listed as a side effect or talk to your doctor.

Keep it straight. When you get an erection, the tissue in and around your penis can expand to three times its flaccid size, says Irwin Goldstein,

M.D., professor of urology at Boston University Medical Center. As some men get into their forties and beyond, the tissue that forms the erectile chambers—the caverns in the penis that fill with blood when you get an erection—can become more brittle, however. In some cases, this brittle tissue can tear during sex. It happens on such a microscopic level, you probably won't even notice it. But if it happens often enough, you will.

Frequent tearing will lead to scarring, and scarring can prevent an erectile chamber from filling completely with blood. When that happens, the chamber essentially develops a kink in it. And when you get an erection, only one side of your penis will become fully engorged, while the kinked side remains at half-mast. The result can be frightening—your penis can develop a marked curve—almost a 90-degree angle in serious cases. This condition is called Peyronie's disease, and while it may scare you and feel uncomfortable, it can be treated if caught early.

Older men can lower their odds of developing Peyronie's disease at all by reducing the wear and tear of vigorous sex, especially sex with their partners on top. "About 75 percent of the men with Peyronie's disease report having sex in that position," says Dr. Mulcahy. "It puts a lot of torque on the penis."

MAKING A HEAD AND HEART CONNECTION

If our penises have a greater enemy than cholesterol, it's our minds. Thinking too much can turn the proudest erection into a pitiful pile of flaccid flesh, and most of us these days have far too much on our minds.

Urologists and psychologists agree that the psychological causes of impotence have been underplayed in recent years because of all the attention being devoted to the physical remedies. "Everybody wants to come into the doctor's office for a quick fix," says Domeena Renshaw, M.D., director of Loyola Sex Therapy Clinic at Loyola University in Chicago and author of Seven Weeks to Better Sex. "But it's not really that simple. There are all kinds of things, mental as well as physical, hanging on to the penis and pulling it down."

The most common form of psychological impotence, especially in younger men or older men recently re-entering the singles scene, is a form of nerves called performance anxiety. Basically, what happens is that the man worries so much about whether he's going to get an erection that he doesn't. His worries become a self-fulfilling prophesy.

Another psychological condition that's driving more and more men into sex therapists' offices might be described as living in the modern world. The emotional and physical costs of simply getting through the day—stress, depression, anger, fatigue—can put a serious damper on our love lives. These are the types of problems that most commonly affect men in their thirties, forties, and fifties, according to Andrew McCullough, M.D., director of the Male Sexual Health and Fertility Clinic at the New York University Medical Center in New York City. "As the complexities of life increase, all sorts of things can impinge on your ability to have sex," he says. "The responsibilities of raising children, divorce, job pressures. When you combine those things with some of the physical problems that slow us down sexually, it can stop a guy— boom!—like that."

A third psychological component is common to all impotence problems, and that's the relationship factor. When a man can't get an erection, it has an impact on his partner as well as himself. Difficulties in the relationship may have contributed to the erection disconnection in the first place, and impotence usually doesn't make relationship problems any easier to deal with. For that reason, communication is almost always the first thing sex therapists recommend for dealing with impotence. "You have to talk about the problem with your partner," says Dr. Manley. "She's going to know about it anyway." If you're not comfortable discussing sex with your partner, counseling may be in order.

There are plenty of other ways to deal with the head trips that contribute to shaky phalluses. Here are a few of them.

Don't panic. If your penis doesn't cooperate once, that doesn't mean your sex life is over. Relax, says Dr. Manley. "Men tend to have an all-or-nothing approach to things," he says, "and many of the patients we see have jumped to some pretty extreme conclusions. Just because you couldn't today doesn't mean that you never will again."

Don't quit. A lot of men interrupt their lovemaking the moment they suspect they're not getting hard. Again, relax. "If you lose an erection, don't quit," says Robert Birch, Ph.D., a psychologist in Columbus, Ohio, specializing in marriage and sex therapy and author of *Oral Caress*. "Back up, play around a little, joke about it. Chances are that it will come back."

Change the focus. A common technique for treating erection problems in couples therapy is to remove the actual act of intercourse from the lovemaking menu for a month or longer. The idea is to learn how to get pleasure out of foreplay and also to take the pressure off the man's penis. "Focus on the process, not the goal," says Dr. Birch. "When you de-emphasize intercourse, you'll be more likely to be able to have it."

Broaden your repertoire. Another way to help yourself relax during sex is to apply all your appendages, not just the one between your legs. "If you're good at manual and oral stimulation," Dr. Birch says, "that will bring your partner pleasure and also take some of the pressure off your penis. And doing that allows the man to respond naturally."

Chill out. If stress is putting a crimp in your erections, take aim at stress by learning to relax. A wide range of relaxation techniques are available today, from meditation and yoga to biofeedback, prayer, and long walks in the woods, points out Kenneth A. Goldberg, M.D., founder and director of the Male Health Center in Dallas. Turning off the noise for a while will do a lot for your penis, and for the rest of you.

The Key Questions

Should I see a doctor or a shrink? That's the first question that a man who's having erection problems may be asking himself. The answer may well be "both" since a majority of erection problems involve some physical component and all have psychological repercussions. Here's a checklist from our experts that can help you track down the most likely source of the problem.

1. Can you get an erection by masturbating?
2. Did your erection problem start suddenly rather than gradually?
3. Have you recently started a new relationship?
4. Are you going through a tough time at work?
5. Are you worried about money?
6. Are you angry at your partner?
7. Do you feel dominated by your partner?
8. Do you follow a religion that has strict rules about marriage and sex?
9. Do you feel tired or overwhelmed?
10. Are you depressed?

If you answered "yes" to one or more of those questions, chances are that the source of your erectile difficulties may be above the neck rather than below the waist. Consistent "no" answers suggest that a physiological explanation is more likely. If the latter is true, ask yourself a few more questions.

1. Have your erections become progressively less hard and less frequent over time?
2. Is your level of sexual *desire* undiminished?
3. Are you taking any medications?
4. Do you have high blood pressure, diabetes, or heart disease?
5. Are you overweight?
6. Has it been a month or more since you last darkened the door of a gym or laced up a running shoe?
7. Has your doctor told you to watch your cholesterol?
8. Is creamed spinach your idea of a fresh vegetable?

"Yes" answers to those questions are further indication of a probable—though not certain—physiological connection.

WHEN TO SEEK HELP

In an age when sex problems are routinely discussed on television, urologists say that a lot of men still wait years before reporting impotence to their doctor. That's a mistake not only because there's no need to be missing out on sex for that long but also because erection problems can be an early warning sign for heart disease. "If it interferes with your sexual function and it's causing you distress, see a doctor," says Dr. Padma-Nathan. "We used to say wait six months before coming in, but 60 to 90 days is a better rule of thumb in my opinion. Early treatment can sometimes get rid of the problem quicker."

Before taking that step, take a self-inventory like the one in "The Key Questions." Then consult your family physician for a referral to a urologist who specializes in sexual dysfunction—according to Dr. Mulcahy, not all urologists do—or a sex therapist.

If you and your doctor decide you need some artificial help getting an erection, there are several treatments from which to choose. By far the most popular is sildenafil (Viagra), the long-awaited impotence pill that revolutionized treatment when it was released in 1998. It works by altering levels of a chemical that controls muscle tissue in the artery walls. "Viagra is unquestionably the most exciting therapy for impotence that has been developed," says Dr. Padma-Nathan. About 15 percent of men taking Viagra reported a side effect of headaches. And taking the pill with nitrate-based heart medication can cause a fatal drop in blood pressure.

"If you need to take Viagra, ask your doctor if you can switch to a heart medication that doesn't contain organic nitrates," says Jay B. Hollander, M.D., associate director of the Beaumont Center for Male Sexual Function in Royal Oak, Michigan. "Also, remind your doctor of all the medications you are taking, including over-the-counter drugs."

Viagra, however, is not a cure-all for impotence. Other erection therapies, including injections, vacuum devices, and implants will be needed to deal with cases of severe impotence, Dr. Padma-Nathan says. Penile injection therapy involves sticking a small needle in the base of the penis when a man is ready for intercourse. Within a few minutes he gets an erection that lasts from a half-hour to an hour or more, depending on the dosage.

The vacuum constriction device uses a hollow cylinder, a pump, and a rubber ring to draw blood into the penis and hold it long enough to have intercourse. The penile implant is a surgically installed device that provides erections on demand, as often and as long as you like. While implants are highly effective and increasingly reliable, the intrusiveness of the surgery alone makes them a last resort.

PROSTATE PROBLEMS

Powerful things can come in small packages. Witness the prostate gland, which is only as big as a walnut yet manages to exert an outsized impact on the psyche of the American male.

This is a relatively recent development. Ten to 15 years ago, guys were clueless about the prostate. But in the past decade, many heroes of the baby boomer generation have succumbed to prostate cancer. Rock stars. Sports heroes. Hollywood celebs. Their tales lead the news, make the front pages. And suddenly, most every man has become aware of the destructive power of this little gland.

The benefits of this newfound awareness are twofold. First, men are willing to get tested more—and once detected, prostate problems are often relatively simple to deal with. More so, all this awareness has helped spark a response from the medical community. This is why there is so much groundbreaking research, so many treatments in development, so much reason to be hopeful about newer, less painful, less complicated ways to control prostate problems.

And if ever a gland needed controlling, it's the prostate. Two things typically go wrong with the gland: It develops cancer or it grows in size. Cancer is the less common but more dire problem. One in five American men will develop prostate cancer in their lifetime, and prostate cancer is now the second leading cause of cancer deaths in men. But for virtually all of us, the discomfort of an enlarged prostate is going to be a growing fact of life as we get older.

"The prostate is definitely something that men need to be aware of, but it's not something to panic about," says Gerald B. Hoke, M.D., chief of urology at Harlem Hospital Center in New York City.

GROWING PAINS

If the organs of the human body had minds of their own, the prostate would be considered the most willful and headstrong of the bunch—once it gets to middle age. Up until that point, this "sex-accessory gland" plays a fairly unglamorous role in your body's reproductive system. Its job: to manufacture much of the fluid that carries sperm. Accordingly, it's situated right in the middle of things, lodged between the bladder and the penis, wrapped around the urethra.

What's nettlesome about the prostate is that at some point in your late forties or early fifties, the darn thing decides, for no apparent reason, to start growing. What was once a walnut can balloon to the size of an orange. The condition is called benign prostatic hyperplasia (BPH for short). If you live long enough, you'll very likely have to cope with BPH yourself. According to W. Scott McDougal, M.D., chief of urology at Massachusetts General Hospital in Boston and author of *Prostate Disease*, studies show that less than 5 percent of men under the age of 40 have BPH. That number rises to 50 percent of men over age 60; by the age of 85, the odds hit 90 percent.

Lots of men have BPH and don't even know it, but eventually that knowledge will trickle into their minds, right about the time their urination is slowing to a trickle. As the prostate grows, it begins to push against the urethra, compressing it from the diameter of a dime to the width a cocktail straw. As a result, you may feel like you have to urinate all the time. Or your stream is weak, you don't feel as though you've completely emptied your bladder, you can't get any flow going, or you feel the need to push the urine forcibly out. These problems are a nuisance but usually not much more than that. BPH is not—repeat, *not*—a sign of cancer, and having BPH does not mean that you're any more likely to develop cancer. The operative term, remember, is *benign*.

TO WAIT OR TO OPERATE?

Most men who have BPH simply learn to live with it, making annual or semi-annual trips to their urologists to keep an eye on the condition. This "watchful waiting" strategy makes sense because in many cases the symptoms don't get significantly worse, and sometimes improve. Still, plenty of men feel bothered enough by BPH to take the more decisive—and incisive—action of treating the problem surgically. In fact, surgery to cut enlarged prostates down to size is one of the most common operations performed in the United States.

Prostate surgery works, but any surgery is serious business with certain risks, which is why drugs like finasteride (Proscar), designed to shrink the prostate, have become increasingly popular. "The first line of approach that most patients choose is either watchful waiting or medications," says Dr. Hoke. "But every individual is different. Some guys don't mind taking a pill every day. Other guys hate that idea; they want to have the surgery and be done with it."

Usually, BPH has no impact on a man's sex life, but there are a few exceptions. One is that for a tiny minority of men (less than 5 percent) the medications used to treat the condition can cause temporary impotence. If you're in that minority, of course, you should talk to your doctor about moving to another form of treatment.

It's also worth noting that roughly three-quarters of the men who undergo prostate surgery suffer an odd sexual side effect called retrograde ejaculation. That means that when you climax, your semen shoots back into your bladder rather than out the end of your penis. This condition harms neither you nor your partner—the semen is simply absorbed into your urine—and it doesn't really change the sensation of orgasm. It does, however, make conceiving a child unlikely, though not impossible.

A more serious concern is the risk that surgery presents to your potency. Because of the prostate's location at the confluence of many muscles, blood vessels, and nerve endings that service the penis, operating on this gland does carry with it the risk of damaging your ability to get erections and feel penile sensation. That risk is between 5 and 10 percent—not high, but not inconsiderable, which is another reason that leading urologists favor treating BPH with drugs wherever possible.

Going with the Flow

When you have prostate troubles, the symptoms don't come in a flood; they trickle in. Experts at the Male Health Center in Dallas have devised a way to chart your urine flow to determine for yourself whether your prostate is starting to act up. Simply answer the questions by circling the number that corresponds to your experience (5 means you experience this quite a bit, 0 means never). This self-exam should never take the place of regular prostate exams or cancer screenings, but it can help you spot trouble early. Over the past month, how often have you...

1. Had a sensation of not emptying your bladder completely after urinating?
       0   1   2   3   4   5

2. Had to urinate again less than 2 hours after urinating?
       0   1   2   3   4   5

3. Found that the flow of urine stopped and started several times?
       0   1   2   3   4   5

4. Found it difficult to postpone urination?
       0   1   2   3   4   5

5. Had a weak urine stream?
       0   1   2   3   4   5

6. Had to push or strain to begin urination?
       0   1   2   3   4   5

7. Had to get up to urinate after going to bed on a typical night?
       0   1   2   3   4   5

Now add your score. If you scored 10 or more points, get to a urologist for an examination.

In addition, a host of new, less invasive prostate-shrinking techniques have been developed. These range from using lasers and super-heated needles to reduce prostate size to employing liquid nitrogen to painlessly freeze and remove pieces of enlarged or diseased prostate. These procedures are just coming out of the experimental phase, says Stanley Bloom, M.D., director of the Men's Sexual Health Center in Livingston, New Jersey. It's too early to know for certain how effective they'll be in the long run. The main point is that the range of treatment options is expanding dramatically.

Meanwhile, if you think that BPH is becoming a part of your life, here are some tips to help you cope.

Rule out infections. If urinating suddenly becomes painful, and that pain is accompanied by a fever, chances are that you have a prostate infection rather than BPH. Such infections are usually treatable with antibiotics, but they may put a damper on your love life in the meantime.

"I don't think many men will want to have sex if they have a 104°F temperature and severe pain in the prostate area," says Drogo K. Montague, M.D., head of prosthetic surgery for the department of urology at the Cleveland Clinic Foundation in Ohio. That said, if you feel at all up to it, try to have sex or masturbate as regularly as you can. It's standard wisdom among urologists that frequent ejaculation can help flush out bacteria in the prostate.

Give your bladder a break. You can reduce the nuisance factor of BPH by reducing your need to urinate, especially at night. Try cutting back on fluids after 6:00 P.M. and having nothing at all after 7:00 P.M. Caffeine, alcohol, cold medicines, and spicy foods can all exacerbate the symptoms of BPH by irritating the urinary tract, adds Dr. Hollander. So go easy on these products.

See saw palmetto. Lots of doctors who favor natural remedies believe that a berry extract called saw palmetto helps reduce swollen prostates. Varro E. Tyler, Ph.D., dean emeritus and distinguished professor emeritus of pharmacognosy of the Purdue School of Pharmacy and Pharmacal Sciences in West Lafayette, Indiana, cites a study of 500 men in which 88 percent of them experienced some relief of BPH symptoms. If you decide to try it, use an oil-based extract—it's the most effective. And seek brands that indicate they're standardized to "85 to 95 percent fatty acids and sterols." Take 320 milligrams a day, suggests Dr. Tyler. Check with your doctor before trying this natural remedy: Saw palmetto may interact with some prostate medicines or affect prostate cancer screenings.

DUCKING PROSTATE CANCER

A sobering statistic from cancer researchers: 30 to 40 percent of men over the age 50 have prostate cancer. The silver lining to that fact is that only 8 percent of those cancers are deemed "significant," meaning dangerous enough to require treatment.

Can there be such a thing as an "insignificant cancer"? Of course not. But where the prostate is concerned, doctors say that there's much less to be concerned about. That's because most prostate tumors grow incredibly slowly, so much so that many men who have it are never troubled by it; live a good, long life regardless; and end up dying of something else. It's often said that more men die with prostate cancer than from it.

Surgery for prostate cancer is becoming more common today, but that's because doctors are learning to catch the disease at an earlier stage in younger men who have longer life expectancies. Research suggests that when surgery is performed to remove the prostate before the cancer has spread beyond it, a man's chance of survival is equal to that of men who have never had prostate cancer at all. "Years ago, most of the cases of prostate cancer that I saw were advanced, and incurable," says Dr. Bloom. "Today, that's completely reversed."

Another major advance in the treatment of prostate cancer is the effect of surgery on sex and continence. In the old days, cutting out the prostate sometimes meant cutting nerves, muscle, and tissue that helped you get an erection or maintain bowel and bladder control. The risk still exists, but it's greatly reduced, especially in light of advances in surgical technique. One of the most successful is loosely but aptly called nerve-sparing surgery. Pioneered by Patrick C. Walsh, M.D., professor and chairman of the department of urology at Johns Hopkins University School of Medicine in Baltimore and co-author of *The Prostate*, nerve-sparing surgery improves doctors' ability to reconstruct the bladder and urethra after surgery, thus helping to avoid postsurgical incontinence. Equally important, the procedure allows surgeons to get a better look at surrounding nerves that support sexual function and thus avoid them whenever possible during surgery. Dr. Walsh says that 90 percent of men in their forties and 75 percent of men in their fifties retain their potency after nerve-sparing surgery.

One thing that medical researchers haven't quite come up with yet is a way to prevent prostate cancer altogether, but they have a number of solid leads. Meanwhile, we've provided some suggestions for keeping your prostate cancer risk to a minimum.

Take the screen tests. The best way to head off prostate problems is to catch them early. The American Urological Association and the American Cancer Society recommend that once you hit 50, you should be getting a digital-rectal exam, where your doctor inserts a gloved, lubricated finger into your rectum and feels or palpates your prostate. As unpleasant as that prospect is, this hands-on approach is one of the best ways for your doctor to detect prostate problems early.

Also at age 50 you should start getting an annual blood test of your prostate-specific antigen (PSA), a protein produced by the prostate. The higher your levels of PSA, the higher the likelihood of developing prostate cancer. If you're African-American or have a family history of prostate cancer, you should have these screen tests done from age 40 on.

Seek soy. Fact: Men in Japan are five times less likely to die from prostate cancer than men in the United States. The reason for that is believed to be their diet, which is lower in fat and higher in fiber than the typical American diet. Also, the soy products so prevalent in the Japanese diet—tofu, soy flour, soy milk—are linked with keeping prostate tumors at bay. One study of 8,000 men of Japanese ancestry found that those who ate tofu on a daily basis were three times less likely to develop prostate cancer than those who ate tofu only once a week or less.

Try tomatoes. In a Harvard Medical School study of more than 47,000 men, researchers found that men who ate the most cooked tomato products had the lowest risk of prostate cancer. By "most," we mean 10 servings a week. It sounds like a lot, but consider that a half-cup of tomato sauce is one serving—and you probably ladle a lot more than that on your spaghetti.

Swallow the alphabet. Some of the leading researchers of prostate cancer believe that vitamin supplements can help prevent the spread of the disease. In one ongoing study, patients are receiving 25,000 to 150,000 international units (IU) of vitamin A, 1,000 to 3,000 IU of vitamin E, and 1,000 IU of vitamin D daily. All three vitamins have been shown to inhibit prostate cancer growth in animals. If taking these doses of the vitamins sounds like something you'd like to try, make sure that you consult your doctor first; these doses are unusually high and exceed government-established safety limits.

Beware the patch. There has been a lot of publicity about how testosterone therapy can boost a man's lust for life in general and for sex in particular. What hasn't been touted quite so loudly is that high levels of testosterone have been linked to prostate enlargement and the growth of prostate tumors, says Domeena Renshaw, M.D., director of Loyola Sex Therapy Clinic at Loyola University in Chicago and author of *Seven Weeks to Better Sex*. If you're already suffering prostate problems, steer clear of the patch. And even if you're not, talk with your doctor about the risk of testosterone therapy before you try to get a prescription for the patch.

Put your mind at ease. If you've had a vasectomy or are thinking about it, have no fear—at least about prostate cancer. A study some years back purported to show that men who had vasectomies were more likely to develop prostate cancer, but subsequent studies have failed to confirm the connection. "If there's any association, it's very weak," says Gerald Chodak, M.D., director of the Prostate and Urology Center at the University of Chicago Hospital. "It's not something to worry about."

SPERM PROBLEMS

How fit are your sperm?

If you're like most men, you imagine your sperm as hordes of tough little tadpoles—the virile action heroes of the microworld. And that Hollywood image isn't so far from the truth. After all, each sperm is designed to set off an explosion of growth: a new life.

But while the hero almost always triumphs in the movies, real life is a different story. Too often sperm just isn't up to the job. Infertility, the ongoing failure to conceive a child, affects millions of men. Fifteen percent of all couples suffer from it. Try as they may, they can't seem to have a baby.

What causes infertility? How can you tell whether you're infertile or just unlucky?

"If you and your partner have unprotected sex for a year and she isn't pregnant, one or both of you may have a problem," says Rebecca Sokol, M.D., professor of medicine, obstetrics, and gynecology at the University of Southern California School of Medicine in Los Angeles. About 40 percent of the time it's a guy thing: a sperm shortage or other problem in the man. That's called male-factor infertility, and it can be one of the thorniest troubles a man faces in life.

There are three ways to measure the health of your sperm: their numbers (sperm count), their shape (sperm morphology), and their ability to swim in a prompt, orderly way (motility). No man gets perfect scores in all three categories—in fact, it's hard to get a perfect score in any of them. Sperm counts vary from month to month, and every man is going to have plenty of sperm that are deformed or that don't move properly. In fact, if 60 percent of your sperm are normal on all scores, you're doing fine.

So what's worse than doubting your own balls?

Taking those doubts too seriously. You see, many—if not most—infertility problems are understood, if not readily solved. And for the truly determined dad-to-be, brand-new medical techniques stack the odds firmly in his favor.

Even if you've been firing blanks, sperm-wise, for years, you'll be glad to know the latest facts. So you should keep reading, but be patient. The scary stuff comes first.

THE TROUBLE WITH SPERM

Each woman is born with a lifetime supply of eggs in her ovaries. Parceled out at a rate of one per month during her fertile years, they add up to between 400 and 600 eggs. In search of these few ova, we men dispatch sperm by the billions. By the time he is 50, a guy produces around 950 billion egg-seeking missiles. The average male climax spews 200 million sperm.

Still, the egg often plays hard to beget.

The struggle to conceive can become daunting, even taking the pleasure out of sex. For afflicted couples, infertility often becomes the central issue in their lives.

And the problem is on the rise. You may have heard about a modern "sperm crisis" in industrialized countries. That scare is largely due to a widely hyped French study in which researchers found an alarming drop in sperm counts, from an average of 89 million per milliliter of semen to 60 million in only two decades. Today's sperm were less vigorous than those of the early 1970s; they also showed more deformities.

Other reports added to the mood of worry. Sperm, it seemed, were practically an endangered species.

Experts blamed bad modern diets, drugs, pollution, even tight jeans and hot tubs. (Your scrotum is designed to keep the testes, your sperm factories, far enough from the body to stay a couple degrees cooler. Saunas, hot tubs, or even tight pants may overheat testes, damaging sperm.)

While many in the scientific community questioned the findings, the alarmists may not be far from the truth. Specialists like Marc Goldstein, M.D., professor of urology and director of the Center for Male Reproductive Medicine and Microsurgery at New York Hospital–Cornell Medical Center in New York City, see men struggling with infertility every day. Many decrease their own chances—risking their reproductive lives—by smoking, abusing drugs, or drinking too much.

A further complication: Dr. Sokol sees social factors, even feminism, affecting modern infertility. "More women these days wait until their thirties before they try to start a family. Biologically, that's late," she explains. And it is simply harder to get a 35-year-old woman pregnant than her 20-year-old sister.

If you've been reading carefully, you would have noticed that every cause mentioned so far for infertility is self-inflicted—things like drugs, tight pants, smoking. That's a part of the picture, but not all. Many causes of infertility are out of your control. Here are a few.

- Undescended testicles. This fairly rare condition occurs in about 1 in 100 male infants. The problem is corrected with routine surgery and may never be mentioned again, but it can damage the testes. If you're unsure about your early surgical history, you may want to check your medical records.
- Genetic factors. These include chromosomal abnormalities.
- Hormonal deficiencies. These are rare and easily treatable.
- Testicular cancer or injury. Both can cause or contribute to infertility.
- Genital infection. Ditto. Prostatitis or the mumps can diminish or, in rare cases, even destroy sperm production.

Fertile to the End

Men are reproductively lucky. Like the aging Hollywood star with a teenage model on his arm, we maintain our fertility far longer than women. The Anthony Quinn effect—studly grandpa sires kids in his golden years—is no fluke.

Yes, fertility does tend to decrease as we age. "But not much," says Rebecca Sokol, M.D., professor of medicine, obstetrics, and gynecology at the University of Southern California School of Medicine in Los Angeles. And not until our years are getting pretty golden. "There is a small decline in sperm concentration in some men over 65, but even that doesn't apply to all men," says Dr. Sokol.

This means that we men can procreate, theoretically at least, even in our last minute of life.

Can you think of a better way to go?

Helping the Tadpoles

Before you panic, before you run to the doctor, there are steps you can take to bolster your fertility. Here are a few.

Do it often; time it right. Even under optimal conditions, the chance of conception tops out at about 20 percent in any given month. Conception can only occur during a woman's ovulation cycle, which lasts a few days per month. Ovulation kits (about $20 at any pharmacy) can identify those lucky days.

Some specialists urge hopeful couples to have intercourse every 48 hours during midcycle when ovulation occurs. Dr. Sokol says you'll enhance the odds by having sex "as often as you're comfortable doing it."

To be fruitful, be fit. Obese men have more sperm-blunting female hormones in their blood, according to reproductive endocrinologist G. William Bates, M.D., executive vice president and chief medical officer of PrincipalCare in Brentwood, Tennessee.

Purify, purify. Many intoxicants harm sperm. Cigarette smoking lowers sperm counts, and according to Machelle Seibel, M.D., medical director of the Faulkner Center for Reproductive Medicine in Boston, the nicotine in cigarettes may change the shape of sperm and lower sperm motility, making it harder for them to get to the egg.

Alcohol is a reproductive toxin. While acknowledging that countless alcoholics sire children, Dr. Goldstein sets an upper limit of two drinks per week. Marijuana is also taboo. "And the effects of pot smoking last 16 days," he says.

Beware prescription drugs. Antidepressants and blood pressure medicines can hamper sperm. Be sure your doctor knows that you're trying to conceive before he prescribes medicine to you.

Get your vitamins. Vitamin C can help sperm. One study showed that 1,000 milligrams of vitamin C per day discourages sperm "agglutination"—clumping, which halts eggward progress. The study found other sperm benefits from vitamin C, particularly for smokers. Larry Lipshultz, M.D., professor of urology for the Scott department of urology at Baylor College of Medicine in Houston, recommends vitamin E and beta-carotene as well, calling them scavengers of the oxidants that can damage sperm.

Check for a "bag of worms" in your scrotum. Such a small, mushy area below the testicle is called a varicocele (pronounced VAR-i-co-seel). It is a swollen blood vessel, the scrotal version of a varicose vein. Varicoceles usually occur on the left side. They restrict sperm production by overheating the area. Some specialists consider them the main cause of male infertility.

About 15 percent of all men have a varicocele. The condition needn't harm fertility but probably has a progressive effect, gradually choking off sperm.

The varicocele cure is microsurgery. Developed in the 1980s by Dr. Goldstein, the procedure is now a half-hour outpatient job.

Planning Your Attack on Infertility

Think you have a fertility problem? First, see a urologist who specializes in male-factor infertility. Get a semen test.

"The test is simple and cheap—anywhere from $50 to $200," says Dr. Goldstein. Semen tests immediately show the number, shape, and vigor of a man's sperm.

"Men are usually not anxious to think that there's a problem with them—with their masculinity," Dr. Goldstein says. "But this easy test can prevent years of problems."

And never forget that there's far more good news than bad in the field of male infertility.

"Ten years ago we had to turn men away," says Dr. Goldstein. Such men were effectively barren: Instead of 70 million sperm per milliliter of semen they had a million or even fewer. "They were hopeless cases. But these days we have revolutionary treatments. We now have men whose sperm count is *zero* successfully fathering children."

About 10 percent of couples struggling with infertility seek advanced techniques such as the three that follow. These methods can be expensive, but for thousands of couples high-tech conception can also be miraculous. Here's how they work.

- Artificial insemination. A doctor delivers healthy sperm directly to the egg inside a woman's body. Donor sperm is an option if yours won't work.
- In vitro fertilization (IVF). Sperm and ovum are combined in a laboratory dish. Fertilized eggs are then placed in the woman's uterus. An IVF attempt costs $7,800 on average, according to the American Society for Reproductive Medicine, and the process can take several tries. Each try only has a 20 percent success rate.
- GIFT and ZIFT. In gamete intrafallopian transfer (GIFT) and zygote intrafallopian transfer (ZIFT), either sperm and eggs or an already-fertilized egg, called a zygote, can be implanted inside a woman's fallopian tubes.

Black-Belt Tactics

"We tried everything. We were the infertility poster couple," says Dane, a Hollywood cameraman. Dane doubted his manhood. He held his wife as she wept, thinking of the baby they would never have.

"Then I decided to go the black-belt route. We were going to get pregnant or go broke trying."

Intracytoplasmic sperm injection (ICSI, pronounced ICK-see) is a technique specialists call revolutionary. ICSI requires only a single sperm, which doctors can sometimes find even in the testes of men whose sperm counts are "zero." That lone sperm is "immobilized by gently stroking the tail with the injection pipette," then micro-injected directly into an egg, leading to fertilization in 58 percent of ICSI attempts, report researchers at Houston's Baylor College of Medicine.

Dr. Goldstein has seen similar success at New York Hospital–Cornell Medical Center. "ICSI is expensive—$10,000 to $15,000 per try—and insurers usually won't cover it. But 44 percent of the time it puts a baby in your hands," he says.

Dane and his wife spent years negotiating the troubled waters of fertility medicine. They spent almost $200,000 before Annie, their "miracle baby," was born.

Dane calls his experience "an expensive miracle."

He also calls it a bargain.

PREMATURE EJACULATION

In a world of overnight deliveries, 3-minute microwave dinners, and lightning-quick computer chips, there are few places where slower is better. The bedroom is one of them.

You already know why. Women need more time and stimulation to become aroused. Sexual chivalry dictates that she should have her orgasm first. Because sex feels so good, we don't want it to end too soon. For these and other reasons, most men place a high premium on controlling when they ejaculate. Nice guys, we're told, finish last.

Sometimes, though, we can't quite regulate the hormonal chain reaction that leads to ejaculation. For most men, this is a once-in-a-while event. But some men struggle on an all-too-regular basis with the frustration of premature ejaculation—and they really don't have to.

AVOIDING THE RAPIDS

Exactly what constitutes "premature" ejaculation is a question therapists have debated for years, as have a lot of men and their partners. Definitions range from not being able to sustain vaginal penetration for a minute or more, to any relationship in which the man ejaculates before his partner more than 50 percent of the time.

Don't focus so much on percentages and timing, says Marilyn K. Volker, Ed.D., a sexologist in Miami. It comes to this: When either partner is dissatisfied with how quickly the man ejaculates, she says, that's a problem. Like many others in her field, Dr. Volker also dislikes the term *premature ejacula-*

tion since it implies something bad about coming fast. "Rapid ejaculation" is the current label of choice. "A lot of men ejaculate quickly," says Dr. Volker. "But if the couple continues to do outercourse—meaning any sex play that doesn't involve penetration—they can still have a satisfying sexual relationship. That's not to say that rapid ejaculation isn't terribly frustrating for a lot of couples."

Why some men are quicker on the trigger than others can be explained in reasons of both body and mind, says Steve Manley, Ph.D., staff psychologist for the Male Health Center in Dallas. Some men are simply born with a hypersensitivity to sex, going from 0 to 60 with no stops in between. The slightest stimulation kicks off the orgasm response and they ejaculate.

Biologically, in fact, rapid ejaculation is standard among mammals. If you've been lucky enough to witness two big animals doing the nasty at a farm or a zoo, then you realize that it's up, in, and—boom!—before you can get the camera out, the action is done. It's survival of the species; males need to plant their seeds efficiently. Well, we're animals, too, and we were once programmed this way. But being thinking creatures as well, we have evolved sex to a higher plateau. We like to take our time, enjoy sex merely for the feelings, work at mastering technique. There's a conflict here. While our minds want sex to last a long time, ejaculating quickly is physiologically normal. This is particularly true for younger lovers—in their teens and twenties—who haven't learned techniques to slow things down.

In some cases, however, rapid ejaculation is a *learned* behavior, imprinted on the mind by rushed or unpleasant early sexual experiences, says Dr. Manley. For these men, anxiety about sex is a major part of the problem, which is why the pattern often starts with younger men who are less confident in bed.

BUILDING UP TO SLOWING DOWN

In either case, experts say a little ejaculatory training can go a long way toward controlling your sexual responses. In some cases, it's entirely possible to unlearn the old behavior that put you in such a hurry in the first place. You can also learn to recognize your limits—the amount of stimulation you can stand before you reach the "point of inevitability" when you must ejaculate. These techniques can help you master the moment, literally.

Pay attention. The first technique you need to unlearn is the old standby of distracting yourself during sex. Focusing on box scores or the Gettysburg Address only removes you from the process of intercourse, and that's the first step toward, ahem, rapid deployment.

"The man needs to keep track of what's happening to his body," says Robert Birch, Ph.D., a psychologist in Columbus, Ohio, specializing in marriage and sex therapy and author of the book *Male Sexual Endurance*. "Nature has wired us to thrust in a way that will bring us to orgasm, so if we go on automatic pilot, we're going to come. We need to be aware of where we are

The Chemical Alternative

In a world as hurried as ours, it shouldn't be surprising that we've discovered a way to speed up the process of slowing down. Not long after the drug Prozac became available to treat depression, an interesting side effect caught researchers' attention: Prozac seemed to delay orgasm. Today, the class of antidepressant drugs which includes Prozac—they're called SSRIs (selective serotonin reuptake inhibitors)—have become the latest treatment option for premature ejaculation, especially among men for whom rapid ejaculation seems to be a physiological problem.

In 1995, Roger T. Crenshaw, M.D., a psychiatrist and sex therapist in La Jolla, California, and one of the founders of the American Psychiatric Association, directed a study in which 60 men who were unable to sustain intercourse for more than 30 seconds were given SSRIs. Virtually all of them, says Dr. Crenshaw, were soon able to stay in the saddle for 6 minutes or more. Of the many patients he has treated with these drugs, Dr. Crenshaw claims that 10 percent need to continue taking them indefinitely, while the remaining 90 percent need take them only intermittently—usually when they know they're going to have sex—or not at all. Other studies appear to confirm Dr. Crenshaw's results.

Although many psychiatrists and urologists are already prescribing antidepressants to treat premature ejaculation, don't rush right out for a pharmaceutical cure-all. For some patients, SSRIs can have undesirable side effects, including a *loss* of sex drive—not the ideal way to overcome premature ejaculation.

sexually so that we can get out of that automatic mode. You can learn when it's time to begin slowing things down."

Test yourself. By yourself or with the help of an understanding partner, masturbation can be a useful, healthy—did we mention fun?—way to learn control. Dr. Volker says by exploring yourself this way, you get a better handle on what feels good and what feels *too* good. By learning what your ultrasensitive spots are, you can communicate to your partner what she should and shouldn't do to you during sex, thereby giving you better control.

Start the stop-start. One of the most common and effective tools for mastering ejaculatory control is the simple "stop-start" method. The idea is to stimulate the penis manually, almost to the point of ejaculation, and then stop. After the man regains his composure, the process is repeated, several times, before he finally allows himself to come. Over time, you can learn to tolerate longer and longer periods of sexual stimulation. Eventually, you and your partner can begin moving closer to intercourse, slowly building the degree of sexual intimacy and intensity as you go.

Try a squeeze play. Famed sex researchers William Masters, M.D., and Virginia Johnson, formerly of the Masters and Johnson Institute in St. Louis, invented a variation on the stop-start technique called the squeeze method. Just before the man reaches the point of ejaculatory inevitability, he or his partner grips the penis just below the head and squeezes firmly. After this temporary turnoff—it shouldn't be painful, by the way—the stimulation cycle can slowly begin again.

Try to be PC. For our purposes, "PC" stands for "pubococcygeal," the muscles in your pelvic region that control the flow of urine (you'll also notice them twitching during orgasm). By doing exercises called Kegels, you can build up these muscles to be strong enough that they can help you control ejaculation, says E. Douglas Whitehead, M.D., director of the Association for Male Sexual Dysfunction and associate clinical professor of urology at the Albert Einstein College of Medicine, both in New York City.

Here's how: Three times a day, simply clench and unclench your PC muscles 20 to 25 times. Do this for about 3 weeks. After that, spend another 8 to 10 weeks doing extended clenches, where you hold each contraction for 2 to 3 seconds; or rapid clenches, where you clench and unclench rapidly 3 times. Work up to 5 or 10 rapid clenches.

By that point, your PC muscles should be strong enough that, when you feel yourself reaching the point of inevitability, you can clench your PCs—hard—to essentially slam on the brakes.

Shift positions. Dr. Birch says that simply stopping and changing positions frequently can give you more control. Every time you stop to shift positions, you're momentarily ceasing the stimulation that puts you past the point of no return. Sex on your side or a position where your partner is on top are two favorites that allow you to enjoy sex but may be slightly less intense so that you can remain in control.

TESTICULAR PROBLEMS

Balls. Nuts. *Cojones.* The family jewels. We probably have as many names for testicles as Eskimos have for snow. It's not surprising, considering the literal and figurative attachments we have to those innocuous little organs dangling between our legs.

Beyond a certain subliminal hyper-awareness, though, it's a safe bet that most of us don't really think or know all that much about our testicles. Elsewhere in this book, we do explain some basics about the function of these precious, delicate orbs. But what happens when something goes awry south of the belt buckle? It's the great male fear and a perennial hazard. Unlike women, whose reproductive organs are nestled safely in their abdomens, a good portion of our generative real estate is literally hanging out there, exposed to a world of dangers that we'd just as soon not think about.

But as a man, you know it pays to be prepared for every contingency, even unpleasant ones. So if ever you be luckless enough to feel a sharp pain in your scrotum—or even just a vague sense that something's not quite right—you don't have to sit around feeling queasy about it. Instead, you can arm yourself ahead of time with a good working knowledge of some common testicular troubles and how to remedy them or avoid them entirely.

CALLING FOULS AND STRIKES

We know it's uncomfortable to think about, but it's worth knowing some of the problems that can befall the hapless testes as they bounce through life. From most common to least likely, here's a brief glossary of testicular ailments.

Trauma. Sure, that's what the doctors call it, but you know it as a kick in the balls. Why is a low blow so extraordinarily painful? "Probably because there's such an ample supply of nerves to that part of our body," says Paul Gleich, M.D., chairman of the department of urology at HealthPartners/St. Paul–Ramsey Medical Center in St. Paul, Minnesota. "Second, I think it has to do with the structure of the testicle, which is basically soft tissue encased in a thick eggshell-type case. That allows pressure to build very rapidly if it gets squeezed, and our body doesn't take well to pressure." We're sweating just thinking about it.

According to Marc Goldstein, M.D., professor of urology and director of the Center for Male Reproductive Medicine and Microsurgery at New York Hospital–Cornell Medical Center in New York City, the best way to protect against testicular trauma is to do what the boxers do: Wear a hard plastic protective cup when playing any contact sport.

Celes. Sometimes trauma can lead to one of the more common testicle maladies, a *cele*, or noncancerous cyst or lump. There are several categories of celes. A hydrocele is a collection of fluid in the scrotum, which can occur from an injury but often can develop for no reason. If that fluid is blood, it's called a hematocele. Fluid-based celes can keep swelling, and after a while, their sheer size can cramp you for space. "Some people walk around for months and come in with swellings as large as grapefruits," says Stanley Bloom, M.D., director of the Men's Sexual Health Center in Livingston, New Jersey. Sometimes errant sperm can form a cyst that you won't notice unless you feel it—that's a spermatocele. Most of these are not life-threatening, but they can be uncomfortable and ought to be taken care of by your doctor.

Varicocele. Although by name it's part of the cele family, a varicocele is not really a cyst but a varicose vein in your scrotum, and it's fairly common. According to Dr. Goldstein, 15 percent of men will develop one at some point in their lives. "Only the big ones are visible," he says. "It looks like a bag of worms inside the scrotum, just above the testicle. It'll disappear when you lie down."

Varicoceles are painless and in most cases harmless, except in men who are trying to have children: Research has shown that they significantly reduce fertility (for more on infertility, see Sperm Problems on page 237). There's nothing you can do to prevent getting one; they're caused by a congenital plumbing problem. Varicoceles are routinely corrected with surgery, but that's something you only need to worry much about if you're planning to have kids.

Epididymitis. There's a delicate mass of coils at the back of your testicles called the epididymis. That's where your sperm goes after it leaves your testicle; it's also a common breeding ground for an infection and inflammation called epididymitis. This condition has lots of possible causes: bacteria from a urinary tract infection, a prostate infection, or a sexually transmitted disease; inflammation caused by trauma or by rigorous exercise; even surgical procedures.

If one or both of your testicles gets inflamed, if it hurts to pee, and if you have a fever, chances are that you have epididymitis. The good news is that this condition is easily treated with a round of antibiotics. Meanwhile, to help ease the discomfort of the condition, Dr. Bloom tells his patients to el-

It's a Grand Old Sag

When it comes to aging, most of us are prepared for thinning hair, deepening wrinkles, and duller memories. What nobody warns us about is sagging scrotum syndrome (SSS).

You see it in steam baths at the YMCA: guys in their seventies and eighties with balls hanging down so low they could probably fling them over their shoulders. You wonder: Will that be me some day? Could be. Alas, it appears that SSS is not a preventable condition.

According to Laurence A. Levine, M.D., director of the male sexual health function and fertility services in the department of urology at Rush–Presbyterian–St. Luke's Medical Center in Chicago, younger men's scrotal sacs remain taut with the help of two sets of muscles, the cremasters and dartos. These are the same muscles that help regulate the temperature of the testicles by moving them closer to the body or further away from it, depending on how hot or cold the surrounding environment is. The goal of all that schlepping up and down is to maintain the optimal temperature for your sperm's survival.

With time, the cremaster and dartos muscles weaken and gravity begins to take its toll. To Dr. Levine's knowledge, no one has yet developed a workout machine to pump up this particular part of the body. And more frequent sex won't keep those muscles strong enough to beat gravity either.

evate their testicles by lying down with a towel underneath them. You can also put an ice pack, wrapped in a light towel or washcloth, on your scrotum two or three times a day until the swelling subsides. You can also take a regular dose of an over-the-counter anti-inflammatory like aspirin or ibuprofen. Although sometimes an errant infection can lead to epididymitis, you can help avoid contracting it sexually by wearing a condom during intercourse. But if you develop signs of epididymitis, do get it looked at, less it gets worse.

Orchitis. This is a more general infection of the entire testicle. It's rarer than epididymitis and more painful. In fact, it can develop from a case of epididymitis that isn't taken care of. Other causes include viral infection—men who get mumps can develop orchitis—and sexually transmitted disease (for more on sexually transmitted diseases, see Sexual Diseases on page 253). To prevent orchitis, says James H. Gilbaugh Jr., M.D., a urologist in Portland, Oregon, and author of *Men's Private Parts*, treat any cases of epididymitis promptly, practice safe sex, and have yourself immunized against mumps.

Torsion. It's rare, but it's nasty and dangerous. And it starts with a sharp, severe pain in your scrotum, seemingly from nowhere. If it happens to you, get it evaluated quickly—it might be a torsion. Testicular torsion happens when the cord from which the testicle hangs gets twisted, cutting off its blood supply. "You have about 6 hours before there's irreparable damage to the testicle," says Dr. Gleich. Don't even waste one—get to a hospital and get that cord unkinked.

Testicular torsion is a rare condition (thank God!) and usually strikes young men between the ages of 12 and 18 who have an inborn predisposition to it. There's no known cure and no known way to prevent it, although wearing a jockstrap when working out or playing sports is recommended.

A YOUNG MAN'S CANCER

Is it a cruel joke of the gods that testicular cancer usually strikes men at the peak of their sexual powers, between the ages of 15 and 39? No, the true reason is much more practical than that.

Men who develop testicular cancer most likely have a genetic flaw that lies dormant through most of their childhood, according to Durwood Neal Jr., M.D., associate professor of urology at the University of Texas Medical Branch in Galveston. "It probably takes a while for the flaw to materialize," he says, "and the chemical changes that occur in puberty probably fuel its growth."

If it's not caught, testicular cancer can take men in their prime, but that fate is becoming increasingly rare. It is, after all, one of the more treatable forms of cancer there is: More than 90 percent of the men who get the disease today survive it. In order to treat testicular cancer you have to find it, though—and the earlier you do that, the better.

The best way to do that is to give your testicles a monthly self-examination. Here's how, according to the National Cancer Institute: The best time for one is after a warm bath or shower. The heat relaxes the scrotum, making it easier to find anything unusual. Having no pants on also helps.

What you're looking for is a lump. Usually, they appear on the sides of the testicle, but some show up on the front. Stand in front of a mirror. Look for any swelling on the skin of the scrotum. Examine each testicle with both hands, rolling it between your thumbs and fingers. Don't worry if one testicle seems larger than the other—that's normal.

If you do find a lump, don't panic: Most likely you've found one of those ubiquitous celes. But you do need to have your doctor confirm that. Make an appointment with your family physician or a urologist.

FETISHES, PHOBIAS, AND ADDICTIONS

One of the diverting things about the Internet is that it can put you in touch with lots of people who have some pretty unusual ideas about sex. Take this posting from a gentleman looking for love at a Web site called the World Fetish Center: "I'm a 34-year-old male, 6'1", 190s. I enjoy wearing tight latex while bound and then being punched in the stomach by a dominant male or female who is dressed in leather or latex, especially tight gloves. Other body abuse is also welcome. E-mail me if this sounds interesting."

What's going on here? Does this man have a fetish? Is he a sex addict? Does he have a sex phobia? Is he a weirdo? Does he need help? For specific answers, we need to start with some basic definitions about fetishes, phobias, and sex addictions.

Fetishism. "Fetishes are focused lust," says Jack Morin, Ph.D., a psychotherapist and sexologist from the San Francisco Bay area and author of *The Erotic Mind* and *Anal Pleasure and Health.* "They are a search for pure genital arousal focused like a laser beam on a particular thing." The intensity of that focus provides a sort of supercharged sexual rush, Dr. Morin says, which is one reason that extreme fetishes are so hard to give up.

You may find yourself attracted to breasts or your girlfriend's sexy, black negligee. But if it isn't required for arousal, then strictly speaking it is not a fetish. It becomes a fetish when it becomes the only way the man can reach orgasm. At that point, relationship troubles often develop: A fetishist's partner can easily feel that he's more interested in his fetish object than he is in her. Many men seek counseling because they're ashamed of their fetish desires.

According to Barry McCarthy, Ph.D., a psychologist in Washington, D.C., and author of *Male Sexual Awareness*, fetishes can be either benign or noxious. A foot fetish would generally be considered benign, unless the fetishist starts stealing women's shoes. Pedophilia, voyeurism, and exhibitionism are noxious: They can cause other people harm and get you arrested.

Fetishists are overwhelmingly men. No one's really sure why that is, although it's assumed that the relative intensity of the male sex drive has something to do with it.

Phobias. "A phobia is an irrational fear that interferes with your life," says Dr. McCarthy. "Most people work around their phobias, but they can become more and more intrusive so that your anxiety and your avoidance behaviors increase to the point where they consistently interfere with your ability to have sex."

Dr. McCarthy defines extreme phobias as aversions. He treated one man whose association with sex became so negative that he developed an aversion to his own semen. Another patient's periodic bouts of impotence caused him such anxiety that commencing foreplay caused him to vomit.

Men are less prone to phobias than women, Dr. McCarthy says, but they do develop them. Often they involve fears of getting a woman pregnant, of contracting a sexual disease, or of being trapped by the vagina.

Sexual addiction. For some men, the song "Addicted to Love" is not a joke. Sex addicts pursue frequent and often promiscuous sexual activity, which they feel unable to control. Some therapists prefer to call this behavior sexually compulsive.

The sex addict, like the drug addict, will become steadily more dependent on his fix, and he'll need more and more frequent fixes to be satisfied, says Mark Schwartz, Sc.D., clinical co-director of the Masters and Johnson Institute in St. Louis. Sex addiction also resembles other addictions in that it's used as an escape. "Whenever there's anxiety or fear in his life, the addict goes to his habit," Dr. Schwartz says. An "addictive cycle" gets started, he adds, when the habit itself becomes a source of anxiety or fear, causing an even greater need to seek relief in the habit.

A GOOD LOOK IN THE MIRROR

Exactly how sexual addictions, fetishes, and phobias get started is a subject of intense debate among sex experts. Most believe that these behaviors can be traced back to traumatic experiences, usually involving physical, sexual, or emotional abuse in childhood. Fear of intimacy is thought to be another common denominator.

While that's all well and good, Albert Ellis, Ph.D., a psychologist and president of the Albert Ellis Institute in New York City, feels that such explanations overlook more obvious possibilities. "The human race is born with

Sex Behavior Test

Sometimes kinky or quirky sexual behaviors can get out of hand. To help determine whether you've crossed that line, Carla Perez, M.D., a psychiatrist in San Francisco and author of *Getting off the Merry-Go-Round: You Can Live without Compulsive Habits*, suggests that you ask yourself the following questions.

- Do you habitually use your sexual indulgences to get through the day or to avoid discomfort?
- Is your sex behavior interfering with the important relationships in your life?
- Are you becoming less discriminating in terms of how, when, where, and with whom you indulge?
- Are you needing more and more sex to feel okay?
- Does your sex behavior cause you to spend time with people with whom you wouldn't otherwise associate?
- Have friends or family members told you they think you have a problem?
- Are you hiding your sexual behaviors?
- Do you continue to indulge in your sexual behaviors even though in honest moments you can see they're having a negative impact on your life?
- Have your behaviors caused you to cross any moral or legal boundaries? Are other people being hurt?
- Do you feel depressed about your sexual behavior? Do you feel trapped by it?

"Yes" answers to a majority of those questions may indicate that your sexual behavior is in control of you and not the other way around.

a tendency to exaggerate the significance of something," he says. "It's only when that tendency involves sex that words like *fetish* get applied." Occasionally, a fetish can be traced back to some childhood trauma, Dr. Ellis believes, but more often it's simply a question of a preference blown out of proportion, or perhaps of a biological predisposition toward obsessive behavior. The latter explanation may help explain why some sex addicts and fetishists have been successfully treated with antidepressant drugs like Prozac, he says.

You needn't rely on drugs, though. If you feel you're suffering from a sexual problem, there are numerous ways you can grab hold of the reins and take back control of the sexual behavior that's controlling you. Here are some useful first steps.

Keep a journal. Because denial and addiction go hand in hand, Carla Perez, M.D., a psychiatrist in San Francisco and author of *Getting off the Merry-Go-Round: You Can Live without Compulsive Habits*, recommends that you chronicle your sex life on paper, in detail, for two weeks (just keep it where no prying eyes can find it). "Each day, try to look at a different way you rationalize your behavior," says Dr. Perez. "That can shoot a lot of holes in denial."

Take the pledge. At the Masters and Johnson Institute, patients being treated for sexual addictions are typically asked to sign an "abstinence contract," agreeing to stay celibate for a month or so. "For most people it's like going cold turkey," says Dr. Schwartz, "which helps them realize how addicted they really are." Many patients who take the abstinence pledge suddenly find themselves experiencing the negative emotions they've been covering up with sex, Dr. Schwartz adds. Usually, that means depression or anxiety. If those emotions feel overwhelming, seek professional counseling.

Reason with yourself. Dr. Ellis believes that it's possible to consciously steer oneself away from developing a fetish, at least in its early stages. "If big breasts are your thing, you can convince yourself that you don't absolutely need them," he says. "Tell yourself that your world won't end if you don't have this." Dr. Ellis adds, however, that at a certain point resisting an obsession only strengthens it. If you find yourself constantly worrying about your sexual behaviors, telling yourself not to worry isn't likely to do much good.

Find a group. There are many 12-step groups dedicated to those with sexual addictions, including Sex and Love Addicts Anonymous, Sex Addicts Anonymous, and Sexaholics Anonymous. Dr. Perez believes that these programs can be especially helpful in addressing the feelings of shame and the obsession with secrecy that characterize so many sexual problems. "Peer support offers something no therapist can offer," she says.

Get help. The sexual problems described in this chapter can be deeply ingrained and their origins deep-seated. If they're causing you or your partner significant dismay, you may need therapy to give them the attention they deserve. Whether you choose a psychotherapist, a psychologist, a pastoral counselor, or a psychiatrist, Dr. McCarthy recommends that you seek out someone who specializes in dealing with such problems.

Don't demonize yourself. Shame and guilt about sexual behaviors can often be more damaging than the behaviors themselves, says Betty Dodson, Ph.D., a sex educator and author of *Sex for One*. "We live in a very repressed culture, and it's too easy to label someone abnormal," she says. "Who's to say that there's a right way and a wrong way to have sex? The sex drive is something we need to value and not try to force into some limited model. Sexual repression is the problem, not sexual expression."

Sexual Diseases

Let's say you're 45 years old, recently divorced, and tonight you have a promising date. You're nervous for two reasons. It has been 20 years since you slept with anyone but your ex, and even if you get lucky, you have no idea how to handle this safe-sex thing you've heard so much about. How worried should you be about picking up more than you bargained for?

Enough to make sure you protect yourself, no matter how awkward that might seem, says Michael Warren, M.D., chief of the division of urology at the University of Texas Medical Branch in Galveston. "There are plenty of sexually transmitted diseases (STDs) out there waiting to attack you," he says. "The rules have changed, and you'd better be ready."

We've learned a lot about STDs in the past 20 years. We now know, for example, that more diseases can be transmitted by sex than we thought. The latest count is about 20 (we explain the main ones in "Hey, Let's Be Careful out There" on page 254). We also know that many of those diseases have no discernible symptoms, which means that lots of people are happily doing the deed without knowing they're passing something on—something potentially incurable or even deadly, like AIDS.

The way to get AIDS or any other STD is to have unprotected sex with a partner whose sexual history you're not sure of. You might think a scared teenager trying to get laid would be more likely to have sex without a condom than an older, more experienced lover—and there is some truth to that stereotype. Teenagers account for one-quarter of the 12 million new STD infections in the United States each year. It would be a mistake, however, to think that only kids have unsafe sex. One study found that heterosexual men 50 years old or older who had some risk of contracting the HIV virus (because they slept with more than one partner, for example) were only one-sixth as likely to use condoms during sex as young adults in their twenties.

Given the number of bugs lurking out there, it's nice to know that a lot has been learned in recent years about how to stop them before they do too much damage. "We have some wonderful new tools to fight STDs," says Judith Wasserheit, M.D., director of the division of STD prevention for the Centers for Disease Control and Prevention (CDC) in Atlanta. "They include diagnostic tests that are more accurate, less expensive, and less invasive than they used to be. We also have better treatments."

The results of these advances can be seen in the CDC's statistics. The number of syphilis and gonorrhea infections in the United States is actually declining, for example, while the growth of HIV has slowed. Still, there's a long way to go. According to Catherine Liu, director of the

(continued on page 256)

Hey, Let's Be Careful out There

There's a whole band of bugs that are just aching to put the big hurt on your sex life—and your health. Here's what you need to know.

AIDS

How Common: It's estimated that as many as 900,000 people in the United States are infected with HIV.

Symptoms: Usually, no symptoms appear in the initial stages of HIV infection, although some people develop a short-lived illness that resembles mononucleosis. Antibodies can be detected in the bloodstream within three to six months. A sizable number of HIV-infected men may not have symptoms for many years. In full-blown AIDS the body's immune system breaks down, opening the way for numerous infections.

Treatment: HIV is still incurable, although new drug therapies hold promise for substantially slowing its progression toward full-blown AIDS.

Prevention: Practice safer sex.

Chlamydia

How Common: The STD that is spreading fastest in the United States, chlamydia now infects as many as four million people each year.

Symptoms: Many people infected with chlamydia have no symptoms. Symptoms that do appear in infected men usually occur within one to six weeks after being exposed to the infection. They include a stinging sensation at the end of the penis, a discharge from the penis, and painful urination. For women, chlamydia can lead to severe abdominal or pelvic pain and infertility.

Treatment: Antibiotics.

Prevention: Practice safer sex.

Genital Herpes

How Common: As many as 40 million people in the United States may have genital herpes.

Symptoms: The initial outbreak usually begins about a week after exposure with tingling and itching around the genitals, followed by the appearance of genital sores or blisters. Subsequent outbreaks are usually milder. Some people may have flulike symptoms.

Treatment: Herpes is incurable. People with severe outbreaks can be treated with one of three drugs, which help minimize symptoms.

Prevention: Practice safer sex.

Genital Warts (also known as human papillomavirus, or HPV)

How Common: Approximately 40 million Americas are infected with HPV, and 1 million new cases are diagnosed every year.

Symptoms: Men usually get genital warts on the penis or scrotum. The warts vary in size and shape from small bumps to larger growths resembling cauliflower. Sometimes they are moist and itchy. They can appear anywhere from a few weeks to several years after exposure, although they are sometimes hard to see.

Treatment: If left untreated, genital warts may go away by themselves, remain unchanged, or grow larger. A doctor can remove them, although the virus that causes the warts is incurable.

Prevention: Practice safer sex.

Gonorrhea

How Common: It's estimated that 1.1 million Americans contract gonorrhea each year.

Symptoms: Generally, symptoms begin one to seven days after infection. They include pain during urination, then yellow discharge from penis. Untreated gonorrhea can cause infertility in both men and women.

Treatment: Antibiotics.

Prevention: Practice safer sex.

Hepatitis B (HBV)

How Common: About 200,000 new infections occur in the United States each year.

Symptoms: Often has no symptoms, although fever, headaches, loss of appetite, vomiting, diarrhea, and jaundice (yellowing of the skin and eyes) may appear. Most HBV cases clear up by themselves, but between 6 and 10 percent of adults develop chronic infections that can lead to serious liver damage.

Treatment: Drug treatments help manage chronic HBV.

Prevention: Vaccines exist for HBV. Safer sex also prevents transmission.

Syphilis

How Common: There are an estimated 120,000 new cases of syphilis in the United States each year.

Symptoms: Between 9 and 90 days after exposure, a shallow, painless ulcer develops at the site of the infection, usually on the penis. It heals after a month or so. If untreated, about six weeks later, a rash appears on the palms or soles of the feet, sometimes on the mouth; swollen lymph nodes and wart-like growths on the genitals may also appear. If left untreated, symptoms disappear and the disease goes into a long, latent stage in which various tissues in the body, from the bones to the brain, can be severely damaged.

Treatment: Antibiotics.

Prevention: Practice safer sex.

CDC's National STD hotline, as many as 55 million Americans are thought to have a sexually transmitted disease. One STD in particular is exploding, she says: chlamydia, which infects as many as four million men and women each year. The number of heterosexual women with AIDS is also on the rise.

America's record on STDs is downright embarrassing compared to other countries in the industrialized world. According to Dr. Wasserheit, the United States has at least eight times the number of gonorrhea cases per capita than Canada, and between 50 and 100 times more than Sweden. Why? There's better access to health care in those countries, she says, and better sex education in their schools. The same reasons help explain why gonorrhea and syphilis rates in the United States are far higher among African-Americans than they are among whites, Dr. Wasserheit believes.

So how can you be smart when it comes to STDs? You can start by reading the chapter in this book on practicing safer sex (see page 201) and keeping in mind the following tips.

Be a professor of history. Any man who has multiple sex partners needs to discuss his sexual history with his doctor as openly and as regularly as he discusses his diet and his exercise regimen. Don't, however, wait for your doctor to raise the subject. "You may need to take the initiative," says Dr. Wasserheit. "Many physicians are not very comfortable taking sexual histories."

Besides the sexual history, an examination of the genitals and other areas of the body for any signs of STDs should also be a part of every checkup routine. Laboratory tests can be conducted if either of those two steps indicate they're advisable.

Be a student of history. Just as you should be forthcoming about your own history, don't be afraid to inquire about a potential partner's history, suggests James H. Gilbaugh Jr., M.D., a urologist in Portland, Oregon, and author of *Men's Private Parts*. It may seem embarrassing or rude to broach the subject, but it's better to be a little embarrassed than a lot infected. To get over the awkwardness, you may want to broach the subject by volunteering your history, leaving her to do the same. And if she doesn't get the hint by then, don't be shy—ask.

Protect each other. Even if you've assured each other you're safe, it would pay to protect yourself by practicing safe sex anyway. This is especially true if you've just met or either of you has had more than one sexual partner recently, says Dr. Gilbaugh. This is not about trust—unless you've just been tested (and even then that's no guarantee; some STDs don't show up in tests for a long time) or have been abstinent for years, neither one of you may know for sure that you're absolutely safe.

Block the viral highway. Having an STD can make you more susceptible to AIDS. That's especially true of herpes or syphilis because those diseases rupture the skin, making it easier for the virus that causes AIDS to get into your bloodstream. Getting treatment helps: Dr. Wasserheit cites a study that found that among people who sought treatment for STD symptoms, the chances of contracting HIV were reduced by as much as 40 percent.

Test at home. Finding out whether you have HIV has been made a lot more convenient than it used to be with the introduction of home test kits. They can be ordered over the phone or purchased at local drugstores and require pricking a finger for a blood sample, which you then mail in for analysis. Other tests that don't require a blood sample are also in the works. For more information, call the CDC's National AIDS hotline at (800) 342-2437.

6

THE TEENS

YOUR CHANGES

Remember when you were a kid, blithely playing baseball, hanging out on the corner, and tormenting girls? And remember how those days of carefree innocence came to a turbulent halt, seemingly overnight? You started getting pubic hair. Zits erupted on your face. Your once-squeaky voice began to resonate with a more manly timbre. And now you wanted to please, not tease, those girls.

What occurred, of course, was the onset of puberty during adolescence. With puberty came not only obvious physical changes, such as the few chin hairs you proudly shaved every three weeks, but the invisible surging of hormones.

Within your once-bitty body your testicles began to release higher levels of these male hormones, or androgens, most notably testosterone, into the bloodstream, says Nitya Lacroix, a sex therapist in London and author of *Love, Sex, and Intimacy*. This, in turn, created a new you. Some of the other physical changes include bigger muscles, wider shoulders, and more body hair, especially on chest and arms.

This all sounds good, but for most of us, growth occurred so haphazardly that we felt that our bodies came right out of a surreal Salvador Dalí painting. Feet grew faster than legs. Hands outgrew arms. But by the time we finished growing—in the late teens or early twenties—almost everything had become more proportionate.

THE RISE OF SEX

Most of all, there were changes inside our shorts. You were now a budding sex machine, and life would never be the same again. You were reacting to all that testosterone, and a lot of transformations—some terribly embarrassing—were occurring. Among them:

- Your testicles began producing sperm.
- Your prostate gland matured.
- Pesky erections began routinely raising their pointy little heads at inopportune times, such as when you were in first period social studies class.
- You joined millions of other adolescents on the wet dream team. These nocturnal emissions were as reliable as Yellowstone's Old Faithful, and nearly as damp.

Little wonder. During potent puberty, young men need little recovery time between erections and can ejaculate several times a day, says Dudley Seth Danoff, M.D., senior attending urologist at Cedars-Sinai Medical Center in Los Angeles and author of *Superpotency*. "In their late teens and early twenties, they are capable of having intercourse all night long," he says.

By the time you were scouring the pharmacy shelves for Clearasil, you probably knew whether it was girls, boys, or something more esoteric with whom you wanted to fulfill your erotic fantasies. In one study of male and female students in middle or high schools, 26 percent of the 12-year-olds were unsure about their sexual orientation, while only 5 percent of the 18-year-olds had doubts.

THE PHASES OF DEVELOPMENT

You may recall adolescence as one short tumultuous period in your life. Actually, it occurred in three protracted stages—early, middle, and late—according to "Facing Facts," a report by the National Commission on Adolescent Sexual Health. Here's what happens in each stage.

• Guys typically pass through the first phase between ages 11 and 15. They are undergoing body changes more rapidly than any time since infancy. Any conflicts with parents will likely reach their peak in this period. They may experiment a bit with sex, but most have their first intercourse during middle or late adolescence, the report found.

• The second stage is from ages 14 to 17. This is when guys undergo the most dramatic changes as they begin—like little Incredible Hulks—to suddenly shed their old bodies and transform themselves from boys into young men.

It's also during this second phase of puberty—around age 15, to be exact—that your penis reached its full adult size. (Look at me, I'm a man!) For most of us, this was 2 to 4 inches long when flaccid, about 6 inches when erect. But for some boys, adolescence also brought a temporary—but mortifying—enlargement of their breasts. (Look at me, I'm...a woman?)

During this period is when boys begin distancing themselves from their family and seek identity from their fellow teens. They feel invincible. They're horny. And they quite possibly will experience for the first time the bittersweet joys of falling in love.

• The final phase of puberty begins at age 17 or older. In late adolescence, young men complete the physical transformation into manhood. They are more apt to be aware of their limitations and how their past actions will affect their future. They are less likely to be influenced by peer group pressure, more likely to have a sexual relationship with somebody to whom they are committed.

At some point during adolescence, most guys calm down a bit and quit being so crazed over sex and just generally combative. This more mellow fellow often emerges after he has had sexual intercourse a few times, suggests Al Cooper, Ph.D., clinical director of the San Jose Marital and Sexuality Centre in California.

"Before you've done it, it's a mystery," Dr. Cooper says. "It means something about you—you're a man, an adult. Once you see what it's about, it's not such a mystery." (For more on puberty's affect on adult sexual attitudes, see Your Sexual Foundation on page 68).

HER CHANGES

Up to puberty, there is not a whole lot of difference between a boy and a girl, physiologically speaking. Sure, the plumbing is different, but the hormonal forces behind the disparities in adult men and women are pretty much in check. But then, the explosion happens. Just as the sudden onslaught of testosterone remakes the male body, a flow of female hormones begins the rapid transformation of a young girl to a fully developed, fertile woman.

This surge in physiological and emotional development can be divided into three stages—early, from ages 9 to 13; middle, between 13 and 16; and late, 16 and older. It's during the middle stage that the most dramatic changes occur. Boys have the same stages, by the way, but each stage occurs earlier for girls. Here, in capsule form, are the key points in the physical transformations, followed by the emotional or mental changes.

THE PHYSICAL CHANGES

At around 9 or 10 years old, girls' ovaries begin to release higher levels of sex hormones, most notably estrogen and progesterone. These hormones instruct their bodies to begin developing in new ways. For starters, their height and weight will grow quickly. Among the other changes that will occur over the next 7 years are these:

- Budding breasts. This is one of the earliest signs that a girl is becoming a woman. And she will become curvier in general as fat deposits under the skin of the breasts, buttocks, hips, and thighs are added.
- The vagina and labia grow larger, and the uterus and ovaries begin to mature.
- Growth of pubic and underarm hair occurs.
- Acne, orgasms while they dream, and insistent sexual feelings begin.
- First menstrual period occurs. It can be a year to 18 months, however, after her first menstruation before a girl starts a regular period and ovulates, or produces eggs.

This timetable is evolving, by the way. Today, most girls start menstruating when they are between 12 and 12½ years old. Evidence suggests that at the time of the American Revolution, girls had their first period when they were about 17 years old.

Like boys, girls have rapid spurts of growth, often with disproportionate results. One breast may start developing faster than the other, for example. "The rate of development of these secondary sexual characteristics can be very uneven," says Shirley Zussman, Ed.D., a certified sex and marital therapist in private practice in New York City. "It's a confusing time because adolescents are always thinking in terms of 'Am I normal?' "

THE EMOTIONAL CHANGES

Concurrent with a girl's physical makeover during puberty are emotional changes that can be difficult for her and her parents. Among them are:

- Sharp mood swings caused by the hormones washing through them and the angst-filled trials of being half-girl, half-woman
- Increasing conflicts with parents as the peer group defines more of her values
- Falling in love for the first time
- Experimenting sexually

This last point, of course, is of greatest interest to teenage boys and causes parents considerable consternation.

Because they mature emotionally and physically faster than boys, teenage girls often have their first sexual experiences with guys a few years older than they. They also tend to wait a bit longer—perhaps, in part, because of a lingering double standard in which adults wink when we guys have our first sexual foray but frown when our sister does the same. Estimates put the average age of first intercourse in the United States at 16 for boys and 17 for girls. Yet a survey by the Alan Guttmacher Institute in New York City found that 30 percent of teens had already had intercourse by age 15.

Whatever the age, a girl who began having sex during her teenage years was more likely to have succumbed to peer pressure than to the allure of your cologne. That's due, in part, to the fact that testosterone is what fuels the sex drive in both genders, and boys are saturated with a lot more of it, says Al Cooper, Ph.D., clinical director of the San Jose Marital and Sexuality Centre in California. All that testosterone makes the guys not only hornier than the girls but also more aggressive, energetic, and outgoing, Dr. Cooper says.

Plus, guys tend to see sex as a way of defining themselves, Dr. Cooper says. Girls define themselves in other ways, such as through friendships and affiliations.

Teenage girls tend to be preoccupied with the concept of sex—being liked by boys and being popular in general—rather than the act itself, says Dr. Zussman.

And while, yes, adolescent girls also rebel against their parents and undergo a sexual awakening, hormones and peer pressure aren't the only factors that determine if they will engage in sex at an early age. Studies show that socioeconomic, educational, and even geographic factors play into the equation of when a woman first becomes sexually active. If you wanted to paint a portrait of a girl more likely to be sexually active at a young age, it would look like this.

1. She would have matured physically at an early age and have low self-esteem.
2. She would have come from a dysfunctional, low-income family living in a large, inner-city community.

3. She would get poor grades in school.
4. Her mother and her sister became pregnant as teenagers, or her father did not live with the family because of death or divorce.
5. She would have tried drinking, drugs, or other risky behavior.

Conversely, a girl with college and career goals and strong religious beliefs is more apt to remain a virgin during adolescence.

WET DREAMS

The stuff is warm, wet, slimy, and just plain there. No denying it. You wake up with this wad of goo in your shorts.

If you weren't expecting this—and many boys aren't forewarned that wet dreams might soon occur—it can be quite startling, yucky, and traumatic, says psychologist Harris Teller, Ph.D., assistant professor of special programs at National University in San Diego. Dr. Teller operates a private practice and has spent 30 years working with teens at Sweetwater Union High School District in Chula Vista, California.

Boys may equate it to wetting the bed and feel horrified and guilty, says Dr. Teller.

The first wet dream is followed by, or closely follows, the first ejaculation during masturbation. The sudden appearance on the scene of ejaculate—whether emitted nocturnally or during full conscious wakefulness—marks a significant physiological passage from boyhood to manhood, and it can come as quite a revelation. For years the old cannon has faithfully just fired blanks, and now the darn thing's starting to squirt. Every time. And the strange stuff it squirts is sticky and stains things. The first wet dream comes early in the onset of puberty, when the sperm system finally gets up and running, so to speak. For most boys, that happens at or shortly after the age of 11.

Sooner or later, nearly all young men have wet dreams. They can hit as often as a dozen times a week during the teen years, though they tend to peter out by the twenties. Still, men can have them occasionally for life, particularly during periods of abstinence and during periods of high sexual activity, says Wendy Fader, Ph.D., a licensed psychologist and certified sex therapist in private practice in Boca Raton, Florida.

Why do they occur? There's no set answer for that. But sex researchers William Masters, M.D., and Virginia Johnson, formerly of the Masters and Johnson Institute in St. Louis, and others theorized that wet dreams are like a safety release valve that flips open when sexual tension is high.

Real Voices

I had my first wet dream at 11. I had a dream that I was with a girlfriend of mine and the next thing I knew, I thought I was peeing in my underwear. I filled my shorts with semen and was totally confused about what had happened. I did not discuss the incident with anyone. It was years later that I found out it was normal.

—Salesclerk, 34, Thief River Falls, Minnesota

Ejaculations, of course, are perfectly normal signs of budding manhood. The Sexuality Information and Education Council of the United States—which helps parents, school districts, and states establish sex education standards and programs—recommends that boys be explained how their sexual gear works well in advance of their first ejaculation or wet dream so that it is not traumatic or worrisome.

SEXUAL CURIOSITY

What is it about a glimpse of a little girl's underpants that makes a little boy crave more? Do we ever outgrow our desire to play "show me yours, I'll show you mine"?

Secretly studying Dad's *Playboy* magazines, conducting free medical exams in the shed, asking your most trusted friend if he can tell you just what exactly a certain sexually implicit term or phrase you heard means—does that make you a weird, maniacal, sexually obsessed kid?

Nope, say the docs. It's all normal behavior. Perfectly normal. All part of the sexual curiosity that helps make the world go round and that you hope you never lose, says Barry McCarthy, Ph.D., a psychologist in Washington, D.C., and co-author with his wife, Emily, of the book *Sexual Awareness* as well as other titles.

We male animals—boys and men—are certainly fascinated with things sexual and with things that cause us to feel sexual sensations. And we enjoy exploring them. The curiosity and exploration start in the crib.

"Boys are going to play with their penises as early as a year old," says Dr. McCarthy. "And when you talk about sex play among children, whether it's doctor or other kinds of games, it certainly occurs and is part of normal sexual development."

PHYSICAL PLEASURES

Interestingly, boys and girls satisfy their sexual curiosities differently, observes psychologist Robert Selverstone, Ph.D., who lectures and publishes papers on sexual wellness and operates a private practice in Westport, Connecticut. Dr. Selverstone says that he asked each group of students in a high school sexuality class he taught for 12 years, "What were your sources for learning about sexuality? How did you get to learn what you learned by the time you got to be 15, 16, 17, 18?"

"And very often young men would talk about unauthorized sources, if you will," says Dr. Selverstone. "That is, they would find Dad's *Playboy*, and they would find an X-rated video that one of their friends had or one of their brothers had. They listened to conversations of their brothers. They would certainly hear dirty jokes."

In contrast, Dr. Selverstone says, girls would cite titles of sex education books and pamphlets geared to young women "and other more or less authorized sources. They would mention serious, sort of formal conversations with parents or big sisters. Whereas the boys would be mostly penis/sex oriented, the girls would be more romance/bigger picture of relationships oriented."

By the time boys are 12, most view sexual acts as primarily recreational and are quite aware that their penises bring them lots of pleasure, says psychologist Harris Teller, Ph.D., assistant professor of special programs at National University in San Diego. Dr. Teller operates a private practice and has spent 30 years working with teens at Sweetwater Union High School District in Chula Vista, California.

The difference in how males and females view sex and express their sexual curiosity doesn't end with teenhood, says Dr. Selverstone. "That got spotlighted for me so wonderfully about three or four years ago when I was invited to a senior center because the seniors there had expressed a desire to talk about issues of sexuality and intimacy and connection," he says. "So I met in the morning with a half-dozen women. The person who set it up wasn't really sure they wanted to talk about sex. So I said, 'The topic is touching, touch, and we translate that in a variety of ways. There is sexual touching, there is affectionate touching, there is emotional touching—as in "that touched me." There is communication touching as in "let's keep in touch." What do you want to talk about?'

"And the women said, 'We want to talk about communication and relationships.'

"In the afternoon I met with the men. And I went through the very same preliminaries, and the men said, 'We want to talk about penises. How come I'm 70 years old and my penis doesn't work the way it did when I was 25?' "

Still curious? Read on.

PERPETUAL HORNINESS

Remember holding a book in front of your crotch while you walked—that is, while you hobbled awkwardly, uncomfortably—attempting to hide a throbbing, aching erection that felt, with each gingerly step, in danger of snapping in two?

Here's what's unfair about that.

First, the old hide-it-with-a-book trick fools no one. Second, no one tells you that the days of incredible, instantaneous, often-beyond-control erections are numbered.

Instead, biology initiates men into the world of full sexuality with the biggest doses of testosterone they'll ever experience in their lives. Spurts of the stuff pulse through the bloodstream in seemingly overwhelming amounts, producing extraordinary sensations and impulses and fantasies—and almost painfully hard erections with virtually no prompting.

A glimpse of thigh, a blouse drawing taut over a breast, a sound, a smell—that's all it takes. Boing! The old soldier, as they say, is standing at attention, twitching a little impatiently, ready for orders. And the mind is off floating through sweet never-never land.

LIFE'S LITTLE LESSONS

We may have excellent penis posture and an especially vivid and lurid fantasy life when we're 13, 14, or 15. But it's another case of all dressed up and nowhere to go, notes psychologist Harris Teller, Ph.D., assistant professor of special programs at National University in San Diego. Dr. Teller operates a private practice and has spent 30 years working with teens at Sweetwater Union High School District in Chula Vista, California.

It's simply not socially acceptable for a young teen boy to act on the urges and impulses—at least with another human being—as often as he might like to, says Dr. Teller. This is one of the great learning challenges of teenhood: developing "internal controls" and learning to cope with our sexual urges in a safe and socially acceptable manner. Adults can help with the lessons, or they can hurt us, says Dr. Teller.

They help when they accept our evolving sexuality and spiking testosterone levels and assist us in understanding it all by providing open, frank, informed communication when appropriate, he says. They can hurt by humiliating, condemning, or punishing us for natural sexual expressions.

Some of us remember a certain teacher with fondness. Dr. Teller vividly and somewhat lividly remembers a cruel teacher "who had an uncanny ability to know when a young male was sexually aroused. At that moment, she would call on him to stand and recite. She was sadistic. Because his erection would be obvious and people would laugh." True story.

The teacher's intention, Dr. Teller assumes, was to teach boys to suppress their sexual responses. It's a lesson we're under enough self-imposed pressure to learn at that point in our lives, says Dr. Teller. Subjecting a young man to ridicule and embarrassment is not a healthy way to speed along the learning, he says. How did you cope with these sorts of embarrassing situations? What lessons were forced on you by possibly well-meaning, or possibly sadistic, elders? How you feel about sex and sexuality today is influenced by these lessons, says Dr. Teller.

A separate lesson—and one nearly all of us get wrong—is self-taught. Because we know nothing else, we assume that manhood is all about a penis that jolts into action at the least provocation.

So, explains psychologist Robert Selverstone, Ph.D., who lectures and publishes papers on sexual wellness and operates a private practice in Westport, Connecticut, "as males age and get to be in their thirties, forties, fifties, sixties, they look down at their penises and say, 'Boy, what's the matter with this thing?' " Because erections increasingly become less automatic as we grow older and, at some point, tend to require physical and emotional stimulation and effort. "And that is what is normal," he says. "The period between, say, ages 15 and 30, when your hormones were so bizarre, was actually abnormal" in the, pardon the pun, long view. "But because it's the first experience we have with our penises, we don't understand that it's unusual. We assume it is the gold standard."

THE STEAM FOGS OUR PERCEPTION OF WOMEN

How men view women is very much affected by how we are biologically initiated into sexuality, notes Barry McCarthy, Ph.D., a psychologist in Washington, D.C., and co-author with his wife, Emily, of the book *Sexual Awareness* as well as other titles. Because we seethe in our juices and are stimulated at the slightest provocation, and learn to relieve the pressure through masturbation, most of us are not innately sensitive to women's needs sexually, he says.

Ask yourself: To what extent are my views of women today shaped by impressions I formed during my brief years of perpetual horniness? Considering this—and adjusting long-held teenage perceptions—can help men become more enlightened lovers, notes Dr. McCarthy. (For more on how we develop our view of women and sexuality during the puberty years, see Your Sexual Foundation on page 68.)

FIRST INTERCOURSE

Is there any greater rite of passage?

The first time. The long-awaited, long-imagined, breathlessly anticipated first time. As hard as we dream, beg, and maneuver for that first taste of the forbidden fruit, for most of us it turns out to be, as they say, just a notch on the bedpost.

It may be incredibly stimulating at the time. We may well walk on air for a few days, experiencing a warm tingle between our legs and suppressing an almost irrepressible smile. But, face it, that first time probably wasn't very good sex. Enjoyable? Likely. But good? Not from the standpoint of Olympic judges. How could it be? No one is a professional fly fisherman the first time he casts his rod. We have no experience, no technique, no skill.

We'll certainly remember it, though, says Barry McCarthy, Ph.D., a psychologist in Washington, D.C., and co-author with his wife, Emily, of the book *Sexual Awareness* as well as other titles. But, he says, it's not at all that uncommon for that first experience to be rather unsatisfactory sex.

Anything as important as "doing it" for the first time has to be a bit frightening: The anticipation and expectation levels are so high, the desire for sex is so great socially, psychologically, and physically, says Dr. McCarthy. Is it a surprise that boys often come just before or just after insertion, or can't get a hard-on, or lose it that first time? If any of those things happened to you, Dr. McCarthy bets that you didn't brag to your friends about that aspect of the experience.

For some boys, none of the shortcomings matter at the time because, fact is fact: You've crossed the threshold, you've done it, you've actually gotten into a female's pants, so to speak. That is a major milestone on the march to manhood. Your friends *will* hear about it. And then some.

Beyond its historical precedence in your existence, the first time just doesn't matter that much to many boys, agree Dr. McCarthy and psychologist Harris Teller, Ph.D., assistant professor of special programs at National University in San Diego. Dr. Teller operates a private practice and has spent 30 years working with teens at Sweetwater Union High School District in Chula Vista, California.

WHEN? WHO? WHERE?

The average age for both sexes to engage in first intercourse is between 15 and 18, according to the researchers for the *Sex in America* survey. That is just an average. Some of us start much younger. Some much later.

Want more proof that males are programmed more for sex than for love? When asked in the *Sex in America* poll what sparked their first intercourse, 51 percent of men responded that they were curious and ready for sex—more

% Sex by the Numbers

Roughly half of all American teenagers have intercourse for the first time between ages 15 and 18. Four out of five have had intercourse by the end of their teens.

SOURCE: *Sex in America*

than double the amount who said they felt affection for the girl. Interestingly, the reasons and percentages are almost perfectly reversed when women were asked about their first time.

Who are men's first sexual partners? Here's what respondents told the *Sex in America* survey folk.

- 10 percent of men had first sex after they were married
- 31 percent of men said that their first partner was someone with whom they were in love
- 49 percent said that it was with someone they knew but were not in love with
- 5 percent said it was someone they had just met
- 3 percent said it was a prostitute
- 1 percent first had sex with a stranger

Want more benchmarks? Twenty-seven percent of first-time sexual encounters were one-night stands, while only 10 percent of men are still with their first partner, according to the *Sex in America* study.

In general, we tend to find sex partners who are similar to us in age, social status, race, religious beliefs, and more. This is true of a first partner as well as the last. By similar in age, the researchers used a guideline of plus or minus five years. While that's close in age in midlife, it may seem quite disparate during the teen years.

And where did you enjoy your first intercourse? We didn't find any serious scientific studies on this, but we heard several expert opinions. A lot of kids first do it outdoors or in cars. Or nowadays, with both parents working away from home full-time in most households, at least some kids have comfortable, private beds available for at least a couple hours after school—and much less risk of getting caught than did those of us from an earlier generation.

"I've heard in my own practice from talking with kids that it's quite varied," says adolescent medicine specialist Donald E. Greydanus, M.D., at Michigan State University/Kalamazoo Center for Medical Studies and editor of the book *Caring For Your Adolescent*. "Basically, the young teen male is ready to get it wherever he can find it, and whenever the opportunity arises, and with whomever it arises, whether it's the older woman, a girl the same age, or a schoolteacher who comes on to him. Wherever, whenever, whoever. The boy just wants to become a man quickly. Girls, though, tend to be more discreet, more discerning."

WHEN IT HURTS

While Dr. McCarthy and Dr. Teller say the first time doesn't have any long-reaching effect on many of us, they also acknowledge that it *can*. The first time can matter if the female berates you or belittles you, if you're raped or injured, or if you're truly not ready emotionally for the experience and feel forced into it. Then, Dr. Teller and Dr. McCarthy say, it can have long-reaching negative effects. And that's one of the problems with the old method of fathers initiating their sons into the world of sex by taking them to houses of prostitution. It did sometimes backfire. A bored or impatient prostitute might treat an inexperienced young man roughly or caustically.

But if all goes reasonably well that first time, it is a celebrated, momentous occasion. You never forget it. But, it's not the sex that you rate all other sex by. It's just a significant blip on your sexual time line.

BRAGGING

Plop yourself into a one-on-one, male-to-male situation with a stranger—we're talking almost any age, now—and in the first couple minutes it happens. Women show up. At least in the words spoken—or in the neck-craning, eyebrow-raising body language.

One or the other of you will mention "the wife" or start talking suggestively about women, or leering at or admiring them. It's an almost-obligatory male ritual that seems to cross caste and class. Why does this happen? It's a several-part answer.

First, it's part of the sizing-up process—a sort of homophobia that has its roots in the locker-room bragging of our teen years, suggests psychologist Robert Selverstone, Ph.D., who lectures and publishes papers on sexual wellness and operates a private practice in Westport, Connecticut.

Bragging about sexual exploits, talking sexually suggestively about women, and subtly or overtly calling one another's attention to the various women in the vicinity and their attractive attributes are ways that men communicate their sexual "normalcy," their heterosexuality, to one another, says Dr. Selverstone.

It's a way of letting each other know, "You can relax around me. I'm not going to come on to you."

A PLAY FOR RESPECT

Next, telling the boys how we slept with 3, or 33, women the night before is "simply an extension of male competitiveness," says Barry McCarthy, Ph.D., a psychologist in Washington, D.C., and co-author with his wife, Emily, of the book *Sexual Awareness* as well as other titles. We're saying, in effect, "Hey, I'm a guy you should respect and admire because I know how to bed down the women."

Males, from teenhood on, "are always in a sexual competition they feel they are losing," says Dr. McCarthy. So they brag.

But male bragging begins even before that. "There is a real focus in male culture on hierarchy and power that I think begins well before issues of sexuality come to the fore," points out Dr. McCarthy. "When you see the 5-year-olds and 6-year-olds and 11-year-olds in terms of, 'What's your batting average,' 'What position do you play,' 'How come you can't catch the ball,' that sort of stuff, you see that sexuality just becomes an additional piece of that."

Another key reason teenagers brag about sex is that males are jerked around by spiking and plummeting testosterone levels during the puberty years, says psychologist Harris Teller, Ph.D., assistant professor of special programs at National University in San Diego. Dr. Teller operates a private practice and has spent 30 years working with teens at Sweetwater Union High School District in Chula Vista, California.

"When they are on the low end, they may feel angry and hurt and then need to do something to build their egos," says Dr. Teller. "They do this by trying to outdo somebody else." The effort can be a tale of an imagined exploit. "Teens have very active fantasy lives," says Dr. Teller. Or it can be a very real competition of some sort.

AT ANOTHER'S EXPENSE

Young women get dragged through the mud when young men start bragging to other young men about how they "screwed" so-and-so, says Dr. Selverstone. "It's a matter of exploiting a female in order to lift your self-esteem. Someone's the screw-er and someone's the screw-ee," he points out.

Is there a more healthful way to fill that need other than talking about our sexual exploits with women?

"Sure," says Dr. Selverstone. "There is a more healthful way to fill the need to feel good about ourselves than through competition, but I think that it would require a major cultural overhaul. We're coming from a culture that puts so much emphasis just on winning. Just on being the best."

That's why sexual bragging—and bragging in general—slops over from male teenhood and into adulthood, say Dr. Teller, Dr. McCarthy, and Dr. Selverstone.

Real Voices

I'm in my mid-fifties and every Sunday morning play softball with a group of guys whose ages go from 17 to 63. And yesterday morning at one point as we were doing batting and fielding practice, I shouted out to nobody in particular, "Isn't this great? The sun is out. We're playing softball with a group of guys. What could be better?" And somebody said, "Getting a blow job at the same time." I shared that with my wife when I came home and said, "I suspect that women playing softball would not have generated that same kind of response."

—Robert Selverstone, Ph.D., a psychologist who lectures and publishes papers on sexual wellness and operates a private practice in Westport, Connecticut

So take control: If you find yourself constantly needing to brag about your exploits, Dr. Selverstone suggests that you ask yourself the following questions.

- Do I look to myself or to others for validation that I'm adequate?
- Do I compare myself to other people, or am I able to say to myself, "I can be my own standard for this. I am good enough and I don't need to look to other people and compare myself to other people."
- What does it mean to have scored? And what's the sense of scoring if scoring means somebody gets scored upon?

GETTING CAUGHT

It hardly seems fair. At the point in life when the sexual urge is the greatest, society conspires to offer us the least opportunities to express it.

Not many teens have their own apartments.

Yet, the comprehensive *Sex in America* survey tells us, 80 percent of American kids these days have intercourse before they graduate from teenhood. So where do they do it? The answer is obvious: Anyplace they can. And sometimes they get caught with their pants down, as the saying goes.

For some, getting caught may be validation. Maybe a hoped-for consequence. The boy wants all his friends to know he is making it with the universally lusted-after cutie. Getting caught is proof and a form of bragging. So he's intentionally careless or even sets up a situation where friends will stumble upon him and his lover in the act.

For some it may be hormones, says psychologist Harris Teller, Ph.D., assistant professor of special programs at National University in San Diego. Dr. Teller operates a private practice and has spent 30 years working with teens at Sweetwater Union High School District in Chula Vista, California. The hormonally driven urges just overpower intellect and logic.

You start making out and getting more and more excited and suddenly making it is about the most important thing in the world. The fact that there are parents in the next room, or police on foot patrol who regularly shine their flashlights in the windows of the cars parked on the hill overlooking the glittery city lights, suddenly are silly, oh-so-distant concerns. What matters is the passion and hunger and the desire thumping and pounding between your legs and pulsing throughout your whole body.

"That is one of the reasons why people get caught," says Dr. Teller. "The sexual tension builds up as they get more and more involved sexually and they become less and less aware of anything that isn't happening somewhere between the navel and the knees."

YOU'LL BOIL IN OIL FOR THAT

In his 1973 book *How I Became an Authority on Sex*, Jim Moran tells how when he was a boy, a Baptist deacon stumbled upon him and a neighbor girl making love in the woods. The deacon physically forced them apart, roared and hollered at them, quoted chapter and verse, painted word pictures of the fiery hell and vats of boiling oil that awaited them if they ever engaged in premarital sex again, and literally instilled the fear of God in Moran. He says he refrained from intercourse for six years after the incident.

Adults these days are much less likely to try to scare kids out of having sex or tell them that sex is wrong, says psychologist Robert Selverstone, Ph.D., who lectures and publishes papers on sexual wellness and operates a private practice in Westport, Connecticut.

"From talking with kids," says Dr. Selverstone, "I know that the message parents communicate most often is not that 'this is a bad thing that you are doing.' It tends to be more along the line of, 'Do it with the right person. Don't take advantage of someone; don't exploit anybody. That's not nice.' But they are told, 'Sex is a good thing.'

"The messages seem to be somewhat different for females than for males. For females the messages seem to be, 'Sex is a good thing, but wait, wait, wait as long as you possibly can.' For males they tend to be, 'Anything you want to do is fine—just don't get in trouble, don't get her pregnant, don't get the disease.' "

And, yes, kids do still get caught. Does it traumatize them? What if their parents scream and cry and yell and ground them? What if the cops drag them down to the station and call their parents, who then scream and cry and yell and ground them? Lasting damage? Lifelong repercussions?

Touchy and embarrassing at the time, for sure, says Dr. Selverstone. But for a boy, he's going to get some long mileage out of it when he gets back with his peers. He has probably just edged up a couple notches in their respectful eyes.

Long-lasting damage? Maybe the contrary, says Jack Morin, Ph.D., a psychotherapist and sexologist from the San Francisco Bay area and author of *The Erotic Mind*. If the experience reinforces an inner idea that sex is somehow naughty or illicit, that can be a tremendous trigger for future fantasy and pleasure. The idea that you are doing something private and sneaky and somehow illicit is a major turn-on for most adults, he says.

If the parents lose it, is that going to sexually or socially inhibit the kids?

"No more than any other time. Parents typically explode many times in front of their children. I don't think that that time is going to be any worse than any time they explode about anything else," says adolescent medicine specialist Donald E. Greydanus, M.D., at Michigan State University/Kalamazoo Center for Medical Studies and editor of the book *Caring For Your Adolescent*.

POINTERS FOR PARENTS

There *are* parents who let their kids and their lovers live together in the family home. There are parents who take a hands-off, eyes-closed approach to their kids' sexual dalliances and pretend nothing is happening, all the while allowing it to happen. And there are parents who forbid their kids to engage in sex.

There is no easy answer to what approach to take, says Dr. Greydanus. It is best to ask your kids how they feel about kids their age having sex, to listen to them, and to explain your feelings about it, says Dr. Greydanus. All in a nonpunitive and nonprobing way.

And when you discover that your kids are sexually active, realize that they are unlikely to quit being sexually active—and that a majority of kids do become sexually active before age 18, says Dr. Greydanus. What you should do, Dr. Greydanus says, is help your kids get the information and tools they need to practice safe sex and healthy relationships and avoid pregnancy and disease.

It may be easiest to take your kids to a good pediatrician, let the doctor know the nature of the visit, and then get out of the way and let the kids and doctor talk, says Dr. Greydanus. What they talk about is confidential, he notes. But at least you'll know they are getting good, accurate information and help.

Dr. Greydanus notes that he is speaking both as the parent of four daughters and as a pediatrician who counsels kids daily. What he does as a pediatrician easily, openly, calmly, he could probably never do with his own daughters, he says.

Establishing good communication with your kids about sex and sexuality issues is important, says Dr. Greydanus. But it is not insurance.

"Even if you do provide good sex education for your children, you still may catch them in the act," Dr. Greydanus says. "Providing sex education does not guarantee that your children will not become sexually active before they should, and the opposite is true as well. Just because you withhold sex education doesn't mean they're not going to become sexually active. So, if you find your child involved in sex, better have a good pediatrician, family doctor, someone you can call and work this through with. Because you may be so angry and upset you won't know what to do. Ideally, what one would do is get both of the participants involved into some kind of contraception immediately. The biggest issue to me is a million-plus teenagers who get pregnant every year and very few of them want to get pregnant at that time. And millions of cases of sexually transmitted diseases. Parents need to realize that, if a child is sexually involved with someone, they have crossed a barrier and they probably will continue to be sexually active. You're not going to stop it."

Ideally, says Dr. Greydanus, if your kids are sexually active, you probably should provide a safe atmosphere for them. "But, as a parent, I wouldn't. I couldn't. I'd be too furious."

Does failure to do this—so the kids must seek sex furtively in the back of cars, in the bushes, in the wilderness, on the sly at home after school—harm the kids' sexual development by sending a message that sex is somehow bad or wrong?

That's probably not really the message being sent, says Dr. Greydanus. Rather, regardless of words used, the message the kid probably gets is: I, as a parent, do not feel it is socially acceptable or appropriate for you, my child, to be having sex at your age. This isn't what I wanted you doing, and I'm shocked and hurt and angry. And I, as a parent, have a right to have those feelings and do not have to help you do something I don't think you should be doing.

And, Dr. Greydanus advises, the parent should make a loving effort to also communicate this message: Knowing you are now sexually active, I have a parental responsibility to help you maintain your health and well-being, regardless of whether I am pleased with the choice you have made about becoming sexually active. (For more on communicating with your kids about sex, see Teaching Children about Sex on page 444.)

CRUSHES

At some point in teenhood we realize we're falling in and out of love about 100 times a day. And that's not counting the really serious, longer-lasting attractions involving four, five, six females at a time—some of whom are 10 or 15 years our senior, some married, some whose names we don't even know.

Like the clerk in the window-coverings department at JCPenney. Suddenly, we find that almost daily we need to buy a curtain ring, rod, or other inexpensive piece of hardware. So we spend, oh, 15, 20, 30 minutes in the department each afternoon after school studying the various forms of window-coverings on display and all the literature describing them.

Who says we outgrow this?

Thankfully, it's not with the same intensity of those roily days of puberty, but most men continue to be drawn to women they find attractive. Often, we momentarily linger in their presence and fantasize about them and treasure every wee bit of attention that such women lavish upon us. But as grown men, hopefully, we aren't quite the lovesick puppies that we once were.

It was the lessons of teenhood that taught us to develop healthy control over such behavior and urges, says psychologist Harris Teller, Ph.D., assistant professor of special programs at National University in San Diego. Dr. Teller operates a private practice and has spent 30 years working with teens at Sweetwater Union High School District in Chula Vista, California.

Through trial and error, success, and embarrassments, we learn ways to actually communicate with—and forge positive friendships and working relationships with—members of the opposite sex to whom we are drawn emotionally and sexually. And we learn that actually communicating is much more satisfying than just swooning in an attractive female's presence and silently fueling a hopeless crush.

The crushes—"they go with the territory" of male teenhood, says Dr. Teller. "You fall in and out of love all the time."

When it happens in later life, you learn to joke about it and not take infatuation so seriously.

When is a crush harmful? What if it goes on for weeks, months, years?

It's only harmful if, because of the crush, you surrender control to the person who is the object of your desires and, as a result, do things that are damaging to your health and well-being, says adolescent medicine specialist Donald E. Greydanus, M.D., at Michigan State University/Kalamazoo Center for Medical Studies and editor of the book *Caring For Your Adolescent*.

Real Voices

"My first big crush was my science teacher. It was right after the war when young attractive teachers came into education for the very first time. She was tall and blond and was unlike anything I had ever seen in all of my entire life. I was 15. I was absolutely and totally and helplessly in love with her. I would have done anything for her. I admired her and I wanted to be around her. I was there all the time. I was cleaning cages and sweeping floors and doing all kinds of things."

—Psychologist Harris Teller, 64, Ph.D., assistant professor of special programs at National University in San Diego

Otherwise, Dr. Greydanus says, a crush can go on for years and perhaps be a bit distracting, but not really be a problem. Crushes are more often a problem for girls than for boys, he says, because under the weight of a serious crush a girl is more likely to accede to pressure for sex and may end up pregnant or with a sexually transmitted disease.

TALKING WITH PARENTS

Stand-up comics have no qualms about it, but talking about sex is something that many of us find awkward. Unless we act like comics—joking about it, bragging, or exaggerating. Or, with a group of men, making crude and lustful talk. That's easy. But talking openly, honestly, intimately, directly about sex is just plain difficult.

This awkwardness may have roots in the family environment in which we were raised, notes psychologist Harris Teller, Ph.D., assistant professor of special programs at National University in San Diego. Dr. Teller operates a private practice and has spent 30 years working with teens at Sweetwater Union High School District in Chula Vista, California.

If our parents were embarrassed or uncomfortable talking, chances are that we developed the same attitude. But it's not one that we want to pass on to our kids. The comfort and ease with which children and teens adjust to their sexuality affects the quality, and ultimately the success, of their adult sexual relationships, says adolescent medicine specialist Donald E. Greydanus, M.D., at Michigan State University/Kalamazoo Center for Medical Studies and editor of the book *Caring For Your Adolescent*.

LET'S TALK SEX

You need to start talking with your children long before adolescence so that the lines of communication are open and stay open during the stormy teen years. You need to be an "askable" parent. Sex educators tell us that it is especially important for adolescents to feel that they can ask questions of their parents and other trusted adults about sexual issues and trust the responses. These days, parents are making greater efforts to facilitate this, says Dr. Teller.

But a rite of teenhood for most boys involves a period during which they don't want to talk to their parents about anything or reveal anything to them about what they are doing. Dr. Greydanus calls this an "almost-catatonic state" that is not rare among teens. There are ways to break through it constructively. (For advice, see Teaching Children about Sex on page 444.)

Not all parents make the effort or know how to open the lines of communication about sex. The best advice is to open those communication chapters early—even before your child hits puberty. Let him know what is about to happen to his body. Then continue the dialogue throughout the teens. It's particularly important that boys be braced for the sudden changes that will slam them when they hit puberty, notes the Sexuality Information and Education Council of the United States. Otherwise, they may be embarrassed or ashamed by perfectly normal events of puberty.

Despite increasing awareness that parents need to be able to communicate well about sexual issues so that their kids will develop healthy sexual attitudes, the onus for sex education continues to fall primarily upon mothers, says Barry McCarthy, Ph.D., a psychologist in Washington, D.C., and co-author with his wife, Emily, of the book *Sexual Awareness* as well as other titles.

"The person who ought to have a more positive influence as a sexual model to boys is the father, but you seldom see that," says Dr. McCarthy. "If fathers say anything at all to their sons, it's about their own extramarital or premarital affairs." Dads, says Dr. McCarthy, tend to take a male locker-room-talk approach with their sons. "They seldom talk about marital sex or problems or dysfunctions. What they tell them is, 'Go for it. Don't get anyone pregnant. Don't get sexually transmitted diseases.'"

Ironically, Dr. McCarthy says, girls generally get a completely different message, one of "wait as long as you can."

The easiest way for a father to instigate substantial, helpful sex talk with his son is "not just to buy him a book but to read it with him and discuss it with him," says Dr. McCarthy.

EARLY MARRIAGE

Few young men march to the altar with the muzzle of a shotgun nuzzling the small of their back these days.

Pregnancy always will be a trauma for unprepared teens, but our society no longer shames pregnant young women to the extent it once did. We don't hide them or ship them off to "homes for wayward girls." Nor do we necessarily feel that an early marriage is the necessary, proper, honorable resolution for an "out-of-wedlock" pregnancy.

Those changes in perception may be two of many factors fueling the decline in teen marriages, notes psychologist Robert Selverstone, Ph.D., who lectures and publishes papers on sexual wellness and operates a private practice in Westport, Connecticut.

Interestingly, kids in general are having sex at younger ages than ever and at the same time are waiting longer to get married.

Incidentally, the rate of teen pregnancy has dropped significantly since the 1950s, reports the National Commission on Adolescent Sexual Health. In 1955, 90 of every 1,000 women between age 15 and 19 gave birth. By 1992 the number was down to 61.

At one time not so long ago, notes Dr. Selverstone, sex in relationships was reserved mostly for those teens who were very seriously involved and/or engaged. "The length of time from holding somebody's hand to going to bed with them was fairly extended. Currently, the process is far more compact. So a kid says, 'I've been going with this girl a long time and we haven't had intercourse yet.' And I say, 'How long has it been?' He says, 'It has been two weeks.' It is astonishing to people from another generation that they're talking weeks instead of years."

The Exam: Are You Ready for Marriage?

Shakespeare knew that "love is blind," but it was centuries before David H. Olson, Ph.D., a family psychologist at the University of Minnesota in Minneapolis, developed a cure.

He created a 125-question exam and follow-up sessions that help couples confront issues essential to a successful marriage but rarely dealt with during courtship. The program helps them assess the character, background, temperament, and attitudes of their potential spouse, plus their strengths and weaknesses as a couple. It also offers help in developing communication and conflict-resolution skills and identifies potential problem areas that need more discussion.

More than 600,000 couples have participated in Dr. Olson's program— PREPARE (which stands for Premarital Personal and Relationship Evaluation)— which is administered by 20,000 trained counselors, clergy, and volunteers nationwide, says syndicated columnist Michael J. McManus, president of Marriage Savers in Bethesda, Maryland, and author of *Marriage Savers*.

On the test, individuals are asked whether they agree strongly, agree, are undecided, disagree, or disagree strongly to statements dealing with expectations, personality traits, communications, conflict resolution, money matters, leisure activities, sex, children, roles, religion, values, and the family environment in which they were raised.

Some typical statements, says McManus, are:

- I can easily share my positive and negative feelings with my partner.
- We have decided how to handle our finances.
- My partner has some habits I dislike.

Increased sexual intimacy among young single people is a factor in the rising failure of marriages as well as in the delay of marriage among young people, contends syndicated columnist Michael J. McManus, president of Marriage Savers in Bethesda, Maryland, and author of *Marriage Savers*.

WHAT COUPLES NEED TO KNOW

Teen marriages, McManus says, are twice as likely as other first marriages to end in divorce. "Basically," he says, "a teenager is not really grown, is not an adult yet, doesn't know who he is, and therefore is not ready to make a commitment to someone else."

More than seventy percent of marriages take place in a church or synagogue, says McManus, but most of them don't prepare couples—young couples or older couples—for marriage. "Most churches are simply wedding machines, wedding factories. They just grind out the weddings without much

- The disagreements we currently have will decrease after the wedding.
- I have some concerns about how my partner will be as a parent.
- At times I feel pressure to participate in activities my partner enjoys.

The test is sent off to be computer-scored, then two feedback sessions are scheduled. At the first, the major issues like money and communications are discussed. At the second, the differences in family backgrounds are reviewed and discussed. This is particularly important, says McManus, "because where each person grew up defines for them what a family is. And they need to talk through what it is they liked about the home they grew up in, what it is they are going to do differently."

Dr. Olson urges counselors to help the couple work through at least one issue during the sessions using the "Ten Steps for Resolving Couple Differences" that they are presented in writing.

To locate someone in your area trained in administering the PREPARE program, write: PREPARE, P.O. Box 190, Minneapolis, MN 55440-0190.

Many Catholic churches administer a similar program called FOCCUS, says McManus. To find out more, call the local diocese or write: FOCCUS, Family Life Office, 3214 North 60th Street, Omaha, NE 68104-3495, or call (402) 551-9003.

There are many other ways to get premarital counseling, adds Shirley Zussman, Ed.D., a certified sex and marital therapist in private practice in New York City. She suggests that you and your fiancée check out the credentials, experience, and goals of any program you are considering. Some programs have very specific philosophies that may not match yours.

Sex by the Numbers

Average age of a groom at the time of his first marriage:

1964 24
1990 27

Average age of a bride at the time of her first marriage:

1964 21
1990 25

SOURCE: National Center for Health Statistics

thought on what it takes to make a marriage work." So McManus has convinced ecumenical councils in 60 cities to implement extensive marital counseling programs that include and require premarital counseling—not just for engaged teens but for all couples considering marriage.

"In part, the problem is that sex gives the illusion of intimacy, makes you feel close to the other person. But if you have not talked through the issues, it is kind of a hollow illusion," McManus observes.

The falling-in-love process is not one of seeking out one another's differences but, rather, glossing over and ignoring them. "You don't confront the disagreements. And the most fundamental issues—like money—are not addressed at all," says McManus.

Suddenly, McManus says, you're married to someone who you realize you don't really understand very well and who doesn't understand you very well. "This comes as a surprise to nearly everyone, it seems. The bloom falls off the rose very quickly," he says.

"One of the answers to that is the premarital inventory called PREPARE (Premarital Personal and Relationship Evaluation)," says McManus. It's a 125-question exam administered by psychologists, clergy, and trained volunteers. McManus urges churches to train happily married members—mentor couples—to administer the exam and discuss its results with engaged couples.

PREPARE profiles each partner's beliefs and feelings about many issues crucial to a successful marriage and gauges the couple's strengths, weaknesses, compatibilities, and conflicts. PREPARE forces reality into the open. The test, McManus says, has a track record of predicting with 80 percent accuracy which marriages will end in divorce.

What's interesting, says McManus, "is that 10 percent of the couples who take PREPARE break their engagements when they see the results."

That number, he says, should be higher. One counselor in private practice, who requires that couples taking the exam commit to at least six counseling sessions at a cost of $350, reports that 42 percent of the couples call off the marriage, says McManus. He encourages churches to also offer extended counseling.

AFTER THE FACT

So you married young? Still married? Congratulations, McManus would say. You made it over some big bumps. But you're not out of the woods. "Every marriage," he says, "needs a midcourse correction" to jolt it back to life, improve communications, and rekindle the flames. And those who marry young may need it a little sooner. (For his precise, one-weekend prescription—and lifelong approach—see Reinventing Romance on page 406.)

Did you miss out on anything by marrying early? Will you regret that you didn't gain greater sexual experience, sniff more roses?

Probably not for most young men these days, says Dr. Selverstone. Because most have experienced more than one partner by the time they are 18 or 20, he says. But if they haven't, then yes, he says, they might sometimes wonder what it might have been like if they had.

Does it become a major issue with young marrieds?

Unlikely, says Dr. Selverstone.

"I haven't seen that either from what I have observed in my own practice nor in any research I've done or read," says adolescent medicine specialist Donald E. Greydanus, M.D., at Michigan State University/Kalamazoo Center for Medical Studies and editor of the book *Caring For Your Adolescent*. "The real issue that arises when people marry too young is that they change over time" and the marriages don't survive the changes, he says.

"You don't hear or see research saying that the people who marry young are resentful or regretful because they didn't have more premarital sexual experience. It's just that the marriages don't last," says Dr. Greydanus.

"It's simply very hard to meet somebody at 17 years of age and hang in there when you're changing all the time," adds Dr. Greydanus. "Even if it's a young woman—say, an 18-year-old girl—marrying a 25-year-old guy. Maybe he doesn't change so much, but she does."

Needs change, expectations change, and the desire to be with someone more compatible and more understanding of the more grown-up you, are the most common issues raised with doctors and counselors by couples who marry too young, says Dr. Greydanus.

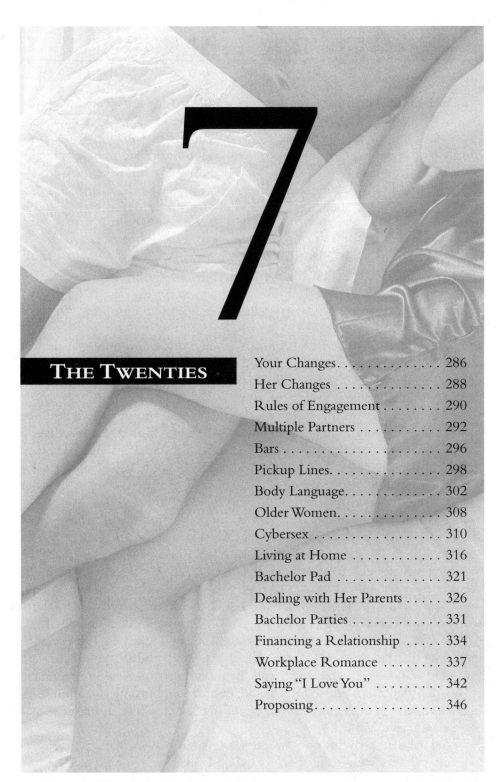

7

THE TWENTIES

YOUR CHANGES

When he was in his twenties, former New York Jets quarterback Joe Namath boasted, "I can't wait until tomorrow...'cause I get better looking every day." Indeed, this is the decade when you are in your physical prime. Your twenties and thirties is when you will add most of your muscle bulk and be at your strongest. But even the swashbuckling Namath's knees were already hurting in his twenties. And for guys who aren't professional athletes, there are other physical changes, real and potential, already occurring in this decade.

SEX-RELATED CHANGES

• Testicular cancer. This form of cancer is rare—only about 3 men in 100,000 per year contract it. But if you're going to get it, odds are that it will be during your twenties. Testicular cancer is the most common form of cancer among guys ages 15 to 35.

What should you look for? A lump on the otherwise smooth, even surface of a testicle. Enlargement of a testicle. A dull ache in the lower abdomen or groin. A sudden collection of fluid in a testicle or in the scrotum. Pain or discomfort in a testicle or in the scrotum.

Testicular cancer is unusual in that it doesn't seem to be caused by poor health habits, like smoking or a high-fat diet. Experts think that it may have a genetic cause or that it may form after a bout of the mumps virus. Another theory is that it is related to a condition found in some babies with undescended testicles. Whatever the cause, the cure rate is nearly 100 percent if the cancer is detected early.

• Sexually transmitted diseases. You're single, you're fit, you're horny, and you're in your twenties. So it follows that this is when you are most at risk to contract a sexually transmitted disease, or STD. In fact, two-thirds of the 12 million new cases of STDs in the United States each year are in people under age 25.

There are more than 20 STDs lurking in the shadows of love. The most worrisome of these diseases, of course, is AIDS. That's because it's usually fatal; AIDS is the leading cause of death among males ages 25 to 44. Other STDs include gonorrhea, herpes, genital warts, crabs, and syphilis—the disease that turned Al Capone into a madman. But the most common STD in America is chlamydia, whose symptoms are a penile discharge, a burning sensation during urination, and sometimes a swelling of the testicles. (For more on sexual diseases, see page 253.)

• Sexual desire. By his mid-twenties, a guy has been as flat-out horny as he ever will be. "Men reach their sexual peak in their early twenties, if not their late teens," says Dudley Seth Danoff, M.D., senior attending urologist at

Cedars-Sinai Medical Center in Los Angeles and author of *Superpotency*. Erections are less frequent, and the refractory period—the time needed to rest between ejaculations—has grown a bit longer. Luckily, this is a slow, gradual decline.

OTHER CHANGES

• Accident proneness. This is the decade for feeling invulnerable and the high-risk behavior that accompanies it, whether it's drinking and driving or diving off the balcony of a hotel into—maybe—the swimming pool. Accidents are the most common cause of death in the twenties, followed by homicide and suicide.

• Other cancers. In addition to testicular cancer, other rare forms of cancer also tend to strike around this age. One of them is leukemia, which forms in the blood, bone marrow, and spleen. Another is Hodgkin's disease. It strikes in the lymphatic system, the nodes and vessels that circulate germ-fighting lymph and filter out germs and assorted crud from the body. And finally, there are brain tumors.

• Hearing. Your high-frequency hearing may begin to deteriorate. But even if that does happen, you likely won't detect much change in your hearing until you reach your sixties. Why? That's when your low-frequency hearing begins to decline, and much of daily audible sound is in the lower frequencies.

• Acne. Our body's production of an oily substance called sebum slows down. This is the stuff of some of the worst teenage angst: acne. We may still get zits, but less often.

• Sports injuries. By age 25 a lot of guys have become "weekend athletes." They have jobs, perhaps a family. They don't have the time for sports and workouts like they once did. And when they do play a weekend game of basketball, touch football, or whatever, their muscles are more likely to cramp, strain, pull, and tear.

• Evaporation. A human embryo is about 90 percent water; a newborn baby is 80 percent. When we become adults, we start losing more and more water, which is essential for life. Those with higher percentages of body fat also have a lower percentage of their total weight made up by body water, says Waneen Wyrick Spirduso, Ed.D., professor in the department of kinesiology and health education at the University of Texas in Austin and author of *Physical Dimensions of Aging*. Some of us who live to be really old may see water account for less than 50 percent of our body weight.

HER CHANGES

It's hard to imagine women looking any better than they do in their twenties. Breasts firm and upward. Skin taut and smooth. Hair that shimmers like a mirage. But women's bodies, like our own, have already become subject to the vagaries of lifestyle and time.

SEX-RELATED CHANGES

• Sexually transmitted diseases. Hey, you're not the only one sowing wild oats in your twenties. And women are even more susceptible than you to sexually transmitted diseases, or STDs, because their vaginas are warm and moist—cozy places for bacteria and viruses to make themselves at home. Guys, on the other hand, urinate away many of these unwanted tenants before they can take up residency in our bodies.

Women are twice as likely as men to contract gonorrhea and chlamydia. These STDs can cause a woman to become infertile, or complicate or lose her pregnancy. As for AIDS, don't think that women are less susceptible just because they make up a minority of total caseload. In fact, women are the fastest-growing group infected with HIV, the virus that is the precursor to AIDS. Roughly 60 percent of heterosexually transmitted cases of HIV are women.

• Urinary tract infections. As young women become sexually active, about 20 percent of them will get at least one urinary tract infection. They often occur as a result of a penis passing on a germ to the urethra. An infected woman has frequent urges to urinate, a burning sensation during urination, and other unpleasant symptoms.

• Vaginal infections. If she escapes a urinary tract infection, a woman may still get a vaginal infection. There are three: yeast infection, bacterial vaginosis, and trichomoniasis. Yeast infections leave a woman with an intense desire to scratch where it isn't polite, and they often produce a discharge. Excessive douching and hormonal changes caused by birth control pills or pregnancy are among the culprits.

Bacterial vaginosis is the most common vaginal infection and often flares up when a woman has several sexual partners. That's not always the case, however. So if a woman gets it, don't assume the worst. The infection occurs when the natural pH balance of the vagina is disrupted. This often produces a fishy odor, especially after sex.

Trichomoniasis is caused by a parasite. The only way a woman can get it is from an infected partner. Symptoms may include a smelly white, grayish-green, or yellow discharge.

OTHER CHANGES

• Arthritis. Rheumatoid arthritis is much less common than osteoarthritis and even more debilitating. It's not clear what causes it. Men and women get the disease about equally, but three times as many women as men develop symptoms severe enough to require medical care. It usually strikes in the prime of life—between ages 20 and 40. Take a look at an x-ray of an arthritic hand—it's gnarled and clawlike—and you get an idea of how crippling the disease can be.

Some doctors, such as Bruce Hirsch, M.D., assistant professor of medicine in the division of infectious diseases at North Shore University Hospital in Manhasset, New York, think that rheumatoid arthritis is an autoimmune rather than a degenerative disease, meaning that the body mistakenly thinks the lining of joints is foreign material and attacks with its own immune system. This causes inflammation, redness, and joint pain, especially in the fingers, Dr. Hirsch says. Patients also appear undernourished and chronically ill.

• Binge eating. This is mostly a female phenomenon. Young women who are on strict diets or who are depressed are thought to be most vulnerable. Though it's not as serious as other eating disorders, such as bulimia and anorexia nervosa, it can cause a woman to become obese and put her at risk for heart disease, diabetes, and other ailments.

By the way, if a woman not only binges but tries to purge the food through self-induced vomiting, overuse of laxatives, or excessive exercise, she may be bulimic.

• Jawbone problems. In their twenties and the next two decades, women are most susceptible to a condition called temporomandibular disorder. It's a malfunction of the temporomandibular joints, the two hinges that connect the jawbones to the bones at the temples.

Men may also be afflicted with this disorder, but usually neither they nor women require medical treatment. In cases where medical help is sought, female patients outnumber males by about five to one.

They complain of headaches, earaches, and facial pain and may hear a clicking or popping noise when they eat, talk, or move their jaws. Some can barely open their mouths.

Most cases are a result of muscular problems created by chewing gum or grinding teeth. Others are hereditary or are caused by an injury to the jaw.

RULES OF ENGAGEMENT

The women's movement. The rise of women's athletics. Increasing sexual equality in the workplace. Growing sensitivity of men. You'd think that with all the ways society has changed, that on the edge of a new millennium, women—particularly young women—would finally be comfortable taking the lead in asking guys out for dates. We might as well have believed that Madonna is chaste.

Certainly our changing times have given women the *option* to take the sexual initiative, says Warren Farrell, Ph.D., San Diego–based author of *The Myth of Male Power* and *Why Men Are the Way They Are*.

The reality, however, is that little has changed. "Women very rarely do anything for men in these initial stages of sexual initiative—taking or asking out—unless it's for a man they sense they are more interested in than is being reciprocated," says Dr. Farrell.

That doesn't mean that the rules of dating a woman in her twenties haven't changed. Women are far more educated, worldly, open-minded, fun-oriented than in decades past. In part 1 of this book, there are chapters that offer universal wisdom regarding where to meet women, how to interact with women, even how to initiate sex. Here (and with each of the "decade" sections that follow) we offer wisdom customized for women in a particular age group. What follows are some general rules of engagement for a woman in her twenties.

WHERE TO MEET WOMEN

So you'd like to ask a woman in her twenties to accompany you skydiving. The problem is that you're not sure where to meet her. Here are some places to hunt.

• At school. A lot of people in their twenties are still attending a college or university. Needless to say, this is a great place to meet attractive women in a natural way.

• Laundromats. They have to wash their laundry, same as you. And some Laundromats now have book racks or video games to make this chore less unpleasant.

• Health clubs. Like college, it's almost impossible not to meet young women here. And since they're working out, they often are in great shape and wearing attire that proves it.

• At your favorite activities. This tip applies no matter what age woman you want to meet. Look in those places that cater to your own interests. If you like bicycling, join a cycling club. If you enjoy cultural activities, visit museums and art galleries. "Always carry business cards with you, and always be prepared to hand out a business card no matter where you are because you might run into someone who has a similar interest to yours," says William F. Fitzgerald, Ph.D., a marital and sex therapist in private practice in San Jose, California, who answers sex questions online for *Men's Health* Daily (the Web site of *Men's Health* magazine).

What Women Want

Okay, now that you've made contact with a woman in her twenties, how do you go about winning her over? By showing her a good time. "They're looking to have a lot of fun and doing really spectacular, stupendous things," says Dr. Fitzgerald. "They're still clawing their way to the top in terms of their careers, but they really want to enjoy life to the fullest." Here are some ideas.

Plan an exotic date. You needn't sleep in hammocks in a guerrilla-infested jungle, but try something more daring than riding the tea cups at Disney World. A mountain hike? A long bike ride? That outdoor international music festival? All good ideas.

Be romantic. Go on a hot-air balloon ride at sunrise, or have drinks and dinner someplace with a view at sunset. Give her flowers for no other reason than you were thinking about her. Single women in their twenties enjoy "being swept off their feet with dramatic, romantic gestures," says Dr. Fitzgerald.

Be spontaneous. A young woman often likes spur-of-the-moment outings. So on Friday night, maybe you suggest that the two of you fly to Las Vegas for the weekend. Or rent a mountain cabin. Or something more modest. "I don't think you need to spend a fortune on her," says Sharyn Wolf, a clinical social worker in New York City and author of *Guerrilla Dating Tactics*. "If you take her to see a meteor shower, you don't have to drop a bundle."

Be patient. Expect that she won't be able to see you as often as you would like. A woman in her twenties may be hitting the books in law or graduate school, or working long hours trying to advance in her career. Don't whine. Be supportive.

Be open-minded. Don't be quick to insist that she be monogamous with you. Like you, she may want to play the field while she's young and before she has a career established. This is perfectly normal. "The lack of monogamy in the twenties is kind of silently accepted by both partners," says Dr. Fitzgerald.

Make dinner for her. A meal in a fine restaurant is nice, but at your own place is even better, says Dr. Farrell. Why? Because it's more intimate. No noisy clatter of dishes or the drone of your fellow diners' chatter. And at home, you control the lighting, the music. "It doesn't have the initial appeal of a restaurant, but that combination creates more long-term intimacy," Dr. Farrell says.

It doesn't matter if you aren't a master chef, Dr. Farrell says. Something simple and not too heavy is the key. "In addition, you pick up a much smaller bill in your home," he says.

Don't praise the obvious. "Women want the portion of them that isn't always complimented, complimented," says Dr. Farrell. So if you're dating a physically beautiful woman who was just crowned Miss Rutabaga at the annual farm festival, don't keep telling her how hot she looks. She's heard it already. A lot.

You'll score more points by praising her intellect or the discipline it took for her to win that beauty title, advises Dr. Farrell. "Focus on things that she doesn't normally get her approval on and that she's more likely to feel insecure about," advises Dr. Farrell. "But be genuine about it. Women, like men, see through the lie."

Go slow when coming on. Offer to give her a back rub. Or really shock her and tell her you like to take things slowly and suggest the two of you just cuddle in front of the television. "That's very refreshing, especially for the young woman who sees all guys as just complete lust machines," says Linda DeVillers, Ph.D., a psychologist and sex therapist in El Segundo, California, and author of *Love Skills*. "But the guy has to follow through on that. It can't be a ploy."

Use your tongue. If and when you do have sex with a woman in her twenties, Dr. DeVillers has a final word of advice for guys. "Younger women definitely expect oral sex," she says. "Women under 35 almost grew up on oral sex. If it isn't delivered, there are going to be problems."

MULTIPLE PARTNERS

Call it sleeping around. Consider it sexuality's equivalent of attention deficit disorder. We like to think of the phenomenon as "sowing your wild oats"—has a nice, wholesome, almost biblical ring to it. However you look at it, though, young men have a unique and, some might say, enviable problem: They can't seem to settle on any one partner for any length of time.

Of course, like most sweeping generalizations, that statement is only partly true. Polygamy, loving more than one woman, is not just a young man's issue.

"But it's probably more prevalent in younger men because they're the ones most likely to act on the urge to sleep with numerous partners," says Helen Fisher, Ph.D., research associate in the department of anthropology at Rutgers University in New Brunswick, New Jersey, and author of *Anatomy of Love*. "It's almost the only time in a man's life when such behavior is socially acceptable." And what's to hold him back? He's single, free to sleep with anyone he wants. Also, in that delicate state between adulthood and adolescence, he's still forming his sensibilities about what's good and bad, moral and immoral. "He's in an experimental phase, and one area of his life where he's going to experiment a lot is with sex," says Dr. Fisher. According to the *Sex in America* survey, by the time they reach their thirties, fully 25 percent of men have had between 5 and 10 sex partners. Ten percent have had more than 20 partners. That's a lot of bed hopping.

We feel the urge to couple with numerous partners for numerous reasons. Sometimes it's a mark of status or sexual prowess. Sometimes we're responding to mysterious, primitive urges. And sometimes we're simply confused and curious and just trying to make our way in the world of sex. As varied as our reasons may be, sometimes they can also lead to some nettlesome internal conflicts. Here we'll examine what the urge for multiple partners does to us as men, as lovers. Recognizing the power our desires have over us is the first step in controlling them, after all. And control them you will, if you want to grow as a person and as a lover of women.

So Many Women...

Scientific curiosity isn't the only force driving us to seek out new partners, nor is it the most powerful. There's also some primitive instinct thrown into that sexual chemical mix.

"On some level, men can make the argument that they're programmed to sleep around. It's part of an old strategy to help ensure that our DNA would live on. The basic survival instinct dictated this sort of behavior," says Steve Manley, Ph.D., staff psychologist for the Male Health Center in Dallas. And chronic bed hopping is a job that men are uniquely qualified for. Consider this: We're able to move around and impregnate numerous women with our genetic code. A woman generally has only one bun in the oven at a time; we can have dozens, hundreds even. Nowadays, getting women pregnant is not the main goal of our numerous trysts—just the opposite, in fact—but that old urge does explain some of our primal desire for more and more sex with many and varied women.

Incidentally, women have their own primal programming on procreation, and it can drive them to seek numerous partners, too. "Women actually have a couple of different mating strategies," says Dr. Fisher. "Men mate to spread their seed; women mate to gather resources. They can do this by mating with one man and drawing resources from him exclusively. But they may also mate with numerous men to increase the amount of resources they can get for potential offspring."

Show versus Meaningful Partners

As we've grown and evolved, those old genetic imperatives have taken a backseat to newer social forces that still cause us to move from one partner to another. "This is less a case of spreading your seed and more a case of choosing a partner based on status," says Dr. Fisher. In short, you seek a trophy partner—someone with undisputed physical attributes who will make you the envy of your peer group.

Jeez, are we shallow or what? And yet Isadora Alman, a sexologist, syndicated columnist of "Ask Isadora," and author of *New Ways to Meet New People*, points out that this is a mating strategy often practiced by younger men who are at an age where appearances mean a great deal. "You're young and good-looking, and you want a similarly young and good-looking woman on your arm," says Alman. Thus, you have your "show" partner. (*Warning:* This sort of behavior may crop up again along about midlife.)

But the show girl comes at a price. Getting someone with supermodel looks may mean that you have to compromise on other qualities: a sharing of similar interests, for example, or a complementary personality.

"The trophy girlfriend is kind of a shallow mating strategy. It's usually short-term because you realize that as good-looking as this person is, or as much as your friends may envy you for having her, she may not excite you at all in other ways. She may not arouse your passion. At least not over the long term," says Dr. Fisher.

That's where the meaningful partner comes in, the soul mate, the woman we pick less for physical appearance and more for other attractive qualities. Her sense of humor, her love of the same music or the same books, her ability to recognize crap when we pull it and to call us on it.

"In short, she fulfills other intangible aspects of the our ideal woman, the woman of our dreams," says Galdino F. Pranzarone, Ph.D., professor of psychology at Roanoke College in Salem, Virginia, who studies how we choose the qualities we look for in an ideal mate. "If you have a woman who fulfills all your requirements in terms of looks but none of the other qualities, eventually you'll find a better match in someone who maybe matches a few appearance requirements but a whole range of other requirements, especially in terms of her interests and attitude and personality."

LIFE WITH ARCHIE

The human mind is a study in paradox, especially when it comes to picking a mate. The fact is that at any given time the urges of polygamy and monogamy are wrestling in our heads and hearts. We want to settle down with one partner. We also want to sleep around with as many partners as we possibly can.

We've come up with a name for it; we call it the Archie Syndrome. Remember Archie? He never could decide between Betty or Veronica. He'd yo-yo between the sweet, adoring nature of beautiful Betty and the sophistication and regal allure of the passionate, hot-headed Veronica. We all have it at some point or another, that conflict when we can't settle on one woman. Or we do, but only until we start to miss the other woman, or women. Then, off we go in search of her. Maybe we find her, or maybe we find someone else. Then we settle down with her until we get restless again.

So, are we practicing monogamy or polygamy?

Well, it's a little of both. "We're both monogamous and polygamous in our nature. And we wrestle with the two urges even after we've settled on somebody," says Dr. Fisher. It's one of the great tug-of-war battles in life, and you'll have to live with the paradox.

Often as not, it's when we lean toward polygamy that we're most likely to get into trouble. If we've caught you in the polygamous stage where you haven't settled on anybody; or if you are with somebody but getting the itch to move on, we'd like to take a couple minutes to give you some important guidelines for living the life of the ladies' man.

Be up-front. Gotta hand it to Archie, he was operating on full disclosure—Betty and Veronica knew their red-headed amour was dating them both. Follow his example. If you're the kind of man who doesn't want to be tied down, don't lead a woman to believe that you're interested in something long-term with her. Be honest about your changing feelings. She may not like it, but on some level she'll certainly respect you for it. Just be aware that the door to polygamy swings both ways. She, too, is perfectly entitled to sleep around with whomever she wants—and will probably have an easier time finding willing male partners than you will finding female ones. How does that make you feel?

Be respectful. Sex is not about scoring the most notches in your bedpost. If you're out on the prowl to see how many women you can bag so that you can brag about it with your Neanderthal pals, then you're out there for the wrong reasons.

"There's nothing wrong with wanting to experience sex with more than one partner. It's only natural to be curious, to want to explore different experiences with different people," says Alman. But it's harmful when you start to focus less on being with the person and more on the act of sex itself. You'll find very quickly that it's a rather empty experience. "And that's what probably turns many men over to monogamy eventually," says Alman. They realize that sleeping around just isn't satisfying enough for them. They need more than sex. Yes, it's true!

Be careful. But before you recognize that truth, while you're sowing your wild oats, take good care to protect your, uh, plow. That means inquiring after a potential partner's history and always taking care to carry condoms—a good ally in the world of casual sex and an effective shield against disease.

BARS

Conventional wisdom tells us that a bar is one of the worst places to meet women—at least the kind of women you'd consider girlfriend or wife material. This is not just public opinion; we have the numbers to back it up. According to the *Sex in America* survey for example, only 10 percent of single folks end up marrying a person they met outside their social circles in a place like a bar.

Even when we're on the prowl, engaged in what anthropologists quaintly call a short-term mating strategy, a bar isn't such a hot venue for satisfying our baser urges. In an age where AIDS, serial killers, and date rape are vivid icons in the cultural landscape, casual sex is dead. These days, no one is looking for Mr. Goodbar.

And yet, despite the conventional wisdom, when we're young or single, we all flock to the bars and taverns of the world—yes, even the women we end up dating and marrying. What's going on here?

PARADOX OF THE PUB

"It does seem like there's a paradox at work. If bars are such an awful place to meet people, why do we keep going?" asks Michael R. Cunningham, Ph.D., professor of psychology at the University of Louisville and a researcher into the science of attraction between men and women. Dr. Cunningham studies mating tactics, and to do it, he and his graduate students often have to venture into bars to gather their data. A demanding job, and one that gives him a unique perspective of bars as a social venue.

"When you look past the concerns of today's society, go back to the historic roots of a bar, you'll begin to realize that this institution serves an important function in the community," says Dr. Cunningham. "Especially for choosing a mate. Not so long ago, it was important for people to marry within their own class and ethnic group. The social institutions of any given neighborhood helped ensure that people could interact with others from their same group. That included churches, social clubs, and the neighborhood tavern."

These days, the neighborhood bar is little more than a piece of history. But Dr. Cunningham says that the same reasons for going to bars still exist. In light of that fact, we're going to turn a deaf ear to conventional wisdom for the moment. Statistics be damned: We'd like to suggest that bars can still be a wonderful, socially acceptable place for meeting women—yes, even women who you might have a long-term mating strategy with. With the help of expert social observers like Dr. Cunningham, we've put together a few arguments for why that might be. Here's our rationale.

It's okay to talk to strangers. When you were in high school or college, you lived in a ready-made social structure where it was easy to befriend attractive strangers and develop relationships with them: They lived down the hall in the dormitory, or you sat next to them in class or at school events. Then school ended and your field for meeting new partners narrowed considerably.

"Once you're out in the real world, how do you meet people? Many do it at work, but that can be fraught with its own risks," says Daniel Kegan, Ph.D., a psychologist with Elan Associates in Chicago and an expert in interpersonal relationships. And many of us quite rightly don't feel comfortable mixing business with pleasure. In that case, all we have left are bars.

"Consider that, as an adult, bars are the only social venue where meeting and talking to strangers is the norm," says Dr. Cunningham. "Without them, you don't have very much opportunity to meet women. It's the most fundamental reason there is for the popularity of bars."

Who Needs Bars?

As a sidebar to our bar discussion, we'd like to suggest some alternative meeting places and watering holes for meeting either Ms. Right or Ms. Right Now. If you're getting tired of your local tavern, consider frequenting one of these venues.

• Coffeehouse. Fast becoming the alternative to the bar scene, the coffeehouse tends to draw a more sophisticated crowd than your average bar. On the other hand, coffeehouses also tend to draw a lot more women than a crowded, smoky sports bar.

• Juice bar. If you're into fitness or repelled by the bar scene, this trendy venue might offer a welcome alternative. And if you catch the eye of some organic wonder down at the end of the bar, you can always send over a smart drink.

• Grocery store. Remember that scene in *National Lampoon's Animal House* where one of the frat boys started talking about his "cucumber" to an older woman in the produce aisle? In some cities, grocery stores even hold singles nights, giving new meaning to the term *checkout lane*. "It mixes two primal needs in the human condition—food and sex," says Michael R. Cunningham, Ph.D., professor of psychology at the University of Louisville and a researcher into the science of attraction between men and women.

• Diner. Hey, it's like a bar: It has stools. It has a long counter you can lean on. It has pert women serving you pie. What more do you need?

• Bookstores. One of the great hangouts of our times. Meet someone at a bookstore and you have safe things to talk about (books, of course), a comfortable place to sit and talk, and increasingly, good food and coffee. Plus, the focus of the place is mind and thoughts. She appreciates that.

There's freedom behind bars. The social construct of the bar gives you permission for other things than just talking to strangers. "I think the atmosphere where there is some anonymity also makes one feel safe, more confident in some ways," says Helen Fisher, Ph.D., research associate in the department of anthropology at Rutgers University in New Brunswick, New Jersey, and author of *Anatomy of Love*. The more safe and confident you feel, the less inhibitions you'll have about, say, approaching a beautiful woman and asking for her phone number.

Lowering inhibitions is an important aspect of meeting people. "Not coincidentally, bars serve alcohol because it does lower inhibitions and make people feel more relaxed. In that sort of environment, it will be easier to meet people," says Dr. Cunningham.

Your bar, your self. While bars do convey a sense of anonymity on the surface, Dr. Cunningham observes that on a deeper level, bars—or more specifically, the kinds of bars you like to frequent—can say a lot about who you are and who you're likely to meet.

"It's the evolution of the neighborhood bar idea. In the neighborhood bar, you had a reasonable expectation of meeting someone who was just like you, ethnically, socially, religiously even," says Dr. Cunningham. Nowadays, with a variety of differently themed bars, especially in big cities, you have an opportunity to choose a bar that suits your personality. So if you like folk music, you go to the pub that has live Irish music every Wednesday. If you dig beat poetry and alternative music, you hang at the Bohemian tavern with the pictures of Jack Kerouac over the urinals. "And you have some reasonable expectation that most of the people who frequent the same place have the same tastes, which is certainly not a bad thing to have in common," says Dr. Cunningham.

So go out and prove the statisticians wrong! Hang at your favorite watering hole with pride. And with an attentive eye for cute female regulars. Odds are that one of them will be the kind of woman who shares your likes and interests—the same kind of women you thought you'd never meet at a bar.

PICKUP LINES

Hey, what's a nice guy like you doing in a chapter like this?

Enlightened male that you are, you must surely know that pickup lines are déclassé—the first resort of churls, cads, and mashers, the sort of men you were put on this earth to rescue women from. If on some enchanted evening you saw a stranger across a crowded room, why, you'd never think of handing her a line.

An "opening gambit," though; you might give that a shot.

Opening gambit—that's what Michael R. Cunningham, Ph.D., professor of psychology, calls it. And he studies mating tactics and the science of attraction for a living. In his research at the University of Louisville, Dr. Cunningham has gathered reams of data about opening gambits, and he says that what you say to a woman is only a small part of a successful approach.

"It's not just what you say. It's how you say it and how you look. There's a real interaction between your words and your appearance," says Dr. Cunningham. In other words, if you're good-looking and sharply dressed, you may get away with a line that would never work if you're sporting five o'clock shadow and a ripped T-shirt. Make no mistake: Part of what makes an opening line successful is how well that line complements other aspects of your sex appeal.

But for the moment, let's focus on the language and intonation of an opening gambit, the building blocks of a successful, respectful verbal approach. What do you say? How do you say it?

"These are really serious questions that every guy has before he approaches a woman. No one wants to be rejected, even by someone who's a complete stranger. So you have to learn what you can and can't say," says John Eagan, author of the 100,000+-selling book *How to "Pick Up" Beautiful Women*. Like Dr. Cunningham, Eagan has studied the mating rituals of the human animal from a unique if not highly clinical perspective—he worked for over 20 years as a bartender at various nightclubs. And after years of watching "from the trenches," he decided to survey the more attractive of his female customers to learn what appealed to or repelled them in the world of verbal approaches. He conducted more than 2,000 interviews. "My goal was to teach men what women respond to, not so you can 'pick up' women per se but so you can introduce yourself to them in a way that's going to put them at ease and make them decide you're worth talking to," he says. (For more on Eagan's findings, see Sex Appeal on page 87.)

What we offer, then, is not a lesson in magic words but a short course in romantic elocution, in talking to a complete—and completely gorgeous—stranger in such a way that you won't come off looking like a goof, a serial killer, or a hopeless barfly. We already know that you're none of the above, but she doesn't. Here's how to put her at ease, without putting your foot in your mouth.

Say it like you mean it. When Eagan was interviewing women for his book, one question he asked them was, "What's the best thing a man can say to you when he first approaches you?" The overwhelming answer, says Eagan, was, "A sincere compliment."

The operative term here is *sincere*. "Nothing you say to a woman—not even an innocent 'Hi'—is going to get you anywhere if you don't mean it," says Eagan. But if you do mean it, even the corniest line will work for you. "Women are far more in touch with feeling," says Eagan. "And if they sense

Say What?

So what are the best lines to use on a woman? After surveying more than 2,000 women in nightclubs, John Eagan, a nightclub bartender and author of the 100,000+-selling book *How to "Pick Up" Beautiful Women*, shares 3 of the top 10 best lines. We've analyzed them for technical and artistic merit.

"Can a beautiful[1] girl like you use some pleasant[2] company?

"It's never easy meeting a complete stranger[3]—especially one as beautiful[4] as you—without being properly introduced.[5] But shall we try anyway?

"A beautiful[6] woman like you should have a great evening. Give me a chance[7] to let that happen. May I join you in a drink?"[8]

1. Building a compliment into the opening gambit is an essential component to its success.
2. Use of the word *pleasant* instead of, say, *terrific* or *well-hung* denotes a certain humility and lack of unattractive and overbearing qualities, which are turnoffs for most women.
3. Honest and sincere—shows that you're a little nervous in the presence of her beauty but compelled to speak to her despite that fact.
4. Although this compliment is used parenthetically, almost as an afterthought, it fulfills the basic requirement of using flattery in an opening gambit.
5. Shows some knowledge of manners, hints of old-fashioned chivalry without being dopey.
6. In case you didn't get it by now, make sure that your opening line includes a compliment.
7. The direct, straightforward approach; preferred by many women over unbearably witty lines like "How do you like your eggs in the morning?" (to which any self-respecting woman would answer "Unfertilized, thanks" and turn her back to you).
8. Polite and nonthreatening. This request also serves another important function: It moves things past the awkward introduction phase, into a realm where normal conversation can occur and the two of you can begin to know one another.

that you feel what you're saying, that's going to get you further with them than anything else you do."

Be honest. Of course, you don't want to tell her any obvious whoppers—what if you start dating and she finds out you really *don't* fight oil fires for a living? But if you want an opening gambit to be successful, honesty needn't keep you from being more interesting to a woman. In fact, you can make honesty work for you to get a woman more interested.

"Going up and introducing yourself to a stranger is an artificial situation;

it's going to make most people feel nervous," says Dr. Cunningham. But you can use that to your advantage. "Admitting that you're nervous or embarrassed is good. It's a direct, honest approach that the women in our research responded to," he says.

Eagan heartily agrees. "It only makes you more sincere if you're honest about how you feel. You don't want to look nervous, but you can go up and say, 'Hey, I feel a little nervous about this, but I just really wanted to meet you. My name is....' "

Don't ask. Most guys have figured out that they shouldn't spend much time talking about themselves—makes you look pompous. Instead, you've learned to ask questions, to make some gesture of interest in her life. "That's the right impulse to have," says Eagan. "It makes her feel important and special." But a lot of men overdo it, he cautions. "They get nervous and they start firing questions off at her. Suddenly, she's on the defensive and she's going to turn off to you." Ask questions about her. Make it clear that you want to get to know her, but keep it light. Comment on the music that's playing and ask her what kind of music she likes. What she does for a living. What kind of car she drives. Don't ask her personal questions like where she lives; she'll take you for a stalker in training.

Build in a compliment. Important ingredient to an opening gambit: a sincere, honest compliment. "Women spend hours picking an outfit, making themselves beautiful before they go out for the evening. They want someone to acknowledge all their hard work," says Eagan. By making sure that your line of introduction includes some appreciation of that fact—"Wow, that dress looks terrific on you" or "I just had to come over and tell you how beautiful you look"—you'll show her that you're a man of distinction and taste. She'll brush your compliment off, of course, but you can bet she'll be pleased, says Eagan.

Crack a smile, not a joke. By now, you've probably heard that women place a high premium on a man's sense of humor. It's important, to be sure, but try not to convey what a laugh riot you are in your first words to her (unless you're really good-looking—we'll discuss why in a minute). In Dr. Cunningham's studies, men who tried a cute or flippant approach to women were successful less than 20 percent of the time (compare this to a simple "Hi," which worked 55 percent of the time). Smile, certainly. Let that mischievous twinkle in your eye show, but don't hand her a gag line. Once you've been introduced, you can spend the rest of the night dazzling her with your wit.

Match your lines to your looks. If you want your opening gambits to have the best chance of succeeding, you have to ask yourself one tough question: How good-looking am I—handsome, average, or nothing to write home about? We hate to get into your personal appearance, but it does play a role in how successful a line is. In his research, Dr. Cunningham found that men who were drop-dead gorgeous, for example, didn't do so well delivering lines that were boastful or showy. "Saying things like, 'I just got a new car.

Words to Live By

That man that hath a tongue, I say, is no man,
If with his tongue he cannot win a woman.

—William Shakespeare, *The Two Gentlemen of Verona*

Want to go for a ride?' was a turnoff," says Dr. Cunningham. "It made the good-looking man seem domineering." By contrast, men with less-than-perfect looks did better with lines of that stripe.

And what worked for handsome guys? "Being self-demeaning or modest seemed to work better. It offset their good looks with humility and made them more appealing all-around," says Dr. Cunningham. Also, remember how we said that only 20 percent of guys did well using a cute or glib line? Well, it turns out most of that 20 percent must have been composed of good-looking guys. "In our studies, good-looking men who displayed a sense of humor did have more success than others who employed humorous opening gambits," says Dr. Cunningham.

BODY LANGUAGE

Before we knew how to say "I love you," we had to show it. In the pre-lingual dawn of mankind, eye contact and a bit of posturing were the fore-runners of the pickup line. Throw in some shifting of the feet, a few nuances with the arms and hands—suddenly, our hairy forebears were going at it hammer and tongs. And the guy didn't have to utter anything. No timeworn lines. No meaningless small talk. No long, one-sided conversations where he had to sit and nod understandingly at key points.

In short, we relied on body language (and maybe a grunt or two), that subtle dance of sexual attraction we've been doing with one another since we first crawled out of the prehistoric brine. As the gentle art of conversation has evolved, the prominence of body language has dwindled. But its meaning as a cue to sexual attraction has not.

"We still use body language all the time to show whether we're interested in one another. Eye contact, lip licking—even the way we sit in a chair. It's all the same thing: a visual cue to show potential partners what we want. We just don't recognize it all the time," says Isadora Alman, a sexologist, syndicated columnist of "Ask Isadora," and author of *New Ways to Meet New People*.

"Certainly men don't. Women are much quicker to pick up on body language, whereas men tend to be a little denser, says Monica Moore, Ph.D., associate professor of psychology at Webster University in St. Louis and a pioneer in the study of women's body language. Dr. Moore says that women tend to be a little more fluent in body language because they use it all the time, not just on men but on each other. As a result, they've developed a large and effective body vocabulary; men just have a handful of physical maneuvers to signal their intentions.

You can recognize and learn to interpret body language if you try, though. In fact, we'd like to suggest that men are singularly well-equipped to pick up nonverbal cues. Throughout this book we've been saying—sometimes in an almost accusatory fashion—how men are visual, women are verbal. We respond quickly and impressively to visual sex cues. That doesn't just mean that some gyrating dancer on the Spice channel puts the lead in our pencil; it also means that when a woman subtly arches her breasts into our airspace, or points a toe at us, our high-tuned visual receptors pick up these signals and route them to the subconscious. Unfortunately, in the subconscious those signals don't do much more than make us horny as hell. But by learning to identify the signals on a conscious level, you can do something about that horniness, such as ask her out for drinks, with a reduced chance of rejection.

READING HER BODY

Okay, she just flipped her hair. Now she's scratching her nose. Okay, now she's taking off her shirt and unhooking her—oh, you know what that body language means. But what do the rest of her cute, quirky movements mean?

"All of her gestures mean something. But you have to learn to read the signals a woman is giving off if you want to act on them," says Dr. Moore. Figuring that out will take time and practice. Reading body language is something of an inexact science because everyone speaks his or her own peculiar dialect of the same root language. So when one woman bats her eyelashes at you, she may be saying, "I want to bear your children," while another woman performing the same exact eye-wise batting may be saying, "I'm wearing new contacts and they're killing me." Your old drinking buddies, Trial and Error, are going to be your inseparable companions should you choose to be a student of the nonverbal language of love. Now, it's time to put on your social anthropologist's hat and do, as the English say, a little bird-watching. To help you along, we've provided the following glossary of terms to cover female body language, head to toe.

Hair: If she primps it, strokes it, plays with it, tosses it, it's a positive sign. In her comprehensive book *Love, Sex, and Intimacy*, London sex therapist Nitya Lacroix says that hair tossing is an overtly sexual gesture. It's also preening, one that many animals share. The instinctive idea is to make your plumage look more attractive, thus edging out competitors in the harsh game of survival. As it is on the African veldt, so it is at the singles bar. *Note:* If seeing you causes her to tear it out by the roots, move on.

Eyebrows: Raising them or raising and lowering them is a universal sign that the human animal has seen something that interests it—in this case, that something is you. Raised eyebrows also indicate an attitude that is receptive and open to an advance. In her studies, Dr. Moore says eyebrow raising and lowering is one of the top flirting gestures exhibited by women, especially when accompanied by a smile and some eye contact.

Eyes: Those baby blues are the windows to her soul, remember. If you repeatedly catch her glancing at you, that's a sign of interest, especially if you glance at her and she holds your gaze for a few moments, says Timothy Perper, Ph.D., biologist, co-editor of *The Complete Dictionary of Sexology,* and an independent researcher who has studied human courtship for two decades. If she bats her eyes demurely, or averts her eyes when you look at her, that, too, may be a sign of attraction.

But the eyes don't always have it. Lacroix observes that very shy or insecure women may look all around the room, in fact, may look at every other man in the room except the one she's interested in. That's why it pays to learn other aspects of body language: If the eyes seem to say "no," the rest of her body may be saying "yes."

Mouth: When you're attracted to someone, you heat up, you get flushed. Your mouth goes dry, your lips feel parched. She feels the same way. So what does she do? She purses her lips. She moistens them. She parts them slightly. "Lip licking is an extremely common flirting gesture," says Dr. Moore. Some researchers think that by incorporating nonverbal mouth action into their body language, women are making subtle reference to the labia, the outer lips of the vagina, which become moist, swollen, and slightly parted as a woman becomes sexually aroused. Just thought we'd pass that along.

Neck: Tell her a joke. If she only laughs, she *might* be interested. If she laughs and throws her head back, then you won't be sticking your neck out very much to show your interest her—because she already has. Stuck her neck out, that is, and shown her interest in you at the same time. The neck is a sensitive and vulnerable part of her anatomy, and she has just exposed it to you. It's a sign of trust, of opening up. Also, by exposing her neck or tilting it to one side, she's going for the swan effect—making herself seem as long and slim and elegant as possible.

Shoulders: When she straightens them, she's showing a definite interest in whatever she's seeing. If she shifts them back a little, that's also a distinct sign of sexual interest since pushing her shoulders back has the effect of making her breasts more prominent—a good thing, yes?

Breasts: Speaking of those good things, any body movement that makes her breasts more prominent is a sign of sexual interest. Aside from pushing her shoulders back, other breast-enhancing poses include arching the back, bending forward to expose cleavage, or raising both hands behind her head or neck (as though she were fixing her hair). If she gets close enough that her breast brushes any part of your body, you don't need us to tell you that's an obvious sign of interest.

If you happen to notice that her nipples are erect, though, don't automatically assume she's interested. While it's true that nipples often become erect when women are sexually aroused, it can also be an involuntary reaction to other conditions, says Dr. Moore. What's stimulating her nipples to erection may not be your charismatic presence but, instead, the simple fact that she's wearing a blouse or bra that's irritating the delicate tissue. Or it could be that she's cold, nervous, or even afraid.

Arms: Even though we were taught that pointing was impolite, we still do it, men and women both. If a woman is interested in someone, she may keep an elbow pointed at the object of affection. Also, if you're chatting a woman up and she's really interested, she may allow her arm to brush yours.

Hands: Like the arms, hands can also point toward something that interests them. When a woman puts her hand on her hip and gazes at you suggestively, think about where that hand is pointing. Also, as a sign of deeper interest in you, she may put a hand lightly on your arm (as she throws back her head and laughs at your lame jokes), says Dr. Perper. Another very serious flirting gesture is when she uses her hands to fondle items nearby: her glass, her keys. In some cases, says Dr. Moore, she may actually touch herself—absently put a hand on her breast or stroke the inside of her thigh, telegraphing a subconscious desire to be touched. (Don't assume this is an invitation for *you* to stroke her thigh or breast. Remember, this is just a signal of interest.)

Hips: Any exaggerated motion of the hips can be read as a sign of interest or an indication that she might be receptive to a man: if she juts them toward you, if the sway of her hips becomes more exaggerated as she walks, or if she moves them in time to whatever music is playing in the background—she's essentially dancing by herself. (In that case, it wouldn't hurt to go up and ask her to dance.)

Legs: Just because she has them crossed doesn't mean that she's not interested. If she crosses and uncrosses them slowly and repeatedly, that's not an off-limits sign. It's a subtle advertisement for the area just beyond all that crossing and uncrossing. Also, it's a universally positive signal if in crossing her legs she happens to hike her skirt a little, exposing more leg. If she's standing, and her legs are wider apart than normal, that's often a positive sign too, signaling sexual receptivity.

Feet: Like hands, the direction her feet are pointing in usually signal where her interests lie. Also, women who are attracted to the guy they're talking to have a tendency to unconsciously slide their foot in and out of their shoe. Hmmm, now what action could that be mimicking?

READING YOUR BODY

Just as women use body language, so do men. We just use a slightly different, slightly smaller vocabulary. Deciphering your own language can help you in your never-ending quest for better communications with the opposite sex. If you catch yourself in some overbearing posture, you can compensate, tone down, not come off as too arrogant. Or maybe you want to exude a sense of better confidence or quiet strength. There are certain gestures and poses that will help telegraph your intentions, aspirations, and unspoken desires subtly. Here's a brief lexicon of the male body language.

Eyes: While there's nothing wrong with giving her a longer-than-normal gaze just to announce your interest, don't stare. Keep your gaze focused on her eyes, her face—no undressing her with your eyes. Also, even though you might be nervous gazing upon such finery as she, don't give in to the old nervous tick of shifting your eyes away from her. By looking all around the room, you give off the appearance of someone who's not interested in her and, well, shifty.

Mouth: Smile, but don't fake it. If the smile doesn't make it up to your eyes, or if you hold that grin for too long, you're not going to look like a nice guy. You're going to look like a predator who's about to go for her throat. Don't smirk—it makes you look smug. Show some teeth.

Shoulders: Like women, we tend to stand up a little straighter when someone catches our eye. That's good. What you want to avoid is walking around slumped over and stoop-shouldered, even if you just came from the worst of all possible days at work. Also, in the presence of desirable women, it's not at all uncommon for men to square their shoulders, trying to make them look as broad as possible. That's fine, but beware of overdoing it: Too much posturing like that and you'll start to look like a swaggering dolt.

Chest: As with the shoulders, we have a tendency to puff our chests up when we're attracted to someone, at the same time sucking in whatever gut we have. It bolsters our confidence, makes us look and feel like a superhero. Try not to be too obvious when you do this, though; you'll look like you're about to try to blow a house down. Another good reason for controlling this common bit of body lingo? Well, try it right now: Puff up your chest. What happened? You had to take kind of a deep breath there didn't you? Now hold that breath as long as possible. At the same time, take sips from a drink and try to carry on a witty conversation. After just a few seconds, you're beginning to see the dilemma—sooner or later you're going to have to exhale, and when you do, your whole appearance will change, for the worse.

Hands: You're at the party, trying to look cooler than cool. You want to be a standout; you want to look original. So you do what every other guy does: You lean against a wall and hook your thumbs into your belt loops or stick your hands in your pockets. In so doing, you're unconsciously signaling your availability for sex—look where your hands and fingers are pointing.

Distress Signals

Women have many ways to indicate their levels of interest in a man, but only a handful of signals to show that the guy who's trapped them at the hors d'oeuvres table is boring them to tears. Here are five sure signs that she's not interested.

General restlessness. Any foot- or finger-tapping, any fidgety shifting, any quick sharp movements are signs that she wishes she—or you—were anywhere but here.

Defenses are up. Folding her arms across her chest, crossing her legs tightly, or resting one arm on the opposite leg are all defensive postures. Guess who she's defending herself from?

The withdrawal method. If her shoulders start to slump or she starts to tuck her chin in toward her chest, she's making like a turtle, drawing into her shell—and away from you.

Moving to the exit. Any gestures away from you are usually signs she wants to exit the encounter. If her torso or hips are swiveled elsewhere, or her toes, breasts, or general body position are starting to orient themselves toward the door or another guy, your chances with her are also exiting fast.

Roving eyes. Unless she's terribly shy, glancing away from you frequently is often a sign that she's casting about for something else to catch her interest—or for someone to come to her rescue. If this happens to you, make a polite exit from her company, then start looking around the room for another woman who is doing this to a man who has her cornered. Go and rescue her.

Genital pointing is extremely common in both sexes. It's not bad. But don't you feel a little obvious now?

Pelvis: Women point toward the object of their attraction with knees, elbows, and hands. We do that, too, along with one another appendage. Of course, men aren't terribly overt about this—they don't whip it out or anything. But if a woman has caught your fancy, you may find yourself arching your pelvis toward her. Kinky, eh? Now that you're aware of this, please don't be too obvious about it—women will think you're walking around like that because you have a load in your pants, which is counterproductive to the image you were probably trying to convey.

Legs: When men want to signal sexual interest in a woman, they expose their genitals, subtly. Sitting or standing with your legs spread wide is one way we present ourselves (discreetly, of course). And, like women, we can signal our interest or disinterest in someone by directing our legs, knees, or feet in a certain direction—either right at her, or toward the nearest exit.

Whew, that's a lot to remember, especially right when you are meeting a new woman. Don't worry about passing a test on body language, says Shirley Zussman, Ed.D., a certified sex and marital therapist in private practice in New York City. Just absorb the general idea that body language says a lot and that you need to tune in to it. But it doesn't always mean the same thing in everyone. Every woman is different, and your reactions are different with each situation. So aim at being open and spontaneous. Chances are that you'll naturally project the right signals anyhow.

OLDER WOMEN

Call it Mrs. Robinson Syndrome, and many is the young man who has experienced it—in their dreams.

It's a classic fantasy: An older woman—be it a sexy manager at work, a lonely widow next door, a worldly, sophisticated college professor—seduces an innocent but lusty young buck (that is, you). Hot, passionate sex of every stripe ensues as this older woman gently, tenderly, patiently leads her young charge deep into the world of sensual pleasures. She makes a man of him, and not just any man, but a man who now knows how to please women.

Beyond the fantasy, there are a chosen few who decide to live the reality: They meet an attractive, experienced older woman who, if she doesn't initiate him into the world of sex outright, certainly can teach him a thing or three about women. But as they share and enjoy this May-December relationship, they may also have to face some unpleasant realities.

STANDING UP TO SOCIETY

Should you be dallying with another generation, or should you be sticking with women your own age? That's not our place to judge. Love, after all, is blind—to looks, to status, and to age.

Alas, society is not. We still live in a world where a generation gap between lovers is smiled on only when it goes one way—older man, younger woman. The reasoning goes that the man has reached the peak of success and power and is somehow entitled to his young, beautiful trophy bride. And in the acquisition of such a prize, the man gains even more status among his peers, while conferring a certain sense of recaptured youth and fertility upon himself.

To date, that same logic can't explain a coupling of an older woman and a younger man. If youth and beauty are such treasures, why would a younger man seek an older woman? Odds are that she has little wealth or power and may even be past the cover girl days or childbearing years that a younger woman can offer. As usual, when society is faced with something it can't understand, it's easier to ostracize and condemn than to accept. But times are changing. Many older women have both wealth and positions of power, and young men may find that attractive, says Shirley Zussman, Ed.D., a certified sex and marital therapist in private practice in New York City. Besides, she adds, older women today are in better physical shape and look better than ever before.

If you enter into such a relationship, you may have to accept certain questions and issues. Not all of them are easy to answer. For example, you remember Kennedy from history class; she remembers where she was when he was shot. You have differing ideas of what's good in culture, music, entertainment. What common ground can you talk about? What do you do when the woman you want to bring home to Mom is one of her peers (or maybe even one of her pals)? What do you do when a younger woman catches your eye—or an older, wealthier, more powerful man catches hers?

LIVING THE AGELESS LOVE

A May-December relationship isn't all about difficult questions and generation-gap dilemmas, though. "If you can get past whatever stodgy old notions society has thrown across your path, you see that the pairing of a younger man and an older woman makes a certain kind of sense, too," says Isadora Alman, a sexologist, syndicated columnist of "Ask Isadora," and author of *New Ways to Meet New People*. In fact, for a young man, there are numerous advantages to having a relationship with an older woman.

They can teach you a lot. Not to put too fine a point on it, but older women are more likely to know what they're doing. They have the benefit of experience. They tend to know their bodies better than a younger woman, and they can teach you valuable lessons that you could never learn from a neophyte. "For example, they can teach you how to take your time and do foreplay right," says Alman. Incidentally, that's especially important for an older woman, who generally requires more time and stimulation to produce enough vaginal lubrication to enjoy sex.

Patience is their virtue. Buying into the notion that youth and beauty are on their side, younger women are less likely to exhibit a lot of time and patience in cultivating a relationship or teaching a lover how to please them. If you can't figure it out during the initial overtures of a high-pressure sexual audition, then they'll happily move on to someone else who can get it right the first time. An older woman is less likely to be as judgmental and more likely to enjoy the time she'll take teaching you everything she knows.

They're easier to please. As a woman gets older and becomes more comfortable and familiar with her own sexuality, she's going to be more relaxed about sex, more liberated. This translates into an increased enjoyment of sex and a greater likelihood of achieving orgasm.

"It has been said that women come into their sexual prime at a later age.

There's truth to that—not because of some physiological change, though. It's just that over time a woman becomes better attuned to her body and her needs, and it follows that she's going to be more sexually responsive," says Doreen Virtue, Ph.D., a relationship expert and psychotherapist in Newport Beach, California, and author of *In the Mood*. According to the survey *Sex in America*, when men and women are in their twenties, there are more of us than there are of them, which is why younger women get to be so choosy. But as time goes on, those numbers shift. In the twenties, the ratio is 105 men for every 100 women. By the time women get into their forties, there are only 98 men for every 100 women. That doesn't seem like much of a gap, but it grows ever wider as time goes on for the simple fact that men die sooner than women. If you're a younger guy who likes older women, it's easy to understand why you might start to feel like a kid in a candy store.

CYBERSEX

The Internet is inescapable. You can't read a magazine, watch the news, or take a business card without noticing that ubiquitous string of letters and slashes in the margins, denoting someone's Web address or e-mail account. It seems as though everyone is wired up—or thinking about wiring up—to that global network of computers and databases. If you have a computer and a modem, you've probably already connected to an online service like CompuServe or America Online at some point. Or maybe you've gone one step further and subscribed to an Internet service provider, giving you direct, unlimited access to the global information network that composes the Internet and its highly graphical, flashy counterpart, the World Wide Web.

As you've been hearing more and more about cyberspace, you've probably also heard—from the media and politicians alike—that the Information Superhighway is just crammed with off-ramps to virtual red-light districts of explicit sexual content. Places where you can see full-color, hard-core sex and nudity. Sites where you can commission various sexual services electronically. Databases where you can read the tawdry musings of millions of horny young men the world over.

VIRTUAL VIRTUES AND VICES

That's all true—such places exist and even thrive on the Web. But when it comes to sex, cyberspace is more than just a cesspool of digital depravity. Just as sex in the real world has its lowbrow and highbrow, so does cybersex have noble aspects to counterbalance its seamy underbelly, says Al Cooper, Ph.D., clinical director of the San Jose Marital and Sexuality Centre in California and an expert in sexuality on the Internet. According to Dr. Cooper, cyberspace is a vast, exciting, informative place where you can fulfill sexual fantasies, pose your own questions and concerns with a certain degree of anonymity, and access a vast store of knowledge on every flavor of sexuality that exists. It's a place that allows you to be the ultimate armchair adventurer, to have brief or prolonged dalliances with women from all around the world. To gape unabashedly at thousands of unclad beauties. To hear the stories and conquests—real and imagined—of people who share the same sexual interests as you.

Of course, trolling cyberspace for sexual information isn't for everyone. If you spend all day working on a computer, you may have a hard time seeing that workstation as a vessel of pleasure. And for many men, the notion of puttering around on the computer, looking up and downloading erotic information, stories, and pictures—well, it sounds a bit nerdy. As though you were somehow unable to satisfy your sexual desires in the realm of flesh and blood. If so, we can understand why you wouldn't see the need to log in to the realm of cybersex.

But you may want to read on anyway because just as many men are curious about what titillating information is flashing and pulsing through the ether of the electronic world. It's not our place to tell you whether sex online is good or bad. Instead, all we present here is a judgment-free primer to that world, highlighting some of the most popular and useful features—and warning you of some of the most common drawbacks—cybersex has to offer.

SURFING FOR SEX

At its most basic, you could see the Internet as the largest repository of sexual data in existence. From stories to photos to meeting places for sexual cybernauts, the online world is chock-full of information and services that anyone with a computer and a connection can tap.

What separates the antisocial nerd from the knowledge-seeking sophisticate is the ability to gather and use those data wisely, says Phyllis Phlegar, a columnist in Boca Raton, Florida, and author of *Love Online*. "There are plenty of people out there who will spend hours viewing pictures, reading messages, or typing explicit comments at other people and never come away with anything they can use in the real world. That's a shame," says Phlegar. Far better—and far healthier—might be to use the sexual resources of the Internet as a way to spice up your real sex life. "There are hundreds of ways to do that," says Phlegar. Here are some examples of what you'll find.

Virtual peep shows. Erotic images and video clips are perhaps the most pervasive and exciting aspect of online sexual data. To find them, all you have to do is go to a search engine (an online service that will search cyberspace for any subject you specify; your computer's Internet software should have a built-in connection to a search engine) and type "sex" or "nudity."

"And be prepared to sift through thousands upon thousands of possible sites," says Nancy Tamosaitis, author of several books about cybersex, including *The Penthouse Guide to Cybersex.* You'll find everything from the latest Playmate of the Month to fan sites devoted to images of the hottest supermodels. You may also stumble across some serious hard-core images of raw sex with all sorts of unlikely people, animals, and objects. Don't say we didn't warn you.

Important note: Before you download any digital cheesecake, make sure that your computer has an up-to-date virus program that's up and running. Scan anything you download off the Net for computer viruses. Just because that Swedish honey looks sweet and innocent doesn't mean she's not carrying some errant bit of code that will turn your hard drive into electronic mush.

Cybersex services. As you surf around to many of these databases, you may find little windows popping up asking you for your password. In an age of increasing concern over children having access to cyberporn, many sexual Web sites are restricting their access and requiring you to be a registered adult member of their database (for which they'll charge you a nominal fee, of course). Many of these services have grown from mere visual databases to all-out sexual service providers, where you can pay for an online striptease act; order sexually explicit toys, books, and videos; or have a "one-on-one" chat with some luscious lass who can type dirty at you as long as you want. Prices for membership and services vary widely, so you should read the terms of service carefully before you decide to subscribe.

Also, be cautious doing any business transactions over the Net. "To pay for these services, most providers will want a credit card number. If you transmit that number to them, there's a chance that someone else can intercept that transmission and use your credit card number," warns Tamosaitis. Check your Web software or talk with your Internet service provider for information about transmitting such sensitive information in protected or secured mode—scrambling your transmission so that a computer hacker can't decipher it.

Seeking advice. Sexual services and peep shows aside, cyberspace also offers numerous sites run by academic and professional sex experts and advisors. "These are places where you can post questions about sex practices or relationships and have a reasonable expectation of getting a thoughtful answer from a qualified expert," says Tamosaitis.

Many of these sites allow interaction from other Net surfers. "This only adds to the level of information you get," says Phlegar. "Someone could read a question you've posed and offer advice and reassurance if they've been in the same situation. That can be very helpful, in a way that no expert could be."

One of the best places to start looking for information is in a newsgroup. These sites are like virtual message boards in the Usenet area of the Internet where people from around the world post questions and respond to queries about every subject imaginable. In the alt.sex area, you'll find dozens of newsgroups devoted to sexual topics. Point of "netiquette": If you have a question, read the file marked FAQ (Frequently Asked Questions) before you pose your query. Nine times out of 10, the question you were thinking of has already been asked and answered, says Tamosaitis.

From the newsgroups, you can branch out to interactive sites on the graphic section of the Internet known as the World Wide Web. As a good starting point, we recommend the sex listings of the site called Yahoo!, at http://www.yahoo.com/Society_and_Culture/Sex/. Other valuable sources of no-nonsense sex information include the Microsoft Network–sponsored site, Feelgood, at http://www.sexualitybytes.com.au, and the home page of the esteemed Kinsey Institute for Research in Sex, Gender, and Reproduction, at http://www.indiana.edu/~kinsey/.

And those are by no means all the resources you'll find for matter-of-fact sex information. All these sites offer links to other related sites. Surf from link to link and pretty soon you'll have enough information at your fingertips to be your own sex expert.

CONDUCTING AFFAIRS ONLINE

Information is only half the equation to cybersex. The other half is interaction, actually having cybersex with someone sitting at their own computer terminal somewhere else in the world.

How can you have sex with someone you've never even met? All you need is access to a "chat room" or using an Internet Relay Chat (IRC) channel—either of these places allows members to type messages to one another instantaneously. Chat rooms are devoted to a broad range of subjects, and many of them exist solely so that people can get together online and type suggestive innuendo at one another. If you find someone you like, you can rendezvous in a virtual private room and get even more explicit, typing things like "I'm unhooking your bra," "I'm sliding my hand into your panties," and so forth. To make cybersex work, you both have to be pretty good at typing one-handed, if you take our meaning.

In one sense, engaging in masturbatory fantasies with a total stranger is a kind of ultimate safe sex. After all, there's no chance that you're going to catch a disease from a casual online encounter.

"It can be fun and exciting, certainly, but there's a downside to this sort of sexual interaction," warns Dr. Cooper. Especially if you're in a relationship in the real world.

"A lot of men have the mindset that if they have an online affair, they're not really being unfaithful since they didn't actually have sex. I don't necessarily buy that argument," says Sherry Lehman, a sex therapist in Cleveland and author of *Seven Days to Better Sex and a More Loving Relationship*. "It's an affair of the mind. It's taking something away from the real relationship, especially if it's something you're keeping secret from your spouse. If you don't believe me, ask yourself how you would feel if you caught your wife or your girlfriend at the computer, typing dirty messages to some other man."

Law on the Electronic Frontier

You've followed the news. You've heard about the Communications Decency Act, the one that's supposed to ban smut in cyberspace. The buzz over this law has made you hesitate to click your mouse and point your browser toward anything sexually suggestive on the Internet. You wonder: Am I breaking the law?

At press time, engaging in cybersex and taking advantage of the sexual material widely available on the Internet is *not* a crime. And it's doubtful that it ever will be.

"There's a wide range of public interest groups fighting any laws proposed to censor material on the Internet. Their main argument is that any censorship violates First Amendment rights," says Nancy Tamosaitis, author of several books about cybersex, including *The Penthouse Guide to Cybersex*. But in the mercurial world of the Internet, that could all change tomorrow. That shouldn't stop your online explorations, but you'll want to proceed cautiously. To that end, here are some suggestions.

• Check the law. Before you go exploring sex sites, visit the Electronic Frontier Foundation, a public interest group dedicated to posting news and information about Internet laws and regulations. You'll find their Web site at http://www.eff.org.

• Don't post your own. If you have your own home page on the Web, keep it free of sexually suggestive material. The Communications Decency Act targets people who distribute sexually offensive material on the Internet. And while posting a nude picture of your favorite supermodel could hardly be called distributing, do you want to take the chance that some computer-savvy kid might find his way to your site—and that picture? We didn't think so. Be conservative: Look, download if you must, but don't put anything explicit up for others to see.

• Protect young eyes. If you have young children and they have access to your computer, make sure that you've protected them from any illicit material on the Web. You can do this by installing filtering software that will prevent anyone without a password from accessing areas of the Internet that contain sexual material. For more information, check out the home pages of the two leading filtering programs, SurfWatch (at http://www.surfwatch.net) and Cyber-Patrol (at http://www.cyberpatrol.com).

But if you're single, or you and your partner have agreed that online flirting is okay, you'll still want to take some precautions to ensure safe cybersex. Here's what you need to do.

Look and listen. Before you ever throw your first line at some online babe, take a few weeks to "lurk"—to watch the interaction between people who are chatting. "This is the best way to learn about developing relationships online," says Tamosaitis. You'll learn all the shorthand, all the slang, figure out the best place to meet people of your similar age group and interests. Then, when you do identify someone you'd like to strike up a conversation with, you won't risk embarrassing yourself or offending her.

Be careful. If you meet a girl in a bar, you're automatically coy, not very forthcoming with tons of personal details, such as your Social Security number or where you hide the key to the back door. As it is in reality, so it is in virtuality.

"When you meet someone online, don't ask for or give out a lot of personal information too soon," warns Phlegar. If you push her for all sorts of vital statistics too soon, she'll feel threatened and turned off. You should, too, if someone pumps you for a lot of personal data early in your liaison. Obviously, you're not going to hand over credit card numbers or office passwords, but don't even proffer phone numbers or addresses until you've spent a long time messaging back and forth.

It seems paranoid, but imagine this: You meet "Gina" online and you both hit it off because of your mutual interests, including a love of coin collecting. You have a few rolls in the virtual hay; you trade addresses and phone numbers. Next week, you hook up again. She mentions that she's going on vacation next week. You share your own vacation plans for next month. You go off on vacation, come back, and find your house broken into, all your valuables stolen—including that coin collection you told "Gina" all about. Phlegar says that this sort of thing, while not frequent, can happen. Remember, you're total strangers—you've never even seen one another. "Take it slow: If you've spent several weeks messaging back and forth, then you might want to move to phone conversation or exchanging pictures. And once you've done that, you may want to meet face-to-face. But you have to give it plenty of time to build trust with one another," she says. Be cool; be coy.

And if you do indeed plan to meet face-to-face, play it safe—meet in public. No matter how comfortable you are with the online person, meeting privately in person is risky business.

Don't be fooled. Since there's no way to see or hear anyone on the Internet, you can be certain of one thing: Nothing is certain. Everything someone tells you about themselves may be the honest truth, or it may be an elaborate lie. In a way, that's what makes the Internet so amazingly liberating. You can tell people you look like Redford. And who's to say you're not? But just as you can adopt a fictitious persona, remember that whomever you're meeting out there can do the same.

"Take everything you see online with a grain of salt. You have no way of knowing whether it's true," says Tamosaitis. While it might be fun to pull the wool over someone else's eyes, imagine how you'd feel if you discovered that the "woman" you've been having cybersex with is, in reality, some horny guy.

You know, just like you.

LIVING AT HOME

Poet Robert Frost once wrote, "Home is the place where, when you have to go there, / They have to take you in."

Sometimes you just have to go back home. According to the Population Reference Bureau, roughly 40 percent of us are or have been "boomerangers"—young adults who return home to live with Mom and Dad after a period of living away. If you're living at home right now, you might be hearing that you're part of a new trend among the slacker, twenty-something set. But you're not. Ever since World War II, about 40 percent of young men return to the nest at some point in their budding adult lives.

"But whatever the reasons for it, the situation of a young adult living under his parents' roof can create some real friction and personal challenges for everyone concerned," says Barry G. Ginsberg, Ph.D., executive director of the Center of Relationship Enhancement in Doylestown, Pennsylvania, and an expert in parent-child relationships. "You're the son, the child, living under their roof, but you're an adult, too. It's a paradox. You want to live your own life, but you have to follow their rules. They know you're an adult—they worked to get you to that point—but they're still your parents, and they have a strong instinct to take care of you and also tell you what to do." You begin to see why there might be conflict, especially when your adult needs and desires conflict with your parents'.

To put it more succinctly: It's nearly impossible to have a normal sex life while you're living with your parents. It reduces you to heavy petting in the rec room; or trying to think of elaborate ways to sneak a woman into your room. If you want to stay over at woman's apartment, that's almost worse since Mom wants you to call if you're not coming home.

If you're living at home or facing the possibility any time soon, consider this chapter a "welcome home" present from us. First, we'll examine what forces have gotten you homeward bound and how to keep a certain measure of your independence—and your sanity—as an adult under his parents' roof. Then, we'll help you to get back out on your own so that you can continue to enjoy all the pleasures of adult life again.

HITTING HOME

As you sit in your old twin bed, looking at the dusty trophies or model airplanes still suspended from the ceiling, you may find yourself wondering how you ended up back here.

"Your parents are wondering, too. They carry a lot of guilt that maybe they didn't do their job, didn't give you everything you needed to make it on your own," says Dr. Ginsberg. This thought may have occurred to you, too.

We urge you to dismiss it. In most cases, there's a legitimate reason—some force beyond your control—that caused you to move back home, say psychologists Jean Davies Okimoto and Phyllis Jackson Stegall, co-authors of *Boomerang Kids: How to Live with Adult Children Who Return Home*. Here are a few of the most likely causes. They're not meant as excuses—experts agree that no matter what brought you home, you can and should work toward getting back out on your own—but they can help you understand how you might have ended up back where you started.

Economics. Financial recession. Unemployment. Cost of living. You name it, it's against you, especially for men who turned 18 in the 1980s and faced significant economic downturns, write Frances Goldscheider, Ph.D., and Calvin Goldscheider, Ph.D., demographers from Brown University in Providence, Rhode Island, who discuss the boomerang phenomenon in *Leaving and Returning Home in the 20th Century*. Sure, you've heard Dad tell you countless times how he was married, had kids, and even owned a house by the time he was your age. Well, hooray for Dad, but he bucked the odds since roughly 40 percent of his generation were living with their parents after adulthood.

"Dad also had a few other advantages that you may not: His dollar stretched further, for one thing, and the cost of living has nearly tripled since he was your age," points out Daniel Kegan, Ph.D., a psychologist with Elan Associates in Chicago and an expert in interpersonal relationships.

We're marrying later. In previous generations it was not at all uncommon for men and women to leave home, go to college, meet each other, get married, and get a place of their own. These days, say Okimoto and Stegall, men and women are marrying later, which means that we're delaying a powerful rite of passage that used to move us quickly into the realm of adulthood.

We're not in the Army now. Right after marriage, the next big rite of passage that motored us out the door was joining the military or being drafted. In an era of downsized military, that's just not happening anymore. So much for the peace dividend.

We're thrifty. Economics aren't always a force keeping us home. Sometimes, we have good jobs and make plenty of money; but we'd just rather stay at home to save that money. Rent costs hundreds of dollars a month, we reason. We could take that money and sock it away for a down payment on a home or pay down car or student loans twice as fast. "Lots of people who live with their parents aren't deadbeats; they're often staying in a rent-free situation at their parents' expense so that they can save what little money they may have starting out. That's not a problem, so long as it's understood by all parties that this is a temporary arrangement," says Dr. Kegan.

We're deadbeats. Okay, so maybe some of us aren't so thrifty. A nasty truth to face up to, but there it is. Plenty of us have learned that, hey, the world is kind of a hard place, where things cost money and people expect you to work. On the other hand, home is the epitome of low-cost and low-responsibility. This is the least noble of reasons for returning home, but it's nothing you can't overcome with a little planning and perseverance. And you should. Remember that home is also a low-sex kind of place, too.

GETTING HOME-FREE

Whatever forced you home, that's not the problem. The real problem, the experts say, is never the situation that made you return home but what happens after you get there. Stay at home long enough, they say, and you'll fall into one of two traps—the Comfort Trap or the Conflict Trap.

"One big area where problems start is where a child moves back home, the parents are glad to have him, maybe Mom dotes on him a little bit," says Dr. Ginsberg. After a taste of the hard life that awaits you out in the real world, you get used to the comfort you enjoyed as a kid. "Then, you don't want to leave," he says. That's the Comfort Trap.

The other side to this behavioral coin is conflict, where you don't feel so comfortable all the time. Maybe you're itching for your bachelor lifestyle to begin again. You're starting to chafe against your parents' rules, which seemed restrictive when you were a kid. Now, as an adult, they're downright intrusive.

Let this fact hit home: It's not good for any of you—parents or offspring—if you stay at home long-term. You're an adult now. Your own nascent sense of self-determination and independence is clashing head-on with the old household rules of calling if you're going to be late and keeping your feet off the furniture.

Meanwhile, you're not the only one who's finding that you can't go home again. While you were away becoming an adult, your parents were changing, too, into people who were looking forward to the time when you would be off living your own life and they could have the place to themselves. They love you and they accept you, but they may also resent you a little bit for coming back. They may never tell you that, of course, but you're an insightful adult now—you've probably sensed this yourself.

You're all living in a tricky, awkward place. But there are ways you can coexist peacefully with your parents. At the same time, you can be working to get yourself out the door and back on your own. Here are some basic rules to live by.

Set a date. When you moved in, you said it would be temporary. Now, here it is six months later and your old room has gotten pretty cozy. You're deep in the Comfort Trap. But you can fix it today. Here's how. Grab a calendar and set yourself a reasonable date for moving out. Don't attach it to situations, like when you get a better job or when you get married. Look at your finances and prospects, discuss it with your parents, and try to set a reasonable deadline for getting out and on your own. "Just setting a date can have wonderfully focusing effect on your efforts," says Dr. Kegan.

Protecting Your Space

Just because your parents set the rules doesn't mean they get to rule over you like they did when you were 10. If you have to move home, you don't have to surrender your rights as an adult. In *Boomerang Kids: How to Live with Adult Children Who Return Home*, co-authors Jean Davies Okimoto and Phyllis Jackson Stegall set some guidelines for hands-off topics—aspects of your life that your parents are not allowed to comment or pass judgment on, things that you as an adult have an intrinsic right to.

What you eat: If you're contributing to the grocery bill, you should have a say in what you want to eat. And if you want to eat when you feel like it, let your parents know up front not to expect you at dinner, unless you ask to join them in advance.

When you sleep: As long as you're fulfilling the obligations you agreed to when you moved in, you should be able to sleep when you want and for as long as you want.

How you look: Your personal appearance is not subject to their approval. If they don't like the way you look, they don't have to go out with you in public. If your personal appearance causes problems for them—if your muddy clothes stain the rug where you left them in a heap or if your sparse grooming habits lead to, say, head lice—then they are within their rights to object.

What sort of friends or lovers you choose: Although your parents may set the rules about when and how you can have visitors, as an adult, you have a fundamental right to consort with whomever you choose. If they don't like the woman you're dating (or the man, for that matter), that's their problem. Exception: If Mom catches your new girlfriend with her hand in the jewelry box, she's allowed to freak.

How you spend your money: The only time your parents should say anything about your finances is when you can't meet whatever obligations you have to them. If you spend all your money on beer and don't have enough cash to pay for household expenses you've incurred or a rent you've agreed on, then they have the right to butt in.

Follow their rules. Parents and adult children clash time and again over the rules of the house. A grown man doesn't want to call in if he's going to be late; or maybe he wants to leave his clothes in a pile on the floor.

We have to point out the obvious for a moment: You're in your parents' house, not your own. If you choose to stay with them, you have to adhere to their rules, just as you'd respect the rules of any host who didn't give birth to you. If they say to call home when you're going to be late, call. If they say that you have to make your bed every morning, get folding, pal. Don't think of it as demeaning; think of it as a sign of respect. Meanwhile, following the rules of another household should only sharpen your resolve to get out and get your own household.

Pitch in. Even as you agree to follow the old rules of the house, you can still assert yourself as an adult. One way is to act responsibly and to make yourself useful. If you can, do it financially. Try to pay a nominal rent to your parents every week or month. It may not even cover the barest household expenses, but you'll both feel better about it. In addition to rent, pay your own expenses wherever possible: That means your own phone calls and whatever groceries you eat. If you have to borrow your parents' car, top off the tank before you bring it home. In addition to financial contributions, make sure that you're on hand to do a man's share of the chores. If there's lawn to be mowed, mow it; if there's firewood to be got, get it.

Budget yourself. Even when they pitch in financially, most live-at-home adults find that they have a lot more money on payday than if they owned an apartment. That makes them a little crazy. They start to think they're loaded and go out and buy a lot of stuff, or find that they can afford vacations that they really couldn't if they were out on their own. This, too, is a bad trap to fall into because you'll start to get accustomed to a lifestyle that you shouldn't realistically expect so early in your adult life. Instead of treating yourself to nightly pub crawls with the guys or expensive stereo equipment, try investing that money or saving it instead—that's the nest egg that's going to help you buy furniture and pay security deposits when you move out. Give yourself a reasonable weekly budget for expenses and entertainment, says Dr. Kegan. Whatever's left over should be put into savings.

Show some restraint. Now for the topic you were beginning to think we forgot about: sex. Living at home, you may have noticed that your love life isn't getting any hotter. Unless you have ultra-progressive parents, they've probably outlawed coed sleepovers. That's assuming that you could find a coed to sleep over with you in the first place. Our research suggests that most women consider the man who "lives with Mom" to be a total turnoff—a mere boy-man who lacks the gumption or resourcefulness to sever the apron strings and get his own life. (Yes, we know this is a terrible generalization and unfair to the man who has a legitimate financial reason for returning to the fold, but there it is.) If you're dating someone, of course, it's okay to take her home for dinner or an evening of TV in the rec room, just like in high school. But they also have to leave at the end of the evening, just like in high school. Don't open yourself to embarrassment by trying to sneak a girl into your room. You're a grown man, for God's sake! Consider this just one more reason to get out and get on your own.

BACHELOR PAD

Where you live should be a place that makes you feel comfortable, that makes you feel at home. It should say something about you. It should also be inviting enough that you'll be able to entertain women there without hearing snide comments about the dish-filled sink; or watching them simply shriek and flee in terror.

If you're out and on your own for the first time, the freedom of your own place can be dizzying. And intimidating. At first, you may have an impulse to outfit your place like you did at college or home. But you quickly realize that's not quite right. You can't tape a few tattered posters to the wall and call it good. You're going to need more furniture than a beanbag, a futon, and a stack of milk crates. You need to decorate. You need to furnish. You need to mark your territory.

"Decorating your very own bachelor pad is one of the great perks of adulthood and an awful lot of fun," says Thomas E. Azzari, Hollywood production designer who has created ideal bachelor apartments for TV shows like *Seinfeld* and *The Single Guy*. Finally, you get to flex some muscle as master of your domain, to exercise your hard-earned right to live however you choose and with whatever you choose.

You may realize that one of the things you'll want to have in your apartment from time to time is a woman. "That means that you'll have to create an environment that not only makes you feel at home but also says something about you: This is my inner sanctum. This is who I am," says Azzari. Done well, a good bachelor's apartment not only displays a facet of your personality but is also a kind of unmoving ambassador of goodwill, inviting, welcoming.

Of course, everyone's taste is different, and what you'll want to do in your place may be different from the next guy. "But there are some general style guidelines that decorators follow that can help add life and style to an apartment—and not for very much money either," says Gerald Tidwell, senior manager of international visual marketing for Pier 1 Imports, whose chain of houseware stores caters to the young, the hip, the low on cash. Here are some general precepts to help you make your place a comfortable, appealing, and above all pretty cool place that women will want to hang out in.

LIVING ROOM

Essentials: If you live in a studio apartment, the living room is also your only room. Your main piece of furniture will likely be a futon or thrift-store foldout couch, and that's okay. You want a big piece of furniture to lounge on, to lend focus to the room, says Tidwell. Also, you can't very well watch TV lying on a hard floor. Even if you live in a multiroom apartment, it's still a good idea to have a large piece of furniture that converts readily into temporary sleeping quarters, for out-of-town visitors you don't want to sleep with; or for the buddy who drank too much to drive home. If it's the couch you and your pals sat on, passed out on, puked on all through college, you might want to invest in a slipcover for it—most major department stores carry them in the linen department. At the very least, go to a store and get a gigantic, neutral-color bedsheet to drape over it, suggests Tidwell.

In this room, a TV is a given. A stereo probably is, too. Make sure that you know where all the jazz and classical stations are on your radio dial (the better for mood music). Display your CDs, tapes, or vinyl in an orderly fashion. They shouldn't be alphabetized (makes you look too anal and controlling) but they shouldn't be in a haphazard pile either. Keep at least one album of girl-oriented acoustic folk music on hand—women are nuts for this genre. Just look for an earthy woman with tousled hair and an acoustic guitar on the cover and you can't go wrong.

Finally, keep a selection of books on display—in a windowsill, next to the couch, anywhere. Books say sophistication, thoughtfulness, sensitivity. Again, don't alphabetize, let them rest in a jumble of fiction and nonfiction. If you're not much of a reader, hit the local book shop and start rummaging through the bargain bins. Stock your shelf with a few thrillers, a book of poetry (an anthology is okay), a biography of someone you admire (or have at least heard of), the baseball almanac that came with your subscription to that sports magazine, and a couple of obscure hardback books. Stash this book in your bedroom, unless you want her to chance upon this chapter.

Extras: Keep a blanket on hand—something draped cavalierly over the back of the couch. Girls get cold easily, even with you around to keep them warm. Having a blanket nearby says that you are thoughtful and considerate. And she'll be obligated to invite you to share it.

Also, get an inexpensive throw rug to put between the couch and the TV. It lends character to the room. Hint: A light-color rug makes a small room seem bigger and brighter; a dark rug makes a big room seem cozier, says Tidwell.

DINING ROOM

Essentials: Recognizing that you may not have a huge place, for our purposes let's call the "dining room" any corner big enough to accommodate two chairs and a flat surface wider than a TV tray. This may be a kitchen alcove, a breakfast nook, or a quadrant of the living room. However you carve it out of the space you have, you do need a designated dining area for those times when you'll want to impress a woman with your culinary skills. If you slave in your kitchen for a couple hours, you want to be able to serve her in a place that's not in front of the TV, where you can actually sit down, gaze into each other's eyes, and share a meal together. If you can afford a nice small café table and some matching chairs, so much the better. If not, a card table and a couple foldout chairs work just as well (when you go to the thrift store for that couch cover, pick up an inoffensive tablecloth. Nothing lacy, nothing in camouflage). This furniture also doubles as an excellent venue for that other staple of bachelor-pad life: poker night.

Extras: Candles. Not masculine, you say? Ridiculous. Go to a good candle shop and check out what's there. Not the spirally, cutesy candles smelling of mulberries—look for the big fat ones sitting on top of wrought-iron pedestals. Tidwell says that you should have one for every room in the apartment—lends a certain medieval machismo to the place. For the dining room table, keep it simple—a couple of thumb-width, foot-long candles in a pair of simple glass or brass holders. The dim light will not only lend an air of romance to the dinner but may also hide any culinary imperfections in the presentation of the meal (remember, everything looks good by candlelight). No fair digging the camp lantern out of your backpack and using that instead.

BEDROOM

Essentials: You already know that you need a bed big enough for two people. A simple frame would be nice, too—something about a bed lying right on the floor makes you look like a squatter in your own habitat.

Right next to the bed, you need a night table. Not a milk crate, but a genuine piece of furniture, with a drawer and a tabletop. "All the bachelors' apartments I've ever designed feature a nightstand in the bedroom," says Azzari. "That's where you store your condoms." Besides providing a convenient storage site for birth control, a bedside table also gives you space for a reading lamp and an alarm clock, while giving her a surface on which to lay jewelry, earrings, diaphragm cases, and so on.

There may be other accessories you normally keep in your bedroom—a suggestive poster, a girlie calendar, the swimsuit issue stowed under your bed. If a woman's coming over and there's even a chance she's going to see the inside of your room, stow this stuff in a closet. You see it as a sort of worship of the female gender; she sees it as disrespectful and insulting. Keep it under wraps.

Extras: Extra pillows and a big, comfy comforter. A woman goes into your bedroom, sees a well-made bed with lots of pillows and a nice comforter, it's only going to confirm her decision to spend the night. Creating a warm, inviting sleeping space as opposed to a dark, foreboding bear's den will also make her want to come back.

BATHROOM

Essentials: Aside from being relatively clean, your bathroom really needs only a couple of vital elements. One is a small trash can, a common oversight in the male bathroom. Anything a man wants to dispose of in the bathroom, he can usually flush. Those he can't—an empty shampoo bottle or soap carton, say—he can always pitch into the big garbage bucket in the kitchen. But women want to be able to throw away any of a number of nonflushable items without carting their refuse through the rest of the apartment to pitch it out. Be considerate.

Other key bathroom elements include more than one roll of toilet paper (stored within arm's reach of the toilet) and more than one set of towels. If you want her to stay over, you're going to want her to be able to bathe in your home and have her own set of dry, warm towels when she does it.

Extras: A box of tissues. A bath mat. Soft toilet paper (trust us, she'll appreciate it). For a real nice touch, keep an unopened toothbrush in the medicine cabinet. If she wonders why you keep new toothbrushes on hand (it may strike her as presumptuous), just tell her you got it last time you went to the dentist (you knew they give them out free after every exam, right?).

KITCHEN

Essentials: Besides whatever cookware you need to make dinner for a date, make sure that you have at least one matching set of dishes, enough silverware to serve two people, and a couple of wine glasses, made from real glass. Everything else can be an eclectic hodgepodge of mismatched dishes, glasses, and cutlery.

For foodstuffs, have a ready supply of ingredients so that you can make a meal from scratch or near-scratch (for a complete list, see "The Perfect Pantry"). Have some meat in the freezer (preferably chicken, fish, or a lean cut of beef) and some real pasta (no elbow macaroni or Chef Boy-Ar-Dee) in the cupboard.

Keep snack food on hand, but make it low-fat, says Chris Rosenbloom, R.D., Ph.D., spokesperson for the American Dietetic Association and associate professor of nutrition at Georgia State University in Atlanta. Odds are that she's eating healthy, and so should you. Instead of mixed nuts and potato chips, buy pretzels, popcorn, or reduced-fat snack chips. Exception: Make sure that there's some form of chocolate in the house, whether it's ice cream or after-dinner mints. Chocolate stimulates pleasure centers in the brain, especially in women's brains. Bring her a plate of truffles after dinner and she won't think of it as dessert; she'll think of it as foreplay.

DOING THE DETAIL WORK

With most of the basics in place, you're ready for Advanced Apartment Decorating—extra touches and details that really put the mark of ownership on your territory. If your apartment is the sort of place where you only stay long enough to sleep and void your bowels, you won't find much here of interest. But if your apartment is something you want to cultivate as a *location*, a destination your pals or your women gravitate to after a night out, then you'll probably take a little more pride in how the place looks.

That being the case, here are a few expert tips for turning the place where you sleep and eat into the place you call home.

Paint your wagon. For less than $100, you can slap a few different colors of paint on your walls and turn a drab flat into a great apartment.

"Most apartments are just off-white. Even painting one wall a different

The Perfect Pantry

She's coming over for dinner, and you're missing, like, five essential ingredients for that chicken à la you dish that you were planning. You can keep that from ever happening again by simply stocking your pantry properly. For a variety of quick, healthy meals, make sure that your kitchen contains the following, suggests Chris Rosenbloom, R.D., Ph.D., spokesperson for the American Dietetic Association and associate professor of nutrition at Georgia State University in Atlanta.

Pantry
Dried and canned beans
Canned tomatoes, tomato
   sauce, and tomato paste
Canned corn
Canned peas
Canned chicken broth
White and brown rice
Quick-cooking grains such as
   bulgur, millet, or couscous
Onions
Ginger
Garlic
Olive oil
Pasta

Refrigerator
A selection of fruits and vegetables
   bles
Mustard
Nonfat yogurt
Nonfat buttermilk
Tortillas

Freezer
Boneless chicken breast
Turkey cutlets
Frozen vegetables

color can really liven it up," says Azzari. Of course, you need to check with your landlord first. Money-saving tip: Spin it as a favor to him. Tell him you think the place needs a new coat of paint, and you'd be willing to do it, if he pays for the paint and gives you a break on that month's rent. If he won't go for that, then at least ask if he has any objections to you painting the place—tastefully. As long as you're not going to throw huge splotches on the wall or paint the place all black, most landlords see a fresh coat of paint as an improvement.

Clean regularly. We hate to be a mom about it, but you have to know that a clean place is going to be the sort of place a woman will want to come back to again and again.

You don't have to sterilize the place from top to bottom, but you should clean your bathroom and kitchen at least every other week. Stuff your dirty clothes in a closet or hamper. If you have carpets, vacuum. If you have hardwood floors, corral those dust bunnies with a weekly mopping. Change your sheets once a week—more if you're having sex between them regularly. Nothing turns a woman off faster than getting it on in grody bedclothes.

Frame it up. No place feels like home until you start putting stuff on the walls. Pictures and prints make all the difference in an apartment, and they can be handy conversation pieces. But put them in frames, okay? Nothing looks more immature than a poster that's taped to a wall, or a handful of curling photos resting on a milk crate. Most frame shops or houseware stores carry a wide variety of pre-made frames, and most prints you'll buy come in standard sizes that these frames fit. Buy one and frame it yourself. Put snapshots in frames of different shapes, sizes, and colors and scatter them around the apartment. Hide the pictures of old girlfriends, but keep a picture of you as a baby on display. Seeing this will amuse her, prove that you don't take yourself too seriously, and may spark some latent maternal instinct in her that will only make her more attracted to you. Like they say, a picture is worth a thousand moves.

Be yourself. Finally, don't feel that you have to create the ideal space based on what she will respond to. Remember, this is your place. "When I design sets, I design them based on the characters who are supposed to occupy them. Take Jerry Seinfeld. He likes cereal, so I make sure that there are lots of cereal boxes on display. He likes Superman, and he's not embarrassed about it—he decorates with Superman statues and magnets."

Whether it's Superman or the Super Bowl, decorate according to your own bliss. The more you display the possessions, color schemes, memorabilia, and artwork that you like, the more you can say about yourself. "It's a way of saying. 'This is who I am.' And if she doesn't like it, well, that may give you some clue that she's not the best person for you and you won't have to waste a lot of time on her," says Azzari.

DEALING
WITH HER PARENTS

Few moments in a relationship are more awkward, more nerve-racking, more suffused with repressed tension than the moment when she brings you home to meet the folks. Walking through the door and into the gaze of the people who created the love of your life, you feel like a chimp in a tuxedo, a knuckle-dragging oddity that everyone's staring at, waiting to see what tricks you can do.

You smile, nod politely, gently clasp her mom's hand. Then you turn, muster your best grip, and grasp the outstretched hand of her father. You look him in the eye. You both mouth noncommittal pleasantries.

You're thinking: I'm sleeping with your daughter.

Dad's thinking: He's sleeping with my daughter.

But this awkward moment passes, and when it does, you begin to realize something. Being introduced to her parents is actually a wonderful compliment. It means you have passed some kind of muster. Your honey considers you important enough in her life that she's willing to show you off to the other people who are important to her. Little wonder that the moment can be auspicious and tense at the same time.

Now, it could very well be you're one of those semi-mythical fellows who immediately, effortlessly endears himself to the parents of the woman he dates or marries—the kind who gets his own tin of holiday cookies from her mom, who plays nine holes with her dad once a month. If so, you have our admiration and our envy. Many guys do not have, and never develop, this kind of hassle-free relationship.

"Sure, there are going to be the boyfriends or husbands who get on so well with her parents that she starts to complain that they like him more than they like their own daughter," says Shirley Glass, Ph.D., a clinical psychologist in Owings Mills, Maryland, who specializes in interpersonal relationships. But most often, says Dr. Glass, relations stay civil at best, or turn chilly or prickly when you reveal a viewpoint, attitude, or habit of life that doesn't meet with their approval. If your relationship is short-term, or your partner doesn't have much contact with her family, it's easy enough to say, "To hell with them!" But if she loves her family, and your relationship with her becomes long-term, you're going to have to deal with these people on a regular basis. Do you want to deal with them as bitter adversaries or as respectful allies?

We suspect the latter, which is why we offer some of the following parental guidance. There are whole books devoted to coping with in-laws but very little information about how to handle that first meeting between the parents and the boyfriend, or how to deal with her parents in that limbo between the first meeting and the time when they become in-laws. This chapter fills that gap. Here, we'll help you get off on the right foot with her parents and lay the foundation for a longer relationship that will help you earn and maintain their respect. Who knows? You might even end up liking each other.

SURVIVING THE FIRST ENCOUNTER

Consider the first meeting of her parents as an unwanted but nevertheless compulsory social function: Since you have to go, you might as well smile, be pleasant, and get it over with as soon as possible. This is not the time to be showing them what an exciting and dynamic person their daughter has latched onto. In a first encounter, exciting and dynamic translates into a parent's mind as ultra-liberal or substance-addicted. If you have any future with this woman, you'll have plenty of time later to show her parents what an odd, wonderful, eccentric genius you are. Meanwhile, get through the preliminaries so that you emerge on the other side with your dignity intact. Meanwhile, if they come away knowing not a lot about you but thinking you're polite and respectful, then the meeting will have been a complete success. Here's how to ensure that outcome.

Talk it over first. Before that portentous first meeting, it may put you both at ease if you talk with your partner first about her expectations and yours. "I'd say it's essential to having a good experience the first time you meet her family," says Dr. Glass. "If you're nervous, you can tell her. You can ask her outright what she expects of the meeting, how you should behave around her family, what topics you should or shouldn't bring up. It seems contrived, but discussing these things ahead of time can help you all have a better experience and will pave the way for good relations." And if you're visiting her parents for an overnighter, this is also the time to confirm sleeping arrangements with her. Odds are that you'll be in the guest room or on the sofa anyway, but it's better to be clear on this fact now than make an embarrassing gaffe later.

Mind your manners. When you're in a tough situation, sometimes it helps to have a set of rules or guidelines to fall back on. This explains why coaches draw up game plans, why the *Boy Scout Handbook* is in its zillionth printing. "And in situations where emotions are running high, it's very helpful to men to have a set of rules to rely on. It helps them cope. It helps them establish a sense of order and control," says Scott Stanley, Ph.D., co-director of the Center for Marital and Family Studies at the University of Denver and co-author of *Fighting for Your Marriage*. When you're meeting parents for the first time, the rules that you should fall back on are the ones of basic etiquette. Let your manners be your shield against whatever happens to you as you enter the parental domain. This will help you in two ways: First, it's a sign of respect. Second, it's excellent public relations for you—good manners under pressure reveal you to be a man of poise and nerve. Parents who see a man with good manners think maybe that man was raised by a couple of people just like them. So how bad could he be?

A quick refresher: Shake Mom's hand first, then Dad's. Put your napkin in your lap. The little fork is for salad. Keep your feet and elbows off the furniture. And don't sit in the recliner or any seat with a remote on the cushion— that's her father's chair.

Be a sponge. Aside from answering direct questions or throwing the occasionally witty comment into the conversation, try to speak less and listen more. Listening is a sign of respect and good manners. So sit there and absorb it all. If her parents are real nightmares, heaping abuse and condescension on you, soak it in with a smile (if it helps, remind yourself that they will die sooner than you). If they render judgments about the world that you don't happen to agree with, don't get sucked into a debate. Just listen with a thoughtful look on your face. "Remember that this is not just an opportunity to make a good impression on them; the reverse also applies. You're trying to learn something about them. The more you learn about them now, the easier it will be to deal with them in the future," says Helen Fisher, Ph.D., research associate in the department of anthropology at Rutgers University in New Brunswick, New Jersey, and author of *Anatomy of Love*.

Show love, not lust. So you love her and you see no reason why the rest of the world shouldn't know it. That's fine—shout your love from the rooftops if you must. But when you're meeting her parents for the first time, keep your hands off her, at least while they're in the room.

"It's important to show your feelings for their daughter. If they see you have a lot of love and respect for their child, then you'll eventually win their love and respect," says Dr. Glass. You do that through nontactile means, though. By looking for opportunities to compliment her on her appearance, her talents, her aspirations; by deferring to her in conversation; by holding doors open for her; by asking her if she needs anything any time you get up to leave the room. But if instead her parents see you pawing her on the rec room sofa or fondling her bottom every time you walk by, they're going to dismiss you as a masher who's taking advantage of their little girl. A dad who sees this sort of lustful behavior isn't trying to remember what it's like to be young and in love; he's trying to remember where he keeps the shells for the shotgun.

OVER THE LONG HAUL

Once the initial meeting is over and her parents start to realize you may be around for a while, you're all going to start letting your guard down a little. This means that you'll see them behave a little more like someone's mom and dad and a little less like a panel of judges. For your part, you'll find that you become more relaxed. You won't be a stiff around them. Occasionally, an elbow or two will make its way onto the table; you might allow her parents to catch you in an amorous clinch. These are all good signs. You're all starting to mesh, to get along when you're together.

But there may still be friction. Maybe you and she are living together now and her parents are so scandalized that they forget their manners when they're around you. Maybe you don't like the way her parents treat her. Or you. Maybe they like you just fine but do or say hundreds of irritating little things that you'd like to call them on just once.

Can you? Should you? Of course.

"It's all well and good to try to make a good impression. But ultimately, you have to be yourself and be mindful of your own needs as well as those of your partner. Her parents may not like it if you start to assert yourself around them, but you can't live your life according to them any more than you could live your life according to your own parents," says Dr. Glass. What's needed is a sense of balance between doing what's right by them and doing what's right for you. Here's how to do it.

Be on her side. With every Sunday dinner, holiday, or weekend you spend with her parents, you'll be brought more into their familial circle. That's good. But beware: You'll also be brought into the family politics. Which, you may remember from your own family experiences, can be cutthroat.

Scenario: You're sitting around the dining room table after a sumptuous feast (and you've dutifully remembered to compliment her mom on the meal). In the midst of after-dinner chat, her mom starts in on your sweetie, suggesting that she might look better if she let her hair grow out a little. You couldn't agree more, by the way. You love the idea of her long, flowing tresses streaming across the bed. (But never mind that right now.) Mom looks to Dad, and now he picks up the ball, agreeing heartily to this change in his daughter's appearance. She gets the hunted look of the hen-pecked daughter. Meanwhile, her mother turns to you. "Well, what do you think? Shouldn't she change her hairstyle?"

Your answer: You look her in the eye and tell her she's absolutely gorgeous just as she is.

What? Even though you're really into the whole long, flowing tresses thing? Yep.

"This is a common trap. Regardless of whether he agrees, if a guy wants to get in good with her parents, he may be tempted to side with them," says Dr. Glass. Big mistake. You're not there to be a yes-man to her parents. You're there to support her. Take your cue from her dad, who sided with his woman right away. "As much as you might want to ingratiate yourself with her parents, your first priority is to be true to your own relationship," says Dr. Glass. You can always tell her on the drive home that you actually wouldn't mind if she grew her hair out.

Learn from them. Just as her parents are learning more about you, you can also learn something from them that will help you in your relationship. "It's all part of observing what they do. How they treat their child. How they treat each other," says Dr. Fisher. These observations will give you glimpses into the future, to see how you'll be with each other.

"And if you see something you don't like, now's the best time to talk to your partner, to see how she feels about this particular trait. It can help you overcome problems before they occur later on," says Dr. Glass.

Show your commitment. You're committed to your partner and she knows that. If you want to be on good terms with her parents, it wouldn't hurt to let them know your feelings, too. When you first met, you were probably pretty reserved around them. But over time, don't be afraid to make it clear to them how you feel about their child, also known as the light of your life.

"Showing your commitment is important for a lot of parents, especially if you and your partner have decided to live together," says Dr. Glass. Many parents frown on that for obvious reasons—not the least of which is that they see living together as a sign that you're not committed. (If you were, you'd marry her, they reason). If you're living together but want to marry her someday, make sure that her parents know it. If you don't believe in marriage but you believe in her enough that you would forsake the glamour of bachelorhood to live with her, make sure that her parents see the dedication in your eyes. "Ultimately, all parents care about is that their children are happy and cared for. If they sense that you are sincere in making their child feel this way, they're going to respond a lot better to you," says Dr. Glass.

Please her, not them. It's a sad truth that there are a certain number of parents out there who believe no man is good enough for their daughter. End of discussion. "If they have made it clear that they can't be won over, no matter what you do, then you have to consider whether it's worth it to keep trying," says Dr. Glass. "Ultimately, they are not the people you have chosen to be with. Your partner is." If she's happy with you, if she knows you've done your best, if she acknowledges on some level that her parents are being jerks, then stop beating your head against the brick wall of their disapproval. Go and live your lives together regardless of what they think.

BACHELOR PARTIES

In days of old, a warrior would gather his best men around him on the eve of his marriage. These men would share an evening of revelry, drinking to the health of the groom, and pledging their unwavering support against all his enemies, including in-laws.

Since then, we've traded in the swords and shields for stogies and stag films, but the bachelor party still serves a time-honored function in the world of men. It gives us a chance to roast and toast a friend before he ventures off into the land of matrimony. It's a time of fellowship and brotherhood, a time to pledge allegiance to a pal good and true. It's also a ceremonial last hurrah when the groom gets to kick back in an estrogen-free environment and celebrate his final hours as a decadent, depraved bachelor.

To that end, bachelor parties should have an element of wildness to them. But a bachelor party is also a social function. And like all social functions, it's bound to certain rules of behavior and etiquette, some of which contribute to the mystique and enjoyment of the event, others which simply drag it down. If you're a best man—or are going to be any time soon—you'll want to know the best way, the right way, to throw a bachelor party nowadays.

Make a list. You already know to invite the groom's pals to this event, but as this is a part of the wedding celebration, there are a few other men besides your usual circle of pals that you'll want to an extend an invite to. This includes any men in the wedding party, as well as the fathers of both the bride and the groom. (Don't worry: If they come at all, they'll probably only stay a short time.)

"Also, if you don't know the bride's family well, it's worth checking with her or her parents to see if there are any other male friends or family members you should invite—brothers, cousins, and so on," says Patty Szabo-Fowler, a wedding planner in Knoxville, Tennessee, and author of the wedding etiquette book *Nicely Done Nuptials*.

Build in recovery time. Although it's not unheard of to hold the bachelor party on the eve of the wedding, consider that throwing such a bash the night before may find the groom doing a little throwing himself the next day. Hungover grooms do not good wedding pictures make. That's why most bachelor parties are scheduled a weekend or two before the wedding—it gives everyone ample recovery time. If the eve of the wedding finds the groom anxious to blow off a little steam, though, there's nothing wrong with rounding up a small group—maybe just the groomsmen and ushers—and taking the groom to a local bar and making one last toast to his bachelorhood. Keep it quiet, keep it low-key. He may remember that more than the actual bachelor party.

Decide who pays. Although the burden of planning a bachelor party usually falls on the best man's head, all the financial obligations shouldn't have to also. Unless the groom or his father has expressed other financial wishes, everyone should pay his own way, except the groom—the guests should divvy up his tab and each pay a share. If you're going to rent a room at a hotel or restaurant, get together a reasonable estimate of what each guest will have to chip in to pay for the room and tell people the amount when you invite them. At that time, you can also make it clear to guests what the financial arrangements will be. "It's not rude to bring up financial matters when you invite a guest to a bachelor party. If you expect guests to pay their share, it's good manners to let them know in advance," says Szabo-Fowler.

Pick a venue. Where you go and what you do will depend largely on the kind of guy your groom is, but it's always nice to plan the evening around his likes and interests. If he's a sports fanatic, throw the party at his favorite sports bar. If he likes the outdoors, plan your party in the woods and camp out overnight. If he's into extreme fun and games, throw your party at a mountain-bike track, with a tailgate party afterward. No one's going to mope if you all go to a bar, drink beer, and smoke stogies. But if you pick a novel venue that has your groom's interests at heart, it's going to be much more memorable.

Roast, don't ruin. A good bachelor party must—simply must—include some good-natured fun at the groom's expense. Once upon a time, that meant taking turns telling embarrassing stories about your soon-to-be-married pal. This is still great fun: Nothing livens up a party like watching the groom squirm while you talk about his old girlfriends or the time he got so drunk that he went blind for a day. But embarrass him within reason. Getting

A Coed Bachelor Party?

Call it a slap in the face to tradition, or call it a new tradition all its own, but rather than segregate the genders into their own separate parties, many modern couples are planning coed parties.

"It's similar to a rehearsal dinner, only much more relaxed," says Patty Szabo-Fowler, a wedding planner in Knoxville, Tennessee, and author of the wedding etiquette book *Nicely Done Nuptials*. "Every one just goes out together and has a good time." You can still incorporate many of the key elements of a bachelor party into a coed party. They may even be a lot more fun. You thought it was fun regaling a roomful of men with tales of the groom's old girlfriends? Watch him squirm when his bride-to-be is sitting at the same table with him.

You can also turn a coed party into an opportunity to blow off some pre-wedding steam. Choose up teams and head to a local softball field. Or have a beach volleyball party. We know one couple who rented a paintball field for an afternoon and played war games—with the bride and groom as opposing generals.

him blind-drunk (again) and then tying him naked to the bride's parents' lamppost is probably overdoing it. And don't even think about taking all his money and putting him on a one-way bus to Toledo. Threatening to do any of the above is perfectly acceptable, of course. But as the best man, be prepared to head off any such attempts should your revelers be overcome by the moment.

Think ahead. Planning a memorable party depends not just on the event itself but also on the infrastructure you build into the event. According to Crys Stewart, editor of *WeddingBells* magazine, you should take a moment to anticipate the needs your guests might have before, during, and after the party and plan accordingly. Examples: "Consider booking a hotel room as a base," says Stewart. "It's a good spot to gather before your night out, and it will provide a place for guests to sleep in the event they're too tired or intoxicated to drive home." Calling a taxi service to provide rides is another option. And if your partying goes into the wee hours, make arrangements to have a late-night round of pizzas or sandwiches delivered. All it takes is a couple phone calls and you come out looking like the guy who was on top of everything, while your groom will simply think of you as, well, the best man.

STRIPPER OR NO STRIPPER: THE GREAT DEBATE

It seems like an unwritten yet unbreakable law that a bachelor party has to include sexual entertainment in order to be a success. In your dad's day, it was the grainy, black-and-white stag films run on a back-room projector.

These days, it seems like anything goes: from an evening around the Playboy Channel to hiring a stripper who lets the groom lick whipped cream off her breasts.

Most etiquette experts we spoke to acknowledge that some racy entertainment at a bachelor party is acceptable but not required. "It's kind of passé," says Szabo-Fowler. "Strippers and porn movies were introduced to bachelor parties at a time when grooms were far less sexually sophisticated than they are now." In an age where your wife was likely to be the only sexual partner you'd ever have, a revealing bachelor party did have some logic. It celebrated and mourned the world of indiscriminate erotic pleasures that the groom would be turning his back on by getting married. "Nowadays, though, both the groom and the bride have usually done quite a bit of sexual exploration before getting married," says Szabo-Fowler. To most latter-day grooms, a nude dancer or a trip to a strip club wouldn't be revealing but embarrassing.

Ultimately, the decision is up to you, depending on what you think the groom would enjoy and whether the bride will go ballistic when she finds out (trust us, she'll find out). But if you're on the fence, our opinion is that hiring erotic entertainment for the bachelor party is in bad taste—hardly something a best man wants to be part of. Remember, you're not just the groom's best man; you're the best man of the entire wedding. As such, it's your job to ensure a certain standard of respect is observed for your pal's union to his honey.

And don't give us that line about tradition. Tradition also used to dictate that the best man had to help the groom break into the home of the bride's family, kidnap the bride, and kill anyone who got in the groom's way—traditions that are nowadays considered bad form, not to mention felony offenses.

FINANCING A RELATIONSHIP

Dating costs money. Forget about dinners out and drinks at the bar. There's cover charges, tickets to shows, gas and tolls for weekends out of town. Flowers, cards, and small gifts add up fast. If the relationship gets deeper and more serious, your debt load gets deeper and more serious to match. Sure, you may start out paying $6 to see a band at the local bar, but see her long enough and you'll be shelling out $200 to a scalper so that you can take her to that sold-out super concert. Once, a handful of hand-picked daisies was a sweet gesture from you. Now, you feel that nothing short of a dozen long-stemmed roses is good enough for her. As your love grows, the stakes and the expenses get ever higher. Suddenly, you're pricing serious high-ticket items, such as vacations in Cancún, diamond rings, and reception halls.

But before that happens, you have to survive the salad years of your dating life—the years when you still want to show your woman a good time, even though you're short on coin. If so, we can help you get the biggest bang for your dating buck.

"A relationship is like any other financial necessity in life—if you want to enjoy it on a regular basis without ever feeling crunched or stressed about it, you'll have to budget for it," says Daniel Kegan, Ph.D., a psychologist with Elan Associates in Chicago and an expert in interpersonal relationships. More to the point, it means learning how to make a total budget for yourself, for your life, then figuring out where to put dating into that budget.

CHEAP DATE, GOOD DATE

A good date doesn't have to break the bank, but it sure seems like that sometimes. "It's true that women tend to look for some sign of resources. It's largely instinctive. They're looking for some sense that the man they're interested in can provide for potential offspring," says Michael R. Cunningham, Ph.D., professor of psychology at the University of Louisville and a researcher into the science of attraction between men and women.

While women respond to a show of financial support or attention, Dr. Cunningham also points out that today's woman is also more sensitive to the fact that you, like she, may be still paying your dues in an entry-level job. As such, you may not have a lot of pennies. The focus then shifts from resources to resourcefulness. How far can you stretch a buck? Or create a memorable night out that costs next to nothing? Here are some suggestions for making dating a high-fun—but not necessarily high-cost—activity.

Plan a picnic. The ultimate cheap date—all you need is a loaf of crusty bread, a hunk of cheese, a bottle of wine, a Swiss Army knife, and a blanket. You can make it part of a bike trek out in the country, or check the paper for free outdoor events that you can plan a picnic around. "It's one of the simplest dates in the world—but also one of the most romantic," says relationship expert Ellen Kreidman, Ph.D., author of *Light Her Fire* and a frequent lecturer on ways men can spice up their relationships, using methods that emphasize creativity, not currency.

Go off-off Broadway. Sure, tickets to the Broadway smash that just hit town are going for scalper's prices. But for a night at the theater, you can opt for something more unconventional and economical. Check out local art house productions or theater troupes; their shows are way cheaper and often a lot more fun for your money than taking in a big show. Plus, by taking her to an offbeat venue, you don't look cheap. You look like an original thinker who doesn't follow the pack. You're conveying the image that you are an eclectic kind of guy who's on the cutting edge of life. Money can't buy that.

Beware a Gold Digger in Training

Despite women's lib and equal opportunity, some women still behave like the 1950s was yesterday. Whether through upbringing or experience, they've come to expect the man to pay his way through the entire relationship. They never offer to split the check or even leave the tip; they never reciprocate in any way financially. And when the well runs dry, they're off to the next meal ticket. Is your girlfriend a giver or a taker? Here's how to tell.

What has she done for you lately? Now, many women do feel uncomfortable picking up the tab or splitting the check—and it's our fault, says Helen Fisher, Ph.D., research associate in the department of anthropology at Rutgers University in New Brunswick, New Jersey, and author of *Anatomy of Love*. "They're afraid that they'll offend their date if they even offer. And many men will be offended. So she'll try to reciprocate in some other way." Before you accuse her of being a mooch, look for that other way. Does she buy you gifts for no reason? Bring you stuff for your apartment—like plants or beer? Does she make you dinner at her place? If so, she's a giver, and a keeper.

Next time your turn? When she thanks you for taking her out to that chic restaurant she always wanted to go to, say, "That's okay. Next time, you can take me to that steak joint across town." Gauge her reaction.

A quiet night where? If she turns you down whenever you say, "Jeez, I can't go out tonight. I'm completely tapped out until Friday. Wanna come over and watch TV?" chances are that she doesn't want to spend quality time with you but with your wallet. This assumes, of course, that you don't say this *every* night that she wants to go out and do something. In which case, she's not a gold digger; you're just a cheapskate.

What did you get for your birthday? The acid test will come at your birthday. If she can't treat you to something—anything—on this of all days, then maybe it's time to look elsewhere, while you can still afford it.

Buy ethnic. Unless it's some four-star gourmet place, ethnic food emporiums tend to be considerably cheaper than standard American fare. Take her out for Indian or go Mexican. While you save a few bucks, you also convey a subliminal message that you are a man of the world who's not afraid to sample the flavor of different cultures.

Cook for her. We don't have to tell you that a sack of groceries and a nice bottle of wine are far cheaper than a night at a posh restaurant. "More important, making a meal for her is a highly romantic gesture, far more so than signing a credit card slip in a restaurant," says Dr. Kreidman.

Let her pay. Now here's a novel way to save some money—but a darn tricky one.

It's true that most women who work—and who were brought up in the era of the women's movement—are more likely to be fair-minded when it comes to pulling their own financial weight. "In fact, they will want to occasionally pay for dinner, or take you out. Or at least split the check. They're very sensitive to the fact that if a man pays for everything that maybe he expects something in return. To combat that a little bit, they'll want to contribute financially to the relationship," observes Helen Fisher, Ph.D., research associate in the department of anthropology at Rutgers University in New Brunswick, New Jersey, and author of *Anatomy of Love*. We don't want to suggest that you should ever insist on it, or even ask. But if she brings up the subject, or reaches for the check after dinner, then once in a while you should let her treat—without making too much fuss. And no, this does not necessarily mean that she expects you to sleep with her (you wish!).

Know when to splurge. Her birthday. Valentine's day. Your anniversary. Anytime she gets a promotion...or shows up on your doorstep bawling. These are the times to momentarily set aside your wise, well-budgeted life and invest in her happiness. Being frugal doesn't necessarily mean cheap, friend. It means being wise, knowing when to save your pennies, and knowing when to recognize that rainy day for what it is—a chance to spend some hard-earned cash on her. If you've been economical most of the time, you should have no problem affording the occasional splurge, whether it's dinner at that fine French restaurant uptown or a weekend at that country inn she's always hinting at.

Don't moan. Even if you are dirt-poor, don't complain about it all the time. Nobody likes a whiner, and nothing turns a woman off faster than hearing a man say he can't afford it or watching him wince every time he opens a menu. Comment about money every time you go out, and she's going to hear, "You're a burden to me. I'm questioning whether you're worth it." And trust us, that's one impression you can't afford to leave.

WORKPLACE ROMANCE

It's a time-honored maxim that you shouldn't mix business with pleasure. But long hours working in close quarters with sharp, beautiful women makes that a hard maxim to follow. Regardless of whether we've acted on it, we've all fallen for a fetching co-worker at one time or another. And many of us have allowed that less-than-professional interest to blossom into a full-blown workplace romance.

Which is great. And completely natural, incidentally. We figure it this way:

Once you reach a certain age—when you're out of school, working full-time, and still single—it only makes sense that work would be the place to meet potential mates. "In high school and college, you picked partners from the pool of people you saw every day—classmates, neighbors in the dormitory. There was a built-in system for meeting people. Once you're out of school, though, that system is gone, and it's replaced by the workplace," says Daniel Kegan, Ph.D., a psychologist with Elan Associates in Chicago and an expert in interpersonal relationships.

Now, you can go out to bars and pick up women or pursue personal interests and meet like-minded women in the course of those pursuits. But many of us still cleave to the old conditioning of looking for love amid the people we see every day. In the *Sex in America* survey, 15 percent said that they met the person they married at work. Your boss probably suspects that, too. In a survey of 200 chief executive officers done by *Fortune* magazine, 51 percent believe that office romances are inevitable. "It's pervasive. If we haven't done it ourselves, we all know someone who met at least one girlfriend in the office," says Dr. Kegan.

WHY WORKPLACE WOOING?

It's easy to say that we date people we work with because we're conditioned for it, but behavioral programming is only part of it. "There are many, many reasons that we date co-workers. And even in this day of political correctness and concerns about sexual harassment, there are still many good reasons for developing a personal relationship with a colleague," says Dr. Kegan. Here are some of the most likely rationales why you and that special someone in the next cubicle might be having some very unbusiness-like thoughts about one another.

Because she's there. Call it the power of proximity: The more time we spend with someone, the more apt we are to like them. "We're very social creatures," says Helen Fisher, Ph.D., research associate in the department of anthropology at Rutgers University in New Brunswick, New Jersey, and author of *Anatomy of Love.* "If we're put in close quarters with someone, we have to learn how to deal with that person. Over time we get to know them and at least develop an understanding of them and a respect for how they do things. But if you find that you have some similar habits and traits, and you're both available, it's only natural over time to start thinking of that person as a potential mate."

You're better than a serial killer. One reason she might be interested in you is simple self-preservation. There's a certain implicit safety in dating someone at work. "If you pick someone up at a bar, for example, you really have no idea about this person," says Dr. Fisher. But with a co-worker—well, at least you know where they work. "You're not a total stranger, even if they don't know you all that well. They've heard you talk on the phone, watched you interact with other people, seen pictures or items that you keep on your

Don't Make a System Error

It's 10:00 A.M. and you love her.

So you decide to take your morning break and compose a little e-mail paean to her beauty. You are rhapsodic, in a workplace sort of way. You find salacious uses for words like *spreadsheet* and *hard drive.* You tell her she has nipples like eraser tips. You tell her you want a piece of her assets. You sign off with a lot of Xs and Os.

And then you accidentally hit the button that distributes your electronic love letter universally. In seconds, every computer from here to the Taiwan office has a copy of your message—including the part about her eraser-tip nipples.

Rule #1 for workplace romancing in the Information Age: Don't send a message; don't leave a message. In these heady days of lightning-fast communication systems, you could all too easily direct a dirty voice mail or e-mail to the wrong person—like your boss.

"Also, remember that your company owns the communication systems you use, and they reserve the right to monitor the use of those systems," says Jonathan A. Segal, Esq., a partner at Wolf, Block, Schorr, and Solis-Cohen law firm in Philadelphia who lectures to companies on sexual harassment issues. So even if you send a private message to her computer or voice mailbox, by no means does that make it confidential. "First, a copy of everything you send through the system is stored somewhere. Second, several people in the company have access to all aspects of the computer and phone systems, including what's in your mailbox," says Segal. If your sweet nothings are found clogging the company's systems, you could conceivably find yourself out of a job: Misappropriation of company resources is a firing offense in some corporate cultures. At the very least, you'd be opening yourself to some serious embarrassment in front of some important people.

If you want your words of love to be private, deliver them the old-fashioned way: in person.

desk," says Dr. Fisher. "They've already picked up valuable information about the kind of person you are, and that helps them make a decision about pairing with you."

She's better-looking than those spreadsheets. File this under "Universal Truths": Sex is more interesting than work. Sometimes when we're pulling 60-hour weeks and bucking for that bigger office, we need a break, a momentary diversion. And that's where an office romance sneaks in—between the cracks of the average workday. "It can be a wonderful distraction. When you're hard at work, taking a moment to have coffee with a co-worker, or even to just notice her as she walks by, is a great stress reliever," says Dr.

Kegan. Over time, you associate that moment of ease with a sense of comfort and familiarity. Things snowball from there.

Instant common ground. Even the best of relationships have to lumber through an awkward getting-to-know-you phase of learning the other's quirks and interests. When you date a co-worker, some of that legwork is a done deal. In an era where we're always crunched for time, this fact alone makes workplace romance highly appealing. "Going in, you may already know you share similar interests," says Dr. Kegan. For starters, you have work in common—although typically, that's not enough. "Usually, you become attracted to someone, not because you work with them but because you find that someone you work with shares other interests with you outside of work," says Dr. Kegan. Either way, you're starting out from a certain comfort level that makes pursuing a deeper relationship easier and more appealing.

HOW TO MAKE IT WORK AT WORK

Understanding how it happens is one thing. Knowing how to deal with it when it *does* happen...well, let's just say there's a knack to juggling the professional and the passionate. Perhaps it has become harder to concentrate on your deadlines, wondering what she's wearing under that suit. Or maybe you're worried about how you'll behave when you're around her. You don't want to be all goo-goo eyed, but you don't want to control yourself so much that you end up snubbing her. Maybe you haven't yet considered what this relationship might mean to a career—yours or hers.

If the love of your life shares office space with you, we're not about to stand in your way. But if you find yourself being drawn to an attractive colleague, we'd like to be the voice of reason and present you with a few, simple guidelines. Consider these your personal company policy for pursuing an at-work relationship.

Be a forecaster. If you're really smitten by a colleague, your heart is likely not going to listen to your head. Nevertheless, take a moment to consider the professional ramifications of pursuing personal interests with a co-worker. "Essentially, you have to ask yourself, 'Can I work with this person after we break up?' Out in the world, when you break up with someone, it's relatively easy to alter your schedule or routine so that you never see her again. But you may see her every day in the office," says Dr. Kegan.

On a more serious note, your dalliances may affect your career. "If you break up with her and she subsequently files a sexual harassment claim against you, even if it's entirely groundless, it could affect your reputation in the workplace," warns Jonathan A. Segal, Esq., a partner at Wolf, Block, Schorr, and Solis-Cohen law firm in Philadelphia who lectures to companies on sexual harassment issues.

It doesn't even have to come to that. It's conceivable that co-workers may view your relationship as a weak link in the chain of command. If you're dating someone a few rungs down the ladder, management may worry that

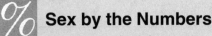

Sex by the Numbers

Percentage of chief executive officers who disapprove of office romances: 12

Percentage who believe that it's none of the company's business: 70

SOURCE: *Fortune*

you're leaking upper-level information—any time a rumor gets out, you might be the scapegoat, regardless of whether it's your fault. If you're dating someone above you, you're not necessarily out of danger either. "It could diminish your reputation. If you get a promotion, your co-workers might think it's because you're dating someone higher up, not because of your excellent job performance," says Dr. Kegan. Even worse, upper management might be hesitant to promote you—even if you deserve it—for fear that co-workers would have that very reaction. "I hate to focus on the negative, but these are very real issues and it pays to think through the implications before you go further," says Dr. Kegan.

Be discreet. As a rule, it's a good idea to keep your relationship low-key at work. Don't lie about it, but don't rub everyone's noses in it either. Your dreamy looks and giggly whispering do not go unnoticed by your co-workers, in case you were wondering. And any overt carrying on really has no place at work. Never mind that it will make co-workers uncomfortable. The bottom line is that it's unprofessional.

Know company policy. Although most companies have few to no restrictions on office fraternization, it pays to know company policy. Some businesses strongly discourage managers from dating their subordinates, for example. "It's a breeding ground for abuse of power or perceived favoritism. It creates ill will among co-workers and may develop into an unworkable situation if you break up," says Segal. In that case, you're probably better off adopting an old military code: If you're an officer, don't fraternize with the enlisted.

Keep it separate. Like church and state, your work life and your love life should be separate spheres. Where possible, you should keep the two at arm's length. "This is more than being discreet," says Dr. Kegan. "This is adopting a mental discipline that maintains a division between your professional and your personal life." If you had a fight with your girlfriend last night, you don't bad-mouth her in front of the boss the next morning. By the same token, don't bring a work disagreement out on a date—it'll just ruin dinner. Between the hours of 9:00 A.M. and 5:00 P.M., when you're in the office and with your co-workers, treat each other fairly, with dignity and respect—no more, no less. And when the whistle blows at the end of the day, you can get on with the more enticing business of being partners in love, not in work.

SAYING "I LOVE YOU"

Some phrases just stick in a man's craw. Small words, a handful of sylla-bles and yet, even when we feel a strong urge to say them, we choke; we hes-itate; we throw in a lot of gulping and swallowing; we let someone else say the words, then nod or grunt our assent. You know these phrases by heart, you've almost said them so many times:

"I'm sorry."

"You were right."

"I need help."

And the hardest of those hard-to-utter phrases: "I love you."

What is it about professing our strongest emotion that turns our speech patterns into so much verbal origami? It's not that you don't love her. You do. You'd crawl over broken glass, take a bullet, go to her brother's wedding, per-form a hundred other selfless acts to keep her safe and happy. But the sight of you covered in glass, riddled with bullets, or doing the hokey-pokey with Aunt Selma isn't enough. She needs to hear the words. You need to say them. Why, for the love of heaven, can't you tell her you love her?

DEEDS, NOT WORDS

Most of the answers to this dilemma of expression can be found in the old conflict of he-versus-she. We do it one way; women do it another. In the case of expressing love, men are bound firmly to the notion of "show, don't tell."

"Men are doers. They'd rather demonstrate their love by doing things," says relationship expert Ellen Kreidman, Ph.D., author of *Light Her Fire* and *Light His Fire*, a series of inventive books and seminars. But remember that women are verbal, says Dr. Kreidman, which means that on her emotional tally sheet, a hundred selfless acts just won't add up to a simple utterance.

"Women need to hear that you love them," says Doreen Virtue, Ph.D., a relationship expert and psychotherapist in Newport Beach, California, and author of *In the Mood*. "They need you to say it. Since men aren't as verbal, they have a really difficult time with this."

The other, deeper problem is that professing love—like apologizing or asking for help—is so hard to utter because it requires us to be vulnerable, if only for a moment.

You're admitting something. You're dropping the shields. "And men are taught from an early age not to show any vulnerability or emotion; they're led to believe that it will somehow compromise their masculinity," Dr. Kreidman points out.

So we aren't so in touch with our emotions. But we are creatures of rea-son. As a reasonable man, you can see the economy of telling her you love her. Proving you love someone costs a lot in time, money, and bodily wear and tear. Saying it takes one second of time, and costs nothing. In fact, you gain something. Respect—both from her and from yourself. You have broken through the male stereotype; you have shown yourself to be a fearless, plain-speaking man. You're not afraid to tell it like it is, and—by God!—this is how it is: You love her.

But breaking male stereotypes isn't exactly work you can accomplish in a day. You have to build to it, wait for the right moment, maybe even psych yourself up a little before you mouth those words. We understand; we've been there. Which is why we've pooled some uncommon wisdom to help you speak your mind and your heart without swerving into the syntactical traps that so often beset the man who wants to tell the world of his love.

Make sure you mean it. Obvious as it sounds, many a man has stumbled over the words "I love you" not because he couldn't say it but because he wasn't quite sure he felt it. Or worse, he felt that he was being pressured into saying it. Let's face it: Often as not, she'll be the first one to say she loves you. If you love her back, this is a nonissue: You can respond with authority and sincerity, "I love you." If you're still on the fence, though, you're in a difficult position. Saying nothing in response only works for so long, and then she'll start to think you're an unemotional pig. Saying "Ditto" or some other lame gesture of reciprocity is almost as bad. But it would be far worse to say you love her and then have to admit later that you didn't mean it. Take some time to think about the relationship and your feelings for her. Do your homework, and you'll be in a better position to give her an answer.

Write it first. Men could do a lot better expressing their emotions if they wrote them down, says James Pennebaker, Ph.D., professor and chairman of psychology at Southern Methodist University in Dallas. "Saying these things to a person can make us tongue-tied. A piece of paper, on the other hand, is far less threatening. You have time to revise, to get your wording just right," he says.

This is why writing "I love you" may be a good first step toward actually saying the words. Best of all, you don't even have to write an actual love letter (although that would sure score bonus points with her). Give her a card with a little note from you, or send flowers and make sure the word *love* appears close to your name on the card. Next time you see her, she'll have already read your profession of amour. Now you've broached the subject—your written words have served as an ambassador, testing the waters before you venture in too deep. From this vantage point, you can gauge her reaction. If she seems standoffish or noncommittal about the card or the flowers, you can mirror her behavior; you don't have to push it. More likely, though, she'll be all cuddly and smiling and will say something like, "I loved those flowers." This gives you the perfect springboard into the subject. You can say something like, "You know, I meant what I said in that card. I love you."

Avoid conditionals. We're so worried about rejection that even when we finally summon the nerve to confess our love, the little editor in our heads

10 No-Brainer Signs You're in Love

For every man, for every relationship, the time to say those three simple words is going to be different. It could be a year after you meet, or a thunder-struck utterance the moment you see her. By and large, there are some clear indicators that you're in love—actions, behaviors, symptoms you'll start to ex-hibit. If you've experienced any of the following, you're in love with her (in which case, now's a good time to clue her in to the fact).

- You can't stop thinking about her.
- Anything you see, hear, taste, smell, or touch—any sensory input at all—reminds you of some cute thing she said or did the other day.
- You feel the urge to call her, just to "check in."
- You perform uncharacteristic acts of kindness or cleanliness because you know she'll like it. For example, sending her flowers, watching her favorite nighttime drama without sneering, cleaning your bathroom (including the gross area behind the toilet).
- You go shopping with her and *actually enjoy yourself.*
- During staff meetings, you write her name over and over again on your legal pad.
- You let her borrow your car.
- You've programmed her work and home numbers into your speed dial and know her e-mail address by heart.
- Every popular love song on the radio seems to apply directly to your rela-tionship.
- Any time you start to *think* you love her. Trust us, if you think you love her, you do.

throws in words and phrases that cushion the impact of the message we're trying to convey. So, instead of a forthright, "Gwen, I love you with the pas-sion of 10,000 white-hot suns!" you end up sounding like a David Cassidy lyric: "Uh, um, you know, I think I love you."

"It's okay to be nervous," says Dr. Virtue. "But you don't want to sound un-certain of yourself." Then, she'll start to question whether you really mean it.

Instead, follow the rules of professional speakers and avoid all "uhs" and "ums." Use no conditionals, especially the words "think," "might," and "maybe." And don't try some glib verbal truncation of the sentiment, such as "Ya know I love ya!" or "Love ya!" or worst of all, "Love ya lots!" Just forget about "ya," will ya? This is not some fraternity pal that you're bear-hugging at a reunion; you're talking to the woman you love. You think such affectations lend a certain casual indifference to the moment, so you can safely retreat if she rejects you. In fact, professing your love in this offhand manner just makes you look like a doof. Remember, these are three simple words here. No need to clutter them up with hoary old add-ons.

Create a mood. Some guys try to sneak in an "I love you" at a moment where the words would be apropos of nothing. While you're shopping. In the middle of that action flick you've been dying to see. In an effort to sidetrack an argument. These are not always the best circumstances under which to profess your deepest held feelings.

Instead, say the words at a time appropriate to the sentiment; let the medium fit the message. "Any moment where you're feeling close to her is a good time to tell her you love her," says Dr. Virtue. Over dinner—take her hand, look into her eyes, say the words. During a slow dance, whisper it in her ear. As you're curled up on the sofa watching your favorite program together; or in bed, in those final moments before sleep, speak your truth. Clearly. Don't mumble. Leave no doubt in her mind.

Be clear-headed. Saying "I love you" while under any kind of external influence or stimulus is no profession of love. Let's be clear about this: Getting drunk and blurting that you love her doesn't count. Neither does saying it at the moment of ejaculation. Because even though you've said it, you've said it under mitigating circumstances, and she can't be entirely sure you meant it. When you tell her you love her, there should be no doubt about it. Otherwise, what's the point in saying it? So tell her when there's nothing else affecting your judgment or your clarity of thought. *Note:* If you did tell while you were drunk or having an orgasm, don't kick yourself. But do reinforce the point at the first sober opportunity you have. Say, "Even though I was blitzed last night, I know what I said. And I meant it: I love you." In the afterglow of sex, hold her close, stroke her hair, repeat what you said earlier in the throes of passion.

Say it again...and again. The funny thing about telling someone you love them is that once you say it, you have to keep saying it, over and over. Their desire to hear you say it does not diminish over time. "In fact, most women want to hear it more often," says Dr. Kreidman. "Every day. Several times a day."

Don't look at this as a can of worms you've opened on yourself. This isn't a problem; this is an opportunity. Love is a celebration, after all. So many men go through life in a loveless state, with no one to care for them, no one they have any strong feelings for. You are one of the lucky ones. Profess that good fortune every day. That means telling her you love her, every day. It will become so easy, you'll wonder why you ever hesitated to say it in the first place.

Now, if only you could do something about that whole admitting-it-when-you're-wrong thing....

PROPOSING

In the old days, proposing was a means to an end. At a time when couples did not enjoy a lot of intimate time together or spend hours discussing "the relationship," a man had to find some way to make his intentions clear. So he would propose marriage.

Nowadays, the act of proposing seems arcane when you look at modern trends. According to the *Sex in America* study, 85 percent of all men born between 1933 and 1942 got married without living together first. But from the baby boom generation onward, more and more men are living with their partners before getting married. Only 34 percent of men born between 1963 and 1974 reported getting married before living together.

"It's an ongoing trend: Couples spend a lot more time together—and get to know their partners a lot better—before deciding to get married. And that's if they get married at all," says Doreen Virtue, Ph.D., a relationship expert and psychotherapist in Newport Beach, California. If you're serious enough about a woman that you want to marry her, she probably knows long before you pop the question. So many men don't even bother. The decision to get married is arrived at mutually, then the couple drive off together to go look at rings. Or their lives are already so intertwined that they skip the ring, dismissing it as a bourgeois symbol that's anticlimactic or fiscally unwise. Who needs an engagement ring when you're both engaged in escrow? Or if you have the money, why not buy something useful—an engagement car or an engagement stereo? The marriage proposal has morphed into a business transaction, a shopping trip.

A MODEST PROPOSAL

To our minds, proposing marriage is one of the great moments in a man's life, and you shouldn't be cheated out of it. In our hearts, we all hope for that moment when we really are larger than life, when we stand in the spotlight and speak our truth and make the world stand still. Done well, a marriage proposal can make all that happen and more. It can be the official launching point into a whole new world of danger, thrills, and high adventure. It can dispel all doubts about your feelings and intentions, doubts that men create left and right by our recalcitrance to discuss our feelings. At its most dramatic, proposing marriage is a formal declaration that you are now changing the course of destiny. And how many times does a man get to do that in his life?

How and when you propose—we'll leave that to you. Meanwhile, we'd like to propose a few guidelines for proposing. If you don't want to follow them, that's okay—we're not, you know, married to them. But they may help you prepare and shape this great moment in life.

Preserve the element of surprise. You're at the point in the relationship where you both know that marriage is inevitable. The proposal is a fait accompli. The only question that remains is: When are you going to do it? Well, that's a question she should have in her mind, right up until the moment you ask. Part of the pleasure of proposing is catching her off guard, you see. Obviously, your proposal isn't going to be out of the blue, but that doesn't mean it can't be a surprise. So keep her guessing. If a big holiday is coming up—holidays and birthdays are always likely times to get a wedding proposal—don't be predictable. Propose the day before Valentine's Day. Or wait until midnight on her birthday, after she's given up hope that you'll ask. Pay a little attention to timing and you'll be able to sneak up on her and pop the question when she least expects it. And won't that be a lot more fun and more memorable than if you played into her hands and proposed on a date and time that she predicts?

Choose a venue. If there's a great debate in proposing marriage, it's whether to do it publicly of privately. Do you take her to a baseball game and arrange to have the question scrolled across the Sony Jumbotron? Or do you have a candlelit dinner at home and hide the ring in the bottom of her champagne glass?

This begs an important question: How well do you know your would-be fiancée? This is something you're doing for her, after all, so you'll want to propose in a venue that she'll appreciate. If she's extroverted and flamboyant and always harping on you because you never even hold her hand in public, then you may well want to make a spectacle of your proposal. Doing so not only complements her outgoing personality; it also earns you bonus points for displaying your affection—big time!—in public. A public proposal tells her: Even though I may be embarrassed as hell to be doing this in front of all these people, it doesn't matter. My love for you is great and wide, and I don't care who knows.

If she's shy or quiet or worried about her appearance in public, then a more subdued proposal—something that just the two of you can share—is probably better. Proposing to her in front of the patrons of your favorite restaurant may only agitate her, disappoint you, and not give either of you much of a chance to savor the moment.

Give her something. Maybe you don't believe in rings. Maybe you don't have the money to believe in rings. That's okay. But when you give her your heart, it's also a good idea to give her some token of your devotion.

"The gesture of giving is very important to a woman. Whether you're handing her a glass of wine at dinner or an engagement ring, the act of giving itself makes her feel close, cared for, loved," says Dr. Virtue. In a proposal, you are giving her something: your undying love and devotion. Since these are intangibles, you need to give her a symbol of your commitment. Exactly what this item could be is entirely up to you. If not a ring, then give her something that has meaning and value to you: an heirloom from your grandmother, a prized possession of yours. Or give her something that is symbolic to your re-lationship. If you met and fell in love at the local coffeehouse, what's wrong with giving her an engagement coffee cup? In the end, it really doesn't matter what you give her, so long as you let her know that this is a token, a mere symbol of your eternal fidelity and unquenchable desire to be with her.

It's never too late to ask. So you're one of those guys who came to a mutual agreement with his honey and never proposed. And after reading this, you're feeling like you missed out. Well, don't even bother—you haven't missed out on an opportunity. Just because you're married doesn't mean that you can't still propose. At your next anniversary, or on her birthday, get down on bended knee and ask her to marry you all over again. She'll think you're the most romantic man alive. And you'll never have to worry about what her answer will be.

8

YOUR CHANGES

Chances are that in the decade of your thirties you're still looking good and feeling good. But slowly, inexorably, changes in your body are beginning in earnest. "At age 30 we begin the aging process," says Bruce Hirsch, M.D., assistant professor of medicine in the division of infectious diseases at North Shore University Hospital in Manhasset, New York.

This doesn't mean that you'll soon be ready for the scrap heap. Far from it. With a good diet and exercise, guys can still look forward to decades of good living and good loving. "A lot of the changes we associate with age are not inevitable," Dr. Hirsch says. "Physiologically, an 80-year-old man can be younger than a 35-year-old man."

With that caveat, here are some changes that men may experience in their thirties.

SEX-RELATED CHANGES

• Less sexual desire. By now, you may have been married for some time and started a family. Perhaps you're a little bored with your partner or irritated with the kids. There are stresses on the job, where you are trying hard not to veer off the career path you are on. With so much turmoil, you're no longer the walking erection you were as a teenager or in your twenties.

"As you get older, you have to work harder at it," says Al Cooper, Ph.D., clinical director of the San Jose Marital and Sexuality Centre in California. "When you're 16, it's a challenge to keep the erection down."

OTHER CHANGES

• More stress. The thirties is the most stressful decade in a man's life. In addition to perhaps getting married and having children, it is during these years that many men buy a home and take on other big-ticket financial responsibilities. High levels of stress can affect not only your sex life but also your overall health.

• Hair loss. Only 12 percent of men are balding at 25, but 37 percent are hair-impaired at 35. If you're among them, you'll eventually have more company. By age 65, nearly two-thirds of all men are bald or balding.

Most hair loss is a result of a hereditary condition called male-pattern baldness, in which the hairline recedes, a bald spot grows on the crown, or both. Doctors think that it comes from a gene that makes you more sensitive to testosterone. In balding men, it's thought that testosterone damages the scalp's hair follicles, foiling their ability to sprout hair.

You can inherit male-pattern baldness from either parent. So if your father has a full head of hair, don't get overconfident. The baldness trait can come from your mother's father or grandfather. On the other hand, just because your father is bald doesn't mean that you will be. It depends on whether you inherited the baldness gene.

A small number of guys who begin balding do not have male-pattern baldness. They may lose hair because of ringworm, use of anabolic steroids, a reaction to stress or certain medications, or a fungal infection.

• High blood pressure. A man's blood pressure usually rises with age. And often it reaches unhealthy heights when you are in your thirties. About 20 percent of men between the ages of 35 and 44 have high blood pressure.

The precise cause of high blood pressure is not easy to determine, but in this age group, African-American and Hispanic men are more likely to suffer from high blood pressure than Caucasian and Asian men and women. Men who are overweight and who have diets high in fat and cholesterol also are at risk.

• Back pain. You are most apt to first suffer back pain in your thirties or forties. Any one of several ailments can make you wince when you bend over or lift an object. The small joints of the back may begin deteriorating at this time. You could develop spinal stenosis, in which a narrowing of the canal in the vertebrae surrounding the spinal cord puts pressure on nerves in the lower back. You might develop a herniated disk. Or just have poor posture that aggravates arthritis and causes disk problems.

More likely, however, you have strained a muscle. This happened because you've become sedentary and out of shape. Maybe you spend most of your time at work anchored to a desk. So now when you pick up your little 2-year-old niece, it feels like you're lifting Shaquille O'Neal.

• Aging skin. Unless you're Dick Clark, your skin will start to age. This is especially true if you work or play outside a lot. "Skin aging is hugely affected by sun exposure and wind and cold," says Waneen Wyrick Spirduso, Ed.D., professor in the department of kinesiology and health education at the University of Texas in Austin and author of *Physical Dimensions of Aging.* "Skiers, tennis players, and farmers—people who are out in the elements a lot—are just going to get a lot of aging." The predominant feature of that aging is wrinkles.

All that sun exposure may take a toll in another way: skin cancer. There are three types: melanoma, basal cell carcinoma, and squamous cell carcinoma. The latter two are common and seldom are fatal. Melanoma, however, spreads quickly and is deadly.

Men are more likely than women to die from melanoma. That's probably because they spend nearly twice as much time in the sun and are four times less likely to use a sunscreen.

• Bones. Bone mass increases until about 35. Bone *loss* likely won't start until your sixties, but it's still smart to be thinking about strong bones this decade. What you do now can lessen the chances of osteoporosis 30 years from now. So get enough calcium in your diet (about 1,000 milligrams a day) along with a maximum of 400 international units of vitamin D (the two work together in your body), do weight-bearing exercises (yes, working out strengthens bones as well as muscle), don't smoke, and limit alcohol intake.

HER CHANGES

Their hairlines aren't starting to recede, and their blood pressure probably isn't rising. But make no mistake about it: Women's bodies are undergoing plenty of changes in their thirties.

SEX-RELATED CHANGES

• Peak desire. Some sex experts say that this is the decade in which a woman's sexual desire reaches it peak. "She's more sure of herself, more assertive, and typically much more demanding in bed," writes sex therapist Theresa Crenshaw, M.D., in her book *The Alchemy of Love and Lust*. If true, it comes as much as two decades after guys reach their peak.

• Sagging breasts. When a woman reaches her thirties, the elastic tissue in her breasts begins to degenerate. The breast fibers will lose resiliency. The result is sagging breasts and perhaps stretch marks, too.

Lots of women, of course, do not have drooping breasts in their thirties. Several factors determine when gravity exerts its inevitable pull. Women with large breasts or who go braless a lot are more apt to sag. So are women who have undergone weight gains and losses, gotten pregnant, and breast-fed.

• Breast lumpiness. It's not uncommon for women to have lumps in their breasts that are perfectly harmless. They tend to wax and wane with the fluctuations of a woman's hormones. Hence, they are more noticeable before her period, less so after. Starting around age 35, fat begins to replace breast tissue, and that oatmeal surface becomes more like Cream of Wheat.

OTHER CHANGES

• Lupus. Ninety percent of those afflicted with systemic lupus erythematosus are women of childbearing age. The disease is especially prevalent between the ages of 30 and 40. The symptoms include fatigue, arthritis pain, fever, and tenderness. Some women get a rash on the face extending from one cheek over the bridge of the nose to the other cheek.

Those who contract lupus have an immune system that is out of whack. Instead of battling infections, it produces too many antibodies and antibodies that are destructive. Researchers aren't sure what causes lupus, but genetics and female hormones are among the suspects.

• Ovarian cancer. The thirties is a good time for a woman to be on the lookout for ovarian cancer. It sometimes strikes in this decade, and the odds keep going up thereafter. Ovarian cancer is one of the leading causes of death among women.

Ovarian cancer is sneaky. Women don't feel any pain until late in the disease. Its only early symptoms are common discomforts: bloating, constipation, and a swollen waistline.

The cause of ovarian cancer isn't clear. Women with a family history are more at risk. So are women who have not given birth. Researchers think that women who ovulate repeatedly year after year without getting pregnant or having been on the Pill may be at greater risk. Ovulation triggers a period of rapid growth in the ovarian cells, followed by cell division. The more times this happens, the greater the chance a mutation might occur.

• Premenstrual syndrome. Women in their thirties and forties are at the age when they are most apt to experience premenstrual symptoms for the first time. It is characterized by bloating or moodiness. Premenstrual syndrome (PMS) is more severe and is characterized by symptoms severe enough to interfere with a woman's ability to function normally in her everyday life. Both are thought to be caused by hormonal shifts in connection with a woman's menstrual cycle. Premenstrual symptoms are a common condition; PMS is not.

• Bones. As with men, bones stop gaining mass around the age of 35. But women face a far greater chance of bone degeneration later in life, so they need to be particularly diligent protecting themselves. How? Weight-bearing exercise like walking or running is particularly important to keeping bones strong. So is getting 1,000 milligrams a day of calcium and a maximum of 400 international units of vitamin D (both numbers go up for pregnant or breastfeeding women). Smoking and excessive drinking both decrease bone strength.

• Raynaud's disease. If your lady can't bear to pick up a cold soda or an ice-cube tray, she may have Raynaud's disease. When she does handle something cold, her skin changes color to white, and possibly to blue, then red. Men also get Raynaud's, but later in life than women and not nearly as often.

There actually are two types of this ailment: Raynaud's disease and Raynaud's phenomenon. The latter is less common and occurs in conjunction with other diseases, such as lupus and rheumatoid arthritis.

It's still not clear what causes Raynaud's or why women are stricken more often. Women's hormones are considered a possible source of the discomfort.

• Back pain. Women are commonly spared the heavy manual labor that hastened the deterioration of men's backs. But by the time they are in their thirties and forties, natural deterioration and pain set in. And they suffer from it for a reason men will never have to worry about—pregnancy. Women in this age range who have babies may have more back pain than younger women if they are not in good shape.

Even for a woman in good shape, carrying a fetus around is no picnic. The weight and size of the budding baby cause a woman's center of gravity to shift forward, so there is more curvature in her lower spinal column. The abdominal muscles that normally support the back are stretched and weakened by the growing uterus.

Also during pregnancy, the body releases greater amounts of a hormone called relaxin. This hormone enables the pelvis to expand as the fetus grows. But it also loosens the ligaments that support the back. When more stress is placed on the lax spine, pain follows. So be extra considerate of a pregnant woman, especially if you are the guy who made her pregnant.

RULES OF ENGAGEMENT

You're dating a woman in her thirties, and you like her a lot. In fact, everything would be perfect if it weren't for that faint but persistent sound that's always present when you're together. Ticktock. Ticktock. Her biological clock.

"Certainly when the woman's biological clock is running, what a lot of guys pick up is becoming a father object, like a woman might pick up becoming a sex object," says Warren Farrell, Ph.D., San Diego–based author of *The Myth of Male Power* and *Why Men Are the Way They Are.*

As their remaining fertile years become fewer, women in their thirties may become increasingly antsy to find not just a date, but a mate. "Some women will be having a certain urgency," says Linda DeVillers, Ph.D., a psychologist and sex therapist in El Segundo, California, and author of *Love Skills.* "If your goal is the same, it's to your advantage. It means that there's not going to be a lot of wasted time. But if the guy is not looking for a serious relationship, he owes it to a woman to be up front about it."

Some thirty-something women may even be looking for a sperm donor if they don't find a man they deem to be suitable as a husband. In one survey, 45 percent of women queried said they either strongly agreed or agreed with the statement: "I would like to become a parent even if I remain single." This is not to say that every unmarried woman you meet in her thirties is scheming to have your baby. Some already have a child. Others don't want one. It's a topic to broach—carefully, gently—early on with a woman so that there are no misinterpretations.

WHERE TO MEET WOMEN

Here are a few places you might go in search of a woman in her thirties.

• Video stores. "Don't just hang out in the violence movie sections," advises Dr. Farrell. "Go to the foreign film section. Go to the more artsy 'chick' film section. If you don't have an interest in those things, get an interest. You'll be better with women if you know more about what women are about—what they're thinking and feeling—and you speak some of their language and overlap with some of their interests."

• Video dating. Although some people look down on it, Dr. Farrell thinks that you can learn a lot about a prospective date by watching her body language and listening to her speak for a few minutes. (For advice, see Matchmaking Services on page 356.)

• At work. This admittedly is a controversial choice and the subject of another chapter in this book (see Workplace Romance on page 337). Dr. DeVillers urges caution but adds, "If somebody looks like they meet your requirements in every other sense, it's silly to put them off-limits. If it's going to be frivolous and you know it's just a roll in the hay, maybe that's not very cool."

Dr. Farrell is less sanguine, however. "If you take an initiative with a woman whom you are working with, you are walking a fine line from being a candidate for a husband and being a candidate for a harasser. Your life can very easily be ruined."

• Grocery stores. Head straight to the produce section to meet the apple of your eye, says Dr. Farrell. When you spot her, grab a cantaloupe and ask her if it's ripe or not. In this way you start a conversation with her in which she can show her expertise rather than you just coming on strong in an obvious pickup ploy, he advises.

"If you want to meet a career woman, you go later in the evening. If you want to meet a homemaker, go in the middle of the day," Dr. Farrell adds.

Supermarkets are a rare example of a meeting place where women usually outnumber men, Dr. Farrell says.

"Men tend to go to places that are comfortable to men, like bars, that don't draw many women," Dr. Farrell says. "Women often go to places like museums and the supermarket that are comfortable to women, but they find disproportionate numbers of men there. So both sexes feel that there are fewer numbers of members of the other sex available than there really are because neither one is going to a place that is relevant."

What Women Want

What a woman is looking for in a relationship in her thirties can differ quite markedly from when she was in her twenties. Here's some age-specific advice.

Be prepared to commit. Whoa, come back. This doesn't necessarily mean a husband, just a guy who's not on the prowl for other women. "They're looking now for monogamy," says William F. Fitzgerald, Ph.D., a marital and sex therapist in private practice in San Jose, California, who answers sex questions online for *Men's Health Daily* (the Web site of *Men's Health* magazine). "That's less of a priority in the twenties."

Be steady. "The key word here is *stability*," says Dr. Fitzgerald. "They're taking their lives more seriously. They're slowing down in terms of their partying." In a man, they're looking for somebody with ties to his community, his family.

Be genuine. Being a braggart, a clown, or a phony won't cut it with most women in their thirties. They've probably had their fill of guys boasting about the size of their bank accounts, their car's engine, or their own anatomy. "They're looking now for more sincerity," says Dr. Fitzgerald.

Be mature. "If you spend a lot of time talking about how the last woman dumped on you or took advantage of you, blaming her without taking any responsibility for what went wrong, that would be a red flag," says Sharyn Wolf, a clinical social worker in New York City and author of *Guerrilla Dating Tactics*.

Be a man with a plan. "Guys in their twenties tend to say to a woman, 'Do you want to hang out?' Women hate that," says Wolf. "A woman wants to feel when you ask her out that you have something in mind."

Be prepared. When it comes to sex and the woman in her thirties, be careful because you might get what you wish for. A lot of women seem to be their most sexual when they hit their late thirties, experts say. It's not a function of hormones or physiology as much as a growing sense of self-awareness and confidence. Meanwhile, some guys have already begun a gentle decline in desire. The most common complaint Dr. Fitzgerald hears from couples in their late thirties and early forties is that the woman wants sex more than the man does. So stay in shape—and amorous.

Practice safe sex. "It may not be the first thing on your mind, but remember the importance of safe sex. By now, probably both you and the woman you are interested in will have had multiple partners," notes Shirley Zussman, Ed.D., a certified sex and marital therapist in private practice in New York City.

MATCHMAKING SERVICES

Bars aren't your scene. Friends can't fix you up. Your strict professional code of conduct prohibits you from drinking at the company well. You're craving female companionship, but you're just too darn tired of going through all the traditional channels. What you need is a hassle-free way to cut to the chase, to identify the right kind of woman for you—without going through the time, frustration, and expense of the dating scene.

Maybe you need professional help.

No, not a therapist. A dating service. Contrary to popular legend, dating or introduction services are not necessarily the last resort of the desperate.

"Far from it. They're a way for busy men to quickly and effectively identify women who meet certain personal tastes and share similar interests," says

Patricia Moore, president of the International Society of Introduction Services in West Hills, California, a trade association for introduction and dating services.

While there are no hard numbers to tell you how successful any of these services are, it makes sense that going through a professional service would increase your odds of meeting a more compatible woman than you might find in a chance encounter at a bar. You can at least have some assurance that the women who use these services are ready and willing to meet men; and many services offer ways that you can get a look at your prospects before you actually have to meet them.

If you're curious but want to know more before you proceed, we've prepared a kind of executive summary of the different services designed to help you meet people. We'll tell exactly what to expect from each type of service and help you figure out which one is right for you.

INTRODUCTION SERVICES

This is the most comprehensive service money can buy. It's also not for the casual dater. With an introduction service, you're essentially contracting to find a long-term partner. To do that, the service will conduct comprehensive interviews with you—some will even have you take personality tests. "It's a very deep interviewing process, much more than simply filling out a form and having that and a picture of you stuffed into a book for others to leaf through," says Moore.

Once they've gotten a clear picture of you and your needs, the introduction service then acts like a kind of private investigator, matching you as closely as it can to female clients who share not only your interests but also your values and your life goals. Many introduction services will not do pictures or videos: Their rationale is that the camera always lies and that the best way to really get a read on someone is to see them in person. You have to trust that an introduction service will follow whatever physical criteria you give them.

And you do have some assurances that they will. Moore says that any reputable introduction service will negotiate a contract with you up front, detailing exactly your terms and what the service provides. They also can provide you with demographics on their female clients and should be able to give you references and an idea of their success rate.

But such personalized service can be costly. In most cities, Moore says, it's not uncommon to pay $1,000 to $5,000 for membership and interviewing and possibly much more if the service actually finds someone you decide to marry. Who says you can't buy love?

VIDEO DATING SERVICES

With a video service, you get to put together your own personal video profile. It can be as simple as sitting in front of a camera and talking about yourself or as advanced as having the service do the personal equivalent of a

Questions and Answers

If you go shopping for a dating service, here are some of the questions you should ask, says the International Society of Introduction Services.

- How many years have you been in business?
- How many clients do you have in my desired age range and gender?
- What is your rate of success? How do you define *success*?
- What is the membership fee?
- How many matches are promised, and over what period of time?
- What is the background of the principal(s) of the service?

If you feel that you have been pressured into making a decision and want to revoke a contract, check your state's consumer protection laws. Most states allow you to cancel a contract within three days of initiating it.

PBS documentary. Of course, you also get to view videos of likely female matches. The advantage of this service is that you get to see what a person looks like before you meet her. And with video, you also get an opportunity to observe a little of how they *are*: their body language, what their voice sounds like.

The downside is that not everyone is comfortable in front of the camera. A person who's stuttering and nervous on video may be the love of your life; and the opposite could be just as true. Video services are for more casual daters—guys who want a sneak preview of next Friday's companion, says Moore. There's certainly nothing wrong with that. Video dating memberships can run from a few hundred to a few thousand dollars, depending on what part of the country you're in and how elaborate your video is. (Go easy on the special effects, okay?)

COMPUTERIZED DATING SERVICES

With a computerized service, you get to scroll through digitized pictures and profiles of female members. Many of these computer dating pools are the height of self-service. Simply sit down at a terminal, plug in your criteria, and get a database search of prospective partners. You'll also have your own image and profile keyed into the system.

While computerized services can be fast, convenient, and inexpensive (in the $200 to $300 range), there are some caveats to be aware of. One is that just because the service is computerized doesn't mean there's a gigantic database stored in a mainframe. Ask up front how many listings you could expect to find in your age range. Also, it's worth knowing how often the database is updated—you don't want to waste your time calling women who are no longer available.

PERSONAL ADS

One of the most pervasive and popular forms of meeting people is also one of the cheapest and most convenient.

Personal ads work two ways. First, you can peruse the personals of your local newspaper or free weekly paper. Most personals include a description of the person as well as a voice mail number. Pick a couple of ads that describe some likely candidates, and trust that when her ad says "pretty" it's not shorthand for "pretty ugly." Then, call the paper's personal line and key in the voice mail number; you'll get a message from that person. If you like what you hear, you have the option of leaving your own message. If you intrigue her, she'll call you back. Otherwise, try someone else.

Or instead of being active, you can be passive and place your own ad. Depending on the paper or service bureau, you might get 20 words for free or up to 50 words for $5 (you can make it longer, but you'll pay for each additional word). In addition to your printed ad, you'll also get a voice mail account, good for the life of the ad (usually two to three weeks). You can leave your own outgoing message that female prospects can listen to. Then, all you have to do is check your voice mail regularly and call back those women who interest you. You get to shop for a date from the comfort of your armchair without worrying about psycho babes getting your home number.

Here's the financial rub: The newspapers and services that post these ads usually don't make money off the pittance you pay for the ad and the voice mail. Their cash cow is the 900 line you dial in on to respond to ads. For each minute that you're in the system, you're charged $1.49 or more. And those minutes add up. Consider this: You dial a woman's voice mail, listen to her message—which could be a few minutes long—then you have the option of leaving a message. You leave one, and then what? You get the option of hearing your message before you actually send it. So you listen, and it turns out you sound like a fool. Of course you're not going to leave that message, so you re-record it. Do this a few times and you start to see how the pennies add up. We've talked to guys who dropped $20—easy—just responding to one or two personals.

That said, it's still not a bad way to meet people. According to men we've spoken to, it can be fun and exciting, and still a bargain, compared to the hundreds of dollars you could spend joining a dating service. Money-saving tip, guys: Don't bother placing your own ad. The men we've spoken to who've gone this route say that you get a disappointing number of replies. As it has been since the dawn of time, you have to be the hunter, going out and seeking your mate while she waits for you to come to her.

INTERNET ADS

We're not talking about logging into "chat rooms" and engaging in seductive keyboard talk with someone else out there in the ether. (For more information on this diverting pastime, see Cybersex on page 310.) Essentially,

Internet personals combine some of the slickness of a computer dating service with the ready availability of newspaper personals. As with printed personals, you can post your own ad (you can even upload pictures in some cases) or troll through the candidates online. Costs vary widely: Some services like Match.Com (at http://www.match.com) charge a monthly fee for access to their comprehensive database. Others, like Cupid's Network (at http://www.cupidnet.com), provide links to places where you can place or peruse ads free. You can contact your chosen through e-mail.

As a new twist on an old format, finding a date online can be incredibly fun. It can also be a tad frustrating. Some of these Internet sites are not yet up to their full potential—ads may be sparse or outdated—or your search may pull up someone whom you can't feasibly have a relationship with. Nothing could be more frustrating than having a search pull up the girl of your dreams, only to find out that she lives in New Zealand.

Finally, this rule of thumb: When meeting a woman from one of these services for the first time, always do so in a public place, says Shirley Zussman, Ed.D., a certified sex and marital therapist in private practice in New York City. First, there can be the problem of misrepresentation—she may not be who she said she was. But a more serious problem could be the potential of a scam. If you meet at her place or your place, you could be at risk for charges of sexual harassment or, worse, rape.

ADJUSTING TO DOMESTIC LIFE

Settling down. Making a home. Being domestic.

When a single man hears these phrases, his gut reaction is a feeling of imprisonment, a sense of loss, a certain remorse for the luckless slobs who have traded in their precious freedom for the comforts of home.

News flash for the single guy: Domestic life is the good life, pal. At least, it certainly is for men. In that moment when you forsake all others to share a lease or a mortgage with your one true roommate, you have signed up for one of the most exciting and life-affirming rides available.

And this isn't just a bunch of married writers and editors trying to justify their life choices. We have science to back us up. In one study on satisfaction with life, University of Florida researchers found that married men with children—the ultimate in male domestication—were happier and more satisfied with their lives than all other groups of men. And the researchers who compiled the landmark *Sex in America* study tell us that guys who are married or living with someone—those poor, domesticated shlubs—get sex more regularly than the average swinging single. In that survey, roughly 40 percent of men who were married or living with their partners had sex two or three times a week. Only 19 percent of undomesticated men were so lucky.

WHY DOMESTIC IS FOREIGN

Like any life change, the shift from single life to domestic life can be a bumpy one. For a lot of men, the re-entry into life at home with another person is a jarring, potentially annoying experience. Not since we left home have we had to contend with someone else's idea of how the bed should be made, how the curtains should hang, how often the bathroom should be cleaned. Now along comes her lovely self, and suddenly we have to learn how to adjust to domestic life.

"It seems terribly traumatic at first. Men are famously set in their ways. And when a woman comes along and challenges their way of doing things with her own routine and habits, it may make some men feel threatened," says Shirley Glass, Ph.D., a clinical psychologist in Owings Mills, Maryland, who specializes in interpersonal relationships.

That tension doesn't have to be permanent, though. By recognizing that this is the sort of thing that happens when two people decide to cohabit, you can work together to live in harmony and preserve your own little patch of domestic tranquillity. Here's how.

Give and take. "In marriage, everything is a compromise. It's not a bad thing," says Scott Stanley, Ph.D., co-director of the Center for Marital and Family Studies at the University of Denver and co-author of *Fighting for Your Marriage.* This goes against a basic tenet of life, drilled into us as far back as Little League: the notion that you should always go for the win. In marriage, though, it's really better to shoot for a tie. "If you feel like you're always doing things her way, or vice versa, one of you is going to be unhappy and feel frustrated in the relationship. And that's going to come back on the other person. But the more you can work to meet each other halfway on various issues, the more balanced the relationship will be," says Dr. Stanley.

Learn to fight. What's this? Yes, our experts say that from time to time you should be prepared to shatter your domestic bliss. "One of the great obstacles couples have to overcome is the fear of disagreement," says Dr. Stanley. "They feel like if they fight, it's a sign that they're not meant to be together. But, in fact, arguing about things—fairly, honestly, with respect for one another—is healthy. It prevents frustration and resentment from building up, and it's one of the best ways couples can come to a resolution about the issues that concern them." If something bothers you, don't bury it, don't explode, but do come right out and say it. *Hint:* Be specific and always come at a touchy issue

A Man's Work

Although we're in an age of equality, there remain some domestic tasks that are universally man's work. You are expected—required, really—to perform these tasks. Sometimes they're nuisances; sometimes they're nasty. But you shouldn't try to palm them off on your sweetie because (a) she'll find out they're not all that hard and (b) she'll think less of you. No need for that. So appropriate these tasks for yourself.

Opening things. Whether it's a jar or a stuck closet latch, it's the man's job to be the opener, the provider of ingress. When it is a jar, the trick is to make it appear effortless. Don't grunt. Smack the jar on the bottom with the flat of your hand, then twist.

Pest control. From sewer rats to carpenter ants, you are expected to step in and decisively—but without too much gore—destroy or remove any bug, critter, or varmint that crosses her path.

If you're required to use deadly force, do not take too much delight in the kill. No need to scream "Gotcha!" or "Look at the guts!" Just stalk it, nail it, and get it out of her way.

---

from the viewpoint of how it makes you feel. Don't say, "You are the most anal-retentive woman on the planet!" Say, "When you tell me I have to arrange the shoes in my closet according to color and style, I feel confined and restricted."

"Explaining how an action makes you feel rather than resorting to a general comment about your partner's behavior is always more constructive and will ultimately be more satisfying," says Dr. Stanley.

Don't be so efficient. Common trap. Guy gets married, sees wife not just as life partner but work partner, too. When the weekend rolls around, he knows there are a dozen things to be done, so he thinks that the best thing to do is divide the work and go off and do it. So you hit the grocery store, drop the dog off at the vet, and pick up the dry cleaning, while she stays home and cleans the bathrooms, rakes the yard, and hauls the trash to the curb. Except as you announce this plan she gives you a sad, lonely look. Why? Because she wants to go with you.

Yes, it's an inefficient use of time and manpower. So what? "You're thinking that if you work to get all your chores out of the way you'll have more time to spend together. But it's important for her to be with you while you're doing chores. She needs that together time. A woman's idea of romance is to spend the whole day with you, even if you're not doing anything necessarily fun," says Louanne Cole Weston, Ph.D., a therapist who counsels patients in Sacramento and San Francisco, and author of the "Sex Matters" advice column in the *San Francisco Examiner*.

Inedible messes. If it's spilled milk or other foodstuffs, either one of you can clean it up. But if it's something lavishly gross—a foot-long hair ball, a decaying squirrel in the chimney, a toilet-based obstacle—it is incumbent on you to don the rubber gloves of honor and do your duty. Make a big deal of washing up after the fact so that she'll have no qualms about getting close to you and rewarding you for your service.

Checking suspicious noises. Whether it's a bump in the night, a hiss in the basement, or a knock under the hood, man is responsible for keeping his ear to the ground of life. Your job is to listen for the signs of trouble and move quickly to cut them off.

Being mechanical. If it plugs in or has moving parts, it's your job to know how to operate it, fix it when it breaks down, or at least shut it off before it blows up. This extends not just to cars (if hers breaks down, she gets yours) but also to water valves, blown fuses, and VCR programming. If something is beyond your capacity to fix, your responsibilities include scheduling a repair and haggling with repairmen.

Do your share. If you do divide the labor, make sure that you hold up your end of the chores. "If one of you feels like you're doing all the work in the house, that's as bad as one of you feeling like you're always compromising or doing things her way," says Dr. Stanley. Draw up a list of things that need to be done in any given week, pick the things you don't mind doing (mowing the lawn, say, or walking the dog), and then take turns doing the less glamorous chores (cleaning the litter box, scrubbing the toilet). If it's feasible, try doing unpleasant chores together.

Synchronize yourselves. She's an early bird; you love to sleep in. Of course, that's only because you love to stay up late, while she's yawning by dinnertime. Having your body clocks set at different times is a common issue between couples, but it needn't be a common problem.

"You can't expect her to stay up and watch the late show, and she can't expect you to get up at the crack of dawn. So what do you do?" asks Daniel Kegan, Ph.D., a psychologist with Elan Associates in Chicago and an expert in interpersonal relationships. All together now: Compromise!

You: Set your wake-up time for a half-hour earlier. Her: Set the time you rise for a half-hour later (If your eyes pop open promptly at dawn, just try to lie there a little while, okay?) That should narrow the gap a little. Meanwhile, try to go to bed at the same time. The night owl can watch TV or read while the other falls asleep, but at least you'll be together. And who knows? Seeing her snoozing might make you sleepy. "The idea is to make an effort to stay on the same schedule so that you can spend more time together," says Dr. Kegan.

Hold on to your hobbies. Even though you've become part of a single, domestic unit, you shouldn't sacrifice your individuality. "It's certainly important to build an intimate bond with your partner, to try to do a lot of things together. But it's also important to maintain your own sense of identity," says Dr. Weston. Remember that you and your partner weren't drawn to each other because of a lack of personality or an ability to mimic the other's behavior. Odds are that she liked you for who you were: a cool guy with a broad range of interests outside of life with her. To that end, make sure that you both have some time alone—at least a few hours each week—to pursue those interests.

Unless your hobby was picking up women.

Designate your own space. When two people share one place, another source of conflict is the sense that each of you is surrendering territory. "You eat together, sleep together, probably share the same bathroom. As much as you need to pursue your own goals and interests, you also need to have a spot to call your own," says Dr. Weston. Your dad knew this: That's why his armchair or den was off-limits. You don't have to rope off forbidden zones in your home, but you can stake your claim on particular rooms or furniture and make them definably yours.

Be open to change. As you learn to live with another person, part of learning how to compromise is being open to a new or possibly better way of doing things. It may just be that organizing the shoes in your closet does make your life easier. We don't know how—but neither will you if you don't at least try it once.

"The point is to at least be receptive to change, to other perspectives and ways of doing things," says Dr. Stanley. "Just as we learned behaviors from our parents or our friends, we can also learn things from our partners, things that can make us better people. It's one of the most exciting aspects of living with or being married to someone. You shouldn't close yourself off to it."

YOUNG CHILDREN

A letter from the front lines: *"Everybody knows that when you've got young kids, sex becomes something that you have to schedule. It's become a cliché.... The fact is that sex itself becomes far more complicated,"* Jack writes us from Boston.

Jack is a 30-ish musician, writer, and now father, with the recent arrival of his daughter, Claire. But in addition to becoming the light of his days, Jack allows that baby Claire is also a tiny harbinger of big change. *"My wife is breastfeeding, so she can't go back on the Pill...plus all the hormonal stuff going on is causing vaginal dryness, which was never a problem for us before. We enjoyed an amazing sex life throughout her pregnancy. The changes in her body really excited us both. But after her delivery…things weren't as relaxed and free as they had been."*

Like millions of American men, Jack could very easily have bought into the standard sexual catch-22 that having sex may lead to more children but having children does not lead to more sex. If you have kids or know people who do, you've probably already heard the old nut that the birth of children can be the death of sex and intimacy with your wife.

Well, it's just not true.

We've heard it from the experts as well as guys in the trenches, like Jack: Young children can enhance all aspects of your relationship. Jack's letter continues: *"If you can get past some of the initial bumps, if you can tune in to what's going on in your house, you start to see that having a baby on the premises infuses the place with a kind of low-level sensuality that's, quite frankly, very sexy."*

YOUR CHILD, YOUR TEACHER

Jack hit the nail right on the head, says Louanne Cole Weston, Ph.D., a therapist who counsels patients in Sacramento and San Francisco, and author of the "Sex Matters" advice column in the *San Francisco Examiner*. "That's a great attitude. It's one that every man should have. Because having children doesn't have to separate you from your partner. In fact, just as you can teach your children how to love, your children can teach you to be better lovers, better partners," Dr. Weston says.

Okay, it sounds weird, but bear with us. If you're looking for specific advice on rekindling a sputtering sex life in the wake of children, this book is loaded with proven methods (check out Sustaining Interest on page 45 and Finding Time for Sex on page 367, in particular) For now, let's focus on making an attitudinal shift from child rearing as work to child rearing as life lesson. Put aside for a moment the bureaucracy of child rearing—burping, rocking, spontaneous eruptions of effluvium, the bottomless pant load of diaper work—and consider the opportunities your shining miracle of a child can offer you. In their own simple, innocent way, here are some examples of how your young children can teach you lessons that strengthen not only your relationship but even your intimacy.

They like touching. Our man Jack noticed early on how tactile his infant daughter is. "Grabbing, patting, doing a lot of weird stuff with her tongue. She can't really talk, of course, so you become acutely aware of other ways that she reaches out to you—literally," he says.

We adults could be a lot more tactile, too. "We all need touching—not necessarily in a sexual way. But we need skin-on-skin contact," says Helen Fisher, Ph.D., research associate in the department of anthropology at Rutgers University in New Brunswick, New Jersey, and author of *Anatomy of Love*. And just touching your wife—on the face, the arm, the back—can be very loving and can keep intimacy alive when you don't have time or energy for anything else.

Show and Tell

It's all well and good to let your children see that you love their mother, but what if they walk in on you and, you know, really see how much you love her?

First, don't freak out. Don't yell or scream. If they haven't run out of the bedroom, ask them, in your calmest voice, to leave. Explain that you'll be out to talk to them pretty soon.

If they're pretty young—preschool-age to around 9 or 10—don't try to explain what was going on. It's okay to be a little vague, to couch it in nonsexual terms. Say how much you and Mommy love each other and sometimes you like to hug in a special way. No need to go into details. But if your kid is precocious or old enough to know what he saw, encourage him to ask whatever questions he may have. Again, don't give him a history of sexual intercourse—no need to tell him how to make a watch when all he wants to know is what time it is.

"In general, it's best to be calm and evenhanded about the whole thing," says Barry G. Ginsberg, Ph.D., executive director of the Center of Relationship Enhancement in Doylestown, Pennsylvania, and an expert in parent-child relationships. "The event won't traumatize your child, unless he senses that you're ashamed or you make him feel ashamed." Then that's the sort of experience that may make him feel that sex and sexuality are bad, shameful things. And you don't want to do that to your kid.

One good thing can come of your child barging in on you. "It's the perfect opportunity to teach them the lesson of privacy," Dr. Ginsberg says. "There's a pretty good chance that they won't walk in on you again."

They like getting naked. You go to bathe a baby or change its diaper, and 9 out of 10 times the kid's going to get a charge out of hanging around in just a birthday suit. And some toddlers act like streakers in training, taking a perverse delight in getting buck-naked and dashing into the yard. In his or her innocent exhibitionism, the young nudist teaches you the value of lowered inhibitions, of taking the time to enjoy what Nature has given you.

They remind you of sex. What? A sticky baby with a loaded diaper and food in his ears can remind you of sex? You betcha. "Remember that your child is the living testimony to love and passion fulfilled, not a constant reminder of a burdensome obligation," says Dr. Weston. In the haze of diaper changing and midnight feedings, it's easy to focus on the negative. But by turning your mind to the more positive aspects of your child's being, you or your partner may be able to find the energy and the desire that you thought you had lost.

They make you better people. A child has an uncanny knack for making an adult out of you. "In a lot of ways, parents try to be on their best behavior with a child. You try not to swear or yell or slam around, for example," says Barry G. Ginsberg, Ph.D., executive director of the Center of Relationship

Enhancement in Doylestown, Pennsylvania, and an expert in parent-child relationships. Of course, being better around your children helps you to be better around each other. Incidentally, you may still have big disputes and little spats. (Remember that conflict is a completely normal part of marriage.) But if you have them in front of your kids, be sure to let your kids see you make up, too. Studies have shown that children who view films of adults fighting are less bothered by what they see if the argument ends with some positive resolution. Let your kids see you kiss and make up—you'll all be better for it.

They follow your example. As a corollary to the above, we'd like to remind you that children have an unnatural ability to absorb and mimic everything their parents do, from the way you walk to that choice epithet you uttered when someone cut you off in traffic. "But children do not just mimic trivial things. They mimic behavior; they learn it, really. How you handle various things in life, how you react to crisis or adversity—these are things they can pick up from you," says Dr. Ginsberg. And one of the biggest traits they can acquire from you is how to love. Let them see you being affectionate with your partner. "And also, let them see that Mom and Dad need their time alone together," says Dr. Ginsberg. Such teaching by doing inculcates your children with a much healthier sense of their own capacity for love. And as they get older and grow more into their own sexuality, your open, loving attitude will help them become stronger, loving people, too.

FINDING TIME FOR SEX

It's one of the oldest clichés in the book, second cousin to the one about marriage being the death of sex. And it's this: Once you're married and raising a family, there's no time for sex.

Like all clichés, that assertion is based in a timeworn but poignant truth: Life is a busy thing and the more you live it, the more you'll have to do. Meanwhile, the day remains fixed at a constant 24 hours, which means between seeing to your careers, maintaining a household, having and raising children, and trying to pursue your own interests as an individual, something's going to get squeezed out of the picture. Often as not, that thing is the intimate time you spend together as a couple.

Now, you'd think recognizing this fact would be the first, best step to remedying the situation. But it's just the tip of the intimacy iceberg.

"Knowing you need to find time for sex creates its own problem, at least initially," says Louanne Cole Weston, Ph.D., a therapist who counsels patients in Sacramento and San Francisco, and author of the "Sex Matters" advice column in the *San Francisco Examiner*. As Dr. Weston explains, the notion of actively seeking out time for sex at first strikes a lot of couples as unnatural, and with good reason. For most people, sex is a spontaneous act. The very idea of penciling it into your schedule seems to diminish it, puts it in the category of a chore, something routine and therefore boring. "But if you're reaching the point where you're having no time for sex, that's not natural or healthy either," says Dr. Weston.

TIMING IS EVERYTHING

Dr. Weston and other experts assure us that finding time for sex, though it may seem awkward at first, can quickly grow more natural.

"The important thing is to at least try it a couple of times," says relationship expert Ellen Kreidman, Ph.D., author of *How Can We Light a Fire When the Kids Are Driving Us Crazy?* If it makes it any easier for you, consider this: Are you sure you aren't already on a sex schedule? A surprising number of couples are on a pretty regular routine—maybe it's every Tuesday night, or every Saturday and Sunday morning. In other words, you make love within a fairly consistent time frame, but it's nothing you consciously schedule. That's all very well, until other events in life start to intrude so that your regular diet of sex goes from feast to famine.

When that happens, don't let your relationship become undernourished. Step in and reset your sexual clock. Reorient your schedule so that you and your partner can set aside time on a regular basis to enjoy one another. Here's how to do that.

Make time to make love. With the frenetic schedules we all keep, you and your partner may very well find that you just don't have a free moment in your day. All your downtime is spent sleeping. Weekends are full of chores. You haven't taken a vacation in four years. When it seems like you can't find a minute to even say a nice thing to your wife, that's when you need to *make* time, wrestling it from your schedule.

"That may mean letting other things slide. So you don't get all the household chores done. So you get to work a few minutes late once in a while. People who say they can't find time to be with their partner often just have a case of misplaced priorities," says Daniel Kegan, Ph.D., a psychologist with Elan Associates in Chicago and an expert in interpersonal relationships. Your marriage should receive priority over almost everything else. It needs time. If you find that you've parceled out all your available time to other commitments and pursuits, then you're going have to give one of those things the short end of the stick once in a while instead of always shafting your relationship.

Schedule it. We're not saying you have to write "Sex with wife" in the 9:00 to 9:15 P.M. slot on your calendar, but you can plan for future sex dates. "It can be fun to sit down at the beginning of the month and just mark down dates ahead of time," says Dr. Kreidman. "And then you can look ahead to the day you've set, which is also fun. Anticipation can be very sexy."

Timesaving Gadgets

If you're in a battle for more time to be with the one you love, you're going to need every tool at your disposal. Here are a few everyday appliances that can help you make the time you need to be with your partner.

Your alarm clock. Set it for the middle of the night, get up and make love. If that's just too jarring an idea, set it a half-hour early in the morning and enjoy one another before you have to get up and get moving.

Your VCR. Like most American households, you probably watch a decent chunk of TV during the week. Instead, pick an hour-long show or two every week that you can record on your VCR for later viewing. The VCR is a great creator of extra time in the schedule. You can make love while it's recording your favorite show. Then you can always watch it together afterward—and fast-forward through the commercials, which will give you even more time. If you have kids, rent them cartoon videos and plunk them down in front of the tube while you go off to the bedroom.

Your answering machine. Just because the phone rings, do you have to answer it? You know pretty much anyone who calls in the early evening is just a salesman anyway. Screen your calls; that way you can take time to ring each other's bells.

Your microwave. Once in a while, don't bother making a big meal from scratch. Keep some "love meals" stashed in the freezer, pop them in, eat them, then have each other for dessert. As a health-conscious publisher, we are compelled to suggest that you stick with some of the low-fat frozen meals that are available. That way, you'll be healthier in both love and life.

Hit the sheets earlier. This common ploy of time managers can also help your sex life. By going to bed—together—just 15 minutes to a half-hour early, you'll gain a couple of advantages, Dr. Kegan says. First, you'll be in bed with your wife at a time when you're still awake. Second, by going to sleep a little earlier, you'll likely wake up a little earlier, which could give you time for an early-morning roll in the hay. Besides, did you really need to see that last 15 minutes of news anyway? If nothing else, be sure to go to bed at the same time. Too many busy couples get in the habit of hitting the hay independent of each other, which is the kiss of death for intimacy.

Make time for other things, too. Maybe, just maybe, the problem isn't that you don't have time for sex. Maybe the real problem is that you're not making time for intimacy.

"In other words, you're not taking the time to talk or interact in all the other ways that are so important," says Scott Stanley, Ph.D., co-director of the Center for Marital and Family Studies at the University of Denver and co-author of *Fighting for Your Marriage*. "I would say that it's as important—maybe more so—to set aside time every day to talk or be with each other as it is to set aside time for sex." To make sure you see to all the aspects of your intimate relationship together, when you look over your schedule, make sure that you set aside time for these things, too.

Every Day

- Make time for at least one hug, one kiss. Tell her you love her. Total elapsed time: 10 to 20 seconds.
- Set aside at least 30 minutes to be with each other, free of distractions. This could be first thing in the morning before you get up, or last thing, after the kids have gone to bed and before you retire. The day is 24 hours long; you can reserve $\frac{1}{48}$ of it for you and your wife.

Every Week

- Set aside a prolonged period of time—more than an hour—where you can be alone together. Take a walk; hole yourself up in the bedroom; run out and rent a spicy movie after the kids have gone to bed.

Every Month

- Set aside at least one evening (two would be better) where you can go out together for a date (remember those?). If you have kids, you already know enough to get a babysitter.

Every Three Months

- Get away for a weekend, or at least an overnight excursion. Go to a nice hotel where you can pamper yourselves and focus on one another.

Every Year

- Take a week-long vacation together. That's right—a week. "In the course of a whole year, this is really not a very long period of time," says Dr. Kreidman. "But you need it. Remember that there's no way you two would have gotten together if you hadn't spent some time alone in the first place." What makes you think you can stay together if you still don't spend time alone?

STRESS AND FATIGUE

If sex and love were to have archenemies, or at least ideological opposites, stress and fatigue would almost certainly top the list. Few real-life villains could match this destructive duo for pernicious perfidy.

We're not talking about the positive stress that comes with tackling a new challenge, or the satisfying fatigue that settles into your muscles after a good workout. This is the species of stress and fatigue that can work you over like a pair of tag-team wrestlers. First, stress—the stress of work, of home, of life— gets you in a headlock, making it hard for you to relax, to enjoy leisure time, to get the rest you need. Then—slap!—here comes fatigue, nailing you with a sleeper hold that tires the body and numbs the mind. Your world shifts slightly out of focus; you fall behind in all of life's demands. As you struggle to pick up the pace—slap!—stress steps into the ring once more.

If you're the guy being pinned to the mat, it's not one bit funny. Permitted to run riot, stress and fatigue can kill men—literally—and turn passionate relationships into mere cohabitation. No matter how much havoc they've wrought in your life, you can beat these villains. But first you have to know a bit about how they operate.

ANATOMY OF STRESS

Like sex, stress is a phenomenon of body and mind. Only it's nowhere near as much fun. Something occurs out in the world, your brain drinks it in, and you have a reaction that is played out in your body. In the case of stress, you could experience either of two events: a physical stressor, such as an upcoming traffic jam, a deer running in front of your car, a woman hurling a shoe at you; or a mental stressor, such as an impending deadline, a criticism from the boss, a vague worry about the future. Either way, your body reacts the same way: The brain sends out an all points bulletin that gets your nervous system a-jangling. The message gets picked up by the systems in your body that govern voluntary physical activity—your muscles, we mean. They start to wind up, getting tighter and tighter, just waiting to spring you into action, the moment your body says "fight" or "flight."

Meanwhile, in the mysterious involuntary reaches of your bodily functions, organs and glands snap on or off with amazing rapidity. Your digestive organs stop what they're doing. Your pituitary and adrenal glands secrete powerful hormones into the body, hormones that raise your heart rate and blood pressure and cause you to breathe faster. Your sensory organs are honed to a razor sharpness. Your mind has prepared your body for battle. And this doesn't just happen once in a while. This happens to us every day, sometimes several times a day. When a blood-curdling scream from the kid's room wakes us up. When the morning commute has us wound in knots. When the boss upbraids us in front of co-workers. When the wife upbraids us in front of the kids for coming home late. When all of the above come crashing in on us and we suddenly find that we can't perform in bed.

As you can imagine, this stress stuff is pretty, well, stressful on the body. It's no wonder that so many of us have high blood pressure, digestive problems, performance issues, or anxiety attacks. But you don't have to be one of those guys anymore.

FORMULA FOR FATIGUE

Fatigue is really about power and the allocation of resources. Your body only has so much energy, and when situations or events cause you to expend that energy, you start to fatigue. When these situations or events continue over long periods of time, your energy levels stay at a low ebb and you can feel fatigued fairly often. The real trick to banishing fatigue, then, is to identify the things that are draining your power or keeping you from replenishing it. Simple, right? Except that uncovering the origins of fatigue can be one of the most complicated and mysterious journeys man can undertake.

"Fatigue is one of the most common symptoms there is. If you go to your doctor because you're feeling run-down, there could be hundreds of reasons why," says Edward B. Blanchard, Ph.D., distinguished professor of psychology at the Center for Stress and Anxiety Disorders at the State University of New York in Albany. These reasons range from something as simple as not getting enough sleep to a more serious ailment, such as an infection, a problem with your body's metabolism—it's even a symptom of cancer.

This isn't to scare you. It's simply to point out that fatigue is almost never a problem so much as a symptom of something else—some condition or situation is draining energy from your body. "It's one of the first warning signs your body gives that something's wrong," says David S. Bell, M.D., a family practitioner in Lyndonville, New York, and author of *Curing Fatigue*. If you're suffering fatigue and low energy levels without any obvious reasons, you definitely should see your doctor.

Most of the time, though, the fatigue you experience is caused by day-to-day stress. After learning about the physiological changes that stress causes, you can see why: Responding to a stressful event burns up a lot of energy, and when the event has passed, you slump. On top of that, mental stress can keep you from getting sleep, that great recharger of the human battery.

FOILING FATIGUE, SLAYING STRESS

Combating stress and fatigue is not a light subject. Whole books are devoted to each of these problems on their own. Our goal here is not to recap the causes of stress and fatigue in glib, Cliffs Notes form. You already know you should be getting more rest, working fewer hours, taking more vacation than you already are. But what's keeping you from doing that?

One factor is your perspective. "I think a lot of men look at stress as a fact of life, or something too big to try to address. And they're right in a way," says Dr. Blanchard. Instead of viewing the stress in your life as one giant wave descending on you, focus on very specific situations that are causing you stress or weariness and attack them. Divide and conquer, as they say.

Here, then, are specific action items, approaches you can take as soon as tomorrow morning to make sure that you get your daily load of stress and its

Serious Stressors

You think tomorrow's deadline is the most stressful thing that has ever happened to you? Sure, it feels like that right now. But just to give you some perspective, here's what researchers say are the top 10 all-time stressors in a man's life.

1. Death of a spouse
2. Divorce
3. Marital separation
4. Death of a family member
5. Going to jail
6. Getting injured or seriously ill
7. Getting married
8. Getting fired
9. Getting back together with your wife
10. Retiring

attendant fatigue down to manageable levels. You'll find that these tips are double-duty directives—useful for both quashing stress and fighting fatigue, no matter where you are during the day.

At Work

A survey conducted by Northwestern National Life Insurance Company found that 4 in 10 American workers said that their jobs are very or extremely stressful. And 15 percent of those questioned in a survey conducted for *Prevention* magazine by Abacus Custom Research of Emmaus, Pennsylvania, said that stress harmed their jobs.

Here's what you need to do to turn down the heat in your office.

Control what you can. Actually, that's good advice no matter where stress attacks. Many times, men worry about things they can't control—traffic, the economy, the boss's attitude. "If you can't control what's causing stress, the best thing you can do is try not to expend energy worrying about it," says Dr. Blanchard. That's a big job, especially for men, who are dyed-in-the-wool control freaks. Instead, try to accept what you cannot control and focus your energy on controlling the stressors that you *can* do something about, says Dr. Blanchard.

Be an early riser. Coming in early may be less stressful on you than staying late. "Staying late makes you feel late, makes you feel time is slipping away, makes you feel more tired when you get home," says Daniel Kegan, Ph.D., a psychologist with Elan Associates in Chicago and an expert in interpersonal relationships. If you set your clock a little earlier and come in before the start of the business day, you may be able to put in the same amount of time. "Plus, any time you work off-peak hours, it's likely to be quieter, you won't be interrupted as much, and there's likely to be less vying for communal resources like printers and photocopiers," says Dr. Kegan. What's more, by heading in early, you may miss traffic on at least one leg of your commute.

Don't stay put. If your 9-to-5 hours are spent jockeying a workstation, you're building up a lot of static stress just sitting there, says flexibility consultant Bob Anderson, author of *Stretching at Your Computer or Desk*. Stop what you're doing and stretch every 30 to 45 minutes. Get up and walk around every hour or so.

Walk at lunch. During your lunch hour, resist the urge to eat at your desk—get outside and get some air. Nothing bashes stress or wakes you up like a little fresh air. "Any kind of exercise you can do will be good for dealing with everyday pressure. And it can give you more energy to get you through the day," Anderson says. If you can manage to get to a health club and do a quick half-hour set, so much the better. (Many companies have corporate deals with fitness clubs that are near the office. Ask your personnel department.) If nothing else, do a brisk couple of laps around the parking lot.

Grab 40 winks. If you've been pulling all-nighters trying to get that project done, or your newborn is keeping you up all hours, a next-day nap may just be the quick fix you need. Studies have shown that taking a 20- to 30-minute nap roughly 30 minutes before you need to be at your best can make you just as sharp as if you'd gotten a full 8 hours the night before. It's true. Aside from finding a quiet place where no supervisor-type can catch you, the main trick to this technique is not to nap longer than 30 minutes. After that, your body goes into deep sleep and you'll wake up groggier than before. And don't use the snooze strategy too often to replace lost sleep: The more you do it, the less effective napping will be for reviving you.

Know when to say "when." Stress quiz: A supervisor asks you to handle a new project in addition to your already-impossible workload. What's your response? If you consider yourself ambitious and eager to advance in the company—like the other 99 percent of us—you probably say yes instantly. And then fret about this new responsibility afterward.

Instead, if you're pushing yourself to the limit as it is, don't be afraid to give your boss a polite but firm "no."

"Some people think that's career suicide. But consider: If you take on too many jobs, you won't be able to do them all with the same level of success or professionalism," Dr. Kegan says. Which is worse: saying no and citing the hundred other things you have to do as the reason; or accepting more work and risking a reputation as a guy who does a slipshod job?

At Home

A man's home may be his castle, but it no longer stands as a fortress against stress. Dueling dual careers, kids, and even something as mundane as who dusts and vacuums can make even the most valiant knight feel like he's under siege.

Here's how to reduce the stress in your home.

Delegate downtime. Although part of your stress in life may derive from the fact that you don't spend enough time with your family, make sure that you give yourself some quiet time away from the kids or other domestic responsibilities. After you've put them to bed, just spend a few minutes sitting and reading something enjoyable. Or before dinner, retire to the basement or your armchair and decompress (just don't spend all evening there). "One of the best ways to cope with stress is to spend some time in relaxation. If you don't give yourself that time, it's going to be very hard to get control of the stress," says Dr. Blanchard.

Keep in touch. In conjunction with having your own personal downtime, make sure that you also spend some time every evening catching up with every member of your family. Nothing wears you down like coming to the end of a hard day and realizing you haven't said two words to your wife or spent any time with your kids besides tucking them in. The idea of "quality time" has become almost cliché, but that doesn't make it any less important in your life.

Look at the big picture. After a long day in the trenches, minor domestic problems can seem magnified. "When little things become big deals, that's a sure sign of stress," says Dr. Kegan. How do you get stress out from under the microscope? Perspective. "When something happens—the kids spill milk or your wife does something you don't like—just take a moment to put it in context before you react," Dr. Kegan says. In the grand scheme of things, how much is that spilled milk going to count for? That's right: squat.

Laugh it off. As part of keeping perspective, make sure that you laugh plenty when the absurd reaches up and slaps you in the face. "As a general stress-buster and fatigue-killer, few things work better than simple laughter," says Joel Goodman, Ed.D., director of the HUMOR Project in Saratoga Springs, New York. *Hint:* Don't have a guffaw at a family member's expense, but don't miss the opportunity for humor in everyday life. You're living in a comedy, pal, so when life seems really crazy, try to pierce that veil of angst and laugh, clown, laugh.

Eat right. Remember what we said about fatigue and energy levels? Well, if you're not pumping your body full of high-octane foods at breakfast, lunch, and dinner, you'll have fewer energy reserves to draw on when you need it.

A proper, high-energy diet should be high in carbohydrates, the preferred fuel of your body, found in pastas and grains, for example. If you aren't already trying to cut back on the amount of fat you eat, start hacking away at it today. Fat slows you down by packing on pounds and narrowing blood vessels, conditions that are both stressful and fatiguing. You should be getting no more than 30 percent of your calories from fat. To figure that out quickly, take your body weight and divide it in half. The number you get is roughly equivalent to the maximum amount of fat you should eat every day (thus a 150-pound man should eat no more than 75 grams of fat a day). And go easy on sugary foods and caffeinated beverages. Although they can provide quick energy boosts, the effect won't last long and you'll crash. Also, these foods can make you more jittery and susceptible to stress.

Work in a workout. There's no better way to raise energy levels or put stress in its place than to follow a regular exercise regimen. "Whether it's a stop at the club on the way home or a workout in the basement before dinner, try to do some exercise every day," says Anderson. At least three days each week, give your body a real workout: Do at least 30 minutes of an aerobic activity like walking, running, or cycling. Follow that up with 15 minutes of weight training. Then finish off with 10 minutes of cooling down and stretching. "You'll feel like a new man," says Anderson.

In Bed

Sex is one of the greatest stress relievers known to man. (Or woman, for that matter.) It also can be one of the greatest stressors in your life. But only if you let it. Here's how to banish stress from the bedroom.

Please yourselves. In the sack, the issue of performing well (read: being the triggerman on your partner's mind-blowing orgasm) is a chronic stressor for modern man. We recognize that even this book can contribute to that. Try not to focus on her orgasm as the Holy Grail of sex.

"Instead, focus more generally on pleasing her: What feels good to her? What makes her feel sexy, attractive?" says William Hartman, Ph.D., a retired sex therapist in Long Beach, California. If you concentrate on doing things that simply please her, everything—including the big O—will fall into place.

Likewise, concentrate on your own pleasure as well. Otherwise, you might find yourself unable to get aroused, says Shirley Zussman, Ed.D., a certified sex and marital therapist in private practice in New York City. After all, there are two things that excite your partner: what you do to her and what she does to please you in return. In a healthy relationship, both partners are considerate of both partners' needs and wants.

And by the way, you may find that on some nights, pleasing her doesn't mean having sex at all. Some nights she may just want to fall asleep in your arms. And how tiring is that?

Come to your senses. A great part of the sexual repertoire—and a great stress-free sexual technique—is called sensate focusing, in which you focus your entire attention on what you're actually feeling. All you have to do is concentrate on your biggest organ—no, not *that*. We're talking about your skin. Drink in the signals that it's sending. When you caress her breasts, really feel the soft rise of flesh, the curious texture of her nipples. When you kiss, close your eyes and concentrate on what your lips are feeling. Instead of anticipating the instant of penetration, focus on the delicious moments when other parts of your bodies touch—when her breasts brush against you, when your stomachs touch. "This sort of focus gives you a much better appreciation of everything else that is going on before and during sex," says Dr. Hartman. It can also be quite, um, diverting from the everyday stress of life.

Take turns. One of you shouldn't have to do all the work all the time. "In seeing surveys and in talking to men, you hear over and over how they wish their partner would take the initiative now and again," says Robert Birch, Ph.D., a psychologist in private practice in Columbus, Ohio, specializing in marriage and sex therapy. That's good advice. Agree in advance to take turns seducing one another. Tonight it's your turn; next time it's hers.

Stay in the game. For the bulk of manhood out there, stress in the bedroom boils down to one simple moment: the act of the erection. "If you can get one, there's no stress. But if you can't..." says Dr. Birch. While it's not the only stress you'll have to face in this life, it certainly is one of the most disconcerting. To help you overcome this particular stressor, we offer two useful, if slightly hackneyed, truths.

1. It happens to everyone (or will).
2. The more you worry about it, the worse it gets.

And when it does happen, don't clam up about it or roll away from your partner. Tell her the truth: This is a quite normal circumstance for men who are under stress. Then continue with your lovemaking. Kiss, caress, stroke, lick. Perfect your technique in other aspects of lovemaking, and believe us when we say that you'll eventually come around. (For more help on quashing this particular brand of stress, see Erection Problems on page 226.)

THE WANDERING EYE

Men are instinctively creatures of observation. We notice things. When something catches our eye—a drop-dead gorgeous woman in a figure-hugging mini-dress, let's say—age-old instincts kick in. Involuntarily, our eyes take note of the bright markings, the decorative plumage, the genetic traits so generously on display. In the space of an instant, the Stone Age mind deep at the core of our Space Age heads has trained visual sensors on the new female that has entered our territory, gathering basic information about the mating potential of this creature. It happens so fast that we're not even aware of it.

Just then, generations of carefully inculcated morality kick in. We remember that, hey, we're married. And that's when we notice something else: the woman we're already with. The one who's glaring us, who's accusing us of having a wandering eye.

LETTING THE EYES HAVE IT

Well, we have to ask: What's wrong with a wandering eye? Just because you're not permitted to touch objects in a museum doesn't mean you can't look at them. And women, after all, are works of art—it would be a sin not to appreciate them in their great diversity. Granted, if the love of your life is talking to you and your attention drifts from her to the skirt that swishes by, it's rude, maybe even a little insulting. But the phenomenon of the wandering eye is also totally natural, especially for men.

We'll state it yet again: Most men are aroused by visual stimuli more than anything else. Women, by contrast, generally respond to more cerebral or verbal stimuli: a man's personality, his emotional qualities, the sound of his voice.

"A man, meanwhile, is more likely to focus on things he can see: her hair, her face, the shape of her body," says Galdino F. Pranzarone, Ph.D., professor of psychology at Roanoke College in Salem, Virginia. Spotting these characteristics helped us zero in on the ideal mate—you know, the one who's glaring at you. The problem is that finding the ideal mate doesn't automatically turn off the reflex of noticing attractive women. It shouldn't either. Because the wandering eye is not just a way of identifying the perfect match for us; it's also the built-in video system that fuels our fantasy life, which is an essential characteristic of the male sexual psyche. (Think we're making that up? Check out Fantasies on page 99.)

"Fantasy is important, especially in marriage. It's a way of keeping your interest alive," says Sherry Lehman, a sex therapist in Cleveland and author of *Seven Days to Better Sex and a More Loving Relationship*. It's also a form of pressure release, a safety valve. Instead of actually running off with another woman and leaving your life and family in tatters, you just play the suggestive scenario out in your mind instead. "It's arousing, it's healthy, it's safe," says Lehman. So in that sense, having a wandering eye can help save your marriage. But not if you continually allow your eye to wander when you're with your partner.

You can temper the primal instinct to notice other women, and in so doing you'll earn a lot more respect from your spouse—and get in a lot less trouble. Here are three simple principles to follow.

Be discreet. Nothing will get you in trouble faster than swiveling your head to follow the track of a beautiful someone at the same time that your own personal honey is talking to you. Control yourself. If you do see someone give her a glance or two, but don't crane and be obvious about it. That just makes you look like an oaf. Exercise some common courtesy: Wait until your woman isn't requiring your immediate attention, then steal a few looks. Never stare, never gawk, and please, don't whistle.

Be honest. Inevitably, discretion will fail you, and she will catch you undressing the waitress with your eyes. When she does, own up to it. The only thing worse than being caught ogling another woman is lying about ogling another woman. And if your wife asks you the dreaded follow-up question, "Do you think she's attractive?" we advocate total honesty. Say, "Well, sure. But I'm much more attracted to you, of course."

Look, don't touch. While there's nothing wrong with being tempted, we have to warn you away from giving in to that temptation. A few choice words for you: anger, betrayal, infidelity, divorce court, visitation rights. You control those Stone Age impulses, not the other way around. If getting an eyeful of a beautiful woman is making you think seriously about getting a handful of the same, we recommend that you close your eyes for a moment and take stock of the situation. Set your sights on confronting the issues and inequities in your current relationship, not on abandoning it in the blink of an eye.

SEXUAL HARASSMENT

Call the rules governing sexual harassment anything you want. Curse them up and down. Decry them as unfair, excessively restrictive, inherently antimale. We're not here to argue the point. We're only here to point out one thing: The law is the law.

And the law says that everyone—man and woman—has a right to work in an atmosphere that isn't hostile to them or their gender, that doesn't make them feel uncomfortable or degraded. And that's fair—work is hard enough as it is without people saying or doing things to make you feel worse.

But what makes men and women feel uncomfortable are often two entirely different things. "You're getting into a real perception question," says Daniel Kegan, Ph.D., a psychologist with Elan Associates in Chicago and an expert in interpersonal relationships. "And men don't always have clear insight into what makes a woman uncomfortable."

Talk about an understatement. But that's one of the reasons why sexual harassment has become such an emotionally charged topic. At worst, some men feel hunted, believing that everything they say or do could be misconstrued as harassing by a gender they don't fully understand. One misstep, one misspoken word and their reputations are forever sullied, their careers over. And some women are only too happy to exploit this fear. Ever vigilant, they look for crude, sexual subtext in every gesture, every office decoration, every passing remark made in a workplace still largely dominated by men.

CONQUERING THE CLIMATE OF FEAR

"There is a certain fear and concern about sexual harassment, and it really makes the whole subject much more difficult to deal with, from a legal and personal standpoint," says Jonathan A. Segal, Esq., a partner at Wolf, Block, Schorr, and Solis-Cohen law firm in Philadelphia who lectures to companies on sexual harassment issues. Such a climate makes people think that sexual harassment is an impossibly complex issue. In fact, to deal with sexual harassment, you only need to know this: Certain behavior in the workplace can create feelings of hostility and discomfort in members of the opposite sex. Communicate more clearly with your female co-workers and you can identify that behavior. Identify that behavior and you can eliminate it. Simple, right?

Well, no. But understanding more about what constitutes harassment and how to prevent it isn't an impossible task either. Here we've provided some guidelines to help you navigate the murky waters between perception and reality—the very breeding ground of sexual harassment. We'll start with the most obvious rules first.

Say no to quid pro quo. This isn't the only form of sexual harassment there is; it's just the most egregious. Quid pro quo happens anytime someone makes sexual overtures to a co-worker and offers advancement or incentive if she complies—or threatens her if she doesn't. Hinting that an employee won't get a promotion if she doesn't perform sexual favors for you is the classic example of quid pro quo—and it's completely unacceptable in the world of civilized men and women.

Don't touch. With the exception of a professional business handshake, your contact with a female co-worker should be strictly hands-off. "Touch carries a lot of meaning in our society," says Dr. Kegan. "And that meaning can be misconstrued." You know that giving someone an encouraging or affectionate swat on the behind is behavior straight out of the Dark Ages. But even patting a female co-worker on the shoulder or back can be a tactile message open to broad interpretation. When you pat her on the back, you may be thinking, "I'm offering encouragement and support." But she may be thinking, "Is he feeling for my bra strap or what?" To keep any innocuous physical gesture from being misinterpreted, your best bet is to make no physical gestures toward her. No hugs, no pats, no squeezes— no kidding.

For that matter, don't look either. Visual creatures that men are, we all too often find ourselves having face-to-face conversations with a woman's chest or thighs. The wandering eye is a natural phenomenon in men, but it's not involuntary—you need to govern it in the workplace. If a female co-worker walks by, don't gawk at her in an obvious way. And when you're face to face with her, make sure you stay that way. Look her in the eye when you talk to her. Or if you tend to look at people for a few seconds then look away, look off over her shoulder, not down to her blouse.

Incidentally, the "don't look" rule also applies to images of women that might be around the office. That co-worker who has the Pamela Lee calendar in his office is skating on very thin ice. (Even a picture of your wife or girlfriend wearing a bikini could create a hostile environment for female co-workers, under the law.) And if you're surfing the Internet on company time, make sure that you don't linger on that Swedish Sex Home Page. "Basically, any images or items that might be offensive are dangerous things to have around the office," says Segal.

Stick to business. It's a bit of a shame, but political correctness is proving to be the death of old-fashioned civility. Once upon a time, it was no big deal to innocently compliment a lovely co-worker on her appearance, but these days it's just not worth the risk. "When you have a conversation with a female co-worker, you're just better off sticking to the business at hand. If you're going to engage in small talk, keep it to neutral topics," says Segal.

Watch it with the guys. With all of these rules and restrictions for proper conduct, you probably consider it a welcome relief to have a moment in the coffee room with a few of the guys, just shooting the breeze. But as long as you're at work—and conceivably within earshot of a co-worker—you still have to be mindful of your conversation.

"Let's say you're sitting around the lunch table and conversation leads to a discussion of sexual fantasies. Or one of you uses language that's derogatory to women. If a co-worker hears you—even if she's not part of the conversation at all—that might be creating a hostile work environment for her," Segal says. By the way, the same holds true even if the group you're chatting with includes members of both sexes.

Develop a "wife filter." Most sexual harassment cases result from differing sensitivities and impressions between men and women. In other words, a man may say or do things that he thinks won't be construed as harassment because it wouldn't bother him if a woman did it to him. "That's the wrong way to look at it," says Segal. "Harassment is about having or not having a certain comfort level at work. Comfort level is a part of perspective and experience. And the experience of being a man is vastly different from the experience of being a woman." So before you say or do anything, don't ask yourself, "How would I feel if a woman said or did this to me?" Ask instead, "How would I feel if some guy said or did this to my wife? Or my sister? Or my mother?"

"Once guys run their behavior through that filter, they become a lot more sensitized to their own actions," Segal says.

Take "no" for an answer. Let's say you are attracted to a woman in your office and you'd like to ask her out. Respectfully. Politely. Is there anything wrong with that? Not at all. "But you'd better not ask unless you're mature enough to deal with the consequences," Segal says. And by that he means *negative* consequences. If she says no, are you professional enough to continue to maintain a good working relationship with her? Or will your ego be so

Ask and Ye Shall Receive

Throughout this book, we've told you how communication between a man and a woman can improve relationships. Well, it may save your career, too.

If in reading over this chapter, you realize you've said or done something recently to a female co-worker that might be construed as harassment, you have an effective tool at your disposal that can save—possibly even enhance—your reputation at work.

"It's called asking someone if you've offended them," says Jonathan A. Segal, Esq., a partner at Wolf, Block, Schorr, and Solis-Cohen law firm in Philadelphia who lectures to companies on sexual harassment issues. "It would be nice if every woman could feel confident enough to tell a man when he has done something that bothers her or makes her uncomfortable, but that's not the case yet." Still, that doesn't mean you can't ask her.

Let's say you have a habit of clapping your co-workers on the back, or standing very close to someone when you talk to them. Or uttering a favorite epithet that happens to have crude sexual connotations. If you've done something questionable recently—within the last few days—there's nothing wrong with being preemptive. Say to your colleague, "Yesterday when I patted your shoulder/swore in your presence/made that off-color remark, I hope I didn't offend you or make you uncomfortable. And if I ever unwittingly say or do anything to make you uncomfortable, I hope you'll tell me so that I won't do it again."

It may seem simpering, but she won't think ill of you. At worst, she'll think that you just came from a sexual harassment seminar. At best, she'll appreciate your professionalism and respect. Then, you haven't gained an enemy but a fan, a supporter who will tell others about what a great, professional guy you are—which never hurts a reputation.

bruised that you'll start to avoid her, snub her—in short, do things that she can claim are creating a hostile environment for her?

And if she says no, can you take that for an answer? For your own sake, you'd better, says Segal. "There's nothing wrong with asking. But if you decide that she didn't mean it and you keep asking her, it could be ruled as harassment," he warns.

Ask for clarification. The best way to avoid any kind of harassment charge is to strive for clarity in your dealings with female co-workers, to make sure that you've understood them and that they haven't misunderstood you.

Let's go back to the above example for a minute. Suppose you ask her out, and she doesn't say no but, instead, says simply that she already has plans. "This is where we get into a gray and dangerous area," Segal says. "Because she may really mean no, but she wants to spare his feelings. But he doesn't know that. So he asks again. And she gives him another excuse. So he asks a third time or a fourth. Next thing you know, she goes to her manager and says, 'This guy is harassing me. He keeps bugging me for a date, even after I told him no.' Who's at fault?"

The most you can do to avoid reaching that stage is to ask for clarification. When she said she was busy, did she really mean no? Make it clear that you're only asking because you don't want to get your signals crossed; you don't want to bother her if she's not interested. She may still waffle (and you'll have to judge whether you should ask again), but at least you tried. (For more advice on dating on the job, see Workplace Romance on page 337.)

Consider the impact. A female colleague whom you respect and admire shows up on the first day of spring wearing a skirt that, though tasteful, still shows off her exquisite legs. You tell her you love it when she wears skirts because she has great legs. And you mean it as a genuine compliment. But that's not what she hears. Instead she feels angry and embarrassed. If she reports you to human resources for sexual harassment, your defense—that you didn't mean it—won't do you a lick of good.

"Why? Because your intent doesn't matter—impact does," Segal says. "You may have meant it as a compliment, but if she perceives it as harassment, it's harassment." The most conservative rule of thumb is not to comment on her appearance at all. But in general, it's another situation where you have to take a moment to ask yourself how the recipient of your comments will feel—even if you have the best of intentions.

Take it seriously. This is an important rule for anyone who is a manager or ever wants to be: If an employee comes to you—female or male—with a sexual harassment complaint, take it *very* seriously. Do not try to downplay it or make light of it. And for goodness' sake, don't ever tell someone they're overreacting or being too sensitive. That's the sort of comment that makes you look highly insensitive if the harassment case goes to court. "You have an obligation not just to address an employee's workplace concerns but also to protect your company. By acting in a serious and decisive manner that demonstrates your sensitivity to a complaint, you may be able to resolve things easily and save everyone a lot of grief," Dr. Kegan says.

MONEY AND ROMANCE

This is a chapter about spoiling yourself.

For the next several hundred words you'll find nothing but permission to take some of your hard-earned cash and spend it on you and your honey. Call it a splurge. Or call it an investment in your relationship. Either way, you've earned it.

Sure, you're no Bill Gates (not just yet anyway). But you are in all likelihood reaching a point in your life where financial stability—and maybe even a wee small bit of excess—is starting to be a reality. You've pulled away from the entry-level pack, started to gain higher positions, greater authority, fatter paychecks. Those student and car loans are getting paid off. Your checking account is starting to show a surplus at the end of the month. You're investing and saving more. You're getting smart about money.

Just don't get too smart.

"This can be a dangerous point in a relationship because it's an age where people are thinking they have to grow up and be responsible. They have to start being like their parents—investing and saving money for their children and planning for the future. But in the process, they stop spending some of their resources on fun and romance," says relationship expert Ellen Kreidman, Ph.D., author of *Light Her Fire* and *Light His Fire*, a series of inventive books and seminars.

Now, we recognize that certain financial realities of life might get in the way of this plan. "Even though this is an age where you're starting to make a decent living, it also just happens to be the time when you're making some serious financial commitments, too, like buying a home or starting a family," says Barry G. Ginsberg, Ph.D., executive director of the Center of Relationship Enhancement in Doylestown, Pennsylvania, and an expert in parent-child relationships. But just as you have those expenses, it's also likely that you have some money earmarked for romancing each other, even if it's only once in a while. When you do find yourself with some extra cash, the adult response is to set it aside, save it for a rainy day. Well, the drops are splashing on the pavement, pal.

Below we've compiled a list of luxuries you should allow yourselves to enjoy. All are luxuries to be sure. But this is about pampering you and your partner, and about showing the woman you love that you know how to spend money on things that will relax you, make you feel good, and give you more time and energy to enjoy one another's company.

DON'T LEAVE HOME WITHOUT THEM

Whether it's a night on the town or a weekend in the country, here are some suggestions for extravagances—both subtle and ostentatious—that you can enjoy.

A babysitter. Actually, where children are concerned, this is more a necessity than a luxury. Consider it money well-spent for an evening out.

Fine dining. At least once a month, make reservations at a fine restaurant (nothing less than three stars). Few things are more luxurious than having people wait on you, pour you wine, and cook for you.

A play. You can go to a movie anytime. So on Splurge Night, why not go to the theater—the real theater? A play is extravagant. Think about it: You get to dress up and go to a cavernous, ornate place. When you get there, people hand you big, creamy programs. They show you to your seat—and it's a mighty cushy seat. Real human beings stand before you and perform their hearts out. There's nothing cheap about it. And for a night, you get to feel like royalty.

Valet parking. When you go out to a play or to dinner, don't get sucked into the frenzy of trying to beat the car next to you for that open meter at the end of the block. This will just wind you up, make you tense. Instead, let someone in a blazer and bow tie park it for you. Your cost: $5 to $10. When it's time to pick up the car, fold a dollar bill in your palm and when you shake hands with the valet, you slip him the tip. Don't you feel debonair?

A suite spot. If you go away for a weekend, don't get a motel room. Get a suite at a hotel or inn, Dr. Kreidman says. Get something with at least one of the following amenities: a Jacuzzi, a fireplace, a balcony with a view, a phone in the bathroom, or mints on the pillow.

Room service. If you have to scramble out of bed to make it down to the lobby for the free Continental breakfast, you're in the wrong place. Instead, when you wake up in the morning, roll over, pick up the phone, and have breakfast brought to you, says Doreen Virtue, Ph.D., a relationship expert and psychotherapist in Newport Beach, California, and author of *In the Mood.* Nothing says "living large" like a bellhop wheeling in a cart of coffee, muffins, a couple of fluffy omelets, fresh fruit, and juice. And don't even think about the price. It's not the food you're paying for, but the experience.

THE HIGH LIFE AT HOME

At least one night a week, Dr. Kreidman says, you should have time alone together, away from the drudgery of everyday life. Giving yourself this extra time is not an extravagance; it's a survival technique.

But once in a while, you should make that one night a week a special time. And these little extras can make the time even more special.

Champagne. Nothing makes her cuddly like a great big bottle of bubbly. Skip the Cold Duck and the sparkling wine. Head for the import section and get some real 100 percent dyed-in-the-wool French Champagne. "If you don't drink, you could always get sparkling cider or juice for something special," says Dr. Virtue.

Food delivered. Having food delivered to you is one of the most obvious sprees you can enjoy from home. And what a bargain! For the price of one delivered meal, you get to spend all the time with your partner you would have spent making the meal and cleaning up. Plus, you don't have to get out of your smoking jacket and silk pajamas and head out into the cold, cruel world to get takeout. Besides ordering pizza or Chinese, check your phone book for other restaurants that deliver, or look for a business called Takeout Taxi—a service that places your order at restaurants that don't otherwise deliver. They then pick up the order and bring it to you.

Fine chocolate. Remember, the operative term here is *fine.* You can buy Hershey bars any day of the week. Go to the candy aisle of your supermarket and look up on the top shelf for the foreign chocolates, the ones with Italian and Swiss sounding names. Yes, now that you mention it, these gourmet chocolates are quite high in calories and fat. But then, it's not like you buy them every day of the week (do you?).

Bubble bath. Granted, it's not very manly, but these bubbles are really more for her than for you. Draw her a warm bath, pour in the suds (bath salts or beads are nonbubble options she may also enjoy). Assign yourself as her bath slave and join her. Then rake in the credit you'll get for treating her so decadently.

Roses. Another extravagance for her, and major romance points for you. Pick them up on your way home from work or, even more extravagant, have them delivered. Mushy Romance Tip Number 412: Take a couple of roses, crush them, and scatter them around the bed. Watch her reaction.

Personal bliss. If none of the above appeals to you and your partner, you should know enough to splurge on something else. If you both hate wine but love beer, buy a case of that pricey microbrew you've been wanting to try. Or get yourselves the fixings for a decadent meal you'd never normally treat yourself to. "The point is to use your money to pamper, to spoil. It will make you both happier and more relaxed," says Dr. Kreidman. And that can only deepen the value of your relationship.

GETAWAYS

As the vise of your life closes ever tighter, lots of the little details of loving one another get squeezed out of the picture. Overwhelmed by demands of jobs and finances, children and chores, you forget to utter that little compliment; fatigue overtakes that urge to make the extra effort with one another. Sex becomes an afterthought or, worse, a bittersweet memory. You feel hemmed in on all sides.

It's a dangerous time and you're desperate people, and when your life is starting to close in on you, that's the time to become the Steve McQueen and Ali MacGraw of love. You need to blow town, break jail, hit the road, go on the lam. In short, you need a fast getaway.

"When jobs and housework and children enter the picture, couples start to lose focus on one another. That can be a real tragedy," says relationship expert Ellen Kreidman, Ph.D., author of *Light Her Fire* and *Light His Fire*, a series of inventive books and seminars.

That's why in her books and seminars she encourages couples to take mini-vacations, short getaways throughout the year that give couples a chance to spend pure, decadent, unadulterated time with one another.

Planning the Perfect Getaway

Maybe you're thinking that you can't afford a lot of vacations, either time-wise or money-wise. But a getaway doesn't have to involve expensive trips. "It doesn't even have to involve leaving town. Or leaving your house, for that matter," Dr. Kreidman says.

Sure, it would be nice if the two of you could schedule a weekend away from home and family. "That's probably the ideal situation. It gives you some excitement, a little novelty, and a physical break from your usual routine," says Carol Cassell, Ph.D., a psychologist in Albuquerque, New Mexico, and author of *Tender Bargainings*. But Dr. Cassell goes on to say that what really matters is that the two of you set aside some amount of time on a regular basis to "get away from it all," be it mentally or physically.

For the moment, we're assuming a best-case scenario—that you can spare a weekend and a few extra dollars to pamper yourself. But where do you go? What do you do? We don't want to specify which hotels, what resorts, what activities—we're sure you can think up a few on your own. But we would like to point out some common themes of the ideal break. Follow these tenets and you'll ensure that your next getaway becomes a great escape.

Go often. Don't wait until your annual two-week vacation to plan a getaway. Both Dr. Cassell and Dr. Kreidman say that couples should go on several mini-vacations throughout the year. "If you have kids, your regular vacation is most likely going to be spent with them, which doesn't give you much time to be together as a couple. By planning a weekend away every two to three months, you make sure that you have alone time," points out Dr. Cassell.

Leave the guilt at home. Many couples, especially those with young children, observes Dr. Kreidman, let guilt restrain them from taking a weekend away from the kids—ever. You need to get over it, she says. "The only real tragedy that will happen if you don't go away once in a while is the loss of intimacy you'll both experience," she says. Let the kids spend a weekend with their best friends, or with grandparents, while you take the opportunity to rekindle the passion that made those little buggers possible.

Plan on no plans. Vacations are too often a time for elaborate planning. But as you may recall from organizing your last one, sometimes it can be more trouble than it's worth. Since the whole point of a getaway is to avoid stress so that you can focus on one another, resolve to make no elaborate plans for your romantic retreat.

"Plan too much to make it perfect and you're opening yourself up to disappointment," Dr. Cassell says. The more plans, the greater the chance that something will go awry and put you or your sweetie in a bad mood. Keep it simple instead: Reserve a room at a hotel and make sure that you have directions to get there. Leave everything else—what you'll do during the day, where you'll go to eat at night—entirely up to whim and random chance.

"You may find it a lot more exciting and invigorating than having everything all laid out," she says.

Take turns. You like making out by a campfire. She likes curling up by the hearth at that bed-and-breakfast upstate. If your ideas of the perfect getaway diverge, you ought to know by now what you can do to resolve any potential conflict: Compromise!

"Look for ways to merge both your interests into the weekend, if that's feasible," says Dr. Cassell. If cycling's her passion and yours is lounging poolside, find a hotel or resort that's close to a cycling trail. Or if she wins the coin toss and you're heading upstate to that bed-and-breakfast, scan the map for nearby parks or a national forest where you could take a romantic day hike—something to satisfy your desires.

But don't push too hard for compromise on every trip. "It's okay, too, if one of you gives in to the other's wishes for a whole weekend," Dr. Cassell says. So let her have her way—and don't grumble about it. Instead, you agree that on the next getaway, you get to call the shots.

Make a weekday getaway. Who says you have to wait for the weekend to plan a getaway? Many busy couples may find it easier to sacrifice a week-

A Working Vacation

Here's one getaway that may be a cure for the seven-year itch. The prescription: Take two weeks. Together. Alone. And work on your marriage.

Doesn't sound like much of a vacation, and yet taking a two-week retreat to work out the assorted kinks of your marriage is something every couple needs after several years together, says Gordon Deckert, M.D., professor of psychiatry at the University of Oklahoma in Oklahoma City. He recommends a two-week working vacation for couples because that long of a getaway gives you just enough time to hash out all the issues that have arisen during your marriage.

Of course, it doesn't have to be all work and no play. "The sheer fun of being away makes the trip really enjoyable for three or four days. Then all hell breaks loose as issues like kids, money, and sex naturally come to the fore," Dr. Deckert says.

The agenda for this 14-day retreat? Draw up a list of issues you frequently disagree on—money, raising the kids, dealing with in-laws, sharing domestic responsibilities, whatever—then tackle them, one at a time.

Whatever you do, be serious about this retreat. Don't blow off the nagging issues that circle your marriage like wolves circling a campfire. And don't let anything or anyone interrupt you. That means not checking voice mail at work. Focus on each other. Focus on your marriage. It may be the best getaway you ever made.

day than a weekend. Take a personal day (you didn't hear it from us, but some couples have been known to call in sick for a weekday getaway). At the very least, you could meet at a local hotel for a long lunch. Or skip the lunch and jump straight to dessert.

GETTING AWAY AT HOME

We recognize that sometimes money's going to be tight. Or personal and professional obligations demand that you stay close to home. Does that mean you still can't plan a getaway? Hardly.

"In a situation like that, you just have to transform your home into a getaway. It takes a little imagination and enthusiasm, but it's still a great way for couples to have time away together—without really going away," Dr. Kreidman says. Turning your familiar environs into a weekend vacation home takes just a little planning and forethought as well as a couple of ground rules. Here are some suggestions.

Kick the kids out. The first step in getting away from it all in the comfort of your home is to ditch the kids, if you have them. Of course, they don't have to know you're kicking them out. You could spin it that you're finally

If you don't think you could survive two weeks alone with your wife talking about your relationship, you might try retreats or weekends run by trained professionals or volunteers. Check with your church, synagogue, or professional counselor, or try these.

- Worldwide Marriage Encounter, 2210 East Highland Avenue, Suite 106, San Bernardino, CA 92404. Call (800) 795-LOVE and they will send you the name of trained facilitators in your area. They offer Marriage Encounter, to make a good marriage better, and Retrouvaille (French for "rediscovery"), if your marriage is in serious trouble.
- PREPARE/ENRICH, P.O. Box 190, Minneapolis, MN 55440-0190. The PREPARE (which stands for Premarital Personal and Relationship Evaluation) program for engaged couples is discussed in Early Marriage on page 279. ENRICH (which stands for Enriching Relationship Issues, Communication, and Happiness) uses the same techniques to strengthen communication after marriage. Send them a self-addressed, stamped envelope and they will send you a list of counselors in your area.
- Marriage and Family Health Center, 2922 Evergreen Parkway, Suite 310, Evergreen, CO 80439. Call them at (303) 670-2630 for more information on their nine-day retreats, three-day weekends, or four-day intensive therapy sessions. Most programs take place in Colorado.

letting them go have an adventure of their own—at Grandma's or a pal's house. Just be prepared to return the favor when the pal's parents want their own weekend away.

Unplug the phone. Just because you're at home doesn't mean you're available. If you were at an island resort, you wouldn't be disturbed by phone calls from friends and neighbors. The same rule applies on a weekend where you've turned your home into a resort. Turn off the ringer and turn on the answering machine. Be incommunicado—let no one disturb the weekend love nest you and your honey have built.

Forget the chores. This is a weekend getaway—laundry, lawn mowing, and cleaning the bathroom have no place here. Forbid one another from doing chores this weekend. If one of you is a compulsive neatnik, then arrange to do your weekend chores on the Wednesday and Thursday nights before the weekend. "Or just put it off. There aren't many chores that won't keep until next weekend," Dr. Cassell says.

Steer clear of the kitchen. Unless your plan is to make a romantic meal together, stay out of the kitchen for the weekend, too. If you want to eat, take yourselves out to a nice local restaurant, just as you would if you were on vacation. At the very least, order out and have food delivered. "If you normally spend time slaving over a meal and cleaning dishes afterward, just ordering a pizza or Chinese takeout can seem very decadent and help you feel more relaxed," Dr. Kreidman says.

Move to a motel. If you can't leave town but can spare a little extra money, one novel spin on the getaway close to home is to leave your house for the weekend but stay in town at a nearby hotel. "There's a hotel 15 minutes from my house that offers a 'Bounce-Back Weekend' for couples," says Dr. Kreidman. "Their motto is, 'Why drive when you can relax in your own backyard?' It's good advice." Dr. Kreidman says that many hotel chains offer weekend specials in the off-seasons, which makes a local getaway even more affordable. Call around to your local hotels to find the best deal.

COUNSELORS
AND THERAPISTS

When we have a physical problem that's beyond our ability to remedy, we may not like the idea much, but most men will eventually see a doctor about it. If it's a relationship that starts to ail, though, are you man enough to see a specialist about it?

We'd like to think so. If you do, you'd be joining thousands of men every year who care enough about their partners and their relationships and themselves to go see a marriage therapist or counselor when things get tough. According to the American Association for Marriage and Family Therapy, 42 percent of the clients a therapist sees are men. You're probably thinking that most men would rather go through a divorce than go through counseling.

Sadly, that's exactly what some unenlightened men do choose, says Sherry Lehman, a sex therapist in Cleveland and author of *Seven Days to Better Sex and a More Loving Relationship*. "And in so doing, they set themselves up for failure in future relationships because they keep hitting the same old stumbling blocks." On the other hand, Lehman says, if they had even tried counseling, they might have found that they didn't have such a bad relationship with that person after all. They could have spent years of their lives being happy with one person instead of falling into the same traps over and over again.

Of course, she *would* tell you that; she is a therapist, after all. But that doesn't change the truth of the matter—counseling and therapy works. In a national survey of therapists and their clients, researchers at the University of Minnesota found that, after therapy, nearly 90 percent of clients reported an overall improvement in their emotional health. Nearly 55 percent were better able to concentrate on their responsibilities at work. And in the specific case of marriage or couples therapy, nearly 77 percent of couples reported an improvement in their relationship after seeing a therapist. The numbers speak for themselves: If your relationship is in trouble, counseling may be the smartest thing you could do. It's a proven, effective, useful tool, a resource that can help good marriages through bad times—or sometimes even resurrect dying relationships.

BRINGING IN THE EXPERTS

Therapists and counselors practice a broad range of specialties within the confines of sex and relationships. If your problem is sexual in nature, then generally a sex therapist or counselor is the one you want to see. They handle problems ranging from impotence to low sexual desire for both couples and individuals. If your problem is more "we" than "me," you'll want to see either a marriage counselor or a therapist who specializes in couples and family issues. Couples therapists also deal with sexual issues as well as broader relationship issues.

For most of us, the hardest thing about seeking outside help isn't knowing the difference between this therapist or that counselor—it's simply knowing when to ask for help.

"As a rule of thumb, any time you feel like you can't handle it on your own or have reached an impasse—where you can't talk about something anymore—that's a good time to seek outside assistance," says Scott Stanley, Ph.D., co-director of the Center for Marital and Family Studies at the University of Denver and co-author of *Fighting for Your Marriage*. Alas, most couples make counseling their last stop before divorce court. You needn't wait until the sit-

Seeking Counsel

When you've made up your mind to see a sex or marriage therapist, you don't want to waste any time reconsidering. In that case, here are two fast resources to help you find the expert you need.

- The Yellow Pages. Look under "Counselors" or "Psychologists." The professionals you want will advertise specialties in family, marital, couple, or sex therapy.
- The American Association of Sex Educators, Counselors, and Therapists (AASECT). Headquartered in Mount Vernon, Iowa, AASECT issues a membership directory and can help you find certified therapists in your state. Send a self-addressed, stamped envelope to AASECT, P.O. Box 238, Mount Vernon, IA 52314-0238.

uation becomes that dire, though. Dr. Stanley says that there's nothing wrong with seeing a counselor if you just have questions or concerns. "If you keep hitting a bump in your marriage, if there's some issue—however small—that you can't get resolution on, there's nothing wrong with seeking counseling for it. Think of it as preventive maintenance: By dealing with the issue when it's a small thing, you nip it in the bud and keep it from becoming a major issue that could hurt your marriage down the line," he says.

Maybe things aren't that clear-cut for you. Maybe you still feel like you're in a gray area. You think things are okay in your relationship, but on some level, you're not quite sure. Most of us have so many things going on in our lives that it's hard to keep tabs on everything, including our personal relationships. But if your relationship is in jeopardy, you can bet that some indicators are going to manifest themselves. Here are a few big ones that should force you to think seriously about seeking some outside, expert advice.

You're not talking. As men, we invented the notion of "comfortable silence." We don't feel the need to fill every moment with conversation, unlike some genders we could mention. But there's silence and then there's the silent treatment. For example, you bring up a touchy subject, and your partner doesn't even respond—just pretends nothing was ever said. Or worse, you stop bringing up the touchy subjects because you already know what the reaction will be. Pretty soon, you stop bringing up any subjects at all.

Talk, in moderation, is what holds your relationship together. "It's the glue to everything," says Steve Manley, Ph.D., staff psychologist for the Male Health Center in Dallas. "If you're to the point where you can't discuss a subject—or you're not talking at all—then that's as good a reason as any to bring someone in who can help you break through the silence. It's absolutely the most important thing, and many couples are going to have trouble communicating at some point in time. Frankly, if men and women could figure out how to communicate with each other all the time, I'd be out of a job."

You're arguing over little things. Maybe you're talking a lot. But it seems like it's always at the top of your lungs. Over the simplest, most stupid things. The way she folds your shirts. The noise you make when you chew. If the tiniest irritants are becoming fodder for explosive arguments, that may be a good reason to seek counseling. "Often, what's at issue is not the little thing. You're harping on that to avoid talking about the big issue, the thing that's so problematic you can't bring yourself to discuss it," says Dr. Stanley. "If you can take a moment to identify what the bigger issue is by yourselves, that's great. But many people can't." That's where a good therapist comes in. They're trained to spot the underlying issues and can help you get them out in the open.

One of you starts counseling. When couples are having troubles they can't seem to resolve on their own, counselors and therapists we talked to say it's common for one-half of the couple to start seeing a therapist.

"This usually happens after they've tried to discuss the issue with their partner but have gotten nowhere," Lehman says. Then they'll start seeing a couples therapist on their own to try to determine what they can do to solve the problem. If you partner admits that she's been seeking therapy to help solve problems in your relationship, consider that a wake-up call. Don't get angry that she went without telling you. Get up and go with her.

Incidentally, if she's the one who won't discuss an issue of concern to you, there's nothing wrong with you going to a marriage therapist by yourself. "Don't think that men won't do that. I get a lot of men coming to me before their wives do. It's not at all uncommon," Lehman says. Once you go, a counselor can give you suggestions and advice about discussing difficult topics with your partner, including getting her to come in for counseling.

You're thinking the unthinkable. Marital troubles are just hell on a person. They can ruin your day, rob you of sleep, interfere with digestion. They can also lead to notions that will have serious repercussions on the relationship. "If you're so troubled that you're contemplating things that were at one time unthinkable—leaving your partner, having an affair, wishing bad things on your partner, that's a clear sign to get some counseling," says Dr. Stanley. Feeling hate, dread, or desperation regarding your partner are also unthinkable. Admit it: Would you ever have thought such feelings possible when you met this person? Any time your feelings about a person undergo a sea change, it's time to get outside help.

WHO YOU GONNA CALL?

So, you've tried to deal with this situation inside the relationship and it's getting you nowhere. You decide to set aside some of that old masculine programming and admit that you need to bring in a specialist and get some counseling. If you have reached that point—or feel like you're getting there fast—you have our congratulations. Not for your marital difficulties, but for being wise enough to know when to ask for help. In so doing, you may have just saved your marriage. At the very least, you may have saved you and your beloved countless hours of frustration and grief.

Having come to this decision, though, you're probably wondering what the next step is. Here are some suggestions, designed to help you keep your pride and your privacy intact while still finding a professional who will help you solve the issues that are vexing your relationship.

Check your benefits. Go to your filing cabinet and look for that benefits package you got when you were first hired at your job. Check for a pamphlet or brochure about counseling services—most employers offer access to some form of counseling as part of their benefits. This is usually an out-of-house, confidential service. Call them up and explain your problem. They should be able to refer you to local experts specializing in the issues concerning you.

If your benefits package doesn't have this information, you could call your company's personnel office and ask—anonymously, if you like—what personal counseling services your company offers. It never hurts to ask, and there are some advantages. One is that you'll find out quickly what forms of counseling are covered by your insurance.

Note: You may find that your insurance covers little or no counseling. Do not let this deter you. According to the American Association for Marriage and Family Therapy, the average length of therapy lasts 9 to 11 sessions, all of which usually costs less than $1,000. That's a heck of a lot less than a divorce, which is what you might be facing if you don't seek help.

Talk to your doctor. If your marital problems are grounded in some physical misery (for example, you're suddenly having a problem getting or maintaining an erection), it's always a good idea to check with your regular doctor. At the very least, he should be able to refer you to a local specialist. At best, he can clear you of any physical problems that might be adding to your marital discord, or he can refer you to a specialist.

Get referrals. If you're having problems in your relationship, odds are that the last thing you want to do is broadcast it to anyone. But if you know someone who has had experience with counselors—a minister, a friend who has gone to marriage therapy and confided in you about it—ask them for a recommendation. And no matter how well-intentioned they may be, don't let amateurs step in and try to help you with your problems. If a pal really wants to help you, he can point you in the right direction and keep his mouth shut. That's all you need ask of him.

Check them out. Once you have a list of names, you'll be familiar with the next part of the process. It's a bit like calling for estimates on plumbing. Certainly, don't just call the first person on the list and make an appointment. Talk to at least three counselors. Most competent therapists will want to talk with you first anyway to make sure that you're going to be a good fit for each other. Be specific about the nature of your problem. Don't hold back: Counselors can't counsel if they don't know what the problem is. If they don't handle your specific problem, good therapists will refer you to someone who can better handle the situation.

But even if the therapist wants you to make an appointment, make sure that you've gotten your questions answered. Don't just settle for someone who hangs out a therapist's shingle and says that he can handle your problem. Make sure that what's bothering you is one of this particular therapist's specialties, something he has plenty of experience handling. Don't be afraid to ask questions about his training and background as well as the nitty-gritty stuff—his rates and schedules.

Tell her. Assuming you and your partner are still talking, and you don't think that telling her would be counterproductive, it's a good idea to let her know that you really think the two of you should go to counseling. Do this before venturing into counseling solo. "Every situation is going to be different, but for the most part it's better if you both are agreed to seek counseling," Dr. Manley says. On one level, it shows her that you're still committed to the relationship. It may also offer some comfort to her that she's not alone. After all, what makes you think you were the only one considering therapy? By telling her, you're serving notice that the relationship is so important to you, you're willing to ask for outside help to make your union stronger. Then, the two of you can start working—together—to make things better.

EVOLVING VALUES

You never stop growing.

From the moment your heart starts to the instant it stops, you're on one big learning curve of personal growth. But growth is another word for change, and change can be scary. At the very least, it can be confusing (remember puberty?). And over time, as you explore the uncharted territory of your married life and getting older, you're going to notice changes in yourself.

For example, it used to be you never gave a thought to the future. Now, with a family in the picture, you're looking into mutual funds and shopping for life insurance. Police used to be the enemy you outwitted through a combination of luck, pluck, and a radar detector. Now, you're on the neighborhood watch, complaining to the local cops about those damn kids speeding up and down your street. Your tolerance levels for loud noise, slow service, and bad manners have reached an all-time low. What's more, you're starting to notice that your thoughts, actions, and advice are all starting to be tinged with just a little bit of wisdom. It's cliché to say you're getting older. That's only the half of it. More to the point, you're changing. Your values are changing.

And nowhere will this change be more evident than in your relationship with your wife.

"Any healthy relationship is going to change over time. Your reactions and attitudes—even your feelings—toward your partner are all subject to change. It doesn't have to be a bad thing; in fact, it's natural. But because so many couples are unprepared for the changes in their relationship with one another, they may get scared. They may start feeling alienated from one another," says Scott Stanley, Ph.D., co-director of the Center for Marital and Family Studies at the University of Denver and author of *Fighting for Your Marriage*. As usual, having some sense of what lies ahead can be terribly helpful and may help you avoid some common pitfalls so often associated with reacting to change. That's why we're going to look at two areas of profound change that can affect married life: changes in your emotional life and changes in your sex life.

BECOMING ATTACHED

As a younger, single guy, you noticed a certain emotional intensity in a new relationship. There was lots of giddy, whiz-bang tension, passion, excitement. The proverbial flame was burning white-hot. And when you broke up with someone, odds are that part of your reasoning was based on the fact that "the passion" was gone. The fire had dwindled to smoldering embers. In short, you were bored.

But then you found a woman who not only inspired unusual heights of passion but also seemed to make some deeper connection with you. Perhaps she had a combination of your favorite personality traits in all the women you had dated. Maybe she was just the first woman to catch you pulling your usual brand of crap and she called you on it. You were so impressed that you developed a new level of respect for her. Whatever happened, you realized that she was The One. You got married.

Here's when your emotional values start to change, says Helen Fisher, Ph.D., research associate in the department of anthropology at Rutgers University in New Brunswick, New Jersey, and author of *Anatomy of Love*. Because once you start down the long road of life together, something gradually begins to happen to that passion. Your heart begins to pound less when you think of her. The spark just doesn't seem to be there. "This is where many men can get hung up. They begin to think something's wrong, that there's a problem," says Dr. Fisher. And meanwhile, they're completely missing some very positive emotional events. The spark hasn't disappeared; it has transformed into something else—devotion. You're getting more comfortable with your spouse, becoming more reliant on her opinions, attitudes, and support. A negative person might look at this as the beginning of a codependent relationship, but in fact, what's happening is the sort of thing that theologians are always going on about when they say that two married people start to become one person.

Psychologists have a term for this, too. It's called the attachment phase, and it's one of the most rewarding aspects of married life, especially for men.

"Because of the comfort level you're beginning to achieve with your partner, this is an opportunity to build a kind of intimate relationship you've never had before," says Louanne Cole Weston, Ph.D., a therapist who counsels patients in Sacramento and San Francisco, and author of the "Sex Matters" advice column in the *San Francisco Examiner*. You might think the more comfortable you are with a partner, the more boring things might get. But in fact, because of that comfort, you have a certain degree of freedom to reveal things about yourself to your partner, things you may not have been able to in the past. "It's the idea of letting it all hang out. The more you reveal to each other your feelings, thoughts, fantasies, the closer you become. And even though you have to be at a certain comfort level to reveal this information, that act of revealing secrets about yourself can be somewhat risky but also exciting, more exciting than anything you've experienced," Dr. Weston says.

On a more practical level, getting your relationship to the attachment phase is going to make things easier on your body and mind. Over time, trying to sustain a constant level of heart-pounding passion is a very stressful thing. And if men need anything, it's less stress—especially at home. Life has conditioned us to be constantly at war with stress, with the world. Having a partner to whom we've devoted ourselves utterly is like having a safe harbor in a storm-tossed world.

"Having that level of devotion, and the sense that you're with someone with whom you've built a bond is a very safe and powerful feeling. And it's something that men really need if they're going to live long and satisfying lives. We're social creatures. We're meant to be with someone, not be alone," Dr. Stanley says.

Changing Your Rhythm

While you're becoming more attached, more emotionally intimate with your partner, you may be a little preoccupied with another changing factor in your relationship. Put simply, sex may have become less of an earth-moving—or even frequent—experience. And it's not necessarily that she's losing interest; it could be that you are, too.

You could dismiss it as part of the "seven-year itch" phenomenon, but spending all your time with the same woman is really only part of the reason why. In life, there are any number of reasons why your sexual habits might change. The demands of job, housekeeping, and children are certainly enough to sap your strength and your libido. But you may also start to notice that sometimes you just don't *feel* very much like sex—or if you do, you'd just rather get to it, get it over with. You begin to wonder what's wrong with you. And the weakest of us think that the only way to solve the problem is to fall into bed with someone else.

"But that won't solve anything because if you stay with a new partner long enough, eventually the same thing will happen again, and then what will you do?" asks Dr. Weston. The problem isn't your partner, and it's not really you, per se. But your sexual values have shifted, and you do need to understand that.

"Essentially, you're trying to run a marathon with a sprint attitude," Dr. Weston says. In other words, you're applying outdated sexual standards to a mature, seasoned sexual relationship. "You think that something's wrong if you can't maintain the same level of passion and desire that you could when you were newlyweds," says Dr. Weston. "But the fact is that no one can." It's a simple pacing issue. Try to maintain a high level of sexual intensity over too long a period of time and you'll both burn out. "You need to be in less of a frenzy about the whole thing. You need to realize that you have plenty of time to be with one another," Dr. Weston says. And the sooner you accept that fact, the sooner you'll get into that long-haul rhythm, and the more normal it will seem that you're making love or feeling physical desire less often.

One final note: Just because you're having less sex doesn't mean that you're not having great sex. "This is the time when couples start to learn the meaning of quality versus quantity. If you can have mind-blowing sex every other week or so-so, routine, mechanical sex more regularly, you're much better off with the mind-blowing sex," says Dr. Weston. But you didn't need us to tell you that; you've probably gotten just wise enough to figure that out for yourself.

9

THE FORTIES

YOUR CHANGES

Middle age is the time when a man is always thinking that in a week or two he will feel as good as ever," American humorist Don Robert Perry Marquis once said.

It's not that bad for most guys, but now that you've reached middle age, you may notice more pains than in the past. Some body parts don't work as efficiently as when you were younger. Other features keep growing and expanding as if you were an inflatable toy.

"All the processes of aging start to accelerate in his forties, fifties, and beyond," says Dudley Seth Danoff, M.D., senior attending urologist at Cedars-Sinai Medical Center in Los Angeles and author of *Superpotency*. "But there are tremendous variabilities between two men at 40." The man who eats well, exercises, takes vitamins, and has a healthy outlook on life will have a far healthier middle age than the guy who doesn't, Dr. Danoff says.

SEX-RELATED CHANGES

• Enlarged prostate. It's likely that during this decade your prostate will begin to grow. Doctors aren't sure why this happens, but it does. It can become a problem, and you'll know it when it does. You wake up several times during the night, feeling the urge to urinate. But when you go, your urinary stream is more like a rivulet. And when you've finished, you still feel like you have to go. (For more details, see Prostate Problems on page 231.)

• Declining sexual desire. A man's libido naturally diminishes after about age 45. There are a number of reasons for this. For one, all those burgers and fries over the years have clogged some of the smaller arteries, including those in the penis, diminishing the flow of blood that is so vital to erections. Testosterone levels also have begun tapering off. The forty-something guy will have a longer refractory period after ejaculation—perhaps needing an hour before he can go again, compared to 20 minutes when he was 30.

OTHER CHANGES

• Weight gain. During this and the next two decades is when men are more likely to pack on extra pounds, says Waneen Wyrick Spirduso, Ed.D., professor in the department of kinesiology and health education at the University of Texas in Austin and author of *Physical Dimensions of Aging*. For men, much of this fat is stored in our bellies, giving many of us an apple shape. Bob Hope said it best: "Middle age is when your age starts to show around the middle." It's around this time, too, that some men will get a double chin as their skin loses some of its elasticity.

• Diabetes. Most men who get diabetes do so between the ages of 45 and 66. It's a serious matter. Men with diabetes are at higher risk to have a stroke or develop heart disease. Some diabetics develop kidney disease; others go blind. As if that's not bad enough, a lot of men who have diabetes become impotent.

Being overweight is a major risk factor for diabetes, which occurs when the body doesn't produce enough or properly use insulin, a hormone secreted by the pancreas that is needed to convert food into energy.

• Cholesterol. Those years of gorging on ice cream and steaks may start taking their toll in your forties in the form of high cholesterol. This waxy substance is produced naturally by the liver. It's essential to human life. But cholesterol also is ingested in the diet, coming exclusively from animal products. Combined with the saturated fat you eat, it can clog your arteries and curtail the flow of blood to your heart. In severe cases it can lead to sharp chest pain, called angina, and a heart attack.

• Heart disease. As we just said, high cholesterol and heart disease go hand in hand like cigarettes and cancer. And heart disease is a killer—the number one cause of death in America, for both women and men.

High-fat, high-cholesterol foods; cigarette smoking; lack of exercise; and obesity are among the factors contributing to heart disease. Needless to say, high cholesterol and heart disease can adversely affect a man's sex life.

• Bursitis and tendinitis. These painful conditions—the inflammation of the bursa, tiny fluid filled sacs in the joint, and the point where your tendons attach to a bone or muscle—hit guys most commonly in their forties. Elbows, hips, knees, ankles, and shoulders are particularly susceptible. The cause is not enough exercise or overdoing a sport or activity, such as tennis or running, especially if there was not enough stretching done beforehand.

• Restless legs. Some guys go to bed at night feeling like they have the brain of Rip van Winkle and the legs of Carl Lewis. It's the legs that are the problem. They just want to get up and go even though the rest of their body feels almost comatose. It's called restless legs syndrome, and it most often plagues guys in their forties.

Men who complain of restless legs say that they have sensations of burning, pulling, and crawling. This, in turn, results in loss of sleep and no small amount of duress. We're not talking here about the occasional involuntary twitches so many of us have during the night. While clearly a nuisance, restless legs usually don't pose a health risk. Doctors aren't sure what causes the condition.

• Healthy immunity. Getting older has its good points. Your immune system is now at its best and will continue to be into your fifties.

HER CHANGES

A century ago, Sir Arthur Wing Pinero, an English dramatist, wrote: "She's six-and-forty, and I wish nothing worse to happen to any woman." What a difference 100 years makes. Being forty-something and female is hardly a forlorn fate any longer. Just look at Kim Basinger. Jessica Lange. Michelle Pfeiffer. Bonnie Raitt. Amy Tan. Women in middle age often are at the peak of their beauty or talent or both. Still, they are undergoing physical changes, some of which can impact sexuality.

SEX-RELATED CHANGES

• Perimenopause. This is the period leading up to menopause. It's something of a dress rehearsal for the real deal—sort of a mini-menopause. What happens is that a woman's estrogen level starts to fluctuate. Her periods become irregular. She probably will feel some hot flashes. She may even experience vaginal dryness and a need to urinate more often.

• Cervical cancer. Studies show that the more sexual partners a woman has had, the more likely she is to get cervical cancer. And there is evidence that the more sexual partners her man has had, the greater her risk, too. Smoking and poor diet are other lifestyle choices that may put a woman at risk. Cervical cancer can be fatal, especially if it has spread beyond the cervix and supporting tissue before it is detected.

• Hysterectomy. Hundreds of thousands of women every year undergo a hysterectomy because of problems they are having with their uterus—the womb. It is second only to cesarean sections as the most often performed surgery in the United States. Hysterectomies are most often done on women in their early forties.

Doctors may perform hysterectomies for a number of problems, including uterine cancer, life-threatening complications during childbirth, pelvic pain, fibroid tumors, and heavy bleeding. Critics say that the surgery is done more often than is medically necessary.

In the most drastic hysterectomy, a woman's uterus, cervix, ovaries, and Fallopian tubes are removed. The result is an inability to have children and the onset of early menopause. Other procedures entail the removal of the uterus and the cervix, or just the uterus. They, too, leave a woman unable to carry a fetus. Some women feel anxiety about resuming sex after a hysterectomy, while others say that it changes how their orgasms feel.

OTHER CHANGES

• Weight gain. Women have a higher percentage of body fat than men, and they store it in different places. As we've noted, men lug most of their fat around in their bellies, giving them an apple-shaped body. Women, on the other hand, tend to store fat in their hips and legs, giving them a pear-shaped body. Like men, they tend to put on pounds from their forties through their sixties, in part, because they are less active than when they were younger. Women's greater fat gives them insulation against the cold but also makes it harder to cool down when it's hot.

• Varicose veins. Women may start developing these knotted, snaking ropes in their legs during their twenties or thirties, but usually it takes until their forties and fifties to become so bad that they seek treatment. Men get them, too—just not nearly as often.

Varicose veins not only look bad; they can be painful. They occur when valves in the leg veins become weakened. When the valves become defective and leak, blood collects in the legs, distending the surface veins. Female hormones are thought to be responsible for the condition.

People with varicose veins also are most likely to get phlebitis, a clot in a vein. Again, women are much more likely than men to develop this, although it was Richard Nixon who brought attention to the ailment when he was stricken during his presidency. With phlebitis, there is a slight chance that the clot can travel to the lung and cause sudden death from a blockage.

• Diabetes. If a woman gets diabetes, chances are that it will be around the age of 40. Just like for men, it's a serious disease that can cause damage to kidneys, eyes, and other organs. Just as the disease can cause men to become impotent, it can cause some women to have reduced vaginal lubrication. Among older people, diabetes is the single most sexually debilitating disease, with half of diabetics experiencing some loss of sexual function, according to *Dr. Ruth's Encyclopedia of Sex*, by Ruth K. Westheimer, Ed.D., noted sexologist, author, and media personality.

• Bursitis and tendinitis. Like men, women feel the aches and pains of bursitis and tendinitis in their forties. And like men, it comes from too little exercise or too much of a good thing, like playing tennis five days a week.

• Gallstones. Yet another malady that strikes women a lot more than men. Gallstones are formed when there is too much cholesterol in the bile that helps digest food, or not enough of the bile salts and detergents that keep cholesterol floating free. Bits of the cholesterol then solidify in the gallbladder. The stones may sit there unobtrusively for years, like a quiet neighbor one rarely ever notices.

Then one day the neighbor decides to move but gets stuck in ducts that lead out of the gallbladder. The gallbladder contracts, trying to expel the intruder. The end result: pain, nausea, or vomiting. The cure: surgery. The culprits: female hormones, obesity, and rapid weight loss.

RULES OF ENGAGEMENT

We need to be honest here. It can be difficult wooing some women in their forties. It is sad and harsh but true that many single women in their forties feel wounded—by fate, by past lovers, by their situation. Not all, mind you. Plenty of single women in their forties are there quite by choice. But for those who aren't, "there can be a little bit of bitterness," cautions Linda De-Villers, Ph.D., a psychologist and sex therapist in El Segundo, California, and author of *Love Skills*.

Unattached women in their forties are far more likely to be divorced than never married or widowed, says Dr. DeVillers. Some of them have recently obtained that status and are none too happy about it. So they distrust or even dislike men at the moment.

It's a condition that Warren Farrell, Ph.D., San Diego–based author of *The Myth of Male Power*, calls First Wife's Syndrome. "The woman in her forties and above grew up in a dream of being swept away," Dr. Farrell says. "When she is divorced, the dream of being swept away is swept away." Men don't grow up with that dream, Dr. Farrell adds.

That's not all that she has to be peeved about. A lot of newly divorced middle-age men are looking to meet what Dr. Farrell calls two twenties rather than one forty—women a lot younger than they. A woman in her forties can seek a younger man, but she isn't likely to have the wealth and power to pull it off, the authors of the survey *Sex in America* concluded. And if she does find one, she's past her most fertile period, so the younger man cannot start a family of his own with her.

It is no wonder that some women in their forties are steamed. But there's more. A divorced woman may have children, which presents problems for her in finding a new mate. A guy may not want to get involved with such a woman for a couple of reasons, Dr. Farrell says.

First, he may not be first in this woman's love. Many other things—children, religion, work—may take priority. As Dr. Farrell notes, "Many men don't like being in fifth place."

Second, he may not want the financial responsibility, especially if he's paying alimony or child support from a prior marriage of his own. Women often misconstrue this as a fear of intimacy by men, when, in fact, it's the prospect of a crushing financial burden that would deter intimacy that makes guys skittish, Dr. Farrell says.

WHERE TO FIND WOMEN

Still, forty-something women may have just the maturity and life experiences that you desire in a woman. But now you wonder, where do I meet them? Here are some possibilities.

• College extension courses. Some schools offer classes on subjects such as flirting and communicating with the opposite sex. "You kind of know people going to those things must also be hunting," says Dr. DeVillers. Or guys can sign up for a class in which there will be more women than men, such as cooking.

• Support groups. Some of these groups, such as Parents without Partners, are likely to have women in their forties attending.

• Sports. "People in their forties still have the physical stamina to do fun things," says Dr. DeVillers. "Doing things that help women feel like they're retaining youth and vitality are really important." Dr. DeVillers has a 72-year-old client who picked up a woman on the golf links. "I had a ton of relationships through tennis," she adds.

• Church or synagogue activities. "Some of the church things are not stodgy," says Dr. DeVillers. "If you're not a particularly religious person, you might nevertheless check out what kind of social activities are offered."

WHAT WOMEN WANT

Once you've met a woman in her forties and are dating her, you may wonder how to deal with that potential anger factor we dealt with at the start of this chapter. Here are some things you can do.

Find out what makes her tick(ed). A guy needs to be sensitive "to not push the same buttons that some previous lover or husband pushed," says Dr. DeVillers. "Learn early on what those issues were."

Compliment her. Always a good idea, but especially now. "I would say in the forties the more a guy can compliment her physically, the more payoff he will get," says Dr. DeVillers. "That's when women start noticing the lines and the sagging. Those former lovers or husbands may have been critical of the woman's appearance, and this would be the time to highlight that she's still a sexy, feminine person." But make sure that your compliments are sincere. If they are not, they may backfire on you.

Honor her femininity. Buy her small, feminine gifts that reinforce the idea that she is a desirable woman. "Don't buy her a set of pliers for her birthday," advises Dr. DeVillers.

Learn together. If she has only recently become single again, she may wish to explore new things by taking a course in photography or painting, or attending auctions and flea markets. If you share any of these interests, join her.

Be a gentleman. Show her that you are attentive, respectful, a good listener, and have a sense of humor. In other words, things that women of all ages value in a man. Courting doesn't change *that* much as we age, you know.

Sexually, be prepared for equality. If she's one of those women in her forties who is distrustful of men, it obviously behooves you to proceed cautiously. On the other hand, sexual experimentation may be another facet of her newfound freedom. In either case, a woman in her forties may very well mesh sexually with a guy of similar age much more easily than when each was younger.

That's because a guy's testosterone is starting to gradually drop now. So is a woman's estrogen, meaning that her testosterone is packing more wallop, says sex therapist Theresa Crenshaw, M.D., writing in *The Alchemy of Love and Lust*. The result is a lessening in the disparity between the genders in this hormone that ignites our sex drives. Dr. Crenshaw writes, "The net effect can produce two most compatible, sexy soul mates."

REINVENTING ROMANCE

Romance is the ethereal substance that finds us, blinds us, binds us—at least temporarily. It's the magical beginning of new love, true love, and even blue love—the kind that leaves you crying. Ah, romance. Sweet dreams are made of this.

True, the heady days of romantic stupor do eventually give way to day-to-day routines and reality in even the best of relationships, observes Hollywood psychologist and sexologist Rachel Copelan, Ph.D., author of *100 Ways to Make Sex Sensational and 100% Safe*. But romance need not die. In fact, it had best not die if we truly crave a lifetime of sex, a lifetime of warmth, a lifetime of love, a lifetime of fascinating new adventures with our partner. And the fact is that we choose—consciously or unconsciously—whether to keep romance alive, says Dr. Copelan. Choose to do it. That's the advice from here.

Too late, you say? Romance *has* gone south in your relationship? Not surprising. Not uncommon for couples in their forties, say the experts. Great news. You can get it back, starting right now. You can develop a mature, living romance that will respark love and bring vibrancy back into your relationship. The payoff is great. Fall in love with your wife again, show it, let her know it. She's going to wonder what has gotten into you, and then, pretty soon, she's going to discover that she likes it, whatever it is. And we all know what that means. After all, we did name this book *A Lifetime of Sex*, didn't we?

RESTORING MAGIC

Reinventing romance is a many-tiered task and involves developing finesse with some matters covered in detail elsewhere in this book. Matters like establishing and maintaining good communication. Learning respect. Avoiding envy and jealousy. Learning foreplay and afterplay and light, loving all-over-the-body touch. It all starts with learning and developing the dynamics of sex and companionship, developing and respecting intimacy—all covered in this book's opening chapter because it's so important. So, re-read the opening chapter anytime you feel intimacy slipping. Hey, read the whole book. It's a primer for making romance, maintaining romance, reinventing romance. Learn to be loving and to be a lover.

What may be the biggest single factor? Communication. You must be able to talk to one another, directly and lovingly. And you must be able to resolve conflicts without gnawing away each other's self esteem. We tell you how in Communicating (page 38). We talk about it in Sex versus Companionship (page 2). We touch on it throughout the book.

Want a short course? Here are easy, almost-magical ways to create and enliven adult romance.

Do the little things. When you first were courting, you did them. You bought cut flowers. You left love notes. You called her at work just to say, "I love you." You bought funny or touching or pretty cards from time to time and left them for her. Then the day came when it seemed like doing these things was kind of corny or getting old and boring—no longer special or original—and you slacked off. This may have been about the same time you started forgetting to always carry out the trash or pick up the dry cleaning or put away the phone book after using it. She noticed. You bet she did, says relationships counselor John Gray, Ph.D., author of the series of mega-selling books with Mars and Venus in the titles.

A woman needs quality attention, says Dr. Gray. When she feels that the quality of attention that you are giving her slip, she believes that your love for her is slipping. She believes that you don't really love her anymore, says Dr. Gray. This is not what we want to have happening, gentlemen. That is why we need to work on the little things. We need not worry about being terribly original or even especially creative. All we need to show is that we are thinking about her. Regularly. Unexpectedly. Always. That we respect her.

How do we do this? Besides I-love-you phone calls, flowers, cards, notes, trash, and dry cleaning, consider noticing when she needs to talk—and encourage her to do so. Click off the TV and listen. Really listen. How about comforting her and holding her when she is frazzled or upset or hurting? How about initiating fun and new adventures that you two can share? How about locating her and giving her a warm hug first thing when you get home—before doing anything else and *especially* if there is company there? Let her know that *she's* important.

Make love all the time. Well, maybe not *all* the time, but at least a lot of the time. Secretly devote whole days to it. When we talk making love here, we aren't talking about intercourse. We're talking being loving, being sensuous, being considerate, being seductive, being appreciative and expressing it. We're talking about being romantic. You think women don't notice these things? Make her feel loved and needed and worshipped and respected. That's the kind of stuff that really turns a woman on and makes her feel wanted, needed, and loved, says Dr. Copelan.

What Women Find Romantic

Hundreds of women responded to a romance survey developed by writers Lucy Sanna and Kathy Miller, reported in their book *How to Romance the Woman You Love—The Way* She *Wants You To!* What did the women say were the most romantic things a man could do? Here are the top six responses in order of priority. You want your women to find you romantic? Learn these; do these.

1. Touch with tenderness.
2. Snuggle after making love.
3. Treat her as the most special person in your life.
4. Be available when she needs help.
5. Be emotionally giving.
6. Share your thoughts and dreams with her.

Also scoring quite high were the following traits.

- You know what makes her happy.
- You are gentle when making love.
- You listen intently. You really listen!
- You are playful with her when the two of you are alone.
- You give her flowers, poems, love notes for no special reason.
- You compliment her.

Practice sweet talk. Sensual talk. Not day-to-day drivel. Show your romantic chops. Recite sensual stuff. Especially thoughts about *her*. About how she tantalizes you. About how she fascinates you. About how you can't get her out of your mind. Some other topics? Music, literature—how about reading romantic or even slightly racy writing in a low sexy voice(?)—art, food, nature, textures, colors. Talking textures is too transcendental for you? Listen, there's at least pseudo-science behind this. Writers Lucy Sanna and Kathy Miller surveyed a broad cross-section of American women about what they find romantic. Hundreds of women responded. Sanna and Miller published the results in a book called *How to Romance the Woman You Love—The Way* She *Wants You To!* The results are clear: Women want us to talk textures.

Your woman likes a soft voice when being seduced. A soothing voice. A loving voice, says Dr. Copelan.

She wants to hear about how much you love and appreciate her body, say Sanna and Miller, Dr. Copelan, and others. The wonderful way it looks, feels, smells. Describe her scent—*her* scent, not her perfume—and what it does for you. Tell her about her touch. How she responds. How much you want her. Stay present. Not future. Not past. *Now.*

Attend a Marriage Encounter weekend. This is the hottest advice for married couples, says syndicated columnist Michael J. McManus, president of Marriage Savers in Bethesda, Maryland, and author of *Marriage Savers*. Marriage Encounter is not for marriages in trouble; it is for marriages no longer in the early, burly days of high romance, says McManus. For one weekend a small group of couples gather in a retreat setting. They listen to two or more mentor couples frankly relate difficulties they encountered on the way to establishing solid, loving marriages. Between talks from the mentors, the attending couples are directed to write a series of specifically oriented love letters and essays. Some of the writings are shared between husband and wife and then discussed privately; some are not. And none are shared with the group. All the writings deal with feelings about various aspects of the couples' relationships. After 20-some years, Marriage Encounter continues to work magic in marriages and win rave reviews from participants.

Make time—take time. Surely, loving your spouse is as important as watching a sitcom or tinkering in the basement. Make time—schedule time, regularly—for you and your woman to just be together. To talk. To touch. To love. And then, during your "special time" or "quality time" appointments, take your time. Don't rush things. Relax. Savor the moments, the experience, the feelings.

Does scheduling time for love rob romance of spontaneity? Not at all, says Dr. Copelan. So much in life is routine, that blocking off time for love is both reassuring and welcome. It gives a couple time to make nonroutine love.

Put it in writing. Write little love notes. They're simple. Start just above the middle of the page. Write the date. What's the nicest thing you've ever called her? Call her that. That's your salutation. Now say something. It doesn't have to be a complete sentence. "In the middle of the marketing meeting and I can't get you off my mind." Then drop down a line or two and add a desirous thought. Maybe, "Would you hold me in your arms? Forever." Then drop down a line or two and tell her that you love her and sign your name. Slip it in an envelope and put her name on it. Leave it on her pillow; on the kitchen table; on her car seat; under the windshield wiper; on her desk at work (make sure you write "CONFIDENTIAL" on the envelope); beneath her breakfast, lunch, or dinner plate; with a gift; with flowers. Use your imagination. Women never, ever get tired of love notes. As another variation (of many), list the top five things you love about her or the top five things you loved about last night—or last year.

Touch her. Emotionally, physically. Specially. Privately. Publicly. Gently. Meaningfully. Remember how magical it felt to lightly stroke the length of the inside of her arm when you first met her? Keep that memory in mind and repeat it. Develop variations on the theme. Often. Remember how wonderful it felt to whisper "I love you" in her ear and watch her face light up? If it has been a while, it may take some practice before the words are guaranteed to work their magic again. But when they do, you'll never be able to say them enough.

Play at romance. Set the mood. Light candles. Put on the right music. Clean up, dress up, clean the car. Pretend it's a first or particularly hot date. Forget that you've been married all those years. Treat her and everything else about the evening like you're just falling in love. Make it a fun game. Ask her questions about herself. Pretty soon you both forget you're playing, says Dr. Copelan.

Don't let sex become a chore. Ever watch *Married with Children* on TV? Remember: Your wife is not Peg, you're not Al Bundy, and your marriage is not the sexless riot that theirs is. Thank God. Don't hide from sex and don't wait till last thing at night, when you've collapsed into bed physically and mentally exhausted, to do your "marital duty." Make sex fun. Make sex special. Make time for sex. Schedule it, says Wendy Fader, Ph.D., a licensed psychologist and certified sex therapist in private practice in Boca Raton, Florida. Create privacy and a beautiful setting. Music? Candles? Luxurious bedding? Massage with nice, naturally scented oils or slippery, less messy cornstarch? Make sex anything but routine if you want magic and romance.

If you find yourself dreading sex or hiding from it, this is a clue. It's a clue that there is a problem. The problem needs attention. Read Communicating on page 38. See a counselor if necessary. Do Marriage Encounter. Solve the problem so that you can enjoy a lifetime of love—and sex. This is *not* a dress rehearsal.

End the nasty behaviors. The top love and lust killers are envy, resentment, and jealousy—and all the mean, hurtful little games that ensue because of them. End them now if you want romance, says clinical psychologist Polly Young-Eisendrath, Ph.D., clinical associate professor in psychiatry at the University of Vermont College of Medicine in Burlington and author of *You're Not What I Expected.*

Make lists. Think, dream, and write down 10 romantic encounters you would enjoy acting out with your partner. Write down times, places, positions, atmospheres. Ask your partner to make a list, too. Then share them. Then make them come true.

Give gifts. Keep them small and simple most of the time. It could be a freshly picked flower with an I-love-you note. All it has to be is a token that shows that you were/are thinking about her. Or, of course, it could be jewelry. Jewelry is always a hit, say Sanna and Miller. What's a no-no? Guess. Okay, we'll give you a clue. If when you think gift, you think household appliance, you might as well call the lawyer now. Household appliances are not romantic gifts. Practical? Sure. Romantic? Not. No matter how expensive, how special, how timesaving. Not even if it's aesthetically beautiful and plated in 24-karat gold. If you *must* give her a blender, take Sanna and Miller's advice. Fill it with flowers. Include a love note. Maybe she won't notice the blender. If you're lucky.

Find romance in the mundane. If all this sounds like too much work and planning for real life, don't despair, says Shirley Zussman, Ed.D., a certified sex and marital therapist in New York City and editor of a newsletter, *Sex Over 40.* In the real world, you can't do much of what is suggested above all of the time, or even most of the time. She suggests that you look for romance in the simple things you do together, like cooking a meal, taking a walk, or going to a concert or a movie. Share your feelings about the experience with each other. Showing an interest in what she does, and even participating in them with her, is a sure way to spark romance.

LOOKING YOUNG

Looking young is not a matter of chasing the latest teenage fashion trend. Show us a man in his forties who can dress like a kid without looking ridiculous.

Much better is to find ways to look vibrant and healthy while honoring your maturity. That's what we'll talk about here. How to look as good as you can in your forties—and how to feel as good as you can about how you look. This involves more than how we dress. It's how we think, how we act, how we take care of ourselves.

The truth is that it's natural and normal for our appearance to start showing wear and tear by our forties. And yet in our youth-drenched society, we choose to beat ourselves up if we don't like how we look.

"You start to see a little droop, a little sag, a little gray hair and it really impacts on your feelings of sexual attractiveness," notes Wendy Fader, Ph.D., a licensed psychologist and certified sex therapist in private practice in Boca Raton, Florida. Then, because we are feeling less attractive, we become overly self-conscious. We are sure that the whole world—and especially the woman who is our lover—must be acutely aware of how sorry we're suddenly looking. Our shoulders start to slump. Our esteem suffers. Pretty soon we're looking really old. And we become inhibited in sex, says Dr. Fader.

There's no reason to, though, because we really *can* do a lot to slow down the clock, look and feel lively, lithe, and youthful for our age—while keeping our manhood and our dignity. How? In a nutshell: We can do a lot cosmetically, short of surgery. We can do surgery. We can put the zip back into our step with attitude and exercise. We can learn to relax and enjoy life. We can burn off the telltale fat that tends to creep up on us and make us less attractive and less healthy in midlife. We can dress with class, even while wearing jeans. We can stand tall and walk proud. We can improve our health and glow with energy. Each of these things shaves years off how we feel and how we look to others.

Then, as Michael J. Coulter, D.D.S., a dentist in private practice in Emmaus, Pennsylvania, notes, when we realize we look good to others, we begin to feel better about ourselves. And that changes our whole outlook on life.

We can do it without looking pathetic or ridiculous. Here's how. We've broken down our suggestions into four categories: personal style, attitude, physical agility and vibrancy, and surface appearance. We'll examine each one in turn.

MAXIMUM STYLE

From top of head to bottom of shoes, how you look sends messages about who you are. If you want people to see you as young and vibrant, how you wear hair and clothes demands some attention.

Get a haircut. For most of us, well-cut, well-styled short to medium-length hair is the right ticket these days, advises Francisco Gavila, senior barber at the Vidal Sassoon Salon in New York City. It keeps us from looking like we made a wrong turn in the 1960s or 1970s and are still lost. Identifying with a generation long past its prime does not make us look younger.

Find a haircutter who works with your natural features and gives you a trim, neat, easy-to-maintain cut time after time, advises Gavila. Shorter hair is especially important if your hair is thinning, receding, or mostly history, Gavila notes. Short hair is light and fluffy and draws the least attention to the vacant land peeking through the ground cover. Clint Eastwood–short and Bruce Willis–short are great examples of how to wear shrinking hair stylishly.

"Cut the hair much shorter, closer to the head," advises Gavila. "That's dramatic and it creates a much younger effect than attempting to comb hair over thin spots." The comb-over. Men, could we please just outlaw the comb-over? Growing hair a foot long just above one ear and then gluing it across the bald dome fools no one. No one. It draws attention to exactly what it's intended to hide. It does not make us appear younger.

Shaved heads? They convey elements of machismo, virility, and confidence and are favored by lots of respected and admired real-world role models—young and old. If you think you're bold enough, if you think you have the machismo, virility, and confidence to pull it off, go for it, says Gavila.

Dress right. The key to youthful dressing for the mature man is quality, says Mark Alden Lukas, creative director for Perry Ellis Tailored Clothing in New York City. Don't chase trends, he advises. Be stylish, but hold the middle ground, not the leading edge. And buy the best you can afford.

"The man in his forties, we would hope, has reached a level in his life where he is able to buy quality clothing. Quality comes through," Lukas says.

GET AN ATTITUDE

Motivational speakers from the Bible's King Solomon on have told us that as a man thinks in his heart, so is he. To be young, you must carry a young attitude with you. Here are two quick ways to juice up your attitude.

Stand tall. Slumping makes you look defeated and old. And it makes you feel that way, too. Take note of your posture. Remember, head up, shoulders back. And while you're at it, smile. A pleasant look is much more attractive than a stern one. And attractive is what we're all about here, isn't it?

"You can take a 70-year-old who stands straight, looks alert, and walks with a steady gait and he'll look decades younger," says Ben H. Douglas, Ph.D., assistant vice chancellor of graduate studies and professor of anatomy at the University of Mississippi Medical Center in Jackson. "And a 40-year-old who slumps and shuffles looks like he's on his way out."

Be positive. "Hang out with people who have active lifestyles," advises Jewett Pattee, who at 73 captained the winning masters team in the 1996 bicycle Race across America.

What's the message here? Think young, stay active, stay interested in life.

PHYSICAL IMPROVEMENTS

How your body looks and how it responds determine whether you look primed for action or just past your prime.

Maximize human growth hormone. Doctors on the questionable edge of anti-aging treatments inject their patients with regular doses of incredibly expensive human growth hormone (HGH), a substance released by the pituitary gland, starting in childhood, and continuing into old age. People who have taken HGH have found it to produce striking improvements in their health, energy level, and sense of well-being. And the list of benefits of HGH seems to be growing with each new study. HGH helps build strength and repair damaged tissue. As with some other hormones possibly remotely or directly linked to aging, production of HGH is highest when we are young and tends to decline as we age. While side effects of injecting HGH can be serious and even life-threatening, most patients report feeling quite rejuvenated and perky while undergoing the treatment. They lose body fat and gain strength and stamina.

We can enjoy the benefits, avoid the risks, and save the $8,000 to $30,000 annual cost of potentially dangerous HGH treatment. How? By producing more HGH naturally. One way is through exercise. High-intensity exercise squeezes more HGH into the bloodstream, say researchers Ronald Klatz, D.O., and physician and biochemist Robert Goldman, D.O., Ph.D., in their book *Stopping the Clock*. They recommend free-weight training several days a week with particular emphasis on the lower body since lower-body workouts seem to stimulate the greatest release of HGH. Sprinting, handball, squash— any particularly intense, strenuous activity seems to work, they say. Long-distance running doesn't seem particularly effective. Check with your doctor before undertaking any strenuous, new exercise program.

Sleep the years away. Another great way to produce more HGH is to sleep. Sleep. That's right. Your body releases the largest concentration of growth hormone during sleep. Get adequate sleep. When you consistently don't, you age in dog years. You look tired. You look worn. "When you get enough rest, you're more likely to perform at optimum levels and to maintain other healthy behaviors, such as exercise and a good diet," says Michael V. Vitiello, Ph.D., associate director of the Sleep and Aging Research Program at

How to Dress in Your Forties

How we dress tells the world how we see ourselves and how it should see us. We have many choices in what we communicate through our clothing. Want to communicate confidence and dignified youthfulness? Here's how, according to Mark Alden Lukas, creative director for Perry Ellis Tailored Clothing in New York City.

• Colors. Consider adding some of the hotter, more fashionable colors to your tie wardrobe. "They can spruce up a solid navy suit. Instead of wearing a gray and navy tie, or a red tie, go with a new-fashion orange," Lukas says. Put a little more spin on the look by wearing a patterned blue shirt under that orange tie. Interpret fashion, but take a more mature, elegant approach to it.

• Patterns and textures. "There is a whole return to elegance right now," Lukas says. "We're seeing the more tailored looks, even in sportswear. We're seeing the heavier chalk stripes come back. We're seeing the richer, more luxurious finishes on cloth—like cashmere blends." Also hot are iridescent finishes—something most guys in their forties should avoid. Rather, buy a high-quality navy or charcoal gabardine with a slight sheen on it. It's not iridescent but has a sense of luster that comes from quality.

• Casual wear. "I think the jacket is the key element," Lukas says. "A man

the University of Washington in Seattle. "Combine sleep with these other behaviors, and all those things we associate with youth—appearance, energy, and attitude—will ultimately improve."

Lose the flab. Middle-age spread is a giveaway. And you can get rid of it. You can. The secret is to burn more calories than you take in. Daily. So watch what you eat. And take off a pound or two a week until you're trim and then stay that way. (For more advice on this, see Less Active Lifestyle on page 418.) Work out with weights. That builds muscle, and muscle burns more fat, around the clock. And for maximum calorie burn, do an aerobic activity—running, biking, skating, skiing. Find a whole-body routine and ease into it, and stick with it. You'll see dramatic changes within six weeks. You'll seem more vibrant and alive to everyone who sees you. That's attractive. That looks young.

Build muscle. It doesn't have to be a lot. Just the outline of muscle showing through your shirt when you flex your arms spells vitality. Vitality is youthful. How to build muscle? See the previous tip.

Be flexible. Stiff and creaky spells old. Flexible and lithe spells youthful. The choice is up to you. Which way do you want to feel? You increase flexibility through stretching routines and other exercise. For a good book showing routines for men at all levels—from the man who has never worked out to the weight lifting monster—and for enhancing performance in all sports,

needs a sport coat or two that can be worn with jeans, khakis, or nice wool trousers. Something with an interesting color mix, like a camel and charcoal. It should be midweight, with a clear surface on the fabric so that it's not heavy looking. That gives you the ability to wear it with a number of things."

Lukas reminds men that the goal for casual wear is comfort. Choose a jacket that's easy to move around in. "With what's happening in the market right now with softer tailoring, the man in his forties can find comfortable clothing that still says, 'I'm dressed and I care about what I look like, and I'm not uptight.' "

• Jeans. "In the fashion circles right now they're either wearing very tightly fitted jeans or they're wearing the rap look—extremely baggy. I think that both are too extreme for a man in his forties," Lukas says. "I suggest a gentleman's cut on a jean—where it's more of a straight leg, not too exaggerated, not too full, but not too slim. Something that is going to flatter the man.

"I think jeans with a fabulous pair of loafers is a great weekend look. And a good sport shirt with a sport coat. And if he wants to be more modern about it, he can wear a boot with jeans. And it doesn't have to be a cowboy boot. Something with a square toe, or a slightly chunkier heel. It shows that the man's thinking about fashion, that he's aware of what's happening around him, and that he's interpreting it for who he is and not what the fashion dictates to him."

pick up a copy of *The Men's Health Guide to Peak Conditioning.* You can order it at your favorite bookstore.

SURFACE APPEARANCE

When people look at you, they see your skin. Your skin is out there. All the time. Dull, lifeless, leathery, cracked, blotched, prunelike skin does not look young. Even if your skin meets all those criteria today, it can look much better in just a matter of weeks. Here are some tips on how to save and salvage your skin, drawn primarily from the advice that New York City dermatologist Nelson Lee Novick, M.D., offers in his book *You Can Look Younger at Any Age.*

Visit a dermatologist. Sure, we know you hate doctors. But look at it as a one-time consultation with substantial long-term gains. Because that's exactly what it is. Ask the doctor to inspect your skin for cancerous and precancerous lesions. Ask him (or her) to look over the exposed parts of your body—face, neck, hands, and so on—and recommend treatment alternatives for any blotches, age spots, "spider veins," light and heavy wrinkling, or other problems marring your appearance. Many of these signs of aging can be erased quickly and effectively, inexpensively in just one or two visits. Insurance covers many of the procedures. Even if it doesn't, a few hundred dollars shelled out for looking great is a few hundred bucks well spent.

Make like Dracula. Avoid direct sunlight, particularly between 10:00 A.M. and 2:00 P.M. When in sunlight, wear a broad-brimmed hat. Wear sunscreen with a minimum sun-protection factor (SPF) of 15. The sorry truth is that tanned skin is damaged skin. Yes, the damage takes a few years to appear. But it *will* appear. It is difficult to repair. While you're at it, stay out of tanning parlors. They do the same thing—destroy your skin.

Clean up. Cut out the smoke, excessive alcohol, and recreational drugs, if you engage in any of those vices. All of them affect your appearance—for the worse.

If dry, moisturize. Know your skin type. If it's oily, you may not need moisturizers. In fact, you may wish to use astringent cleansing pads to clean away oil a couple times. If your skin is dry, though, you need to moisturize. Aging skin is prone to dryness. A moisturizer is designed to draw natural moisture from deeper layers of the skin to the surface layers and to retard its evaporation. Which moisturizer? That depends on your skin type. Water-based or oil-free are best if you have oily skin. Light, hypoallergenic moisturizers are good if you have normal, sensitive, or slightly dry skin. If your skin is very dry, a heavier, oil-based cream may be necessary. The most expensive ones and those with 2,001 herbal extracts and vitamins probably are not much better than the $2 generic bottle. Apply moisturizer while your face is still damp from cleansing.

Experiment with products. Many moisturizers, sunscreens, and the like cause rashes, acne, and other problems. Different people's skin reacts differently. Regardless of whether the products say they are "comedogenic," "hypoallergenic," or "nonacnegenic," expect some trial and error to find the right one for you.

Eat wholesome food. In a balanced diet. It feeds your skin, providing the needed vitamins, nutrients, and minerals. The U.S. Department of Agriculture food pyramid is a good guide.

Work out. Regular exercise improves blood flow to your skin, making it healthier and giving it a rosier glow.

De-stress. Periodic calm, deep breathing; relaxing; visualizing a peaceful scene—anything that works for you to wipe away the tension throughout your day will make you feel and look younger. Stress also triggers or aggravates acne, flushing, eczema, psoriasis, and other unwanted skin conditions.

Use alpha hydroxies. Moisturizers listing alpha hydroxy acids (AHAs) moisturize the skin, plump it up, dissolve the "glue" holding dead cells on the surface of the skin together, and help restore the skin. Most over-the-counter alpha hydroxy products do not list the percentage of AHAs they contain. To be sure you are getting a reasonably potent one, buy only those that list the AHA as one of the first five ingredients. Or ask a dermatologist for a prescription for a guaranteed 12 percent to 15 percent strength product. Skin should begin looking better within two months of daily use. Wrinkling should decrease after six months or a year of daily use.

Professional Repairs

Self-maintenance just not getting your facial skin to where you want it to be? Here are professional fixes available to you.

• Peels. In a peel, the doctor applies an acidic solution to your face, then neutralizes it at the proper time. This causes the surface layers of skin to peel off over a couple weeks. The application and peel is done either lightly in a series of sessions or more heavily in one or two sessions. The treatment cost can range from $1,500 to $3,000.

• Dermabrasion. In this procedure, a doctor anesthetizes your face, then freezes it a part at a time. While firm and frozen, he uses a rotary sanding or cutting device to plane away imperfections. You're then bandaged for 24 hours; complete healing takes about three weeks. Expect to pay from $2,000 to $3,500.

• Laser abrasion. This process costs from $5,000 to $8,000. While it heals more quickly than conventional dermabrasion, it does not produce better results, says New York City dermatologist Nelson Lee Novick, M.D., author of *You Can Look Younger at Any Age*.

• Buffing. This is a kinder and gentler repair. A doctor uses a handheld abrasive material and buffs or sands manually. This process requires no bandage and takes about two weeks to heal. The cost is usually between $1,800 and $2,500.

• Facelifts and other procedures. Qualified plastic surgeons can eliminate double chins and wrinkles and facial sags—at a substantial price and risk. Results are always iffy. It's your face. You decide.

Renovate with Renova. Ask your doctor for this prescription cream, which helps smooth and repair wrinkles and lighten brown spots. It is formulated with a potent derivative of vitamin A, the same active ingredient as Retin A, but is said to work deeper in the skin.

Wash your face. Do it gently. Not with a scrubby. Not with a washcloth. Use your fingertips, warm water—not hot—and a relatively gentle cleansing bar or cleansing lotion. If you have sensitive, dry skin, try a soap-free cleansing lotion. If you have oily skin, try stronger bar soaps. And if your skin is extremely oily, experiment with astringent wipes as well. Use the tips of your fingers to lather and rinse. Pat dry with a towel.

Brighten your smile. As we get older, our teeth wear down, lose enamel, lose their brightness. Cosmetic dentistry offers a number of options for improving your smile, notes Dr. Coulter.

• Tooth bleaching. "This gives you a revitalized smile," says Dr. Coulter. It costs from $300 to $400.

- Bonding. "If a person's teeth are completely broken down, or a little malformed or misshapen, porcelain veneers are a solution," says Dr. Coulter. A bright, light-reflecting, properly shaped piece of porcelain is bonded to the front surface of the tooth. Porcelain is substantially more durable than the plastics once used in bonding, he says. The cost ranges from $270 to $350 per tooth.
- Adult orthodontics. Clear bands and braces can be attached to the inside of the teeth, so these days you can have your teeth straightened without looking like a kid with a "metal mouth."

Consult an orthodontist for latest treatments and prices.

LESS ACTIVE LIFESTYLE

Middle-age spread is not a set of odds offered by a sports bookie. You can bet the bank that unwanted weight gain is a sure shot for most men once they leave the active days of youth behind, says Roger T. Crenshaw, M.D., a psychiatrist and sex therapist in La Jolla, California, and one of the founders of the American Psychiatric Association.

Bad news: The sedentary lifestyle and the concomitant weight gain add up to a more sluggish sex life, Dr. Crenshaw says. There are many reasons. We'll look at the biggies—and what we can do about them—later.

A precise reason why men put on weight as we age is unknown, says Dr. Crenshaw. It might be related to hormonal changes. In many cases it certainly is lifestyle-related. In most men, metabolism slows down as we age. Most likely, Dr. Crenshaw says, middle-age weight gain is a combination of those factors and possibly others.

"Every male I've ever seen will tell you that he never had a problem with weight gain up until a certain point in his life; then after that, everything sticks," says Dr. Crenshaw. "Some men start putting it on in their mid-thirties, some in their forties, some in their fifties. But rarely does anyone get past their fifties without having a weight-management difficulty. It just increases as we get older."

We need to emphasize here that, despite the conspiracy of physiology, lifestyle, and aging, no man needs to surrender his self-esteem and sexual satisfaction to a lifetime of disappointing decline. We *can* beat the odds and conquer middle-age spread. We *can* remain sexually active. We'll tell you how.

First, though, let's look at how too much TV, too much junky fattening food, too little basketball, and an ever-expanding belly can affect our sex lives.

THE NOT-SO-SEXY TRUTH

Sedentary, simply put, means "less active." It means that we sit and stand and maybe even shuffle around a bit. But it means we aren't regularly engaging in sustained, intense physical activity. "To me, sedentary means not only obese but out of shape," says Dr. Crenshaw.

As the years add up and work and family responsibilities pile onto us, we tend to become more sedentary. We are more likely to skip the morning jog, afternoon handball game, evening softball or volleyball. We're more likely to drive than walk. And, most of all, says Dr. Crenshaw, we probably sit in front of the TV set for hours each night.

This is not good, says Dr. Crenshaw. "There is a direct correlation between males who are in good physical shape and males with a good sexual life," he says.

Overweight and out of shape spell high cholesterol, gummed-up arteries (including those feeding the penis), a less vibrant and upbeat attitude, and often, poor self-esteem. All of those things are downers on our sexual functioning, says Dr. Crenshaw. Gummed-up arteries, in particular, lead to severe softening of erections, he says.

Single men in their forties tend to be in better shape than married men in their forties, says Dr. Crenshaw, but not by much. Both usually need some work to get back into prime physical and sexual shape. The improvements are both physical and psychological, he notes.

"I will see many males coming in feeling badly about themselves because they are no longer physically attractive," Dr. Crenshaw says. "This even happens with men who have been married 20 or 30 years."

While getting active improves health and trims pounds for all men, middle-age single men, in particular, need "to get into what I call dating and mating shape," says Dr. Crenshaw. Being in shape, he says, really affects their self-esteem and, consequently, "their ability to approach an unknown female. Now, self-esteem is directly going to affect their choices of whom they ask out and when they ask them out and how far they will go in the relationship. So sexually, it is a very important aspect." Not to mention that women respond to the physical shape of a man and that, usually, lean is the thing if you want a positive response.

Regular physical activity boosts moods and energy levels, notes Dr. Crenshaw. Both are important to our sexual functioning.

WHAT TO DO

We can overcome the degeneration and debilitating effects of the less active life, says Dr. Crenshaw. Here are the major ways.

Exercise regularly. The antidote to the inactive lifestyle is—what else?—to get active. You don't need to pay money for advice like that. But the issue does run deeper. Men often don't realize that there is an art and science

How to Tell if You're Too Sedentary

For starters, says Roger T. Crenshaw, M.D., a psychiatrist and sex therapist in La Jolla, California, and one of the founders of the American Psychiatric Association, count the hours you watch television each week. Many men watch 3 hours or more a night, he says. Active men may only watch 2 hours per week. The closer you come to the active man's viewing pattern, the less likely it is that you are sedentary.

Also, he says, ask yourself: Do I get outdoors? When I'm out, do I exert myself, or do I lounge? If golfing, do I walk the course and carry my bags, or do I hire a caddie or rent a cart?

Ask yourself if you're getting a minimum of 20 minutes' worth of physical exertion at least three times a week. Anything less is a symptom of creeping couch potato-ism.

to exercising effectively. They think they can just be guys—play some softball, go for a jog, lift some weights in the basement—and get back to health. They think that by doing situps you can flatten your belly. Wrong.

Not that exercising smart is complicated or miserable. In fact, the top advice any good fitness coach will tell you is only to do things that you enjoy. Being active is a lifelong commitment, and if you choose exercises you don't enjoy, you are sentencing yourself to either quick failure or, well, a life of unhappy exercise.

That said, here are some quick points to help get you exercising smartly, for life.

• You'll need to school yourself some before you can be effective. What does weightlifting do to your body, your metabolism, your fat? How's that different from running? How much exercise is enough? How do I measure my effectiveness? What's right for my body, my health and fitness goals? To get answers, you have lots of choices. You can read (we, of course, recommend our own *The Men's Health Guide to Peak Conditioning*; it's comprehensive, easy to understand, and filled with programs for every goal and lifestyle). You can hire a personal trainer. You can get on the Internet. You can ask the trainers at your local gym. Your doctor can give you an important lesson or two.

• You'll need to start slowly. The goal is not to be panting or sweating or nauseated or sore. The goal is to slowly, carefully, pleasantly, painlessly raise your body's capacity for physical activity. Walking is the best way to start, in fact. After dinner, go for a 30-minute stroll three or more times a week. After a month, you'll be ready and willing for more.

• You'll need to achieve a balance. A well-conceived fitness regime has three components: stretching, strength training, and aerobic exercise. For weight loss, the most important is aerobic exercise—running, bicycling, stairstepping, swimming, or any activity that raises your heart rate and breathing levels for a sustained period. It is the most efficient way to burn calories and also conditions your heart and lungs. But you still need to increase your flexibility for healthy joints, limber muscles, and an injury-resistant body. And strength training has a zillion benefits as well, ranging from greater round-the-clock calorie burn (muscles consume more calories than flab, even while you sleep) to a palpable feeling of power and vitality. A smart guy builds a program around all three.

• You'll need to prioritize. Being active doesn't mean just three hour-long exercise sessions per week and the rest of the time in your usual habits. The active lifestyle is 24 hours a day. It's an attitude that says, "I like to move; I like being active; I like the way my body feels when it is energized and strong." It means opting for the stairs rather than the elevator. It means not hassling to find the closest parking spot but just putting the car in the distant open area and walking the extra 200 feet to the door. It means jumping on the bike or going for a walk, and dragging your family with you, whenever the weather is unusually nice. It means choosing active vacations, not lie-around vacations.

• You'll need to invest. Not a lot, but some money. For a bicycle, some good shoes, a basic weight setup, maybe a membership to the YMCA. Sometimes putting out a few hundred dollars is good incentive to get active. Who likes to throw away money?

Gravitate toward low-fat, high-fiber foods. It is an extremely simple equation: Burn more calories in a day than you consume, and you lose weight. There are two ways to do that: Burn more calories through exercise, and choose foods that are less dense in calories. And fat is the most calorie-dense food there is. Moreover, low-fat, high-fiber foods have other crucial strengths, including their ability to reduce clogging in your arteries. One great piece of advice: At any meal, split your plate (mentally) into four quarters. Your meat portion should take up just one-quarter of the plate; a second quarter should go to a carbohydrate like rice, noodles, or potatoes; the rest of your plate should be vegetables or fruit. Follow this, and you are off to a great start in cutting down fat, increasing fiber, and improving your overall mix of nutrients.

Be calorie-conscious, but don't make your diet too stringent or punishing, warns Dr. Crenshaw. If you do, it will be too hard to follow. Shoot for weight loss of no more than 5 pounds a month and you should be able to stick with it for life—and you won't have to miss Christmas and Thanksgiving dinners.

Set realistic, specific, short-term goals. Goal setting is tricky business. Make your goals too long-term or sweeping or vague and chances are that you'll get discouraged. Our best pieces of advice: Make your goals short-term (run a mile nonstop within a month) rather than long-term (run a 10-kilometer race in under 45 minutes by next summer). Make your goals task-oriented (I will ride my bike three times a week) rather than outcome-oriented (I will lose 5 pounds this month). Keep your goals focused on yourself (I will run the race faster than my last race time), not on others (I will place in the top 20 of the race). Have more than one goal (I will ride my bike three times a week and will increase the amount I can bench-press every two weeks for eight consecutive weeks).

Use your newfound vigor. There's a payoff to all this activity: You can do *more* activity, particularly the things you like most. Like sex. Or going out with friends. Or finally joining a softball league. Or volunteering. Or wrestling with the kids. Or sex.

MIDLIFE CRISIS

Sometime between our late thirties and our early fifties, we experience a period of tumult, a time of intense personal questioning, reassessing, disillusionment, and ultimately, new growth. The depth and seriousness of the transition varies from man to man. Some coast through. Some crash and burn and then, like a phoenix, arise from the ashes and soar.

Why call this a midlife crisis? It is a necessary period of pruning and preening; an essential check of the coordinates and a flick of the wheel to assure that we are on the straightest, most effective course. A soulful search for what is truly important and worth our precious time and effort and love and attention. We should feel honored that we are allowed this midlife checkup, that we receive this wake-up call, says Frederic Hudson, Ph.D., president of the Hudson Institute in Santa Barbara, California, and author of *The Adult Years* and other books.

But the truth is that most of us are a bit frustrated and embarrassed by it, says Ross Goldstein, Ph.D., a San Francisco psychologist and author of *Fortysomething*.

We will not belabor the issues here. They are thoroughly covered in Disillusionment (page 491). We do suggest that you turn there for more detail if this is a current fascination. Here we will hit a few essential highlights.

WAKE-UP CALLS

We face three realities at midlife, says Dr. Goldstein. One is mortality; one is career; one is family. Each confrontation and realization comes as something of a shock. A friend dies or our health fails, and suddenly, we realize that we aren't going to live forever, notes Dr. Goldstein. We realize that our life is probably half over, if we're lucky enough to live a long life. We realize that the clock is running down, time is running out. We freak.

"We say, 'Hey, that may be me there in the ground before too long,' " says

Maximize Your Forties

You can truly turn the angst of midlife into a positive, productive time of transition. Here are four suggestions from Frederic Hudson, Ph.D., president of the Hudson Institute in Santa Barbara, California, and clinical psychologist Pamela D. McLean, Ph.D., drawn from their book *Life Launch: A Passionate Guide to the Rest of Your Life*.

1. Learn to rearrange your busy life around your basic values and what you perceive to be your natural essence and strengths.
2. Become your own best friend.
3. Develop and nurture your sense of connectedness with nature and the universe; or, if religious, with your concept of the higher presence; or, if comfortable with the term, with your spirituality.
4. View your life in terms of time remaining rather than time already spent.

Daniel Beaver, a marriage and family therapist from Walnut Creek, California, and author of *Beyond the Marriage Fantasy* and *More Than Just Sex*.

Turn the page and our career is in our face. We either made it to where we thought we would and find that it isn't the be-all and end-all fulfillment we had expected, or we realize that we've gotten about as far as we're going to get and it's far short of what we had planned, says Dr. Goldstein. Neither feels great.

Turn the page and there's our family staring back at us. And it doesn't look a bit like the Nelsons did on *Ozzie and Harriet*. No. Our family has foibles and flukes and flub-ups and some tattered baggage, some hard feelings, some serious flaws. Our marriage may be teetering and unsatisfactory and holding together simply because that's easier than splitting it apart. Or it may be dying from lack of attention and affection. Or it may be good, but adrift. Each situation requires action if we are to grow.

In every one of these confrontations with reality, we are likely to demand that things change for the better. We may throw away that which no longer works for us; we may alter it; we may exchange it. It is in response to that first wake-up call—the realization that life is fragile and ours might deteriorate or end at any time and certainly will sometime—that men are likely to do the sorts of things that make them the butt of jokes about midlife crisis. They may chase lost youth, as Calvin A. Colarusso, M.D., clinical professor of psychiatry at the University of California, San Diego; an adult and child psychiatrist and psychoanalyst in La Jolla, California; and author of *Fulfillment in Adulthood*, puts it. That is, dump the aging wife, color what's left of the graying hair, dress and talk and walk like a teenager, latch on to a fetching young lady who makes the 19-year-old boys' tongues hang out, and otherwise try to pretend they are anything but a 40-something-year-old man.

Only a few men actually act that out, says Dr. Goldstein, but nearly all of us may ponder it briefly. More likely we will make changes that may confuse our family and friends but that clearly improve our quality of life, says Dr. Goldstein.

We may begin exercising and eating better. We may switch jobs or departments or try to make our work more meaningful some other way. We may deal more lovingly or directly with family members, says Dr. Hudson. We may focus much more on matters of lasting and deeper value and importance. We may become kinder and gentler, Dr. Hudson says. And all those developments clearly are positive in nature. How can we achieve them? That's what we'll look at next.

NAVIGATING THE RAPIDS

Here are some tips for making the most of our midlife opportunity and inclination to reassess and refine.

Be nice. To yourself. Seventy-five percent of the work of making it through the midlife transition productively is "having an accepting attitude toward oneself that is relatively forgiving and encouraging. Then you don't denigrate into character assassination and self-loathing," says Dr. Goldstein.

Assess reality. Identify those things you *can* work on, those areas in your life where you have some control, advises Dr. Goldstein. What does this mean? What are areas over which you have control? Here are some examples from Dr. Goldstein.

• Health: "Get started on a fitness program, eat wisely, take care of your body as though you are going to live a long time instead of saying, 'I've smoked and I've overeaten, so all is lost. I might as well give up the fight.'"

• Work: "The old notion that you could get your degree and you were set for life is no longer operant. Get on a learning curve. Accept the notion that survival in today's work world demands lifelong learning. Get in some kind of lifelong learning program."

• Relationships: "Diversify. You need a lot of different friendships, a lot of different kinds of people in your life. One of the benefits is that it keeps you in touch with a lot of segments of the world around you, and that's a key to staying youthful and useful." And it keeps you from becoming too rigid and judgmental, he says.

• Curiosity: Keep it alive. "Be experimental, be challenging, be accepting. Engage in some trial and error. Try some different ways of dressing and different ways of thinking."

• Field of vision: The tendency as we enter the afternoon of life is to look at the big picture, "a tendency to start thinking in kind of an oceanic, global, metaphorical way, and we lose sight of the little victories we have each day." However, he says, noting and celebrating "the small victories we have each day is important to our well-being and wholeness and acceptance of ourselves."

• Communication: "Men have lots of preconceived notions about what men do and do not talk about." And that inhibits us. We figure that we cannot talk about feelings. Really we can't usually, at least not the way women do—face to face. "Men do side-by-side bonding," says Dr. Goldstein. "The metaphor is two guys bent over the fender of a Chevrolet working on the engine. The focus is on the engine. But they are bonded by the activity." Then, he says, if a man talks about what's on his mind, about a feeling or emotional conflict, he may be surprised to find that the other man shares his concerns.

RE-ENTERING THE SINGLES SCENE

More than half of us get a second chance at the being-single thing. For many of us, the second chance comes when we're in our forties. We may not immediately recognize it as an opportunity.

Yes, bright, intriguing new possibilities do lie before us. And yes, we may not see them at first because we may be confused and hurt and have some serious mourning or sorting out to do. The sorting process is necessary, says Allan J. Adler, M.D., a psychiatrist in San Diego and co-author of the book *Divorce Recovery*.

Not to bring you down, but usually we find ourselves single again for rather depressing reasons. The most common is divorce. Divorce happens. Sometimes a marriage crashes and burns. Sometimes it simply fades away. But all the time it hurts. Regardless of whether we show it, a failed marriage rips us apart inside, challenges our core beliefs and self-image, and forever changes how we intimately relate with others. Rough as this sounds, ultimately, it is an enlightening and positive process, says Dr. Adler. Some of us, though, are tempted to shortcut the process.

A quick-rebound relationship may seem the perfect antidote to post-marriage blues. It may seem reaffirming and healing, but it usually isn't, warns Dr. Adler. Rushing into a new, exciting relationship often is just a way of burying and postponing the hurt and the serious reassessment and healing work that needs to take place, says Dr. Adler. It's your life. Would you rather learn from your mistakes or hide from them?

If you choose to rush into a rebound relationship, enjoy it. But understand what you're doing and expect that you'll need to make time later for real healing, says Dr. Adler.

Our first bit of advice? Before fixing yourself up with another woman, take time to fix yourself up with you. Man, heal yourself. Although less common than divorce, the death of your spouse is another reason for becoming single again in midlife. (For more on this, see Death of a Spouse on page 542.)

WHAT'S A SCENE?

Before we go any further, let's dispel any misimpression we may have conveyed by the heading on this chapter: "Re-entering the Singles Scene." In the chapters Where to Find Women (page 14) and How to Find the Right Woman—And Avoid the Wrong One (page 18), we've made it clear that no real "singles scene" exists—at least not geographically. Of course, there are singles bars. But most singles don't frequent them. The real and most healthy singles scene is a state of mind that you wear out there in the real world. The real world where you will meet real women with whom you might really want to share real life. We tell you in those earlier chapters how to steer yourself into corners of the real world where it is more likely that you will meet available—and compatible—women. The advice applies to men of all ages.

Because the real world is the real singles scene, it is important that you always be your best you—not just on Friday nights when you slick your hair back and dress up and head to the Ice Cream Social or Community Barn Dance. It is important that you always project your self-confidence and positive traits. Following the end of a marriage, some restoration work may be in order before you feel completely at ease doing this.

RESTORING THE SELF

In any long-term coupling, each partner loses some of their identity—they surrender it to the partnership. This can be beneficial or disastrous. When a marriage ends through death or divorce, many of us find that we have lost or misplaced much of the inner strength we called upon when we were single and tackled the world alone. We feel damaged, defective, uncertain whether we can function effectively. We may feel insecure sexually, physically, emotionally, financially, notes Jane K. Burgess, Ph.D., sociology professor emeritus at the University of Wisconsin in Waukesha and author of *The Single-Again Man* and *The Widower*.

How do we best deal with that?

Take time to review, sort, and reassess, urges Dr. Adler. Discover and rediscover your basic values: what really matters to you, what makes you happy, what makes you feel you are contributing positively to the world. Think about what you need in a relationship. Think about what you did wrong in the last one, what went wrong, and what you allowed to go wrong.

Many men will not date for a year or two after a marriage ends, says Dr. Adler. And those who do may find that they experience erection problems and depression, he says. It's okay to take the time off from the pressure of relationships and partner sex, he says, and just work on coming to terms with yourself and the world. Many men need time to mourn the loss.

Here are two more top tips.

Sex by the Numbers

So when do you first get to sleep with her? Sex educator Sari Locker surveyed 500 young people (ages 19 to 29) about this. The singles culture is ruled by the young, so these responses may well set the standard for those of us in our forties. Here's what Locker found.

The percentage of couples that first sleep together:

On their first date?	13%
Beginning on their fourth to seventh date?	24%
Within two weeks to one month?	19%
Within one month to three months?	17%
Between the third month and the sixth month?	16%
Within six months to one year?	10%
Once they're married?	1%

SOURCE: *Mindblowing Sex in the Real World*

Work on yourself. Your health, your self-esteem, your direction, your skills, your fitness, your appearance. This summarizes some of the best advice from 50 or so men that Dr. Burgess interviewed and followed through their successful emergence from divorce. Starting over is cool. You have a chance to do things better. This is an opportunity to do things that are good for you. Don't allow yourself to dive into booze, TV, and junk food, said Dr. Burgess's men. Treat yourself to a great new life and a solid course of self-improvement. Rediscover sensitivity and romantic skills if they may have rusted.

Get support. Find a support group for divorced or widowed singles. You *do* need to talk, say Dr. Burgess and Dr. Adler. You do need to see, hear, and accept that other people are going through the exact same anger, pain, confusion that you are, say the doctors. It's reassuring. It's nonthreatening. It brings friendship into your life. It's a transition into the world of adult singles. Private therapy helps, too, if you can afford it, notes Dr. Burgess.

Then, when you're ready, when you like yourself again, gently venture into the more traditional singles scene.

MAKING THE SCENE

When ready for a partner or partners, know what you're looking for. A gentle, deep, sharing relationship? A pretty woman to pal around with? Uncommitted sex? And there are many shades and combinations in between. Most of us find that detached, uncommitted, purely sexual pairings are rarely fulfilling. We recommend that you seek a loving, caring relationship. Our focus here assumes that that is what you want.

Let us again suggest that, when you're ready, you should turn to the chapters Where to Find Women (page 14) and How to Find the Right Woman— And Avoid the Wrong One (page 18), along with all the Rules of Engagement chapters. We offer explicit details, lots of helpful suggestions and strategies for meeting women. We won't repeat them here. We're going to assume you're thoroughly versed in where to go to meet the kind of partner you're looking for. Here we'll just offer some quick tips for midlife singles.

Give. Be a supplier of love, care, praise, concern, advises Seattle psychologist Arthur Wassmer, Ph.D., author of *Making Contact* and other books. "Human beings need admiration," he says. "They need respect. They need attention. They need affection. They need a sense of importance.... Hold the awareness that all human beings need those things high in your consciousness, and then behave as a supplier of those things, and you'll rapidly become an important person to other people." Remind yourself, before entering a social environment, "I have something to give." Then do it. Practice this with people and you will find potential partners drawn to you, says Dr. Wassmer.

Look good. Visit a beauty college regularly for an inexpensive hair trim and manicure, recommends R. Don Steele in his book *How to Date Young Women for Men over 35*. And dress nicely, in quality, age-appropriate clothes, he advises. (For more advice on how to dress, see Looking Young on page 411.)

Exchange cards. To keep things easygoing and lightly businesslike when meeting a potential partner, hand her your business card when you introduce yourself, advises Sharyn Wolf, a clinical social worker in New York City and author of *Guerrilla Dating Tactics* and *50 Ways to Find a Lover*. And ask for hers. Do this early in the conversation, casually, not later at the point when normally you would be working up the tact and courage to ask for her phone number, says Wolf. If you don't have a business card, have one made, she says. Cite your hobby or an area of expertise if you do not want to put your job title on the card, she says.

Focus on now. Keep your eye on the prize: the woman you are with. Talking about your past loves is a no-no, warns William Perkins, author of *How to Pick Up Women in the 90s.*

Also, mentioning a recent divorce doesn't help any either, says Steele. Women, Steele says, figure you're a basket case for at least two years after a divorce.

Most women know or have heard that dating a man on the rebound from a broken heart is troublesome and often ends in pain and suffering, notes Dr. Adler.

The woman you are with wants to feel like she is the only woman in the world who matters to you, says Perkins. Talking about other women—even saying bad things about them, shows her that other women are on your mind, he says.

Don't force it. Let love flow, says Hollywood psychologist and sexologist Rachel Copelan, Ph.D., author of *100 Ways to Make Sex Sensational and*

100% Safe. Move very slowly and gently in any new relationship, she says. Get to know one another. Don't push for sex. Develop "communicative intimacy," she advises. Friendship, she says, is the best basis for a lasting, meaningful relationship.

It's not uncommon for both widowed and divorced men to suffer from erectile difficulties and other sexual problems, says Shirley Zussman, Ed.D., a certified sex and marital therapist in New York City and editor of a newsletter, *Sex Over 40.*

Called the widower's syndrome by sex researchers William Masters, M.D., and Virginia Johnson, formerly of the Masters and Johnson Institute in St. Louis, it is caused by guilt, depression, and anxiety over performing with a new partner.

Practice what Dr. Copelan calls outercourse as you and your partner become comfortable touching one another. That is, make love through touch and caress and words and sounds while fully dressed. She calls this pleasure without penetration. Slow-motion foreplay that can last for hours. This helps you get completely comfortable with each other. It builds anticipation. Builds responsiveness. Proves that you are a caring person and not a lust-charged, love-starved baboon. Also, it sets a nice pace for the full sexual-contact lovemaking that it likely eventually will lead to. It can conjure a spiritual, or trancelike, bonding that leads to other worldly sex, she says.

Get blood tests. Before first engaging in intercourse with a partner, take an HIV blood test. Most cities have clinics that will draw blood on a walk-in basis and provide results in about two weeks. The cost ranges from $15 to $50, although at government-funded clinics no one is denied testing because of inability to pay. Then, once a sexual relationship is begun, practice monogamy, Dr. Copelan says.

YOUNGER WOMEN

He's 45 going on 19. She is 19. What's wrong with this picture?

Listen to what Calvin A. Colarusso, M.D., clinical professor of psychiatry at the University of California, San Diego; an adult and child psychiatrist and psychoanalyst in La Jolla, California; and author of *Fulfillment in Adulthood*, says about this: "I always have two or three men like this in my practice. They're saying to the world, to themselves first of all, 'I'm not old. I'm not old. I'm still young. I'm still young enough to attract younger women.' They're saying, 'Sexually, I'm as good as I used to be.' Both are lies. They're trying to go back and re-create a lost youth that they have not successfully mourned for and they're struggling to accept their position in life physically, psychologically, and sexually. They're warding off the growing preoccupation with aging and dying."

Maybe they also don't want to be as intellectually challenged as they would be by someone closer to their own age and worldly experience level?

Not the case, says Dr. Colarusso. "They want the tight body and the beautiful woman who is interested in them. It makes them feel young. That's what they want."

They aren't seeking someone who looks up to them for wisdom?

"You don't find that in that type of relationship," says Dr. Colarusso. "They're looking for somebody who looks up to them for their masculinity."

Men who have lost interest in sex with their aging partner often find themselves revivified with a younger woman, says Galdino F. Pranzarone, Ph.D., professor of psychology at Roanoke College in Salem, Virginia. "Their erections pop right up," he says. They find the experience validating, he says. See, they're all right after all. But the reason they can perform and feel so good about themselves with a younger woman is that while their bodies have aged, their concepts of what is sexually desirable has not. They still desire the beautiful young girl with the tight body, says Dr. Pranzarone.

Problems with following up on this? Allan J. Adler, M.D., a psychiatrist in San Diego and co-author of the book *Divorce Recovery*, thinks so.

"A 45-year-old guy gets out of a marriage where he has not been getting enough sex and, thinking only with the tip of his penis, marries a 25-year-old. And now getting enough sex is not a problem—they're in bed all the time," says Dr. Adler. "But he's not thinking ahead. Fifteen years down the line, he's 60 and his sex drive has slowed tremendously. But she's 40 and raring to go. Now she's the one who's not getting enough sex."

Do these relationships work?

"Sometimes they do; most of the times they don't," says Dr. Colarusso. "Sometimes they lead to marriage and the creation of a second family and they continue as long as the man's physical and psychological health last. But obviously, the age difference excludes the whole process of the children and the couple growing old together, and so on. Many times the relationships don't last because either the man or the woman comes to his senses. He comes to his senses and realizes that the age discrepancy, the social discrepancy, all the other discrepancies don't work. Or the woman comes to her senses and realizes that he may have a lot of money or prestige or whatever, but that's not enough to sustain a relationship."

HOW TO DATE YOUNG WOMEN

Many cultures have looked quite favorably upon May-December relationships, particularly ancient Chinese cultures, which celebrated the concept in Tao erotic texts. Of course, that was then and this is now, and the give-and-take equation of relationships has changed dramatically over the years.

Still, if you put psychological and moral issues aside, and look strictly from the sexual perspective, there are good things to say about older men bedding down with younger women. From the woman's perspective, you get an experienced, worldly, unselfish lover who doesn't climax after 30 seconds, like the young colts of her age. From the man's perspective, you get a youthful body that is highly exciting, and a well-lubricated vagina that is more accepting of a penis that is not always rock-hard.

So you're going to chase this dream, even after reading what the experts say? Okay. We understand. May we recommend a book? The language is a bit crude and attitudes a little chauvinistic, but the advice is solid. Buy a copy of *How to Date Young Women for Men over 35*, by R. Don Steele.

Steele has made a career of dating women in their twenties and advising other men how to do it. His step-by-step program starts with getting fit and trim. His book tells in detail how to dress, how to talk, which young ladies are most likely to be interested in older men, which ones to avoid, where to look, and on and on and on. We'll offer a few highlights here, the ones Steele says are the biggies.

Look good. That means that you are slim, trim, clean, neat, well-dressed (slightly on the casual side), well-groomed. It means that you aren't trying to look like a 20-year-old but like a man who has his act together and enjoys life. Get in shape. Wear your hair short. No beards, no ponytails, no bandannas tied around your forehead.

Be a man. Not a boy. She expects you to be mature, relaxed, confident, and experienced.

Take your time. Slow and easy does it. Be casual. She needs to feel comfortable with you. Don't be obvious. Exhibit absolutely no lust. Don't stare at her breasts—until she offers them to you. Don't mention sex.

Learn her language. That is, know what's important to a 19- to 24-year-old (assuming that's your target age) and be conversant in it. Watch the TV shows she watches, read the magazines she reads, listen to the radio stations she does. Read and leave *Cosmopolitan* and *People* on your coffee table.

STEPFAMILIES

She has a couple kids from the previous marriage. You do, too. Or maybe you don't. Or maybe she doesn't and you do. In any case, you love each other, you remember *The Brady Bunch*, and you figure you can all move in together and be one big happy family. Go figure. Again.

"Forty-six percent of all marriages involve someone who has been married before and involve children from the previous marriage—either hers or his," says syndicated columnist Michael J. McManus, president of Marriage Savers in Bethesda, Maryland, and author of *Marriage Savers*.

"These marriages are explosions. And the explosions begin the very first week of the marriage. The stepchildren inevitably resent the stepparent. They manipulate the two partners to drive them apart," McManus says.

True, says Allan J. Adler, M.D., a psychiatrist in San Diego and co-author of the book *Divorce Recovery*. Your children may like your new wife and hers may like you. But, unknown even to themselves, the kids have a deep, underlying desire to sabotage the relationship. They want things to return to the way they were before the marriage when they had their natural parent's undivided attention and devotion, says Dr. Adler.

The kids may even encourage the adults to wed and then, after the wedding, do everything they can to make the stepparent feel unwanted and unappreciated and to divide the couple, Dr. Adler says. A subtle undercurrent of tension pervades the household. The parent and stepparent are played one against the other. Accept that this will happen if you enter this kind of relationship. Expect it and you'll be better equipped to deal with it, say the experts.

Expect to spend from two to seven years of concentrated effort overcoming problems to create a successful, effective blended family, says Dr. Adler.

McManus advises that it often takes longer than that. Five to 10 years is common, he says. The length of time varies based on any number of variables among them the age of the children, the emotional state of those involved, the trauma level of the previous breakup.

We'll look at the typical problems that arise—and why—and talk about how best to handle them.

WHAT THE KIDS SEE

Couples with children invariably enter marriage with the best of expectations and intentions. Even though they may carry reasonable fears and concerns, in their hearts, they still see their two families melding beautifully into one great loving family. That rarely happens, say the experts.

In the best of situations, says Dr. Adler, family members realize that it takes much more than love, hope, and intention to build a new healthy family. It takes constant communication and work. Family members must commit to a long course of identifying problems, comprehending them, and together, working to resolve them. They must create new rules and new routines. The various personalities must learn to meld and adapt to each other and to the new environment. There must be an understanding that things are different now, that there's no going back.

That's a lot of change to force onto kids who already have dealt with a lot of unsettling change. Now the kids enter a completely new environment. The long-established relationships and behavior patterns that recently were dis-

Kids Have It Hard

Here are some common problems kids have adjusting to stepsiblings, as identified by Allan J. Adler, M.D., a psychiatrist in San Diego and co-author of the book *Divorce Recovery*.

• Territoriality. Who wants to share their room, their chair, their space, their parent with some strange new human being forced upon you whom you are supposed to treat with love and respect?

• Loss of rank. Maybe the oldest kid now is the second-oldest. Maybe the youngest now has a younger sister who is getting more attention. Such shifts cause a change in identity among children.

• Differing parental values and expectations. Dr. Adler gives the example of a teenage boy who since earliest childhood was assured he was destined for college and graduate school and always was an exemplary student, studying late into the night, attending weekend enrichment programs and cultural events. Now the new father has no respect for "eggheads," complains about the cost of sending the boy to extracurricular activities, refuses to turn down the TV while the boy studies, and urges the stepchild to "get real" and think about training for a trade.

• Relatives favoring biologically related kids. Sometimes they're downright hostile to the stepchildren.

• Interference from the other parent. The one who does not have custody resents and undermines the new family life, routines, values during his or her times with the kids.

rupted and modified or discarded because of the divorce now are being altered again—because of you, explains Dr. Adler. Kids look to their parents for stability, he says. They are uneasy with change. Now they face lots of change and the unsettling realization that suddenly you are more important to their mother than they are. And that's just not the way they think it should be.

What can you do about this?

Establish priorities. Solidify your couple relationship first, says Dr. Adler. Show the kids that it is good, real, important; that it holds the highest priority and is going to last; and that they'll have to get used to it. Treat each other with respect when in front of the kids. Dr. Adler is not alone in recommending this approach. It was supported by several other experts we spoke with as well.

Listen to what Daniel Beaver, a marriage and family therapist from Walnut Creek, California, and author of *Beyond the Marriage Fantasy* and *More Than Just Sex*, says: "My advice is that the couples really have their couple act together. If they do and they are really a strong unit, then they can deal with the adversity of the blended family and the second family issues; they can

% **Sex by the Numbers**

50 percent of U.S. children under 13 are living with one biological parent and that parent's partner.

60 percent of second marriages fail.

SOURCE: Stepfamily Foundation

deal with the kids. If the couple is not really together, it can get ugly. The problem in those cases is that the parents tend to cater too much to the kids. They compensate for the guilt of the divorce. The kids take on a power that they shouldn't have. The couple relationship becomes secondary. Whenever that happens, it is done. That screws up any marriage. First, second, third, or fourth."

Ease in. Realize that you cannot become an instant parent and that a newly married couple cannot function smoothly as co-parents right out of the starting gate. It can take years of effort and communication. Don't expect stepkids to treat you like their "real" dad. Children never really detach from their biological parent, even if they are very young when the divorce occurs, says Dr. Adler. They may really like the stepfather. But he's always going to be the stepfather, and they're likely always to hurt about their real father, Dr. Adler says. The same goes for how they feel about stepmothers. A stepparent never replaces the biological parent. Don't even try. Instead, create a unique and special relationship with the stepchildren.

Do not force togetherness. In fact, force some separateness, advises Dr. Adler. Make sure that you establish routines and schedules that allow you and your wife some private time together, and allow the children to spend private, quality time with their natural parent, with the whole family, and with the stepparent.

Lighten up. Don't discipline the stepchildren at first unless you are the only parent around. Let the natural parent handle the discipline and observe the dynamics that have been established. View yourself as an aunt or babysitter, says Dr. Adler. Do discuss ground rules with your spouse.

WHAT TO EXPECT

Just how do stepkids try to sabotage marriages? McManus recalls, "One woman told me, 'When I take a shower at 6:30 in the morning, my stepdaughter takes a shower downstairs so that I get no hot water. If I shift my time to 6:15, she does, too.' See what I mean? That's diabolical. The woman said, 'She treats me like a chair. She walks past me and only talks to her dad.'

"Now, the man can't understand why his wife can't get along with his daughter because *he* does. And the daughter is all sweetness and light to him. And what she does to his wife is largely all behind his back. This is a formula designed to explode the family.

"People enter into second marriages thinking they are like first marriages. 'All I have to learn to do is, you know, take my wife out on dates and spend more time with her and everything will be fine. Because I ignored my first wife, but this time I'll pay attention to her.' But there's a whole new formula here. A whole new avenue for the fiercest arguments, which wasn't present in the first marriage, and it's totally baffling to most of these couples. That's why first marriages last longer than second marriages. And why second marriages have much higher divorce rates than the first."

WHERE TO GO FOR HELP

If you're about to blend a family, or already are in the midst of it, you need some good, qualified help. Some options include individual or family therapy. McManus and Dr. Adler both recommend stepfamily support groups. Peer support groups exist for both parents and children.

The best, says McManus, are those that are facilitated by couples who have already "been there, done that" successfully. "Who have created a genuine blended family," he says. "Those people have learned tricks that can be helpful to those people who are new to it," he says. The next best suggestion is to read *Willing to Try Again: Steps toward Blending a Family* by Dick Dunn.

How does a support group work? Remember the scenario McManus offered in which the woman described the problems she was experiencing with her stepdaughter? McManus reports that the couple went to a stepfamily support group where the woman told of how her daughter waits for her to get into the shower to take her own so that they fight for hot water.

"Group members said, 'Sounds normal to us,' " says McManus.

"Normal? It sounds abnormal," says McManus. "But it is normal to stepfamilies. And that in itself was reassuring to hear. Then she said, 'Well what do you do about this?' And one guy said, 'Well, I find different ways to build up

Help Is a Phone Call Away

These two organizations offer phone counseling and can refer you to organizations and counselors near you.

Stepfamily Association of America, 215 Centennial Mall South, Suite 212, Lincoln, NE 68508. Phone: (402) 477-7837 or (800) 735-0329.

Stepfamily Foundation, 333 West End Avenue, New York, NY 10023. Phone: (212) 877-3244. Visit their Web site at http://www.stepfamily.org.

respect for my wife in the eyes of my children. So if my kid asks me if he can spend the night somewhere, I say, 'Wait a minute, let me ask Sue.' Then I come back and say, 'Sue thinks it's a great idea.'

"See, you would not think of that if you had not lived in the situation. There is experiential wisdom in the group that we are deprived of because of the glass walls that we place around each of us as couples, the sense that we can go it alone. And men are particularly vulnerable to this. Because it is in a man's character to want to do it alone, by himself, without asking any expert for advice. And if he tries to go to counseling, he gets frustrated and he sees this counselor as a rip-off artist who is making him come back for more $90 sessions." But there is "no pecuniary motive" in stepfamily support groups, says McManus. "They're only going to try to help you."

Don't be too big to ask for help.

CAREER CHANGES

As we peer into the *Men's Health* crystal ball, we must inform you that there is a very good chance that you are going to change jobs—and possibly in the near future.

Of course, you don't need a sex book to tell you that constant change is the way of the work world these days. That a single skill can no longer carry you through a career. That long-term loyalty between companies and their workers is all but dead. That more and more people are working temporary jobs, working from home, entrepreneuring. That suddenly, whether you are plumber, a lawyer, or salesclerk, your work is inextricably linked to a computer.

No. But you *do* need a sex book to tell you that all this career hell can have a big impact on your sex life. More than you realize.

Career upheaval and uncertainty can damage our sexual self-image and performance, says Daniel Beaver, a marriage and family therapist from Walnut Creek, California, and author of *Beyond the Marriage Fantasy*.

The problem, he says, is that we men still tie our sense of identity, worth, and manliness to our jobs. Then, when the job heads south—or overseas to a Third World country, we're likely to feel limp, beaten, maybe even castrated, says Beaver. From a sexual standpoint, this is not good. Our penis may respond in kind, he says.

Even those men who boldly set out on their own, establish their own business midlife, or retrain and turn to an entirely new career are likely to suffer some sexual difficulty as a result, says Wendy Fader, Ph.D., a licensed psychologist and certified sex therapist in private practice in Boca Raton,

Florida. The problem, she says, is the extreme amount of pressure that such efforts pose—the incredible hours one must put in to build a new career. Expending all your energy trying to make it in the business world can leave you just too tired to make it in the bedroom, she says. Her advice? Pace yourself. Schedule pleasant, quality, relaxation time for sex.

DEALING WITH CHANGING TIMES

Don't live in denial. All this workplace change is real, and it is a rare man who can sidestep it. Today we *must* prepare for, expect, and learn to handle midlife career changes, say the experts. We must do this for our financial, family, emotional, and sexual stability, says Beaver.

Just living under the threat of losing one's job—or the possibility of failing at a business you've started—is enough to throw men into depression, says Beaver. And depression kills sex.

"The pressure has a major impact on everything emotional, on sex, on intimacy," Beaver says. Self-esteem suffers.

The solution is found in understanding the problem, Beaver says. "The problem is putting all your identity into a job, then having it blown out," he says. "Then it is like, who are you? A lot of times men look for escapes in alcohol and in other women and stuff."

That, though, is not the healthy alternative.

The advice? "Work on building an identity around your work, if necessary, that is not tied to your job or your company," says Beaver. "That is, if I am an environmental engineer for Lex Luther Industries, I should build my image around being an environmental engineer, and not around Lex Luther Industries," says Beaver.

How to do that? Hobnob with others in your field. Join environmental engineering associations, write papers, attend conferences, network in those circles. Volunteer community services based on your expertise, not based on your association with your company.

Keep up with the latest changes and trends in your field. Keep your skills and education up-to-date, advises management consultant William N. Yeomans in his book *Seven Survival Skills for a Reengineered World*.

Also, Yeomans says, "Work on building strong friendships." Strong friendships give us a healthy sense of self-worth that is not tied solely to our employment, he says.

FAMILY MATTERS

The family man today can't just come home and announce, "Great news! We're moving to California. Start packing." Chances are that our spouse works and contributes heavily to the household income. Her job, her house, her friends are all important to her. Particularly if she has built a career. Our kids are loyal to their school, their friends, their soccer team, their piano lessons, and so on. So, when career changes are imminent, we must consider

The Necessary Skills

What can you do to maximize your viability as a worker? Here are six simple but crucial steps, gleaned from professional career counselors.

- Stay abreast of trends.
- Plan on lifelong learning.
- Keep your skills brushed up.
- Change with the ever-changing technologies and needs in the workplace.
- Be ready for new challenges. Be flexible. Be creative.
- Communicate effectively.

the family. We must talk to everyone and consider everyone's needs and feelings, advise James C. Cabrera and Charles F. Albrecht Jr., co-authors of *The Lifetime Career Manager*.

Should we face a layoff or substantial cutback in income, we need to explain to the family, right off, what it means to the family, what the alternatives are, and how each person can help.

Here are some specific steps to take when a career crisis hits.

Plan the finances. Draw up a tentative, belt-tightening six-month budget, in consultation with your wife. Discuss it in detail with the whole family and enlist their cooperation. The kids may well think of ways to cut expenses and pitch in other ways. Best you all work as a team, suggests the 40-Plus Organization.

Plan your attack. Discuss in detail with your spouse all the job-hunting options and agree on a strategy. As we said, dual careers must be taken into consideration—is your wife's career flexible enough that it could move to another part of the country should you get an offer there? Or should you look only locally? If you are looking outside the area, let the kids know. If you've promised them you won't move until they graduate from high school, discuss this with them and see how strongly they feel about that. For family cohesion it might be best to take a lower-paying job locally for a couple years until the kids finish school and then seek the perfect job in another state, say career counselors Cabrera and Albrecht.

Keep the work habit going. Can you set up an "office" in your home to which you report to work each day and develop your job hunt and make contacts and do freelance (or contract) work if any is available? Or can you rent a desk in a friend's office? For many it is important that they maintain their work routines so that they don't slide into despondency and lose self-esteem. For all of us, it is important to maintain contact with professionals in our field—they'll help us find work if they see us regularly and know our strengths and know what we're seeking.

Stay in contact. Keep up friendships and socializing Just don't spend extravagant amounts on socializing—keep it within the budget. You need your friends and contacts, says the 40-Plus Organization. Don't withdraw.

Tend to your appearance. Keep fit, trim. Dress neatly. Stand tall. Keep your hair cut neatly. These all add to your self-esteem as well as make you more salable. As Beaver said, maintaining your self-esteem is key to sustaining strong, healthy sexuality through the challenge of career upheaval.

TRAVEL AND SEX

From "On the Road Again" to "Travelin' Man," pop music has no shortage of odes to the road, tales of mysterious strangers, laments to the lonesome despair of the working man whose job takes him from city to city, hotel to hotel. If you're a traveling man, you know the words, you know the music. Of course, Ricky Nelson's hit recording, "Travelin' Man," was upbeat. In every port, he owned the heart "of at least one lovely girl." That, though, is not the case with most traveling men, say psychological counselors.

Most traveling men who are single have trouble starting romantic relationships. Women meet these guys and see only a one- or two-night stand, says Wendy Fader, Ph.D., a licensed psychologist and certified sex therapist in private practice in Boca Raton, Florida. Sometimes that's enough for both parties. But women eager for one- or two-night stands are rarely interested in more than that, she says. And when a traveling man does succeed in starting a romance, they are tough to keep going because the man isn't around to stoke the fires, Dr. Fader says.

Then there's the married man—or the man in a serious relationship. The traveling life creates terrific strain and resentment on the domestic front, says Dr. Fader.

The luckier travelers, agrees Dr. Fader, are those who traverse a regular weekly circuit, always jetting between just a few set destinations. The consistency of that kind of arrangement gives them the opportunity to form support networks and lasting relationships in each destination. But even that can be a strain, she acknowledges. Particularly if they are married and have a mistress or mistresses on the road.

"Mistresses are very common with men who make the same circuit," she says. "And very easy to maintain. Logistically, it's easy; emotionally, it's not. Because generally, if it's a relationship of long standing, there's a lot of emotional attachment. Very much it's like having two different families or two different wives.

"It's easy to maintain the secrecy, and that's an allure to all of this also. It's very exciting," Dr. Fader adds. "Very often if the wife finds him out and kicks him out, the other relationship goes down the tubes, too, because it's no longer taboo. And now it's 100 percent of the time, and a lot of people can't handle those kinds of relationships. Too intense. They crave the variety."

IT'S A FAMILY MATTER

A road-hardy man bent on maintaining his marriage (or a living-together relationship) faces a different set of challenges in many ways from the living-alone-single man on the road. Let's look at the attached man's plight first.

We use the term *road-hardy* loosely. You might be a Navy man. You might be a merchant marine. You might work oil rigs off the shore of Santa Barbara—or Houston. You might be an airline pilot. You might be a sheepherder, sleeping in the fields with your flock. You might rarely see a road and still be away from home most of the time for days, weeks, months on end. If so, and if you're married, this is for you, bud.

You think *you* get lonely. What about the little lady back home?

"Women get pretty horny, too," says Dr. Fader. So the couple, in their anticipation, in their fantasy, in their visions, in their longings, imagine a warm, wild, wonderful, passionate homecoming, says Dr. Fader. But often it doesn't happen, she says. Because they're strangers in a way. "They have to get to know each other again."

A man can't just show up and pop into a chauvinist, white-knight, head-of-the-household role if he has left the wife to care for things on the home front for months or weeks or even several days a week every week. "The woman has had to handle everything on her own in his absence, and a lot of that will get played out in the bedroom," says Dr. Fader. To avoid facing resentment, the man needs to recognize all the responsibility the woman has taken on and respect it. Listen to her discuss and bring him up to date on matters she is dealing with, says Dr. Fader. Don't start second-guessing or berating her decisions or overruling her if you want her to welcome you warmly into her arms and between the sheets, says Dr. Fader.

Other disappointments can dampen the homecoming fantasy, says Dr. Fader. Perhaps the man is tired from traveling, jet-lagged, bummed by a business deal that just fell through, sick. Maybe the wife is frazzled from domestic emergencies. Or her job has her down, too. Remember that warm, lonesome goodbye hug? That was then. This is now. Rarely can you pick up where you left off, says Dr. Fader. Then there's the nasty stuff they show films about in the military.

Dr. Fader has treated wives of sea captains and wives of Navy men. Yes, she says, boys will be boys. "The men are out to sea and overseas for anywhere from four to six months at a time, then home four to six months at a time," she says. "The problem is that a lot of times, the guys end up going to prostitutes overseas. Then they come back and give the wife an STD (sexually transmitted disease), and it all blows up in their faces." How's that for a home-coming surprise? Or just as bad: catching an STD from your wife.

Here's some advice specifically for traveling men maintaining marriages or similar relationships.

Be handy. "What these men have to do if they are committed to a monogamous relationship is learn to masturbate in a way that is going to ful-fill them on a regular basis. Otherwise, they are going to get themselves and their partners into a lot of trouble," says Dr. Fader. There's some basic, hands-on, do-it-yourself advice.

Go online. The best thing for men to do, if they travel a lot and have computers, is have e-mail sex with their spouse. That's something a lot of couples do and enjoy," says Dr. Fader.

Talk, talk, talk. Budget for plenty of long-distance calls and call home, lovingly, regularly. Keep in touch. Make sure that your wife (or life partner) knows your basic itinerary and how to reach you in an emergency, or just to chat, says Dr. Fader. Maintain a feeling of connectedness even when distance separates you. Be accessible.

In addition, much of the advice Dr. Fader gives single men, applies to the committed man as well.

THE SINGLE MAN

You think holding together a marriage while living on the road is hard, try living on the road and being single, says Dr. Fader. The road life may have a certain romantic aura, but most perpetual travelers don't find much ro-mance in reality, she says. The myth of the traveling man leaving behind a string of broken hearts may hold a wee bit of truth for rock musicians, but it's fiction for the rest of us.

"Basically, if you're a healthy man or healthy woman, you're going to have physical and emotional needs for intimate contact. And to suppress them is a problem. It's a problem because there aren't such great solutions," says Dr. Fader.

Many men—and women—give up the road life because of the loneli-ness, the difficulty in establishing or maintaining meaningful relationships, the forced separation, the difficulty of planting roots, Dr. Fader says. "That's why so many people do it for only a short period of time and then say, 'I can't do this anymore,' and stop," she says.

But you want to make it work. You don't want to give up. Not yet. So here are some things that help.

Stay in contact. Keep in touch with friends you do have—wherever they are in the world. Use the phone, use e-mail, send notes and postcards, visit when you're near, says Dr. Fader.

Get a life. "Keep yourself busy when you're away, and as distracted as possible," says Dr. Fader. One way is to visit gyms, sports fields, or basketball courts and work your way into games, she says. Find sports partners among people you regularly see in various cities, and schedule games with them when you're in town, she says.

"Any kind of regular exercise program is helpful," Dr. Fader says. Take up activities that work off energy and frustration, make you feel better, improve your sense of esteem. These are good, helpful diversions for the traveling man, she says.

Get back often. Those who are wealthy should fly home often and fly their girlfriends or partners to where they are, says Dr. Fader. That's one of the luxuries of wealth well worth enjoying, she says.

Partner smartly. Ultimately, if you are contemplating marriage—or re-marriage—you might seek a woman who also is intensely career-oriented and whose career keeps her on the road a fair amount. She is likely to be more un-derstanding of separations, and to intensely value the time you can spend to-gether, says Frederic Hudson, Ph.D., president of the Hudson Institute in Santa Barbara, California, and author of *The Adult Years* and other books.

In a situation like that, adds Dr. Fader, you may be able to arrange work in the same cities at the same times occasionally and meet for conjugal visits and adventure on the road.

TEENAGE KIDS

Teenagers know what sex is all about. They know what you and Mama Bear are doing in the next room. Maybe they're cool with it. Maybe they're not. How do you handle this one?

When they were still young and naive, you just needed to tell them that you and she-bear were taking a nap and needed some privacy. So you locked the door.

Continue to lock the door when you want privacy so that you have no unannounced visits to the bedroom, says Daniel Beaver, a marriage and fam-ily therapist from Walnut Creek, California, and author of *Beyond the Marriage Fantasy* and *More Than Just Sex*. "This boundary," says Beaver, "is really more psychological. What is going on in their parents' bedroom is none of their business, and they can guess and joke all they want. The message is that we the parents want to be alone. That's all they need to know."

Hopefully, says Beaver, you and your spouse have established a "couple identity" long before the kids reached teenhood. If so, the kids are used to you and your spouse being alone together. If so, "the parents go out together to dinner or to a movie or go away together for the weekend. So when the cou-ple goes to their bedroom together, it's just part of the whole package," he says.

"The mistake so many couples make is that they always think 'family, family, family' and no couple time. So when the couple is alone together, it's a big deal," Beaver observes.

Still, he acknowledges, "I know it's difficult to be lovers in a house of teens and be able to relax and have a great sexual experience. That's why I make it an important imperative to get my wife out of the house and spend the night with her at a hotel or bed and breakfast. How far away is not important, but get out of the house from time to time, with the kids being supervised, if necessary."

There's actually less chance of getting surprised when a couple's kids are teens than when they are younger, says Wendy Fader, Ph.D., a licensed psychologist and certified sex therapist in private practice in Boca Raton, Florida.

"Teens," Dr. Fader says, "certainly understand closed doors better. Teenagers themselves basically close their doors and don't come out too much." That, Dr. Fader says, gives parents more opportunity, more time to themselves. Then the kids begin to drive. They're out of the house a lot, and that, too, provides more opportunity for parental privacy, she says.

Dr. Fader agrees with Beaver that parents need not wait until the kids are asleep to have sex. But, she says, parents need to be respectful. "I wouldn't expect my teenage son to have loud sex in the next room while I was home. The same standard should apply for me," she says.

THE TOUGH QUESTIONS

And what about the questions teens ask? What if they want to know the intimate details of your sex life or of your past?

"It's all very subjective; there's no black and white," says Beaver.

"It's very individual and really depends upon the kind of relationship you've had already with your kids," adds Dr. Fader. "I'm basically all for honesty. But you can couch the honesty a little bit differently. In the sense of 'I did this, and it was a mistake.' Or 'I did this, but now looking back on it I would have been better off if I had waited.' Or 'I did this, but things were different then.'

"Most parents with teens now were teenagers themselves in the 1960s and 1970s, and sexually, things were a lot different then," says Dr. Fader. "So most of the parents I know are not at all comfortable about talking about what they did. Because there was a lot more freedom then and there wasn't that much risk. So I think that's somewhat of a turnaround. A lot of parents feel that it is the ultimate in hypocrisy if I did one thing and tell you to do another thing."

Do be careful what you say, says Dr. Fader. "If you have a teenager who is really impulsive, they are going to jump on anything you say you have done and might act out on it. If you have a more thoughtful or more mature kid, they'd be able to digest that. I really think you have to tailor what you have to say to who is getting the message. There is a vast difference between a 13-year-old hearing this and a 17-year-old hearing this. Those few years of maturity really make a big difference."

But what if they ask really intimate questions about your sex life?

"I'd wonder where they were coming from with these kinds of questions," says Beaver. He would only answer when he felt that it was appropriate to do so, he says.

Yes, says Dr. Fader, "What if all of a sudden they say, 'Well when was the first time Mom gave you a blow job?' Maybe you never want to talk to your kids about that. Maybe you never want to talk to your kids about the very private kinds of things. And everyone's definition of private is different. For some parents, any sort of talk about sex is private. Basically, people have to gauge their own comfort level. The worst thing they can do is talk about something they are very uncomfortable with because the kids will wonder why there is so much anxiety associated with sex."

What if they ask you about an affair you've had?

No, says Shirley Zussman, Ed.D., a certified sex and marital therapist in private practice in New York City. They don't need the details. The only reason you should discuss an affair with your teenage children would be if they were already aware of it, by hearing it from your spouse, overhearing gossip, or finding out about it themselves. In that case, says Dr. Zussman, the discussion should involve both parents and needs to focus not on the details of the affair but on your children's reaction to it, such as their fears about divorce. Often, she adds, it is the deception surrounding the affair rather than the affair itself that is so disturbing to children

TEACHING CHILDREN ABOUT SEX

Want to talk major responsibility? This is it. How we communicate about sex and sexuality to our kids, to a great extent, shapes their attitudes about sex and sexuality—for better, for worse, for life.

We're not talking about stuttering and stammering and blushing your way through the big talk come the 12th birthday. We're talking full-time job here. From the time children first can see and hear and think till they graduate from teenhood, they are forming impressions about sex and sexuality. Because we *are* sexual creatures, we are communicating information about sex and sexuality both verbally and nonverbally all through those years. If we can communicate open, honest, accurate information comfortably and directly, day in and day out, we are giving our kids an immensely positive lifetime gift.

So says psychologist Harris Teller, Ph.D., assistant professor of special programs at National University in San Diego. So says adolescent medicine specialist Donald E. Greydanus, M.D., at Michigan State University/Kalamazoo Center for Medical Studies and editor of the book *Caring For Your Adolescent*. So say the Sexuality Information and Education Council of the United States (SIECUS) and the National Commission on Adolescent Sexual Health.

Now, we know this is all easier said than done. But here are some ideas. The National Commission on Adolescent Sexual Health identified parental behaviors that seem to contribute to sexually healthy adolescent children. Among the ideal behaviors outlined by the commission are these that follow. The parents:

- Demonstrate that they value, respect, accept, and trust their children
- Exhibit sexually healthy attitudes in their own relationships
- Avoid a punitive stance about sexuality
- Are knowledgeable about sexuality
- Discuss sexuality with their kids
- Make an effort to understand their children's points of view
- Ask questions about the adolescent's friends and romantic partners
- Stay involved, actively, in their kids' lives
- Help their kids understand and develop values
- Establish and maintain limits for activities outside school, including dating
- Create and maintain a supportive and safe environment for their kids
- Help their kids plan for the future
- Help kids assess health care options

That's a lot to teach. But remember, you have nearly two decades to cover it. And it should be taught bit by bit, day in and day out, by example as much by discussion. So where do you start? Here is some advice for breaking the ice and opening up sexual communication with your kids.

Know what you're talking about. Step one is to be informed. Read up-to-date, reliable literature about adolescent sex and sexuality. Know what physical changes your child will go through. Know how to answer questions that come out of the blue. And do your best to answer them calmly, encouragingly—that is, so that the kids feel that you're glad they asked. Answer authoritatively so that they know they've gotten good, straight information. If you don't know an answer, admit it and promise to find some good information about it, and then do.

Parental sex education classes are available in some communities, notes the report of the National Commission on Adolescent Sexual Health, *Facing Facts: Sexual Health for America's Adolescents*. School counselors, sex education teachers, pediatricians, clergy, and others might be able to steer you to such classes, says Dr. Greydanus.

Start teaching when they're infants. As your child sees babies coming into the world, discovers physical differences between boys and girls, and so on, your role as educator is paramount, says the American Academy of Pediatrics. Readily, openly provide accurate information appropriate to the child's age, recommends the academy.

Read to your kids. Get some great books about sexuality, recommends Barry McCarthy, Ph.D., a psychologist in Washington, D.C., and co-author with his wife, Emily, of the book *Sexual Awareness* as well as other titles. And as your kids raise questions and as they cross into puberty, read them aloud with them and discuss them. Not all kids are into this, however, so don't force it.

Get comfortable talking about sex. Gerald F. Kein, certified clinical hypnotherapist, of the Omni Hypnosis Training Center in De Land, Florida, which trains doctors, counselors, and others in techniques of hypnotherapy, advises students to get comfortable with talking about sex. It's good advice for parents as well. One exercise Kein urges is to practice when

Read Some Good Books

Here is a reading list of authoritative and helpful books about adolescent sexuality recommended by the American Academy of Pediatrics and the Sexuality Information and Education Council of the United States. You might request these titles at your library.

- *It's Perfectly Normal: Growing Up, Changing Bodies, Sex and Sexual Health*, by Robie H. Harris (Candlewick Press, 1994)
- *What We Told Our Kids about Sex*, by Betsy and Michael Weisman (Harcourt Brace Jovanovich, 1987)
- *Let's Talk about...S-E-X*, by Sam Gitchel and Lorri Foster (Planned Parenthood of Central California, 1994)
- *500 Questions Kids Ask about Sex and Some of the Answers*, by Frances Younger (Charles C. Thomas Publisher, 1992)
- *Talking with Your Child about Sex: Questions and Answers for Children from Birth to Puberty*, by Mary S. Calderone and Eric W. Johnson (Ballantine, 1983)
- *The Family Book about Sexuality*, by Mary S. Calderone and James W. Ramey (Harper and Row, 1990)
- *Learning about Sex: The Contemporary Guide for Young Adults*, by Gary F. Kelly (Barron's, 1986)

This one is nominated for inclusion on this list of parental resources by those of us here at *Men's Health* Books.

- *Everybody's Doing It: How to Survive Your Teenager's Sex Life (and Help Them Survive It, Too)*, by Andrea Warren and Jay Wiedenkeller (Penguin Books, 1993)

you're alone in your house or office. Just start by saying the word "sex," he says. Say it to the lamp. Say it to the wall. Put it in sentences and say them out loud. And add other proper but explicit terms. Practice saying them daily until you're completely comfortable with them. Until you can say them naturally, comfortably, without hesitation, without strange emphasis, without embarrassment. That, he says, will go a long way toward helping you become comfortable discussing sex and using such terms with your kids—and others.

Talk casually about sexual issues. Ask your teen children if they know kids their age who are engaging in sexual activities. Ask them how they feel about that. But don't probe deeply or directly into their personal experiences, advises Dr. Greydanus. Everybody, including your kids, deserves some privacy, he says.

Accept that sex is natural. Natural and fun. Communicate that to your kids. Explain that it also carries lots of emotion and responsibility. Talk about unwanted pregnancy and prevention. Talk about unwanted sexually transmitted diseases (STDs) and protection. Offer to take your child to a doctor who can answer more questions and provide and explain birth control devices and condoms. Explain why you feel kids should not rush into partner sex, advises Robert Selverstone, Ph.D., a psychologist in private practice in Westport, Connecticut.

Keep religion out of it. Dr. Greydanus says that he is a member of a conservative church and admits that he sometimes gets into trouble with his church brethren for saying that. But, he says, kids who are told that God wants them to "maintain purity" and behave a certain way sexually often come to him confused and troubled. A problem with bringing God's desires into the equation is that different people seem to hear God saying different things, he notes. That confuses adults as well as kids. Is that really what we want to do? Further, Dr. Greydanus says, a late 1980s study of religiously oriented, abstinence-based sex education found that it does tend to delay the onset of teen coital activity—but only by a few months at best. That's all.

Other surveys show that kids given sexual instruction focused primarily on abstaining tend to be just as sexually active as those who are not, reports SIECUS. What's important, says Dr. Greydanus, is that the kids know how to protect themselves and that the parents understand that we all are sexual creatures. If we need to bring God into it, he says, understand that God created us with strong, natural sex drives. The sex drive tends to be strongest when we're just coming of age.

A positive approach toward abstinence education is found in this statement from the findings of the National Commission on Adolescent Sexual Health: "Society should encourage adolescents to delay sexual behaviors until they are ready physically, cognitively, and emotionally for mature sexual relationships and their consequences. This support should include education

What to Tell Kids at What Age

This advice is from Félix E. Gardón, outreach coordinator for the Sexuality Information and Education Council of the United States (SIECUS). Kids look to their parents for attitudes and accurate information about sex and sexuality at all ages. These guidelines suggest what to expect and what is appropriate at various ages.

• *Birth to 2 years old:* Kids are watching you and soaking in signals from birth about how to trust and relate to others. The toddler years are a time of discovery. Teach your children the proper names for all their body parts: knee, penis, elbow, and so on. How you hold them, look at them, and talk to them communicates values. They also are watching the girls, boys, and men and women in their lives relate and are learning from this.

• *3 to 4 years old:* Here we teach kids about washing their hands, bathing, brushing their teeth, eating wholesome foods. They also are quite likely to surprise you with sexually specific questions—like why Mary doesn't have a penis; why Daddy doesn't have large breasts. The best thing to do, according to SIECUS, is maintain a home environment where they are free to ask questions about their health, body, and sexuality—and get serious, accurate answers. This tells them that sexuality is an open topic in your home and with you. This tells them that they are welcome to come to you with their questions.

• *5 to 8 years old:* Kids in this age range are curious about birth, death, families, diseases, health, relationships. From TV and friends, they may hear about sexually transmitted diseases and HIV/AIDS. They may have fears about sex. They are ready to hear about your feelings about some of these matters.

about intimacy; sexual limit setting; resisting social, media, peer, and partner pressure; benefits of abstinence from intercourse; and pregnancy and STD prevention."

Don't try to scare kids out of sex. Don't punish them for sexual thoughts, talk, activities. Don't tell them that they'll catch syphilis and their penises will rot, dry up, and fall off—that you saw it happen to an Army buddy. Do discuss what is appropriate in various social settings. And do encourage your kids to talk about how they feel or see these things, says Dr. Greydanus.

Expect that your kid will argue at times. They'll blow up. They may tell you you're completely out of touch with reality. That you're a social dinosaur. That's okay, say doctors at the American Academy of Pediatrics. It means that they heard and are thinking about what you had to say. It means that there is two-way communication. It means that your child is mulling over values and will develop some. On his own. Of his own.

They are ready to hear about how a woman gets pregnant, how a fetus develops in a woman's body, why men don't get pregnant.

- *9 to 12 years old:* Puberty hits in these years, usually. Kids are terribly concerned about what is normal, how they look to others, what is happening to their bodies. They are coming alive sexually. It is crucial, says Gardón, that you understand these influences in their lives and give attention to their needs. Strong social pressures and sexual pressures begin in this period. You want to keep the lines of communication open. Encourage your child to ask questions, to come to you with worries and problems. Communicate that intercourse has consequences and is not appropriate for young people. Teach about preventing pregnancy and disease. Tell them about how sexually transmitted infections and HIV are passed. Tell them about how to use condoms and other protective methods. Explain your values and encourage them to talk about what they're feeling and hearing about these things. Let them know that they can always come to you.

- *13 to 19 years old:* It is okay for you to tell your kids that you feel they should wait until they are adults to become sexually active. To let them know that abstinence is the only sure way to avoid pregnancy and sexually transmitted infections. Be clear about your values. But also understand that teens frequently do not wait until they are adults to become sexually involved—regardless of parental values and desires. About 50 percent of U.S. boys and slightly less than 50 percent of girls have had intercourse by their 17th birthday, according to the *Sex in America* survey. So, advises SIECUS, it is important that your kids know how to protect themselves from pregnancy and disease.

Talk about peer pressure and ways to resist it. Discuss the importance of thinking for oneself and forming bedrock values.

Don't brag. Dads, in particular, need to be thoughtful about what they say to their teenage sons, says Dr. McCarthy. Far too many men treat their sons like drinking buddies and brag about their own sexual prowess and their extramarital and premarital exploits, says Dr. McCarthy. Often fathers are jealous of a son's youth and opportunity and feel sexually competitive with him, he says. Restrain these urges and behaviors, he advises. Put yourself in the role of helpful, supportive, trustworthy parent and authoritative teacher instead, says Dr. McCarthy.

Talk about false impressions. TV and media paint a very false picture of sexuality for teens, and teens are immersed in 23-plus hours of television a week, says Dr. Greydanus. Parents need to help teens and kids distinguish between media and reality. A study of sex on television revealed that sex between unmarried partners is 24 times more common than between people

Is My Child Gay?

The most comprehensive sex survey ever done in America exploded the myth that 10 percent of us are homosexual. When University of Chicago social scientists asked men and women whether they considered themselves homosexual or bisexual, 2.8 percent of men and 1.4 percent of women said yes. But, interestingly, when the researchers asked if the respondents had ever engaged in homosexual sex since puberty, 9 percent of men had. About 4 percent of women said that they had sex with another woman after the age of 18.

These findings, reported in the book *Sex in America*, indicate that most male homosexual experimentation takes place during the puberty years. While 9 percent of men report having had homosexual sex since puberty, only about 5 percent say they have engaged in homosexuality since age 18 and only about 5 percent say they have in the past five years. The figures for women are lower; generally, women are not as likely to have their homosexual experiences in adolescence and, in fact, are usually 18 or older when they have their first same-sex encounter.

The point is that a certain percentage of the population is gay and that the greatest amount of experimentation with sexual orientation takes place before

who are married, says Dr. Greydanus. That's not the way it is in the real world. Tell them that in the biggest survey ever done, 86 percent of married people said they had sex at least a few times a month, compared with only 48 percent for single men and women not in a steady relationship.

ARE YOUR KIDS SEXUALLY HEALTHY?

An adolescent's sexual health is a complicated matter. It's not just how they feel about themselves sexually. Or how they feel about others sexually. It's much more involved than that, according to the National Commission on Adolescent Sexual Health.

The commission, funded by grants from the Ford Foundation, Henry J. Kaiser Family Foundation, and the U.S. Public Health Service, assembled an impressive panel of medical doctors, psychologists, and sex educators to explore issues of adolescent sexual health and make recommendations to policy makers. The commission's findings were issued in 1995 and endorsed by 48 national organizations, including the American Medical Association, National Association of School Psychologists, SIECUS, and the YWCA of America.

The commission identified the precise characteristics of a sexually healthy adolescent. We're going to repeat those findings here for your consideration. An adolescent's sexual health revolves around the following factors, according to the commission.

age 18 for men. Such experimentation does not necessarily denote a lifetime orientation.

Most kids who determine that they are homosexual will not identify themselves that way until their late teen years. They may realize, in retrospect, that they felt "different" since childhood. But gay males only tend to begin to believe that they are, in fact, homosexual at an average age of 17, reports the National Commission on Adolescent Sexual Health. For women, it's 18. And they generally do not share this realization with others until adulthood.

When a child announces that he or she is homosexual—comes out of the closet—parents often are devastated and wonder if they somehow are to blame, notes adolescent medicine specialist Donald E. Greydanus, M.D., at Michigan State University/Kalamazoo Center for Medical Studies and editor of the book *Caring For Your Adolescent*. They may be tempted to reject the child. That is not what they should do, he says. Sure, they may need some time to absorb and accept the news, but they need to realize that neither they, nor their child chose this, he says. And they need to realize that the child is probably having an extremely hard time coming to terms with his sexuality and needs his parents' love and support.

- Self-esteem and self-responsibility
- Relationships with parents and family members
- Relationships with peers
- Behaviors with romantic partners

In each of those areas, the commission identified specific behaviors that denote healthy sexuality. We'll look at some of them. (For the complete 32-page report, *Facing Facts: Sexual Health for America's Adolescents*, write SIECUS, 130 West 42nd Street, Suite 350, New York, NY 10036, Attention: Publications Department. The price at this writing is $12.95. Some SIECUS publications and fact sheets are available free, online, at its Web site http://www.siecus.org.)

Self-awareness and self-responsibility. According to the commission, a sexually healthy adolescent:

- Is comfortable with his/her body
- Understands the changes of puberty and accepts them as normal
- Takes responsibility for his/her behavior
- Can distinguish personal needs/desires from those of peer groups
- Recognizes self-destructive behaviors and seeks help with them when necessary
- Is able to enjoy feelings of sexuality without always acting upon them

- Understands his/her own sexual orientation and gender identity—and realizes they may, in fact, be different
- Is knowledgeable about sexuality issues and seeks more information when needed

Family relationships. The commission says that a sexually healthy adolescent, among other things:

- Communicates effectively about issues, including sexual matters
- Is able to balance family responsibilities and roles with an increasing need for independence
- Is respectful of adults and siblings
- Seeks understanding of parents' and family's values and considers them as he/she develops values of his/her own

Relating to peers. The commission's findings showed that a sexually healthy adolescent:

- Has both male and female friends and treats them appropriately and with respect
- Respects confidences and privacy
- Identifies and avoids exploitive relationships
- Relies on own beliefs/values when they conflict with peers'

Behavior with romantic partners. A sexually healthy adolescent:

- Can distinguish love from sexual attraction
- Views partners as having equal rights and responsibilities in matters of love and sex
- Is able to communicate desire to avoid sexual behavior and is able to accept partner's refusals. Can discuss and negotiate limits
- Makes sexual decisions in respectful consultation with partner
- Uses effective contraception and protection from STDs

These behaviors, for the most part, apply also to sexually healthy adults, says the commission. None of us demonstrate all of these behaviors all the time, the commission recognized. They "represent an ideal to strive toward," to use the commission's language.

TESTOSTERONE ISSUES

Throughout this book, you have read or will read references to testosterone. It's impossible to write a definitive book about sex and not discuss the hormone that gives guys' rockets the fuel they need for liftoff. Back in the chapter Understanding Sex Drive (page 122) we discussed how testosterone gets made and how it affects sex drive. In this chapter we'll explore in more detail this hormone that is the essence of maleness, and whether having too much or too little is a problem.

Testosterone is almost mythical in its purported powers. So combustible a chemical that it supposedly causes men to make love and war with equally reckless abandon. So full of macho mystique that Team Testosterone Sportswear was created. So reviled that in her book, *The Alchemy of Love and Lust*, sex therapist Theresa Crenshaw, M.D., describes the high-testosterone man as one who "might turn into a temperamental monster with high blood pressure, explosive tantrums, a wandering eye, and a hairless head."

Guys have a higher opinion of the hormone since they associate it primarily with sex drive. So they quite naturally wonder: Do I have enough Big T? And now that I'm in my forties, am I losing a lot of it?

HOW MUCH IS ENOUGH?

There is a wide range in the level deemed normal—between 275 and 850 nanograms of testosterone per deciliter of blood, says Adrian S. Dobs, M.D., associate professor and vice chair of the department of medicine clinical research at Johns Hopkins University School of Medicine in Baltimore. The mean level of a 40-year-old man is about 500.

The thing is that if you measured testosterone levels in a man first in the morning, then in the evening, the numbers could be vastly different. Like all hormones, testosterone levels in your bloodstream ebb and flow through the day, with the greatest levels usually being the morning. Similarly, testosterone levels change over the years. In your teens, testosterone seethes in your blood. At some point, though, testosterone levels begin to fall. "If you had to pick an age, I would probably have to say there begins to be a drop in the forties," says Dr. Dobs. "I think that might be the time that many men feel it but don't say anything about it."

A guy who wants to jump-start his sputtering sex drive may think a boost of testosterone is what he needs, but it's not that simple. He may not, in fact, have a low libido for other physiological or psychological reasons. This is one reason that you should see a doctor when sex drive plummets; never assume that flagging testosterone levels is the culprit. In fact, giving extra testosterone to a guy with a normal level of the hormone can be harmful. For men truly deficient in testosterone—and some estimates put the amount at one in five men over 50—replacement of the hormone usually results in increased sexual desire and functioning. Candidates for testosterone replacement therapy need to be tested first for prostate cancer, since the extra hormone can worsen the condition.

Those men who do get medically approved testosterone supplements typically do so by wearing a patch or getting injections. The patch costs about

When You're Low on Fuel

How do you know if you have an abnormally low testosterone level? Here are eight symptoms, courtesy of Adrian S. Dobs, M.D., associate professor and vice chair of the department of medicine clinical research at Johns Hopkins University School of Medicine in Baltimore.

1. Low sex drive
2. Few erections in the morning and erectile troubles during sex
3. Osteoporosis, thinning of the bones, repeated fractures
4. Depression
5. General fatigue
6. Loss of body hair—for example, you don't need to shave as often
7. Increase in the pitch of your voice
8. Putting on more fat around your hips

Of course, you may be suffering bone loss because of your strict diet of pork rinds. You might be depressed because your honey does more heavy petting with her cat than with you. And, hey, even Mike Tyson could sing soprano. The only way to know for sure if your testosterone is low is to have a doctor test it.

The testosterone you need to be concerned about is called bioavailable free testosterone. It's the stuff that has separated from binding proteins and flows freely in your blood. It usually is not necessary for you to get the more complicated and expensive test that measures free testosterone because a general test is a good barometer, says Dr. Dobs. The exceptions are men with borderline testosterone levels and those who have protein abnormalities, such as in AIDS.

$100 a month, says Dr. Dobs. Research also is being done on developing a testosterone cream.

"I don't think it will become as common as estrogen because not all men have a drop in testosterone, as opposed to all women," says Dr. Dobs. "But I think it will become quite common."

MALE MENOPAUSE

You've heard this term, but is there really such a thing? No. "It's just a myth," says Dr. Dobs. When a woman's capacity for childbearing ends, there is a drastic hormonal shutdown, he explains. It is a major physiological shift with significant implications for a woman's moods and functioning. Men face no such transition, however. Testosterone levels decline gradually and, in some men, imperceptibly.

Okay, so men don't have a true menopause like women do. But much is made of a midlife crisis experienced by many guys. The stereotype is that of an angst-ridden guy in his forties or fifties who reaches a crossroads in his life, dumps his wife, starts dating younger women, marries one of them, and starts a new family. What about that?

"We can't find any evidence of that," says Alan Booth, Ph.D., professor of sociology and human development at Pennsylvania State University in University Park. "We looked at large samples of data, and we can't find that the divorce rate is any higher at 40, 45, or 50 than it is at 35. As far as we're concerned, there is no special midlife crisis or menopause."

Of course, others dispute the point, saying that it is natural for men to undergo an intense personal reassessment at some point in midlife. We have detailed chapters elsewhere in this book on dealing with midlife challenges such as disillusionment and career distress. But the doctor's point is well taken: From a physiological standpoint, testosterone loss doesn't cause a male menopause. But just what are the benefits and drawbacks of testosterone?

THE GOOD

As we know, testosterone ignites a guy's sex drive. A woman's, too, although she has much less of it. Studies also have shown that testosterone helps maintain bone density, and testosterone replacement therapy can be used to treat osteoporosis. And the hormone helps us increase muscle mass.

"One thing that is clear is that testosterone provides an improved sense of well-being," says Dr. Dobs. Men who receive testosterone replacement feel better, she says.

Testosterone also pushes men to excel. Researchers have studied competitors in events ranging from wrestling to chess. "We find that in anticipation of competition, testosterone goes up, and in fact, those elevations of testosterone have a positive effect on performance," Dr. Booth says. "They tend to do better, they have more stamina, better visual acuity, and a lot of other things."

What happens next depends on whether you won or lost your match. "Individuals who win, their testosterone level goes even higher or stays at a high level," Dr. Booth says. "Those who lose, it drops off quickly. We think this has beneficial effects. Very often if you win, your position is going to be challenged quite soon after competition, so having that high testosterone level pays off in terms of subsequent competitions. Whereas if you lost, you don't need it. In fact, it's better if you're not still feeling competitive because, having lost, you may be injured or not in a position to be competing again."

Other research also suggests that testosterone-saturated men are more theatrical. "We found that trial lawyers were a little higher than the non-trial lawyers," says James M. Dabbs Jr., Ph.D., professor of social psychology at Georgia State University in Atlanta, who has been studying the effects of testosterone for years. "We also found that actors were higher in testosterone than others. Putting on a show is what it amounts to."

THE BAD

Another study conducted by Dr. Dabbs found that men with higher testosterone levels are more likely to be unemployed or working in lower-status occupations. "The differences are not large, but they are statistically significant," says Dr. Dabbs. He suggests that high-testosterone guys tend to be more unmanageable and have more difficulties in school, and hence are less educated.

Dr. Booth also conducted a study that showed that men with high testosterone levels were less likely to marry and more likely to physically abuse their wives if they did marry.

Dr. Booth found no magic threshold at which men with testosterone at a certain level were more likely to be bachelors or brutes. "It's a very linear relationship," he says. "A person who is below average in testosterone is less abusive and more likely to marry than a guy who is average."

This is not to say that women ought to start demanding to see guys' testosterone test results before marrying them. "One has to take into account that there are many men with higher levels of testosterone that have wonderful marriages and never commit a criminal act in their life and are successful," Dr. Booth says. "There is some segment of the population where you find that negative relationship. We don't know exactly what explains it yet."

Dr. Dobs doesn't think that there is any connection. In other studies, men have been given high doses of testosterone, she says, and they did not turn into wild-eyed bar bouncers—or even trial lawyers.

"Men do sense something with a high level of testosterone," says Dr. Dobs. "They can feel an anxiety or an irritability. It's very difficult to measure, though. We don't have the good tools to look at aggression or quickness to anger."

Testosterone Plus

It's doubtful that in the history of mankind a guy has ever complained of having too much testosterone. You don't hear of doctors prescribing testosterone-*reduction* therapy. But in case you're wondering, here are some signs that you might have too much T in your tank.

1. Acne
2. Baldness
3. Leanness
4. Restlessness
5. Difficulty maintaining relationships
6. High interest in sex (applies to most guys we know)

Testosterone combined with environmental factors probably makes us what we are, says Dr. Booth. The hormone may give us a predisposition to act in certain ways, but our environment can alter that script.

Testosterone also affects women. One study concluded that women with higher-than-normal testosterone levels were more likely to get into male-dominated careers. They also were less interested in having children and had fewer children.

"Whether this translates into poor motherhood or not, we don't know," Dr. Booth admits. "We're involved in a study now that will tell us more about that."

THE UGLY

Violent criminals often have more testosterone than their nonviolent colleagues, Dr. Dabbs concluded in another study. High-testosterone guys aren't necessarily violent, he cautions. "I think that if you're a criminal, you're a little more likely to trend toward that kind of crime," he says.

Dr. Dobs is skeptical, however. She says that research linking high testosterone with criminal behavior fails to take into account socioeconomic and education factors.

Some women, of course, readily believe that testosterone is at the root of society's ills. "They look at two men and they have no idea what the testosterone difference is, and they conclude the worse one is higher in testosterone," says Dr. Dabbs. "That's pretty much nonsense.

"Would you like men to have no testosterone? They'd probably all be depressed. They'd never amount to anything. Women want resources, so they want resourceful men. That probably means men who can outdo other men in the mating game."

BACK PAIN AND SEX

Until you experience it, you'll never understand the helplessness, the pain, the disability of your back giving out on you. The sad news is that you likely will experience it. Eight out of 10 people do at some time in their lives, says Lauren Andrew Hebert, a physical therapist who wrote the book *Sex and Back Pain* as well as numerous patient education manuals on back problems and tendinitis. The book, accompanying video, and physical therapists' instruction manual are used nationwide by back doctors and pain clinics, the publisher says. They teach people suffering from back injuries how to maintain a sex life.

If every movement, every swivel of the hips, is excruciating, imagine what attempting sex might feel like—if you don't have professional help and instruction. Most people with chronic back problems just give it up. That puts a strain on their relationship, notes Hebert.

What follows is some of Hebert's best advice on enjoying sex and sexual sensations, even with a painful, troublesome, unpredictable back. You may need to experiment a bit to find which works for you—or for your spouse, if she is the one who has the bad back. And Hebert emphasizes that you should talk to your doctor about the best positions for your particular situation.

Assume the basic position. The injured partner should lie on his or her back on a firm surface, legs resting on pillows (this alleviates pressure on the lower spine). Place a folded or rolled hand towel under the lower back to give it a comfortable arch. From this supported passive position, the other partner can carefully, gently engage in romantic and sexual play that does not involve any spinal movement—things like touch, oral sex, massage. The injured partner also can, within limits of the injury, participate as giver as well as receiver, says Hebert. The key is patience, Hebert says. And if the injured can stand a little motion, the uninjured partner can kneel atop the injured partner in a variety of intercourse positions.

Go slow. Merely the fear of pain can hinder orgasm and pleasure. The key to sex with an injured back is patience and gentleness. Move slowly, both during the sexual encounters and in the progression of activities from one encounter to the next. Find what is and is not comfortable.

Talk about it. "Your fear of hurting yourself and your spouse's fear of you hurting yourself are very disabling," says Hebert. The answer? "Communication. The couple must communicate about the issue. Sex is an issue that people usually don't talk about. If you don't talk about it, you can be doomed. And, of course, the loss of sex is going to feed into all kinds of other interactions between the couple. The feedback that I have received over the years is that the back problem led to communicating about the other issues, which led—once the back got better—to a sex life that was markedly improved from what it was before the back injury."

Be her missionary. If the woman has back pain, cautious, careful sex in the missionary position—with a folded towel supporting the arch of her back, may work well, says Hebert.

On the other hand, a man with back pain may not be able to tolerate the traditional missionary position. But by placing one or two pillows under the woman's back and bottom, she may be raised enough that the man can enter her comfortably while kneeling between her legs.

Hebert's books and video are available from IMPACC USA, One Washington Street, P.O. Box 1247, Greenville, ME 04441. You can call (800) 762-7720 for credit card orders and current pricing information, or visit the World Wide Web site at http://www.impaccusa.com.

The book is available in two versions. A 108-page bookstore version gives lots of information about overcoming back pain. A shorter version dealing primarily with sexual positions, sells for about half the price. The books and the companion video all are titled *Sex and Back Pain*.

LUBRICANTS

If you haven't had this experience before, you probably will. During lovemaking, you've become accustomed to the pleasures of Slip Sliding Away. But now you and your partner are suffering through Skin Tight. Instead of that wonderfully wet and warm feeling you both savor, it's as if your genitals are now coated with sandpaper. The expression "rough sex" suddenly takes on a whole new meaning.

Vaginal dryness often is an age-related problem, but not always. When women approach or reach menopause, many suffer from a loss of lubrication caused by a sharp decline in their estrogen levels. It has been estimated that as many as 60 percent of women over the age of 40 have some problem with dryness.

But younger women also may have difficulty lubricating. Twenty percent of women of all ages surveyed by the authors of *Sex in America* said this was a problem. Some women simply don't get all that wet even when they are sexually aroused. For others, the causes can include:

- Fluctuating hormone levels during menstrual cycles
- Recently giving birth or breastfeeding
- Side effects of medications
- Psychological reasons, such as stress, fear, and anxiety
- Marathon lovemaking sessions that cause chafing

There are a few things a woman can do to try and enhance lubrication, says Andrew Weil, M.D., author of *Eight Weeks to Optimum Health*. In his newsletter, *Dr. Andrew Weil's Self-Healing*, he recommends that she drink 1 to 2 quarts of water every day and avoid alcohol and caffeine. She can occasionally apply an estrogen cream after consulting with her doctor and take 500 milligrams twice a day of borage or evening primrose oil to moisturize tissues, writes Dr. Weil. And regular sexual activity, including masturbation, can also help.

Still, you and your partner may decide to use a lubricant to ensure that your lovemaking goes smoothly. The question is, which one?

BUYING A LUBRICANT

Unless you are getting a cream or jelly for masturbation, you should buy a water-based lubricant. Oil-based substances will destroy a latex condom, permitting your sperm to impregnate your partner and leaving you vulnerable to the HIV virus and other disease.

Here's another reason to avoid oil-based lubricants. They don't dissolve as quickly in a woman's vagina, leaving her more susceptible to vaginal infections.

Don't confuse water-based with water-soluble. "Water-soluble will sometimes have oil in it," advises Anne Semans, one of the owners of the adult store Good Vibrations in San Francisco and co-author of *The Good Vibrations Guide to Sex*.

The downside to water-based lubricants is that they dry up faster than the oil-based, but this can be remedied, Semans says. Simply keep a cup of water or a plant mister bedside. A spritz of water will have your willy slick again in no time.

You can find some water-based lubricants, such as K-Y jelly, in any drugstore. Or you may opt for something with a more exotic name like Probe or Astroglide. A number of people opt for the latter, Semans says.

"Astroglide was developed by a former NASA employee who was inspired by the fluid used to lubricate O rings on the space shuttle," Semans says. "Apparently, his wife was going through menopause and decided there should be a good lubricant out there. That's actually our most popular lube."

In deciding what kind of lubricant to buy, here are some things to consider.

• Texture. Some brands are stringier than others.
• Thickness. "Another thing to consider is whether you are going to use it anally or vaginally," Semans says. "If you want to use it anally, you want a thicker lube." One such product is Embrace, she says.
• Odor. While some lubricants claim to be odor-free, this isn't always so and the smell may not be pleasing to a couple.
• Taste. Some creams and jellies also claim to be tasteless but often have a slightly sweet or bitter taste. "For oral sex purposes, some people like to use flavored lubes," Semans says. "You can buy lubes now that come in flavors like cherry cinnamon."
• Price. You don't have to spend a lot of money to find the one best for you. "In our store we have a bunch of samples where people can actually put a little on their fingers and do the sticky finger test if they want to," says Semans. "A lot of times you can find very small bottles or even samples that you can try."

Of course, if you're looking for a lubricant solely for solo sex, you needn't concern yourself with whether the product is water-based. Oil-based standards like Vaseline are still okay, as are some of the newer products. "There's actually a really good oil-based lube out now called Men's Cream that is designed specifically for male masturbation, and it's just selling like hotcakes," Semans says.

MORE ON LUBE JOBS

Okay, now that you and your partner have decided to try a lubricant, you may wonder whose genitals to apply it to. "I think a lot of people tend to put it on penises or condoms, partly because condoms need lube to make them slippery," Semans says. "But a lot of other people put them on vaginally. It's really kind of a personal preference." Unless, of course, you and your partner have opted to use one of the vaginal moisturizers on the market such as Replens.

And while women around menopause tend to lose lubrication, it's younger men and women—"probably a pretty even split"—who buy most of the creams and jellies, Semans says. "A lot of people use them to enhance their regular sex play," she says. "With a little bit of lube you can keep the intercourse going longer. Anything you insert, whether it's a penis or a sex toy, is going to be more comfortable with lube."

10

THE FIFTIES

YOUR CHANGES

A man turns the big five-oh and often finds that it's not such a traumatic age after all. During this decade, he may have established himself in his career to the point where he can relax a little. The kids are out of the house, and he has more time for himself and his partner. Yeah, fifty can be nifty. Of course, our bodies go right on changing.

SEX-RELATED CHANGES

• Prostate cancer. Men are most likely to get this cancer after they turn 50, when it becomes the most common cancer among American men. About one man in eight will eventually contract prostate cancer. There are no symptoms in the early stages when it is treatable, which is why regular exams are important.

Prostate cancer is unpredictable—it can spread rapidly or take years to advance. At high risk are men who have had a father, brother, or son afflicted by the disease, men who eat a high-fat diet, and African-American men.

Surgery, hormone therapy, and radiation therapy are among the treatments for prostate cancer. All three can leave a man impotent. Some men who are still capable of having intercourse after transurethral prostate surgery experience retrograde ejaculation, in which their ejaculate goes back into their bladder rather than out the penis during orgasm. This is harmless, unless the guy is hoping to father more children.

• Less libido. As you age, your desire for sex continues to decline, steadily but not dramatically. By age 50, most men will notice slower, less intense sexual responses. It will take them longer to become erect. When they ejaculate, it may feel like they are expelling semen less forcefully. Orgasms may feel less intense. The refractory period also will increase to perhaps 24 hours. Whereas, when he was young, a guy would get an erection just thinking about a beautiful woman, now he needs direct stimulation of his penis by a woman.

Sometimes men in their fifties will get only partial erections, and the angle of the erection will be less acute than when they were younger because of changes in the elasticity of the connective tissue in the penis and in the blood flow to the organ, says Domeena Renshaw, M.D., director of Loyola Sex Therapy Clinic at Loyola University in Chicago and author of *Seven Weeks to Better Sex*.

Sex experts stress, however, that this is simply a normal part of aging. Sex hasn't become inferior or less enjoyable, they say. Just different.

OTHER CHANGES

• Colon cancer. This is the third-leading cancer killer among men after lung and prostate cancer. It is most likely to show up after age 50, which is when you should start getting annual fecal blood tests. Colon cancer is caused by bumps called polyps that sometimes develop into tumors in the colon. Regular medical exams can detect them before they become a problem.

• Stroke. Starting at age 55, the number of strokes suffered by men doubles each decade. Ischemic strokes make up 80 percent of all strokes. They occur when blood flow to a part of the brain is cut off, causing brain cells to die from lack of oxygen. A common cause is hardening and blockage of the arteries that transport blood to your head.

Hemorrhagic strokes account for the other 20 percent. These strokes are caused by bleeding from an artery on the surface of the brain or in the brain itself. These are deadlier than ischemic strokes, with nearly half of those stricken dying.

• Gray hair. You might have started going gray in your thirties or forties. Even earlier if you're like Steve Martin. But by age 50, 50 percent of men will be 50 percent gray. (We're guessing the other 50 percent are bald.) Gray hair is not a sign of any medical maladies. It's simply a genetic quirk. Now is the time to start repeating the gray-haired man's mantra: "It makes me look distinguished. It makes me look distinguished...."

• Excess hair. It's one of life's cruel little jokes: As we grow older and balder, agonizing over our naked noggins, we start growing hair where we don't want it. During their fifties, many men look in the mirror one day to see a face staring back with enough new nose and ear hair to weave a rug. Eyebrows have become bushier, too. Why does this happen? Genes again.

• Snoring. Even if you've never snored in your life, you might start in your fifties. The frequency and intensity of snoring gradually increase with age. By the end of their fifties, about 60 percent of men are snorting while they slumber.

These nocturnal rumblings occur when tissues in the upper airway that are taut during the day relax during sleep. As air passes through the narrowed opening, it causes the tissues to vibrate against each other. Snoring increases with age because we put on fat and the muscles and other tissues in the throat become less firm. Being overweight may mean you have an even greater likelihood of driving your bedmate into another room.

• Cholesterol. It finally levels off in this decade. Have a glazed donut and celebrate. But only one. For too many guys, you are leveling off at an unhealthily high level.

HER CHANGES

After puberty, most of a man's sexual and other physical changes occur slowly, almost imperceptibly. Not so, a woman. For many, their bodies will undergo a transformation during their fifties so dramatic that we guys can only guess what it feels like.

SEX-RELATED CHANGES

• Menopause. This is the event that causes the great physiological and psychological upheaval in women. For the average woman, menopause occurs at age 51. They stop producing an egg every month. Their periods end. Most significantly, their production of estrogen drops way off.

These changes can have a big impact on a woman's—and her partner's—sex life. The decrease in estrogen may cause the lining of her vagina to become thin, creating dryness, followed by burning, irritation, and painful intercourse. Some women report a loss of sexual desire, insomnia, hot flashes, depression, and other unpleasant symptoms. Hormone replacement therapy can help alleviate these symptoms, but it's a controversial topic.

Menopause isn't all bad news, however. For some women, sex is now better than ever. That's because they no longer have to worry about an unwanted pregnancy. By now, all the children may be out of the house, so there is more privacy. "There's a new freedom for many women that contributes to their sexual interest," says Shirley Zussman, Ed.D., a certified sex and marital therapist in New York City and editor of a newsletter, *Sex Over 40*.

"Hormones really are an important part of what happens to a person sexually, but you can't count out how emotions and feelings and conditioning affect the sexual functioning," adds Marilyn Fithian, Ph.D., a sex researcher and retired sex therapist in Long Beach, California. "Ninety-nine and nine-tenths percent of what happens sexually is in the head."

• Breast cancer. Most breast cancers occur in women over 50, and the odds keep going up with age. It's thought that estrogen, that most feminine of hormones, is linked to tumors in these most feminine mammary organs. This is the second most fatal cancer among women in the United States.

Among the women at highest risk are those who have never had a child or who gave birth for the first time after age 30. Also high at risk are women who started their first period early or began menopause late in life. Being on estrogen replacement or supplements also can raise the risk of breast cancer. So can having a mother or sister who contracted breast cancer.

Breast cancers often are discovered when a woman finds a new lump on a breast or as a result of a mammogram test. Treatment can include a mastectomy—removal of the cancerous breast—or a lumpectomy, which removes only the tissue around the lump, followed by radiation.

OTHER CHANGES

• Heart disease. Men tend to be plagued by heart disease considerably earlier in life than women. With the onset of menopause, women start to catch up. After age 75, they finally do. "When they begin to lose estrogen, they start being as susceptible as men," says Waneen Wyrick Spirduso, Ed.D., professor in the department of kinesiology and health education at the University of Texas in Austin and author of *Physical Dimensions of Aging.*

In addition to the loss of estrogen, several other factors can contribute to heart disease, which by far kills more women than any form of cancer. Among them are smoking, high blood pressure, a poor diet, being overweight, and a sedentary lifestyle.

• High blood pressure. After age 55, women actually are at higher risk than men to have high blood pressure, also called hypertension. Once again, hormonal changes are to blame. High blood pressure has no symptoms, so a woman may be unaware that she has a problem unless she gets it checked periodically. Left unchecked, it can make a woman more vulnerable to stroke, heart attack, and congestive heart failure. Preventive medicine includes exercising, reducing fat and salt in the diet, and seeing your doctor for blood pressure checks.

• Bone deterioration. Estrogen seems to protect not only a woman's heart but also her bones. After menopause, she may start losing bone density rapidly, says Dr. Spirduso. This is even more true if she gets little weight-bearing exercise—such as running, walking, and aerobic dancing—and has low levels of calcium and vitamin D in her diet. Women, in particular, can ill afford rapid bone loss. They start life with bones less dense than those of men, so they have less to lose.

• Gastric ulcers. If your woman gets a burning feeling or vague uneasiness in her stomach, perhaps accompanied by nausea, she may have a gastric ulcer. They strike women more than men, usually after the age of 50.

Gastric ulcers are often caused by over-the-counter medications such as aspirin and anti-inflammatory drugs. These drugs inhibit the production of mucus and acid-neutralizing agents, and aspirin also can weaken the stomach lining and cause bleeding. By the way, the other type of ulcers, duodenal ulcers, are more common in men and generally strike between ages 20 and 40. They often are caused by smoking.

• Excess hair. This is yet another change brought on by menopause in some women—new hair growth on the upper lip or elsewhere. It won't be so coarse that she can dress up as Charlie Chaplin without makeup, but it can be noticeable, especially if she is a brunette. This hirsute appearance may occur because when estrogen drops, the effects of the male hormone androgen, already present in a woman's body, become more pronounced. The androgen then is free to spur more hair growth.

RULES OF ENGAGEMENT

For certain people, after 50, litigation takes the place of sex," according to Gore Vidal. And sure, when you hit your fifties you have to make certain concessions to age. This chapter is aimed at ensuring that your briefs turn up in a bedroom, not a courtroom. If we use the word *court*, it will be only as a verb, not a noun.

WHERE TO FIND WOMEN

Figuring out where to meet women can be a daunting prospect in your fifties, especially if you're new to the single life. Older men who are unattached are enough of a novelty, however, that sometimes they are approached by women first, says psychologist Matti K. Gershenfeld, Ed.D., adjunct professor of psychoeducational processes at Temple University in Philadelphia and author of *How to Find Love, Sex, and Intimacy after 50*.

"They won't say, 'I want to date you.' They'll say, 'It's probably hard since your wife died. Why don't you come to my house for dinner on Thursday night?' It's a way to get to know him better. Older women are very aggressive that way."

Still, you can't count on women breaking down your door. Here, then, are some ways of meeting women in their fifties.

• Introductions by friends and relatives. There are more single women than men in their fifties, so chances are that friends and relatives will offer to introduce you to some of them or invite you to soirees where you can meet women.

• Weddings, anniversaries, bar mitzvahs—even funerals. All are places you may meet single women around your age, advises Dr. Gershenfeld.

• High school and college reunions. A great place to catch up with women you knew years ago, some of whom may be unattached.

• Organizations devoted to your interests. Whether it's politics, environmental causes, or playing tennis, you can probably find a club or organization of other people with the same interests.

• Conventions or professional affiliations. This is a good way to meet colleagues and peers in a social setting, says Dr. Gershenfeld. Plus, the people you meet will have similar interests and goals.

WHAT WOMEN WANT

A woman in her fifties has far different expectations from a man than a woman in, say, her twenties. Here are ways to interact smartly with the mature woman.

Socialize in crowds. Ask her to an event at which other people, especially singles, are present. If the woman you are interested in is newly widowed or divorced, the thought of dating again may strike terror in her heart. But at a company picnic or a party she can mingle with other people, too, and not feel that every move she makes is being scrutinized by you.

Be worldly. Impress her with the breadth of your life experiences. She has reached an age where she'll be relieved to learn that you have had a rich life and aren't still hankering to date a Dallas Cowboys cheerleader or join the merchant marine. As at any age, however, the old admonitions about not talking excessively about yourself apply.

Make it clear that you value her maturity. Quite a few women by this age fear losing a man to a much younger woman.

Be nice to her kids. Her children are probably adults now, but if you meet them, still work to make a good impression. One or more of her kids may be a close confidant, and odds are that she cares greatly as to what they think about the man in her life.

Don't dress like an old man. She's in her fifties, not her eighties. She's in no hurry for the rocking chair and doesn't want to be around a guy who looks like he is. Don't dress like a boy either unless you are one.

Initiating Sex

By the time you've reached your fifties, initiating sex brings with it a host of concerns that you probably didn't have when you were younger. Above all else, go slow. Sex still matters to most women in their fifties, but 4 out of 10 women between the ages of 55 and 59 had no sexual partner in the previous 12 months, the authors of *Sex in America* found.

The older woman wants "someone who will hold your hand, or put his arm around you, not big heavy stuff. Just gentle, caring nice stuff," says Dr. Gershenfeld. "What a woman likes is to be courted. He should definitely not try and get sexual right away." There are emotional and physical reasons why caution is advised.

• Emotional concerns. A woman who is recently widowed or divorced may be anxious about having sex again. She may wonder if she's adequate in bed, especially if she has been with only one man for the past 20 or 30 years. And she may fear rejection because her body is not as firm and taut as when she was younger. Men often have the same fears.

"One of the major differences in sex when you're young and sex when you're middle-age or older is that in the younger period there's a lot of chemistry and a lot of spontaneity—feeling more comfortable with your body," says Dr. Gershenfeld. "As you get older and you feel pouchy or 40 pounds overweight, the spontaneity is much more the embarrassment: How will I be, and what will she think of me?"

• Physical concerns. Even if the spirit is willing, there is the question of the flesh. After menopause, a lot of women have difficulty lubricating. Men don't get erections as reliably as when they were younger, nor are the erections as firm.

Couple that with a guy's nervousness and discomfort if he only recently has become single again, and you have the potential for the dreaded limp noodle syndrome. "He has to take his time," says Dr. Gershenfeld. "They ought to kiss or hold each other. Don't do the bedroom scene for a while."

When doing "the bedroom scene" does seem imminent, Dr. Gershenfeld advises a man to fess up if he's feeling anxious or hasn't been with another woman since Reagan was in the White House. "He needs to explain because if she's somebody who has been out there dating for the past five years, she will have more experience, even though they are both the same age," says Dr. Gershenfeld.

Similarly, if a man needs a bit of time to get aroused, he should say so, telling his partner what turns him on and encouraging her to share the same information about herself, says Dr. Gershenfeld. "It's about overcoming anxiety," she says. "If you get to know one another over time, how it goes at the beginning is nothing. It gets better over time."

APPROPRIATE EXPECTATIONS

What can you expect to get out of sex in your fifties? Pretty much what you got out of it in your forties—or thirties or twenties, for that matter. Studies keep showing that the best indicators of sexual activity in later years are your patterns of sexual activity in earlier years. You, the insatiable stud at 30 and 40, can therefore expect to be in service considerably more often than your take-it-or-leave-it contemporary.

But not quite as often as before. And not quite in the same way.

As pleasurable as before, yes. As satisfying, absolutely. As important, in all likelihood. As good, sure, and often better. But as frequent as before? Probably not. And with the same heart-pounding intensity? It's unlikely.

Therein lies the difference in sexual outlook between a 25-year-old and a 55-year-old. The middle-age warrior, assuming that he has adapted well to maturity, sees himself having a pleasurable, satisfying, and skillful sex life and therefore considers himself lucky to have been born on this still-green earth. The youngster can only say, "Less often? So middle age really does suck!"

Of course, if you're in your fifties, what matters is what you think, not what Junior thinks. And studies show that healthy older men—from their forties to their sixties—are sexually satisfied, thank you. The landmark 1994

Massachusetts Male Aging Study, for example, found steady satisfaction levels at all ages from 40 to 70 even while demonstrating that frequency of intercourse declines with age and episodes of erectile dysfunction increase.

THE TRUE PICTURE

What it comes down to is this: Your fifties is a period of adjustment for a lot of things, including sex. Just as your psyche now demands a more introspective, wisdom-driven attitude about life, so your body dictates a more contemplative, less urgent, smell-the-roses approach to sex. And what guys in their fifties find out is that this alternative way of going about things opens up new vistas of sexual pleasure.

"This is when you start getting into quality," says Judith Seifer, R.N., Ph.D., professor of sex research at the Institute for Advanced Study of Human Sexuality in San Francisco and past president of the American Association of Sex Educators, Counselors, and Therapists (AASECT). "You're not just accumulating notches on your belt anymore."

Should you expect some erection problems in your fifties? The Massachusetts study notes that about 50 percent of all men between 40 and 70 experience some trouble, with the incidences increasing with age. But we're not necessarily talking about permanent power failure here. What's happening is that men in their fifties begin to experience a vascular slowdown that translates to a sexual response slowdown. Combine that with any one of a myriad of factors such as illness, stress, medication—all of which are more likely to happen the older you are—and erectile dysfunction can result.

But men who play their cards right can translate all that into better sex. "When couples accept the fact that they have to go slower, they engage in more foreplay," says Marion Hart, M.D., a psychoanalyst and professor of psychiatry at the Cornell Medical Center in Westchester, New York. "If you have trouble with an erection, she can find ways to help you maintain it, and you can be more patient if she has trouble achieving an orgasm. All this enhances the sexual experience."

And it's always worth mentioning that the same blood flow issues that may delay erection also delay ejaculation. So you last longer. Few men (and fewer women) complain about that. You may feel less urgency to ejaculate each time, adds Shirley Zussman, Ed.D., a certified sex and marital therapist in New York City and editor of a newsletter, *Sex Over 40*. It's not a problem; it's a physiological fact.

There's another thing you can expect from your fifty-something sex life: freedom of choice. Women have always been able to put conditions on sex ("Not now, sugar, *ER* is coming on"), but guys are always supposed to be on full-stage alert, ready to rock and roll as soon as they're smiled at by something female. That comes to a blissful end by your fifties, and well-adjusted middle-age men see that as the liberation it is. You haven't lost interest in sex; you're simply putting some reasonable conditions on when and where.

"The breeze can blow and a man of 20 is erect and ready to go; he has no choice in the matter," says Leonard Felder, Ph.D., a Los Angeles psychologist and author of *The Ten Challenges.* "By the time you're in your fifties, you're able to impose conditions. And if they're not right, then you're simply not in the mood. And that's how it ought to be. You're just exercising your freedom of choice."

HELPING YOU ALONG

Let's tote up the score. On one side: possible occasional erectile dysfunction, slower arousal and probably not quite as much sex as before. On the other: enough sex to satisfy, slower sex, longer-lasting sex, more cooperative sex, more quality-conscious sex, new sexual exploration, and sex when you want it rather that when some Darwinian imperative demands it.

Those are odds you can take. And you can stack them even more in your favor without much effort. Here's how.

Ban the heavy booze. If you've been drinking heavily all your life, you run a serious risk of irreversible organic impotence sometime in your fifties, according to Debora Phillips, Ph.D., a behavior therapist in Beverly Hills, California, and New York City who wrote the book *Sexual Confidence.* "Stopping in your fifties is too late," she warns. "If you're 48, stop the heavy drinking now." Occasional social drinking doesn't qualify as "heavy drinking," but you don't have to be a knock-down drunk to run the risk of altering your liver to the point that hormonal output is affected. "A few strong drinks most every night can do it," Dr. Phillips says.

Take two. Dr. Phillips also suggests keeping the pre-lovemaking alcohol consumption down to two drinks maximum. Penalty for going over the limit: Your penis may give considerably less than a stand-up performance. "You have to remember that you're not 20 anymore," Dr. Phillips says. "Alcohol has more of an effect at your age."

What Dr. Phillips is proposing is an awareness of alcohol's performance-weakening effects, not teetotaling. In fact, a little of the romantic bubbly can help things along under the right circumstances. "A half-glass might lower inhibitions, especially in an atmosphere of romance, with candles and flowers and music," she says. "But the two-drink limit holds. Nobody in his fifties should have three glasses of champagne before making love."

Assess your stress. Before you blame middle age or your partner or Congress for any apparent decline in your sex drive, take a look at what's going on in your day-to-day life. "A decline at this age can have a lot to do with stress," says Dr. Zussman. "The fifties can be a time when you're really fighting hard in your work, either to maintain your position with the threat of downsizing or to move ahead while you still can."

Get happy. Find sources of fulfillment that aren't about your job or income. That's essential advice for a successful middle age in general, but it's good for your sex life, too, according to Dr. Felder. "Being in a dead-end job and feeling stuck or without respect translates into the biochemistry of nonarousal," he says. "On the other hand, if you're tutoring a low-income kid in reading or helping a young entrepreneur get started, you're going to feel potent from that stuff. That translates into the biochemistry of arousal."

Exercise for better sex. Engage in regular vigorous exercise and watch your sex life soar. That's as true at 50 as any other time of life. Want proof? A team of University of California at San Diego researchers put 78 sedentary middle-age men (average age 48) on an exercise program and then monitored their sex lives (with diary entries, not hidden cameras). The results couldn't have been more convincing. The subjects reported more frequent intercourse, more reliable sexual functioning, and more satisfying orgasms. And those whose fitness improved the most were those whose sex lives improved the most. So what are you waiting for?

Nurture your relationship. Married life is where most middle-age sex resides. And, says Gene D. Cohen, M.D., Ph.D., director of the George Washington University Center on Aging, Health, and Humanities in Washington, D.C., "one of the biggest factors that's going to influence your sexual interest and satisfaction at this point in your life is the strength of your relationship." Putting a little time and effort to making things work on the home front, then, is a wise sexual investment.

Sounds obvious, but apparently it's not. "There are a lot of men who spend more time with their buddies on the golf course than they do with their partner," Dr. Seifer says. "And then they wonder why the sex doesn't work so well."

BOOSTING SENSITIVITY

They say your biggest sex organ is between your ears, and who's going to argue? But even if your brain is the five-star general, the frontline work goes to a dozen or so of your dangling extremities—more if you've found ways to use your toes. And those good soldiers of sex begin to show some battle fatigue when you hit your fifties. They can still win the wars with vigor and valor, but you're going to have to adjust your strategy.

Technically speaking, the intensity in which your body responds to sexual stimulation has declined steadily since around your 18th birthday. It just never mattered before. But as you climb into your fifties, things reach a kind of critical mass. You start to notice some unrest in the realm of the senses.

Most of the problem here is vascular. The sluggish blood flow (including to the aforementioned extremities) that virtually defines sex for men over 60 already affects men in their fifties. That means you'll need more than a wink to get lots of blood to your penis. "It will take more direct genital stimulation for a longer period of time to achieve that consistent, reliable erection you used to get spontaneously," says Judith Seifer, R.N., Ph.D., professor of sex research at the Institute for Advanced Study of Human Sexuality in San Francisco and past president of the American Association of Sex Educators, Counselors, and Therapists (AASECT).

More direct stimulation by her of your genitals? You can live with that. Hell, most of us have been living *for* it. But now it's mandatory. And that's the key to all of the shifts brought on by your new sexual sensitivity. "They're not worse or better," insists Dr. Seifer. "Just different."

Some sensitivity changes fall into the "so what?" category, such as the decrease in intensity of your ejaculations. When's the last time you checked how far it would fly across the room anyway?

Others have obvious advantages, such as the decreasing urgency of climax. "Some men have ejaculatory control for the first time in their life in their fifties," Dr. Seifer points out. "That's one less thing to worry about."

That can go even further. "You can have that strange and wonderful-feeling experience of thoroughly enjoying sex but not having to ejaculate at all," Dr. Seifer says. So sometimes the trip's not half the fun, but all of it.

On the downside, when ejaculation does come, the intensity of your orgasm will probably drop a few notches in your fifties, but again, who's measuring? The satisfaction's still there. You also might find that that welling-up pre-orgasmic tension is less pronounced. Sometimes you just come without any preliminary drum roll.

A SENSE OF DECLINE

What might take a little more getting used to is the occasional disappearing erection. Those things, as you know, tend to come and go and come back again. But now, if you lose it for any one of a million reasons during lovemaking, it just might not come back again in time to do anything about it. It's not because you're worried about it, as may be the case for younger men.

"It's a blood flow issue," says Debora Phillips, Ph.D., a behavior therapist in Beverly Hills, California, and New York City, and author of *Sexual Confidence*. "It may not occur until your sixties, but it can happen from 50 upward." Dr. Phillips calls this little quirk a false refractory since it mimics the time period needed between ejaculations, even though there's no ejaculation. Your true refractory period, by the way, does indeed lengthen in your fifties over your forties, as it will in your sixties over your fifties.

Your other senses are shifting as well, most pertinent of them being your sense of sight. It's not necessarily that you need glasses. It's just that the visual thing doesn't turn you on like it used to. "Seeing your regular sex partner nude isn't as exciting," says Shirley Zussman, Ed.D., a certified sex and marital therapist in New York City and editor of a newsletter, *Sex Over 40*, "unless there is direct genital stimulation." This is one of lots of ways male and female sexuality begin to merge in later years. Women have always been more excited by the message than the sight.

We talk at length in this book on how to stay mentally up for sex throughout a lifetime. What can you do to keep your body's capacity for physical stimulation equally high? We'll tell you.

Explore new routes. You experimented with your body when it was changing some 40 years ago. Now it's encore time, with pleasure the goal again. "Your body is sending you some very clear messages that it's needing something different," Dr. Seifer says. "Adjust. Recognize that you don't need as much of this or you need some more of that. Find other ways of achieving the same things."

Figure it out. Do a little detective work, advises Dr. Seifer. When the sex is great, reconstruct the event and try to see what was different from when it wasn't so great. Maybe you didn't have wine with dinner last night. Maybe you were less stressed. And let your partner be Watson to your Holmes. If it was great, say so and ask her what was different. "Partners can trigger that kind of self-assessment," Dr. Seifer says. "But she may not even think about it unless you ask her."

Exploit the synchronicity. Remember that she's going through similar sensitivity shifts, too. "She's needing to be touched in different ways, and she doesn't always know what they are," Dr. Seifer says. Explore your new sexuality together, she suggests. A lot of it, you'll find, works together quite nicely. *Hint:* It may take longer for her to reach orgasm, just as it may take longer for you to ejaculate.

Open up. Women are pretty intuitive, we know. But let's face it: If she catches on that seeing her nude is no longer an automatic turn-on for you, she's not going to conclude that you need more direct genital stimulation. She's going to think there's something wrong with her. Help her out. "Unless you get this stuff out in the open, you're both going to start catastrophizing the situation," says Dr. Seifer.

Use an opening line. Getting it out in the open means talking about your sexual sensitivity shifts. The important thing is to open the door, Dr. Seifer says. Two door openers include "Hey, you know, it's just not working the way it used to. What do you think is going on?" and "You know, what I do doesn't seem to feel as good to you anymore. Is that right?"

Chatter in flagrante. Conversation right in the act is another communication device. More door openers from Dr. Seifer include "Let me touch you like this and tell me how that feels," "It would feel better if you touched me like this," and "That's what I need a lot of."

Take out some reassurance. You can be the best-adjusted 53-year-old on earth, and there are still going to be times when a slow-rising erection gets under your skin, so to speak. "The best antidote for that is a partner who gives you support," Dr. Seifer says. "When you do get a good erection, she can say 'Wow, that was really great. We have to package that one.'" But *asking* for an ego boost defeats the purpose of the thing. Instead, suggests Dr. Seifer, cast your bread upon the waters. Tell her, "Boy, you were wet and turned on last night. What a treat."

"When it's good," says Dr. Seifer, "celebrate it out loud."

WHAT? MORE CHANGES?

Adjusting to changes in your sexual sensitivity is the easy part. It's the mere fact that your body's changing at all is what most guys in their fifties find hard to accept.

You did everything you were supposed to do to adjust to midlife. You fixed your priorities. You adjusted your career goals. You broadened your mental horizons. Now you have to reinvent the wheel when it comes to sex? What *is* this?

"Men think that it all ought to be just fine now, and then they get blind-sided by a physical transition," says Dr. Seifer. "You talk about it and you know it's going to happen, but it's still a profound experience when it comes to you personally."

It doesn't matter that these "changes" have been advancing for decades. Or that they're less pronounced than they will be in your sixties. "It hits men harder in their fifties than their sixties because of the shock," says Dr. Zussman. "Men in their sixties have had more time to get used to it."

It's like the Kennedy assassination. Every man can tell you where he was and what he was doing the first time he decided that he would just as soon not climax after a healthy round of sex. Or when he realized that his penis was asserting a new independence of thought when it came to erections.

You feel like your body is failing you. It's not. The changes are natural and normal. Adapt, and decades of sexual pleasure lie ahead. Don't adapt and...well, you don't have any other choice, do you?

And that's exactly what rankles us about the physical aspects of our fifties, according to Dr. Seifer. "That's where anger and bitterness creep in," she says. "You're thinking that you have no choice, and you feel like you weren't necessarily prepared for what's happening."

But we usually end up doing just fine. You don't wake up one morning and decide it's a nice day to explore your new sexual sensitivity for maximum benefits. But you do it. Here are two suggestions for maintaining the right attitude toward your body's changes.

Avoid blame games. Don't blame your partner for the changes in your sexual sensitivity. "In your forties and before you may have seen it as a matter of changing partners if the sex wasn't working," Dr. Seifer says. "By your fifties you better figure out what to do with what you have and get the most out of it."

Remember the wonder years. Dr. Seifer suggests looking back on when you were 13 and recognize that some of the same unpredictable things are going to be going on with your body for a while. "You're going to have to get reacquainted with this body of yours," she says. "You've done it once as an adolescent and you survived. Try not to make a catastrophe or pathology out of a period of change."

An Empty House

Having all the kids out of the house offers the same advantages for your sex life at 55 as having your parents out did at 17. But it also poses the same potential danger as that earlier freedom: They might come back any time.

"Chances are that your children won't be gone completely," says Frank Pittman III, M.D., a psychiatrist and family therapist in Atlanta and author of *Man Enough: Fathers, Sons, and the Search for Masculinity.* "They still need you for things."

It's an increasingly common sight: the 31-year-old raiding his folks' refrigerator before crashing out in the same room he learned to play checkers in. Society is tough on young adults today, so don't consider your kid a failure if he needs to live at home for a while. If this is an issue at your house, read the chapter Living at Home on page 316. It'll give you some perspective on your kid's state of mind, plus provide some ground rules for housing an adult child (a wonderful oxymoron, isn't it?).

Still, the time will come, usually in your fifties, when the last of your issue, along with his empty pizza cartons, bombastic music, and Kilimanjaros of dirty laundry, moves out.

Then the light turns green and stays there. You have more time alone for sex, more freedom to indulge yourselves noisily, more choice of venue. All the obvious sexual advantages of the empty nest are real. You can stay in bed on a Saturday morning and have sex instead of getting up to watch them play soccer. Or, just as delicious, you can feel free *not* to have sex, knowing, unlike before, that this won't be your only chance of the day.

Your house is an unsupervised sexual playground. You're newlyweds again. Paradise regained. A time for your relationship to soar.

Or nose-dive.

The Truth of Aloneness

"If you have a decent relationship, it can get better now," says Judith Seifer, R.N., Ph.D., professor of sex research at the Institute for Advanced Study of Human Sexuality and past president of the American Association of Sex Educators, Counselors, and Therapists (AASECT). "If you have a lousy relationship, it's going to go into crisis pretty quickly."

That's because a lot is going on at this time in your life. Your body's changing, your sexuality is shifting gears, your goals are in flux, and your kids are gone. The hub of this many-spoked wheel of fortune is your relationship with that long-term love of your life.

"If you're feeling that there's a sexual issue in your life at this time, it's probably a relationship issue," says Samuel Osherson, Ph.D., a psychologist in Cambridge, Massachusetts, specializing in midlife issues and author of *Wrestling with Love*. "That's what sexuality really comes down to—relationship issues. You're changing, and your relationship or relationships are changing, too."

In other words, the admission price into the sexual paradise that your newly underpopulated household promises is some serious maintenance work on your marriage, which has some miles on it. Finding yourselves suddenly alone together, the need is indeed crying, "Get thee to a relationship repair shop."

"Raising kids was duck soup compared to maintaining a marriage after they're gone," Dr. Seifer says. "But now you have the chance to develop a new appreciation for this person you've spent maybe half your life with. You simply have more time to do that."

One thing you'll need to appreciate is her new point of view. Her child-bearing and child-rearing days may have ended virtually simultaneously, and she feels like she has her life back. She may just want to keep it. That can create some disparities in approach, to put it nicely. You: "Isn't it nice, honey, that we can smell some roses together at last?" She: "Don't bother me with that stuff now. I have some glass ceilings to break."

PREPARING FOR TOGETHERNESS

Now, there should be nothing mutually exclusive about personal growth goals and relationship renewal. But it takes some spade work, with both of you wielding shovels.

"You end up renegotiating your relationship in your fifties," Dr. Seifer says. "You might agree to grow apart, but you also might decide you're going to be absolutely the most important thing in one another's lives from here on out. Either way, it's essential to do the renegotiating." Here are some approaches.

Be friends again. "Be kind to one another now that you're not overwhelmed by the confusing needs of your children," Dr. Pittman suggests. Kids, you may have noticed, consider it their earthbound duty to divide and conquer their parents. And parents tend to second-guess one another—if not outright blame each other—for anything their children do. "Now there's no reason for that," Dr. Pittman says. "You can be friends again."

Don't live through your kids. Know any seniors who grew up during the Great Depression, who saved every penny, worked every moment, so that their kids "could have the life we couldn't"? The problem is that, once they retire, they have no life other than their children or grandchildren. But that's not fair to the kids, and it's a rather hollow way to live your last few decades. Don't be like that. When your kids grow up and move out, let go. Don't make your house a shrine to your kids and their kids; don't plan your life around their visits and phone calls. Take up hobbies, volunteer, renew friendships. Get a life all your own so that you don't have to get theirs.

Renew your vows. Younger couples tend to see "commitment" as keeping your pants zipped outside the home. In your fifties, you know that it's much deeper, and potentially more beautiful, than that. Your last child's departure is the time to renew that commitment in an explicit, tangible way, according to Dr. Seifer. Some couples even formally renew their vows on their 25th or 30th wedding anniversary.

"You see that recommitment manifest itself in all kinds of ways, including in the bedroom," says Dr. Seifer. "The couples who prioritize their commitment to one another have a much easier time dealing with her hot flashes or his occasional erectile dysfunction or lack of a need to ejaculate. They're going to take those things in stride."

Call a cease-fire. 1. Don't sweat the small stuff. 2. Learn to forgive the big stuff. Couples who've made it this far should have learned those things by now, according to Dr. Seifer. Some of the big stuff, though, can be pretty darn big—long-simmering resentments that can poison your later years. "But if you both find that ability to forgive, you can get really close again," Dr. Seifer says. "On the other hand, if you're still trying to make a point, or if it's more important to you to be right than it is to be close, then you're about six months away from Prozac."

Do something together. Nature photography, anyone? A little linguistic history? Develop a skill together. Take a course together. If nothing else, you'll have something to talk about. But there *is* something else. "It helps a relationship when there's a mutual interest in something," says Marion Hart, M.D., a psychoanalyst and professor of psychiatry at the Cornell Medical Center in Westchester, New York. "And it can help your sex life. The closer a couple feels to each other, the better their sexual life is going to be."

COPING WITH ILLNESS

You could mount a pretty good argument that fear of 50 has a lot more to do with dread of disease than with slowing of sexuality. After all, tardy or less rigid erections don't preclude amorous encounters. But early death can absolutely ruin your sex life.

Not that your chances of such a fate are anywhere near as great as the chances of occasional erectile dysfunction. But, as Irwin Goldstein, M.D., professor of urology at Boston University Medical Center, says, "something dramatic happens between ages 50 and 60: Diseases start kicking in."

Some of those doing the kicking are killers. Heart disease and cancer—especially lung and prostate cancer—account for more than half of all deaths. Other lung diseases, stroke, and diabetes also loom over the lives of 50-plussers.

Other illnesses are content to inflict pain rather than death. It's in your fifties when you need to start guarding against chronic back pain, arthritis, and increased susceptibility to injury.

Eat right, exercise, and get lucky and you can avoid all these things in your fifties. But even if illness isn't *in* you, it's all *around* you. A friend goes down. A parent dies. Your doctor's tone of voice changes when he tells you to get more exercise. Or you read somewhere that a prominent urologist says that your fifties is when "diseases start kicking in."

All this tends to crumble that mental wall you constructed against illness in your youth. "And it begins to crumble *significantly*," says Ross Goldstein, Ph.D., a San Francisco psychologist. "The notion of 'it couldn't happen to me' starts to break down."

FEAR OF ILLNESS

As any female can testify, we men are funny animals, emotionally speaking. At the same time we're recognizing serious illness as a real threat, we still refuse to believe it could happen to us. "That's not really contradictory," Dr. Ross Goldstein says. "Your awareness that it can happen to you is always fighting with your denial that it ever will."

That's because men in their fifties deal with health concerns via a three-step process. First there's denial that anything bad can ever happen to you. Then there's despair with the realization that it really can. Finally, there's your goal: acceptance. Those who bounce back and forth between the first two—denial and despair—can have a rough time. But if you accept the possibility of illness and then face it as you did the challenges of every other stage of your life, then you're ready for the good things that your fifties have to offer.

Control what you can and accept the rest. Carve yourself a niche between your fantasy of controlling everything and a blind acceptance of the aging process, advises Dr. Ross Goldstein. In other words, take control over those things that you can control, but not over those you can't, such as the fact that illness is a threat. "That means managing your health risk," he says. "Be effective, but not obsessive."

Monitor your prostate. One way to take control is to include screenings for prostate cancer in your yearly checkups. That means at least two things, according to Dudley Seth Danoff, M.D., senior attending urologist at Cedars-Sinai Medical Center in Los Angeles and author of *Superpotency*. One is a PSA test, which is a blood analysis looking for prostate-specific antigens. The other is a digital rectal examination, which is the old finger pokeroo that men dread. But look at it from another perspective. Are a few minutes of discomfort too high a price for detecting cancer on time? "It's the single most important thing that can be done," says Dr. Danoff. "There are very few cancers that we can discover at an early and curable stage; prostate cancer is one of them."

Take a hint from your penis. It's not very likely that impotence in a 50-year-old is psychological. Rather, blood just isn't getting into your penis for some physical reason. Which means if you can't get it up, you could be at risk for coronary disease. "Blood supply problems cannot be localized," says Fran E. Kaiser, M.D., professor of medicine and associate director of the division of geriatric medicine at St. Louis University's Health Sciences Center and director of the university's Sexual Dysfunction Clinic. "What you find in the penis may be occurring in the coronary arteries."

Roll up your sleeve. You could be one of perhaps 50 million Americans with high blood pressure (also known as hypertension) and never know it until a simple blood pressure test gives it away. Or you can wait for a stroke or heart attack to let you know. That's because there are usually no symptoms of hypertension. You feel fine, even though your blood pressure isn't. The condition is controllable, but you have to know that it needs controlling. So have your blood pressure checked regularly and pay attention to the results.

Take Mom's advice. "Eat sensibly" is Dr. Danoff's sensible advice to men in their fifties. Mom could have told you that—and probably did. But with prostate cancer the scourge of your fifties, your diet takes on additional significance. Regardless of whether cutting the fat is a proven risk reducer, evidence for the link is accumulating. Dr. Irwin Goldstein points out that there's little prostate cancer in Japan but plenty among Japanese-Americans. "That has to be an environmental difference," he says. "And the most obvious difference is what Americans eat, their high-cholesterol, high-fat diet. I don't think there can be a lot of controversy about that."

Most guys in their fifties have been advised to eat sensibly for five decades. "But they smoke and drink and eat steak and french fries," says Dr. Irwin Goldstein. "And you can't tell me they're unaware that these things cause problems." So why do they do it? Simple. Because they've gotten away with it. Or at least they have the impression that they've gotten away with it.

No more. "You start feeling the effects between 50 and 60," Dr. Irwin Goldstein says. "The cigarette smoking and all that cholesterol start kicking in at this age."

And, of course, the result is cardiovascular chaos. Among other things. "If we abuse ourselves the way 15-year-olds abuse themselves, we'll be dead," says Dr. Danoff.

Grab the lion's share. You already know that regular, vigorous exercise, especially cardiovascular exercise, lessens your health risks, improves your sex life, and boosts your self-esteem. What may help you get started in your fifties is the knowledge that most of these benefits come with the initial efforts. Sure, there's more to be gotten in advanced stages, but the first 30 percent of effort is where 70 percent of the benefits are. "It's better to take a moderate approach and get the lion's share of benefits than to try for that last 30 percent and have trouble staying with it," says Dr. Ross Goldstein.

Practice preventive sex. Regular sexual activity is known to help prevent inflammation of the prostate (or prostatitis, yet another prostate-related problem pestering men over 50). But it may do more than that. Sex relieves stress, and stress not only is damaging in and of itself but also suppresses your immune system. So sex can be a weapon in your disease-prevention arsenal.

Know your family. Undertake a little oral history. Are there precedents of heart disease in your family? Did a parent or grandparent die of a heart attack in his fifties?

If so, "you're going to need to be more vigilant about heart disease," says Jeffrey Metter, M.D., chief medical officer for the National Institute on Aging's Baltimore Longitudinal Aging Study.

Snuff the Snickers. You don't have to be a diabetic to have trouble with sugar, according to Dr. Metter. In fact, some studies show that glucose intolerance is a risk factor for cardiovascular disease, even among nondiabetics. So those three-Mars-bars lunches are probably not a good idea, regardless of whether they're tax-deductible. "Older people have more difficulty managing large loads of sugar," Dr. Metter says. "And that's something that seems to start in middle age."

And the subtraction of empty calories when you cut out extra sweets doesn't hurt your cause either. "Latent diabetes can show up in your fifties, especially if you've put on poundage," Dr. Danoff says.

WHEN DISEASE STRIKES

As much as we may be aware that illness is a factor of our fifties, men are shocked—*shocked*—that such a thing could happen to them when it does. "Men in their fifties don't ordinarily expect to come down with anything serious," says Robert S. Weiss, Ph.D., senior faculty associate in the Institute of Gerontology at the University of Massachusetts in Boston. "And that's one of the problems when they do."

So a 55-year-old man is likely to consider a diagnosis of prostate cancer an insult to his sense of justice. Who can blame him? Often the target of disease is a guy who thought he was in pretty good shape and taking care of himself reasonably well. And, for crying out loud, he's only 55. Precisely because you're still not old, you have more at stake in dealing with these things in such a way that your quality of life stays high. And that includes the quality of your sex life.

Erection difficulties are, as they say, a rising problem with age. But remember that it isn't age per se that causes impotence. It's other conditions that may be increasingly common with age—usually illnesses—that do the dirty work. Absent illness, there's no reason why you shouldn't have efficient erections till your dying day.

Most threatening by its presence is cardiovascular disease in all its incarnations—from coronary artery disease to clogged arteries and high blood pressure. By definition, all variations of cardiovascular disease inhibit your blood flow. And since it takes a fivefold increase in blood flow to get an erection, you can see what the hang-up is, sexually speaking.

Next on the list is prostate problems, which have become the very symbol of male midlife and late-life illness. "It's definitely a fifties thing," Dr. Danoff says. Cancer of the prostate was once synonymous with impotence (if not death) since the surgery required to remove it also removed essential nerves. That's not always true anymore. But while the chances of developing prostate cancer are just one in five if you live to a ripe old age, according to the American Cancer Society, virtually all men will eventually experience benign enlargement of the supposedly tiny prostate gland. And that puts the clamp (quite literally) on sexual functioning. Suspect that you have it if you drink a beer in the first quarter of a Chicago Bulls game and you're still dribbling away feebly in the men's room by the time Michael Jordan has wrapped up his triple double. The problem can often be taken care of medically these days, but even if surgery is required, the operation rarely results in impotence.

Then there's diabetes, a notoriously early impotence instigator. Men in their forties, not to mention their fifties, can often trace erectile dysfunction to diabetes, a body-ager if there ever was one. Diabetes hits your sex life from two directions: It can damage the nerves and, therefore, block messages to the penis. And it can damage the vessels charged with delivering erection-essential blood. Result: Some 50 to 60 percent of men over 50 with diabetes suffer from erectile dysfunction.

Chronic back pain and arthritis take a different route to sexual sabotage. Neither affects potency per se, but pain has a way of ruining the mood, to say the least. "If you're hurting, there goes your sex drive right down the tubes," Dr. Kaiser says.

Remember, though, that illness is there to be fought and defeated. Part of the fight is to maintain your sex life, and there's no reason why you shouldn't.

Get it early. Overcome that age-old male reluctance to get your prostate checked regularly. That means overcoming macho misconceptions but also overcoming fear. "Men worry that if we find something, they'll never have an erection again," Dr. Danoff says. "But if we diagnose prostate cancer at an early stage, we can preserve potency." But not if you don't go in.

Speak up for your sexuality. With modern nerve-sparing procedures, surgeons can often take out your prostate without taking out your sex life.

But put the issue of sexuality on the table when you discuss any prostate operation with your doctor. And don't cut corners when picking a surgery site. "The skill of the surgeon makes a tremendous difference in any procedure involving the genitalia, prostate, or bladder," says Dr. Weiss, who has worked with recovering prostate patients. "In this area, a so-so surgeon really can screw people up."

Watch what you take. The medications prescribed for hypertension and depression (and lots of other problems) can do as much harm to your sex life as the condition itself. Again, make sexual function part of the discussion when your doctor takes out his prescription pad. (For more on this, see Medications on page 538.)

Run a tub for two. Taking a warm bubble bath together never hurt anybody's romantic mood, especially if the tub is a tad too small for two. But even if you soak alone, a warm bath before the main attraction can make for pain-free sex if you're an arthritis sufferer, says James H. Gilbaugh Jr., M.D., a urologist in Portland, Oregon, and author of *Men's Private Parts*. A swim in a heated pool or applying heat to the area around the hurting joints also helps reduce pain.

Place pillows strategically. Some positional experimentation can alleviate pain during sex if you've had heart surgery or any other kind of surgery. The American Heart Association recommends that stroke recoverers use pillows to help support their affected side. And there are even medical devices that help provide support or balance if you have any kind of weakness or paralysis.

Suck it up. You can do a lot to alleviate back pain by making your stomach muscles stronger, according to Dr. Metter. Choose abdominal exercises that don't strain your back.

Don't smoke. If the increased risk of heart disease couldn't get you off cigarettes, once you get it, the following finding from the Massachusetts Male Aging Study might inspire you: There is a 700 percent increase in erectile dysfunction among men with cardiovascular disease who smoke. "It's the most noxious combination there is," says John B. McKinlay, Ph.D., senior vice president and director of the New England Research Institutes in Watertown, Massachusetts, and principal investigator of the study. "Your level of erectile dysfunction shoots straight up." And it will be the only thing you have that shoots straight up.

Stay in the game. Keep having sex in order to keep having sex? Your introductory logic professor would let you have it for such a tautology, but it's good advice anyway. For one thing, sexual inactivity bequeaths more sexual inactivity since the relevant blood vessels need action to maintain their readiness for even more action. For another, sex is a painkiller of sorts, either through the release of "pleasure chemicals" (endorphins) or by simply altering your attitude. And remember that unfounded fear is a lousy reason for depriving your body and mind of the sexuality they deserve. The risk of sexual activity triggering a second heart attack or stroke is so minuscule as to be virtually meaningless. (For more on this, see Heart Health and Sex on page 534.)

COPING WITH MORTALITY

Give us all an Oscar. Throw in a Grammy, an Emmy, a Tony, and whatever other little statue they make. Invent a new award called the Grim Reapies. When it comes to dealing with our own mortality, we men know how to act, sing, and dance.

We talk about death with bravado, and nobody complains that it doesn't ring true. We indulge in black humor. We laugh and pretend not to notice how forced the laughter is. Outwardly, we do everything but voice the truth.

What's the truth?

"The truth," says Ross Goldstein, Ph.D., a San Francisco psychologist, "is that this stuff shakes men down to their boots."

And it shakes us all. "Everybody can tell you when he has experienced that crisis of mortality for the first time," says Judith Seifer, R.N., Ph.D., professor of sex research at the Institute for Advanced Study of Human Sexuality in San Francisco and past president of the American Association of Sex Educators, Counselors, and Therapists (AASECT). "You're trotting down the path of life and things are going fine, and all of a sudden, this awareness strikes you on a very gut level that someday you're not going to be here and the world is going to go on without you."

THE PAINFUL TRUTH

That mortality awareness, for lack of a better term, usually comes only after four decades of blissful, I'm-going-to-live-forever denial. After it introduces itself rather rudely, it sticks around as a fuzzy companion that occasionally sits on your shoulder and makes mischievous little ticking sounds to remind you that the clock is running. Or it can be a clinging gargoyle, its claws around your neck, intent on having its say about everything you try to do.

Whatever shape it takes, you won't go through your fifties without it.

"Your sense of mortality may begin at about 40, but it's much stronger in your fifties," says Debora Phillips, Ph.D., a behavior therapist in Beverly Hills, California, and New York City, and author of *Sexual Confidence*.

Or as Dr. Seifer puts it, "If you haven't had that experience and put it into perspective before, you will by your mid-fifties. The universe will force you to look at it by your mid-fifties."

There's a logical explanation for that. Middle age isn't the virtual battle-field older age resembles, when friends drop away one by one and lots of guys read the obituary section before the front page. But in your fifties, sobering things do begin to happen.

You may lose a friend more or less your age. A serious illness in your peer group may jolt you. Your parents may be approaching the end of their lives. "Those things bring death into your life in a way that takes it out of the abstract and into the real and tangible," Dr. Goldstein points out.

There's another thing—your own health. Not that your fifties need to be disease-ridden by any means. But health is much more of an issue for you, and those annual physicals are no longer without some suspense. "You feel like you're spinning the wheel of fortune," Dr. Goldstein says. "You never know what's going to come up."

And you don't actually have to be sick to get those subtle little messages about your own mortality. Petty injuries? How they nag more than they used to. Doctor tells you your cholesterol level's too high? Blood pressure up? Troublesome before, vaguely ominous now.

"Lots of things can set off a chain of anxiety about your own mortality," Dr. Phillips says.

One thing about mortality awareness: The worries it can cause don't nec-essarily include a sense of impending death. "People make some sort of esti-mate early in life about how long theirs will last," says Frank Pittman III, M.D., a psychiatrist and family therapist in Atlanta and author of *Man Enough: Fathers, Sons, and the Search for Masculinity.* "Most guys base it on the age their grandfather or father dies, or perhaps an uncle. They may revise it from time to time, but most guys in their fifties expect to live a lot longer."

So the issue isn't the sand in the hourglass running out. It's the knowledge that the hourglass exists. And like midlife issues, it's something you can use to improve your life.

TAKING CONTROL

So how do you deal with this crazy little thing called mortality? You can do what some guys do, which is run around with a lot of younger women. "The terror of mortality can lead some men to deny it by having multiple af-fairs to reaffirm life," says Marion Hart, M.D., a psychoanalyst and professor of psychiatry at the Cornell Medical Center in Westchester, New York.

That approach may or may not be a lot of fun, but it's hardly recom-mendable as a method of dealing with death's demons. The giveaway phrase in Dr. Hart's observation is "deny it." Denying your mortality isn't going to cut it in your fifties. You need to confront it.

"But don't confront it as Mortality with a capital M," says Dr. Goldstein. "What you have to confront are the subtle and profound ways you can take control over it. A sense of control is of the essence."

So now that you know you're not going to live forever—really know it—

make a productive promise to yourself: "I'm going to live as long as I can as well as I can." That's not that old river in Egypt they call denial. That's taking control. Here are some specific ways to do that.

Just do it. Let your new sense of temporal limitation inspire you to do those things you always knew you should have been doing. Sure, some personality types tend to see inevitable death as a reason not to bother to do anything. But your response should be to become a better person, to watch what you eat, take care of your body, enrich your mind.

"That's the healthy response," Dr. Goldstein says. "It's a strategy you have available to increase your sense of control."

Not to mention feel better, look better, and think better.

Take your time. Mortality awareness can work like a good trainer. It's there to see you get things done sooner rather than later. If you don't start in on that exercise regimen now—or wine collection or European tour or addition to your house—just when are you going to get it done?

But don't overdo it. Panic is a lousy trainer.

"A moderate dose of time urgency is a great motivator," Dr. Goldstein says. "But too much will actually keep you from getting things done. Guard against that false sense of your demise being right around the corner."

Be upbeat. By definition, mortality awareness means that there will be times when you're going to be thinking about the end of your life. The ultimate downer? It doesn't need to be. Dr. Phillips advises diving right into what is, after all, one of the great philosophical questions facing humanity. Go ahead and think about it.

"But not in a depressing way," Dr. Phillips says. "Deal with it philosophically, humanistically—or theologically if you're so inclined. Read what other people have to say about it."

Take care of business. Speaking of dying, this is a good time to make sure that your will and all other matters relating to your legacy are in order. "Do it now while you're healthy and vital," Dr. Phillips says.

Dr. Phillips also suggests that you make out a living will, in which you give instructions about your death, when to pull the plug, what extreme measures should or should not be taken, that sort of thing. "Deciding how you want to die is a positive thing," she says. "It gives you a sense of control over the issue."

Enjoy your vitality. Sometimes the Hallmark doggerel is right on. If you're now more aware than you care to be that you're not going to live forever, is it really so corny to want to savor every one of the 10,000 or more days you probably have left? Now that you know how precious a commodity time is, treat it that way. Dr. Phillips even suggests living each day as though it were your last. "Don't mourn your mortality," she says. "Enjoy your vitality."

LOVE WITHOUT SEX

If you remember only one thing after you close the covers of this book, we hope it is this: There's no reason for any reasonably healthy man of any age not to enjoy a rich, satisfying, wholesome sex life.

But actually, there *is* one reason: if he doesn't want to.

Sex isn't compulsory. It just seems that way. Who knows how many Americans shun it? Some say 10 percent. As for sexless marriages, even sex researcher William Masters, M.D., of Masters and Johnson fame once confessed he had no idea how many there are. But they're out there.

"Sure, there are couples who go from middle age on with little or no sex and are okay about it," says Judith Seifer, R.N., Ph.D., professor of sex research at the Institute for Advanced Study of Human Sexuality in San Francisco and past president of the American Association of Sex Educators, Counselors, and Therapists (AASECT). "They're saying, 'Sex, schmex. What's the big deal?'"

The big deal is the "okay about it" part. Sex therapists, while admittedly biased (after all, they make their living helping couples *have* sex), suspect there are more restlessly sexless couples than happily sexless couples.

"I think the chances are limited that both partners are satisfied," says Shirley Zussman, Ed.D., a certified sex and marital therapist in private practice in New York City. "Even if one is thanking God she doesn't have to be part of that thing anymore, the other might be wondering what he's missing."

Dr. Zussman suggests fantasy checks for determining if you're really content in your chaste ways. "Fantasies are probably the key to it," she says. "It's hard for me to believe that couples are really satisfied without sex if they're fantasizing about it."

Satisfied are not, by middle age couples find all kinds of routes to sexlessness. Some might be conducive to happy sexlessness. Others clearly aren't. Here are some of the paths to no sex.

I'm Hansel, you're Gretel, we're happy. There are married couples who've never had sex together and never intended to. Dr. Zussman calls it the Hansel and Gretel syndrome—just two nice people living together like brother and sister. But it's not always as comfy as it seems. Dr. Zussman says that many younger Hansel-and-Gretel couples eventually come to her because they want children. "And once you get into it, you discover pathology," Dr. Zussman says.

Okay, have it your way. Then there are marriages that are sexless even though at least one of the partners isn't. "There are lots of people who manage to keep living together in a marriage despite a disparity in taste," says Dr. Seifer. "Vegetarians live with guys who eat meat. It can be the same way with sex."

Ban Sex

Want to spice up your sex life? Try banning intercourse. We're talking total prohibition here. Fool around all you want, but no scoring.

We're also talking only for a week. Or some other set period of time. And we don't mean doing this while miles apart from your regular partner. In fact, according to Debora Phillips, Ph.D., a behavior therapist in Beverly Hills, California, and New York City, and author of *Sexual Confidence*, who recommends this gambit, it's important that you use the downtime in as romantic a way as possible.

"Have champagne by candlelight, shower together," Dr. Phillips suggests. "But no intercourse."

Touching is allowed. "Kiss and neck like when you were 17," Dr. Phillips says. "Make out in all kinds of ways. But no intercourse."

Actually this sounds a *lot* like the rules of the game at 17. But remember how exciting the prospect, however remote, of going all the way was in the context of all that preparation? That's what you're recapturing here.

The intercourse-ban treatment is often used for younger men with performance anxiety as a way of taking the pressure off. But it's also effective for couples in their fifties, when your less insistent sex drive can sometimes sink into lethargy. "You want newness and freshness," Dr. Phillips says.

And there's nothing like prohibiting something to make it more urgently desirable. In fact, the self-imposed teasefest often ends sooner than it's supposed to. In other words, you cheat. "Couples often break the ban," says Dr. Phillips. "The arousal is so unbearable that they just have to."

You can ask any country/western songwriter what happens when a man (or woman) doesn't get what he wants at home. Or you can ask a sex counselor: "He'll get out to get it somewhere else," Dr. Seifer says. "Or he'll masturbate or climb onto the Internet or call a 900 sex number or watch porn flicks. He'll find some other sexual outlet, but that doesn't always destroy the marriage."

When's tee time? Erectile dysfunction is more common the older you get, right? So why are urologists' waiting rooms filled with men in their early fifties instead of in their later fifties or sixties? It is sometimes the partner's fault, thinks Irwin Goldstein, M.D., professor of urology at Boston University Medical Center, since women can be less interested in sex after menopause. "As women start becoming less and less interested in whatever sexual dysfunction their partner may have, men become less and less seen in the office," Dr. Goldstein says. "They play golf instead."

In other words, some couples in their later fifties fall into sexless marriages because she stops giving him encouragement—or orders, as the case may be—to get things in working order. She's not even bothering to put her own sexual house in order. "There's no question that a lot of the motivation was female-driven," Dr. Goldstein says. "And when the female stops driving, golf becomes important."

Keeping your head. Sometimes, according to Dr. Seifer, your other "head" is making better decisions for you than the one on top of your shoulders. And that may be especially true when your relationship has gone irredeemably sour. Your second head's refusal to stand up and salute may be its way of telling you that your other half is no longer worth saluting. "Why would you want to get it up and stick it in somebody who'll bite your (other) head off?" says Dr. Seifer. "Maybe it doesn't want you to put yourself in harm's way anymore."

The penile message: Who needs sex with *her*? "And if you don't believe in fooling around, it becomes, 'Who needs sex, period?' " Dr. Seifer says. "That's an option." Love without sex? Hardly. But for some it's better than hatred *with* sex.

Negotiated sexlessness. As they renegotiate their relationship in their fifties, some couples bargain themselves right out of the bedroom. Autonomy is agreed to and, next thing you know, she's out buying her own individual retirement account while he's running in social circles that don't include her. "They're going to take the same power struggles to bed," Dr. Seifer says. "How can two people have sex together when they're both only in it for their own thing?"

Often they don't. The only thing they do together is argue. These are the couples you can't play bridge with, the ones that can't even share a dessert without fighting over it. "Think about what that's like in bed," Dr. Seifer says. "It's like batting your penis against a brick wall. It just gets easier to withdraw from sex and intimacy."

A mature and mutual decision. One thing about being 55 is that you can't fool yourself anymore. If sex just isn't doing it for you, you can cut through the imposed notion of what it means to be a man and take action to stop the action. If she feels the same way, you have the basis for an agreement. "If you both happily decide to have a life without sex, then you both have a happy life without sex," Dr. Seifer says.

The medical imperative. Dudley Seth Danoff, M.D., senior attending urologist at Cedars-Sinai Medical Center in Los Angeles and author of *Superpotency*, tells of a man in his late fifties with prostate cancer who had to put up with regular testosterone-blocking shots for years and years. With the injection routine straining his marriage more than the cancer, he eventually told Dr. Danoff to simply cut off his testosterone supply at the source, the old-fashioned way—castration. Afterward, his wife of 30 years came in to thank Dr. Danoff for making them both happier.

This is extreme, admittedly. But the point is that sexlessness in a marriage can be the result of a choice that would seem to be agonizing but may actually be easy if you (1) face medical reality bravely and (2) have a deep, loving relationship. Love without sex, for this couple, is surely a gift.

That said, however, most of us feel better for having sex. It's the physical complement to the emotional intimacy that's so fundamental to men's lives. And, as Dr. Danoff puts it, "it's the best way I know of to have fun without paying for it."

DISILLUSIONMENT

If disillusionment means being freed of illusions, your fifties thankfully are full of it. True, some cherished dreams die hard. But most illusions are better off dissed. And that includes the pernicious youthful misjudgment that somehow your fifties are doomed to be a sexless and spunkless decade of defeat and resignation.

The fact is that most men in their fifties are as happy as they ever were. Researchers have confirmed this by the simple expedient of asking them. "We did a big national survey asking people if they had a 'midlife crisis,'" says Ron Kessler, Ph.D., a sociologist formerly at the University of Michigan's Institute for Social Research and now at the Harvard Medical School. "There's not a great deal of it. Life has worked out pretty well for people in their fifties."

One reason for the rosiness, says Dr. Kessler, may be simple relief. What in simpler times was a strictly adolescent anxiety about not making it in life now keeps nagging us into our thirties since careers and families are so much slower to develop these days. So there you are at 35, still starting out in life at an age when Mozart and Alexander the Great were dead. And looming just ahead is what threatens to be a middle age of no achievement. Hence, the fear of 50 is so much worse than the reality of 50 that your mature years seem positively bursting with satisfaction.

But there's another reason: Your fifties really are a golden decade. "It's when you reap the rewards of everything you've done before," says Frank Pittman III, M.D., a psychiatrist and family therapist in Atlanta and author of *Man Enough: Fathers, Sons, and the Search for Masculinity.* "You devoted your twenties to learning, your thirties to learning how to apply what you learned, and your forties to clawing your way to a position where you could take advantage of those things. Your fifties is when it all pays off."

You're old enough to be wise, young enough to be healthy. If you're industrious, you're in your peak earning years. If you're smart, you've stayed in good shape. If you're lucky, you have your friends and family. If you're typical, you've maintained a robust and satisfying sex life and will continue to do so. What's not to like about being in your fifties?

And it keeps getting better. As Dr. Kessler puts it, "For men's mental health, late middle age seems to be the best years in life."

SURVIVAL SKILLS

But let's be clear here. The fact that "most men do pretty well," as Dr. Kessler puts it, doesn't mean that your fifties offer a free ride. We're talking about a time of confronting life's limitations, facing up to your own mortality, perhaps losing your parents, most likely seeing your kids bolt the house, and most assuredly dealing with the indignity of declining physical prowess. That's a full load of change, the likes of which you haven't tackled since adolescence. And besides, doing "pretty well" isn't good enough for you. You want to take this decade for all the riches it has to offer.

Here's the crux of the matter when it comes to your second half-century: Up to now, you've probably thought of your life as an upward line on a graph, with the future always promising more—more money, more achievement, more success. Somewhere around your 50th birthday, you sense that that line is going to flatten out. Maybe not tomorrow, but the mere realization that it will is staggering.

"Suddenly, there's a whole bunch of things you have to make peace with if you want to feel good about the second half of your life," says Leonard Felder, Ph.D., a Los Angeles psychologist and author of *The Ten Challenges*. "That's a tough concept for American men because we don't like to talk about that stuff. We like to talk about unlimited growth."

One thing you have to make peace with is that most of your goals won't be reached. Coming in your sixth decade, such a reality injection can be, well, disillusioning. Why? Because you've always based your self-esteem on your achievements and the external praise they bring. That's threatened now. Even if your goals have been more or less arrived at, this is an age you may wonder if it was worth it. Is this what it was all about?

The solution is obvious: Find other sources of self-esteem. "The healthiest men are those who go into their fifties with a fairly rich variety of things on which they can rely to feel good about themselves," says Ross Goldstein, Ph.D., a San Francisco psychologist.

That means you look inward for self-worth, to your personal values, to your interpersonal relationships, to how you go about doing things rather than what you accomplish. Find value in you the person instead of you the performer.

If you don't make that shift, the price can be high. "Many middle-age men take a torturous route characterized by alcohol and substance abuse, divorce, courting 'trophy' women, and wild financial risk taking," says Robert E. Simmons, Ph.D., a clinical psychologist at the Alexandria Psychotherapy and Consultation Center in Alexandria, Virginia. "Some give up, lose hope, and believe that all satisfaction, including sexual pleasure, has escaped their grasp."

Another essential later-life survival skill, according to Dr. Goldstein, is what you might call intellectual flexibility. "If you draw a line between those men who feel good about middle age and those who don't, the first group would be men who are curious, who reach out, engage other people, try new experiences, learn new things," Dr. Goldstein says. "The others shrink their world down and perceive it as a place of threats and diminishing opportunities."

But you know what? It's that second group that's doing what comes naturally in middle age. The inertia is toward abandoning experimentation, closing down the learning process, becoming judgmental—all the things you *shouldn't* do if you want a fulfilling later life. "So you have to do something that's really counterintuitive," says Dr. Goldstein. "That's where most men have the greatest difficulty. But you must at least make the effort or you end up alienated and detached from the world."

FREED OF ILLUSIONS

Is it a contradiction that at the same time you're expanding your horizons and re-creating yourself you should also reach a certain self-acceptance? Maybe so, but that's your best strategy for dealing with what Dr. Goldstein calls the three wake-up calls of midlife.

1. You're not going to live forever.
2. You're not going to make vice president (or if you have, you realize that it's not as rewarding as you thought it would be).
3. Your family life won't turn out like *Ozzie and Harriet*.

"In your fifties, you really have to make peace with these things," Dr. Goldstein says. "Self-acceptance—understanding that you have faults and flaws and aren't just the victim of life's slings and arrows—is one of the lubricants that slide you through the transition."

Here are some specific ways to avoid the pain and punishment of disillusionment.

Keep your eyes open. Even from youth, you're always getting little clues here, little hints there, about your life's limitations. Pay attention to them. "People who have crises in midlife tend to have lived in a fantasy world," says Dr. Kessler. "They just wouldn't let reality in until it came rushing in all at once." So keep your eyes open, he advises, and constantly make small adjustments to your expectations of life. "It's easier to get your priorities in shape when you confront reality daily," he says.

Ditch those dusty dreams. Remember when it dawned on you that you'd never pitch a no-hitter in Game 7 of the World Series? It's even more important to unload impossible dreams now, according to Dr. Simmons, who says that "a successful passage through your fifties means charting realistic expectations." Making the Senior Tour is probably not a realistic expectation. Constantly improving your golf game is.

Dr. Kessler worked on a study that asked people if they had given up on a dream recently. Many had and were glad they did. "They felt that they had been living for the dream rather than for themselves," Dr. Kessler says. "They felt that this enormous burden had been taken off their shoulders."

Mix the right cocktail. We know what you're thinking. All this talk about jettisoned dreams and calm self-acceptance sounds suspiciously like an anti-success formula, a recipe for resignation. Rest assured, nobody's advising you to put out the fire. "Success enables you to connect with pride to the world," Dr. Pittman says. "You have to have it. But guys who think that it's central are missing the point, which is to achieve enough success to stop competing in life, to savor your relationships and your experiences."

Says Dr. Goldstein, "It's a matter of mixing a cocktail with the right proportion of dreams and reality. Every person settles into a different place in that mix, but the important thing is to have a mix. All self-acceptance without dreams is as poisonous as all dreams with no recognition of one's limitations."

Seek truth. You're too young to be an old man at 55, but not for the old man syndrome. You know the shtick: "Things aren't as good as they were in my day. The world's changed, so to hell with it." Need we mention that it's best to avoid that? "You have to pull the reins in on your natural tendency to be judgmental about things that are new and different," Dr. Goldstein says. "How? Develop a certain amount of intellectual curiosity about the world around you."

Says Dr. Felder, "In your fifties, you have to change your view of how it's supposed to be. Rather than feeling resentful that what you thought was true turns out not to be, find out what is true."

Know thyself. According to Dr. Simmons, that life of "compulsive, macho competition" you've probably led up to now has atrophied the "emotional attunement" you need for self-esteem. It's time to get in touch with yourself again.

As Dr. Goldstein puts it, "Take some of that new intellectual curiosity you're developing and use it to learn about yourself. Understand how you're changing."

How do you get to know the inner you better? Not, as you might think, by pure introspection. "You learn more about yourself by engaging the outside world and then bringing those lessons inward than you do by just staring at your navel," says Dr. Goldstein. "In other words, you have to have a variety of stimulating experiences, encounters, and conversations to push yourself outside your comfort zone."

Don't covet. So the guy you hated in college now has a prettier wife? Bigger house? Better-behaved kids? Envy doesn't cut it at any age and causes problems at 50. "Coveting leads to a sense of disempowerment and a loss of enthusiasm for everything, including sex," says Dr. Felder.

If someone else appears superior to you, it only means that you've dealt with a different series of events. Wishing your life were more like his is a logical absurdity, not to mention waste of time. "It's more empowering to notice how well you've handled the challenges in your own life and how well you're taking on the challenges that are on your plate right now," says Dr. Felder. "That's where you get a sense of meaning and mastery and potency—all things that translate to health and sexuality."

LOSING PARENTS

When one of his parents dies, the average man grieves and then feels sorry for himself. The healthy, potent man grieves, and then draws strength from crisis and moves ahead as a better person.

That's not to minimize the trauma of the thing. The loss hits you quickly and it hits you hard. It can happen at any age, of course, but simple arithmetic holds that sometime in your fifties you're very likely to face this particular major life crisis.

And the effects go a lot deeper than a sense of loss. "Your self-image changes, your sense of mortality deepens, your relationship with your own children is affected," says Ross Goldstein, Ph.D., a San Francisco psychologist. "It's just a very profound event in your life."

They say celebrity deaths happen in threes, but two's plenty when it comes to parents. It doesn't get any easier the second time. In fact, the loss of the second parent can be even more devastating because it touches that inner suspicion that you're ultimately alone here on this earth. You feel isolated, solitary.

"You can get the feeling you've been orphaned," says Debora Phillips, Ph.D., a behavior therapist in Beverly Hills, California, and New York City, and author of *How to Give Your Child a Great Self-Image*. "Everybody, no matter what age, wants a mommy and a daddy. There's something in all of us that calls out for that."

The first thing you need to know, according to Dr. Phillips, is that your behavior is going to be immediately, though temporarily, affected after the death of a parent. Bereavement is related to depression, and that causes some changes. And yes, one of them can be an inability to get an erection. "You need to expect this as part of your grieving," Dr. Phillips says. But not for too long, she says. If that or any other symptom of depression lasts for more than two months, you should seek some help, according to Dr. Phillips.

COMING OUT AHEAD

The grieving part is difficult and necessary. But painful as it may be, it's not your final task. "The loss of a parent is the opening of a chapter in your life, not an ending," Dr. Goldstein says. "The real work comes after the grieving."

That's because there are three issues to work out with every big-time change. One is how you feel about it. Another is what you think about it. The third is what you do about it. It's psychology's ubiquitous double-play combination: emotional to cognitive to behavioral. The first two are natural and helpful. But it's the third that will get you places.

"You may feel sad and you may come to some kind of intellectual understanding," Dr. Goldstein says of dealing with a parent's death. "Now what do you do about it? That's much more important, but the grieving process is as far as some men get."

This kind of death comes in different flavors. If a parent was particularly inhibited and disapproving of sex—or at least gave that impression—you might feel a sense of liberation, a new permission. Often the death is so expected, the terminal illness so lingering, you might even feel a sense of relief. The impact of it may not hit you till next Thanksgiving, when you're the one up there carving the turkey as the eldest male in the family.

And the death of your father and mother will often generate different shades of grief. The death of your mother—the nurturer, the unconditional love giver—is often a purely emotional experience for you. While the death of your father—emotional as well, of course—can be a rite of passage, establishing you finally as a man, even at age 50. "It can also be a practical burden," says Judy Tatelbaum, a grief workshop leader in Carmel, California, and author of *The Courage to Grieve* and *You Don't Have to Suffer.* "Sometimes you're suddenly responsible for family finances or taking care of your mother. That can be overwhelming."

But sooner or later, you need to translate this inevitable event from a tragedy into something more empowering. You can't resurrect your father's life, but you can improve your own.

Reflect. "Reflect on the situation and ask yourself what you want to change in your life as a result of losing a parent," advises Dr. Goldstein. Pondering the nature of life and death can be interesting, but that's not the kind of reflection we're getting at here. You'll benefit a lot more from posing concrete questions about what you'll actually do from now on. Here are some that Dr. Goldstein suggests.

- How does this change my life?
- What lessons do I want to take away?
- What decisions do I want to make?

And then get specific.

- Do I want to change my line of work?
- Do I want to work less? More?
- Do I want to devote time to volunteer activity?

"The palette is pretty open," Dr. Goldstein says. "What's important is to actually *do* something as a result of your reflection."

Keep it going. Ever ride out an earthquake? Walked away from a car accident? Miscalculated the break of a 20-foot wave? Whatever happened to that vow you made afterward? You know, the one that went: "Man, this thing called Life is fleeting. I better make my life more fulfilling."

That in a nutshell is the kind of thing you should be saying—and doing—after the death of a parent. But not for just a few days, like after that earthquake. For a lifetime. "The challenge is to hang on to that way of thinking," says Dr. Goldstein. "Day-to-day living tends to erode your resolution. Don't let yourself fall back into the same old patterns."

Be a man. We men are pretty sure that when a crisis hits, we'll have the *cojones* to deal with it. If the entire cockpit crew goes down, we'll volunteer to land the 747 if nobody else does. The death of a parent is a more profound—and more likely—crisis that calls for a sturdier kind of bravery. "When you lose a parent, you see that you're alone," Dr. Goldstein says. "The healthy response to that is to take control of the course of your life. The weak response is to start searching for somebody else to take care of you."

Taking on a new responsibility in your life doesn't happen automatically. You have to make a decision and act on it. "You're at a crossroads," Dr. Goldstein says. "But most 50-year-olds have reached the point where they can stand up and be a mensch."

Judge not thy brother. "Expect differences in the way your siblings react to a parent's death," says Tatelbaum. "No two people in a family grieve alike." In fact, the events surrounding the funeral can be a veritable variety show. One sibling may cry nonstop. Another gets angry. Both of them may resent the "fixer" who deals with his grief by attending to all the funeral details. All three of them may be confused by the sister who just cooks away though it all. And the entire brood finds it hard to forgive the brother who doesn't even show up for the service. "But it may be he simply couldn't face the pain," says Tatelbaum. "Don't be judgmental. Have compassion."

Come together. It's not like you're going to cap off your father's funeral by blurting out to your brothers and sisters, "We ought to get together like this more often." But you ought to get together. "The grieving process is an opportunity to enlist your siblings in your support system," Tatelbaum says. "Be willing to share yourself with them and it can carry on in life."

Actually, a parent's death, especially the second one, can move a family apart as likely as together. For siblings who were never close to each other, the passing of parents provides a kind of permission to drop all pretenses of being close. "But you'd rather have that support system than not," Tatelbaum says. "It's better to try to work it out because you can get something special."

Pop for a beer. "Sharing yourself" with a brother you hardly know anymore may be the last thing you want to do as you deal with your parent's death. But it's not the only way to get closer. "If you can't talk, at least hang out together," says Tatelbaum. "Sometimes just sitting next to each other and drinking a beer in these circumstances can restore some of the relationship."

Cut her some slack. You're not the only one in the family with parents. If your wife loses her mother or father, the best thing you can offer is patience, says Tatelbaum, not help. As you observe it from the outside, her grieving process may seem overly long to you. It isn't to her, so ride it out and avoid the temptation to nudge her out of bereavement. "Don't try to 'fix' her," advises Tatelbaum. "Just pass the Kleenex."

Take care of them. Coping with the death of your parents is easier if you've taken care of them at the end of their lives. If you have the opportunity to care for your aging parents, do it, says Frank Pittman III, M.D., a psychiatrist and family therapist in Atlanta and author of *Man Enough: Fathers, Sons, and the Search for Masculinity*. Don't leave it all to your sisters or wife or strangers.

"It gives you a feeling of giving back what you've gotten," Dr. Pittman says. "In a sense, you pay your debts by doing it, and that leaves you free. You own yourself after you've been able to take care of the older generation. And it gives you the opportunity to forgive them for everything you've been blaming them for all your life."

CHANGING SOCIETAL STANDARDS

Talk about a shifting status. Just a few decades ago, if you were in your fifties, you were *past* middle age as far as most of the scientific literature was concerned. Middle age was a 35 to 49 thing. And being "old," you naturally had no sex life at all, as far as society was concerned.

Or look at it another way. A century ago you weren't even *alive* at 50, statistically speaking.

Simply put, 50 just isn't considered old anymore. "The notion of 'act your age' is out the window," says Ross Goldstein, Ph.D., a San Francisco psychologist. "We've had a real breakdown in terms of what the 'appropriate' ages are for various markers in life. That has very definite implications for sexuality."

Those implications are good ones. A generation ago, you turned 50 and the culture made jokes about your supposedly lost sexuality. Now it uses sex to sell you things. "It's a very positive time," notes Shirley Zussman, Ed.D., a certified sex and marital therapist in New York City and editor of a newsletter, *Sex Over 40*. "There's much more of an expectation of sexuality for people in their fifties and older. And the more that gets across, the more they can enjoy sex."

If you're in your fifties, then, and seek an active, healthy sex life, you're no longer swimming against the cultural tide. Whom do we thank for this happy sea change? Well, there's the longer life expectancy and medical advances. And, as Dr. Zussman points out, "50-year-old men are in a lot better physical shape than they were 30 years ago."

But we all know what's really going on. The baby boom generation—that howling, clamoring mass of humanity born between 1946 and 1964—is marching into the fifty-something era and hauling the sexual revolution with it. "Just compare the sexual attitudes of this group with their parents at the same stage of life," Dr. Goldstein says. "Their sexual activity is much higher, more creative, more varied than it was for their parents."

And it's probably going to stay that way. "Baby boomers have had the numbers to redefine every stage of life they go into in their own image," Dr. Goldstein says. "Why should it be any different when we talk about sexuality? They'll bring those same attitudes of exploration and rebellion into their fifties when it comes to sex."

But wait a minute. Isn't there something called AIDS these days? Isn't there also a sexual backlash? A conservative trend? A counterrevolution?

Obviously, there's all that. But AIDS affects sexual behavior more than sexual attitudes, sexologists say. And there's nothing in the current cultural winds that's going to blow away 30 years of change. "These are mini-trends versus a macro-trend," Dr. Goldstein says. "The backlash has probably had a greater effect on Generation X than on baby boomers."

GETTING PERSONAL

So you have the sexual thumbs-up from society. That's one barrier smashed. What matters now is your own thumbs-up. Your fifties demand a new sexual liberation, and this time it's personal.

After all, who were those people who 20 to 30 years ago ridiculed the fifties as too old for sex or almost anything else? Look in the mirror and hum a song from The Who, pal. Now you know better, but you may still have to convince the inner you.

"It's not that men see themselves as trying to be sexually active in a sexually conservative society," says Samuel Osherson, Ph.D., a psychologist in Cambridge, Massachusetts, specializing in midlife issues and author of *Wrestling with Love*. "Rather, men in their fifties are faced with reinventing their own sexuality as they try to understand the kind of rhythmic changes that aging brings."

If you're 50 and single, the personal challenge is even scarier. Society may make you feel more welcome in the dating world than before, but you still have to find your place in it. "You have to reactivate vulnerable parts of yourself," Dr. Osherson says. "You have to relearn and redo the whole sexual thing with another partner. That's much more significant than any cultural attitude."

But it helps that, while making the transition, you don't have to worry so much about finger wagging from society's standard bearers. All in all, this era is kinder to your quest for a sexually fulfilling middle age.

BEYOND SEX

This issue of changing standards goes two ways, of course. It's not just how society copes with you as a 50-plus guy; it's also how you cope with society. Consider this.

Rap music. Absurdly baggy pants. Drugs. Gangs. Ludicrous hairstyles. Internet sex. Horrible youth TV programming (Beverly Hills 90210). Ultra-skinny, over-hyped supermodels (Kate Moss).

This is how kids want to live today? Unbelievable. Pathetic. Pitiful. Let me tell you about the good days of being young, 30 years ago.

Psychedelic music. Absurdly wide bell-bottoms. Drugs. Hell's Angels. Ludicrous hairstyles. Free sex. Horrible youth TV programming (The Partridge Family). Ultra-skinny, overhyped supermodels (Twiggy).

Get the point? The reality is that each generation has its own personality, and while you may be partial to the generation you grew up with, none are inherently better or worse than the next. Society marches on, and you had better, too.

There is nothing sadder in these wondrous times we live in than to meet an old-timer whose mind is completely stuck in the old days. Remember this piece of wisdom, friend: The good days are *any* days that you are alive and healthy, and your *best* days should be those about to happen. Here's how to adjust your attitudes—sexual and otherwise—if the past has too strong a hook on you.

Stretch your role. A generation ago, you spent time diapering and even the little guy you were changing looked up and wondered, "Aren't you s'posed to be out earning money, Daddy?" Times have liberated us, so take advantage of it because assuming roles other than breadwinner is key to midlife success. "Fortunately, the women's movement has forced men to get good at things we weren't allowed to do before," points out Leonard Felder, Ph.D., a Los Angeles psychologist and author of *The Ten Challenges.* "Things like caregiving, parenting, friendships, volunteer activities—they give you a feeling of potency."

Plug yourself in. In today's climate, you don't have to negotiate your way through the changing landscape of middle age in a social vacuum as your forefathers did. "It's very important not to get socially isolated," Dr. Osherson says. "Don't try to solve it all on your own. Go out and get information."

From a sexual standpoint, that could mean talking with your doctor, reading books like this, communicating with your loved ones.

Culturally, that means reading magazines other than *Modern Maturity*, watching TV channels other than American Movie Classics. It means getting good at computers, listening to new music, keeping an eye toward what's happening in the culture around you. It's paying attention to your kids' interests. We're not saying *be* a 20-year-old again, but at least have some knowledge of what being 20 is like today.

Develop an ally. "Find a buddy who's willing to talk about what he's struggling with," Dr. Felder says. "There's a breakthrough for men when they discover they're not the only ones going through what they're going through."

Again, talking to a pal about sexual or other midlife issues—anything other than work, sports, or dames in the lusty sense—was virtually unheard of in ancient times, like the 1960s. But even today, you have to speak English. "Ask him what his 'feelings' are, and you're not going to get an answer," Dr. Felder points out. "Ask him what has been going on lately, and you might get somewhere."

11

60 AND ABOVE

YOUR CHANGES

Time was when a guy was 60 and older, his sex life was considered as dormant as Mount Saint Helens. No longer. "As a man gets older, he can become an even better lover because the orgasmic experience isn't as important as the lovemaking," says licensed psychologist William R. Stayton, Th.D., professor of human sexuality at the University of Pennsylvania in Philadelphia and president of the American Association of Sex Educators, Counselors, and Therapists (AASECT).

Skeptical? Convinced that as you age you and your penis will be as listless as a deflated balloon? Maybe you need a role model, an inspiration to persuade you that it ain't so, Joe. How about actor Anthony Quinn? In his late seventies, he impregnated his thirty-something lover. Or South Carolina senator Strom Thurmond? Between the ages of 68 and 73 he fathered not one, but *four* children.

That's not to say that when we're 70, we'll be trysting the night away three times a week. Our erections will be fewer and less firm. We will continue to need more time after orgasm before we can get aroused again. Here are some other physiological developments.

SEX-RELATED CHANGES

• Less testosterone. Beyond the ages 60 to 70, as many as one-third of men lose the ability to get and maintain an erection because of low testosterone levels.

• Medication side effects. It is medications, not flagging testosterone, that are the most frequent culprits in erection difficulties experienced by older men. Blood pressure medicine, tranquilizers, sedatives, and antidepressants can all keep your flag dangling at half-mast.

• Prostate cancer. The risk of contracting this disease continues to rise with age. More than 80 percent of prostate cancers are diagnosed in men over age 65.

• Less intense orgasms. It takes older men longer to come, and when they do, there will be less ejaculate and a less intense feeling.

OTHER CHANGES

• Arthritis. Roughly one-half of people 65 or older suffer from arthritis. "Osteoarthritis is almost universal," says Bruce Hirsch, M.D., assistant professor of medicine in the division of infectious diseases at North Shore University Hospital in Manhasset, New York.

This degenerative disease of the joints occurs when the cartilage that normally covers the ends of the bones, reducing friction and absorbing shock, wears away, exposing the bone to the surface of other bones at the joint. It is very common in the lower spine and joints of the fingers, and also flares up in the hip and knee joints.

It is no mystery why so many seniors get osteoarthritis: After decades of life and abuse, the joints just wear down, simple as that. The disease is a normal part of aging. Old injuries or abuse to joints, such as from playing sports or work activities, can hasten its development.

• Bone deterioration. Men have denser bones than women and don't suffer as much bone loss as they age. But they do lose some, so consequently, in old age we are apt to be a little shorter and more stooped than when we were young. Men also may suffer from osteoporosis in their later years, especially those who have low testosterone levels.

• Weakening immunity. Diseases you could ignore in your twenties are potentially life-threatening as your near age 70. That's because the thymus gland, the central command of your immune system, has by now shrunk to $\frac{1}{10}$ the size it was when you were born. And white blood cells—the body's primary defense against infections—also aren't what they used to be.

• Weight loss. After years of trying to shed pounds, you now find yourself losing weight without even trying. This is probably true in your sixties, and it accelerates between 70 and 80.

There are several reasons why. You are losing muscle mass, and muscle is heavier than fat. You also may have cancer, depression, ulcers, or other conditions that account for the thinner look. But in about one case out of four where older folks start losing weight rapidly, it's not clear why, says Waneen Wyrick Spirduso, Ed.D., professor in the department of kinesiology and health education at the University of Texas in Austin and author of *Physical Dimensions of Aging*. "As people get older, they eat less, and as they eat less it becomes more important that what they eat has the right nutrients in it," Dr. Spirduso says. "When you eat a lot, you cannot worry about that because you're bound to get your daily minimum requirements."

• Muscle loss. Men start losing their strength fairly rapidly after they turn 60, but Dr. Spirduso says that until age 70 this happens mostly because of disuse, not aging. By age 65, upper body strength and muscle tone will decrease by 20 percent compared to when a man was young.

• The brain. Fat makes up a large amount of your brain tissue. So the next time somebody calls you a fat head, accept it as fact. Unless you are old. Your brain began losing neurons in your thirties. If you live to be 80, it will weigh about 7 percent less than it did when you were 25.

Fewer neurons and a small brain have little effect, however, on mental functioning. Fluid intelligence—problem solving that requires abstract, nonverbal mental nimbleness and a knack for quickly assessing new situations and refiguring old ones—peaks in early adulthood, then begins to decline.

But crystallized intelligence—verbal and mathematical skills and the use of accumulated knowledge—improves throughout life. Researchers think that staying mentally challenged keeps your brain functioning at its peak.

HER CHANGES

It's true that women will outlive us men by about seven years on average. But there is a downside for the women. They are more apt to have lingering, chronic illnesses, while we guys just drop dead one day and get life over with. And older women are less likely than older men to enjoy good mental and physical health, and three times more likely to eventually live in nursing homes.

Rather than death and decay, however, we prefer to think about women in their sixties and older who remain vibrant and lovely. There are plenty of them. Lauren Bacall. Sophia Loren. Elizabeth Dole. Jane Fonda. Heck, even Tina Turner is pushing 60. And as Tina herself might put it: What's age got to do with it?

"Aging is extremely individualistic," says Waneen Wyrick Spirduso, Ed.D., professor in the department of kinesiology and health education at the University of Texas in Austin and author of *Physical Dimensions of Aging*. "People age at much different rates, depending on their genetic makeup and their lifestyle." Her advice to women and men: Eat right, exercise, don't smoke, and drink in moderation.

Here are some changes that women in their sixties and older might encounter.

SEX-RELATED CHANGES

• Orgasms. Women still have orgasms as they age, but they are less intense. And they have fewer multiple orgasms. Since a man now takes longer to reach orgasm, a man and woman's sexual response times are more in sync than they've ever been.

• Sexual desire. A woman's libido lessens with age, same as a man's. In one study, half of the women interviewed over the age of 65 said they had no desire or interest in sex. Maybe they just needed a live man to woo them, because in another study of healthy people between the ages of 80 and 102, 71 percent of the women said they fantasized about sex.

• Medications. Just as with men, various medications that women take as they age can douse their ardor.

OTHER CHANGES

• Bones. The rapid bone loss that women experience after menopause continues, but at a slower rate. Still, by the time a woman is elderly, the cumulative loss over the years can be considerable. Women may lose 2 to 3 inches in height by the time they are in their eighties as a result of bone loss and collapsing vertebrae, Dr. Spirduso says. Men shrink, too, she says, but much less.

Older women have four times as many broken bones as men do. They also suffer two to three times as many hip fractures, and many of these women will never again regain their full mobility, Dr. Spirduso says. The earlier a woman goes through menopause, the greater her risk of osteoporosis.

• Stroke. Women are most apt to have a stroke after they turn 65. They aren't stricken as often as men, yet women are more likely to experience a type of hemorrhagic stroke in which an artery bursts and bleeds into the area between the skull and brain tissue.

A woman's stroke may be caused by high blood pressure, smoking, lupus, migraine headaches, and several other conditions and activities.

• Arthritis. As we've already seen, women are more apt to contract severe cases of rheumatoid arthritis when they are younger. They also are far more likely to get the more common osteoarthritis.

It's not clear why women are more prone to this inflammation, swelling, and pain in the joints. Experts think that hormones, obesity, heredity, and mechanical problems—in addition to injuries incurred in sports and accidents—may be factors.

• Skin. The facial skin care market is more than $2 billion a year and growing, but there is no stopping Mother Nature's work on a woman's face. Her first laugh lines and crow's feet probably appeared in her late twenties or thirties. Now she has aged a bit more and has the additional wrinkles to prove it.

The bulk of skin wrinkling comes from sun damage. The second-biggest culprit is smoking. Besides the inevitable lines and wrinkles, her skin may betray her age if her eyelids crease into heavy folds or she has wrinkly bags around the eyes. The gradual loss of bone along the jaw and of soft tissue beneath the cheeks is another sign of the advancing years.

Yes, she's older now. And so are you. It doesn't have to mean the end of passion. Sex therapist Theresa Crenshaw, M.D., sums up the sentiments of many sex therapists regarding aging in her book, *The Alchemy of Love and Lust*. She writes, "The bottom line on aging is this: Barring debilitating disease, there is no reason a man and woman can't enjoy love, romance, intimacy, and sex as long as they live."

RULES OF ENGAGEMENT

The women at a retirement complex were all atwitter at the arrival of a new male resident. Giddily, they all primped and fluffed before going outside, where the new man sat poolside.

"Where did you live before you came here?" one of the smitten women asked the man.

"I was in prison," he replied.

"Why were you in prison?" asked a second woman.

"I murdered my wife," he replied.

A third woman trilled: "Oh, does that mean you're single?"

Okay, it's a bad joke. Older women aren't really so desperate for a man that they would pursue a murderer. But as with all humor, there is a kernel of underlying truth. And the truth is that the pickings are slim for women in their sixties and above. From the perspective of older women, senior men who are single, divorced, or widowed are more coveted than a ticket to a Tom Jones concert.

"They will be made much of wherever they go," says psychologist Matti K. Gershenfeld, Ed.D., adjunct professor of psychoeducational processes at Temple University in Philadelphia and author of *How to Find Love, Sex, and Intimacy after 50.* "If they didn't do well in their twenties, they'll do well in their sixties."

In the chapters that follow, we'll give detailed advice on how to maximize your appeal to women as well as how to keep your sex life active, whether with a new partner or old. But to start you on the path, here we give you some overview advice for courting a senior lady.

WHERE TO FIND WOMEN

They'll find you. They really will. "As soon as the world hears that someone is a widower or divorced, every woman he ever knew—even his cousin's next-door neighbor—has someone to fix him up with," says Dr. Gershenfeld.

And yet you may want to be the hunter, not the hunted. And if you are new to this, you might be tempted to try one of the many singles dances, mixers, and the like that are aimed at people in your age group. A word of caution: A lot of women sum up the type of man who goes to these events in one word—loser.

The perception is that with so many women pursuing the paucity of available men in this age group, there must be something wrong with a guy who has to schlep around at a singles scene, says Dr. Gershenfeld. "The guys who go—and the women will tell you this—are the same losers all the time," she says.

Still, some men are uneasy with blind dates and prefer to meet a woman on their own terms, so they will go. "I always tell women to go because you might find somebody who is going for the first time. He'll be a different type than is in the regular crowd," says Dr. Gershenfeld.

The experience also can be good for a newly widowed or divorced man. "It's very good for ego gratification," says Dr. Gershenfeld. "If you're not feeling very terrific with women, or you're having a hard time making small talk, by all means go to one of the singles things.

Women will come and talk to you. It makes it easier if you need to get started."

Want some other places to look for women in your age group? Try these.

- Piano bars. They are more congenial and less blatant of a meat market than singles bars.
- Auctions. People attending tend to be chatty and sociable, explains Dr. Gershenfeld.
- ElderHostel. This outfit puts on classes and programs at colleges and universities throughout the United States and abroad for people over 60.
- Jogging or dog walking. Especially in the morning hours, a good, casual way to meet others.

What Women Want from You

By the time they reach this age, women don't ask a lot from a man. "Really, all he has to be is pleasant and polite," says Dr. Gershenfeld. And a few other things, she adds.

- Reasonably healthy. A woman doesn't want to be your nursemaid. If she's a widow, she may already have had to care for a man in faltering health.
- Reasonably wealthy. No, your name doesn't have to be Rockefeller. But older women are leery of dating a guy with less money than they for fear that he is a gold digger.
- Reasonably self-sufficient. She doesn't want to be your maid, cooking all your meals, cleaning your house, and washing your laundry.
- Reasonably sociable. More than anything, an older woman wants a man who is a good companion. Somebody who will ask about her day and tell her about his. "What they really want is affection," says Dr. Gershenfeld.

So Many Women, So Little Time

With so many women to choose from, you would think that older guys would be in dating heaven. And some are. But there are land mines on the battlefield of love that are unique to this age group and must be tiptoed over. If you encounter any of the following, you need to think it through, perhaps discuss it with your lady. Any of the these could ruin a budding relationship—or land you in one that is not healthy for you or for her.

- Deification. A widow sometimes remembers her late husband as she wishes he were, in effect, deifying him. Nobody can live up to his memory, and she shouldn't expect you to be a replacement. You are a unique person, and should be considered as such.
- Betrayal. Similarly, some widows and divorcees feel like they are betraying their late or former husband by going out with another man. Guilt is not a good emotion to launch a relationship upon.

• Rigidity. Chances are that an older woman is less flexible—not as likely to try things she might have when younger. So don't ask her to go inline skating unless she says she likes this.

• Your own rigidity. An unattached man over 60 can play the field for some time, he has so many women available in his age range. But many do not. They are so flattered by the first woman to pay them any attention and so intimidated by dating that they often stick with the first woman they date, Dr. Gershenfeld says.

"If they find somebody that's reasonably comfortable, they will stay with her," Dr. Gershenfeld says. "More for the comfort and more for the fact that she will cook meals and they'll watch television together. It's like a continuation of their former life."

INITIATING SEX

The axiom of taking it slow and easy when you were younger is even more pertinent now. With the advancing years, men and women may both have anxieties about how they look and how they will perform sexually. Another thing that hasn't changed is that the man is expected to initiate sex, but often only does after the woman signals her willingness.

"The man should initiate, but in reality what happens, the woman initiates," says Dr. Gershenfeld. "The woman will give clues. 'You can come over to my house. Why don't you stay over?' The woman will initiate by saying that she's ready for it or that she's willing to go further in the relationship."

HER DECREASED DESIRE

It happens. You want it and she doesn't. Your longtime partner in passion just doesn't seem to care for sex anymore. Or that relatively new object of your desire resists consummating your romance.

What do you do? Shrug it off because she's "old"? Hardly. Age alone is not a sex-ender for her any more than it is for you.

How many women over the age of 60 stay sexually active? "There are little data about older women," notes Fran E. Kaiser, M.D., professor of medicine and associate director of the division of geriatric medicine at St. Louis University's Health Sciences Center and director of the university's Sexual Dysfunction Clinic. But in an article published in *Urologic Clinics of North America*, she cites one study that found 55.8 percent of married women over 60 engaging in sexual activity. And that's despite lingering social myths that discourage senior sex.

Interestingly, notes Dr. Kaiser in the article, while women over 50 may have less vaginal intercourse than they did before, they masturbate just as much as ever. Obviously, the fires are still burning. And while it's true that men over 60 have more frequent intercourse than women do, that's a constant at all ages. And remember that women over 60 have a partner problem since they live longer. By the time they reach 85, there are only 39 men for every 100 women.

So if your partner is unwilling, don't just kiss it off to age. There are usually addressable reasons. Your mission is to discover what they are and deal with them. Consider it intelligent, compassionate seduction.

HER PLUMBING CHANGES

Your body has changed. So has hers. But the big difference is that her lowered levels of estrogen, the female hormone, wreaks more havoc than testosterone reduction does for men. And what's affected most is the vagina. You don't need to be a gynecologist to figure out that a dryer, smaller vagina can diminish her eagerness for sex. "If she has a dry vagina that hurts and bleeds, she's not going to feel very sexy," says Domeena Renshaw, M.D., director of Loyola Sex Therapy Clinic at Loyola University in Chicago and author of *Seven Weeks to Better Sex*.

Again, vaginal atrophy does not mean that she can't have sex with you anymore. "The vagina is usually capable of accommodating a man's penis until the day you die," says Theodore R. Brooks, M.D., a geriatric specialist and professor of family practice at the King/Drew Medical Center in Los Angeles. "She can engage in sex, but it may not be comfortable."

There are ways, fortunately, to get her comfortable—and willing—again.

Rub it in. How simple can you get it? Her vagina's dry, so get it wet. "Using lubricants makes sex a lot more pleasant for her," says Dr. Brooks. "They're really simple to buy, and they really help an older couple."

As at any age, make sure that you use a water-based lubricant. Petroleum jellies such as Vaseline can lead to infections. K-Y jelly is fine, but other water-based lubricants on the market, such as Astroglide, don't have the antiseptic, institutional feel associated with K-Y. And they're sexier.

Use it or lose it. For women, as with men, sex is the best stimulator for sex. "Women who maintain an active sex life have greater expandable capability in the vagina than women who are not having sex," Dr. Kaiser says. So if you have maintained a reasonable sexual pace to date, don't stop now.

Start slow. Okay, the years have slipped away, as they tend to do, and for her, pain-free sex has slipped away with them. Get back in the game, a little at a time. "I advocate going very slowly," Dr. Kaiser says.

If she's hesitant, dust off that old ploy from your youth: Tell her that you just want to put one finger in. This time, though, you mean it. "Learn to stretch the vagina with fingers, yours and hers," says Dr. Kaiser. "When you

The Young and the Lustless

When a senior man speaks of an unwilling partner, most of the time he is referring to a postmenopausal woman. But what about when a considerably younger sexual partner turns unwilling?

"For older men with younger partners, things are usually okay when they start," says Wulf H. Utian, M.D., Ph.D., a gynecologist, chairman of the department of reproductive biology at Case Western Reserve University in Cleveland, and executive director of the North American Menopause Society. "But at some point the age factor is going to come into play."

The upside is that, by definition, postmenopausal hormonal factors aren't a problem with premenopausal women. What's at issue are *your* changes and her need to adjust to them. If, for example, she doesn't understand that your slower response time is healthy, natural, and a potential advantage, she may jump to some damaging conclusions about her ability to turn you on—or your ability to be turned on. Next thing you know, she's keeping her distance. Obviously, that's what you want to avoid. And you can.

Clue her in. Make sure that she knows what you know about your new sexual patterns, Dr. Utian advises. Give her the course in Senior Sexuality 101. With a positive approach and some well-timed show-and-tell, the learning process

can get three fingers in without discomfort, she is probably ready for intercourse."

Get the hormones back. The best way for her to overcome the negative effects of lost hormones is to find them again. Hormone replacement therapy—orally, transdermally, or topically—restores the tissues of postmenopausal women. "Once you replace the hormones, you pretty much put the lady back to where she was at a younger age," says Dr. Brooks. "It's tremendous for making sex—and life—better for older people. And it's very common."

Pills, patch, or cream? That's a doctor's call, of course. But, says Wulf H. Utian, M.D., Ph.D., a gynecologist, chairman of the department of reproductive biology at Case Western Reserve University in Cleveland, and executive director of the North American Menopause Society, "the cream gives a higher concentration. The interesting thing is that you can take a woman of 80, give her vaginal estrogen, and the vagina will look almost as healthy as it was at age 40."

Be aware that hormone replacement therapy is a hot button in the women's health arena. There are risks, including a heightened chance of developing uterine or breast cancer. In other words, while you might suggest it to your partner and help in the research, let her make the final call and respect her choice.

itself can be exciting. When her doubts about your sex life turn to eager antici-pation of new routes to sexual happiness, she has graduated with honors.

Convert less to more. Make her an offer she can't refuse: less frequent sex in exchange for more satisfying sex every time. That's exactly what your longer refractory period and delayed ejaculations make possible. "The issue is mutual adjustment," Dr. Utian says. "Two or three times a week, say, instead of two or three times a day is a minimal sacrifice for good quality."

Expand your horizons. "Build your relationship on more than the simple issue of sex frequency," says Dr. Utian. "There are other ways of being intimate, other ways of showing interest. If you do a lot of things that you both enjoy, the sex will come out of that."

In other words, when full-fledged, penetrating intercourse is temporarily on hold, be intimate anyway. Never let her conclude that you're not interested in her. She won't assume the fire has gone out if you keep her on simmer. "Sex isn't a one-note experience," says Helen Fisher, Ph.D., research associate in the department of anthropology at Rutgers University in New Brunswick, New Jersey, and author of *Anatomy of Love*. "It's a symphony. You can play it in many different ways."

MAKING HER FEEL SEXY

You may be a silver fox, but "silver vixen" is not in the lexicon. The sad truth is that it's much harder for a woman to maintain a sexy self-image in a youth-oriented society. Her unwillingness to have sex may be the result of not liking the way she looks, or at least not considering the image conducive to sex. Surgeries such as mastectomies or colostomies—though not physically im-pairing, sexually speaking—can make things rougher for her psychologically.

"There are women who are desperately trying to hold the aging process back," Dr. Utian says. "They may look at themselves in the mirror, and, well, they may not want to look at themselves in the mirror."

She needs sexual self-esteem therapy, and you're the one to provide it.

Stroke her. Never underestimate the power of kind words. "You have to reassure her," says Dr. Utian. "You have to say, 'Hey, you know I married you for better or worse and for life. I'm with you all the way, so let's not get up-tight about this. I love you how you are.'"

Be supportive. Let her know you like what she has and are grateful for what she's doing to stay attractive. "You can make it tough for a woman who's does her best if you don't show any appreciation," says Dr. Utian.

Be honest. You didn't choose a dummy for your sexual partner. So you're not going to do anything for her self-esteem by telling her she looks the same as she did 30 years ago. "That's the wrong thing to say because she

Talking the Talk

If sex advice professionals had their way, we'd convert our bedrooms into talk-show studios. Or espresso bars. Nothing in the world of sex, it seems, can't be improved by talking about it. Changes with aging? Talk about them. Time has altered your taste? Communicate it. Your partner has turned unwilling? Discuss it. Sometimes you wish everyone would just shut up.

The problem is that they're right. Sex is mysterious enough at any age; when you're over 60 and dealing with a changing sexual landscape (not to mention the ever-present mythology of the sexless senior), silence is dangerous. "I've had patients whose marriages are at the point of breaking up," says Wulf H. Utian, M.D., Ph.D., a gynecologist, chairman of the department of reproductive biology at Case Western Reserve University in Cleveland, and executive director of the North American Menopause Society. "They've simply not spoken to each other, so they're not aware of the mutual changes that come with age."

Talking doesn't just help you learn what's going on. More important, it keeps you from imagining things. "Communication is important because if you're not aware of the changes a woman is going through, you may interpret her unwillingness as rejection," Dr. Utian says. And, of course, that works both ways.

Still, knowing you should talk about sex with your partner is one thing. Doing it is another. For a lot of us, those vocal cords stop vibrating when the topic is sex. And it doesn't get any easier with age. "If it has always been difficult for you, it will continue to be," acknowledges Sandra Scantling, Psy.D., assistant clinical professor of psychiatry at the University of Connecticut

knows you're lying," Dr. Utian says. Instead, tell her you're just as excited by her as you were 30 years ago. That's true, isn't it?

Don't falsely flatter, but don't be cruel either. This won't help: "Look, I don't care if you're wrinkled and overweight. You turn me on," says Dr. Utian, "You have to have some charm and tact."

BE A LOVER, NOT A SEX PARTNER

Your sex life is taking place—or not taking place—in the context of a relationship. All right, that's not always true. But it is always true that it takes two of you to have sex. That means that her feelings and desires count as much as yours. And they may have changed with age, just as yours have. Or, you may have forgotten with age some of the details that fan her flames. That cold shoulder you're getting may simply be her reaction to an unaddressed new reality. It's time to reassess your technique.

Survey the scene. Find out what she likes these days and what she doesn't. That thing you did may no longer do the trick. If she assumes that

School of Medicine in Farmington and co-author of *Ordinary Women, Extraordinary Sex*, "unless you do something to face up to it."

Like what? Take a tip from that eminent authority on sexuality, the Chinese philospher Lao-tzu: "A journey of a thousand miles must begin with a single step." Dr. Scantling puts it this way: "Begin somewhere, but begin. Take baby steps, talking about things that are easy. Slowly get into the mindset of talking about your likes and dislikes."

How? Unlike in some conversations, beating around the bush is an advantage in sexual discourse. "If you have difficulty talking about rear-entry penetration, don't start there," suggests Dr. Scantling. "Talk about how you like your back scratched a little harder. Create a win-win situation for yourself."

Remember that it can be as hard for her to listen as it is for you to talk. "Some people don't even like to hear that you want a little more salt in your soup," Dr. Scantling warns. "They think, 'What? You don't like my cooking the way it is?' The whole notion of making a suggestion about anything is tough."

So Dr. Scantling suggests using an exercise metaphor. "If you haven't worked out for a long time, you're not going to start with anything too heavy. If you do, you get sore or injure yourself and you won't want to go back. The same thing is true when it comes to expressing sexuality."

This means to start with light weights—that is, an observation or suggestion that isn't overwhelming. Increase gradually. And, says Dr. Scantling, "don't measure yourself or her against what you think other people might be doing. Use yourselves as the standard."

sex with you will include things she no longer likes—and not what she currently likes—she'll naturally lose interest. Let her know you aim to please.

"Sometimes after menopause, women find that certain textures are now uncomfortable on their skin," says Sandra Scantling, Psy.D., assistant clinical professor of psychiatry at the University of Connecticut School of Medicine in Farmington and co-author of *Ordinary Women, Extraordinary Sex*. "Or maybe that Old Spice smell she used to like doesn't smell good to her anymore."

What's true for smells and textures can also be true for sexual techniques. Her sexual tastes have changed. To what? Try asking her. Is there something you can wear? A position she'd prefer? A change of pace? Satin sheets? Showering together? Carpenters music in the background (hey, you'll do anything)?

"Sometimes it's the smallest thing that can make her feel really sexy," Dr. Scantling says.

Make yourself desirable. If sex doesn't stop at 60, neither does its attendant prerequisites. That means keeping yourself attractive to her. It's easy to fall into off-turning habits in your golden years. Don't do it. She may be unwilling because you're unappetizing.

Dr. Brooks relates some common complaints of his women patients about their men: They come home smelling of cigars and alcohol and don't bother to brush their teeth. They pay no attention to their mates until they want sex. No foreplay. Slovenliness. Laziness. Of course, these are common (and legitimate) complaints at any age. But many seniors think they deserve impunity. You don't if you want sex.

In fact, go further and improve yourself to show that you care. "Lose those 10 pounds that she has been grumbling about for 40 years," suggests Helen Fisher, Ph.D., research associate in the department of anthropology at Rutgers University in New Brunswick, New Jersey, and author of *Anatomy of Love*. "Or there's a whole lot of sex technique books on how to please a woman. Buy one."

Surprise her. Now, we'd never advocate outright bribery to turn an unwilling partner around. But unsolicited gifts work as well in sex as they do in politics. "In cultures around the world, men give women a little present in order to get sex," Dr. Fisher says. "The little extras are exciting for women. Older men who've been married for a long time forget these little things."

Of course, what's at work here is not bribery but gestures from the heart. The idea is to slay the monster of ennui that has had decades to grow. Flowers here, compliments there, a little extra time together—those are powerful weapons. "It's the little touches that get you to the big places," Dr. Fisher says.

Pitch the woo. "Women of any age are turned on—sexually turned on—by a man who courts her," Dr. Fisher says. She didn't jump into bed with you when you first met her, did she? You had to court her then. Court her now. The only difference is that you're probably a lot better at it these days. "Younger men overlook many of the standard techniques of courtship, but an older man knows how to cultivate them," says Dr. Fisher.

What techniques? Well, courtship is corny when you talk about it but an aphrodisiac when you actually do it. It's holding her hand at the movies—not mechanically, but like you really mean it. It's an evening walk on the beach, kissing her by the waves. It's candlelight dinners and close dancing. Sure, they're clichés, but how do you think they got to be clichés? They work.

"Women are fools for romance," says Dr. Fisher. "And older men can be terribly romantic. Just let it go."

WHEN NO IS NO

There are times, of course, when technical difficulties beyond your control cause her to resist intercourse despite your best efforts. An extreme example might be a serious disease like advanced cancer, which tends to reorder life priorities. As Dr. Renshaw put it, "The dying process puts a pretty heavy deep freeze on sexual desire." Even without such a disease, though, her unwillingness may persist. The answer may be a nonnegotiable no.

But sexuality doesn't end even if sexual intercourse does. "There's a hell of a lot more to sex than just intercourse," points out Dr. Kaiser. "There are plenty of other ways to express sexual intimacy." Those other ways are available to all age groups and are especially handy for older seniors. In her articles, Dr. Kaiser cites a study that found that 83 percent of men and 64 percent of women over 80 engaged in "touching and caressing without intercourse."

So touch and caress. Focus on sensuality. "Ask her to do alternatives," suggests Dr. Renshaw, "like stimulating you manually while you stimulate her. You can do a lot of kissing and hugging and fooling around." It's not intercourse, but it's sex. And better yet, it's love.

How to Stay Attractive to Women

Movies and television would have you believe that young, muscular, slightly dangerous men are the true magnets of women. But as it usually is on matters of sex, Hollywood has it all wrong. When it comes to possessing the specific qualities that women are genetically programmed to pursue, senior men have the game won. Women know it, and 60-plussers find out fast.

"Women are attracted to men with resources and status," explains Helen Fisher, Ph.D., research associate in the department of anthropology at Rutgers University in New Brunswick, New Jersey, and author of *Anatomy of Love*. "And men have acquired those things by their sixties or seventies."

We are talking universal truth here, too. A researcher at the University of Michigan studied the mating choices in 37 different countries. Conclusion: Sexual attraction has a lot more to do with biology than society. And these traits are the aforementioned resources and status.

And who is the most likely to have resources and status? Successful senior men.

Candidly substituting dollar signs for the concept of "resources," Dr. Fisher concludes, "A rich, healthy man could probably have a different partner every night."

This is probably not what a man over 60 wants, of course. But the point is this: Whether you're trying to attract a new woman into your life or re-attract the one you've loved for decades, the fact that you look different than the typical cover boy is irrelevant. The fact that you have experience, wisdom, patience, perspective—and perhaps plenty of cash in your wallet—isn't.

OTHER SENIOR BENEFITS

There's more good news: Just by being alive, you have a mathematical edge in finding a companion. "Women live longer than men and remain in very good health," Dr. Fisher says. "A man over 60 or 70 has an enormous pool of potential partners of all ages to choose from."

All ages? Yes, your expanding landscape of sexual opportunity includes May-December romances, which even get the Darwinian seal of approval (that is, the resourceful older man, the fertile younger woman). But in the real world, Dr. Fisher points out, men are attracted to women only somewhat younger than they are. "Most men in their sixties and seventies don't want a 29-year-old girl," she says. "But they do prefer a woman in her fifties to a woman in her eighties."

The reason is simple: Men are more compatible with women relatively close in age. For example, if you're at a point in your life where you want to stop and smell the roses, can you deal with a partner who's fighting her way up the corporate ladder? "You can get younger women, but you're going to have to keep up with them," warns Dr. Fisher. "Do you really want to do that?"

So if you are over 60 and looking for a companion, this is our message

The Beauty of Bald

Co-owner of Miano-Viel Salon and Spa in New York City Damien Miano sums up the situation with admirable directness: "A lot of guys in their sixties don't have a hell of a lot of hair." You can't argue with that. But you can debate what to do about it.

Especially for an older man, baldness is a look, not a condition. Still, if you're typical, you think about "solutions." Here are some considerations.

• It's not coming back. "Now's the time to give up all remedies for baldness," Miano tells men over 60.

According to Barry Resnik, M.D., a clinical instructor of dermatology at the University of Miami School of Medicine, it's not so much age as the advanced state of your baldness that keeps minoxidil, the only proven baldness treatment, from working.

• You can comb, but you can't hide. "There are certain cuts and techniques that can help disguise thinning hair," Miano says. But combing hair over bald spots isn't one of them. "If you want to scream out that you're uncomfortable being over 60, then just do that," he says.

• Want hair? Try your face. "If you want to draw attention away from your baldness, grow facial hair," Miano advises. But whatever you grow on your

number one: Figure out exactly what you want of your companion, and determine what age and lifestyle best fits those needs. Chances are that you'll be after a women who is not that different in age from you.

HOW TO BE A CLASSY SENIOR

On to the chase. If women want men with resources and status, it seems pretty obvious what to do: Show off your resources and status. But that isn't nearly as easy as it sounds. Here's some wisdom on how to stay attractive to women, no matter how many years young you are.

Show off modestly. Nature has dealt you some aces. Play them. But that doesn't mean flashing a wad or bragging about your portfolio. You want to send signals, not missiles. But you do want to send them. "Wear your Rolex watch," says Dr. Fisher. "Continue to drive the nice car."

You don't have to be Ted Turner rich to be attractive to women. But if she senses that she can order anything on any menu when she's with you, you're ahead of the game. "Exhibit your resources and you're likely to get women of all ages," Dr. Fisher says.

Listen up. "Women aren't just looking for a meal ticket," Dr. Fisher says. "They want a companion." A companion doesn't try to dazzle with knowl-

face—a mustache, a full beard, a goatee—must be meticulously groomed. And, he warns, "it's more work to maintain facial hair properly than to shave."

• Beware the cheap rug. Burt Reynolds has always been up front about what's up top. And, yes, he's in his sixties. "Somebody like Burt Reynolds looks okay in his toupees," says Christina Griffasi, style director at the Minardi Salon in New York City. "But you have to remember those are custom-made, natural-hair toupees that cost thousands of dollars apiece. Artificial toupees are horrible."

• It's expensive to replant. Hair transplants, which move healthy growing hairs from one part of your head to where they're needed, have come a long way in recent years, according to Dr. Resnik, who performs them. The receptor areas for the grafts are now so small and numerous that you can't see them. Also, the grafts are now placed at various angles on the scalp, rather than perpendicular to each other, as before. "The look is more natural," Dr. Resnik says. "No more corn rows." Still, you're talking about surgery here, not a step to be taken lightly...or cheaply.

• Nothing is something. The best advice comes from Griffasi: If you're balding, be bald. "An attractive man in good shape shouldn't worry about it," she says. "If you're a striking person, women always appreciate the natural amount of hair."

Saving Your Skin

The assorted spots, splotches, wrinkles, and dryness that can bedevil an older man's appearance are mostly sun-induced and usually treatable, says Barry Resnik, M.D., a clinical instructor of dermatology at the University of Miami School of Medicine. So are dental deficiencies. Here's a quick look at what ails your well-worn hide.

• Liver spots. They have nothing to do with your liver and often disappear with chemical peeling agents administered by dermatologists, Dr. Resnik says. Peeling (which is less drastic than it sounds) also works for other spotting, some of which is precancerous, so take heed.

• Wrinkles. They're hereditary, so the best way to avoid them is to have an unwrinkled mother and father. Otherwise, says Dr. Resnik, moisturizers with alpha hydroxy acids (AHAs), which are available in buffered form over-the-counter, can help.

• Rough skin. "What shows up in older men is dry skin, rough skin, and a deepening of the smile lines and creases around the eyes," says David Nap, vice president of creative services at Aramis, the men's grooming care com-

edge. Sure, you have a lifetime of war stories to share, but that doesn't mean that she wants to hear them. At least not all at once. The occasional nod and the well-timed interjection during a conversation controlled by her say a lot more about your acquired wisdom than any of your monologues would. "Women like to do the talking, and they're better with words than men are," says Dr. Fisher.

Here again, your years give you an advantage. As your levels of testosterone go down, says Dr. Fisher, estrogen in your system is unmasked. Estrogen being the dominant female hormone, you may find that you're getting pretty good at those "feminine" virtues, such as nurturing. That, says Dr. Fisher, makes older men much better active listeners, if they'll just give it a shot.

"Active" listening is shrinkspeak for not just letting her talk but actually hearing what she says. Don't just politely wait for her to finish so you can say your piece. When the appropriate time comes, respond to her words and on her terms. Pay attention.

The payoff? "Women are attracted to men who are interested in them," Dr. Fisher says.

Get in shape. So why is Sean Connery the embodiment of mature male attractiveness? Okay, besides being rich, handsome, a terrific actor, and forever associated with 007, the perfect male human being. Take a look. The man's in superb shape.

pany in New York City. "Once you accept the notion that *moisturizer* is not a feminine word, the AHAs can soften the lines and smooth the roughness."

• Paleness. Suntans are famously attractive on men over 60. But the sun is your skin's enemy (always use a strong sunscreen with a sun protection factor of at least 15, says Dr. Resnik, or stay out of the sun altogether) and tanning machines emit the same damaging rays, according to Dr. Resnik. But the newer self-tanning products get Dr. Resnik's safety approval, and they're much better than their predecessors if you follow the directions. "They don't make you orange," he says.

• Crooked teeth. "The new 'invisible' braces make it popular for older adults to use the appliances," says Robert Bray, D.D.S., spokesperson for the American Association of Orthodontists. Ceramic braces are tooth-colored; "lingual" braces work from the inside and don't show at all.

• Missing teeth. There's no longer a reason for it, says Dr. Bray. With implant techniques, teeth are saved (or replaced) one by one. "No longer do you have to take partial dentures in and out of your mouth," says Dr. Bray.

There are lots of reasons to stay fit after 60. Let's add another to the list: It's attractive to the opposite sex. "It's not that women don't love men with the big guts," says Pepper Schwartz, Ph.D., a sociologist at the University of Washington in Seattle and author of *American Couples* and *Love between Equals*. "But they love you in spite of it, not because of it."

A muscled, trim body at 65 or 70 isn't going to resemble a 24-year-old's ("It would be bizarre-looking if it did," muses Dr. Schwartz), but an older man who can take his shirt off with pride has two things going for him, according to Dr. Schwartz. One, he's simply more pleasing to look at, something that's always important to women. And he's sending the right message, which is that he hasn't given up, that he wants to look good for women and for himself. "That," says Dr. Schwartz, "is pretty sexy."

LOOKING LIKE YOU MEAN IT

One reason you're a virtual babe magnet after 60 (besides the fact that you'd never use the term *babe magnet*) is that it's the real you that's exerting the pull. Appearance blunders weaken the force. Trying to look 35 when you're 70 is an appearance blunder. Letting yourself slide into the geezer stereotype is another. Getting sloppy is the worst.

Strictly speaking, your dress and grooming goal is not to attract women. It's to provide a conduit for the inner you, which is what does the attracting. In Dr. Schwartz's words, "Projecting that strength about who you are that has evolved with the years is a very attractive quality." Here are some pointers then for projecting the unique you.

Dress your age. Mistakenly assuming sexual attractiveness to be a young man's game, men old enough to know better squeeze into tight clothes designed for 20-year-olds with zero body fat. Who are they kidding? Not women.

"Dressing younger than your years reads to the opposite sex that you're trying to recapture something lost," says *Men's Health* magazine's clothing and grooming editor Warren Christopher. "It's not a wise decision."

There are lots of ways to project that youthful vigor you feel inside. Putting on some kids' clothes isn't one of them. "You don't want to look like mutton dressed up as lamb," says Jarlath Mellett, senior vice president and design director for Brooks Brothers in New York City. "It just doesn't work."

Play the classics. So what does work? "You want to dress more classic once you reach your sixties," says Stanley Tucker, vice president and fashion director at Saks Fifth Avenue in New York City. "Lean toward the classic silhouette, the classic clothes. You don't want to be too far left or too far right—just well-dressed."

"Classic" covers a broad territory that might include such tried-and-true clothing choices as three-button pullover shirts, blue sport coats, navy pinstriped suits, brown loafers, or pressed khaki trousers. The idea is to project a quiet tastefulness and let your personality do the shouting. "Don't take any fashion leaps," says Christopher.

But classic, Christopher emphasizes, doesn't mean hopelessly out of it. "You have to take your cues from what's happening now," he says. "You want to look like you're in the know, even as you're quietly elegant."

You pull off that sartorial balancing act, says Mellett, by simple things like putting on a pale yellow sweater with your khakis, or brightening the tie under your classic suit. "Nothing radical," Mellett says. "Respect your classic style, but just twitch it a little bit."

Trim it. No matter how much hair you still have, keep it shorter than you used to. "At your age, the better groomed you are, the better you look," says Damien Miano, co-owner of Miano-Viel Salon and Spa in New York City. "Long hair looks like you're trying too hard. It's really best to stay classic."

Of course, there's short and there's short. Christina Griffasi, style director at the Minardi Salon in New York City, recommends for heavier men a bit of layered length on the sides and in back to tone down the jowliness and longer ears (yes, longer ears) that often accompany maturity. "But if you're thin and trim," she says, "cut the hair shorter, even if it's balding."

Don't use your hair to show how hip and creative you are. The ponytail behind the bald pate sends the wrong message. "When you try to look funky, you end up looking merely unkempt," says Miano.

Cut the other hair. Maybe it's nature's sense of symmetry. Once over 60, you tend to lose hair where you want it (your scalp) and gain it where you don't (the eyebrows, nose, ears, and back of the neck). Get the wayward hairs cut off. And between haircuts, do it yourself with an electric trimmer. They even make tiny trimmers for nose hair.

"Clean up all those spare hairs in the ear area," says Griffasi. "And learn to trim your own neckline in back. No woman likes to see hair creeping out of a man's collar."

Color it…a little. Your gray hair is your pride. Keep it. But taking it back just a shade or two toward its original color isn't cheating. "When your hair gets too white, it doesn't look natural and you lose any frame for your face," Griffasi says. "Just a slight deepening of your hair is excellent at age 60 and beyond."

You can't do it with over-the-counter dyes. "It has to be done professionally, using acid-balanced, semipermanent hair color," Griffasi says. "Otherwise, it's a mess."

Stay clean. The only thing that a woman of any age dislikes more than a sloppy man is a sloppy older man. What may be ill-advised bohemianism at 30 comes off as inexcusable laziness after 60. "Around the world women are interested in two things," says Dr. Fisher. "A creature that's healthy and a creature that's clean."

Clean also means neat. "Women are not turned on by a man who's slovenly," Dr. Fisher says. "You tend to get more casual as you get older. Casual's fine, but neatness and cleanliness are essential."

GETTING MOTIVATED FOR SEX

Need a sex-after-60 pep talk? Try this: It makes you happy. It's satisfying. It's natural. And a hell of a lot of guys your age are doing it.

Happy? In 1992, Andrew Greeley, who may be the world's only living priest/sociologist/fiction writer, reviewed current data on the topic and concluded, "The happiest men and women in America are married people who continue to have sex frequently after they are 60."

Satisfying? A more recent study of changes in healthy men from 45 to 74 published in the *Journal of Sex and Marital Therapy* confirmed that men enjoy sex equally at any age. "One parameter didn't change with age," says Raul Schiavi, M.D., former director of Mount Sinai Medical School's Human Sexuality Program in New York City who led the study, "and that was sexual satisfaction."

Natural? "There is no age at which sexual activity, thoughts, or desire end," wrote Fran E. Kaiser, M.D., professor of medicine and associate director of the division of geriatric medicine at St. Louis University's Health Sciences Center and director of the university's Sexual Dysfunction Clinic, in a medical journal.

How many are "a hell of a lot"? Putting numbers on sex is a tricky business, and in the case of seniors, a sketchy one. Dr. Kaiser cites one study giving the percentage of sexually active married men over 60 as 73.8 percent. Greeley's study notes that 37 percent of 60-plus married men and women have intercourse frequently—at least once a week. Of course, those numbers can shift downward if you include unmarried men, or upward if you limit the data to healthy guys.

That last point is key because it's only the increased probability of disease—and not the aging process itself—that can be a sexual deal-buster. "Erectile dysfunction should not be considered 'normal aging,' " insists Dr. Kaiser. "It's pathologic. You should be able to get erections until the day you die."

INFORMATION, PLEASE

Given that senior sex is certifiably healthy, satisfying, and common, the old canard of the asexual older man is hardly worth mentioning, let alone refuting. But if nothing else, the big lie serves to underscore the importance of information in your sex life. "Accurate information is the number one way to challenge the fallacies about aging," Dr. Schiavi says.

Why? Well, a compendium of the sexual changes that come with age is full of words like *decrease*, *less*, *slower*, and *reduced*. Those are good things if you know what's going on but scary words if you don't. For example, if you begin to notice that your erections take longer to develop—and you're not aware that it's a natural blessing—the myths about aging and sex may seem less mythical, and you can create a self-fulfilling prophecy.

"The mythology that you're over the hill can affect the reality," says Sandra Scantling, Psy.D., assistant clinical professor of psychiatry at the University of Connecticut School of Medicine in Farmington and co-author of *Ordinary Women, Extraordinary Sex*. "It's your own perspective that you're over the hill that pulls you in that direction."

So get smart. The secret to great sex in your older years comes down to understanding the changes your body is going through and adapting them to your advantage. "These changes are natural," Dr. Schiavi says. "You compensate for them with different strategies."

Slow down. Your erections take shape more slowly than even men in their fifties. What does that do to your sex life? It makes you better in bed.

"You tend to be more into kissing and touching and taking your time," says Pepper Schwartz, Ph.D., a sociologist at the University of Washington in Seattle and author of *American Couples* and *Love between Equals*. "That's what women have been asking you for the past 40 years of your life."

So instead of worrying about it, use the extra time for extra pleasure—for you as well as for her. For example, the direct stimulation of the penis you now need to help the slower-moving blood along is just what you've been asking *her* for the past 40 years. Enjoy it.

"Allow yourself to see this as a benefit," Dr. Scantling says of the longer opening act. "I mean, what the heck is all this rushing about? As long as you're focusing on having fun, everything will take care of itself."

Forget the finish line. If you're like most men, you've spent your entire sex life considerately trying to delay your ejaculation. Now nature does it for you. "As you get older," says Dr. Scantling, "the urge to ejaculate subsides some. And that's really good news, especially if you were a rapid ejaculator when you were younger."

Savor the staying power you now have instead of worrying that you've "lost" something. That should be easy if you remember that ejaculation and orgasm are not the same thing. "The force of your ejaculation does diminish with age," says Dr. Scantling, "but the intensity of your orgasms, that pleasurable rush, doesn't need to diminish at all."

The now-standard advice not to set ejaculation as a "goal" of sex is even more useful for an older man whose refractory period (the time it takes to have another ejaculation, though you may have another erection sooner) may have skyrocketed to perhaps several days. "But, frankly, who cares?" says Dr. Scantling. "If you're not trying to impregnate your partner, do you actually care if you don't ejaculate? Why not sit back and enjoy the whole experience?"

Sometimes you may thrust away for an hour and never come (you read that right: the 60-year-old man is sometimes the legendary 60-Minute Man). In fact, try it. You'll have ended up with an hour of great sex with a grateful partner, and still be that much closer to your next ejaculation.

Use what works. Partial erections are part of your sexual tool kit. Less rigidity is a natural result of your more sluggish blood flow, and any one of a number of conditions common in older men can take out more starch.

"You're going to have some expectable partial erections," says Domeena Renshaw, M.D., director of Loyola Sex Therapy Clinic at Loyola University in Chicago and author of *Seven Weeks to Better Sex*. "But if you're ready for them, you can use what you do have."

Of course, what you might consider wobbly another man might envy. Either way, a partial erection can get the job done. Don't think of one as half-soft. Think of it as hard enough.

Let it grow. As with younger men, your semi-firm erection will often upgrade itself once home. "It's helpful for the woman to manually assist penile insertion," suggests Dr. Schiavi. "Once the penis is inside the vagina, it often increases its rigidity as the woman begins thrusting."

Focus on pleasure. Use semi-rigidity as a reason to experiment with more partial erection–friendly ways of having intercourse. "Adjusting the mechanics can be helpful," says Dr. Schiavi. "There are certain positions that facilitate insertion." What are they? That's for you to find out. "They change with the individual couples," Dr. Schiavi says. "There are no magic bullets."

Enjoying the occasional (or frequent, as the case may be) partial erection is a microcosm of the world of great senior sex. Dr. Scantling's advice in her popular videos *Ordinary Couples, Extraordinary Sex*: "Focus on pleasure, not measure" is especially applicable to men over 60 since quantitative standards are based on hard-bodied youngsters. "Pleasure is what turns you on," Dr. Scantling says. "Measure is how hard, how long, how big. It's the kiss of death."

Keep it up. Pun intended here. Since, as Dr. Scantling puts it, "the mechanisms of sexual functioning are pretty much a matter of plumbing," your sex life improves by, of all things, having sex. "The more often blood flows into your penis, the better it is," she says. "If you don't exercise, your muscle tone shrinks. The same thing is true with erections."

That's why Dr. Kaiser, Dr. Scantling, and others believe that the best predictor of a great sex life in your sixties and seventies is a great sex life in your thirties, forties, and fifties. That does not mean, however, that you can't get back in the game if you've been on the bench for whatever reason. For that, it helps to prime the pump. How? Masturbation.

"Self-pleasuring brings blood flow into the genitals, and that's important," says Dr. Scantling. "Masturbation is really key. It's so much better to wear out than to rust out."

Remember, though, that with your longer refractory period, reaching climax alone in the afternoon may preclude getting there with a partner in the evening. So plan your pump priming wisely. And there's no law saying that you have to masturbate to ejaculation.

MIND AND MOTIVATION

The decrease in your libido with age is only that—a decrease. As you've surely noticed, it doesn't disappear. But again, sexual lethargy can set in if you misinterpret natural changes as signals to cease and desist instead of to adapt and enjoy. "You can't discount the psychological overlay of not being able to do as easily something that you think should come naturally," says Dr. Kaiser. "That's a real issue for men."

Bogus reasons for giving up sex are all around you if you want to find them. But do you? As Dudley Seth Danoff, M.D., senior attending urologist at Cedars-Sinai Medical Center in Los Angeles and author of *Superpotency*, puts it, "You don't have to stop having sex as you get old, but you get old if you stop having sex."

The advice is the same for men of any age in need of a libido lift: Perk up your sex life. For men over 60, it's no different. Only the methods change.

Take inventory. What turns you on at 65 probably isn't the same as what turned you on at 45. It's time to update your data. Go back to the sexual menu and reorder. How can you tell her what you really want if you're misinformed yourself?

"Identify what you like," advises Dr. Scantling. "How? Well, think about it. Look at some movies. Read some erotica. Allow yourself to fantasize about what might be an ideal sexual situation for you. The way to develop arousal is to find out what turns you on."

What you come up with can be anything from increased attention to hitherto neglected areas of your (or her) anatomy to previously taboo sexual practices to rechoreographed playfulness. Whatever the changes, you'll now be dealing in current reality.

Indulge your imagination. Fantasy is another road to a renewed sense of sexual adventure in your later years. Honest introspection may reveal that you find the thought of making it with Hillary Clinton on the White House lawn an incredible turn-on. It is not recommended that you actually do that. Rather, says Dr. Scantling, "allow your mind to sort of float to your fantasy as you're making love."

It may strike you as something of a betrayal, this thinking of somebody else while you make love with your partner of four decades. "But there's nothing wrong with it," insists Dr. Scantling, "because the whole key here is to learn what's pleasurable."

Rent a movie. Dr. Schiavi recommends erotic films or reading material to increase arousal and improve the sex life of older couples. "A good many men in their sixties and seventies resist the idea," he acknowledges. "That initial negative bias has to be addressed." There's no reason for erotica to be more socially acceptable to younger couples than to older couples, other than the absurd "dirty old man" stereotype. Besides, if you want proof of respectability, points out Helen Fisher, Ph.D., research associate in the department of anthropology at Rutgers University in New Brunswick, New Jersey, and author of *Anatomy of Love*, "you can buy them through the *New York Times Book Review*. You don't have to go to seamy porno shops. And they will stimulate your sexual energies."

Of course, you don't see much golden-years sex on celluloid or videotape. "You may compare yourself to those thirty-something hunks and think you're over the hill," smiles Dr. Schiavi. But let's face it: Few people of any age perform like those carefully selected, editing room–enhanced sex machines you see in erotic videos. The idea is to watch the movies, not star in them. Erotica is a source of stimulation and ideas for adults of any age.

RETIREMENT

Think of retirement as an aphrodisiac. Your capacity for intimacy, the electric current of good sex, expands after retirement. Your sexual attractiveness is deeper, your sexual skills more polished, your sexual pace more pleasing. Most important, retirement is a time when you concentrate on the quality of your life. And as Fran E. Kaiser, M.D., professor of medicine and associate director of the division of geriatric medicine at St. Louis University's Health Sciences Center and director of the university's Sexual Dysfunction Clinic, puts it, sex is "one of the most important quality-of-life issues in older adults."

Don't take our word for it. Study after study uncovers a swarm of satisfied, happily adjusted, and lusty retirees.

"Most people who retire are satisfied with their retirement," says Erdman Palmore, Ph.D., professor emeritus of medical sociology at the Duke University Center for the Study of Aging in Durham, North Carolina, and author of *Social Patterns in Normal Aging, Retirement*, and *Ageism*. "In fact, the majority report that, if anything, they are happier than ever—and that spills over into the sexual area."

Researchers actually keep score, and the pro-retirement squad has an insurmountable lead. "Marital satisfaction scores of people who are retired are astronomical compared to what they're like when people are in their forties," says Robert C. Atchley, Ph.D., distinguished professor of gerontology and director of the Scripps Gerontology Center at Miami University in Oxford, Ohio.

Glory days? Sure. But like any other major undertaking, retirement requires adjustments. You have to play it right, avoid the pitfalls, and exploit the opportunities.

PREPARING FOR THE BIG DAY

Dr. Atchley, who's conducting an ongoing study of older people's life adaptations, scoffs at the common notion of retirement as a sex life–devouring monster. "You find very few real problems associated with retirement," he says. "You have all these apocalyptic predictions about what happens to people when they retire, and it doesn't work that way. Even people who think they're not going to adjust to it very well do adjust to it very well. It's one of those great cases where the self-fulfilling prophecy doesn't happen."

But that doesn't mean you can just breeze into such a major change of life without thinking about it, not if you want to keep your sex life healthy. After all, retirement is one of life's major crises (in the not-necessarily-malignant Greek sense of the word), on a par with puberty, marriage, and the death of a family member. You have to prepare for it.

Men run into trouble when they simply approach retirement as a kid does summer vacation, says Myrna Lewis, assistant professor of community medicine at Mount Sinai School of Medicine in New York City and co-author with Robert N. Butler, M.D., of the book *Love and Sex after 60*. "If you don't think through how you're going to live your life after retirement, you tend to feel aimless or at a loss," she says. "That gets reflected in your feelings of well-being, which can impact on sexuality."

As Sandra Scantling, Psy.D., assistant clinical professor of psychiatry at the University of Connecticut School of Medicine in Farmington and co-author of *Ordinary Women, Extraordinary Sex*, puts it: "Retirement itself is neither a positive nor a negative thing. It's an opportunity to create something wonderful or to make what you have better."

To do that, approach retirement as a deep, rich, new (and sex-filled) life adventure. Plan it like a voyage. "Let retirement be a stimulus to think about your life," says Dr. Atchley. "It provides a window of opportunity to think about what your lifestyle is going to be and how to ensure that you're going to be healthy and active and satisfied."

HOW TO ENJOY IT

Here are other considerations for becoming a happily sexed retiree.

Be financially prepared. There's no shortage of pros who'll help you with your retirement income, which isn't irrelevant to your sex life. A common factor among study subjects reporting postretirement marital satisfaction, according to Dr. Atchley, is "incomes that essentially sustain their lifestyles." But he has an encouraging word: "Even if income drops some, a lot of people are still pretty much able to maintain the structure of their lifestyle. You may not be able to afford to do exactly the same things you did before, but you can find satisfying substitutes that allow you to maintain a sense of continuity."

Retire, but don't be retiring. "Retirement can lead to inertia, boredom, and stagnation," says Dudley Seth Danoff, M.D., senior attending urologist at Cedars-Sinai Medical Center in Los Angeles and author of *Superpotentcy*. Those are apt adjectives for a bum sex life as well as life in general. The trick is to avoid them.

How? "Always stay active," says Dr. Danoff. Commonsense advice, you say, but isn't retirement an antonym of "active"? Most emphatically, no.

"If you think of work as the expenditure of energy toward goals, you don't stop working, ever," says Dr. Atchley. In other words, you're retiring from a job—or a career, if you prefer—but not from productivity.

"Think of it as becoming self-employed," says Dr. Atchley. "Whether it's for pay or not depends on your preference or perhaps opportunity, but you get just as much satisfaction out of doing, say, community service as you do out of a job."

Do what you do. Being active and involved after retirement—and hence sexually robust—doesn't mean that you have to radically alter your interests. You can if you want to, of course, but Dr. Atchley's research indicates that happy retirement marriages don't need that. In fact, after looking at more than 1,100 people for 20 years, the youngest of them age 50 at the start of the study in 1975, he didn't come across a single case of somebody who picked up a sustained new interest in retirement. "They all kept doing what they had been doing," he says.

If you plan to use your retirement to read the classics, chances are that you've had an interest in reading—if not the time to do much of it—all your life. On the other hand, if you've never cared about the classics, don't feel that you're wasting your retirement by not reading them. It's still your life.

"The interests you've had may become more prominent in your retirement," says Dr. Atchley. "They may get noticed more, but they've been there all along."

OF TIME AND SEX

Time seems to be the very stuff of which retirement is made. There's now so much of it. And with that surplus comes new opportunities for your scheduling of sex. Your sex life can improve. But not automatically.

"With retirement there can be just more time to do whatever you've been doing or not been doing," says Dr. Scantling, "If you've not been having sex, then you have more time to not be having sex, which is going to be kind of anxiety-provoking."

So your new time allotment and the slackened work pressure are two-edged swords. "The freedom, the opportunity, and the other positives are sharper than the negative side," says Dr. Atchley. "But that doesn't mean that the negative side doesn't exist."

Time and leisure can be your sexual allies, but only if you show them who's boss.

Use it. If your gut reaction tells you that retirement means more time—and different times—for sex, congratulate your gut. You should take advantage of the longer days to vary the routine.

"There's a positive repercussion in your sexuality in that you have more time after retirement," says Lewis. "You have more flexibility during the day. And you don't come home exhausted and drop into bed sound asleep."

It's not just the amount of time but the kind of time that helps if you make the effort. "With the pressures of day-to-day living off your back, the sex can get a lot better," Dr. Danoff says.

Fill it. But don't think of your retirement time as one big sexual ice cream cone. A vacuum in the rest of your life is a proven libido-buster. One key to a fulfilling, well-rounded sex life is a fulfilling, well-rounded life, period.

"Time takes on a different importance in retirement," Dr. Scantling says. "You have to adjust, learn how to use it differently than you did. Before, it was all about getting it fast and quick and hard. Now you need to slow down and rediscover what it is you really like, to taste your food and your life."

Next thing you know, there's not as much time as you thought. "The thing that surprises guys the most about retirement is that they don't have anything like as much spare time as they thought they'd have," Dr. Atchley says. "There's a lot of stuff that needs doing around the home that you blew off because you had to go to work. And a lot of people increase their involvement in community organizations. It's not like you sit at home looking out the window."

So fill out your dance card. It will pay dividends, in the bedroom and everywhere else. "Prepare to use your time after retirement," says Lewis. "If you don't think about it, it will suddenly be there upon you, and you won't be able to use it productively and in a way that makes you feel good."

RELATIONSHIPS AND RETIREMENT

Witty essayists have a field day with how retirement supposedly shreds the lifelong peace treaty you've made with your wife. Suddenly there you are...together...all day...every day...My God! "Who's going to make lunch?" becomes a metaphor for the perils of proximity.

How real a danger is it? It's real, all right, but not necessarily dangerous unless the danger was there to start with.

"Retirement can be the straw that breaks the camel's back if your marriage has a shaky foundation that can't take much change," says Dr. Atchley. "But most people have developed pretty robust marriages by retirement age."

Like everything else in retirement, intensified togetherness is what you make of it. Sure, it can be stifling for both of you if you let it. But it can also be a sexual boon if you master it. Since when is closeness per se a bad thing for your sex life?

Move in. There's a reason that "getting intimate" is a favorite euphemism for having sexual intercourse. Intimacy and sex are mutually sustaining. "Sex," says Dr. Kaiser, "is probably the most intimate connection you will ever experience with another person."

Use retirement's imposed closeness to develop more intimacy, more emotional closeness with your sexual partner. You won't be the first to do it. "There tends to be a lot more sharing of self with each other in retirement," says Dr. Atchley. "What that usually leads to is greater intimacy."

There are skills to employ in developing that intimacy, and you have them. Part of it is hormonal; your lower levels of testosterone (though normally not low enough to affect your sexual performance, despite popular misconceptions) liberate your capacity for connecting with your woman at intimate levels. Far from being unmanly, this subtle change reads to her as a definite turn-on.

"But it's not all physiological," says Pepper Schwartz, Ph.D., a sociologist at the University of Washington in Seattle and author of *American Couples* and *Love between Equals*. "In your life experience you've learned more empathy and compassion. You've taken some knocks. Now you're retired. You're no longer the hot-shot partner in your firm, so you understand a little bit more about what it's like to be marginal. You're a better companion."

To nurture intimacy, develop what Lewis calls the second language of sex. "Learn how to listen and empathize with her rather than immediately leaping to take action and solve the problem," she says.

The fact that men want to act and women want to talk has made relationships counselor John Gray, Ph.D., author of the mega-selling book on the

You Gotta Be You

Conventional wisdom maintains that your self-esteem shrinks with your last paycheck, that the transition from a savvy veteran in your chosen field to "just another retiree" is depressing (sometimes even in the clinical sense), not to mention libido-reducing.

But sometimes conventional wisdom is so, well, conventional. Not to say that conventional wisdom always is *wrong*. These aren't myths; there's some truth in most conventional wisdom. But it might help to look at some examples of retirement-related conventional wisdom in unconventional ways.

• *Retirement lowers your self-esteem.* "I think men get a bad rap on that," says Sandra Scantling, Psy.D., assistant clinical professor of psychiatry at the University of Connecticut School of Medicine in Farmington and co-author of *Ordinary Women, Extraordinary Sex.* "Just because you were Mr. Big Banker until you were 65 doesn't mean that your self-esteem gets flushed down the toilet all of a sudden when you're not Mr. Big Banker anymore."

You see, your worth as a human being has to do with more than your professional position. Self-esteem problems erupt with retirement only when you fail to understand that.

"Our culture encourages men to pretty much identify with whatever it is they do for a living, rather than with their relationships with people," says Myrna Lewis, assistant professor of community medicine at Mount Sinai School of Medicine in New York City and co-author with Robert N. Butler, M.D., of the book *Love and Sex after 60.* "So it's very important to have thought through what you're going to be using to replace your work as a form of self-expression."

• *You miss power when you retire.* "That only applies to people who ever had any power," says Robert C. Atchley, Ph.D., distinguished professor of gerontology and director of the Scripps Gerontology Center at Miami University in Oxford, Ohio. "And even then I think the loss is more than offset for a lot of people by the release from responsibility. Yes, you can't make people do things anymore. But on the other hand, you may be real tired of doing that and of the lonely-at-the-top thing that goes along with it."

subject, *Men Are from Mars, Women Are from Venus*, a rich man. Retirement offers the best atmosphere to bridge the gap.

"In later life the wanna-talk part is very important for men to learn," Lewis says. "The best aging seems to be when men and women learn from each other whatever they were strong on earlier in life."

Share and share alike. The best answer to the who's-going-to-make-lunch question is...both of you. Take turns or do it together. Despite the ubiquitous humor on the subject, this arrangement is not often a problem, according to Dr. Atchley. "By the time people get to retirement, they've devel-

- *Retirement can cause depression.* "If there's such a thing as retirement-related depression, I've never found it," Dr. Atchley says. "I believe the people who say that folks come to them because they say they're depressed about retirement. But I wonder if they didn't jump upon retirement as an easy answer to why he's depressed when it can be caused by a lot of other things."

- *The suicide rate goes up after retirement.* Sure it does, says Dr. Atchley, at least for White men (though not for White women, or Black men or women). "But it's not connected to retirement," he says. "If you follow a cohort of people over time, the suicide rate goes straight up from the age of 14 on. So the highest rate is with White men in their eighties. But you cannot contribute that to retirement because most of them have been retired for 20 years."

- *Retirement reduces your sex appeal.* If you think your sex appeal goes down with age, you haven't been reading this book carefully enough. If you think it suffers because you no longer occupy a position of status in the workplace, you should know that with retirement you enter a culture in which status is defined by who you are, not what you do.

"People overlook what you used to do for a living," says Helen Fisher, Ph.D., research associate in the department of anthropology at Rutgers University in New Brunswick, New Jersey, and author of *Anatomy of Love*. "You could have been a plumber all your life, but in the retirement world you can play the part of a more high-status person."

Says Pepper Schwartz, Ph.D., a sociologist at the University of Washington in Seattle and author of *American Couples* and *Love between Equals*, "There's something cute about boys, but there's something quite wonderful about men. You're happy with who you are, you're not defensive, you're not as narcissistic, you're not as impulsive."

And retirement only enhances those attributes. "You're not posturing anymore," Dr. Schwartz says. "That's a very attractive thing."

oped a lifestyle of living together," he says. "In middle-class marriages nowadays there's a lot more sharing of responsibilities. Most of the changes you have to make in terms of household routines were made when you had your children."

If that didn't hold true for you—you worked, she cooked, like you think nature intended—let retirement lead you to enlightenment. Don't consider sharing the household chores a capitulation; rather, think of it as what it is— a strategy for smoother cohabitation, a way to turn your time together toward intimacy rather than confrontation.

"It's very important for men to learn practical survival skills, including household maintenance," says Lewis. "Be able to switch back and forth with your female partner."

And—surprise—most retired men do just that. "Generally, retired men do become more involved around the house," Dr. Atchley says. "They often discover what a pain in the butt it is and argue for hiring a housekeeper."

Get sociable. There's another division of labor that gets blurred in the happiest retirements. During the early and middle part of most marriages, according to Lewis, it's the woman who generally takes charge of the nonwork-related social organizing. She organizes the dinner parties.

Retirement's a good time to change that, for at least one very good reason. "Social network skills are life-enhancing," Lewis says. "The men who live the longest tend to learn them. Men who don't learn these social skills tend to have shorter lives."

Change the mouse. Dr. Danoff tells of some experiments that led to what's fondly known as the same-old-mouse theory. It seems that if you put a male mouse in a cage with a female mouse in heat, the male will mount the female repeatedly, to the point of exhaustion. But if at that very point of exhaustion you switch the female for another, also in heat, the male mouse's vigor miraculously renews itself and the mounting begins afresh.

The same-old-mouse theory has implications for a retired couple's sex life, according to Dr. Danoff. No, he's not advising you to trade in your wife for a fresh mouse in heat. Keep in mind that researchers got the same results—that is, a reinvigorated male mouse—when they simply dyed the first mouse another color, or even sprayed perfume on her. The lesson: Variety and fresh approaches to sexuality are vital for retirement-age couples.

"The more you're with somebody, the more important it is to keep it interesting," says Dr. Danoff. "Do it in the living room, in the kitchen, in the garden. Make it new and exciting. The kids are out of the house; you're out of the rat race. Your sex life should be better than ever."

HEART HEALTH AND SEX

A heart attack can strike anyone, any time, at any age.

But very rarely during sex. And almost *never* because of sex.

Who knows how many senior sex lives have been curtailed by the fantasy that intercourse triggers heart attacks? Those notions aren't just the product of fertile imaginations. The movies have magnified the myth; Goldie Hawn and Kirstie Alley are just two actresses whose characters found themselves postcoitally quite alone when their partner suffered "the big one" in flagrante. Doctors, too, helped create the problem by their erstwhile habit of counseling heart attack survivors to avoid sex (and exercise, for that matter). They don't do that as much anymore because the facts are in.

The most pertinent of those facts come from a study headed by researchers from Harvard and published in 1996 in the *Journal of the American Medical Association.* The topic: What is sexual activity's role in triggering heart attacks? Conclusion: Not much.

The study found that sexual activity doubles the risk of heart attack. But in a healthy person the risk is increased from one chance in a million per hour to two in a million, and then only for the 2 hours following sex. For those subjects who've had a heart attack before, the risk is a still-minuscule 20 chances per million per hour.

"The likelihood of dropping dead from a heart attack during sex is about the same as having a piano fall on your head," says Fran E. Kaiser, M.D., professor of medicine and associate director of the division of geriatric medicine at St. Louis University's Health Sciences Center and director of the university's Sexual Dysfunction Clinic. "It's really rare."

THE REAL FEAR

The same Harvard study that put the kibosh on the notion that sex triggers heart attacks acknowledged that the fear of that very thing does indeed exist. It's not a healthy fear. Not only can it reduce your sexual interest and capacity, but also it can do bad by the thing you're trying to protect—your heart. In the study's words, "Fear of sexual activity...often prevents complete rehabilitation from cardiovascular disease."

With cardiovascular disease being the number one killer of men over 65, it's natural for you to be concerned about your ticker. But channel that concern to where it will help—a healthy diet, exercise, and good medical care—rather than worry needlessly about sexual activity.

If you find yourself in a fear-of-sex mode, get informed. Reread the first paragraphs of this chapter. And talk about it with your doctor. If he won't bring up sex, bring it up yourself. As Dudley Seth Danoff, M.D., senior attending urologist at Cedars-Sinai Medical Center in Los Angeles and author of *Superpotency* says, "Discuss your sex life with your cardiologist as candidly as you would your exercise routine."

Just because heart attacks are almost never triggered by sexual activity doesn't mean that it's not within the realm of possibility for them to occur during sex. "Any time" includes whoopee time, so if you think you're experiencing cardiac symptoms, don't ignore them just because you happen to be in the throes of passion.

"You need to be smart about these things," says Dr. Kaiser. "If you get chest pains when you're having intercourse, you need to stop. Take nitroglycerin if that's what you're doctor said to do. Go to an emergency room."

IF YOU HAVE HEART DISEASE

"If you can climb stairs, you can perform sex" is a phrase experts often use to reassure heart patients. But if you've had any kind of heart disease, you'll be given a stress test that's somewhat more sophisticated than being shooed up a flight of stairs. That test marks a passage in your sexual recovery.

"If you've had a heart attack or coronary bypass surgery, you should pass a stress test before resuming intercourse," cautions Dr. Kaiser.

But let's say it again. Heart disease, a heart attack, heart surgery, or stroke does not end your sex life. Listen to none other than the American Heart Association (AHA): "After the first phase of recovery is complete, patients find that the same forms of lovemaking that were pleasing before are still rewarding."

There are things you can do to smooth the transition back into sex. The AHA has issued some guidelines for couples resuming sex after a heart episode.

- Choose a time when you are rested, relaxed, and free from the stressful feelings brought on by the day's schedules and responsibilities.
- Wait 1 to 3 hours after eating a full meal so that digestion can take place.
- Select a familiar, peaceful setting that is free from interruptions.
- Take medicine prior to sexual relations if prescribed by your doctor.

Both of you will need to be tolerant of your emotions. Mood swings, even depression, are common after heart attacks or strokes, and they can make whatever previous sexual problems you might have had loom larger. Teach your soul the virtue of patience. In 85 percent of the cases, mood swings or depression disappear within three months.

Here's some more wisdom for heart patients regarding their sex lives.

Ponder positions. There's no "heart-safe" position for intercourse. Even if there were a danger of erotic exertion triggering a heart attack—which there isn't—changing positions wouldn't reduce it. Your heart beats fastest during orgasm, and, as Dr. Kaiser puts it, "an orgasm is an orgasm is an orgasm in terms of maximum heart rate. So it doesn't matter if you're side by side or if you're on the top or the bottom or if you're hanging by a toenail from a chandelier."

There are position considerations for heart attack or stroke survivors, but they have to do with comfort, not safety—and chandelier hanging isn't one of them. If you've had recent bypass surgery, Dr. Kaiser advises using the side-by-side, "two spoons" position to minimize pain at the surgical incision. If you've had a stroke, the AHA suggests using pillows to support your affected side during lovemaking.

Exercise from the heart. With blood flow being the principal issue in sex over 60, it makes sense to help it along with cardiovascular exercise. But won't aerobic exercise put your heart at risk? On the contrary, it's one of the best things you can do for your heart.

In fact, that's one of the conclusions of the Harvard study. The researchers maintain that regular exercise not only appears to prevent triggering of heart attacks; it also is associated with decreasing risk.

That should be stimulus enough to get you started on a good fitness program. But will it really improve sex at your age? "You bet," says Dr. Kaiser. "Along with good health and good nutrition."

Use sex as therapy. Looking for a painless and fun exercise to help your heart? How about sex itself?

"Sex is actually a healthy part of your rehabilitation," says Myrna Lewis, assistant professor of community medicine at Mount Sinai School of Medicine in New York City and co-author with Robert N. Butler, M.D., of the book *Love and Sex after 60.* "Patients are encouraged to return to their usual sexual habits fairly soon after having a heart attack. It's part of their general conditioning program."

And, writes Dr. Danoff in *Superpotency,* "it is not only a terrific form of exercise; it is unsurpassed in lifting the spirit of a man who has suffered the trauma of heart disease."

Listen to your blood. Blood supply problems can't be localized. What's happening in your penis may be occurring in your coronary arteries. Very often, the first clue about heart problems is impotence. So pay attention because if it's caught early, it can often be reversed.

"If you're having sexual problems more than a quarter of the time—less than that is considered run-of-the-mill and will take care of itself—get a physical exam," offers Lewis. "Blood flow problems very often show up first in the genital area."

Stop smoking. You're probably not reading this book to be told again about the ill effects of smoking. You know that it's bad for your heart. And you know that it's bad for your sex life.

But here's another reason to quit, if you need one. According to Robert C. Atchley, Ph.D., distinguished professor of gerontology and director of the Scripps Gerontology Center at Miami University in Oxford, Ohio, it's lung disease—heavily linked to smoking—that does in your sex life more than just about anything.

Dr. Atchley analyzed the effects of debilitating diseases on older people's life satisfaction and concluded that, outside of Alzheimer's, emphysema and chronic obstructive pulmonary disease are the cruelest.

"People with heart disease, diabetes, arthritis, amputations—things you'd consider pretty serious—were actually able to compensate in one way or another and maintain their life satisfaction," Dr. Atchley says. "But if you have lung disease, you basically can't do anything. It's the major cause of folks essentially dropping out of life."

So if you need another reason to quit smoking, consider Dr. Atchley's conclusion: "If you quit smoking, the likelihood that you'll become disabled in a way you can't adapt to is reduced substantially."

MEDICATIONS

If you're over 60, who can blame you for suspecting a conspiracy against your sex life? First you might find yourself working around the effects of a myriad of illnesses that are often the unwelcome companions of age. Then you realize that the very medications you take for those diseases can put your flag at half-mast.

"Medications are a huge issue because so many older men are on them," says Fran E. Kaiser, M.D., professor of medicine and associate director of the division of geriatric medicine at St. Louis University's Health Sciences Center and director of the university's Sexual Dysfunction Clinic. "They can really do you in in terms of erectile function."

Dr. Kaiser cites studies indicating that medications play a role in 25 percent of all men suffering from impotence. And, she points out, "older men need more drugs."

This can put you in a classic catch-22 situation. "Take depression, for example, one of the most prevalent disorders in older men," says Raul Schiavi, M.D., former director of Mount Sinai Medical School's Human Sexuality Program in New York City. "Depression itself certainly can affect sexual function, so using an antidepression agent improves that function. But the antidepressant agent may create other problems, such as ejaculatory problems or reduced sexual drive. You need to know to what extent the sexual problem you're having is due to the condition itself or the medication."

What's an older guy to do? Plenty.

Complain. Stand up for your right to have sex. There was a darker age when doctors would ignore sexual side affects as irrelevant for seniors. But, as Dr. Kaiser puts it, "it is no longer acceptable to tell a patient that impotence has occurred because he is too old." If you suspect that a medication is affecting your sexual functioning, chirp up. And insist that the doctor do something about it. When he prescribes a medication, ask point-blank if it will affect your sex life.

Don't be foolish. Far be it from us to insult your intelligence by pointing out the obvious: Don't decide on your own to stop taking prescribed medicine. But, says Schiavi, "it's less obvious than you think. A lot of men just discontinue the medicine because they're embarrassed to discuss sexual problems."

So keep your priorities. "If the choice is not getting a stroke from hypertension or getting an erection, most people would prefer not to have the stroke," says Dr. Kaiser. "Erection problems are fixable, but you can't fix a stroke."

So talk to your doctor before discontinuing a medicine. There are solutions to medication-induced sexual problems. Here are some that he might suggest.

Get in sync. Schedule your medication around sex, and vice versa. "You can make love the furthest time away possible from taking the needed medication," says Domeena Renshaw, M.D., director of Loyola Sex Therapy Clinic at Loyola University in Chicago and author of *Seven Weeks to Better Sex*. "For example, if you take your blood pressure pill in the morning, you can make love at 9:00 in the evening. Or make love in the morning before you take your medication."

Wait a bit. Try the most time-honored crisis-management technique—do nothing and wait for the problem to go away. Dr. Schiavi calls it persuasion compensation for pesky medications. "In some instances," he says, "the erectile function improves with time even though you haven't changed the medication. Your body adapts."

Take less. It's certainly not uncommon for doctors to change the dosage of any medicine to compensate for side effects, once you tell him what they are. The same goes for sexual side effects. "Sometimes the problem is dose-related," says Dr. Schiavi. "A slight adjustment of the dosage can have profound effects on sexual function."

Change the medication. Modern medicine is nothing if not versatile. If changing the dosage doesn't get rid of a drug's downside, have your doctor change the drug itself. "We have a smorgasbord of options," says Dr. Renshaw. "Some are less of a culprit on erections than others. There are alternatives."

Fight fire with fire. Dr. Schiavi suggests a final resort: "The use of other drugs to modify the problem, while maintaining the original medication. The use of some other drugs a few hours before intercourse might facilitate sexual activity."

De-stress yourself. Stress and fatigue make you more vulnerable to adverse drug effects, Dr. Kaiser says. So take it upon yourself to make it harder for the drugs to do their dirty work. Exercise to combat stress. Rest to combat fatigue. In the long run, work on your lifestyle. In the short run, advises Dr. Kaiser, "it may help to change the timing of sex to periods of least stress or fatigue."

THE MAIN CULPRITS

There's no Chinese-menu approach to fingering the offending medications. The one from column A may wilt one guy and not another. And no normal human being can be expected to make sense out of the dizzying dictionary of generic and brand names for drugs—the building blocks of a veritable Tower of Babel. Your best resources are your own self-observations and your doctor's advice. Here, though, is a far-from-exhaustive list of some of the categories of prescription drugs that should send up red flags.

• Blood pressure pills. Hypertension, or high blood pressure, is a ubiquitous bugaboo of maturity. And, says Dr. Kaiser, "all of the antihypertensives without exception can cause erection difficulties." They're often responsible for partial erections, delayed ejaculation, no ejaculation, total erectile dysfunction, and lowered libido.

Social but Not Sexual

Call them what you will—social drugs, recreational drugs, or venial sins—their negative effect on sexual function is universally acknowledged. Here's a rundown.

• Tobacco. Smoking lowers your hormone levels, restricts blood flow to your penis, and pollutes your lungs. What does the last have to do with sex? "It cuts down your capacity for expression in sexual intercourse," says Diana Galindo, M.D., clinical assistant professor of medicine at the University of Miami School of Medicine. In other words, few love a lazy lover.

• Alcohol. Simply put, it's the Great Numb Maker. "Its effect on sexuality is the same as a sedative," says Dr. Galindo. And remember that your tolerance for alcohol's dulling effect on your central nervous system diminishes with age.

• Marijuana. "You know that cotton-mouth feeling you get?" says Sandra Scantling, Psy.D., assistant clinical professor of psychiatry at the University of Connecticut School of Medicine in Farmington and co-author of *Ordinary Women, Extraordinary Sex.* "Well, other things can be drying up, too."

• Cocaine. Some think that cocaine produces a strong desire for sex. It more often produces a strong desire for more cocaine. Other things it can produce include erectile dysfunction, lower sperm count, unsatisfying orgasms, and lost libido.

• Opiates. They're associated with impotence, says Fran E. Kaiser, M.D., professor of medicine and associate director of the division of geriatric medicine at St. Louis University's Health Sciences Center and director of the university's Sexual Dysfunction Clinic. Among other things, they go right after the hormones.

Why do they do such bad things? "Remember the reason you're on antihypertensives in the first place," says Dr. Kaiser. "You probably already have narrowing of the blood vessels. You think that's only in the arm where they check the blood pressure? It's probably in the penis, too. And then when the blood pressure is lowered, it's lower in the penis, too." Less blood flowing through narrower vessels equals erection problems.

Here's a partial roster of antihypertensives agents: the beta blockers, such as propranolol (Inderal) and atenolol (Tenormin); methyldopa (Aldomet, Aldoclor, or Aldoril); clonidine (Catapres); guanethidine (Ismelin); prazosin (Minipress).

• Diuretics. Thiazide diuretics are also used to treat hypertension, and according to Dr. Kaiser, they're the most common impotence-causing drugs. Other diuretics prescribed to assist urine flow also can cause problems. "They're associated with impotence," says Diana Galindo, M.D., clinical assistant professor of medicine at the University of Miami School of Medicine. "We're not sure why. Maybe it's electrolyte imbalance or just going to the bathroom all night. But I make sure to tell my patients that diuretics may affect their sexuality."

• Drugs for depression. Here a tightrope act is sometimes required because depression itself causes sexual problems. "Actually," says Dr. Galindo, "if you're depressed and use antidepressants, your libido will improve. But at the same time, antidepressants have been noted to cause a decrease in potency."

That includes Prozac (fluoxetine), the recent glamour drug. "Everybody was on the Prozac bandwagon a couple years ago," says Robert C. Atchley, Ph.D., distinguished professor of gerontology and director of the Scripps Gerontology Center at Miami University in Oxford, Ohio. "But nobody talked about the fact that Prozac, for a fairly substantial minority of people, basically eliminated their sex life."

SSRIs, the class of drugs that includes Prozac, are the antidepressants most commonly associated with sexual difficulties, according to Dr. Galindo. For the record, the initials stand for "selective serotonin re-uptake inhibitors."

Others kinds of antidepressants that could affect your sex drive include amitriptyline hydrochloride (Elavil), phenelzine sulfate (Nardil), and desipramine hydrochloride (Norpramin).

• Anti-androgens. "They're what we use for patients with prostate problems, a common condition in the elderly," says Dr. Galindo. "Androgens are an important factor in the libido part of sexual function. So when you use anti-androgens, you cut down sexual desire."

• Anti-inflammatory agents. The nonsteroidal version of these include such over-the-counter medicines as aspirin, Advil, and Motrin, all of which can affect the libido. You can also put ulcer medications such as cimetidine (Tagamet) in this category.

• Tranquilizers. These include the popular favorites diazepam (Valium) and alprazolam (Xanax). "There's a role for anti-anxiety agents with older men," says Dr. Galindo. "But they can cause confusion and decrease the libido." They're also orgasm inhibitors.

Partial roster: Besides diazepam and alprazolam, watch out for meprobamate (Equanil, Miltown), among others.

• Antipsychotics. Drugs used to treat paranoid delusions can also bring down your erections. Some of the more time-honored culprits are chlorpromazine (Thorazine) and haloperidol (Haldol) as well as thioridazine (Mellaril) and thiothixene (Navane).

• Anticonvulsants. These seizure-preventers are commonly prescribed to older men. "Their main function is to control hyperactive neurons in the brain," says Dr. Galindo. "But as they control that, they control everything, including sexual urges."

Here's a partial roster: carbamazepine (Tegretol), ethosuximide (Zarontin), primidone (Mysoline).

DEATH OF A SPOUSE

Maybe it's a tribute to human compassion that so much has been studied and written about coping with the death of a spouse. Or, if you want to be cynical, maybe a lot of people just know where an inevitable market lies. Either way, among the welcome abundance of scientific research, popular books, and World Wide Web pages offering help at your time of loss, almost nothing is ever mentioned about the issue of sexuality.

The most charitable explanation for the omission would be that the sexual aspect is simply taken as a given. After all, the person you lost was, among other things, your sexual partner. And your status as a sexual human being doesn't end with the death of your wife.

So as you run across the frequent phrase "move on" in coping with the death of your spouse, it's not stretching things to interpret that to mean, in part, "have sex again if you're so inclined." Reattaining sexual satisfaction is part of what it means to recover. And the road to recovery, experts say, is well-traveled. Most men reach their destination. Here's how you can, too.

THE ELEMENTS OF GRIEF

You suffer differently than women after the loss of your spouse. "Men feel totally bereft at first," says Helen Fisher, Ph.D., research associate in the department of anthropology at Rutgers University in New Brunswick, New Jersey, and author of *Anatomy of Love.* "Men are apparently more deeply connected in their marriages than women are. If you ask men and women if they're happily married, more men than women say yes."

The loss hits men directly at one of our weak points. "Most men at that point in their lives don't really have anybody in their close social network," explains Morton A. Lieberman, Ph.D., a psychologist at the University of California, San Francisco, and author of *Doors Close, Doors Open: Widows Grieving and Growing.* "The person you really relied on for emotional support was your wife."

Also, it must be said that you suffer on a practical level. "When your wife dies, a great many daily supports vanish," Dr. Fisher says. "You may not have done much cooking, cleaning, washing, shopping, and organizing of household affairs."

That's not as callous a consideration as it might sound. It's part of what goes into what you're feeling. "It can make you feel quite adrift," says Dr. Fisher.

HOW TO RECOVER

At the beginning, probably the last thing on your mind is starting over sexually. Bereavement—grieving for your lost spouse—is a natural and necessary response to what is, medically speaking, a form of stress. It takes priority. "Get through with your grieving before you move on," says Robert C. Atchley, Ph.D., distinguished professor of gerontology and director of the Scripps Gerontology Center at Miami University in Oxford, Ohio.

Medical research identifies three stages of bereavement. The first they call numbness, as do many new widowers. It can last anywhere from a few hours to a few weeks. Then comes depression, with depressive symptoms dominating the picture. Recovery follows and, again, varies in duration from one person to another.

Clearly, the first two stages are hardly conducive to sexual activity. How long before recovery sets in? "Essentially, at the point where your lost wife is no longer in your consciousness all the time, you're ready to move on," says Dr. Atchley. "Some men get there in two or three months, some in two years. I've seen people whose spouse died and it took them seven or eight years before they develop a relationship with somebody else. It's a very individual thing."

At the other end of the spectrum, a protracted illness can result in a much shorter bereavement period. "With Alzheimer's disease, for example, the grieving can take place before the spouse dies," Dr. Atchley says. "You might even develop a new relationship before she dies."

The bottom line is that you do recover. "A substantial majority of our subjects recovered from their grief reaction within a year, usually within a few months," says Erdman Palmore, Ph.D., professor emeritus of medical sociology at the Duke University Center for the Study of Aging in Durham, North Carolina, and author of *Social Patterns in Normal Aging*. "And they reported the same or higher levels of life satisfaction after a year."

FIXING THE PAST

A key to recovery can actually consist in some after-the-fact problem solving. That's because research is showing that more problematic relationships result in longer mourning periods. "It's really an extended period of trying to deal with unresolved issues," says Myrna Lewis, assistant professor of community medicine at Mount Sinai School of Medicine in New York City and co-author with Robert N. Butler, M.D., of the book *Love and Sex after 60*.

So it helps to retroactively assess your relationship, especially if you can't seem to move on after an extended period. "If you're preoccupied with your previous mate, there are probably unresolved problems," Lewis says. "You can still resolve them in your mind, even if she's not there anymore."

And if your marriage was good? "The mourning period is still intense after good relationships," says Lewis. "But because it was unproblematic, you can pick up and move on without feeling conflicted."

Beyond grieving, but simultaneous with it, you have another mental task in the recovery process. It has to do with what Dr. Lieberman calls existential issues. Simply put—perhaps too simply put—it's time to ask, "Who am I?"

Says Dr. Lieberman, "Your self-image is largely based on the messages you get from the reflecting mirrors around you. And the most salient mirror was your spouse. So one of the tasks of widowerhood is dealing with such self-image issues as who you are, with growth, with expanding your horizons."

Curiously, women tend to do that more than men, according to Dr. Lieberman, who conducted a study of some 100 widows and widowers over a seven-year period. "Men don't stop and reflect," he says. "They just jump ahead very quickly."

But you should stop and reflect. "There's no question that it's healthier for men to deal with these issues," Dr. Lieberman says. "The task is uncomfortable, but the payoff is pretty good."

LISTENING TO YOUR BODY

A good navigator for your sexual recovery journey is your first mate, your penis. "As a widower, you'll have a rough time at first," says Domeena Renshaw, M.D., director of Loyola Sex Therapy Clinic at Loyola University in Chicago and author of *Seven Weeks to Better Sex*. "In penis language, the message may be, 'I'm scared of trying again.' That's just for a period of adjustment."

Then, says Dr. Renshaw, you might start getting morning erections, which are normal and message-packed. "Morning erections are not to be dismissed," she says. "Your penis is telling your head, 'Good morning, head. I'm fine down here. How are you up at the other end? Pay me a little attention.'"

That initial attention can be masturbation, suggests Dr. Renshaw. "You need to practice," she says. "And you also need to be patient with yourself."

Of course, recovery is one thing. Actually getting back in the ball game is quite another. You, the wise and sophisticated mature gentleman, can feel like a timid teenager. That's normal. "A lot of widowers and divorcees are insecure about new relationships," Dr. Renshaw says. "They get pretty nervous."

So what do you do? Don't dive into the deep end; test the waters with your toes. "Take it slowly," Dr. Renshaw counsels. "Make friendships first. Don't expect to jump into bed."

Instead of desperately seeking sex, simply open yourself up to female companionship. The sex will come. "If you start to pursue women," Dr. Fisher says, "you're eventually going to find one who's interested in sex. And she will begin to galvanize your own sexuality."

LINGERING FEELINGS

Even with mourning behind you, clinging to your past can ruin your present. Feeling guilty about a new relationship isn't inevitable, but it happens.

Sometimes the problem is right on the surface. "I've worked with a couple that uses the same house and the same bed (as his dead wife)," Dr. Renshaw says. "It's like they're being watched; they have a ghost."

The solution is simple. "Get a new house," Dr. Renshaw says. "If you don't have the money, buy a different bed, or at least change the bedroom around."

But the ghosts of relationships past can inhabit deeper regions, where they can even cause problems with potency, according to Lewis. "From clinical experience, you can see there are men who create a shrine to their lost wives," she says. "They can't accept sexual involvement with anybody new. They get caught up living in the past."

What to do? "If you're comfortable with that, leave it alone," Lewis says. "But if it's interfering with your quality of your life, then it's important to examine where you want to go with your life and what the death of that close relationship meant to you. If you feel guilty for having sexual feelings or thoughts, you just might not be ready emotionally. You need time to talk it all through with somebody."

Letting a "shrine" to your ex-wife keep you from new relationships is not necessarily a testimonial to your devotion to her. Remember that it's those from a happy relationship who most comfortably adjust to widowerhood. Adds Lewis, "One of the signs of maturity is to be able to love the person you lost and move on to a new love at the same time."

REMARRIAGE

Most widowed men over 60 remarry. Most widowed women over 60 don't. It sounds like a mathematical absurdity, but mathematics itself explains it. There are a lot more single women over 60 than men. Women tend to live longer, so much so that by age 85 there are about 100 women to every 39 men. Between the ages of 65 to 74, widows outnumber widowers by almost four to one.

But there's more than numbers at work here. "You also have many cultural reasons," says Erdman Palmore, Ph.D., professor emeritus of medical sociology at the Duke University Center for the Study of Aging in Durham, North Carolina, and author of *Social Patterns in Normal Aging.* "For example, there's a double standard in our society that says older men can marry younger women but not vice versa. It's an example of sexism combined with ageism."

Also, men over 60, especially widowers, are simply more eager to remarry than women are. "The widowers I studied felt kind of lost, and they more or less ran into another marriage," says Morton A. Lieberman, Ph.D., a psychologist at the University of California, San Francisco, and author of *Doors Close, Doors Open: Widows Grieving and Growing.*

Remarriage is certainly a doable deed for widowed or divorced men over 60. But though your reasons for getting married again probably won't be too different than they were the first time, your situation is different.

FINDING A WIFE

A man of 30 assumes (usually correctly) that single women his age are looking to get married. Not so at 60.

"A lot of older women are very gun-shy about remarriage," says Dr. Lieberman. "They have other agendas."

So don't assume divorced or widowed women can't wait to marry you. You could be in for a rude surprise. Knowing why they're hesitant may help. "Women are especially reluctant to remarry in later years if they had a difficult caregiving duty with their previous husbands," says Myrna Lewis, assistant professor of community medicine at Mount Sinai School of Medicine in New York City and co-author with Robert N. Butler, M.D., of the book *Love and Sex after 60*. "They don't want to get into that caregiving stuff again. Been there. Done that."

Dr. Lieberman offers another reason. "A lot are college-educated, but they came from traditional settings in which you stay home and raise the kids," he says. "So they have needs to fulfill—careers, study, writing, painting, traveling, or God knows what. That becomes very important to them, perhaps more important than a relationship with a man."

Money is another factor, according to Dr. Lieberman, who conducted a study of 100 widows and widowers over seven years. "For those women who did remarry, economics played a role," he says. "But if they're economically comfortable, many women are just not interested in getting re-married."

That doesn't mean that you should give up on the object of your desire. But to make marriage attractive, you have to bring something to the party. "If you're just looking for a caregiver, you better be straightforward about that," says Lewis. And she adds, only half-kidding, "Maybe if that's all you're looking for, you should just hire somebody to do it."

SEXUAL COMPATIBILITY

Yes, some senior marriages are sexless. "But most of them are not," says Dr. Palmore. Even fewer are sexless if you broaden the concept of sex, which many older couples do. "Sex can be massaging, caressing, or just lying in bed together holding each other," Dr. Palmore says.

Those who assume that most senior marriages are sexless are simply wrong. "It's a myth," says Lewis. "Older people are about the same as they were when they were younger in terms of their sexual interests. Some are actually more interested in sex in later life than younger. Some less. You can't generalize."

According to Dr. Palmore, you get married at 65 for all the same reasons

Have It Your Way

Be warned: There are weird people out there who think there's something silly about sex and marriage after 60. And their destructive opinions might be the unwelcome companion of your new romance. It's like a moth in the bedroom—annoying, out of place, but essentially ignorable. Things are supposedly getting better as baby boomers are passing 50, but there are those who still smirk at the idea of senior marriages and laugh out loud at the thought of a senior wedding. Like a lot of notions, it's media-fed.

"The media, in general, still does a lot of making fun of the sexuality of people over 60," says Myrna Lewis, assistant professor of community medicine at Mount Sinai School of Medicine in New York City and co-author with Robert N. Butler, M.D., of the book *Love and Sex after 60*. "So weddings are just a part of that humor. I think that's unfortunate."

But there's a convenient synchronicity that presents itself. The very target of the guffaws—your maturity—is your most powerful tool for disarming the guffawers. You know what you want, and you're comfortable with it. All but the most insensitive should eventually see that it's no different from what they want.

"All of us want the same romance," says Lewis. "That doesn't change at all with age. You also want the same respect and same understanding as anybody."

You may ask how you make sure that your wedding is dignified, as befitting an older couple. Wrong question. Age is simply not a factor on the dignified-wedding scale, save for in the minds of the misinformed. If a younger "friend" brings it up, you might remind him how many of his generation tie the knot at Elvis's Love-Me-Tender Chapel of a-Hunka-Hunka Burning Love, or some such thing. But why bother?

"Do what you want to do and be as romantic and as fun as you want to be," advises Lewis. "Plan it exactly as you wish."

It's your wedding. If there is dignity to be displayed, it will emanate from you and your bride-to-be. Whatever anybody else thinks is his problem. "Don't even think about whether anybody is going to laugh," Lewis says. "If people are going to laugh, all it means is that they are insensitive. Who needs friends like that?"

So maybe the best way to deal with those whom you fear won't take your wedding seriously is by exercising your ultimate prerogative: Don't invite them.

you do at 25, raising a family excepted. "All the same motivations are there as when you were younger, except the urge to procreate," he says.

That would include sexual compatibility. It doesn't really matter if others assume that your new marriage will be sexless. But it matters a lot if your bride-to-be assumes that it will be and you don't—or vice versa.

"One extreme stereotype is that no older people are interested in sexual relations," Dr. Palmore says. "The other extreme is that everybody ought to have a lot of intercourse for their own good. Neither extreme is valid, and both can result in misery."

OTHER CONSIDERATIONS

Here is some other advice as you go out in search of wedded bliss.

Don't expect miracles. Marriage is a wonderful thing. But it doesn't solve your personal problems, be they an unsatisfying retirement, a fear of death, or merely a need for sex. If you've found Ms. Right-the-Second-Time, marry her. If you're confronting life's problems, work on them. But don't mix the two things up.

"How much does remarriage make a difference? In terms of adjustment, happiness, and well-being, it's not that impressive," Dr. Lieberman says.

While studying widows and widowers, Dr. Lieberman looked at those who opted for remarriage and those who didn't. "You can't make a real case for saying that remarriage solves problems," he concludes. "That doesn't mean that relationships are unimportant nor that marriage is harmful. It's just that the formal, marital thing isn't critical. You just don't get that clear-cut finding that marriage is the way to go."

Consider living together. There are a number of considerations that have nothing to do with your actual relationship that can complicate remarriage after age 60. To name a few: family assets, your children's inheritance, your pension situation, social security, community property.

"You should decide based on your circumstances whether it makes sense to get married," Lewis says. "What are the advantages and disadvantages of marriage? You should look at that right straight in the eye."

And if you blink? Is living together without marriage a viable option for an older couple?

"I think so," Lewis says. "You should have the same options as younger people."

And, according to Helena Lopata, Ph.D., a sociologist at Loyola University in Chicago, it's not uncommon. "Very frequently, older couples move to a cohabiting relationship considering that it has more advantages than remarriage," she says.

And, Dr. Lopata says, there are variations on the theme. "What often happens is that if a sexual relationship develops, the question becomes in whose place they will live," she says. "Sometimes, though, they get together only on weekends, sometimes sporadically. A lot are afraid of permanence."

Others are afraid of going through the loss of a partner again, or becoming the caretaker for an ailing spouse, adds Shirley Zussman, Ed.D., a certified sex and marital therapist in New York City and editor of a newsletter, *Sex Over 40*.

Value your confidante. Whether you choose to get married, live together, or maintain an ongoing your-place-or-mine relationship, give it the priority it deserves. It's more than emotionally rewarding. It's downright healthy.

"Studies have found that having a confidante, regardless of whether you're married, is very important for older people's health," says Dr. Palmore. "There's something almost magical about having somebody who loves you and cares for you and listens to you. It keeps you mentally and physically healthy."

So the romantic poets and June-moon songwriters were on to something, even in a medical sense. The same good old, from-the-heart reasons for getting hitched at 25 apply at 65 or 75. "In fact, you may need those things even more," Dr. Palmore says. "You may not have a career or children around to distract you. What's left in life that's more important than companionship and love?"

Be open. You're not sparing anybody's feelings by making your first marriage a taboo topic with your new spouse. "People who reveal truthfully their feelings about their earlier relationships have better second marriages," Lewis says. "Keeping secrets doesn't help a marriage."

GRANDCHILDREN

Liberate yourself. As you may have noticed, you didn't stop being a human being the day your first grandchild was born. You should let your grandchildren notice that, too. "Getting into that I'm-the-grandparent thing can really lock you in to one role in life," says Myrna Lewis, assistant professor of community medicine at Mount Sinai School of Medicine in New York City and co-author with Robert N. Butler, M.D., of the book *Love and Sex after 60* "It's an important role, but it shouldn't be your only one."

One of those roles, according to Lewis, is as a model for growing old. You should be living proof to your grandchildren that they will be entitled to the same things in their later years that you want for yourself. You can show them the value of the freedom to be yourself. "And that includes sexuality," Lewis emphasizes.

If being a role model for mature sexuality strikes you as somehow treasonous to grandfatherdom, ask yourself if there's a more suitable person to project a healthy respect for sexuality. You're not corrupting a youngster by showing him life's riches in a positive way.

"Not only is it not corrupting, it's life enhancing," says Lewis. "Sexuality is part of the exhilaration of being a human being. To have that capacity for intimacy with another person is one of life's great pleasures."

But don't flaunt it either. A role model is not the same as a pitchman. You're not trying to sell sex to your grandkids. Rather, says Lewis, "they should see that you're comfortable with your sexuality so that they can feel comfortable with it themselves."

Comfortable doesn't mean obsessed. Keeping senior sex a shameful secret doesn't help your grandchildren, but neither does turning it into a circus sideshow. Lewis, a grandmother of six, tells how she finds the middle ground: "I don't flaunt it in front of grandchildren, but I don't hide it either. And I try to be frank in answering their questions."

WHEN THEY GET OLDER

As you reach your seventies, maybe even your sixties, those little grand-tots may suddenly be young men and women. That brings on new opportunities for the grandfather—and for them.

"As they reach their twenties, begin to encourage them to see you more as a complete person, not just as Grandpa," Lewis suggests. "Let it become more of an adult-to-adult relationship with give and take in both directions."

Of course, you never completely relinquish the grandparent role, but it's healthy for both of you to go beyond it and let your personalities interact. "You can do some of the grandparenting when there are crises," Lewis says. "But it's more interesting to also encourage them to see the equality there of two adults. Prepare them for their own old age by taking on the role of a fellow adult in their minds."

THE REAL YOU

Dealing with your grandchildren, where the difference in years is probably the most pronounced of all your interpersonal relationships, tends to throw into sharp relief one of the more debilitating misconceptions about aging in America. That would be the curious (and false) popular concept that older adults are intrinsically different animals than the rest of the human species.

If you're typical, that concept clashes with you're inner self-perception. "People identify with their thirties and forties all the rest of their lives," Lewis says. "A lot of people in their seventies and eighties, when asked how old they feel, say that internally they feel somewhere around 30 or 40."

But you're aware of the contradiction. "It's often hard to look at your body, especially if disease has worked fast changes, and identify with it in terms of how you feel internally," says Lewis.

One secret to satisfying maturity—and that includes satisfying sexuality—is to accommodate the body but live the inner you. And you need to let others do the same. "They should make an end run around appearance and look to the person inside you," Lewis says. "They'll find that there's not much real difference among people at any age."

That can be a tough task in our country, with its chronologically strati-fied social pockets. Teenagers seem to live in one world, young adults in an-other, middle-age adults in yet another, and seniors out on the edge somewhere. Sometimes it seems as if they hardly talk to one another, let alone interact.

But it doesn't have to be that way. And, indeed, sometimes it isn't. Lewis points out what often happens when older persons are thrust together with young ones as equals in, for example, a seminar, an adult-education class, or traffic school. "At first everybody is very aware of the age differences," she says. "But that all melts away quickly, and people end up just relating to each other as personalities."

So don't isolate yourself in the geezer ghetto. Don't let prejudices or dif-ferences in appearance stifle the inner you. You have a life to live. Live it.

INDEX

Underscored page references indicate boxed text. **Boldface** references indicate primary discussion of topic. *Italic* references indicate illustrations. Prescription drug names are denoted with the symbol Rx.

<u>Underscored</u> page references indicate boxed text. **Boldface** references indicate primary discussion of topic. *Italic* references indicate illustrations. Prescription drug names are denoted with the symbol Rx.

Underscored page references indicate boxed text. **Boldface** references indicate primary discussion of topic. *Italic* references indicate illustrations. Prescription drug names are denoted with the symbol Rx.

Underscored page references indicate boxed text. **Boldface** references indicate primary discussion of topic. *Italic* references indicate illustrations. Prescription drug names are denoted with the symbol Rx.

Underscored page references indicate boxed text. **Boldface** references indicate primary discussion of topic. *Italic* references indicate illustrations. Prescription drug names are denoted with the symbol Rx.

Underscored page references indicate boxed text. **Boldface** references indicate primary
discussion of topic. *Italic* references indicate illustrations. Prescription drug names are denoted
with the symbol Rx.

Underscored page references indicate boxed text. **Boldface** references indicate primary discussion of topic. *Italic* references indicate illustrations. Prescription drug names are denoted with the symbol Rx.

Underscored page references indicate boxed text. **Boldface** references indicate primary discussion of topic. *Italic* references indicate illustrations. Prescription drug names are denoted with the symbol Rx.

Underscored page references indicate boxed text. **Boldface** references indicate primary discussion of topic. *Italic* references indicate illustrations. Prescription drug names are denoted with the symbol Rx.

Underscored page references indicate boxed text. **Boldface** references indicate primary discussion of topic. *Italic* references indicate illustrations. Prescription drug names are denoted with the symbol Rx.

Underscored page references indicate boxed text. **Boldface** references indicate primary discussion of topic. _Italic_ references indicate illustrations. Prescription drug names are denoted with the symbol Rx.

Underscored page references indicate boxed text. **Boldface** references indicate primary discussion of topic. *Italic* references indicate illustrations. Prescription drug names are denoted with the symbol Rx.

<u>Underscored</u> page references indicate boxed text. **Boldface** references indicate primary discussion of topic. *Italic* references indicate illustrations. Prescription drug names are denoted with the symbol Rx.

Underscored page references indicate boxed text. **Boldface** references indicate primary discussion of topic. *Italic* references indicate illustrations. Prescription drug names are denoted with the symbol Rx.

Underscored page references indicate boxed text. **Boldface** references indicate primary
discussion of topic. *Italic* references indicate illustrations. Prescription drug names are denoted
with the symbol Rx.

Underscored page references indicate boxed text. **Boldface** references indicate primary discussion of topic. *Italic* references indicate illustrations. Prescription drug names are denoted with the symbol Rx.

Underscored page references indicate boxed text. **Boldface** references indicate primary discussion of topic. *Italic* references indicate illustrations. Prescription drug names are denoted with the symbol Rx.

Underscored page references indicate boxed text. **Boldface** references indicate primary discussion of topic. *Italic* references indicate illustrations. Prescription drug names are denoted with the symbol Rx.